Development Through Life
A Psychosocial Approach FIFTH EDITION

Development Through Life
A Psychosocial Approach   FIFTH EDITION

Barbara M. Newman

Philip R. Newman

The Ohio State University

Brooks/Cole Publishing Company
Pacific Grove, California

Brooks/Cole Publishing Company
A Division of Wadsworth, Inc.

Printed in the United States of America
10   9   8   7   6   5   4   3

Library of Congress Cataloging-in-Publication Data

Newman, Barbara M.
    Development through life : a psychosocial approach / Barbara M.
Newman, Philip R. Newman. — 5th ed.
      p.   cm.
    Includes bibliographical references and indexes.
    ISBN 0-534-15396-8
    1. Developmental psychology.   I. Newman, Philip R.   II. Title.
BF713.N48   1991
155—dc20   90-25467
                                                                CIP

Project Development Editor: *Vicki Knight*
Editorial Assistant: *Heather L. Riedel*
Production Editor: *Penelope Sky*
Production Assistant: *Micky Lawler*
Manuscript Editor: *Barbara Salazar*
Permissions Editor: *Mary Kay Hancharick*
Interior and Cover Design: *Lisa Thompson*
Art Coordinator: *Lisa Torri*
Interior Illustration: *Precision Graphics; Judith Macdonald*
Photo Editor: *Ruth Minerva*
Typesetting: *Graphic Typesetting Service*
Cover Printing: *Phoenix Color Corporation*
Printing and Binding: *R. R. Donnelley & Sons*

Cover: *Pablo Picasso, "Woman with Raised Arms," 1936. SPADEM/Art Resource, N.Y. Copyright 1990 ARS, N.Y./Spadem.*

Credits continue on page 691.

To our parents and our children.
We thank you for our past and our future:
for the great gift of continuity.

Preface

Between the first and the fifth editions of this text, we have developed from early to middle adulthood. When we first published *Development Through Life,* we attempted to build conceptual bridges from the metaphors of Erikson's work to the barely emergent field of human development. Since then, Erikson's work has continued to evolve, the field has matured, and we have achieved a new sense of ourselves: as husband and wife, as parents, as scholars, as teachers, and as citizens. We are pleased to welcome you to this fascinating journey.

Perspective

Development Through Life is a general introduction to the study of human development, from conception through very old age. The text treats physical, intellectual, social, and emotional growth in each of eleven stages. It emphasizes that development is a product of the interdependence of these areas at every stage. Special attention is given to the conditions that promote optimal development throughout life.

Psychosocial theory provides a conceptual framework for the text, as we highlight the continuous interaction of individual competencies with the demands and resources of culture. Development is viewed as a product of genetic, maturational, societal, and self-directed factors. There are several advantages to applying this integrating perspective to an analysis of human development. First, although the subject matter is potentially overwhelming, the psychosocial framework helps us identify meaningful directions of growth across the life span. Second, the framework helps us assess the influence of experiences during earlier life stages on later development, and the impact of expectations about later development on the course of earlier stages. It helps readers understand some of the ways that their own past, present, and future expectations are systematically connected to the lives of those older and younger than they. Third, the framework allows us to take a hopeful outlook on the total life course: the promise of continuous growth validates many of the struggles of adolescence, and of early and middle adulthood.

Organization

The basic focus and organization of the text have been retained in this edition. However, we have thoroughly updated the material and added new sections. The first chapter establishes the orientation and assumptions of the text, and introduces the scientific process through which a systematic study of development becomes possible. Chapter Two presents a detailed discussion of the basic concepts of psychosocial theory, including an analysis of its strengths and weaknesses. Briefly, this theory argues that human development can be conceptualized as a sequence of stages from conception through very old age. At each stage a number of major tasks require new kinds of learning; at each stage there is also a major developmental conflict, or psychosocial crisis, which can be resolved gradually or suddenly but which does require resolution. This conflict results from a discrepancy between our competencies as we enter a particular stage, and the demands of the environment—family, school, or community. Development occurs in an ever-changing social context. Successful conflict resolution and task accomplishments at one stage allow us to face and cope with the new demands imposed by the culture and by members of our immediate social groups at the next period of life. At each new stage we redefine ourselves and our relationships with others. Continuity and change, whether in response to internal pressures and environmental demands or as a result of our own choices and commitments, are both products of development.

Chapter Three outlines significant ideas about change and growth from other theoretical perspectives, including, for the first time in this edition, systems theory. These concepts provide the intellectual structure for later discussions of physical, cognitive, social, and emotional development. They help readers analyze apparent conflicts among the maturational, societal, and individual forces toward growth. In presenting a variety of theoretical perspectives, we also offer a multidimensional source of information about individual behaviors and patterns of change.

In Chapter Four, fetal development is studied in relation to the pregnant woman and her social environment. The recent flood of research on behavioral genetics led us to include a detailed treatment of this material. We believe that students of human development must achieve a high level of comprehension about the basic genetic processes as they pertain to the life span.

Chapters Five through Fourteen cover the remaining stages of human life: infancy, toddlerhood, early school age, middle school age, early adolescence, later adolescence, early adulthood, middle adulthood, later adulthood, and very old age. Each chapter traces basic patterns of normal growth and development. We consider how individuals organize and interpret their experience, noting changes both in their behavior and in the environmental demands they face. Each chapter begins by examining four or five of the critical developmental tasks of the stage under discussion. These tasks reflect global aspects of development, including physical growth and sensory and motor competence, cognitive maturation, social relationships, and self-understanding. We consider the psychosocial crisis of the stage in some detail. We show how the successful resolution of a crisis helps us develop a prime adaptive ego quality, and how unsuccessful resolution leads to a core pathology. Although most people grow developmentally, albeit with pain and struggle, some do not. People who acquire core pathologies lead withdrawn, guarded lives; for the most part they are not psychologically healthy and often are not physically healthy either.

We conclude each chapter by applying research and theory to a topic of societal importance at the given life stage. These discussions may seem controversial, and often provide a productive transition from gathering new ideas and information to the more active practice of applying these ideas to difficult social issues. Table 2.7 (pages 64–65) contains an overview of the basic tasks, crises, and applied topics.

The Fifth Edition

The changes in this edition do not affect the basic structure of the book. Many new sections bring clarity or a fresh way of thinking to a topic. We have increased the material about cultures other than our own, and introduce the issue of ethnic identity in several places in order to emphasize that there are many subcultures within our society. These additions strengthen the text by raising questions about which aspects of development are universal and which are shaped by society; they have also increased our appreciation of the importance and wonder of human diversity.

In this edition we have emphasized the theme of genetic and environmental interaction. This is most evident in the chapter on prenatal development, but it is relevant to our discussions of temperament, skill development, puberty, parenting, and optimal functioning in later life.

In several places we summarize good solid advice discovered in our research, including Erik Erikson's remarks on aging and Dr. Chester Pierce's comments on the process of achieving integrity as a black American.

Our work on this edition required substantial reviewing and rethinking of basic concepts; the resulting updating brought a new vibrancy to the text. We are extremely pleased by the continuous increase in well designed, well executed research into so many facets of psychosocial development. This made our job more difficult and more stimulating intellectually.

Acknowledgments

We express our appreciation to many students, colleagues, and friends who shared their ideas with us. Our children, Sam, Abe, and Rachel, made constructive comments about the content, appearance, and tone of the book. It is wonderful to be at a time in our family's development when a project such as this can benefit from so many points of view. Two special friends, Judy Woodall and Helen O'Leary, helped us prepare the manuscript. The fifth edition was produced under the guidance of a superior editor, Vicki Knight. Finally, we acknowledge the thoughtful, constructive comments and suggestions of the following reviewers: Sheldon Brown, North Shore Community College; Agit Das, University of Minnesota at Duluth; George Holden, University of Texas at Austin; Boaz Kahana, Cleveland State University; Raymond Lish, Western Michigan University; Robert McLaren, California State University at Fullerton; Ann Nihlen, University of New Mexico; Suzanne Pasch, University of Wisconsin at Milwaukee; Virginia Paulsen, University of Washington; Ronald Sabatelli, University of Connecticut; and Anne Stanberry, Friends University.

Barbara M. Newman
Philip R. Newman

Brief Contents

Brief Contents

Contents

Development Through Life

A Psychosocial Approach   FIFTH EDITION

Chapter One

The integrating theme in our analysis of the life span is psychosocial theory. Our goal is to describe the dynamic interaction of the developing person and the socio-cultural environment.

The Development Through Life Perspective

In this book we attempt to bring you the most accurate information and the newest, most thought-provoking ideas about human development so that you will be able to continue to chart your own course as you travel through life. Human development is very puzzling and relatively unexplored. If we are to understand it, we must explore the way people integrate beliefs and experiences at each stage of development in their efforts to make sense of their lives. This process is as individual as each person's life story. Yet common threads of organization and understanding allow us to know one another, care for one another, and contribute to one another's well-being.

Assumptions of the Text

Our perspective on development through life embraces four assumptions that are critical to the organization and focus of this book. They are a product of our psychosocial orientation and our awareness of the significance of the societal and historical contexts in which behavior occurs.

1. *Growth occurs at every period of life, from conception through old age.*
2. *Individual lives show continuity and change as they progress through time.* An awareness of processes that contribute to both continuity and change is central to an understanding of human development.
3. *We need to understand the whole person, because we function in an integrated manner on a day-to-day basis.* To achieve such an understanding we need to study the major internal developments that involve physical, social, emotional, and thinking capacities and their interrelationships. We also need to study actions, the many forms of observable behavior.
4. *Every person's behavior must be analyzed in the context of relevant settings and personal relationships.* Human beings are highly skilled at adapting to their environment. The meaning of a given behavior pattern or change must be interpreted in light of the significant physical and social environments in which it occurs.

A Psychosocial Approach

Erik Erikson (1963, p. 37) has written that human life as the individual experiences it is produced by the interaction and modification of three major systems: the somatic system, the ego system, and the societal system.

The *somatic system* includes all those processes necessary for the functioning of the biological organism (Figure 1.1). Our sensory capacities, motor responses, and respiratory, endocrine, and circulatory systems are all somatic processes. Somatic processes develop and change as a consequence of genetically guided maturation, environmental resources such as nutrition and sunlight, encounters with accidents and diseases, and life habits related to the use of drugs, daily exercise, eating, and sleeping.

The *ego system* includes those processes central to thinking and reasoning (Figure 1.2). Our memory and perception, our problem-solving, language, and symbolic abilities, and our future orientation are all ego processes. Like the somatic processes, the

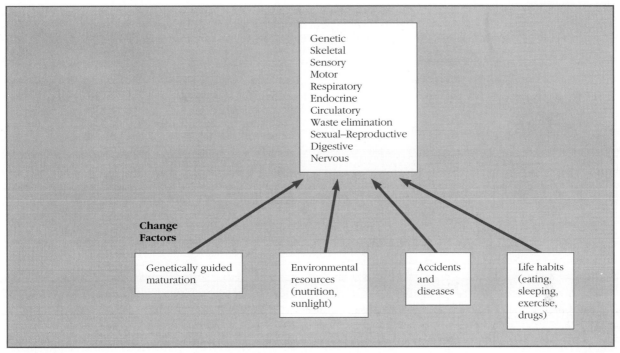

Figure 1.1   Some Elements of the Somatic System

ego processes develop and change over one's life span. Change is guided in part by genetic information. The maturation of intellectual functioning, for example, appears to be directed by a genetic plan. A number of genetically transmitted diseases result in intellectual impairment and a reduced capacity for learning. Change results from the accumulation of experiences and encounters with various educational settings. Formal schooling, of course, is a major element of this experience. Numerous other life experiences, however, also enhance ego processes. Sports, camping, travel, reading, and talking with people all enrich a person's thinking and reasoning. Finally, change can be self-directed. A person can decide to pursue a new interest, for example, or learn a foreign language, or adopt a new set of ideas. Through self-insight or perhaps psychotherapy, one can begin to think about oneself and others in a new light.

The *societal system* includes those processes through which a person becomes integrated into society (Figure 1.3). Societal processes include social roles, rituals, cultural myths, social expectations, leadership styles, communication patterns, family organization, ethnic subcultural influence, political and religious ideologies, and patterns of economic prosperity or poverty and war or peace. Much of the impact of the societal system results from interpersonal relationships, often relationships with close or significant others.

The societal processes, too, can change over one's life span. One of the most striking instances of such change occurs when a person moves from one culture to another. In this case, many of the fundamental assumptions about the self and social relationships are modified.

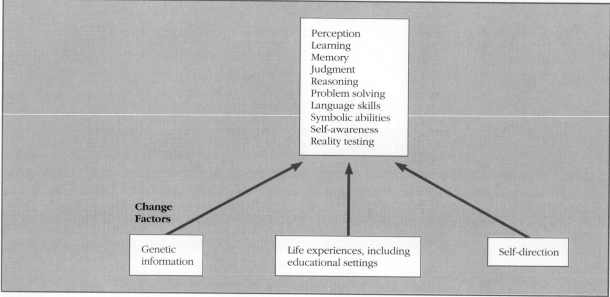

Figure 1.2   Some Elements of the Ego System

Historical events—conditions of war or peace, being the victor or the vanquished, prosperity or poverty—influence the way people in a given culture perceive themselves. For example, the conditions of World War II—forced military service, decreases in the availability of resources and the resulting system of rationing, the increased involvement of women in the labor market, the bombing of European cities, the unveiling of unprecedented human atrocities, the explosion of the first nuclear bomb over Japan—made a lasting impact on the values and ideology of the people who lived through that period, even if they took no part in the war itself.

Even in less extreme cases, the influence of society on an individual can change over the life course. Entry into new roles brings new demands and behaviors. Most societies have changing expectations for competence and participation of members at each period of life. These expectations can be in harmony or in conflict with the maturation of the somatic and ego processes.

The *psychosocial approach* focuses on the internal experiences that are products of interactions among the somatic, ego, and societal processes. When we consider somatic processes, we focus on the effects of physical attributes and physical changes on our personal sense of self and our relationships. When we focus on ego processes, we examine our internal representations of information and relationships, on the way we categorize and interpret experience. When we focus on societal processes, we examine the way our membership in one kind of group rather than another affects our thoughts, feelings, and actions. Figure 1.4 illustrates how changes in one of the three systems—somatic, ego, and societal—generally bring about changes in the others.

We can see how the three systems interact when we consider the problems facing Rose, a 60-year-old woman who has been having serious attacks of dizziness and

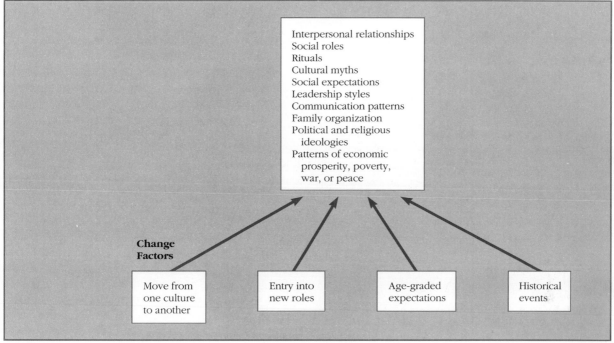

Interpersonal relationships
Social roles
Rituals
Cultural myths
Social expectations
Leadership styles
Communication patterns
Family organization
Political and religious
   ideologies
Patterns of economic
   prosperity, poverty,
   war, or peace

**Change
Factors**

Move from
one culture
to another

Entry into
new roles

Age-graded
expectations

Historical
events

Figure 1.3   Some Elements of the Societal System

shortness of breath as Thanksgiving approaches. Rose is normally active and energetic. Usually she looks forward to entertaining her family, which includes three married daughters, one married son, and their children. However, recently her son has been divorced. Feelings between him and his ex-wife are bitter. Any attempts on Rose's part to communicate with her daughter-in-law or granddaughter meet with outbursts of hostility from her son. Rose knows she cannot invite her former daughter-in-law and granddaughter to a family gathering that includes her son.

Rose's daughters suggest having the dinner at one of their homes in order to avoid further conflict. They hope this solution will take some of the pressure off their mother and ease the attacks. Rose agrees, but her attacks are not relieved.

All three systems are involved in this situation. The somatic system is the one in which the conflict is being expressed—through the symptoms of dizziness and shortness of breath. It is important to realize that the demands of a situation may call forth responses from the somatic system, as they commonly do in people under stress. Although the solution to the problem must be found in the ego system, often the somatic system alerts the person to the severity of the problem through the development of physical symptoms.

Rose's ego system is involved in interpreting her son's behavior, which she views as forcing her to choose between him and her daughter-in-law and granddaughter. She might also use ego processes to try to arrive at a solution to the conflict. Here we sense that Rose has not identified any satisfactory solution to the problem. Although

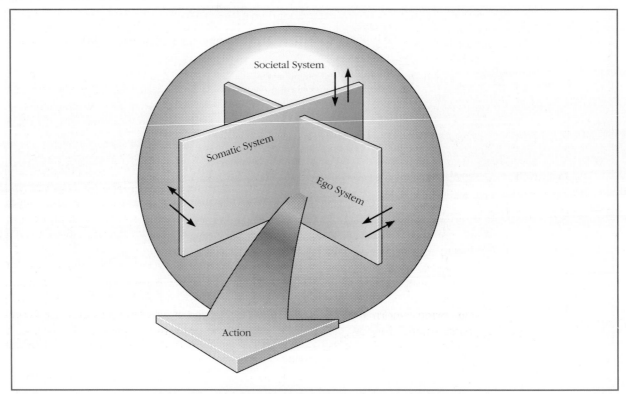

Figure 1.4   The Interrelationships of the Somatic, Ego, and Societal Systems

she can avoid the conflict most of the time, the impending Thanksgiving dinner is forcing her to confront it directly.

The ego system is involved in Rose's self-concept and in the way she views her role within her family. Through memory, Rose retains a sense of her family at earlier periods, when they enjoyed greater closeness. Having to face a Thanksgiving dinner at which she will feel angry at her son or guilty about excluding her daughter-in-law and granddaughter places her in a fundamental conflict. The Thanksgiving meal is also a symbolic event, representing Rose's idea of family unity, which she cannot achieve.

With respect to the societal system, the situation can be viewed from several levels. First, there are the societal expectations regarding the mother role: Mother is nurturing, loving, and protecting. But Rose cannot exercise the nurturing role without sending messages of rejection to her son or to her daughter-in-law and granddaughter.

Second, our society has no clear norms for relating to various family members after a divorce. How ought one to behave toward the former spouse, the noncustodial parent and child, and extended family members, especially grandparents? Rose is confused about what to do.

Third, the Thanksgiving celebration has social, religious, and cultural significance. This family ritual has been performed in Rose's home since she was a child, and she has carried it through in her own home as an adult. Now, however, she is being forced to pass the responsibility for this festival to her daughter before she is ready to do so. Rose is likely to feel a special sense of loss if she has to give up her role in this cultural ritual. She will also lose the sense of family unity that she has tried to preserve.

To grasp the importance of the cultural component of the societal process, think how a Japanese person might react to being unable to celebrate Thanksgiving. Thanksgiving is not a Japanese holiday. It has no particular emotional or historical significance within the Japanese culture. The importance of Thanksgiving to Rose is linked to her cultural identity.

Fourth, specific interpersonal dynamics are at work here. Rose and her son have a history of conflict that continues to interfere in her other family relationships.

This case illustrates how conflict in the societal system can result in symptoms in the somatic system. Ordinarily, one would expect a person to use the ego system to create a solution to the conflict. Perhaps because of Rose's past socialization, her age, and her personality, she seems to be expressing the conflict somatically but is unable to use ego processes to resolve it. The psychosocial approach highlights the continuous interaction of the individual and the social environment. At each period of their lives, people spend much of their time mastering a relatively small group of psychological tasks that are essential for adaptation within their society. Each stage brings a normative crisis, which can be viewed as a tension between one's competencies and the new demands of society. The resolution of each crisis provides a new and basic social ability that influences the person's general orientation to the next stage.

Throughout life, several relationships occupy a person's attention. Some of these relationships are more important than others; but their quality and diversity provide a basis for the study of a person's psychosocial development. As individuals progress through the stages of life, they develop an increasing capacity to initiate new relationships and to innovate in thought and action so as to direct the course of their lives.

Human beings strive to make sense of their experiences. The meaning they derive depends on their beliefs about themselves and about their relationships with others. This meaning changes over their lives as a result of the maturation of their somatic and ego systems and their increased participation in the societal system.

Take the concept of love. In infancy, love is almost entirely physical. It is the pervasive sense of comfort and security that one feels in the presence of the caregiver. By adolescence, the idea of love includes loyalty, emotional closeness, and sexuality. In adulthood, the concept of love may expand to include a new emphasis on companionship and open communication. The need to be loved and to give love remains important throughout life, but the self we bring to a loving relationship and the signs of love change with age.

We humans struggle to define ourselves through a sense of connectedness with certain other people and groups and through feelings of distinctiveness from others. We establish categories that clarify whom we are connected to, whom we care about, and which of our own qualities we admire. We also establish categories that clarify those to whom we are not connected, those whom we do not care about, and those of our qualities that we reject or deny. These categories provide us with an orientation toward certain kinds of people and away from others and toward certain life choices and away from others. It is important to be sensitive to the existence of these categories in your own mind and to be aware of the fact that they can change.

The Scientific Process

The *scientific process* allows us to create a body of knowledge. Essentially it is a method for developing information that contains within it procedures for ensuring that the information is correct. The process involves several distinct steps.

Scientific thinking usually begins when one attempts to reason systematically about a puzzling idea or observation. The observer tries to figure out how the observation might be explained, and thinks about what leads to what and which things cause other things to happen. As a result, one develops a set of interrelated ideas to account for the observations. These ideas, often referred to as *assumptions, hypotheses,* and *predictions,* constitute a theory. The theory is not an end in itself—it is a way to get going.

The second step of the scientific process is to test the theory. Testing is conducted through experimentation and observation. If a theory is good, it will contain specific predictions about cause and effect. After stating the theory, one must figure out how to test whether or not its predictions are accurate or the hypothesized relationships can be observed.

One must *operationalize* the concepts of a theory so that they can be tested. In other words, one must translate an abstract concept into something that can be observed and measured. If one decided to measure personal attraction, for example, one could think about the various ways in which people show they are attracted to each other. One might observe that people who are mutually attracted tend to look each other in the eye rather than off to the side. The amount of eye contact is a way of defining the concept of attraction so that it can be observed and measured. Eye contact thus becomes an *operational definition* of personal attraction.

Often the theory is not tested by the same person who develops it. One reason is that the theorist may have some personal investment in demonstrating that the theory is correct. The scientific process usually involves the ideas of more than one person. Sometimes people with different points of view engage in a debate as they try to refute positions they find flawed. At other times two or more people work on different phases of theory building, experimentation, and evaluation.

Working in this way, as a community of scholars, helps to ensure that a theory is not confirmed simply on the basis of the theorist's personal biases. For example, Erik Erikson was not the person who tested his psychosocial theory. Researchers such as James Marcia, Ruthellen Josselson, Alan Waterman, and Jacob Orlofsky have pursued some of Erikson's hypotheses about identity development. They have developed a variety of strategies for operationalizing Erikson's concepts, especially the psychosocial crisis of personal identity versus identity confusion. Their work has clarified Erikson's concepts and supported many of his views about the relation of personal identity to subsequent development.

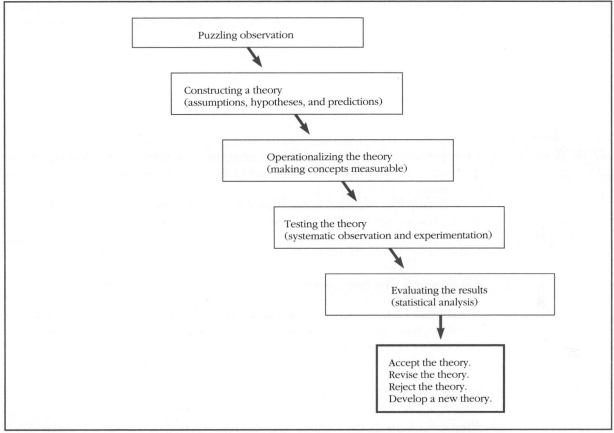

Figure 1.5   **The Scientific Process**

The final phase of the scientific process involves an evaluation of the experiment and the theory. Statistical techniques help us determine if the results of a series of observations could have happened by chance. If our observations could have been produced by chance factors, we have no reason to assume that any systematic causal mechanism was operating. These results will not confirm the theory. We may decide to test it further and perhaps modify it. If the observations have a low probability of having occurred by chance, we may assume that something other than chance factors must have been operating to cause what we have observed. If the results occur in the direction that the theory predicts, we are likely to accept our observations as providing support for the theoretical explanation. We may still be skeptical, though, and go on to test the theory through further experimentation.

In summary, the scientific process consists of creating a theory, testing it through experimentation, and modifying, rejecting, or accepting it. To the extent that a theory is confirmed by the scientific process, it helps us to interpret many of our observations about reality (see Figure 1.5).

The section that follows provides an overview of the basic principles of the research process as it is applied to the study of human development. In reviewing these principles, you will begin to grasp the challenge of trying to arrive at a systematic body of knowledge about the patterns of continuity and change in the life course. At the same time you will encounter concepts that will improve your ability to ask critical, analytic questions about the research discussed in subsequent chapters and elsewhere.

Scientific Observation

Scientific observation is somewhat different from personal observation. Scientific observation in human development, as in other areas of social science, is characterized by three essential qualities. It must be objective, repeatable, and systematic. These qualities may or may not be characteristic of the way you use observation to test your own personal theories.

Objectivity means that the observations accurately reflect the events that are taking place. They are not unduly influenced by what the observer expects or hopes to see. Suppose that you want an objective assessment of your physical attractiveness. You cannot just go up to some friends or relatives and ask them to tell you whether they find you attractive. Because they know you, and presumably would not like to insult you, they may slant their answers.

A more objective approach might be to include your photograph with photographs of 100 other people chosen at random. You would then ask another student to give the photographs to ten people who do not know you and have each of them rate the photographs for physical attractiveness. You might or might not like the outcome, but at least your method would be objective! It would reveal what other people thought of your attractiveness, without being biased by any feelings about you.

Repeatability means that someone else could approach the task of research and observe the same things as the original investigator. To satisfy this requirement, the investigator must carefully define all procedures used in the research study, describe all the essential characteristics of the subjects (such as age, sex, and social class), and describe the setting or situation where the observations were made.

Systematic means that research is done in a comprehensive, orderly way. Systematic observations focus on behaviors that are relevant to a basic relationship. Scientific research does not poke here and there at unrelated events. Scientists have a framework of essential questions that they strive to answer thoughtfully, in a logical order.

Theory and scientific observation are intimately connected in the scientific process. Theories can be used to guide research in areas that are important for study. They generate hypotheses that can be tested or evaluated by means of systematic observation. Research can support theories and produce observations that challenge theories. As we noted earlier, the outcome of research efforts sometimes leads to the revision of a theory or the formulation of a new theory.

Research Design

Numerous methods are used to carry out research in human development. Research investigations are designed just as cars, bridges, and buildings are designed. How should you go about designing a research study to answer a question you have?

In formal scientific work, small groups of highly trained professionals often meet to try to identify the most absolutely foolproof methods available for finding out the answer to a question. Scientists know that the information they gain from conducting research will be heavily influenced by the way they gather their data and the characteristics of the subjects who are involved in their study. In the same way that theories are critical for drawing our attention to essential concepts and causal relationships, research design is critical for building a body of evidence that is objective and readily interpreted.

A research design includes the method that is selected to gather information, the sample that is selected to participate in the study, the frequency with which data are gathered, and the statistical techniques that are used to analyze the data.

Selecting a Sample

Sampling is the method of choosing subjects for a study. The particular subjects who participate in any study and the way they are selected will have some influence on the nature of the results. Studies of human development, just like studies in any other area of social science, are vulnerable to problems of sampling. The way an investigator selects the subjects is related to the kinds of questions being asked. If the study is about some universal principle of development, it would be ideal to include as wide a range of subjects as possible. Studies of normal language development, for example, might include children of various ethnic, racial, social class, and cultural groups. If a pattern of growth is expected to be universal, it should apply to children of a wide variety of family and societal backgrounds.

If a study is intended to focus on the effects of certain life conditions on development, then people who have experienced those conditions will be compared with people who have not experienced those conditions. Sometimes it is hard to decide on the best or most appropriate comparison groups. If you wanted to understand the impact of divorce on young adults, what would be a good comparison group? Older adults who have experienced divorce? Young adults who have not divorced? Young adults who have lost a spouse through death? Each of these comparisons would allow one to answer a slightly different question. Children and adolescents are typically embedded in at least two settings: family and school. If researchers study children in their school setting, they may capture something about the school environment that influences the way children respond. Similarly, if researchers study children in their home setting, they may capture something about the home environment that will influence the children's responses. One cannot assume that behavior observed in one context, whether it is school, home, playground, or laboratory, would also be observed in the others.

The sample and the population from which the sample is taken determine which generalizations may be made from the research findings. If the sample for a study is selected from only middle- and upper-middle-class male college students, can the findings of the research be applied to women, to people who are not college students, to younger or older people, or to people of lower or higher social classes? The answer to this type of question is not always clear. Strictly speaking, we cannot generalize beyond the population from which a sample was selected. Nevertheless, we often do generalize. The validity of a generalization beyond the sample's population depends partly on the type of research question that is being investigated.

Some research questions require relatively little attention to the character of the sample. If we were interested in the firing of neurons in the cortex, for example, we might assume that any human subjects who were not brain-damaged would give us comparable information. For some physiological issues this may be true. Even here, however, the age of the subject might influence the firing time, so the sample probably should include subjects of various ages. Then we would be more confident in generalizing the results to all people.

Research questions that focus on attitudes, motives, or beliefs absolutely must include a consideration of the background of the subjects. We simply cannot assume that all subjects will bring the same basic attitudes or values to the research question. Attitudes are shaped by a wide range of socialization and sociohistorical factors. It would be unwise to assume that attitudes of members of racial and ethnic minorities are the same as the attitudes of white subjects.

How, then, is sampling done? Four methods are frequently used:

Random sampling: Each person has an equal chance of being included. The researcher may ensure equal opportunity by putting everyone's name on a slip of paper and then choosing some of the slips blindly, or by selecting names from a list based on a table of random numbers.

Stratified sampling: Subjects are deliberately selected from a variety of levels or types of people (strata) in the population. For example, the proportions of upper-, middle-, and lower-income groups in the sample may be selected to correspond with their proportions in the population. Within each level, however, subjects are selected at random.

Matched groups: The researcher selects two or more groups of subjects who are similar on many dimensions.

Volunteer sampling: Subjects are selected from among people who volunteer.

Random sampling and stratified sampling are used to ensure that a sample is representative of the population from which it is drawn. Then one can be confident in generalizing from the sample to the population. The ratio of men to women, for example, can be approximately the same in the sample as in the population from which it is drawn. Either method can ensure the same representativeness in regard to any characteristic of the subjects, such as race, income, or educational background. Matched groups are sometimes used in experiments, when the purpose is to administer different conditions to otherwise similar groups of people.

The method that places the most limits on generalization is volunteer sampling. One never knows what type of person will volunteer for a study. Thus the researcher cannot tell how far to generalize the results. Reliance on volunteers can also produce special problems. People who volunteer for a study on obedience, for example, may be especially obedient, so that the results are slanted. Nevertheless, volunteer samples are used frequently. Often this is the only way to begin to understand the attitudes and behaviors of a particular group. People who are undergoing treatment for a certain kind of problem, for example, are often asked to volunteer to participate in research about that problem. Without their voluntary cooperation, a researcher would have no way to begin to document the background characteristics, attitudes, coping strategies, or course of recovery related to the problem.

In clinical studies, data may be obtained directly from a patient during a regular office visit as well as from patients' records.

You will undoubtedly read some studies that are referred to as *clinical studies*. The term usually indicates that some of the participants or an entire family has been involved in some type of treatment program or is on a waiting list to receive clinical treatment. This treatment may be related to (*a*) health, as in studies of low-birth-weight infants, asthmatic or diabetic adolescents, or older adults who have Alzheimer's disease; (*b*) mental health, as in studies of child abuse, autism, schizophrenia, or suicide; (*c*) handicapping conditions, such as blindness, deafness, or learning disabilities; or (*d*) developmental delay resulting from genetically transmitted diseases or from abusive or negligent family environments.

These studies are especially important for understanding the causes of clinical conditions, the developmental path along which these conditions travel, the effects of certain interventions, and the long-term consequences of these conditions for adaptation. At the same time, one must be careful not to generalize findings from clinical studies to the population as a whole. Theories that are developed to account for the causes of these clinical conditions or to propose treatments for them cannot necessarily be applied to individuals and families who are not seeking such treatment. Interventions that might make sense and be effective in working with clinical populations are not necessarily appropriate or relevant for other groups.

Research Methods

A variety of methods have been used to study development. Each one has its strengths and weaknesses, allowing the investigator to focus on some set of behaviors at the expense of others. The choice of method must fit the problem under study. Five general categories of developmental research are described here: observation, experimentation, surveys and tests, case studies, and interviews.

Observation

Direct observation of children in their home and school environments is one of the oldest methods for studying development (Kessen, 1965). Researchers have used mothers' diaries and observation logs to gather information about intimate settings that could not be known in any other way. Jean Piaget was guided by the naturalistic observations of his own children in the formulation of his theory of cognition. Today some researchers conduct observations in homes, schools, day-care centers, and nursing homes. Others bring individuals, sometimes including their families or friends, into homelike laboratory settings where they can watch behavior under somewhat more constant and controlled physical conditions (Kochanska, Kuczynski & Radke-Yarrow, 1989).

Naturalistic observation, or the careful monitoring of behavior without any other kind of manipulation, provides insight into the way things occur in the real world. Sometimes, researchers go into a setting to observe the full range of interactions and behavior patterns. On the basis of their field notes, they begin to develop hypotheses about important relationships. Then they may test these hypotheses through more focused observation or through more controlled experimentation.

In other instances researchers use naturalistic observation to examine a specific behavior or relationship. They may be looking for various forms of peer aggression, patterns of social cooperation, or conditions that promote cross-gender interaction. In these cases, the observers have a predefined focus and limit the scope of their observations to behaviors that are relevant to their concern.

One strength of naturalistic observation is the ability to capture naturally occurring responses as they take place. Another strength is the ability to allow the actual behavior that is taking place to guide the researcher's conceptualization. Rather than setting up a specific task or a group of questions and asking individuals to respond, the observer examines the full range of relevant behaviors.

Naturalistic observation also has some limitations as a research method. First, it is often difficult to establish agreement between observers about exactly what occurred. Often two or more observers' codings of the same situation are compared in an effort to determine whether their ratings of the situation are reliable. When such *interobserver reliability* is high, several people can make observations simultaneously. When interobserver reliability is low, the researcher must determine why and correct the differences found in observation techniques, usually through training.

A second difficulty with the observational method is that in some settings so much activity is going on that it may be difficult to observe it all accurately. Finally, if you are interested in studying a particular behavior or sequence of behaviors, you cannot be assured that this target behavior will take place within the limitations of a realistic period of observation.

The technology of videotaping gives us a powerful tool that has relevance for naturalistic observation as well as for experimentation. A videotape can be reviewed over and over again. Several observers can watch a tape, stop it, and discuss what they saw. The same events can be observed from several points of view. Researchers inter-

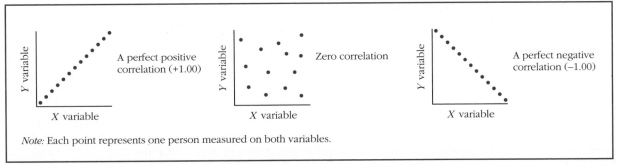

Note: Each point represents one person measured on both variables.

Figure 1.6   **Positive, Zero, and Negative Correlations between *X* and *Y***

ested in children's play, for example, might videotape a child's free play in three or four settings—perhaps at a preschool, at a park, at home, and at a friend's house. Several observers might review the tapes, each looking for a different aspect of behavior, such as creativity, peer interaction, complex motor skills, or language use. Without interfering with the child's behavior, the videotaped record offers us a vehicle for detailed and repeated analysis.

Observational studies lend themselves to an examination of correlation rather than causation. *Correlation* refers to the degree to which knowing the value of one variable, such as age, allows one to predict something about another variable, such as helpfulness. Observational researchers can ask many types of questions. Do children who play alone often show more creativity in their play? Do adolescents who are most aggressive with others have parents who use a lot of physical discipline strategies? Do older adults who receive a lot of help and support from their children have higher self-esteem than those who do not receive much help from their children?

A statistic called a *correlation coefficient* is calculated. A correlation coefficient tells you whether there is a mathematical relationship between variables and what the relationship is like. Many of the research findings reported in studies of development are reports of correlations. A correlation coefficient can range from a value of $+1.0$ to -1.0.

Let us take the correlation between aggression and school performance. If higher levels of aggression are associated with better school performance, the correlation between the two dimensions is positive (toward $+1.0$). As one increases, so does the other. If higher levels of aggression are associated with lower school performance, the correlation is negative (toward -1.0). As one increases, the other declines. If there is no systematic relationship between aggression and school performance, the correlation will be close to 0. The strength of the association between variables is reflected in whether the correlation is closer to 0 or closer to $+1.0$ or -1.0. Figure 1.6 shows a perfect positive, a zero, and a perfect negative correlation.

A high positive or negative correlation between two variables shows only that there is an association between them. It indicates nothing about causation. A strong association between aggression and low grades in school does not mean that being aggressive causes children to get poor grades. Perhaps low grades cause children to be aggressive. Or perhaps some other factor, such as a short attention span or low motivation for school success, accounts for both aggression and low grades.

Experimentation

Experimentation is a method best suited for examining unidirectional, causal relationships. In an experiment, some variable or group of variables is systematically
manipulated while others are held constant. The variable that is manipulated by the
experimenter is called the *independent variable*. The variable defined by the subjects'
responses or reactions is the *dependent variable*.

In some experiments, one group of subjects has a certain set of experiences or
receives information (usually referred to as a *treatment*) that is not provided to another
group. The group that experiences the experimenter's manipulation is called the
experimental group. The group that does not experience the treatment or manipulation is called the *control group*. Differences in behavior between the two groups
are then attributed to the treatment. In other experiments, the behavior of a single
group of subjects is compared before and after the treatment or across several treatments. Once again, systematic differences in behavior before and after the treatment
are attributed to the experimental manipulation. In this case each subject serves as
his or her own control.

Control is the key to successful experimentation. The experimenter must exercise
control in selecting the individuals or groups who participate in a study. The participants must be able to bring equivalent competences to the situation. If this condition
is not met, one cannot assume that differences in behavior between groups are due
to the treatment.

The experimenters must control the way a task is presented to the participants
so that such factors as the ability to understand the instructions, the order of events,
and the degree of comfort and familiarity with the setting do not interfere with the
subjects' behavior. Control ensures that changes in the subjects' behaviors do in fact
result from the experimental manipulation.

Suppose we are interested in the impact of unemployment on children and adults
at various ages. We cannot (nor do we want to) cause some people to lose their jobs
and keep others at work. We can, however, compare children of about the same age
and social class whose parents have experienced unemployment with children whose
parents have not. We can compare adolescents and adults who are unemployed with
those who are working.

Assignment to a "treatment" occurs as a result of real-world events. It is the task
of the scientist to compare some of the consequences of this treatment—the experience of unemployment—and to deal with the limitations that are imposed on the
results by the way the individuals arrived in one treatment group or the other to begin
with. The researcher is able to compare children, adolescents, and adults who have
experienced unemployment with those who have not but is not able to say that
unemployment is the only factor that might account for the differences in outcome
that are observed.

The *experimental method* has the advantage of providing conclusions about causal
relationships. If we can show that subjects' behavior changes only when something
about the experimental situation changes, we can conclude that the manipulation has
caused the changes in behavior.

Experiments also have limitations. We cannot be certain about how applicable a
controlled laboratory situation is to the real world. Would the behaviors that are

observed in the laboratory also be observed at home, at school, or at work? Through studies of attachment (which is discussed in chapters 5 and 10) we have learned that infants and young children do not behave the same way in the presence of their mothers as they do when their mothers are absent. This research makes us aware that experimental research with young children that does not allow mothers to be present may produce behavior that differs in quantity, quality, and sequence from the behavior that would be observed under more normal conditions, when the mothers were present.

Experimental studies tend to suggest that event *A* causes response *B*. In many domains of development, however, a multifaceted, reciprocal process promotes change. Just think a moment about the development of romantic relationships among college students. Falling in love depends on many domains and on the two partners' fit or lack of fit in each domain. Romantic attachments may be influenced by physical appearance, shared values, capacity for emotional expressiveness, abilities, temperaments, intelligence, and the reactions of parents and friends, just to name a few factors. Each person reacts to the other, building toward new levels of affection and closeness or pulling away. This is reality. The development of a romantic bond is a complex process. A love relationship is a system. It is sustained and promoted by continuous feedback and interaction between the partners as well as by many other factors, not by one or two external factors that can be said to promote or inhibit romantic attachments.

Many studies of human development are *quasi-experimental;* that is, the researchers study the variable in which they are interested but they do not actually manipulate it. We are interested in studying the effects of certain life events on infants, children, adolescents, or adults, but it would be unethical to deliberately introduce those events into people's lives.

Surveys and Tests

Survey research is a means of collecting specific information from a large number of participants. If people are to respond directly to surveys, they must be able to read and write, unless the survey questions are read to them. The survey method is most commonly used with middle school children, adolescents, and adults. Survey information about infants and toddlers is often collected from parents, child-care workers, physicians, nurses, and others who are responsible for meeting the needs of these young children. Thus surveys have contributed a great deal to our knowledge about the way adults perceive the behaviors and needs of young children.

Survey methods can be used to collect information about attitudes (Do you believe teachers should be permitted to use corporal punishment with their students?); about current behaviors and practices (How many hours per day do you watch television?); about aspirations (What do you hope to do when you graduate from high school?); and about perceptions (How well does your mother/father or son/daughter understand your views?).

Survey questions are prepared in a standard form, and the responses are usually coded according to a prearranged set of categories. In well-designed surveys the questions are stated clearly and offer response choices that are not ambiguous or overlapping. In the most powerful surveys, the sample of subjects is carefully selected to be representative of the population under study. Surveys may be conducted by telephone, through the mail, in classrooms, at work, or in the participants' homes.

Tests are often similar in form to surveys. They consist of groups of questions or problems the person is expected to answer. Usually tests are designed to measure a specific ability or characteristic. You are no doubt familiar with the kinds of tests that are typically given in school. You are presented with a group of items and asked to produce the correct answer or to select the correct answer from among several choices. Intelligence tests and achievement tests are of this nature. A researcher might give these tests along with some other measures in order to learn how intelligence relates to social life, emotions, or self-understanding.

Other tests are designed to measure a variety of psychological constructs, such as creativity, conformity, depression, and extroversion. Some tests are administered to assess whether a person has some form of mental illness, learning disorder, developmental disability, or handicap.

In order to be of use, psychological tests must be reliable and valid. Tests are *reliable* when they provide approximately the same score or the same diagnosis each time a person takes the test. This is not to say that the test should not indicate change when change has occurred. But a person who takes a reliable test on two consecutive days should get approximately the same score on both days unless some deliberate training or intervention has been introduced between them. There ought to be a positive correlation (toward +1.0) between the two scores.

Tests are *valid* when they measure what they claim to measure. The people who design the tests have to define what it is they are trying to measure. They also have to provide evidence that their test really measures this construct (Messick, 1989). Consider the various tests that have been designed to measure intelligence in infants and very young children. The results of these tests are not very closely related to the results of tests of intelligence given in adolescence and adulthood (Bayley, 1970). In other words, correlations between intelligence tests given to infants and those given to the same subjects when they are older tend to be low (nearer to 0.0 than to −1.0 or +1.0). Perhaps the underlying components of intelligence differ in babies and in adolescents and adults. Or perhaps intelligence evolves in so many ways that the intelligence of the adult bears little relation to that of the infant. Or perhaps these infant tests are not really tests of broad, adaptive intelligence, but are measures of sensory processing and central nervous system coordination.

Surveys and tests have certain advantages that make them widely used in developmental research. They allow us to compare the responses of large groups of respondents. Surveys and tests have been designed to address a wide variety of topics. With a prearranged coding or scoring system, many tests can be administered and evaluated without difficulty.

These methods also have limitations. Some surveys create attitudes where none existed before. For example, you might ask sixth-grade children questions about their satisfaction with their school curriculum. The students may answer a lot of questions on this topic, but they may not have given much thought to the issue before. Another problem is the gap between answers to survey questions or scores on tests and actual behavior. Children may say they would rather read than watch television, but in real life they may watch television most of the time and rarely read. Similarly, parents may

In the comfortable atmosphere of their preschool environment, Native American children demonstrate advanced language abilities that might not be evident under the competitive conditions of standardized testing.

say that they allow their children to participate in family decisions, but when it comes to real family decisions, the parents may not give their children much voice.

The use of tests to determine school admissions and placement has come under serious attack (Weinberg, 1989). Some tests have been criticized for putting unfair emphasis on knowledge derived from a white, middle-class, Eurocentric cultural perspective. Some tests have been criticized for putting at a disadvantage children whose first language is not English. Some tests have been criticized for being insensitive to different learning styles and modes of synthesizing information.

Intelligence tests in particular have been criticized because they are used to decide children's educational placement, but they do not encompass the full array of psychological factors associated with social competence and adaptive behavior. Psychological tests continue to be used in research to explore the relationship among developmental domains. Their use in settings such as schools and treatment facilities is becoming increasingly controversial.

Case Study

A case study is an in-depth description of a single person, family, or social group. The purpose of a case study is to describe the behavior of only that person or group. Case studies are usually carried out to describe in detail the experiences of a single person or to examine a phenomenon that does not conform to theoretical predictions. Case studies have been used to examine the sequence of life events that have led up to a certain crisis or major decision. They have been used to document the course of mental disorder and treatment. In some instances, they have been used to illustrate a theoretical construct (Runyan, 1982).

Case studies can be based on a variety of sources of information, including interviews, therapy sessions, prolonged observation, logs, letters, diaries, remembrances, historical documents, and talks with people who know the person or group under study.

Some case studies document the lives of great individuals. In *Gandhi's Truth,* Erik Erikson (1969) analyzed the life of Mohandas Gandhi. Erikson considered Gandhi's childhood, adolescence, and young adulthood as they contributed to Gandhi's personality, to his moral philosophy, and to his behavior as a powerful social leader.

Other case studies describe clinical problems. Sigmund Freud used cases to clarify the origins of some mental disorders. He showed through his cases how the method of psychoanalysis could be used to identify the conflicts that were at the base of the patient's symptoms. In one of his classic cases, Freud analyzed a strong irrational fear of horses in a 5-year-old boy he called Little Hans (Freud, 1909/1955). The boy's fear was so strong that he refused to go out of his house because he thought that a horse in the street would bite him. Freud reasoned that Hans's fear was actually an indirect way of expressing strong psychological conflicts about sex and aggression that the child could not admit to his conscious mind. Freud worked from careful notes kept by the boy's father, who was a physician. Many of these notes are published in the case. Little Hans was treated by his father under Freud's guidance.

Case studies can also focus on social groups, families, and organizations. One of Anna Freud's most famous cases described the attachments that developed among a group of orphans who had lived together in a concentration camp during World War II (Freud & Dann, 1951). The study focused on the children's attachments to one another and their strategies for maintaining their sense of connectedness once they were placed in a more normal social environment.

Case studies have the advantage of illustrating the complexity and uniqueness of individual lives. Studies carried out with large samples often identify general relationships. Case studies provide concrete examples of how these relationships are experienced by specific individuals. Some cases give the details of an experience that is rare or unusual and therefore might not lend itself to a large-scale study. Sometimes the case study brings a problem to the attention of researchers, who then pursue it through other methods.

Case studies have been criticized as unscientific. They are obviously not representative of large groups of individuals. One must be cautious about generalizing the conclusions drawn from a case study to other individuals or groups. If the information that provides the basis of the case study is gathered in a biased or subjective way, the results or conclusions of the study may be of little worth. Finally, critics argue that case studies lack reliability. Two people who do case studies of the same individual may come up with very different views of the events and their significance.

These limitations suggest that one must have a very clear idea of the purpose and a systematic approach to gathering information in order to conduct a case study that meets the standards of scientific observation. At the same time, vividly written, compelling case material has consistently stimulated theory and research in the field of human development.

Interviews

Many case studies are based largely on face-to-face interviews. This method can also be used also to gather data from large numbers of individuals and from people in clinical settings.

Interviews can be highly structured, almost like a verbal survey, or very open-ended, allowing the subject to respond freely to a series of general questions. The success of the interview method depends heavily on the skill of the interviewer. Interviewers are trained to be nonjudgmental as they listen to a person's responses. They try to create rapport with the person by conveying a feeling of trustworthiness and acceptance. In unstructured interviews, the interviewer must make use of this rapport to encourage the person to say more about a question and to share thoughts that may be private or personal.

The interview method has traditionally been associated with clinical research, and it is becoming a major method in the study of cognition and language as well. Piaget's structured interview technique (Piaget, 1929) provides a model for the investigation of conceptual development (see Box 1.1). The researcher who uses this technique asks a child a question, (say, "Are clouds living or dead?") and then follows up on the answer with questions about how the child arrived at his or her conclusion. In other studies, Piaget asked children to solve a problem, and then asked them to explain how they arrived at the solution. The child becomes an informant about his or her own conceptual capacities. This approach has been adapted in the study of moral development, interpersonal development, and prosocial behavior. The interview method has the advantage of allowing individuals to contribute their own views on the topic being studied. They can tell the interviewer what is important to them, why they might choose one alternative over another, or what they think is wrong with the investigator's view of the situation. People may also, of course, present themselves in the way they want the interviewer to see them; when they do, they are said to be exhibiting a *self-presentation bias*.

A person's responses are vulnerable to influence by the interviewer. By smiling, nodding, frowning, or looking away, the interviewer can deliberately or inadvertently communicate approval or disapproval. There is a fine line between establishing rapport and influencing responses.

The advantages and disadvantages of the five research methods are summarized in Table 1.1.

Designs for Studying Change

The primary concern of developmental research is to describe and account for patterns of continuity and change. Four research approaches have been used to examine change: retrospective studies, cross-sectional studies, longitudinal studies, and cohort sequential studies.

Retrospective Studies

A researcher engaged in a retrospective study asks the participants to report on experiences from an earlier time in their lives. Many early studies of child rearing used parents' recollections of their parenting techniques to evaluate patterns of child care. Researchers who studied the effects of stress during pregnancy often asked women to recall their emotional states before, during, and after their child was born. Investigators of personality development use retrospective data by asking adolescent or adult subjects to recall important events of their childhood.

Box 1.1   Piaget's Interview Method

Piaget's use of the clinical interview method to pursue a young child's cognitive reasoning can be seen in two excerpts from his works. In the first, Piaget is exploring a 5-year-old child's understanding of dreams.

> *Where does the dream come from?*—I think you sleep so well that you dream.—*Does it come from us or from outside?*—From outside.—*What do we dream with?*—I don't know.—*With the hands? . . . With nothing?*—Yes, with nothing.—*When you are in bed and you dream, where is the dream?*— In my bed, under the blanket. I don't really know. If it was in my stomach(!) the bones would be in the way and I shouldn't see it.—*Is the dream in your head?*—It is I that am in the dream: it isn't in my head(!) When you dream, you don't know you are in the bed. You know you are walking. You are in the dream. You are in bed, but you don't know you are.   *[1929:97–98]*

Here Piaget is describing a 7-year-old child's understanding of class inclusion:

> *You present the child with an open box that contains wooden beads. The child knows they are all wooden because he handles them, touching each and finding that it is made of wood. Most of these beads are brown, but a few are white. The problem we pose is simply this: are there more brown beads or more wooden beads? Let us call A the brown beads, B the wooden beads: then the problem is simply that of the inclusion of A in B. This is a very difficult problem before the age of 7 years. The child states that all the beads are wooden,*
> *states that most of them are brown and a few are white, but if you ask him if there are more brown beads or more wooden beads he immediately answers: "There are more brown ones because there are only two or three white ones." So you say: "Listen, this is not what I am asking. I don't want to know whether there are more brown beads or more white beads, I want to know whether there are more brown beads or more wooden beads." And, in order to make it easier, I take an empty box and place it next to the one with the beads and I ask: "If I were to put the wooden beads into that box would any remain in this one?" The child answers: "No, none would be left because they are all wooden." Then I say: "If I were to take the brown beads and put them into that box, would any be left in this one?" The child replies: "Of course, two or three white ones would remain." Apparently he has now understood the situation, the fact that all the beads are wooden and that some are not brown. So I ask him once more: "Are there more brown beads or more wooden beads?" Now it is evident that the child begins to understand the problem, sees that there is indeed a problem, that matters are not as simple as they seemed at first. As we watch him we observe that he is thinking very hard. Finally he concludes, "But there are still more brown beads; if you take the brown ones away, only two or three white beads remain."   [1963: 283–299]*

Source: "The attainment of invariants and reversible operations in the development of thinking," by J. Piaget, *Social Research*, 30, 283–299. Reprinted by permission.

This approach produces a record of what a person has retained of past events. We cannot be certain if these events really occurred as they are remembered. For that matter, we cannot be certain that they occurred at all. Piaget described a vivid memory from his second year of life:

> *I was sitting in my pram, which my nurse was pushing in the Champs Elysees, when a man tried to kidnap me. I was held in by the strap fastened around me while my nurse bravely tried to stand between me and the thief. She received various scratches, and I can still see vaguely those on her face.*   [Piaget, 1951:188]

Table 1.1   Advantages and Disadvantages of Five Methods of Developmental Research

Method	Definition	Advantages	Disadvantages
Observation	Systematic description of behavior	Documents the variety of ongoing behavior; captures what happens naturally, without experimental intervention	Time-consuming; requires careful training of observers; observer may interfere with what would normally occur
Experimentation	Analysis of cause-effect relations by manipulation of some conditions while others are held constant	Permits testing of causal hypotheses; permits control and isolation of specific variables	Laboratory findings may not be applicable to other settings; focuses on unidirectional model of causality
Surveys and tests	Standard questions administered to large groups	Permits data collection from large samples; requires little training; very flexible	Wording and way of presenting questions can influence responses; response may not be closely related to behavior; tests may not be appropriate for use in schools or clinical settings
Case study	In-depth description of a single person, family, or group	Focuses on complexity and unique experiences of individual; permits analysis of unusual cases	Lacks generalizability; conclusions may reflect bias of investigator; hard to replicate
Interviews	Face-to-face interaction in which each person can give a full account of his or her views	Provides complex first-person account	Vulnerable to investigator bias

Thirteen years later, when Piaget was 15, the nurse joined a religious order. She wrote to his parents and returned a watch they had given her for protecting Jean from the kidnapper. She confessed that she had made up the story even to the point of scratching her own face. Piaget believed he had created the visual memory from the story his parents had told him about the incident.

In retrospective studies, participants are asked to describe past experiences. In this study, the interviewer asks a couple how their lives have been influenced by changes in their neighborhood during the past ten years.

The passage of time may change the significance of certain past events in a person's memory. There is also some evidence to suggest that as we gain new levels of cognitive complexity or change our attitudes, we reorganize our memories of the past in order to bring them into line with our current level of understanding (Goethals & Frost, 1978).

Cross-Sectional Designs

Studies that compare people of different ages or different social backgrounds or different school or community settings at one point in time are called cross-sectional designs. Such designs are quite commonly used in research on child development. Investigators may compare children of different levels of biological maturity or different chronological ages to learn how a particular developmental domain changes with age.

One such study explored differences in the way children aged 7, 9, and 12 were able to reason about problems in which more than one outcome was possible (Horobin & Acredolo, 1989). Even though the younger children were aware that there were multiple solutions, they were more likely than older children to settle on one solution and insist that it was correct.

The limitation of the cross-sectional method is that it blurs the pattern of individual development. With respect to the study on reasoning, the cross-sectional approach tells us that most 12-year-olds are more flexible in their reasoning than most 7-year-olds. It does not tell us how the children who were the most flexible at age 7 perform at age 12 in comparison with those who were at least flexible.

Longitudinal Studies

A longitudinal study involves repeated observations at different times. The time between observations may be brief, as immediately after birth and two or three days after birth. Or observations may be repeated over the entire life course, as in Leo Terman's longitudinal study of gifted children (Terman, 1925; Terman & Oden, 1947, 1959; Oden, 1968).

Longitudinal studies have the advantage of allowing us to consider the course of development of a group of individuals. We can discover how certain characteristics of children in infancy or toddlerhood relate to those same characteristics when individuals reach adolescence or adulthood. We can also learn whether certain qualities of childhood, such as intelligence or outgoingness, are relevant to overall social adjustment or life satisfaction in later years.

Longitudinal studies can be very difficult to complete, especially if they are intended to cover a significant age period, such as the years from childhood into adulthood. Over this span of time, participants drop out of the study, investigators lose funding or interest in the project, and methods become outdated. Questions that once seemed important are no longer seen as vital. One of the greatest limitations of these studies is that they focus on only one generation of subjects. Historical and social factors that may influence the course of this group's development will be inextricably intertwined in the observations. You cannot tell if all people growing up at all times in history exhibit the pattern of changes that characterize this one particular group.

Cohort Sequential Designs

A cohort sequential design combines the cross-sectional and the longitudinal approaches into one method of study (Schaie, 1965). Groups of participants, called cohorts, are selected because they are a certain number of years apart in age. For example, we might begin with a group of adolescents who are 11, 14, and 17. Every three years, this group would be interviewed until the 11-year-olds have turned 17. In addition, every three years a new group of 11-year-olds would be added to the study.

This combination of a longitudinal and a cross-sectional design is a very powerful developmental research method. It produces immediate cross-sectional data, longitudinal data after three and six years, and a comparison of children who were the same age (11, 14, or 17) at three different times. This third comparison permits us to identify social and historical factors that may influence age-related differences. The elements of a cohort sequential design are seen in Figure 1.7.

Evaluating Existing Research

In addition to collecting new data, social scientists give considerably scholarly effort to reviewing and evaluating existing research. Statistical techniques allow us to compare the findings of a variety of studies so that we may identify patterns of results. As a student, you may be asked to review research findings on some topic that is of interest to you. Such a review gives one a broader point of view that one could get by concentrating on a single area of observation. Most researchers use this method to keep well informed on the research being reported in their subject area and analyze the work of others to generate well-founded conclusions about something of interest for study. The study, analysis, and evaluation of the current research literature constitute a special skill in its own right.

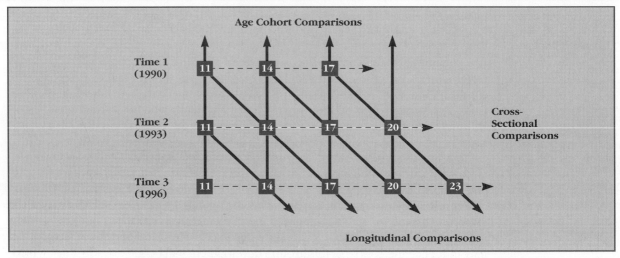

Figure 1.7   Elements of a Cohort Sequential Design

Ethics

In conducting research with living beings, and especially with children, social scientists continually confront ethical questions. *Ethics* refers to principles of conduct that are founded on a society's moral code. As part of their professional socialization, researchers are obligated to maintain humane, morally acceptable treatment of all living subjects.

Ethical guidelines for research with human subjects encompass a variety of considerations. Because we are concerned with subjects' right to privacy, the identities of individual subjects must be kept confidential. Subjects must not be coerced into participating in a research project, and a refusal to participate should have no negative consequences. If children in a classroom, for example, decide that they do not want to participate in a research project, or if their parents do not give permission for them to participate, these children should not be shamed, given an undesirable alternate assignment, or given a lower grade.

Researchers must protect subjects from unnecessary painful physical and emotional experiences, including shame, failure, and social rejection. Researchers must weigh the benefits of the new information they may discover in a particular study against the potential risks or harm to the subjects. Two questions must guide the researcher's decisions:

1. How would you feel if you, or one of your family members, were a subject in this study?
2. Can the problem be studied in ways that do not involve pain, deception, or emotional or physical stress?

The American Psychological Association has published a guide for researchers titled *Ethical Principles in the Conduct of Research with Human Participants* (1982).

Table 1.2	Average Remaining Lifetime at Various Ages, 1900–1985						
Age	*1985*	*1978*	*1968*	*1954*	*1939–1941*	*1929–1931*	*1900–1902*
At birth	74.7	73.3	70.2	69.6	63.6	59.3	49.2
65 years	16.7	16.3	14.6	14.4	12.8	12.3	11.9
75 years	10.6	10.4	9.1	9.0	7.6	7.3	7.1
80 years	8.1	8.1	6.8	6.9	5.7	5.4	5.3

Source: U.S. Bureau of the Census, *Demographic and socioeconomic aspects of aging in the United States,* Current Population Reports, series P-23, no. 138 (Washington, DC: U.S. Government Printing Office, 1984), p. 59, and *Statistical Abstract of the United States, 1988,* 108th ed. (Washington, D.C.: U.S. Government Printing Office, 1987).

This guide requires that human subjects be told about all aspects of the research that might influence their decision to participate. They must be free to withdraw from the study at any time. They are entitled to a full explanation of the study once it has been completed. When the subjects are children, their parents must be given this information and must approve their children's participation. Most schools, day-care centers, hospitals, nursing homes, and other treatment centers also have their own review procedures to determine whether or not they will permit research to be carried out with the people in their programs.

The scientific process is complex and requires the efforts of large numbers of people who are committed to the task of gathering information to guide their thinking. Theories are often difficult to understand and test. However, a good theory points us in the direction appropriate for making observations. By exploring theories of human development and evaluating the empirical evidence available for testing them, we should arrive at a clearer understanding of the nature of our own development. A combination of theory and research is the most effective way we know to build our knowledge base concerning human development in general and our personal development in particular.

The Life Span

The task of mapping one's future depends on how long one expects to live. Naturally, we can make only rough predictions. We know that our lives may be cut short by a disaster, accident, or illness. However, our best guess about how long we will live is based on the average life expectancy of others in our group.

Table 1.2 presents data on the average life span of people in the United States during seven time periods. Look first at the top row of the table, labeled "At birth." The average life expectancy of people born at the turn of the century was about 49 years. For people born at the time of the stock market crash and the beginning of the Depression, the average life expectancy appears to be about 59 years. The average life expectancy of people born at the beginning of World War II is around 64. The average life expectancy of people born in 1978 is approximately 73 years, and rises to almost

Table 1.3   Projections of Life Expectation at Birth and at Age 65, by Sex, Prepared by the Social Security Administration, November 1981 (Figures in parentheses represent alternative low and high projections.)

Age and Sex	1980* (Base Year)	2000	2050	Increase 1980–2000	Increase 1980–2050
At birth:					
Male	69.8	72.9(71.4–75.9)	75.0(72.4–80.2)	3.1(1.6–6.1)	5.2(2.6–10.4)
Female	77.7	81.1(79.4–84.9)	83.6(80.6–90.6)	3.4(1.7–7.2)	5.9(2.9–12.9)
Difference†	7.9	8.2(8.0–9.0)	8.6(8.2–10.4)	0.3(0.1–1.1)	0.7(0.3–2.5)
At age 65:					
Male	14.3	15.8(15.0–17.4)	17.3(15.7–20.8)	1.5(0.7–3.1)	3.0(1.4–6.5)
Female	18.7	21.1(19.8–24.2)	23.2(20.8–29.3)	2.4(1.1–5.5)	4.5(2.1–10.6)
Difference†	4.4	5.3(4.8–6.8)	5.9(5.1–8.5)	0.9(0.4–2.4)	1.5(0.7–4.1)

*Assumed to equal the estimated figures for 1979.
†Excess of female over male figure.
Source: U.S. Social Security Administration, Office of the Actuary, *Social Security Area Population Projections, 1981,* by Joseph F. Faber and John C. Wilkin, Actuarial Study no. 85. (Washington, D.C.: U.S. Government Printing Office, July 1981, Table 18.

75 years for those born in 1985. As we look across these generations, it is quite clear that the length of life has been increasing for more and more people.

The next few lines in Table 1.2 show us something else. People who had reached advanced ages (65, 75, and 80) in each of the time periods (1900–1902, 1929–1931, 1939–1941, 1954, 1968, 1978, and 1985) had a much longer life expectancy than people who were born in those time periods. Thus someone who was 65 at the turn of the century (born in 1835) lived to be 76.9; someone who was 75 at that time (born in 1825) lived to be 82.1; and someone who was 80 years old during that period (born in 1820) lived to be 85.3. These figures suggest that hazards during the early and middle years of life shorten the average life expectancy at birth. Infant mortality was a major factor in limiting the life expectancy at the turn of the century. Many women in their early adult years died in childbirth. Respiratory diseases were a serious threat to life during the middle adult years. If one survived these common killers, one's chance for a long later life increased.

Using these kinds of statistics to estimate the life span, we are able to compute rather accurate projections of changes in its length. The average person born in 1985 can expect to live 25.5 years longer than one who was born in 1900. The average life expectancy of people born in 1985 is 74.7. At the extreme end of the life span, however, we find no dramatic increase in life expectancy. People who were 65 in 1985 (born in 1920) will live to be about 82; people who were 75 in 1985 (born in 1910) will live to be 85.6; and people who were 80 in 1985 (born in 1905) will live to be 88.1.

The Social Security Administration makes projections of life expectations that are quite reliable. These data, showing the life expectations for men and women separately, are seen in Table 1.3. They show that overall, men do not live as long as women. They die younger around the world as well as in the various regions of the United States. In the appendix you will find data on national patterns of life expectancy by race and sex as well as regional patterns within the United States and international comparisons.

You can see that according to the government statistics, the life span of both men and women is expected to increase from 1980 to 2050. The question arises as to whether this increase will continue or whether there is an upper limit to the length of the life span. There are theories supporting both sides. Bernice Neugarten (1981), a noted human development scholar, argues that if the rates of advance in such fields as medicine and nutrition proceed for the next 40 years at the rate at which they have progressed for the last 60, by 2020 many people may be living to be 120 years old. Others point out that the primary killers of infants, adults, and aging persons have already been brought under control and that there is little room left for expansion in the human life span, which they view as genetically limited. They argue that the best we can hope for is a healthier, rather than a longer, period of life.

When you try to estimate your own life expectancy, you must consider projections for people in your country, region, and state and in your age, educational, racial, and sex groups. The more careful your comparisons, the more accurate your estimate is likely to be. Individual lifestyle factors are also associated with longevity. In a study of longevity among healthy older men, the strongest predictors of survival into old age were smoking patterns and complexity of daily life (Rosenfeld, 1978). Men who had never smoked or had stopped smoking by the time they were in their late 60s and 70s were more likely to be among the survivors. The daily lives of survivors were characterized by high levels of organization and complexity. Both of these factors are largely a matter of personal control, suggesting that the individual does play a part in influencing his or her longevity.

Many of our most important life decisions are made with either an implicit or explicit assumption about how long we expect to live. The way we feel about ourselves, our activities, and our relationships is often guided by underlying assumptions about the point we have reached in life.

Consider a black American male born in 1986; he can expect to live to age 65. A white American female born in 1986 can expect to live to age 79. The black male will grow up looking at the years after about age 55 or 60 as old age. The white female will probably not consider herself to be in old age until she reaches about 70. These differences in outlook, coupled with actual differences in health and resources, will affect the way these two people regard themselves and go about their daily activities in middle and later life. The best advice one can give here is to make as accurate an estimate as possible while you explore the implications of various possibilities.

☐ Chapter Summary

Psychosocial theory emphasizes interaction among the somatic, ego, and societal systems. As a result of maturation and change in each of these systems, individuals' beliefs about themselves and their relationships are modified. Although each life story is unique, we can identify important common patterns, allowing us to anticipate the future and to understand one another.

Scientific process results in a body of knowledge that informs our understanding of human development. Scientific observation must be objective, repeatable, and systematic. Five principal research methods are naturalistic observation, experimentation, surveys and tests, case studies, and interviews. Each has its advantages and disadvantages, but all provide special insight about continuity and change over the life span. Research design is also important to the study of change. Four significant designs are retrospective studies, cross-sectional designs, longitudinal studies, and cohort sequential designs. The method and design of research have a powerful effect on how the findings are interpreted.

Demographic information about the life span stimulates thought about one's own life expectancy. In the United States, average life expectancy has increased by almost fifty percent in this century. This dramatic change affects how each of us views our own future. We need to study human development within a constantly changing context. We can never be satisfied that the information established in earlier periods will hold true for future generations.

References

American Psychological Association (1982). *Ethical principles in the conduct of research with human participants.* Washington, D.C.

Bayley, N. (1970). Development of mental abilities. In P. H. Mussen (ed.), *Carmichael's manual of child psychology* (3rd ed., vol. 1). New York: Wiley.

Erikson, E. H. (1963). *Childhood and society* (2nd ed.). New York: Norton.

Erikson, E. H. (1969). *Gandhi's truth: On the origins of militant nonviolence.* New York: Norton.

Freud, A., & Dann, S. (1951). An experiment in group upbringing. In R. Eissler, A. Freud, H. Hartmann, & E. Kris (eds.), *The psychoanalytic study of the child,* vol. 6. New York: International Universities Press.

Freud, S. (1955). An analysis of a phobia in a five-year-old boy. In J. Strachey (ed.), *The standard edition of the complete psychological works of Sigmund Freud,* vol. 10. London: Hogarth Press. (First German ed. 1909).

Goethals, G. R., & Frost, M. (1978). Value change and the recall of earlier values. *Bulletin of the Psychonomic Society, 11,* 73–74.

Horobin, K., & Acredolo, C. (1989). The impact of probability judgments on reasoning about multiple possibilities. *Child Development, 60*(1), 183–200.

Kessen, W. (1965). *The child.* New York: Wiley.

Kochanska, G., Kuczynski, L., & Radke-Yarrow, M. (1989). Correspondence between mothers' self-reported and observed child-rearing practices. *Child Development, 60*(1), 56–63.

Messick, S. (1989). Meaning and values in test validation: The science and ethics of assessment. *Educational Researcher, 18,* 5–11.

Neugarten, B. L. (1981). Growing old in 2020: How will it be different? *National Forum, 61*(3), 28–30.

Oden, M. H. (1968). Fulfillment of promise: 40 year follow-up of the Terman gifted group. *Genetic Psychology Monographs, 77,* 3–93.

Piaget, J. (1929). *The child's conception of physical causality.* New York: Harcourt, Brace. (Originally published in French in 1926).

Piaget, J. (1951). *Play, dreams, and imitation in childhood.* New York: Norton.

Piaget, J. (1963). The attainment of invariants and reversible operations in the development of thinking. *Social Research, 30,* 283–299.

Rosenfeld, A. H. (1978). *New views on older lives.* DHEW Publication no. ADM 78–687. Washington, D.C.: U.S. Government Printing Office.

Runyan, W. M. (1982). *Life histories and psychobiography: Explorations in theory and method.* New York: Oxford University Press.

Schaie, K. W. (1965). A general model for the study of developmental problems. *Psychological Bulletin, 64,* 92–107.

Terman, L. M. (1925). *Genetic studies of genius.* Stanford, Calif.: Stanford University Press.

Terman, L. M., & Oden, M. H. (1947). *The gifted child grows up: Twenty-five years' follow-up of a superior group.* Stanford, Calif.: Stanford University Press.

Terman, L. M., & Oden, M. H. (1959). *The gifted group at mid-life: Thirty-five years' follow-up of the superior child.* Stanford, Calif.: Stanford University Press.

Weinberg, R. A. (1989). Intelligence and IQ: Landmark issues and great debates. *American Psychologist* (special issue: Children and Their Development: Knowledge Base, Research Agenda, and Social Policy Application), *44*(2), 98–104.

Chapter Two

Psychosocial theory emphasizes the natural tension between the individual and the environment. At each stage of life, new strengths emerge and a new balance is struck.

Psychosocial Theory

What Is a Theory?

A *theory* is a logical system of general concepts that provides a framework for organizing and understanding observations. The sciences have their formal theories, and we all have our informal, intuitive theories about our social lives. In this chapter we will define the concept of theory and introduce the basic concepts of psychosocial theory, which provides the integrating framework for our analysis of human development.

Usually theories are built from questions that are raised about observations. For example, your friend Janet tells you she has decided she is not going to go to a party with you. She says she just doesn't feel like it. You find her explanation incomplete and her behavior out of character, because Janet is usually very sociable. You may generate a hypothesis of your own about why Janet is not going to the party. A *hypothesis* generally makes a prediction on the basis of an underlying theory. If a hypothesis is tested and found to be correct, the theory from which the hypothesis is derived is supported. Your hypothesis will be linked to your intuitive theory of social behavior. You may believe that people choose their behavior in an effort to avoid rejection or win acceptance. With this theoretical orientation, you may hypothesize that Janet is avoiding the party because she does not want to be rejected by someone who will be there.

Theories are constructed to organize and interpret observations about which people desire more knowledge. Theories help us identify orderly relationships among many diverse events. They guide us to those factors that will have explanatory power and identify those that will not. In the area of personality development, for example, one theory may point to dreams and slips of the tongue as data worth observing, while another may direct our attention to goals and aspirations. Different theories are likely to address the same observation from a variety of perspectives. Some theories about development emphasize social roles, some emphasize cognition, and others emphasize motivation.

Individuals experience life as an integration of all of these factors. An adequate theory of human development should emphasize the interrelationships of the somatic, ego, and societal systems, discussed in Chapter 1. It is the way these systems function together that exerts the greatest influence on human behavior. To evaluate a theory we must answer three questions.

1. *Which phenomena is the theory trying to explain?*   If a theory is being used to explain intellectual development, it may include hypotheses about the evolution of the brain, the growth of logical thinking, or the capacity for symbolism. We are less likely to expect such a theory to explain fears, motives, or friendship.

Jean Piaget (1950) offered a developmental theory of the origins of logical thought. He described a predictable sequence of naturally occurring stages, each with its unique strategies for making meaning out of experiences. His theory has helped us to understand how young children differ from adults and how they interpret and explain events. The theory is generally not used to explain why certain fears persist or how couples achieve a sense of intimacy.

Understanding the focus of the theory helps to identify its *range of applicability*. This is not to say that principles from one theory will have no relevance to another area of knowledge. Usually, however, we begin to evaluate a theory in terms of the events it is intended to explain.

2. *What assumptions does the theory make?*   *Assumptions* are the guiding premises underlying the logic of a theory. In order to evaluate a theory, you must first understand what its assumptions are. Charles Darwin assumed that lower life forms "progressed" to higher forms in the process of evolution. Freud assumed that all behavior was motivated and that the unconscious was a "storehouse" of motives and wishes.

The assumptions of any theory may or may not be correct. The assumption that the sun is the center of the solar system leads to different explanations than does the assumption that the earth is the center of the universe. Assumptions may be influenced by the cultural context, by the sample of observations from which the theorist has drawn inferences, by the current knowledge base of the field, and by the intellectual capacities of the theorist.

3. *What does the theory predict?*   Theories add new levels of understanding by suggesting causal relationships, by unifying diverse observations, and by identifying the importance of events that may have gone unnoticed. Theories of human development offer explanations regarding the origins and functions of human behavior and the changes that can be expected in it from one period of life to the next.

We expect a theory of human development to provide explanations about four issues:

1. What are the mechanisms that account for growth from conception through old age, and to what extent do these mechanisms vary across the life span?
2. What factors underlie stability and change across the life span?
3. How do physical, cognitive, emotional, and social functions interact? How do these interactions account for the mixture of thoughts, feelings, health states, and social relationships?
4. How does the social context affect individual development?

The Psychosocial Perspective

Psychosocial theory provides a rich, thought-provoking structure within which to explore major issues of growth and development across the life span. It combines three powerful features that are not clearly articulated or integrated in other analyses of development.

First, the theory addresses growth across the life span. It identifies and differentiates among issues of central importance from infancy through old age.

Second, the theory assumes that we are not totally at the mercy of biological and environmental influences; we have the capacity to contribute to our own psychological

Biographical Sketch

Erik H. Erikson   1902–

Erik Erikson   Joan Erikson   Sigmund Freud   Anna Freud

Erik Erikson was born in Frankfurt, Germany, in 1902. His Danish parents were divorced before his birth. Erikson's mother married his pediatrician, Dr. Homburger, before Erikson was 5. Erikson grew up in the home of this prosperous physician. In early adulthood he would serve as teacher, student, and patient in the household of another physician, Sigmund Freud.

At age 18, after completing gymnasium (a German secondary school that prepares students to study at a university), Erikson traveled around Europe for a year. He spent several months on the shores of Lake Constance, reading, writing, and enjoying the beauty of the setting. When he returned home, he enrolled in art school, and he pursued this study for the next few years. He traveled to Florence, Italy, where he concluded that he was not going to succeed as an artist. He and some of his friends, including Peter Blos, wandered around for a time, searching for a sense of themselves and their personal resources (Coles, 1970).

Erikson and Blos accepted an invitation to teach in a private school that had been founded by Anna Freud for the children of students at the Vienna Psychoanalytic Society. In Vienna Erikson studied the techniques of psychoanalysis and underwent a training analysis with Anna Freud. His decision to become an analyst was encouraged by the supportive, influential analysts of the Psychoanalytic Society, who were eager to help promising people enter the field they had created. Erikson's admission to training was unusual in that he had neither a university nor a medical degree.

After analytic training and marriage, Erikson set off for America. He became a child analyst on the faculty of the Harvard Medical School. Three years later he went to Yale, and two years after that he went off to study the Sioux Indians in South Dakota. After completing his research observations on the Sioux, he opened a clinical practice in San Francisco. During this time he also conducted a study of the Yurok Indians. In 1942, Erikson became a faculty member at the University of California at Berkeley.

In 1950 he left Berkeley and became an analyst on the staff of the Austen Riggs Center in Stockbridge, Massachusetts. In the late 1950s Erikson became a professor of human development at Harvard. He retained this position until his retirement. Today, in their late eighties, he and his wife, Joan, continue to expand their analysis of human development. Their book *Vital Involvement in Old Age* (1986) probes the life histories of a number of octogenarians and examines issues associated with a fully developed humanness in old age.

Erikson's major theoretical work, *Childhood and Society,* was synthesized while he was at Berkeley and published in 1950, when he was 48. In this work Erikson presents a psychosocial theory of development. A revised edition was published in 1963. He has expanded and revised his theory in many other books and papers. In two biographies he has applied the principles of psychosocial theory to analyses of the lives of Martin Luther and Mohandas Gandhi (Erikson, 1958, 1969).

Erikson's life story reveals him to be a person who took a personal route to realize his potential. His writings blend compassion, keen observational skills, a poetic synthesis of ideas and experiences, and a persistent questioning about the interrelationships of individual lives and societies. In the course of his own intellectual development he has mastered several disciplines, including psychoanalysis, cultural anthropology, psychology, theology, and history. In his search for deeper understanding he remains open to all human behavior that will inform his questioning mind, drawing on life histories, clinical cases, and fictional characters.

As observations from his clinical practice raised questions that the research literature was unable to answer, he turned to the study of traditional cultures and historical figures. He followed his ideas, pursuing observations that would help him clarify his analysis of human development. Through his clinical and theoretical writings, he demonstrates that the evolved structure of each individual, although very complex, can be studied and understood. He identified a process, the psychosocial crisis, that links individuals and the societies they create in a fundamental way that produces development.

Erikson has won the Pulitzer Prize and the National Book Award. In 1984 he received the G. Stanley Hall Award from the Division of Developmental Psychology of the American Psychological Association for distinguished contributions to developmental psychology. ■

development at every stage of life. The theory assumes that people integrate, organize, and conceptualize their own experiences in such a way as to protect themselves and direct the course of their own lives.

Third, the theory takes into consideration the active contribution of culture to individual growth. At each life stage, cultural goals and aspirations, social expectations and requirements, and the opportunities that the culture provides make demands on individuals. These demands draw forth reactions. These reactions influence the systems within the person's capabilities which will be developed. This vital link between the individual and the world is a key mechanism of development.

Societies encourage patterns of parenting, provide unique opportunities for education, and communicate values and attitudes toward basic domains of behavior, including sexuality, intimacy, and work. These patterns develop to preserve and protect a culture. Each society has its own view of the qualities that enter into maturity. These qualities are infused into the lives of individuals and help determine the direction of human growth within the society.

One of the great theorists who identified and developed psychosocial theory is

Erik H. Erikson. Erikson initially was trained as a psychosexual theorist. An interest in the effects of sexuality on functioning and in the ideas of the biologist Julian Huxley led Erikson to focus on the influence of social instincts on functioning.

Basic Concepts of Psychosocial Theory

Psychosocial theory represents human development as a product of the interaction between individual (*psycho*) needs and abilities and societal (*social*) expectations and demands. The theory accounts for the patterns of individual development that emerge out of the more global process of psychosocial evolution.

Julian Huxley (1941, 1942) used the term *psychosocial evolution* to refer to those human abilities that have allowed us to gather knowledge from our ancestors and transmit it to our descendants. Child-rearing practices, education, and modes of communication transmit information and ways of thinking from one generation to the next. At the same time, people learn how to develop new information, new ways of thinking, and new ways of teaching their discoveries to others. Through this process, according to Huxley, psychosocial evolution has proceeded at a rapid pace, bringing with it changes in technology and ideology that have allowed us to create and modify the physical and social environments in which we live.

Psychosocial evolution has its basis in the biological system. Over millions of years, humans have evolved complex mechanisms with which to create and adapt to social conditions. We would extend Huxley's definition of psychosocial evolution to include all the biologically driven processes that have led us to build civilizations and create our own lives in relationships with others. The biological system is of fundamental importance in determining how people experience life, what they are capable of, and how their potential may be directed. Biology often has a great deal to do with what we experience psychologically and when we experience it.

The theory of psychosocial development offers an organizational framework for considering individual development within the more all-encompassing perspective of psychosocial evolution. The transmission of values and knowledge across generations requires the maturation of individuals who are capable of internalizing knowledge, adapting it, and transferring it to others. People change and grow systematically, enhancing their potential for carrying their own and succeeding generations forward.

Psychosocial theory, as we view it, is based on six organizing concepts: (1) stages of development, (2) developmental tasks, (3) psychosocial crisis, (4) a central process for resolving the crisis of each stage, (5) a radiating network of significant relationships, and (6) coping—the new behavior people generate to meet the challenges and build the relationships of their lives. Figure 2.1 shows development as a building process. The structure grows larger as the radius of significant relationships expands and as the achievements of earlier stages are integrated into behaviors of the next stage of development.

At each stage the accomplishments from the previous stages serve as resources to be applied toward mastery of the challenges presented by the mixture of developmental tasks, central process, psychosocial crisis, and significant relationships. The

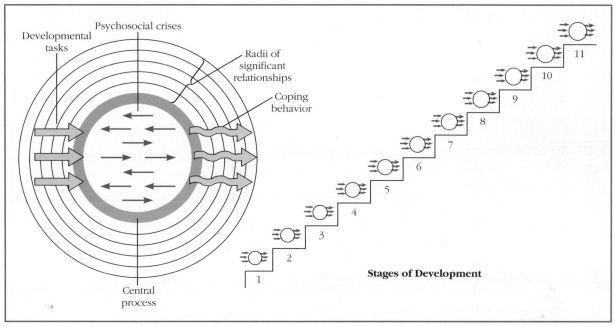

Figure 2.1　　Six Basic Concepts of Psychosocial Theory

interplay of these factors provides the experiential base for new learning, and therefore for development. Each stage is unique and leads to the acquisition of new skills related to new capabilities.

Stages of Development

A *stage of development* is a period of life that is characterized by a specific underlying organization. A wide variety of behaviors can be viewed as an expression of the underlying structure of each stage. Every stage has some characteristics that differentiate it from preceding and succeeding stages. Stage theories propose a specific direction for development. Each new stage incorporates the gains made during earlier stages (Davison et al., 1980; Fischer & Silvern, 1985; Flavell, 1982; Levin, 1986; Miller, 1989).

The stage concept suggests areas of emerging competence or conflict that may explain a range of behaviors. To some extent, you can verify the stage concept through your analysis of your own past. You probably can recall earlier periods when you were very preoccupied by efforts first to gain your parents' approval, then to win acceptance by your peers, and later to understand yourself. These concerns may have appeared all-encompassing at the time, but eventually each gave way to a new preoccupation. At each stage the person is confronted with a unique problem that requires the integration of personal needs and skills with the social demands of the culture. The end product is a new orienting mode and a new set of capabilities for engaging in interactions with others.

	1	2	3	4	5	6	7	8
8. Maturity								Ego integrity vs. Despair
7. Adulthood							Genera-tivity vs. Stagnation	
6. Young Adulthood						Intimacy vs. Isolation		
5. Puberty and Adolescence					Identity vs. Role confusion			
4. Latency				Industry vs. Inferiority				
3. Locomotor–Genital			Initiative vs. Guilt					
2. Muscular–Anal		Autonomy vs. Shame, doubt						
1. Oral–Sensory	Basic trust vs. Mistrust							

Figure 2.2   Erikson's Psychosocial Stages
Source: Erik H. Erikson, *Childhood and Society,* 2nd ed. New York: Norton, 1963, p. 273.

Erikson (1950/1963) proposed eight stages of psychosocial development. The conception of these stages can be traced in part to the stages of psychosexual development proposed by Freud and in part to Erikson's own observations and rich mode of thinking.

Figure 2.2 is the chart Erikson produced in *Childhood and Society* to describe the stages of psychosocial development. The boxes identify the main psychosocial ego conflicts of the various stages. These ego conflicts produce new ego skills.

The concept of psychosocial stages of development is very good as far as it goes, but Erikson's roadmap seems incomplete. If the idea of psychosocial evolution has any validity—and we believe it does—new stages can be expected to develop as a culture evolves.

We have identified 11 stages of psychosocial development, each associated with an approximate age range: (1) prenatal, from conception to birth; (2) infancy, from birth to 2 years; (3) toddlerhood, from 2 to 4 years; (4) early school age, 4 to 6 years;

(5) middle school age, 6 to 12 years; (6) early adolescence, 12 to 18 years; (7) later adolescence, 18 to 22 years; (8) early adulthood, 22 to 34 years; (9) middle adulthood, 34 to 60 years; (10) later adulthood, 60 to 75; and (11) very old age, 75 until death.

By discussing a prenatal stage, two stages of adolescent development, and very old age, we are adding three stages to the ones Erikson proposed. This revision is a product of our analysis of the research literature, our observations through research and practice, discussions with colleagues, and suggestions from other stage theorists.

The elaboration of psychosocial theory by the addition of three new stages provides a good demonstration of the process of theory construction. Theories of human development emerge and change within a cultural and historical context. Patterns of biological evolution and psychosocial evolution occur within a cultural frame of reference. The extension of the adolescent period, for example, is a product of changes in the timing of onset of puberty in modern society, the expanding need for education and training before entry in the world of work, related changes in the structure of the educational system, and the variety of life choices that are available in our society in regard to work, marriage, parenting, and ideology. Our observations relating to the life circumstances and preoccupations of certain age groups lead to the clarification of new stages of development.

Figure 2.3 shows the 11 stages of psychosocial development we have identified. The age range of each stage is only an approximation. The person moves from one stage to another after psychosocial events have occurred rather than because of chronological age. Each person has his or her own timetable for growth.

An assumption of this and other stage theories is that the psychological development that takes place at each stage will have a significant effect on all subsequent stages. The stages are viewed as a sequence. Although one can anticipate issues that will occur at a later stage, one passes through the stages in an orderly pattern of growth.

Erikson (1963) proposed that the stages of development follow the *epigenetic principle;* that is, a biological plan for growth allows each function to emerge in a systematic way until the fully functioning organism has developed. There is no going back to an earlier stage—experience makes retreat impossible. In the logic of psychosocial theory, the entire life span is required for all the functions of psychosocial development to appear and become integrated.

The concept of life stages permits us to consider the various aspects of development at a given period of life and to speculate about their interrelatedness. It also encourages us to focus on the experiences that are unique to each life period—experiences that deserve to be understood in their own right and in terms of their contribution to subsequent development.

When programs and services are to be designed to address critical needs in such areas as education, health care, housing, and social welfare, the developmental stage approach is very helpful in keeping attention focused on the needs and resources of the population to be served.

The main caution we would offer is to avoid thinking of stages as pigeonholes. The mere fact that a person is described as being at a given stage does not mean that he or she cannot function at other levels. It is not unusual to anticipate issues applicable

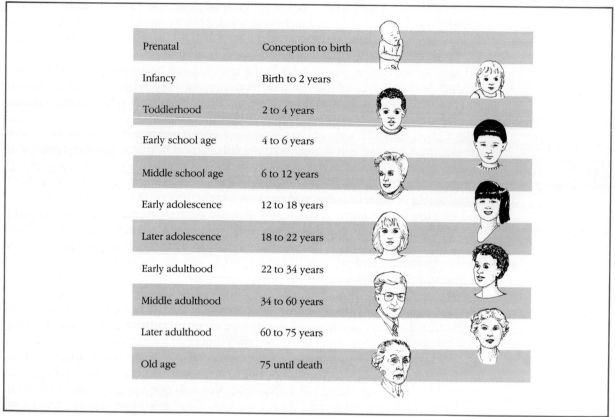

Prenatal	Conception to birth
Infancy	Birth to 2 years
Toddlerhood	2 to 4 years
Early school age	4 to 6 years
Middle school age	6 to 12 years
Early adolescence	12 to 18 years
Later adolescence	18 to 22 years
Early adulthood	22 to 34 years
Middle adulthood	34 to 60 years
Later adulthood	60 to 75 years
Old age	75 until death

Figure 2.3   **Eleven Stages of the Life Span and Approximate Ages**

to a later stage before they become dominant. Many children of toddler and preschool age, for example, play "house," envisioning a husband or wife and children. You might say that in this play they are anticipating the issues of intimacy and generativity that lie ahead. While some elements of the central psychosocial skills can be observed at all ages, it is the intensity with which they are expressed at certain times that brings them to our attention in our study of development and marks their importance in the definition of a stage. Erikson puts it this way:

> *The epigenetic chart also rightly suggests that the individual is never struggling only with the tension that is focal at the time. Rather, at every successive develop-mental stage, the individual is also increasingly engaged in the anticipation of tensions that have yet to become focal and in reexperiencing those tensions that were inadequately integrated when they were focal; similarly engaged are those whose age-appropriate integration was then, but is no longer, adequate.* [Erikson et al., 1986, p. 39]

As one leaves a stage, the achievements of that stage are not lost or irrelevant to later stages. Erikson warns us to take care not to become too structural in our thinking.

... certain misuses of the whole conception would have to be avoided. Among them is that the sense of trust (and all other positive senses postulated) is an achievement, *secured once and for all at a given stage. ... The assumption that at each stage a goodness is achieved which is impervious to new inner conflicts and to changing conditions is, I believe, a projection on child development of that success ideology which can so dangerously pervade our private and public daydreams and can make us inept in a heightened struggle for a meaningful existence in a new, industrial era of history.*   [Erikson, 1963, pp. 173–174]

The idea of life stages should be used to highlight the changing orientations toward self and others that dominate periods of the life span. The essential idea is that the ways in which one perceives and experiences one's life vary qualitatively from stage to stage.

An alternative approach in the study of human development is to trace single processes or systems across the life span. We might, for instance, consider changes in emotional functioning across the life span, from infancy through later life. This approach might provide greater detail regarding the emergence and modification of each system. It would not, however, contribute as much to an understanding of the interaction of systems within the person or of the ways in which integrated individuals experience their lives. If you wish to study the continuity and change within a particular system across the life span, you may wish to refer to the sections of each chapter that deal with the theme of interest to you.

To our minds, movement from one stage to the next is the result of changes in several major systems at the same time. The new mixture of needs, capabilities, and expectations is what produces the new orientation toward experience at each new stage. In our view, one can identify the important systems of each stage by looking at what researchers have identified as the major unique preoccupations of each period. Generally, the developmental tasks reflect areas of accomplishment in physical, cognitive, social, emotional, and self development.

Developmental Tasks

Developmental tasks, the second organizing concept of psychosocial theory, define what is healthy, normal development at each age in a particular society. The tasks form a sequence: success in learning the tasks of one stage leads to development and greater chances of success in learning the tasks of later stages. Failure at the tasks of one stage leads to greater difficulty with later tasks or may make later tasks impossible to master.

Robert J. Havighurst believes that human development is a process in which people attempt to learn the tasks required of them by the society to which they are adapting. These tasks change with age because each society has *age-graded expectations* for behavior. "Living in a modern society is a long series of tasks to learn" (Havighurst, 1972, p. 2). The person who learns well receives satisfaction and reward; the person who does not suffers unhappiness and social disapproval.

Although Havighurst's view of development emphasizes the guiding role of society in determining which skills need to be acquired at a certain age, it does not totally ignore the role of physical maturation. Havighurst believes that there are *sensitive*

Biographical Sketch

Robert J. Havighurst   1900–

Robert J. Havighurst was born on June 5, 1900. He received his Ph.D. in chemistry in 1924 from The Ohio State University. He was a member of the Committee on Human Development at the University of Chicago through his adult life. At his retirement in 1974 he was named Professor Emeritus in Development and Education.

Havighurst is known for many contributions in the fields of psychology, sociology, and education. In the 1950s he guided a major research project that demonstrated how children who are unsuccessful in school become socially alienated. At that time, he and his colleagues estimated that about 30% of adolescents were drifters and socially alienated young people of all social classes, though their backgrounds were predominantly lower middle class and working class (Havighurst et al., 1962). This is one of the few estimates of the number of disaffected youth in American society ever offered.

Havighurst proposed the concept of developmental tasks in 1952 and applied this concept to a life-span analysis of development. Many theoretical systems have been built around this idea because of its relevance for understanding the basic process of human development. Havighurst also proposed the idea of the "teachable moment," a time when a person is most sensitive to the learning related to a particular task.

periods for learning developmental tasks. These are times when the person is maturationally most ready to acquire a new ability. Havighurst called these periods *teachable moments*. Most people learn developmental tasks at a time and in the sequence appropriate for their society. If a particular task is not learned during the sensitive period, learning it may be much more difficult later on.

Learning during a sensitive period may enhance learning and performance in this task area later in life. Initially skills are developed in a sensitive period when much is happening both internally and externally to stimulate that area of growth. Once the sensitive period has passed, however, learning may still continue. Language skills, for example, do not cease to develop after toddlerhood. New and complex ways of using language expand throughout the life span. Gerontologists are discovering that motivation plays a great role in increasing linguistic skills in elderly people who wish to learn a new language before a trip to Europe.

The basic tasks we identify differ from Havighurst's. Our choice of tasks focuses on general areas of accomplishment that are critical to psychological and social growth at each stage within a modern, technological culture. We believe that a relatively small number of extremely important psychosocial tasks dominate a person's problem-solving efforts and learning during a given stage. These new competences enhance

Pablo Picasso, *Maternity,* 1921. The period of entry into parenthood is a teachable moment. At this important life transition, adults are usually open to new information and willing to try new behaviors in order to be effective in their parental roles.

the person's ability to engage in more complex social relationships. To our way of thinking, a successful culture stimulates behaviors that help its members learn the things they need to know for both their own survival and that of the group.

In our view, developmental tasks consist of a set of skills and competences that contribute to increased mastery over the environment. The tasks may reflect gains in physical, intellectual, social, or emotional skills, or in self-understanding. One of the developmental tasks of infancy, for example, is the creation of an attachment with the caregiver. This task presents itself early in the person's development and must be mastered at this time of life. The person's ability to develop intimate relationships in adult life is built on an initial sense of attachment to a caregiver during infancy.

Keep in mind that the person is changing on several major levels during each period of life. Tasks involving physical, emotional, intellectual, social, and self growth all contribute to the person's resources for coping with the challenges of life. Table 2.1 shows the developmental tasks we have identified that have major effects on the life experiences of most people in modern society and the stages during which each set of tasks is of primary learning value.

Mastery of the developmental tasks is influenced by the resolution of the psychosocial crisis of the previous stage. It is this resolution that leads to the development of new social capabilities. These capabilities orient the person toward new experiences, aptitude for relationships, and feelings of personal worth as he or she confronts the challenges of the developmental tasks of the new stage. In turn, the skills learned during a particular stage as a result of work on developmental tasks provide the tools

Table 2.1 Developmental Tasks Associated with Life Stages	
*Life Stage**	*Developmental Tasks*
Infancy (birth to 2 years)	Social attachment Maturation of sensory, perceptual, and motor functions Sensorimotor intelligence and primitive causality Understanding of the nature of objects and creation of categories Emotional development
Toddlerhood (2 to 4)	Elaboration of locomotion Fantasy and play Language development Self-control
Early school age (4 to 6)	Sex-role identification Early moral development Group play Self-esteem
Middle school age (6 to 12)	Friendship Self-evaluation Concrete operations Skill learning Team play
Early adolescence (12 to 18)	Physical maturation Formal operations Emotional development Membership in peer groups Sexual relationships
Later adolescence (18 to 22)	Autonomy in relation to parents Sex-role identity Internalized morality Career choice
Early adulthood (22 to 34)	Marriage Childbearing Work Lifestyle
Middle adulthood (34 to 60)	Nurture of the marital relationship Management of household Parenting Management of career
Later adulthood (60 to 75)	Promotion of intellectual vigor Redirection of energy toward new roles and activities Acceptance of one's life Development of a point of view about death
Very old age (75 until death)	Management of physical changes of aging Development of a psychohistorical perspective Travel through uncharted terrain

*We do not consider the concept of developmental tasks to be appropriate for the prenatal stage.

available for the resolution of the psychosocial crisis of that stage. Task accomplishment and crisis resolution interact to produce individual life stories.

Psychosocial Crisis

A *psychosocial crisis,* the third organizing concept of psychosocial theory (Erikson, 1950/1963), arises when the person must make psychological efforts to adjust to the demands of the social environment at each stage of development. The word *crisis* in this context refers to a normal set of stresses and strains rather than to an extraordinary set of events. At each stage of development, the society and social groups make demands on the individual.

Societal demands vary from stage to stage. The individual experiences these demands as mild but persistent guidelines and expectations for behavior. They may be demands for greater self-control, further development of skills, or stronger commitment to goals. Before the end of each stage of development, the individual tries to achieve a resolution, to adjust to society's demands and at the same time to translate those demands into personal terms. This process produces a *state of tension* that the individual must reduce in order to proceed to the next stage. It is this tension state that produces the psychosocial crisis.

A Typical Psychosocial Crisis   The psychosocial crisis with which you are probably most familiar is that of identity versus identity confusion, associated with later adolescence. An *identity crisis* is a sudden disintegration or deterioration of the framework of values and goals that a person relies on to give meaning and purpose to daily life.

An identity crisis usually involves strong feelings of anxiety and depression. The anxiety occurs because the person fears that without the structure of a clear value system, unacceptable impulses will break through and the person will behave in ways that might be harmful or immoral. The depression occurs because the person suddenly feels worthless. When our previously established goals come to seem meaningless, we are likely to be overwhelmed by feelings that our actions have no purpose or value to ourselves or to others.

A college student's identity crisis may be intensified under two conditions, both of which demand rapid, intense examination of value issues. First, the identity crisis may be heightened in students who attend a college that departs significantly from their own value orientation and where they frequently interact with faculty members. These students realize that the people with whom they have frequent interactions and with whom they are supposed to identify have values that are quite different from their own. They suddenly feel at a loss when significant adults challenge their values. They believe they should admire and respect adults, especially their professors. Yet they may try desperately to sustain their old value system in order to maintain a sense of control.

This kind of conflict can occur when students who have very traditional values and a clear career agenda attend a highly selective and prestigious private college. A student may want to attend Harvard or Yale, say, because of its status and reputation.

Yet the student may be totally unprepared for the strong socialization pressures that such schools exert—pressures to examine ideas objectively, to open oneself up to new views, and to experiment with many roles. Going to a prestigious liberal arts college is not the same as buying a Mercedes Benz or a Brooks Brothers suit. It is more than a status symbol; it is a life experience that can create intense conflict in students who are not prepared for it.

The identity crisis may also be heightened in students who are exploring and experimenting if external demands force them to make a value commitment while they are still uncertain or confused. The need to make a decision about selecting a major, to make a commitment to a love relationship, or to take a stand on a campus controversy will convince some students that they do indeed know what they want. They will be reassured to find that their values are more fully shaped than they had realized. Students who make this happy discovery will move in the direction of identity achievement. Other students, however, may be thrown into even greater confusion by demands for commitment. Students who are uncertain about which values and goals are best may feel overwhelmed when sudden demands for commitment send the existing tentative value structure into disorganization.

Psychosocial Crises of the Life Stages   Table 2.2 lists the psychosocial crisis of each stage of development from infancy through very old age. The crises are expressed as polarities—trust versus mistrust, autonomy versus shame and doubt. These contrasting conditions suggest the nature of an underlying dimension along which each psychosocial crisis is resolved. According to psychosocial theory, most people experience both ends of the continuum. The inevitable discrepancy between one's level of development at the beginning of a stage and society's push for a new level of functioning by the end of it introduces the experience of at least a mild degree of the negative condition. Even within a loving, caring social environment that promotes trust, an infant will experience some moments of frustration or disappointment that introduce sentiments of mistrust. Even the most industrious, skillful child of middle school age will encounter some tasks that are too difficult or some sense of inferiority in comparison with a more talented peer.

The outcome of the crisis at each stage is a balance or integration of the two opposing forces. For each person, the relative frequency and significance of positive and negative experiences will contribute to a resolution of the crisis that rests at some point along a continuum from extremely positive to extremely negative.

It should be noted that the likelihood of a completely positive or completely negative resolution is small. Most individuals resolve the crisis in the direction of the positive pole. That is, for most people the weight of experience combined with natural maturational tendencies supports a positive resolution of the crisis. At each successive stage, however, the likelihood of a negative resolution increases as the developmental tasks become more complex and the chances of encountering societal barriers to development rise. A positive resolution of each crisis provides new ego strengths that help the person meet the demands of the next stage.

If we are to understand the process of growth at each life stage, we have to consider the negative pole of each crisis as well as the positive. The negative poles offer insight into basic areas of human vulnerability. Experienced in moderation, they

Table 2.2 Psychosocial Crises of the Life Stages

Life Stage*	Psychosocial Crisis
Infancy (birth to 2 years)	Trust versus mistrust
Toddlerhood (2 to 4)	Autonomy versus shame and doubt
Early school age (4 to 6)	Initiative versus guilt
Middle school age (6 to 12)	Industry versus inferiority
Early adolescence (12 to 18)	Group identity versus alienation
Later adolescence (18 to 22)	Individual identity versus identity confusion
Early adulthood (22 to 34)	Intimacy versus isolation
Middle adulthood (34 to 60)	Generativity versus stagnation
Later adulthood (60 to 75)	Integrity versus despair
Very old age (75 until death)	Immortality versus extinction

*We do not consider the concept of developmental tasks to be appropriate for the prenatal stage.

foster clarification of ego positions, individuation, and moral integrity. While a steady diet of mistrust is undesirable, for example, it is important to a trusting person to be able to evaluate situations and people for their trustworthiness. One must be able to recognize the cues that are being sent about the safety or danger in an encounter. It is certainly an advantage to be able to anticipate that in some relationships, others may not be concerned for one's needs or welfare. However, a person who tends to mistrust others and who would recommend being careful in all relationships must also be able to evaluate people's trustworthiness if he or she is to have a feeling of hope. In every psychosocial crisis, the experiences that are relevant to the positive and negative poles contribute to the total range of a person's adaptive capacities.

Why conceptualize life in terms of crises? Does this idea adequately portray the experience of the individual, or does it overemphasize conflict and abnormality? The concept of crisis implies that normal development does not proceed smoothly. The theory hypothesizes that tension and conflict are necessary elements in the developmental process. According to the theory, crisis and its resolution are basic, biologically based components of life experience at every stage—in fact, they are what drive the ego system to develop new capacities. "Growing pains" occur at every stage of life. Those who expect their problems to be over after adolescence will be sorely disappointed.

The term *psychosocial* adds another dimension to the concept of developmental crises. These crises are the results of cultural pressures and expectations. The theory suggests that in the process of normal development, individuals will experience tension regardless of their culture because of the society's need to socialize and integrate its members. Although the tension itself is not a result of personal inadequacies, failure to resolve it can seriously limit future growth. To some extent, psychosocial theory attempts to account for failures in development that appear at every stage in the life span. The concept of crisis implies that at any stage something can interfere with growth and reduce the person's opportunities to experience personal fulfillment.

The exact nature of the conflict is not the same in all stages. Few cultural limits are placed on infants, for example; the outcome of the infancy stage depends greatly on the skill of the caregiver. In early school age, the culture stands in fairly direct

The psychosocial crisis of industry versus inferiority is suggested as a child develops a new level of competence in language skills in full view of a younger peer. The desire to achieve new levels of mastery develops in a cultural context of peer comparison and social evaluation.

opposition to the child's initiative in some matters and offers abundant encouragement to initiative in others. In young adulthood, the dominant cultural push is toward the establishment of intimate relationships; yet an individual may be unable to attain intimacy because of cultural norms against certain forms of interaction.

Psychosocial theory suggests that crisis is a predictable part of growth. At every life stage, we can anticipate that some tension will arise from the discrepancy between the skills that are developed at its beginning and the expectations for growth during the stage. In addition to these predictable crises, any number of unforeseen stresses can arise during a lifetime (Brim & Ryff, 1980; Klein & Aldous, 1988; Lazarus & Folkman, 1984). The parents' divorce, the death of a sibling, the loss of a job, and widowhood are life crises that can come at any point. The need to cope with such unpredictable crises may overwhelm a person, particularly if several occur at the same time.

However, unanticipated crises may also lead to new growth and the emergence of new competences at any point in the life course. In other words, the picture of predictable developmental stress that is emphasized in psychosocial theory must be expanded to include the possibility of unanticipated crises (Kaplan, 1983). These chance events may foster growth, but they may also result in defensiveness, regression, or dread. The impact of an unpredictable crisis will depend on whether or not the person is in a state of psychosocial crisis at the time.

The Central Process for Resolving the Psychosocial Crisis

Every psychosocial crisis reflects some discrepancy between the person's developmental competences at the beginning of the stage and societal pressures for more effective, integrated functioning. Under normal circumstances, the person is ready with certain new skills and capacities for social relationships. Our society is organized in such a way as to make age-related demands on individuals that are communicated by their significant social relationships. For example, the law requires that all 6-year-olds go to school, but it is parents who actually send them there. The law requires that people remain in school until they are 16, but it is peers, teachers, parents, and adolescents' own aspirations that ensure their continued attendance.

The demands exerted on a person by all elements of the social world make up what Erikson (1982) refers to as the *social system*. Part of a person's ego includes a social processing system that is sensitive to social expectations. The demands of the world around you serve as natural stimulators of your social processing mechanisms.

We have offered an extension of psychosocial theory by identifying a central process through which each psychosocial crisis is resolved. The *central process,* the fourth organizing concept of psychosocial theory, unfolds through a mechanism that links the individual's needs with the requirements of the culture at each life stage. Significant relationships and relevant competences change at every life stage. Specific modes of psychological work and specific modes of social interaction must occur if a person is to continue to grow.

For example, imitation is viewed as the central process for psychosocial growth during toddlerhood (2 to 4 years). Children expand their range of skills by imitating adults, siblings, television models, playmates, and even animals. Imitation appears to provide toddlers with enormous satisfaction. Through imitation they can increase the similarity between themselves and admired members of their social groups. They can begin to experience the world as other people and animals experience it. They can exercise some control over potentially frightening or confusing events by imitating elements of those occurrences in their play.

The movement toward a sense of autonomy in toddlerhood is facilitated by the child's readiness to imitate and by the variety of models available for observation. Imitation expands the range of behaviors in which children engage. Through persistent imitative activity, children expand their sense of self-initiated behavior and control over their actions. Repetitive experiences of this kind lead to the development of a sense of personal autonomy.

Imitation is more dominant in the behavioral repertoire during toddlerhood than at any other time in life, although it is often used as a learning and social strategy at other stages. Also, one can sense the society—in this case, through the significant relationship with the parents—telling the child, "That's good, Robbie. Now watch Daddy, and do it just like him." Not only are this child's tendencies toward imitation internally motivated; his society is telling him, "Imitate! It will help you learn."

Table 2.3 shows the central processes that we predict lead to the acquisition of new skills, the resolution of the psychosocial crisis, and successful coping at each life stage. Each of these processes appears to take on heightened significance in the course of a particular stage. Each one can be encouraged through the organization of significant social relationships.

The central process for coping with the challenges of each life stage provides both personal and societal mechanisms for taking in new information and reorganizing existing information. It also suggests the means that are most likely to lead to a revision of the ego system so that the crisis of the particular stage may be resolved. Children of age 5 or 6, for example, incorporate many of their parents' beliefs into

Pablo Picasso, *Paulo, Aged Two,* 1923. Paulo, Picasso's son, is shown in deep concentration sketching at his desk. The central process of imitation is beautifully illustrated in this painting. It is not surprising that a toddler would choose this behavior as a way of imitating a parent who is an artist.

their own world view through the process of identification. They begin to value many of the same goals and behaviors that their parents do. Thus their ego system is reorganized in a way that emphasizes the importance of some goals over others. Images of an ideal self take shape in relation to newly internalized values. Each central process results in an intensive reworking of the ego system, including a reorganization of boundaries, values, and images of oneself and others.

Table 2.3 The Central Process for Resolution of the Psychosocial Crisis

Life Stage*	Central Process
Infancy (birth to 2 years)	Mutuality with caregiver
Toddlerhood (2 to 4)	Imitation
Early school age (4 to 6)	Identification
Middle school age (6 to 12)	Education
Early adolescence (12 to 18)	Peer pressure
Later adolescence (18 to 22)	Role experimentation
Early adulthood (22 to 34)	Mutuality among peers
Middle adulthood (34 to 60)	Person-environment fit and creativity
Later adulthood (60 to 75)	Introspection
Very old age (75 until death)	Social support

*We do not consider the concept of developmental tasks to be appropriate for the prenatal stage.

At each stage of development we have a radius of significant relationships. Those closest to us are the people who stand out in our thoughts, toward whom we experience intense emotions, and with whom we enjoy a sense of understanding, companionship, and loyalty.

Radius of Significant Relationships

Erikson (1982, p. 31) points to a *radius of significant relationships* at each stage of development (see Figure 2.4). Initially a person focuses on a small number of relationships. During childhood, adolescence, and early adulthood, the number of relationships expands and they take on greater variety in depth and intensity. In middle and later adulthood, the person often returns to a small number of extremely important relationships that provide opportunities for great depth and intimacy. Most of the demands made on a person are made by people in these significant relationships.

In infancy, the significant social relationship is with a maternal or nurturing person. Most often the mother is the significant other. However, father, siblings, or a substitute caregiver may also provide this significant relationship. One significant relationship is necessary, but it is possible for an infant to have more than one.

Most toddlers establish relationships with a widening circle of caregivers. In early school age, relationships with family members, including siblings and grandparents as well as parents, become stronger and deeper. More relationships with friends and teachers become important.

At middle school age, significant relationships are found with a widening circle of people, including acquaintances in the neighborhood and at school. In early adolescence, the peer group, clubs and organizations, work, and religious groups provide new relationships that help people define themselves.

In later adolescence, the radius of significant relations expands to include mentors, leaders, and models for leadership as people struggle to create an integrated personal identity. In early adulthood, partners in friendship, sex, competition, and cooperation provide significant relationships. There is a new focusing on depth of relationship. In addition, for most people, children emerge as significant relations at this time.

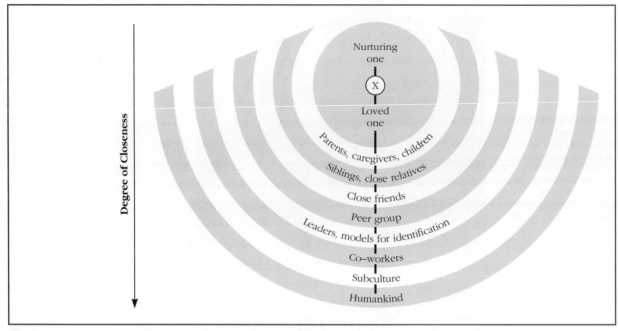

Figure 2.4   Radius of Significant Relationships

In middle adulthood, significant relations are based on family, work, and/or community. Relationships may extend to friendships established in other cities and countries. Adults are influenced by social relationships that have an impact on the lives of their children and parents as well as on their own lives, In later adulthood and very old age, the significant relationships become more abstract as a person develops a more general relation to humanity and at the same time more focused as a person develops a new level of caring for the few close relatives and friends who are still living. These are the relationships that transmit the messages of society and that produce states of tension.

According to Erikson's formulation, readiness to engage in this ever-changing network is a result of the epigenetic plan. Each person has a network of significant relationships at each stage of life. This network determines the demands that will be made on a person, the way he or she will be taken care of, and the meaning that the person will derive from relationships. The relationship network varies from person to person; but each person has a network of significant relationships and an increasing readiness to enter into a widening social arena (Duck, 1988; Grusec & Lytton, 1988; Higgins, Ruble & Hartup, 1985).

Coping Behavior

Coping behavior, the sixth organizing concept of psychosocial theory, consists of active efforts to resolve stress and create new solutions to the challenges of each developmental stage. Robert White (1974) has identified three components of the coping

Robert W. White

process: (1) the ability to gain and process new information, (2) the ability to maintain control over one's emotional state, and (3) the ability to move freely within one's environment.

Coping behavior is an important concept in psychosocial theory because it allows us to explain how new, original, creative, unique, and inventive behaviors occur. In addition, it allows us to predict that individuals will behave in original, spontaneous, and successful ways in their active social lives. Coping behaviors can be understood as those that allow for the development and growth of an individual as opposed to the maintenance of equilibrium in the face of threat.

White calls our attention to high school seniors' strategies for coping with the challenge of college. Those who go to the campus, talk to the students there, start reading for courses they will take, or take summer jobs in which they will be interacting with college students are doing more than maintaining their current level of functioning or reestablishing equilibrium. They are devising coping strategies that will lead to increased information about the setting and increased competence in it.

Individuals create their own strategies for coping with life challenges. The variation in coping styles reflects people's talents and motives as well as the responses of relevant others to a particular strategy. Think of the first day of kindergarten for a group of 5-year-olds. Some children are just sitting, shyly watching the teacher and the other children. Others are climbing all over the equipment and eagerly exploring the new toys. Still others are talking to the teacher or the other children, finding out names, making friends, or telling about the bus ride to school. Each of these strategies can be understood as a way of gathering information while preserving a degree of autonomy and integrity in a new and potentially threatening environment. No one way is right or even best except insofar as it serves the person by allowing access to information, freedom of movement, and some control over the emotions evoked by the new challenge.

An individual's characteristic style of coping appears to be influenced by a variety of factors, including gender, available resources, the nature of interpersonal relationships, and accumulation of life experiences. In addition, personality provides some consistency to the person's coping style. Children who are temperamentally difficult, for example—that is, children who are irritable and fearful, who have difficulty establishing regular eating, sleeping, and toileting patterns, and who have high activity levels—have been found to adapt less readily to change and are more vulnerable when they encounter such a misfortune as divorce or family economic hardship (Hetherington, 1989; Rutter, 1987).

Everyone's coping style undergoes some developmental transformations. With increased maturity, people approach stressful events more philosophically. They are less likely than the young to use simplistic forms of coping, such as escape, denial, and blaming others for their misfortunes. They are able to reconceptualize negative events, finding some positive consequences in them or redefining them in a more positive light. Adults who have reached a high level of maturity seem to be able to determine when it is best to try to take action and when it is best to accommodate to the situation (Folkman et al., 1987; Labouvie-Vief, Hakim-Larson & Hobart, 1987).

Prime Adaptive Ego Qualities   Erikson (1978) has postulated *prime adaptive ego qualities* that develop as a result of the positive resolution of the psychosocial crisis of a given stage and provide resources for coping in the next. He describes these qualities as mental states that form a basic orientation toward the interpretation of life experiences. A sense of competence, for example, permits a person to feel free to exercise his or her wits to solve problems without being weighed down by a sense of inferiority.

The primary ego qualities and their definitions are listed in Table 2.4. The ego qualities contribute to the person's dominant world view. Throughout life, an individual must reformulate this world view to accommodate new ego qualities.

Core Pathologies   Accompanying each potential ego strength is a potential *core pathology,* or destructive force (Erikson, 1982). Each core pathology serves as a guiding orientation for behavior (see Table 2.5). It is the result of a severe negative resolution of a psychosocial crisis. In the extreme, it tends to prevent further exploration of the interpersonal world and stands in the way of resolution of subsequent psychosocial crises. The energy that would normally be directed toward mastering the developmental tasks of a stage is directed instead toward resisting or avoiding change. These core pathologies are not simply passive limitations or barriers to development; they are energized strategies that protect the person from further unwanted association with the social system.

Evaluation of Psychosocial Theory

Although we believe that psychosocial theory provides a useful theoretical framework for organizing the vast array of observations in the field of human development, we recognize that it has weaknesses as well as strengths. We must not lose sight of either

Table 2.4 The Prime Adaptive Ego Quality at Each Psychosocial Stage

Stage	Ego Quality	Definition
Infancy	Hope	An enduring belief that one can attain one's deep and essential wishes
Toddlerhood	Will	A determination to exercise free choice and self-control
Early school age	Purpose	The courage to imagine and pursue valued goals
Middle school age	Competence	The free exercise of skill and intelligence in the completion of tasks
Early adolescence	Fidelity (I)	The ability freely to pledge and sustain loyalty to others
Later adolescence	Fidelity (II)	The ability freely to pledge and sustain loyalty to values and ideologies
Early adulthood	Love	A capacity for mutuality that transcends childhood dependency
Middle adulthood	Care	A commitment to concern for what has been generated.
Later adulthood	Wisdom	A detached yet active concern with life itself in the face of death
Very old age	Confidence	A conscious trust in oneself and assurance about the meaningfulness of life

Source: Adapted from Erik H. Erikson, "Dr. Borg's Life Cycle," in *Adulthood,* ed. Erikson, pp. 1–31 (New York: Norton, 1978).

Table 2.5 Core Pathology of Each Life Stage

Stage	Core Pathology	Definition
Infancy	Withdrawal	Social and emotional detachment
Toddlerhood	Compulsion	Repetitive behaviors motivated by impulse or restrictions against the expression of impulse
Early school age	Inhibition	A psychological restraint that prevents freedom of thought, expression, and activity
Middle school age	Inertia	A paralysis of action and thought that prevents productive work
Early adolescence	Isolation	Lack of companions
Later adolescence	Repudiation	Rejection of roles and values that are viewed as alien to oneself
Early adulthood	Exclusivity	An elitist shutting out of others
Middle adulthood	Rejectivity	Unwillingness to include certain others or groups of others in one's generative concern
Later adulthood	Disdain	A feeling of scorn for the weakness and frailty of oneself and others
Very old age	Diffidence	Inability to act because of overwhelming self-doubt

Source: Adapted from Erik H. Erikson, *The Life Cycle Completed* (New York: Norton, 1982), pp. 32–33.

Table 2.6   Evaluation of Psychosocial Theory

Strengths	Weaknesses
The theory provides a broad context, linking development in various stages of life to the resources and demands of society.	The basic concepts of the theory are abstract and difficult to operationalize.
The theory emphasizes ego development and directions for healthy development across the life span.	Mechanisms for resolving crisis and moving from one stage to the next are not well developed.
It provides a useful framework for psychotherapy.	The specific number of stages and their link to a genetic plan for development have not been adequately demonstrated, especially in adulthood.
It emphasizes the dynamic interplay between a genetic plan and the forces of culture and society in guiding individual development.	The theory is dominated by a male Eurocentric perspective that gives too much emphasis to the emergence of individuality and not enough emphasis to social competence and social needs.
The concept of normative psychosocial crises provides an effective set of constructs for examining the tension between the individual and society.	The specific way in which culture encourages or inhibits development at each life stage is not clearly elaborated.

its strengths or its weaknesses if we are to be sensitive to the ways in which the theory itself may influence our thinking. The strengths and weaknesses of psychosocial theory are listed in Table 2.6.

Strengths

Psychosocial theory provides a very broad context within which to study development. The theory links the process of child development to later stages of adult life, to the needs of society, and to the ability of societies to interact with one another. Although many scholars agree that such a broad perspective is necessary, few other theories attempt to address the dynamic interplay between individual development and society.

The emphasis of psychosocial theory on ego development and ego processes provides insight into the directions of healthy development across the life span. At the same time, the theory is useful as a framework for approaching psychotherapy and counseling in that it provides a guide for identifying the tensions that may disrupt development at each life stage. It also offers a therapeutic outlook that recognizes the contributions individuals make to their own well-being.

The theory offers a dynamic picture of the interplay between a genetically guided plan for development and the powerful forces of culture and society in shaping the course of development at every life stage.

The concept of normative psychosocial crises is a creative contribution of the theory. It identifies predictable tensions between socialization and maturation throughout life. Societies, with their structures, laws, roles, rituals, and sanctions, are organized to guide individual growth toward a particular ideal of mature adulthood. If individuals grew in that direction naturally, as a result of an unfolding, genetically guided plan, presumably there would be no need for these elaborate social structures. But every society faces problems when it attempts to balance the needs of the individual with the needs of the group. All individuals face problems when they attempt to experience their individuality while still maintaining the support of their group. Psychosocial theory gives us concepts to explore these natural tensions.

Weaknesses

One weakness of psychosocial theory is that its basic concepts are presented in language that is abstract and difficult to examine empirically (Crain, 1985; Miller, 1989). Such terms as *initiative, personal identity,* and *generativity* are hard to define and even more difficult to translate into objective measures. Nonetheless, efforts have been made along this line, beginning with the work of James Marcia. Alan Waterman, Anne Constantinople, and others have contributed to a rather extensive literature that examines the construct of personal identity. Other researchers have tackled the concept of intimacy, and still others have tried to operationalize the concept of generativity. These studies suggest that deliberate testing of the implications of psychosocial theory requires ingenuity but can be quite productive. In addition to studies that start out to test psychosocial theory, many studies have a bearing on its constructs. In each of the stages of life that we will be examining, you will find an analysis of research that has a clear link to the constructs of psychosocial theory.

Another weakness of the theory is that the mechanisms for resolving crises and moving from one stage to the next are not well developed. Erikson does not offer a universal mechanism for crisis resolution, nor does he detail the kinds of experiences that are necessary at each stage if one is to cope successfully with the crisis of that stage. We have addressed this weakness by introducing the concepts of developmental tasks and central process for each stage. The developmental tasks suggest some of the major achievements that permit a person to meet the social expectations of each stage. The central process identifies the primary social context within which the crisis is resolved. Using these two vehicles, we are beginning to glimpse the answers to many questions in regard to the way development takes place.

The specific number of stages and their link to a biologically based plan for development has been criticized (Crain, 1985), most notably in discussions of the stages of adulthood. Other human development theorists, such as Robert Peck, Robert Gould, Daniel Levinson, and Marjorie Lowenthal, take a more differentiated view of the stages of adulthood and later life. We have responded to these criticisms by treating adolescence as two distinct stages and by adding a stage of adulthood, very old age. You will also read about the important developmental issues of the prenatal period, a stage that Erikson's theory does not consider, but one that clearly plays a central role in setting the stage for a lifetime of vulnerabilities and resources. In our view, these revisions present no threat to the usefulness of the theory. Rather, they demonstrate the natural evolution of a theoretical framework as it encounters new observations in a new historical era.

Finally, the theory has been criticized as being dominated by a male, Eurocentric, individualistic perspective (Gilligan, 1982). With its emphasis on ego development and ego identity, the theory does not go far enough to explore how such capacities as empathy, helping, altruism, the ability to take the point of view of the other, and cooperation emerge during childhood, and how these critical aspects of social competence contribute to effective functioning in adulthood. Although the theory addresses the role of society in shaping the individual and the role of the individual in directing the course of his or her own development, we humans seem to have such a wide range of capacities for social interaction and such a deep need for social connectedness that they must be elaborated in greater detail.

☐ Chapter Summary

Psychosocial theory offers a life-span view of development. Development is a product of the interactions between individuals and their social environments. The needs and goals of both the individual and society must be considered in conceptualizing human development. Predictability is found in the sequence of psychosocial stages, in the central process involved in the resolution of the crisis at each stage, and in the radius of significant relationships. Individuality is expressed in the achievement of the developmental tasks, in the development of a world view, and in the style and resources for coping that the person brings to each new life challenge.

At the beginning of this chapter we discussed the three questions you must ask in order to evaluate a theory. Let us now answer these questions with respect to psychosocial theory.

1. *Which phenomena is the theory trying to explain?* The theory attempts to explain human development across the life span, especially patterned changes in self-understanding, social relationships, and world view.
2. *What assumptions does the theory make?* Human development is a product of three factors: biological evolution, the interaction between individuals and social groups, and contributions individuals make to their own psychological growth.
3. *What does the theory predict?* There are 11 distinct stages of development. Developmental tasks are dictated by the interaction of biology and culture during each stage. A normal crisis arises at each stage of development, and a central process operates to resolve it. Each person is part of an expanding network of significant relationships that convey society's expectations and demands. These relationships can also provide encouragement in the face of challenges. New behaviors continue to be possible throughout life.

Development will be optimal if a person retains the ability to create new behaviors and relationships as a result of skill acquisition and successful crisis resolution over the course of each stage of growth. Lack of development and core pathologies are the result of tendencies that restrict behavior in general and new behaviors in particular (especially social behaviors). The mechanism for positive and negative development is diagrammed in Figure 2.5.

The basic concepts of psychosocial theory provide the framework for analyzing development across 11 life stages. Each chapter from 4 through 14 is devoted to one life stage. With the exception of Chapter 4, on pregnancy and prenatal development, each starts with a discussion of the developmental tasks of the stage. As we trace

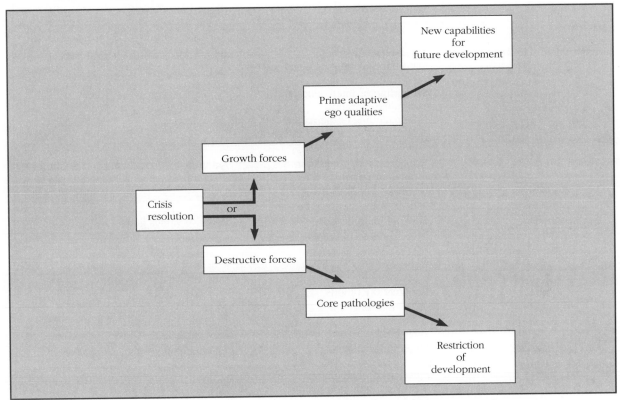

Figure 2.5   Mechanism for Positive and Negative Psychosocial Development

developments in physical growth, emotional growth, intellectual skills, social relationships, and self-understanding, you can begin to appreciate that development is simultaneous and interrelated in several dimensions during each period of life.

In the second section of each chapter, we describe the psychosocial crisis of the stage under discussion, accounting for the tension by examining the individual's needs and personal resources in light of dominant societal expectations. In addition to defining the crisis, we conceptualize the central process by which it is resolved. Some crises involve interaction with significant others, as in the case of trust versus mistrust or intimacy versus isolation. Others reflect private, internal reorganization, such as the crisis of individual identity versus identity confusion, or integrity versus despair. The resolution of crisis at each stage develops either new ego strengths or new core pathologies.

At the end of each chapter we use the material we have discussed to analyze a selected topic that we consider relevant and of persistent concern to our society. These topics are controversial: they may generate sentiment as they deepen understanding. We intend these sections to stimulate the application of developmental principles to other real-world concerns.

Take a moment to study Table 2.7. You can use this table as a guide to the major themes of the text. It may help you to see the connections among topics within a

(Text continues on page 66.)

Table 2.7   Organization of the Stages

Life Stage	Developmental Tasks	Psychosocial Crisis
Prenatal (conception to birth)		
Infancy (birth to 2 years)	Social attachment Maturation of sensory, perceptual, and motor functions Sensorimotor intelligence and primitive causality Understanding of the nature of objects and creation of categories Emotional development	Basic trust versus basic mistrust
Toddlerhood (2 to 4)	Elaboration of locomotion Fantasy and play Language development Self-control	Autonomy versus shame and doubt
Early school age (4 to 6)	Sex-role identification Early moral development Group play Self-esteem	Initiative versus guilt
Middle school age (6 to 12)	Friendship Concrete operations Skill learning Self-evaluation Team play	Industry versus inferiority
Early adolescence (12 to 18)	Physical maturation Formal operations Emotional development Membership in peer groups Sexual relationships	Group identity versus alienation
Later adolescence (18 to 22)	Autonomy in relation to parents Sex-role identity Internalized morality Career choice	Individual identity versus identity confusion
Early adulthood (22 to 34)	Marriage Childbearing Work Lifestyle	Intimacy versus isolation
Middle adulthood (34 to 60)	Nurture of the marital relationship Management of household Parenting Management of career	Generativity versus stagnation
Later adulthood (60 to 75)	Promotion of intellectual vigor Redirection of energy toward new roles Acceptance of one's life Development of a point of view about death	Integrity versus despair
Very old age (75 until death)	Management of physical changes of aging Development of a psychohistorical perspective Travel through uncharted terrain	Immortality versus extinction

Table 2.7   (continued)

Central Process	Prime Adaptive Ego Quality	Core Pathology	Applied Topic
Mutuality with caregiver	Hope	Withdrawal	Abortion The role of parents
Imitation	Will	Compulsion	Discipline
Identification	Purpose	Inhibition	The impact of television
Education	Competence	Inertia	Sex education
Peer pressure	Fidelity (I)	Isolation	Adolescent alcohol use
Role experimentation	Fidelity (II)	Repudiation	Career decision making
Mutuality among peers	Love	Exclusivity	Divorce
Person–environment fit and creativity	Care	Rejectivity	Adults and their aging parents
Introspection	Wisdom	Disdain	Retirement
Social support	Confidence	Diffidence	Meeting the needs of the frail elderly

chapter, or to trace threads of continuity over several periods of life. You may also use this table in constructing a life map for yourself, which will reveal levels of tension and major psychosocial factors that may be affecting your self-concept and your relationships with others.

References

Brim, O. G., Jr., & Ryff, C. D. (1980). On the properties of life events. In P. B. Baltes & O. G. Brim, Jr. (eds.), *Life-span development and behavior* (pp. 368–388). New York: Academic Press.

Coles, R. (1970). *Erik H. Erikson: The growth of his work.* Boston: Atlantic–Little, Brown.

Crain, W. C. (1985). *Theories of development: Concepts and applications* (2nd ed.). Englewood Cliffs, N.J.: Prentice-Hall.

Davison, M. L., King, P. M., Kitchener, K. S., & Parker, C. A. (1980). The stage sequence concept in cognitive and social development. *Developmental Psychology, 16,* 121–131.

Duck, S. (1988). *Handbook of personal relationships: Theory, research, and interventions.* New York: Wiley.

Erikson, E. H. (1950/1963). *Childhood and society.* New York: Norton.

Erikson, E. H. (1958). *Young man Luther.* New York: Norton.

Erikson, E. H. (1968). *Identity: Youth and crisis.* New York: Norton.

Erikson, E. H. (1969). *Gandhi's truth.* New York: Norton.

Erikson, E. H. (1978). Reflections on Dr. Borg's life cycle. In E. H. Erikson (ed.), *Adulthood* (pp. 1–32). New York: Norton.

Erikson, E. H. (1982). *The life cycle completed: A review.* New York: Norton.

Erikson, E. H., Erikson, J. M., & Kivnick, H. Q. (1986). *Vital involvement in old age.* New York: Norton.

Fischer, K. W., & Silvern, L. (1985). Stages and individual differences in cognitive development. *Annual Review of Psychology, 36,* 613–648.

Flavell, J. H. (1982). Structures, stages, and sequences in cognitive development. In W. A. Collins (ed.), *The concept of development* (pp. 1–28). Hillsdale, N.J.: Erlbaum.

Folkman, S., Lazarus, R. S., Pimley, S., & Novacek, J. (1987).

Age differences in stress and coping process. *Psychology and Aging, 2,* 171–184.

Gilligan, C. (1982). *In a different voice.* Cambridge, Mass.: Harvard University Press.

Grusec, J. E., & Lytton, H. (1988). *Social development: History, theory, and research.* New York: Springer-Verlag.

Havighurst, R. J. (1972). *Developmental tasks and education* (3rd ed.). New York: David McKay.

Havighurst, R. J. et al. (1962). *Growing up in River City.* New York: Wiley.

Hetherington, E. M. (1989). Coping with family transitions: Winners, losers, and survivors. *Child Development, 60,* 1–14.

Higgins, E. T., Ruble, D. N., & Hartup, W. W. (1985). *Social cognition and social development: A sociocultural perspective.* New York: Cambridge University Press.

Huxley, J. (1941). *The uniqueness of man.* London: Chatto & Windus.

Huxley, J. (1942). *Evolution: The magic synthesis.* New York: Harper.

Kaplan, H. B. (1983). *Psychosocial stress: Trends in theory and research.* New York: Academic Press.

Klein, D. M., & Aldous, J. (1988). *Social stress and family development.* New York: Guilford Press.

Labouvie-Vief, G., Hakim-Larson, J., & Hobart, C. J. (1987). Age, ego level, and the life-span development of coping and defense processes. *Psychology and Aging, 2,* 286–293.

Lazarus, R. S., & Folkman, S. (1984). *Stress, appraisal, and coping.* New York: Springer-Verlag.

Levin, I. (1986). *Stage and structure: Reopening the debate.* Norwood, N.J.: Ablex.

Miller, P. H. (1989). *Theories of developmental psychology* (2nd ed.). New York: W. H. Freeman.

Piaget, J. (1950). *The psychology of intelligence.* New York: Harcourt, Brace; London: Routledge & Kegan Paul.

Rutter, M. (1987). Psychosocial resilience and protective mechanisms. *American Journal of Orthopsychiatry, 57,* 316–331.

White, R. W. (1974). Strategies of adaptation: An attempt at systematic description. In G. V. Coelho, D. A. Hamburg, & J. E. Adams (eds.), *Coping and adaptation* (pp. 47–68). New York: Basic Books.

Chapter Three

How does the young person become the old one? The theories discussed in this chapter provide a variety of answers to this question.

Theories of Change

When we view human development across the life span, it is important to be able to move from a general overview of the pattern of development to an explanation of specific processes of change. Psychosocial theory provides the conceptual umbrella for our approach to the study of human development, but we need other theories to explain behavior at different levels of analysis. If we are to account for both stability and change across the life span, we need theoretical constructs that will help account for global evolutionary change, societal and cultural change, and individual change. We need concepts that will help explain the contributions of life experiences, maturational factors, and a person's own constructions of experience to patterns of physical, cognitive, social, emotional, and self development.

This chapter introduces the basic concepts of seven major theories: evolutionary theory, cultural theory, psychosexual theory, cognitive developmental theory, learning theory, social role theory, and systems theory. The use of several theoretical perspectives helps us to maintain flexibility in interpreting behavior and facilitates our understanding of the integration of individuals and social systems.

Biological Evolution

The theory of evolution explains how diverse and increasingly more complex life forms come to exist. Evolutionary theory assumes that the natural laws that apply to plant and animal life also apply to humans. This theory is important to the study of human development because it integrates human beings into the vast array of life forms. Evolutionary theory emphasizes the importance of biological forces in directing growth and the gradual modification of species as a result of biological adaptation to specific environments.

Natural Selection

Darwin believed that unchanging laws of nature apply uniformly throughout time. This assumption, called *uniformitarianism,* had been advanced by Charles Lyell (1830/1833). The challenge that it posed was to discover the basic mechanism that accounts for species change from the beginnings of life to the present. The mechanism that Darwin (1859) discovered is *natural selection.*

Every species produces more offspring than can survive to reproduce because of limitations of the food supply and natural dangers. Darwin observed that there was quite a bit of *variability* among members of the same species in any given location. Some individuals were better suited than others to the immediate environment and were more likely to survive, mate, and produce offspring. The offspring were also more likely to have characteristics appropriate for that location. Overall, the species would change to become more successful, or it would evolve into a new species. If the environment changed (in climate, for example), only certain variations of organisms would survive, and again species would evolve. Forms of life that failed to adapt would become extinct. It is important to understand that it is the variability within a species that ensures the species' continuation or its development into new forms. Variability arises through genetic mechanisms.

The law of natural selection has been referred to as the principle of "survival of the fittest." Herbert Spencer (1864) first referred to it in this way. This phrase often calls up images of head-to-head combat between members of a species. This is not what Darwin's principle says. Darwin describes the process in the following way:

> *It may metaphorically be said that natural selection is daily and hourly scrutinizing, throughout the world, the slightest variation; rejecting those that are bad, preserving and adding up all that are good; silently and insensibly working, whenever and wherever opportunity offers, at the improvement of each organic being in relation to its conditions of life. We see nothing of these slow changes in progress, until the hand of time has marked the lapse of ages, and then so imperfect is our view into long-past geological ages, that we see only that the forms of life are now different from what they formerly were.* [Darwin, 1859/1979, p. 77]

Adaptation

Adaptation is the process that underlies evolutionary change—the process by which living things develop characteristics that enable them to thrive in a particular environment. Adaptation can operate at the biological level, as a change in some physical characteristic over generations. Adaptation can also operate at the behavioral level, as a change in some pattern of behavior.

Biological Adaptation

Biological adaptation can be seen in the coloration of the peppered moth. The original silvery-flecked color of these moths provided excellent camouflage when they were at rest on lichen-covered trees. Lichen is a simple plant form that grows on rocks and trees. In areas where air pollution has killed the lichen and blackened the tree trunks, however, a black variety of the peppered moth has an adaptive advantage. The black variety has almost totally replaced the silver form in many industrial areas.

Behavioral Adaptation

Behavioral adaptations are learned. They do not influence genetic information that offspring inherit from their parents. We humans pass on our behavioral adaptations through child-rearing practices, schools, and other culture bearers. With our remarkable capacity to develop behavioral adaptations, we can survive and thrive under quite varied environmental conditions.

Behavioral adaptation is seen in the patterns of dress that have emerged in the world's various climates. We do not wear the same kinds of clothing in a hot tropical climate, a hot dry climate, a temperate climate, and an arctic climate. This type of behavioral adaptation is essential for survival of the individual. Other behavioral adaptations, such as courtship rituals and rules that determine who is a permissible marriage partner, influence an individual's chances to reproduce.

As their environment became increasingly polluted, the silvery peppered moths were more readily seen and eaten, but the dark peppered moths survived.

Evolution and the Human Species

"If one sets January 1 as the origin of life on earth, marine vertebrates would then first appear on November 24, dinosaurs on December 16, and man at 10:15 P.M. on December 31" (Lerner & Libby, 1976).

The evolution of the family of humans began about 2 million years ago with the species *Homo habilis* and *Homo erectus.* Anthropologists have two opposing views of the origin of modern humans, *Homo sapiens.* The two theories can be described very roughly as the "candelabra" model of evolution and the "Noah's Ark" model of evolution. The *candelabra model* suggests that modern humans evolved simultaneously in several parts of the world. This view argues for continuity in evolution from ancient *Homo erectus* ancestors to modern *Homo sapiens,* with a gradual transformation of features and characteristics. From this perspective, racial differences among Asian, African, European, and Australian people are very ancient, having arisen early in the transformation from *Homo erectus* to *Homo sapiens* in each geographic area.

The *Noah's Ark theory* suggests that modern humans have evolved from a group of common ancestors, *Homo sapiens,* who most likely had their origins in Africa about 200,000 years ago. This group of advanced humans then dispersed throughout the Old World and replaced the more primitive populations. In this view, there was no continuity from ancient to modern humans, but a rapid extinction (*rapid* meaning somewhere between 1,000 and 13,000 years) of one group and expansion of the other. This theory leads to the conclusion that the racial differences we observe today are not based in very ancient local differences, but evolved after the establishment of *Homo sapiens* in many parts of the world.

Biographical Sketch

Charles Darwin   1809–1882

Charles Darwin was born in 1809 into an educated family with a long-standing tradition of belief in the concepts generated by the theory of evolution. Darwin's grandfather Erasmus Darwin was one of the pioneers in the development of evolutionary theory. As a schoolboy Darwin rebelled against the classical pattern of learning by rote memorization. He preferred to spend long periods of time outdoors, exploring nature and puzzling over its mysteries.

As a young man Darwin was sent to study medicine. He found the lectures boring and the work distasteful. He left medical school, gravely disappointing his father. Darwin was then sent to Cambridge to study theology in preparation for entering the clergy, but he found this study even less interesting than medicine. He continued to spend much of his time outdoors, exploring nature.

In 1831 an opportunity arose that allowed Darwin to indulge his passion in a personally and professionally acceptable way: he became the resident naturalist on *H.M.S. Beagle*. The crew's mission was to sail to South America and survey its coast and the islands of the Pacific in order to map this region and document its plant and animal life. The voyage lasted from 1831 to 1836. During those years Darwin demonstrated unbounded energy in his exploration of the natural phenomena that he encountered.

After he returned to England, Darwin settled down to work on the samples he had collected and to reflect on his observations. He was painstaking in his attention to details. Over a period of twenty years, he gradually developed his theory of how species can change and evolve into new plant or animal forms. However, he postponed writing about his views while he searched for examples that would support his argument. It was not until 1859, when he learned that another naturalist, Alfred Russell Wallace, was about to introduce a very similar argument, that Darwin felt compelled to publish *The Origin of Species*. ■

From an evolutionary perspective, the future of a species depends on the capacity of individual members of the species to mate, reproduce, and rear their young to the age when they can mate and reproduce.

A combination of fossil evidence and genetic evidence provides strong support for the Noah's Ark theory (Lewin, 1987; Tattersall, Delson & Van Couvering, 1988). The similarities in features of fossil evidence found in many parts of the world are so great that it seems unlikely that these humans could have evolved independently along such a common course without having had a recent common ancestor. With techniques from molecular biology it is possible to trace characteristics of mitochondrial DNA which show that the modern humans found in various areas of Europe, Asia, and America are quite similar to one another, suggesting common genetic ancestry. The DNA would not be so similar if they had evolved independently from local primitive ancestors.

Thus the picture that is taking shape is one of a common modern ancestor, whose offspring migrated throughout the world and dominated other human species. This domination was probably subtle, not a case of open warfare or competition. Some superiority in hunting skills, toolmaking, and planning could have given the modern species an evolutionary advantage by enabling them to establish dependable sources of high-quality food. Assuming that the two forms of humans, modern and archaic *Homo sapiens,* lived side by side for a time in the same geographic area, one analysis suggests that a 2% increase in the mortality rate of the more ancient species could lead that species to be replaced by the more modern form in as few as 30 generations (Zubrow, cited in Lewin, 1987).

Humans have characteristics that link them to the larger group of *mammals* from which they descended. Humans produce live young. The mothers feed their young

Box 3.1   Evolutionary Theory and Emotions

Through his study of the links between human behavior and that of related animal species, Darwin (1872/1965) became interested in the adaptive functions of emotions. He suggested that emotional expressions were originally a form of preparation for such critical survival behaviors as attack, locomotion, defense, breathing, and vision. Through evolution, these expressions have become elements in a system of communication. Emotional expressions, especially facial ones, reveal the inner state of the individual to others in the social group.

The frown is an expression with clearly adaptive origins. It originated as an intense stare directed at an object close to the face. Many species—including dogs, Capuchin monkeys, and humans—typically lower their eyebrows when they frown. This move perhaps helps focus the eyes on the object, reduces glare, and protects the eyes should the object's position suddenly change. In most animals, a direct stare is a good indication of concentrated interest and little or no fear. Often a stare and frown immediately precede an attack. The frown has become an expression of confidence and assertive threat in monkeys, apes, and humans.

The evolutionary perspective suggests that some of the basic emotions are innate patterns, emitted without a need for practice or imitation of others. Some evidence for this view can be seen in the emotional development of infants. The startle, grimace, smile, and expression of disgust are all reflexive responses that have been observed in early infancy. Of course, the interpretation and expression or inhibition of emotions in childhood and adulthood depend on the cultural context and the individual's cognitive capacity.

on milk produced by the mammary glands. Our bodies are covered with skin, which is protected by hair. We also have some characteristics that link us to other *primates,* the class of mammals that includes humans, apes, monkeys, lemurs, and tarsiers. Primates share ten major characteristics:

1. Progressive movement of the eyes toward the midline of the head and consequent development of stereoscopic (three-dimensional) vision.
2. Retention of five-digit extremities and of the major bones of the arms and legs—clavicle, radius, and fibula.
3. Progressive development of the digits, particularly the thumb and big toe, which allows for increasing dexterity.
4. Development of flattened nails, instead of claws, and also of sensitive pads on the tips of the digits.
5. Progressive shortening of the snout, reduction in the size of the apparatus for smell, and consequent reduction in olfactory acuity.
6. Great increase in the size of the brain.
7. Prolongation of prenatal and postnatal development.
8. Decrease in the number of teeth and retention of a simple molar system.
9. Overall increase in body size, progressive development toward upright stature, and increased dependence on the hind limbs for locomotion.
10. Development of complex social organizations.

Each of these characteristics contributes to the essential quality of human behavior. The structure of our hands permits the flexible manipulation of objects as tools.

Reduced reliance on smell and relatively greater reliance on vision influence our mode of exploring the environment. Perhaps the most critical item on the list for human beings is the size, structure, and complexity of the brain. The prolonged period of prenatal and postnatal development characteristic of human infants provides the evolutionary basis for our work in the study of development.

All human beings, regardless of culture, share characteristics that tie them together as a species. They can mate and produce living children who in turn are capable of reproducing. They produce spoken symbolic language. They store information and pass it on from one generation to the next. They are self-conscious; that is, they raise questions about their origin and anticipate their death.

Ethology

Ethology is the comparative study of the biological bases of behavior from an evolutionary perspective. Its roots lie in Charles Darwin's ideas on the evolution of "instincts." These ideas were further developed in the 1930s by the European zoologists Konrad Lorenz and Niko Tinbergen. Ethology uses observation, experimentation, and the comparative method to investigate the proximal causes of behavioral acts, the relative contribution of inheritance and learning to these acts, and the adaptive significance and evolutionary history of various patterns of behavior within and across species. Ethologists emphasize the importance of studying behavior in natural settings (Blurton-Jones, 1972; Eibl-Eibesfeldt, 1975). Laboratory experiments are used to discover answers to questions derived from these observations.

Evolutionary theory focuses our attention on those capacities and behavior patterns that contribute to the long-term survival and continued adaptation of the species. From this perspective, the study of individual behavior and development focuses on how a particular behavior contributes not just to the future growth and development of the individual but to the adaptation and continuation of the species.

The future of a species depends on the capacity of its individual members to survive, mate, reproduce, and rear their young. Some of the factors that contribute to the vigor and continuity of a species are the health of the individuals when they attain reproductive capacity, the characteristics of the environment that promote or inhibit procreation, and the capacity of sexually mature partners to rear their offspring.

From Darwin's interest in the evolution of species grew the biologist's interest in those behaviors that are central to the species' survival, including feeding efficiency, competition among males for breeding females, and cooperation among males in warding off predators and competing primates. The field of ethology has emerged as the study of evolutionarily significant behaviors that appear to be innate and specific to a particular species. These behaviors are commonly associated with eating, mating, and protecting a species from harm.

Two early contributors to the field of ethology, Konrad Lorenz (1935/1981) and Niko Tinbergen (1951), focused on *innate behaviors* and how they are expressed under natural conditions. Innate behaviors are present in some standard or shared form in all members of a species. They are expressed without previous learning and remain relatively unchanged by experience. Innate behaviors include *reflexes,* which are simple responses to simple stimuli. A baby's grasp of a finger or other object that is placed in its palm is a reflex. Many infant reflexes disappear by the end of the first year. Some provide the basis for learned habit patterns.

Table 3.1 lists three kinds of infant reflexes: (1) reflexes that serve some adaptive function for the survival of the newborn, (2) reflexes that are adaptive for the survival of genetically related species over the period of evolution, and (3) reflexes whose functions are not known. The third group includes patterned behaviors that are either remnants of more complex patterns in other species or perhaps latent resources for future adaptations of which we are not yet aware.

Some innate behaviors, called *fixed* or *model action patterns,* are more complex than reflexes. Birds build nests, squirrels bury nuts, and goslings follow their mothers. These behaviors are genetically guided sequences that are prompted by a particular stimulus pattern that releases or signals the behavior. The *releasing stimulus* may be a certain odor, color, movement, sound, or shape. It may require a special relation between stimuli.

In recent years some ethologists have turned their attention to the study of human behavior. Lorenz (1943) first hypothesized that certain aspects of an infant's appearance stimulate positive emotional responses in adult caregivers. The quality of "cuteness" or "babyness" that Lorenz identified includes a head that is large in proportion to the body, large eyes, and round, pudgy cheeks.

John Bowlby (1958, 1988) has been influential in bringing the ethological perspective to bear on development through the study of attachment. Bowlby describes the *attachment behavioral system* as a complex set of reflexes and signaling behaviors that bring about caregiving responses from adults. These responses in turn shape an infant's expectations and help to create an inner representation of the parent as a caring, comforting person.

The infant's innate capacities for smiling, cooing, grasping, and crying draw the adult's attention and provoke a sympathetic response. The adult's gentle cuddling, soothing, and smiling establish a sense of security in the child. Attachment, viewed in this light, is an innate behavior system that promotes the safety of offspring in infancy and provides the basis for the trusting social relationships that are necessary for mating and parenting in adulthood.

Bowlby argues that attachment behavior serves a basic survival function: protection.

> *Whilst attachment behaviour is at its most obvious in early childhood, it can be observed throughout the life cycle, especially in emergencies. Since it is seen in virtually all human beings (though in varying patterns), it is regarded as an integral part of human nature and one we share (to a varying extent) with members of other species. The biological function attributed to it is that of protection. To remain within easy access of a familiar individual known to be ready and willing to come to our aid in an emergency is clearly a good insurance policy—whatever our age.* [Bowlby, 1988, p. 27]

William Charlesworth (1988) has focused on the importance of social interaction as a mechanism that allows humans to obtain resources from the environment at any point in the life span. He has suggested that the resources required to resolve the crises of the psychosocial stages vary with the stage. The infant may require protection,

Table 3.1   Some Reflexes of the Human Infant

Reflex	Evoking Stimulus	Response
Reflexes that facilitate adaptation and survival		
Sucking reflex	Pressure on lips and tongue	Suction produced by movement of lips and tongue
Pupillary reflex	Weak or bright light	Dilation or constriction of pupil
Rooting reflex	Light touch to cheek	Head movement in direction of touch
Startle reflex	Loud noise	Similar to Moro, with elbows flexed and fingers closed
Swimming reflex	Neonate placed prone in water	Arm and leg movement
Reflexes linked to competences of related species		
Creeping reflex	Feet pushed against a surface	Arms and legs drawn under, head lifted
Flexion reflex	Pressure on sole of foot	Involuntary bending of leg
Grasp reflex	Pressure on fingers or palm	Closing and tightening of fingers
Moro reflex	Infant lying on back with head raised— rapidly release head	Extension of arms, head thrown back, spreading of fingers, crossing arms across body
Springing reflex	Infant held upright and slightly forward	Arms extend forward and legs drawn up
Stepping reflex	Infant supported under the arms above a flat surface	Rhythmical stepping movement
Abdominal reflex	Tactile stimulation	Involuntary contraction of abdominal muscles
Reflexes of unknown function		
Achilles tendon reflex	Blow to Achilles tendon	Contraction of calf muscles and downward bending of foot
Babinski reflex	Mild stroke on sole of foot	Fanning and extension of toes
Tonic neck reflex	Infant on back with head turned to one side	Arm and leg on side toward which head is facing are extended, other arm and leg flexed

food, or attention; the toddler may require a toy or someone to talk to; the child of middle school age may need tools and materials for work; and the early adult may need a mate.

Charlesworth suggests that the tasks of obtaining resources change with development. Infants learn to signal their needs by crying or fussing. As they get older, children acquire an increasingly diverse set of strategies to use in their efforts to get the resources they need. Both aggressive and help-giving behaviors are strategies designed to elicit needed resources.

Other areas of interest in the ethological study of development include peer-group behavior, especially play behavior; altruism; aggression and dominance; communication of emotions, especially through facial expressions; and naturally occurring problem solving.

Implications for Human Development

Human beings are the products of evolution. Evolutionary theory focuses our attention on the biological bases of behavior. A genetic plan, shaped through hundreds of generations, guides infants' predispositions, capacities, and sensitivities. Evolutionary theory points out that infants come into the world with a range of innate capacities and potentials. They are not hunks of clay to be molded and shaped by parents, teachers, and other caregivers. Rather, they have competences that permit them to establish social contact, to organize information, and to recognize and communicate their needs.

An organism is most vulnerable during childhood; children require care if they are to survive to reproductive age. It is important to understand that biological capacities and the environments in which they can be expressed operate together to produce behavior. Childhood experiences shape the future of the human species by providing the context for the establishment of attachments, meaningful social competences, and problem-solving capacities, all of which have a bearing on an individual's behavior in adulthood.

From an evolutionary point of view, the future of a species depends on the capacity of its individual members to mate, reproduce, and rear their young. The factors that contribute to the vigor and continuity of a species are the health of individual members when they attain reproductive capacity, an environment that is conducive to mating, and the capacity of sexually mature partners to rear their offspring. During adolescence, when sexual activity emerges and attitudes about marriage and parenting are being formulated, the quality of life for young people is critical to the future of human beings of every cultural group.

The evolutionary perspective draws attention to the importance of variability for a species' survival. Individual differences contribute to the vigor of the species. Human beings are genetically designed to permit wide variations in size, body shape, coloration, strength, talent, intelligence, and personality. This variability contributes to our capacity to adapt successfully to a wide variety of environmental conditions. It also protects the species as a whole from extinction.

One of the unique aspects of the human species is that it is capable of modifying the environment in significant ways; we not only adapt to the environment but alter it to suit our needs. We all hope that we will alter the environment in ways that will enhance our species' survival. However, some of the environmental risks to which pregnant women, young children, and the rest of us are exposed alert us to the fact that not all human modifications of the environment are beneficial, and to the grave responsibilities we all face to ensure that the species will not become a victim of its own inventiveness.

Cultural Differences

Ruth Benedict was one of the first cultural anthropologists to argue for a diversified view of human development. There are many cultures on the earth, each one celebrating its own holidays, following its own religion, defining its own version of family, and prescribing its own pattern of roles and role expectations. According to Benedict (1934/1950), the course of individual development is predominantly a product of cultural expectations.

Cultural determinism refers to the power of culture to shape individual experience. This perspective is in striking opposition to the evolutionary view. Biological factors are considered to be relatively insignificant in comparison with the role of culture in governing patterns of personality development.

Benedict recognized that some experiences are universal. One major common thread is the transformation of a person from a dependent child into a relatively independent, responsible adult. But Benedict observed that the path one follows in changing from a child to an adult varies from one culture to another. The degree to which the transitions are experienced as emotionally stressful or smooth depends on whether the cultural conditioning is continuous or discontinuous.

Continuity is found when a child is given information and responsibilities that apply directly to his or her adult behavior. For example, Margaret Mead (1928/1950) observed that in Samoan society, girls of 6 or 7 years of age commonly took care of their younger siblings. As they grew older, their involvement in this caregiving role increased; the *role expectations,* however, were not substantially changed.

Discontinuity is found when a child is either barred from activities that are open only to adults or forced to "unlearn" information or behaviors that are accepted in children but considered inappropriate for adults. The change from expectations of virginity before marriage to expectations of sexual responsiveness after marriage in American society is an example of discontinuity. Sexuality and sex play are viewed as inappropriate behavior for young children but appropriate for adults.

Benedict suggested that the degree to which behaviors appear to occur in stages depends on the degree of discontinuity in cultural conditioning. Cultures that have discrete, age-graded expectations for individuals at different periods in the life span produce a pattern of development in which age groups have distinct characteristics and appear to function at different skill levels. These societies are marked by public ceremonies, graduations, and other rites of passage from one stage to the next. Cultures that are permissive and open and recognize few distinctions between the respon-

Within the Orthodox Jewish culture, men and women do not dance together. This tradition is preserved during the wedding celebration, highlighting the power of culture in shaping gender roles.

sibilities of children and those of adults do not produce age-graded stages of development. In those societies, development is a much more gradual, fluid transformation in which adult competences are built directly on childhood accomplishments.

The idea of cultural determinism has been critical in guiding cross-cultural research on basic issues of human development, especially questions about the universality of certain characteristics of individual development, family life, and gender-role differences. In one of the most ambitious cross-cultural studies of child development, Beatrice Whiting and Carolyn Edwards draw on systematic observations of 12 cultural communities to examine "the processes by which the culturally determined environment affects the development of sex-differentiated behavior during the childhood years" (Whiting & Edwards, 1988, p. 3). These investigators link the development of male and female children to the status of men and women, the division of labor among men and women, the extent of the mother's daily workload, and the amount of social support available to the mother during the child's early years. In societies where men have much higher status than women, boys begin to distance themselves from women, including their mothers, between the ages of 5 and 10.

Ethnic Subcultures

Although societies can be characterized by certain shared cultural characteristics, it is important to recognize that most modern societies comprise a large number of subcultures. Because of its relative youth among the nations of the world, and because of the way it has been and is being populated, the United States is especially rich in ethnic subcultures.

An ethnic group has been defined as "a collectivity within a larger society having real or common ancestry, memories of a shared historical past, and a cultural focus

Biographical Sketch

Ruth Benedict   1887–1948

Ruth Benedict was born in New York City in 1887. She studied English literature at Vassar College. Benedict maintained a strong interest in the contributions of a culture's literature, religions, language, and aesthetic dimensions to the overall impact of the culture on its members. She studied anthropology at Columbia University under Franz Boas and completed her Ph.D. in 1923. Her dissertation focused on the concept of the guardian spirit among North American Indians. She expressed her interest in the religious and aesthetic dimensions of life through her poetry, which she wrote under a pseudonym until the early 1930s.

Benedict became an assistant professor at Columbia University in 1930 and was promoted to full professor in 1948, the year of her death. In her professional life, she studied the folklore and religion of several American Indian tribes. She elaborated the concept of cultural determinism in her book *Patterns of Culture,* in which she illustrated the great diversity of cultural forms.   ■

on one or more symbolic elements defined as the epitome of their peoplehood" (Schermerhorn, 1978, p. 12). Individual members of an ethnic group can vary in the intensity with which they identify with this subculture, but they generally share some common values, beliefs, preferences or tastes, and norms in regard to behavior. They also share a sense of loyalty to the ethnic group, which is likely to become heightened if the security of the group is threatened. Some ethnic groups are defined in part by a common racial ancestry, and therefore may be referred to as racial subcultures. Ethnicity, however, is the more general, overarching concept. It encompasses many aspects of shared experience, including racial similarities, that contribute to a sense of group identity (See & Wilson, 1988).

Identification with an ethnic subculture introduces another layer of influence in the process of cultural determinism. Persistent ethnic stereotypes or prejudices can influence the self-concept of members of an ethnic subculture. Preferences for contact with members of one's ethnic subculture can affect the kinds and amount of contact one has with members of other subcultures. Ethnic subcultural values shape one's outlook on such critical areas of life as child-rearing practices, educational aspirations, and gender-role definitions. These aspects of one's world view can be in conflict or in harmony with values held in the workplace, school, and larger political community (Horowitz, 1985).

Implications for Human Development

According to the concept of cultural determinism, the events of the various stages of development will be experienced as stressful or calm depending on how they are noted by the culture. This contrast is seen in the ways in which different cultures mark

Pablo Picasso, *Two Brothers,* 1905. This painting of two brothers suggests the theme of cultural continuity. The older brother assumes responsibility for the protection and care of his younger sibling. We can imagine that when he is mature he will extend this love toward his own children.

an adolescent girl's first menstruation (Mead, 1949/1955). The people of some societies fear menstruation, and treat the girl as if she were dangerous to others. In other societies she is viewed as having powerful magic that will affect her own future and that of the tribe. In still others, the perceived shamefulness of sex requires that the menstruation be kept as secret as possible. The culture thus determines how a biological change is marked and whether the transition will be perceived as significant in the child's eyes.

Societies vary in the extent to which they expect people to make significant life decisions during each period. They also vary in the range of choices they make available. American adolescents are asked to make decisions regarding sex, work, politics, religion, marriage, and education. In each of these areas, the alternatives are complex and varied. As a result, adolescence is prolonged and the risk of leaving this period without having found a solution to these problems is great. In cultures that leave fewer choices open and provide a clearer path from childhood to adulthood, the period of adolescence may be quite brief.

Human development must be approached with appreciation for the cultural context. Cultural expectations for the timing of certain life events, such as schooling, work, marriage, childbearing, and political and religious leadership, influence the tempo and tone of one's life history. Cultures also vary in the personal qualities they admire and those they consider inappropriate or shameful. A society's standards of beauty, leadership, and talent determine how easily an individual can achieve status within it.

An individual's life course is influenced by his or her identification with subcultural norms and values, as well as by the overarching norms and values of the dominant culture. It is difficult to assess the relative contribution of subcultural influences to a person's development. Much depends on the intensity of the person's loyalty to the subcultural group and on the way the group is viewed or treated within the larger society. However, as we consider the dynamics of normative development across the life span, we must keep in mind that people of various ethnic subcultures may have unique views on such issues as the definition of successful maturity, the value of marriage and childbearing, and the proper balance between individual achievement and responsibility to family and community.

Psychosexual Development

Freud's (1933/1964) psychoanalytic theory focuses on the development of the person's emotional and social life. Although much of this theory has been revised, refuted, or repressed, many of Freud's original assumptions persist in contemporary personality theories. Freud focused on the impact of sexual and aggressive drives on the individual's psychological functioning. He distinguished between the impact of sexual drives on mental activity and their effect on reproductive functions. As an observer of human behavior, Freud recognized the influence of sexuality on the mental activity of children. He argued that although children are incapable of reproduction, their sexual drives operate to direct aspects of their fantasies, problem solving, and social interactions.

Freud suggested that all behavior (except that resulting from fatigue) is motivated. This is a profound assumption. It carries with it an implicit need for a psychology of behavior. Behavior has meaning; it does not occur randomly or without purpose.

Much of Freud's work was an attempt to describe the processes by which motives prompt behavior. Freud hypothesized that there are two basic psychological motives: sexuality and aggression. His interpretation of all psychological events is based on this hypothesis. Every behavior, by its very nature, is in part an expression of sexual or aggressive impulses.

Pablo Picasso, *Caricature of the Artist,* 1903. In each of us the id is the source of instincts and impulses. At age 22 Picasso drew this devilish caricature of himself, suggesting his impulsive, primate nature.

A second hypothesis of psychoanalytic theory is that there is an area of the psyche called the *unconscious:* a storehouse of powerful, primitive motives of which the person is unaware. Unconscious as well as conscious motives may simultaneously motivate behavior. Thus behaviors that may appear to be somewhat unusual or extremely intense are described as *multiply determined*—that is, a single behavior expresses many motives, some of which the person can recognize and control and others of which operate unguided by conscious thought.

Domains of Consciousness

One of Freud's most enduring contributions was his analysis of the topography of mental activity. Freud thought the human mind was like an iceberg. *Conscious processes* are like the tip that protrudes out of the water: they make up only a small part of the mind. Our conscious thoughts are fleeting. We can have only a few of them at any one time. As soon as energy is diverted from a thought or image, it disappears from consciousness.

Freud thought there was an area analogous to the part of the iceberg near the waterline, in which material could be made conscious if attention were directed to it. He called this area the *preconscious.* Preconscious thoughts are readily accessible to consciousness through focused attention. You may not be thinking about your hometown or your favorite desserts right now. But if someone were to ask you about either of them, you could readily recall and discuss it.

The *unconscious,* like the rest of the iceberg, is hidden from view. It is a vast network of content and processes that are actively barred from consciousness. Freud hypothesized that the content of the unconscious, a storehouse of wishes, fears, impulses, and repressed memories, plays a major role in guiding behavior even though we cannot account for it consciously. Behaviors that are unusual or extremely intense may not make sense if they are explained only in terms of conscious motives.

A young patient of Freud's who had recently been married sometimes forgot his wife's name. Freud hypothesized that consciously the man felt he loved his wife and thought they were happy together. Freud used the evidence of forgetting the name as a clue to the content of the man's unconscious. In his unconscious, the man had unacceptable, negative feelings about his wife. Freud reasoned that since the young man could not express them directly, they found expression by blocking the wife's name from his consciousness.

Over the past thirty years, scholarly interest in cognitive processes has resulted in renewed attention to the notion of the *cognitive unconscious,* the range of mental structures and processes that operate outside awareness but play a significant role in conscious thought and action (Kihlstrom, 1987). It is becoming evident that conscious thought, just as Freud argued, accounts for only a small proportion of our capacities to identify, analyze, recall, and synthesize information.

One model of the way humans process information suggests that there are a large number of processing units or modules, each devoted to a specific task or category (Rumelhart & McClelland, 1986; Gazzaniga, 1989). Activation of one unit may excite some units and inhibit others. Information about an object may be found in a number of units. The concept of an apple, for instance, may be represented in units related to things that are red, fruits, teachers, health (an apple a day keeps the doctor away), and other, more idiosyncratic units (such as a fear of bees that swarm around rotting apples or a pleasant memory of the family outing gathering apples or the smell of applesauce cooking in Mother's kitchen). Many mental functions, including language, memory, and planning, could be operating in response to the presentation of an apple as a stimulus, although most of them would be occurring unconsciously. This view of the way the brain is organized gives a major role to unconscious processing, which accompanies all types of conscious activity.

Three Structures of Personality

Freud (1933/1964) described three components of personality: the id, the ego, and the superego (see Figure 3.1). The *id* is the source of instincts and impulses. It is the primary source of psychic energy, and it exists from birth. The id expresses its demands according to the *pleasure principle:* we are motivated to seek pleasure and avoid pain. The pleasure principle does not take into account the feelings of others, society's norms, or agreements between people. Its rule is to achieve immediate discharge of impulses. When you lie to a friend to protect your own image, or when you cut ahead of people in line so you won't have to wait, you are operating according to the pleasure principle.

The logic of the id is also the logic of dreams. This kind of thinking is called *primary process thought.* It is characterized by a lack of concern for the constraints of

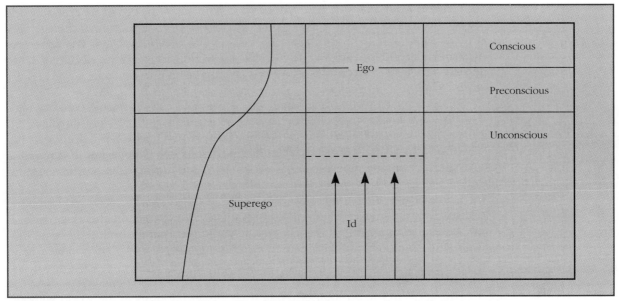

Figure 3.1   **Freud's Model of the Structure of Personality**

reality. In primary process thought there are no negatives. Everything is yes. There is no time. Nothing happens in the past or in the future. Everything is now. Symbolism becomes flexible. One object may symbolize many things and many different objects may mean the same thing. Many male faces can all represent the father. A house may be a symbol for one's mother, a lover, or the female genitals as well as for a house.

Ego is the term for all mental functions that have to do with the person's relation to the environment. Freud thought the ego begins to develop in the first six or eight months of life and is well established by the age of 2 or 3. Of course, much change and growth occur after this time as well. The ego functions include perception, learning, memory, judgment, self-awareness, and language skills. The ego responds to the demands from the environment and helps a person function effectively in the world. The ego also responds to the demands of the id and the superego and helps the person satisfy needs, live up to ideals and standards, and establish a healthy emotional balance.

The ego operates according to the *reality principle.* Under this principle, the ego protects the person by waiting to gratify id impulses until a socially acceptable form of expression or gratification can be found. In the ego, primary process thought becomes subordinated to a more reality-oriented process, called *secondary process thought.* This process begins to dominate as the ego matures.

Secondary process thought is the kind of logical, sequential thinking that we usually mean when we discuss thinking. It allows people to plan and act in order to engage the world and to achieve gratification in personally and socially acceptable ways. It enables people to delay gratification. It helps people test plans by examining whether they will really work. This last process is called *reality testing.*

The *superego* includes the moral precepts of one's mind—the *conscience*—and the ideals in regard to one's potential as a moral person—the *ego ideal*. Freud's work led him to conclude that the superego does not begin to develop until the age of 5 or 6, and probably is not firmly established until several years later. The superego determines a good measure of one's ideas about which behavior is proper, acceptable, and to be striven for and which behavior is improper and unacceptable. It also defines one's aspirations and goals as a "good" person.

The superego psychologically punishes a person for unacceptable behavior and rewards a person for acceptable behavior. The superego is harsh and unrealistic in its demands. It is as illogical and unrelenting in its search for proper behavior as the id is in its search for pleasure. When a child thinks about behaving in a morally unacceptable way, the superego sends a warning by producing feelings of anxiety and guilt.

The superego is developed through a process called *identification*. Motivated by love, fear, and admiration, children actively imitate characteristics of their parents and internalize their parents' values. Through identification, parents' values become the ideals and aspirations of their children. Parents and others in the environment may make demands that a child does not internalize as part of the superego. The ego deals with these demands as well as with the superego's internalized demands.

The ego is in the position of trying to gratify id impulses in the world without generating strong feelings of guilt in the superego. In one sense, the ego serves both the id and the superego: it strives to provide gratification, but to do so in personally acceptable ways. In another sense, the ego is the executive of personality. The strength of the ego determines the person's effectiveness in meeting his or her needs, in handling the demands of the superego, and in dealing with the demands of reality. If the ego is strong and can establish a good balance among id, superego, and environmental demands, the person is satisfied and free from immobilizing guilt and feelings of worthlessness.

When id and superego are stronger than ego, the person may be tossed and turned psychologically by strong desires for pleasure and strong constraints against attaining those desires. When environmental demands are strong and the ego is weak, a person may also be overwhelmed. In Freud's psychoanalytic theory, it is the breakdown of the ego that leads to mental disorder.

Much of the relationship of the id, the ego, and the superego is played out at an unconscious level. In the early years, aspects of basic drives and primary process thought are noticeable in a child's consciousness. This is an indication of the conscious presence of the id. As the ego grows stronger, it is able to push the id's desires and fantasies into the unconscious, so that the person can attend to the exploration and demands of the external world. Freud thought that the superego also operated mostly at the unconscious level. He thought the ego, however, functioned at both the conscious and unconscious levels.

Much of the ego's work involves mediating the conflicts between the id's demands for gratification and the superego's demands for good behavior. This work is conducted outside the person's awareness. When unconscious conflicts threaten to break through into consciousness, the person experiences anxiety. If the ego functions effectively, it pushes these conflicts into the unconscious and thereby protects the

When the ego fails to find acceptable ways of expressing impulses, society has to step in with external controls.

person from unpleasant emotion. The ego proceeds to satisfy desires in acceptable ways by directing behavior and social interaction.

Strong, unresolvable conflicts may leave a person in a state of constant anxiety and symptoms of conflict may emerge. A person who feels a desire that is thought to be very "bad," such as an unconscious wish to harm a parent or to be sexually intimate with a sibling, may experience anxiety without recognizing its source. The ungratified impulse continues to seek gratification. The superego continues to find the impulse unacceptable, and the conflict continues to produce anxiety in the person's conscious experience. The unpleasant emotional state may preoccupy the person and make it difficult to handle the normal demands of day-to-day life.

Defense Mechanisms

If the conflict continues to cause anxiety, the ego makes efforts to reduce it. Defense mechanisms are used to protect the person from anxiety so that effective functioning can be preserved. They distort, substitute, or completely block out the source of the conflict. They are usually initiated unconsciously.

Often the defense mechanism used depends on a person's age and the intensity of the perceived threat. Younger children tend to use denial and repression (pushing thoughts from awareness). A more diverse set of defenses, requiring greater cognitive complexity, becomes available in the course of development. In situations of greatest threat, denial is often the initial defense used, regardless of age.

For Freud, the basic defense mechanism was *repression:* unacceptable impulses are pushed into the unconscious. It is as if a wall were constructed between the

Biographical Sketch

Sigmund Freud   1856–1939

Sigmund Freud was born in Freiberg (now Pribor), Czechoslovakia, in 1856. Both his grandfather and great-grandfather had been rabbis. One of Freud's early memories was of a strong resentment toward his baby brother, who had been born when Freud was 19 months old. Freud was filled with guilt over his angry feelings when the infant died at 8 months of age.

Freud was trained as a neurologist in Vienna during the 1870s. His early research focused on the functions of the medulla, the conduction of nerve impulses in the brain and spinal cord, and the anesthetic properties of cocaine (Freud, 1963). In 1882 Freud's interest turned from physiology to psychology because of his association with Josef Breuer. Breuer and Freud developed a theory of hysteria in which they attributed certain forms of paralysis to psychological conflict rather than to physiological damage (Breuer & Freud, 1895/1955).

As a physician, Freud continued to develop his scientific interests in psychology by keeping careful notes on his patients. In many of his writings he presents cases from which he derived his theory of psychological functioning.

In 1905 Freud published his theory of infantile sexuality and its relation to adult life. His ideas on this topic produced a fury of insults and criticism. His medical colleagues could not accept the idea of childhood sexuality. They considered his public lectures on the topic crude and distasteful. Freud was denied a professorial appointment at the University of Vienna primarily because of these lectures and writings. Even Breuer, his longtime colleague and collaborator, found Freud's preoccupation with sexual motives offensive and terminated their association.

In response to his exclusion from the medical community, Freud helped to form the International Congress on Psychoanalysis. There he developed his psychosexual theory and taught the principles of psychoanalysis to his followers. Freud was very intolerant of any questioning of or deviation from his views. Alfred Adler and Carl Jung broke away from the congress to establish their own schools of thought after repeated unsuccessful attempts to get Freud to modify his theory in the direction of their ideas.

Toward the end of his life, Freud, like Albert Einstein in Germany, was forced to leave Austria to protect himself and his family from the threat of extermination by the Nazis. In the 1930s Freud and Einstein corresponded regarding their perceptions of anti-Semitism (Einstein & Freud, 1933/1964). They shared their experiences as men of science who had been subjected to the same form of bitter attack.

Freud died of cancer in England in 1939. He devoted the last years of his life to extensive writing that furthered the pursuit of his theory by other analysts and scholars. ∎

unconscious and the conscious mind, so that anxiety-provoking thoughts and feelings cannot enter consciousness. With unacceptable thoughts and impulses far from awareness, the person is protected from uncomfortable feelings of anxiety and may devote the remaining psychic energy to interchange with the interpersonal and physical environments.

The following are defense mechanisms:

Repression: unacceptable wishes are barred from conscious thought.

Projection: unacceptable wishes are attributed to someone else.

Reaction formation: unacceptable feelings are expressed by the opposite feelings.

Regression: one avoids confronting conflicts and stresses by reverting to behaviors that were effective and comforting at an earlier life stage.

Displacement: unacceptable impulses are expressed toward a substitute target.

Rationalization: unacceptable feelings and actions are justified by logical or pseudo-logical explanations.

Isolation: feelings are separated from thoughts.

Denial: parts of external reality are denied.

Sublimation: unacceptable wishes are channeled to socially acceptable behaviors.

According to Freud, all normal people resort to defense mechanisms at various times in their lives. These mechanisms not only reduce anxiety but may lead to positive social outcomes. Physicians who use isolation may be able to function effectively because they are able to apply their knowledge without being hindered by their feelings. Children who rationalize defeat may be able to protect their self-esteem by viewing themselves favorably. The child who projects angry feelings onto someone else may find that this technique stimulates a competitive orientation that enhances performance.

Some people rely more on one or two defensive techniques than on the others. The resultant *defensive style* becomes part of an overall personality pattern. It permits one to regulate the impact of the environment and to perceive experiences in ways that are compatible with one's needs.

When defense mechanisms are used to excess, however, they may indicate a deeper psychological problem. The use of defense mechanisms draws psychological energy from the ego. Energy that is used to prevent certain wishes from entering conscious thought is not available for other life activities. A person whose energy is devoted to defensive strategies may be unable to develop other ego functions and to use those functions adequately.

Psychosexual Stages

Freud assumed that the most significant developments in personality take place during five life stages from infancy through adolescence. After that time, according to Freud, the essential pattern for expressing and controlling impulses has been established. Later life serves only to uncover new modes of gratification and new sources of frustration.

Pablo Picasso, *Silenius Dancing,* 1933. Freud emphasized the role of sexual impulses in directing and shaping personality and inter-personal life.

The stages Freud described reflect his emphasis on sexuality as a driving force. Freud used the term *sexuality* quite broadly, referring to the full range of physical pleasure, from sucking to sexual intercourse. He also attached a positive, life-force symbolism to the concept of sexuality, suggesting that sexual impulses provide a thrust toward growth and renewal. At each stage, he taught, a particular body zone is of heightened sexual importance. The five stages Freud identified are the oral, anal, phallic, latent, and genital stages.

During the *oral stage,* in the first year of life, the mouth is the site of sexual and aggressive gratification. Freud characterized infants as dependent, incorporative, and poorly differentiated from others. As infants learn to delay gratification, the ego becomes more clearly differentiated and they become aware of the distinction between the self and others.

In the *anal stage,* during the second year of life, the anus is the most sexualized body part. With the development of the sphincter muscles, a child learns to expel or withhold feces at will. The conflict at this stage focuses on the subordination of the child's will to the demands of the culture (via parents) for appropriate toilet habits.

The *phallic stage* begins during the third year of life and may last until the child is 6. It is a period of heightened genital sensitivity in the absence of the hormonal changes that accompany puberty. Freud described the behavior of children at this stage as bisexual. They direct sexualized activity toward both sexes and engage in self-stimulation. This is the stage during which the Oedipal or Electra complex is observed. The *Oedipal complex* in boys and the *Electra complex* in girls result from ambivalence surrounding heightened sexuality. The child has a strong, sexualized attraction to the parent of the opposite sex. The child may desire to have the exclusive attention of that parent, and may fantasize that the other parent will leave, or perhaps die. At the same time, the child fears that amorous overtures toward the desired parent may result in hostility or retribution from the parent of the same sex. The child also worries that this beloved parent will withdraw love. Parental threats intended to prevent the child from masturbating add to the child's fears that sexualized fantasies are going to result in punishment or withdrawal of love.

Freud believed that once the Oedipal or Electra conflict is resolved, the child enters a period of *latency*. During this stage, which lasts from about 7 years until puberty, no new significant conflicts or impulses arise. The primary personality development during this period is that of the superego. Other theorists, particularly Harry Stack Sullivan (1953) and Erikson (1963), perceive these years as a time of significant growth in social relationships and achievement.

Freud described a final stage of development that begins with the onset of puberty: the *genital stage*. During this period, the person directs sexual impulses toward someone of the opposite sex. Adolescence brings about a reawakening of Oedipal or Electra conflicts and a reworking of earlier childhood identifications. Freud explains the tension of adolescence as the result of the sexual threat that the mature adolescent poses to the family unit. In an effort to avoid this threat, adolescents may withdraw from their families or temporarily devalue their parents. With the selection of a permanent sex partner, the threat of intimacy between young people and their parents diminishes. At the end of adolescence, a more autonomous relationship with one's parents becomes possible.

Freud believed that the psychological conflicts that adolescents and adults experience arise from failure to satisfy or express specific wishes during childhood. At any of the childhood stages, sexualized impulses may have been so frustrated or overindulged that the person continues to seek their gratification at later stages of life. Freud used the term *fixation* to refer to continued use of pleasure-seeking or anxiety-reducing behaviors appropriate to an earlier stage of development. Inasmuch as no person can possibly satisfy all wishes at every life stage, normal development depends on the ability to channel the energy from those impulses into activities that either symbolize them or express them in a socially acceptable form. This process is called *sublimation*.

During adolescence and early adulthood, patterns of impulse expression, fixation, and sublimation crystallize into a life orientation. From this point on, the content of the id, the regulating functions of the superego, and the executive functions of the ego rework the struggles of childhood through repeated episodes of engagement, conflict, and impulse gratification or frustration.

Freud's psychoanalytic emphasis on early childhood gave an enormous boost to the study of young children. Unfortunately, this much-needed impetus to consider the early years of development may have distracted psychoanalytically oriented psychologists from considering the relevance of later development.

Modern scholars in the psychoanalytic tradition have begun to direct their attention to developmental issues of the adult years (Greenspan & Pollack, 1980). Of particular relevance for life-span development is the expanded interest in ego development as expressed in the focus on self, self-understanding, and self-other relationships, referred to as *object relations* (Goldberg, 1988; Stern, 1987; Gardner, 1983). In addition, feminist criticism of Freud's analysis of the psychosexual development of women, especially his view of the Electra complex and his obviously sexist perspective on the female body, has led to a new psychoanalytic approach to issues of gender and the psychology of women (Fast, 1984; Westkott, 1986; Alpert, 1986). Finally, the focus on early object relations has been expanded to examine experiences of bereavement and loss in adult life (Parkes, 1987; Viorst, 1986).

Implications for Human Development

Psychoanalytic theory emphasizes the importance of interpersonal demands and intrapsychic demands in the shaping of personality. The ego develops skills for dealing with the realities of the interpersonal world. It also develops skills for satisfying personal needs and for imposing personal standards and aspirations on the way these needs are satisfied. The expectations of others, particularly parents, are internalized and given personal meaning in the formation of the superego. Once the superego is formed, the person must respond to constraints on impulse that represent the expectations and interactions that become part of the person's psyche. By developing this idea, Freud was able to show how a person translated the demands of the interpersonal world into his or her own personal way of functioning. At the same time, new demands and experiences continue to play a role in the development of personality. Freud focused on the effects of sexual impulses on personal and interpersonal life. Erikson extended Freud's thinking by emphasizing that many psychoanalytic concepts also shed light on the effects of social impulses and experiences on personal and interpersonal life.

One of the major early contributions of psychoanalytic theory was the identification of the influence of childhood experiences on adult behavior. Psychoanalytic theory was unique in its focus on stages of development, family interactions, and unresolved family conflicts as explanations for ongoing adult behavior. The emphasis Freud gave to the importance of parenting practices and their implications for psychosexual development provides one of the few theoretical frameworks for examining parent-child relationships. Many of the early empirical studies in developmental psychology focused on issues that derived from his theory, such as child-rearing and discipline practices, moral development, and childhood aggression.

The psychoanalytic approach recognizes the importance of motives, emotions, and fantasies to human behavior. Within this framework, human behavior springs at least as much from emotional needs as from reason. The theory suggests that underlying motives and wishes explain behaviors that otherwise might not make sense. Psychoanalytic theory recognizes domains of thought that may not appear to be logical to the observer, but that make sense from the point of view of the individual. Many domains of mental activity, including fantasies, dreams, primary process thoughts and symbols, and defense mechanisms, influence the way people derive meaning from their experiences. Through the construct of the unconscious, Freud provided a means for conceptualizing explanations for thoughts and behaviors that appear irrational, self-destructive, or contradictory. The idea that development involves efforts to find acceptable outlets for strong, often socially unacceptable impulses still guides therapeutic intervention with children, adolescents, and adults.

Another critical point is Freud's open recognition of the role of sexual impulses during childhood. Freud believed that a sexual relationship with a loving partner is important for healthy adult functioning. He concluded that sexual impulses have a direct outlet in behavior during adult life. Freud recognized that children have sensual needs for stimulation and satisfaction, but they seemed to have no acceptable means to satisfy those needs. Today we are more aware of a child's need for hugging, snuggling, and physical warmth with loving caregivers, but most adults in our society still find it difficult to acknowledge or permit the expression of more direct, sexualized behaviors on the part of young children. Childhood wishes and needs, bottled up in the unconscious by defense mechanisms, guide behavior indirectly through symbolic expression, dreams, or, in some cases, the symptoms of mental disorders. We need only look at a daily newspaper to recognize widespread concern about the expression of sexual impulses in modern society. Controversies over sexual dysfunction, sexual abuse, rape by strangers and acquaintances, sexual harassment in the workplace, sexually transmitted diseases, contraception, abortion, infidelity, and homophobia reveal the difficulty with which Americans deal with the expression of sexual impulses. The relationship between changing sexual needs and behavior during adulthood and aging still requires research in the study of development over the life span.

Cognitive Development

Cognition is the process of organizing and making meaning of experience. Interpreting a statement, solving a problem, synthesizing information, critically analyzing a complex task—all are cognitive activities. The modern approach to understanding cognitive development has been stimulated by the work of Jean Piaget.

According to Piaget, every organism strives to achieve equilibrium. *Equilibrium* is a balance of organized structures, whether motor, sensory, or cognitive. When these structures are in equilibrium, they provide effective ways of interacting with the environment. Whenever changes in the organism or in the environment require a revision of the basic structures, they are thrown into disequilibrium (Piaget, 1978/1985). Piaget focused both on equilibrium with the environment, achieved through the formation of schemes and operations that form systematic, logical structures for comprehending and analyzing experience, and on equilibrium within the schemes and operations themselves.

In this theory, knowing is an active process of achieving and reachieving equilibrium, not a constant state (Miller, 1989). Knowing is a product of continuous interaction between the person and the environment. We approach new situations with expectations that have developed in the past. Each new experience changes those expectations somewhat. Our ability to understand and interpret experience is constantly changing as we encounter diversity and novelty in the environment.

Piaget assumed that the roots of cognition lie in the infant's biological capacities. Intelligence unfolds in a systematic fashion provided the environment offers adequate diversity and support for exploration. Among the concepts that inform Piaget's theory, three are of special relevance here: scheme, adaptation, and stages of development.

Self-Portrait, 1896

Yo Picasso, 1901

*Self-Portrait with a
Palette,* 1906

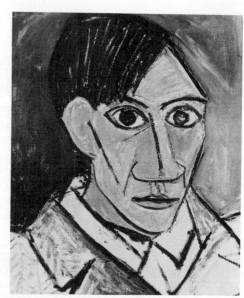

Self-Portrait, 1907

The self-concept is a complex scheme that undergoes continuous revision and modification. In these four self-portraits, completed at ages 15, 20, 25, and 26, Picasso shapes and revises not only his artistic techniques but his self-image.

Scheme

Piaget and Inhelder (1969) defined *scheme* as "the structure or organization of actions as they are transferred or generalized by repetition in similar or analogous circumstances" (p. 4). A scheme is any organized, meaningful grouping of events, feelings, and related images, actions, or ideas. Piaget preferred the term *scheme* rather than *concept* because it is more readily tied to actions as opposed to words. He used the word to discuss the counterpart of concepts and conceptual networks during the period of infancy before language and other symbolic systems are developed.

Schemes begin to be formed during infancy through the repetition of regular sequences of action. Two kinds of schemes emerge in infancy. The first guides a particular action, such as grasping a rattle or sucking on a bottle. The second links sequences of actions, such as climbing into the high chair in order to eat breakfast or crawling to the door to greet Daddy when he comes home (Uzgiris, 1976). Infants differentiate between people who are familiar and those who are unfamiliar. They differentiate between playful sounds, such as cooing and babbling, and sounds that will bring a caregiver, such as crying and screeching. They differentiate between foods they will eat readily and those they reject. Such groupings suggest schemes, developed by a mental coordination process that evolves with an infant's repeated transactions with aspects of the environment. Schemes are created and modified continuously throughout the life span.

Adaptation

Piaget (1936/1952) views cognition as a continuously evolving process in which the content and diversity of experiences stimulate the formation of new schemes. People are constantly striving to attain equilibrium both with the environment and in the cognitive components of their mental structures. According to Piaget, knowledge is the result of *adaptation,* or the gradual modification of existing schemes to take into account the novelty or uniqueness of each experience. You can see the similarity between this use of the term *adaptation* and its use in evolutionary theory. Piaget extended the concept of adaptation, suggesting that it works to produce modifications in the capacity for logical thought. "It is by adapting to things that thought organizes itself," he says, "and it is by organizing itself that it structures things" (1936/1952, pp. 7–8).

Adaptation is a two-part process in which the continuity of existing schemes and the possibility of altering schemes interact. One part of the adaptation process is *assimilation*—the tendency to interpret new experiences in terms of an existing scheme. Assimilation contributes to the continuity of knowing. For example, Karen thinks that anyone who goes to the private high school in her city is a snob. When she meets Gail, who attends the private school, she expects Gail to be a snob. After talking with Gail for five minutes, she concludes that Gail really *is* a snob. Here we see assimilation: Karen interprets her interactions with Gail in light of an existing scheme about the kinds of students who attend the private school.

The second part of the adaptation process is *accommodation*—the tendency to modify familiar schemes in order to account for new dimensions of the object or

Pablo Picasso, *Maya Sleeping,* 1938. Adaptation involves two complementary processes, assimilation and accommodation. Through assimilation, we apply familiar schemes to new experiences. Through accommodation, we modify schemes to take into account the new aspects of experience. Babies use the sucking scheme to assimilate new objects. They accommodate by modifying the sucking scheme to provide comfort as well as nutrition.

event that are revealed. For example, if Karen and Gail were to spend a little more time together, Karen might discover that Gail is not rich and is attending the private high school on a scholarship. She and Karen actually have a lot of common interests. Gail is quite friendly and wants to see Karen again. Karen decides that not everyone who goes to the private school is a snob. She realizes that she has to postpone judgment about people until she gets to know them a little better. Here we see accommodation: Karen is modifying her scheme about the students who attend the private school in order to integrate the new information she is receiving.

Throughout life we gain knowledge gradually through the related processes of assimilation and accommodation. In order to have a new idea, we must be able to relate a new experience, thought, or event to some already existing scheme. We must also be able to modify our schemes in order to differentiate the novel from the familiar. On the one hand, we distort reality to make it fit existing cognitive structures. On the other hand, when current cognitive structures are inadequate to account for the new experiences, we adjust them to take into account the demands of reality. According to Piaget, cognitive development proceeds in small steps. Moderately discrepant experiences can be accommodated, but if discrepancies are too different from our current level of understanding, we will gain no new understanding.

Stages of Development

Piaget was interested in understanding how we arrive at our knowledge. He was interested in *knowing* as an active process, a means of constructing meaning, not in the specific content of our knowledge. He therefore focused on the abstract structures

Biographical Sketch

Jean Piaget   1896–1980

Jean Piaget was born in Switzerland in 1896. Much like Darwin, he showed talent as a naturalist early in childhood. He observed and studied birds, fossils, and seashells, and at the age of 10 contributed a note on the albino sparrow to a scientific journal. While in high school he began to publish papers describing the characteristics of mollusks. His work in this area was so impressive that he was invited to become the curator of the mollusk collection at the Geneva Museum. He earned his doctorate from the University of Neuchâtel in 1918; his dissertation was on the mollusks of Vallais.

For cognitive psychology the most direct consequence of Piaget's training as a naturalist was his sense that the principles of biology could be used to explain the evolution of knowledge. And the observational skills he had honed would serve him well as he developed his theory.

After several further years of research, Piaget was able to define a set of problems and methods that would guide his program of research and theory building. Between 1918 and 1921 he worked in the laboratory of Theodore Lipps, whose research focused on the study of empathy and aesthetics. He spent some time working at Eugen Bleuler's psychiatric clinic near Zurich, where he learned the techniques of psychiatric interviewing. He went to the Sorbonne in Paris, where he had the opportunity to work in the laboratory of Alfred Binet. Binet's laboratory was actually an elementary school in which studies on the nature of intelligence were being conducted. Here Piaget investigated children's responses to reasoning tests. He devised a clinical interview technique to determine how children arrive at their answers to reasoning problems. He became interested in the patterns of thought revealed by their incorrect answers. In essence, Piaget focused on how children think rather than on how much they know.

Piaget's observations provided the basis for his first articles on the characteristics of children's thought processes. One of these articles brought him to the attention of the editor of *Psychological Archives,* who offered him the job of director of studies at the Institut Jean-Jacques Rousseau in Geneva. There Piaget began to investigate children's moral judgments, theories about everyday events, and language. It was not until the period from 1923 to 1929, when Piaget conducted experiments and systematic observations with preverbal infants, that he began to unravel the basic mysteries of the growth of logical thought. This work was significantly enriched by observations of his own children.

Piaget produced a massive quantity of research and theory about cognitive development, logic, the history of thought, education, and the theory of knowledge (epistemology). In 1969 the American Psychological Association gave Piaget the Distinguished Scientific Contribution Award for the work that had revolutionized our understanding of the nature of human knowledge and the development of intelligence. He continued his work on the nature of children's cognitive development until his death in 1980, at the age of 83. ∎

The outdoor environment is a rich source of stimulation for sensorimotor exploration.

that underlie the way children approach experiences. As he worked with children he was more interested in seeing how they arrived at the answers to the problems they were solving than in the answers themselves.

From this perspective Piaget developed a theory of basic stages of cognitive development. He was working to describe a fundamental pattern of cognitive maturation, a universal path along which the human capacity for logical reasoning unfolds. The stages he described therefore encompassed abstract processes that could be applied to many content areas and that could be observed at roughly the same chronological age periods across cultures. Piaget was not trying to explain why some children know more about mathematics and others know more about history. He was not trying to explain why some children learn more readily through talking and listening (auditory modes) while others learn more readily by reading (visual mode). He was not trying to explain why some children can solve a problem at age 8 and others cannot solve that same problem until 8 years, 6 months. In other words, his theory focuses on the epigenesis of logical thought—that is, the development of new structures for thought—not on explanations for individual differences in knowledge and reasoning or on differences that might result from cultural and subcultural experiences.

Piaget viewed intelligence as following regular, predictable patterns of change. He posited four stages of cognitive development. At each new stage, the competences of the earlier stages are not lost but are integrated into a qualitatively new approach to thinking and knowing.

The first stage, *sensorimotor intelligence,* begins at birth and lasts until approximately 18 months of age. This stage is characterized by the formation of increasingly complex sensory and motor schemes that allow infants to organize and exercise some control over their environment.

The second stage, *preoperational thought,* begins when the child learns a language and ends about age 5 or 6. During this stage, children develop the tools for representing schemes symbolically through language, imitation, imagery, symbolic play, and symbolic drawing. Their knowledge is still very much tied to their own perceptions.

The third stage, *concrete operational thought,* begins about age 6 or 7 and ends in early adolescence, around age 11 or 12. During this stage, children begin to appreciate the logical necessity of certain causal relationships. They can manipulate categories, classification systems, and hierarchies in groups. They are more successful at solving problems that are clearly tied to physical reality than at generating hypotheses about purely philosophical or abstract concepts.

The final stage of cognitive development, *formal operational thought,* begins in adolescence and persists through adulthood. This level of thinking permits a person to conceptualize about many simultaneously interacting variables. It allows for the creation of a system of laws or rules that can be used for problem solving. Formal operational thought reflects the quality of intelligence on which science and philosophy are built.

Later, when we explore these stages in greater depth, we will find evidence that both supports and conflicts with Piaget's cognitive developmental theory. The importance of understanding the development of the human capacity for reasoning and knowing has understandably led to an enormous amount of scholarly research. We now have an extensive literature that examines many of Piaget's conclusions and another body of literature that extends his theory in new directions. Evidence in support of qualitatively unique developmental levels of the sort Piaget described is quite impressive. At the same time, evidence that culture, experience, and conditions of learning affect one's performance at each stage is also compelling. Individual factors, too, introduce variations in timing, sequence, and performance (Fischer & Silvern, 1985).

Implications for Human Development

At the earliest stage of development, children depend on their senses and motor skills to "know" the world. Each subsequent stage frees them somewhat from their dependence on sensation. Through repeated interactions with the environment, children and adolescents discover logical bases for organizing and interpreting experience. They develop language as a means of communicating and testing their interpretations (Chomsky, 1972; Lorenz, 1935/1981). By adolescence they are capable of explaining some phenomena through a series of logical hypotheses, whether or not they have observed the phenomena or performed the actions of any of the hypotheses. Their thought processes become increasingly effective at analyzing experience.

In addition to describing the characteristics of thought at various stages, Piaget contributed to the methodology of research with children. His theory of intelligence during infancy (sensorimotor intelligence) was based primarily on careful observations and slight manipulations of his own children's behavior (1936/1952). His theory of intelligence during toddlerhood (preoperational thought) was based on children's answers to questions about their dreams and familiar life events, such as what makes things alive and what causes day and night (1924/1952, 1926/1951). He carried out his research on characteristics of the school-age child's thought (concrete operations) and the adolescent's thought (formal operations) by posing a variety of problems, watching subjects solve them, and questioning them about their solutions (1941/1952, 1950, 1954). The emphasis of these studies was on how the person arrived at the answer rather than on the answer itself. The subjects became collaborators, providing Piaget with some insight as to the meaning of the problem and the path toward a solution from their own points of view.

Interest in cognitive development has taken several directions. Neo-Piagetians, while accepting the concepts of stages and sequences in the development of cognition, are shifting their focus to changes in the information-processing capacities that underlie changes in development (Case, 1985; Case et al., 1988) and changes in skills linked with specific domains, such as mathematical reasoning and role taking (Fischer, 1980; Resnick, 1989).

Research on moral reasoning, guided by Lawrence Kohlberg's analysis of stages in the development of judgments about moral dilemmas, is a direct outgrowth of Piaget's theory (Kohlberg, 1978, 1984; Haan, Weiss & Johnson, 1982; Smetana, 1989). This work has linked the ability to make moral judgments to certain conceptual changes in the understanding of intentionality, justice, and reciprocity. Moral reasoning appears to follow a stage sequence, especially if one focuses on the period from preschool through early adolescence (Walker, 1989).

Another area of interest has been social cognition. Researchers have been concerned about the development of knowledge about the self and others. They have traced the development of the ability to take the point of view of another person by studying performance on a variety of tasks that challenge the person's own perspective. Studies on role-taking ability, communication skills, and friendship have used the social-cognitive perspective. Among the many social concepts that have been studied, the concept of gender has received particular attention. Research has focused on how children develop an understanding of gender, and on the attributes they associate with gender (Bem, 1989; Fagot & Leinbach, 1989; Levy & Carter, 1989). The quality of social relationships and self-understanding are intimately tied to underlying qualitative changes in a person's capacity to conceptualize about rules and regularities that apply to social life.

An important new direction in cognitive developmental research addresses the development of *metacognition,* or thinking about thinking (Ruffman & Olson, 1989; Moore, Bryant & Furrow, 1989; Flavell, Green & Flavell, 1989; Sternberg & Smith, 1988: Neisser, 1987; Cole & Means, 1986). What do individuals know about the way their own reasoning capacities operate and how information is organized? How does this knowledge develop? How do we achieve a sense of concepts such as certainty about our understanding? How do we come to distinguish reality from belief and opinion? How do we assess how well we understand something or what strategies would help us understand it better?

Cognitive theorists are just beginning to document the direction of developmental changes during the stages of adulthood. Research on adult problem solving and reasoning has been inconclusive. Some studies have shown that adults tend to be practical rather than hypothetical in their approach to tasks. Others have emphasized adults' increasing capacity to maintain opposing ideas and to find solutions that are adaptive in a given context (Labouvie-Vief, 1980; Denney, 1982; Kosslyn, 1986; Cornelius & Caspi, 1987).

Learning

Learning theories have proposed mechanisms to account for the relatively permanent changes in behavior that occur as a result of experience. The reason that humans have such an extensive capacity to adapt to changes in the environment is that they are so well equipped to learn. Four theories of learning have made significant contributions to the study of human development: (1) classical conditioning, (2) operant conditioning, (3) social learning, and (4) cognitive behaviorism. As you read about these theories, you will begin to appreciate that the term *learning* encompasses a wide variety of processes.

Classical Conditioning

The principles of classical conditioning, sometimes referred to as Pavlovian conditioning, were developed by Ivan Pavlov (1927/1960). Pavlov's work focused on the way control over a response can be shifted from one stimulus to another. In much of his work, he used the salivary reflex as the response system. He carried out an extensive body of research in an effort to understand the conditions under which other stimuli in the environment would elicit or inhibit salivation.

The model for classical conditioning is seen in Figure 3.2. Before conditioning, the bell is a *neutral stimulus* (NS). It elicits a response of interest or attention, but nothing more. The sight and smell of food are *unconditioned stimuli* (US) that elicit salivation, the *unconditioned response* (UR). During conditioning trials, the bell is rung shortly before the food appears. The dog is said to have been conditioned when it salivates to the sound of the bell, even before the food is presented. The bell, therefore, comes to control the salivation response. Salivation that occurs in response to the bell alone is called the *conditioned response* (CR).

Modern research on Pavlovian conditioning has demonstrated that conditioning is a means by which the learner identifies structure in the environment (Davey, 1987; Rescorla, 1988). The pairing of two events, such as the sound of a bell and the presentation of food, becomes significant because one stimulus becomes a signal for the other. The CS does not always have to occur before the US. The CS may occur frequently with the US, but if there is no systematic relationship between the two, conditioning will not take place. The light may be on in the kitchen whenever the telephone rings, for example, but since there is no predictable relationship between the light and the telephone, the light does not become a signal that the telephone is going

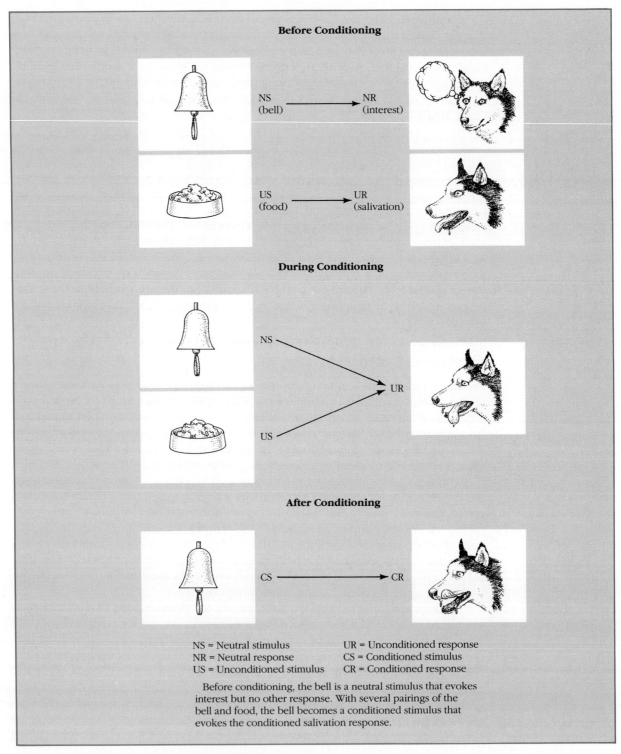

Before Conditioning

NS (bell) → NR (interest)

US (food) → UR (salivation)

During Conditioning

NS
US → UR

After Conditioning

CS → CR

NS = Neutral stimulus   UR = Unconditioned response
NR = Neutral response   CS = Conditioned stimulus
US = Unconditioned stimulus   CR = Conditioned response

Before conditioning, the bell is a neutral stimulus that evokes interest but no other response. With several pairings of the bell and food, the bell becomes a conditioned stimulus that evokes the conditioned salivation response.

Figure 3.2   Classical Conditioning

to ring. Conditioning is not an artificial paradigm; it is an actual process by which one stimulus provides information about another.

Conditioning does not take place randomly between any two events linked in time. A conditioned response is established to the degree that there is a "meaningful" relationship between the CS and the US. Furthermore, the CS itself is not totally neutral. A visual stimulus such as a colored light will prompt visual orienting, for instance, whereas an auditory stimulus may simply increase attention or arousal. In a conditioning experiment, the learner builds many associations simultaneously. Although the focus of a particular experiment may be on establishing a link between one CS and one US, the learner will build links among many elements of the environment—its visual, auditory, and olfactory components, including the US. Pavlovian conditioning provides a model for understanding how multiple associations can be established and triggered in the process of concept formation, memory, and problem solving (McClelland & Rumelhart, 1986; Rumelhart & McClelland, 1986).

Implications for Human Development

Classical conditioning can account for a great deal of the associational learning that occurs throughout life. When a specific symbol is paired with an image, emotional reaction, or object, that symbol takes on new meaning. The associations that are made through classical conditioning may involve labels and concepts, but they do not necessarily require language skills. During infancy and toddlerhood, a variety of positive and negative emotional reactions are conditioned to people, objects, and environments as the child develops attachments. Our reactions to the taste of a certain type of food or the feel of a particular material may be the result of conditioned learning that has persisted until adulthood. Similarly, fears can be the results of classical conditioning. Many people recall at least one frightening experience, such as nearly drowning, being beaten, or falling from the top of a slide. The association of fear or pain with a specific target may lead to systematic avoidance of that object for the rest of one's life.

Operant Conditioning

E. L. Thorndike (1898) studied a different type of learning called *operant conditioning*. He observed cats as they figured out how to escape from a cage. Thorndike described a process of trial-and-error learning in which the cats made fewer and fewer random movements and increasingly directed their behavior to the correct solution (pulling a string to release a latch). Operant conditioning emphasizes the role of repetition and the consequences of behavior in learning.

One of the best-known American psychologists is B. F. Skinner. Skinner had the benefit of reviewing Pavlov's work on classical conditioning and Thorndike's work on trial-and-error learning. In an early paper Skinner (1935) summarized the essential differences between the two kinds of learning.

1. In classical conditioning, the conditioned reflex can begin at zero level; that is, it is not present at all. In trial-and-error learning, the response must be made if it is to be reinforced or strengthened.
2. In classical conditioning, the response is controlled by what precedes it. In trial-and-error learning, the response is controlled by what follows it.

Biographical Sketch

B. F. *Skinner*   1904–1990

Burrhus Frederic Skinner was born in 1904 in Susquehanna, Pennsylvania. As a child he liked to build such mechanical creations as roller-skate scooters, steerable wagons, and rafts. He was an eager explorer and enjoyed biking and canoeing with his friends along the Susquehanna River.

Skinner studied English literature at Hamilton College and graduated in 1926. After graduation he tried to develop a writing career. Despite a letter of encouragement from Robert Frost, Skinner came to the conclusion that he had nothing important to say.

In 1928 Skinner enrolled in the graduate program in psychology at Harvard, where he studied animal behavior. He described his life as a graduate student as highly focused:

I would rise at six, study until breakfast, go to classes, laboratories, and libraries with no more than fifteen minutes unscheduled during the day, study until exactly nine o'clock at night and go to bed. I saw no movies or plays, seldom went to concerts, had scarcely any dates, and read nothing but psychology and physiology. [1967, p. 398]

Skinner received his Ph.D. in 1931 and stayed at Harvard as a research fellow for five more years. He began his faculty career at the University of Minnesota, where he wrote *The Behavior of Organisms* (1938). During World War II he was a research scientist, working on a project to train pigeons to pilot torpedoes and bombs. Although this project was never implemented, Skinner continued to conduct much of his research with pigeons. He created unique experimental equipment that allowed pigeons to make complex responses. He even taught pigeons to play table tennis! After two years as a Guggenheim fellow, Skinner became chairman of the psychology department at Indiana University. In 1947 he returned to Harvard, where he remained until his retirement.

A major emphasis of Skinner's work was his empirical approach to understanding behavior. He searched for explanations that were tied to observed relationships between behaviors and their consequences. In the process he devised a number of remarkable inventions, including the Skinner box, an apparatus in which animal behaviors could be modified, monitored, and recorded; a temperature-controlled mechanical crib that was intended to provide the ideal environment for an infant; and the teaching machine, which provided step-by-step instructions and immediate reinforcement. In addition to his experimental contributions to the field of learning, his utopian novel, *Walden Two* (1948), and his extension of behaviorist principles to social criticism in *Beyond Freedom and Dignity* (1971) provided strong arguments for the powerful role of the environment in determining and controlling behavior. ∎

3. Classical conditioning is most suitable for internal responses (emotional and glandular reactions). Trial-and-error learning is most suitable for external responses (muscle movements, verbal responses).

Skinner's work followed along the lines of Thorndike's. His focus was on the modification of voluntary behaviors as a result of the consequences of those behaviors.

In the traditional operant conditioning experiment, the researcher selects a response in advance and then waits until the subject makes the desired response (or at least a partial response). Then the experimenter presents a reinforcement. *Reinforcement* is operationally defined as any stimulus that makes a repetition of the response more likely.

There are two kinds of reinforcers. Some, such as food and smiles, increase the rate of response when they are present. These are called positive reinforcers. Others, such as electric shock, increase the rate of response when they are removed. These are called negative reinforcers.

In one such experiment, a researcher places a rat in a cage. An electric grid in the floor of the cage is activated. As soon as the rat presses a bar, the electric shock is turned off. Soon the rat learns to press the bar quickly in order to turn off the shock. The shock is a negative reinforcer because its removal strengthens the response of bar pressing.

Suppose a mother gets upset whenever she hears her baby cry. She may try a number of things to stop the crying—rocking, feeding, talking, changing the baby's diapers. If one of these behaviors leads to an end to the noise, it is reinforced. The mother is more likely to try that behavior the next time. The baby's cry is a negative reinforcer because when it stops, the specific caregiving response is strengthened.

A stimulus can be considered a positive reinforcement only if it in fact makes some behavior more likely to occur. In the process of socialization, parents may offer a reward that fails to strengthen a response because it has no reinforcing properties for the child. For example, a parent may offer a new bicycle if the child can stay dry during the night for two weeks. If bed-wetting is an expression of the child's persistent wish to be babied and protected, the bicycle, which would permit greater mobility and distance from the parent, may fail to serve as a reinforcement for staying dry.

Operant conditioning refers to the development of behavior patterns that are under the learner's voluntary control (Davey & Cullen, 1988). The person can choose to make a response or not, depending on the consequences associated with the behavior. In many instances, however, the behavior to be learned is one that has never been performed before. How can you be reinforced for making a complex response if you have never done it? The answer lies in reinforcing behaviors that are in the direction of the final complex behavior, until eventually the behavior is emitted.

Shaping

One means of developing a new complex response is *shaping*. Here the response is broken down into its major components. At first a response that is only an approximation of one element of the behavior is reinforced. Gradually new elements of the behavior are added, and a reinforcement is given only when two or three components

Box 3.2   Operant Conditioning and Superstitions

Do you have a "lucky" shirt? Do you avoid walking under ladders? Have you ever noticed that some baseball players talk to the ball before they pitch or swing in a certain way before they bat? All these oddities are instances of superstitious behavior. We can usually see a logical connection between a behavior and its intended consequence: we wash our hands in order to remove dirt; we put on a jacket in order to stay warm on a chilly day. Some behaviors, however, are repeated even though they are not clearly tied to some observable consequence.

According to the operant conditioning view, superstitious behavior is the result of the accidental pairing of a behavior and a reinforcement. Suppose that just before a batter gets up to bat, he knocks the mud from his cleats. On this at-bat, he hits a triple and scores the winning runs for his team. The next time he gets up to bat he knocks the mud from his cleats on the chance that he may hit a triple again. If the behavior is followed by a positive consequence every once in a while, that will be enough to maintain it. Here we see an intermittent reinforcement schedule in action.

Some people fear that something undesirable will

If you have ever known a child who has a "lucky hat" you know that there is no point in arguing: the hat is going to stay put!

happen if they do not perform some behavior—that they will have bad luck, say, if they fail to hold their breath as they pass a cemetery. They reduce the fear by performing the ritual. The fear reduction in itself is reinforcing, and the ritual continues to be performed.

Behaviors that appear illogical to an observer may be tied to a reinforcement history that maintains them.

of the response are linked together. Once the person makes a complete response, earlier approximations are no longer reinforced.

Parents often use the shaping process to teach their young children such complicated behaviors as using the toilet, table manners, and caring for their belongings. Parents may begin toilet training, for example, by reinforcing children when they behave partially in the desired way, such as telling the parents that they have to go to the bathroom. Eventually the children receive rewards only when they have completed the entire behavior sequence (including wiping, flushing, adjusting clothing, and washing hands).

Schedules of Reinforcement

Much research has been devoted to efforts to establish which conditions of learning result in the strongest, longest-lasting habits since Ferster and Skinner first addressed the topic in 1957. *Schedule of reinforcement* refers to the frequency and regularity with which reinforcements are given. A new response is conditioned rapidly if reinforcement is given on every learning trial. This schedule is called *continuous* reinforcement. Responses that are established under conditions of continuous reinforcement are very vulnerable to *extinction*—that is, if the reinforcement is removed for several trials, performance deteriorates rapidly (see Figure 3.3).

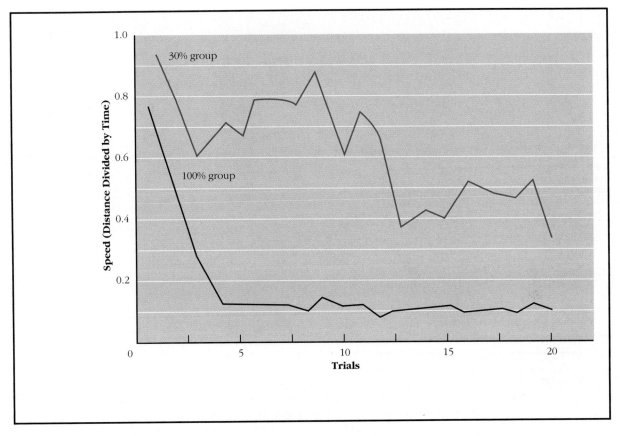

Figure 3.3

Continuous versus Intermittent Reinforcement
This figure shows runway speeds for two groups of rats once reinforcement has been discontinued. One group previously has been reinforced on every trial; the other has been reinforced on only 30% of the trials. Running speed declines rapidly for the group trained under continuous reinforcement. The group that has been trained under intermittent reinforcement continues to run quickly for the first ten trials and remains above the 100% group for all 20 trials.
Source: Adapted from H. Gleitman, *Psychology* (New York: Norton, 1986), p. 111.

Some schedules vary the amount of time or the number of trials between reinforcements. This procedure is called *intermittent* reinforcement. The learner responds on many occasions when no reinforcement is provided but does receive reinforcement every once in a while. Such schedules result in the most durable learning. Intermittent reinforcement lengthens the time an operant behavior remains in the learner's repertoire after reinforcement has been permanently discontinued (Ferster & Culbertson, 1982).

A variable reinforcement schedule is probably truer to real life. It would be very difficult for anyone to learn a behavior if every instance of it had to be reinforced. A person often exhibits a new response when no observers are present, when teachers are attending to other matters, or in the context of other behaviors that are followed

Pablo Picasso, *Courtesan with Jeweled Collar,* 1901. Imitation is the process through which much of social learning occurs. Imitation is a common strategy for the development of artistic style. This painting of a courtesan, done when Picasso was 20 years old, shows the strong influence of Toulouse-Lautrec.

by a negative consequence. Research on operant conditioning demonstrates that conditions of intermittent reinforcement are precisely those under which the longest-lasting habits are formed.

Implications for Human Development

The principles of operant conditioning apply whenever the environment sets up priorities for behavior and conditional rewards or punishments for approximating a desired behavior. People change whenever their operant behaviors adapt to changes in environmental contingencies. The environment controls the process of adaptation through the role it plays in establishing and modifying contingencies (Skinner, 1987). Behavior can be modified in the desired direction as long as the person who is guiding the conditioning has control over the distribution of valued rewards. We believe that these principles are especially applicable to the learning that takes place during toddlerhood (2 to 4 years) and early school age (4 to 6). Children of these ages are unlikely to be able to conceptualize about the existing framework of reinforcement. Once individuals can interpret a reinforcement schedule, they may choose to adapt to it, resist it, or redefine the environment in order to discover new sources of reinforcement.

There is no doubt that operant conditioning occurs at all ages. Reinforcement schedules set by work, spouse, and self operate on much of an adult's behavior. Reinforcement conditions determine the behaviors that will be performed. Conditions of learning influence how long a given behavior will persist once the reinforcement for it is removed.

Social Learning

The concept of *social learning* evolved from an awareness that much learning takes place as a result of observing and imitating other people's behavior (Bandura & Walters, 1963). We have emphasized the role of *imitation* as the central process in resolving the crisis of autonomy versus shame and doubt in toddlerhood. At that age, imitation provides a mechanism for the rapid acquisition of new behaviors. Think about all the things a child of 4 can say or do. It would be impossible for parents to deliberately teach a child every single behavior—they would have no time left to eat, sleep, or work. Children must acquire much of their knowledge by observing and imitating others. Adults provide the *models* for many activities. They express feelings, voice attitudes, perform tasks, and enact their moral values. By observing and imitating many of these behaviors, children become socialized into their family's and community's way of life.

A great deal of research has been devoted to identifying conditions that determine whether or not a child will imitate a model (Bandura, 1971, 1977, 1986). Children have been found to imitate aggressive, altruistic, helping, and stingy models. They are most likely to imitate models who are prestigious, who control resources, or who themselves are rewarded. The concept of social learning highlights the relevance of models' behavior in guiding the behavior of others. These models may be parents, older siblings, entertainment stars, or sports heroes. Insofar as new *identifications* may occur at any life stage, new learning through the modeling process is always possible.

Implications for Human Development

The principles of social learning theory are assumed to operate in the same way throughout life. Observational learning may take place at any age. Exposure to a certain array of models and a certain pattern of rewards results in the encouragement to imitate some behaviors rather than others. The similarity in behavior among people of the same ages reflects their exposure to a common history of models and rewards.

Cognitive Behaviorism

One objection that is frequently raised to classical and operant conditioning as theories of learning is that they have no language or concepts to describe events that occur in the learner's mind. Learning is described as a relationship between environmental events and individual responses. Edward Tolman (1932/1967, 1948) discussed the notion of an intervening set of responses that influence learning. He said that the learner develops a *cognitive map,* which is an internal mental representation of the learning environment. Individuals who perform a specific task in a certain environment attend primarily to that task, but they also form a representation of the rest of the setting. This internal representation forms the cognitive map. The map includes expectations about the reward system in operation, the existing spatial relationships, and the behaviors accorded highest priority. An individual's performance in a situation represents only part of the learning that has occurred. The fact that people respond to changes in the environment indicates that a complex mental map actually develops in this situation.

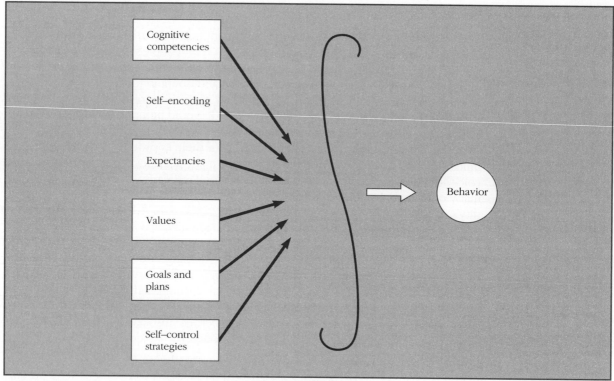

Figure 3.4   Six Cognitive Dimensions That Influence Behavior

Cognitive behaviorists study the many internal mental activities that influence behavior. According to Walter Mischel (1973, 1979), at least six cognitive factors must be taken into account if a person's behavior is to be understood: cognitive competencies, self-encoding, expectancies, values, goals and plans, and self-control strategies (see Figure 3.4). *Cognitive competencies* consist of knowledge, skills, and abilities. *Self-encoding* is the evaluation and conceptualization of information about the self. An interesting finding in this area is that depressed people tend to evaluate themselves more realistically than those who are not depressed. Mischel (1979) argues that "to feel good about ourselves we may have to judge ourselves more kindly than we are judged" (p. 752). In other words, most people who are not chronically depressed may bias their evaluations of themselves in a self-enhancing way.

Expectancies here refers to expectations about one's ability to perform, the consequences of one's behavior, and the meaning of events in one's environment. *Values* consist of the relative importance one places on the outcomes of situations. One person may value high levels of task performance, while another may value success in social situations. One's behavior in a situation is influenced by how one values its possible outcomes. *Goals and plans* are personal standards of performance and the strategies one develops for achieving them. Obviously individuals differ in their goals and plans; these differences will lead to considerable variation in behavior. *Self-control strategies* are the techniques an individual develops for regulating his or her own behavior. *Self-control* helps us to understand how we may leave the realm of stimulus control in order to gain control over our behavior. The more aware we are of the effects of stimuli on our behavior, the more effectively we may overcome, channel, or eliminate their influence.

Of these six areas, one that has received considerable attention among those interested in learning and performance is the area of expectancies. People's judgments about how well they expect to perform, or whether or not they expect to improve their skill level through training, have a clear impact on their performance. Albert Bandura (1982, 1989) has identified self-efficacy as a key element in the cognitive basis of behavior. *Self-efficacy* is defined as the sense of confidence that one can perform the behaviors demanded by a situation. According to Bandura, the decision to engage in a situation, as well as the intensity of effort expended in the situation, are dependent upon a person's confidence about success.

> *Those who have a high sense of efficacy visualize success scenarios that provide positive guides for performance and they cognitively rehearse good solutions to potential problems. Those who judge themselves as inefficacious are more inclined to visualize failure scenarios and to dwell on how things will go wrong. Such inefficacious thinking weakens motivation and undermines performance.* [1989, p. 729]

Bandura points out that adjustment depends on one's judgment about the outcome of the situation. If a woman with a strong sense of self-efficacy is in an environment that is responsive and rewards good performance, she is likely to behave in a self-assured, competent way. If this same woman is in an environment that is unresponsive and does not reward accomplishment, she is likely to increase her effort and even try to change the environment. People who judge their efficacy to be low give up and become apathetic in unresponsive environments. In responsive environments they may become more depressed and self-critical as they see others who appear to be similar to themselves succeeding.

The concept of self-efficacy clarifies how people adapt when they enter new roles or new situations. The successes and failures we observe in others and the encouragement we receive from others influence our expectations. Coping behavior can also be influenced by a history of prior efficacy.

Implications for Human Development

Cognitive behaviorism suggests that through the processes of classical conditioning, operant conditioning, and observational learning, the learner acquires cognitive structures that influence subsequent learning and performance. We might say that the learner acquires an outlook on the learning situation. This outlook may influence the learner's feeling of familiarity with the task, motivation to undertake the task, optimism about performing the task successfully, and strategies for approaching the task. In addition to everything a parent, a teacher, or a supervisor might do to structure a learning environment, one must always take into account the outlook the learner brings to the task. Differences in judgments of self-efficacy, self-control strategies, values, and goals all influence the way people approach a learning situation.

Table 3.2   Four Learning Processes

Classical Conditioning	Operant Conditioning	Social Learning	Cognitive Behaviorism
When two events occur very close together in time, they acquire similar meanings and produce similar responses.	Responses that are under voluntary control can be strengthened or eliminated, depending on the consequences associated with them.	New responses can be acquired through observation and imitation of models.	In addition to new responses, the learner acquires a mental representation of the situation, including expectations about rewards and punishments, the kinds of responses that are appropriate, and the physical and social settings in which they occur.

Summary of Learning Theories

All four of the learning theories contribute insights into human behavior (see Table 3.2).

Classical conditioning can account for the extensive network of associations that are formed between symbols and stimuli, enduring emotional reactions to one's environment, and the organization of learning associated with reflexive patterns. Operant conditioning emphasizes the acquisition of behavioral patterns on the basis of their consequences. Social learning theory adds the important element of imitation. People can learn new behaviors by watching others. Finally, cognitive behaviorism suggests that a complex set of expectations, goals, and values can be treated as behavior and can influence performance. While information or skills can be learned, they cannot be expressed in behavior unless expectations about the self and the environment justify their enactment. This perspective highlights the person's capacity to guide the direction of new learning.

Social Roles

Another approach to conceptualizing the effect of the environment on development is suggested by such social psychologists as Orville Brim (1966) and such sociologists as Talcott Parsons (Parsons & Bales, 1955). They trace the process of socialization and personality development through the person's participation in increasingly diverse and complex social roles. A *role* is any set of behaviors that has a socially agreed-upon function and an accepted code of norms (Biddle, 1979; Biddle & Thomas, 1966; Brown, 1965). The term *role* was taken from the context of the theater. In a play, actors' behaviors are distinct and predictable because each actor has a part to play and follows a script. Role theory applies this same framework to social life (Biddle, 1986). The three elements of concern to role theory are the patterned characteristics of social behavior *(role enactment)*, the parts or identities a person assumes *(social roles)*, and the scripts or shared expectations for behavior that are linked to each part *(role expectations)*.

Social roles serve as a bridge between the individual and the society. Every society has a range of roles, and individuals learn about the expectations associated with them. As people enter new roles, they modify their behavior to conform to these role expectations.

An infant has few roles that have socially agreed-upon functions. In our own culture, the roles of an infant may include that of child, sibling, and grandchild. At successive life stages, the person plays a variety of roles within the family as well as within the context of other social institutions such as school, business, and community.

The concept of role highlights the importance of the social context in the developmental process. Individuals bring their own unique temperaments, skills, and values to bear on the interpretation and enactment of the roles they play. Nonetheless, most roles exist independently of the people who play them. For example, our expectations about the role of a teacher guide our evaluation of each new teacher we meet. Those same expectations influence the way people who perform the role of teacher actually behave in this role. Knowledge of the functions and norms associated with any given role will influence both the performance of the person who assumes it and the responses of a whole network of people associated with the performer (Goffman, 1959; Biddle, 1979). Each role is usually linked to one or more related, or *reciprocal,* roles. The student and the teacher, the parent and the child, and the salesperson and the customer are in reciprocal roles. Each role is partly defined by the other roles that support it. The function of the role is determined by its relation to the surrounding role groups to which it is allied.

Four Dimensions of Social Roles

Social roles can be seen as having four dimensions. First, one must ask about the *number of roles* in which a person is involved. As that number increases, the person's appreciation of the social system as a whole increases. Cognitive complexity, social perspective taking, and interpersonal problem-solving ability can be expected to increase with the number and diversity of social roles. In fact, Parsons (Parsons & Bales, 1955) has argued that the process of socialization can best be understood as an outcome of participation in a growing number of increasingly diverse and complex social roles. People who resist involvement in new roles can be viewed as forestalling their development by closing off access to new responsibilities as well as new demands.

A second dimension along which roles vary is the *intensity of involvement* that they demand or that a person brings to them. Sarbin and Allen (1968) offer an eight-point scale of role involvement, from 0, or noninvolvement, to 7, at which the self is indistinguishable from the role. At the low end, they give the example of a person whose membership in a club has lapsed for a number of years. Such a position holds no immediate expectations for behavior, although the person could resume involvement at any time. At the high end, they give the example of a person who believes he or she is the object of witchcraft. The total being is so involved in the role that death can result.

The role of close friend is an example of a social role that usually has high emotional intensity and low structure. Friends establish any role expectations they wish in order to ensure a satisfying, intimate relationship.

The more intense the role involvement, the greater the investment of attention and energy, the greater the emotional commitment to the role, and perhaps the greater the anxiety about failure to meet role expectations. As a person becomes fused with a role, his or her personality comes increasingly to be influenced by the socialization pressures that are tied to it.

A third dimension of the social role is the *amount of time the role demands*. This dimension is important because a time-consuming role sets up the basic structure for many daily interactions. The role of gas station attendant, for example, may not involve high intensity, but it may require so many hours per day that the person has few opportunities to enact other roles. In fact, a low-intensity role may be a source of constant personal frustration if it continues to demand a large number of waking hours.

The fourth dimension of a role that influences its impact on personality is the *degree of structure* specified for it. Social roles vary in the extent to which expectations are specified and in the degree of consensus about how they should be performed. Some social roles, such as member of Congress, police officer, and college president, have written criteria for their enactment. Such public figures are generally held accountable for their performance of the services they were elected, hired, or appointed to provide. The role performer and the audience agree upon certain behaviors as being appropriate to the role. Even less public roles, such as secretary, bookkeeper, and salesperson, have written criteria stating a specified degree of structure. Like public figures, these workers are expected to perform the services for which they were hired.

Other roles are much less clearly articulated. They may be defined by cultural myths (for example, the role of explorer) or by community norms (such as the role of neighbor). Enactment of some roles is quite private—viewed only by members of the immediate family or a few close friends. In these instances, one is free to define and to enact the role as it suits the few people who are involved. Lovers, siblings, close friends, and marriage partners can develop relationships along a variety of paths without coming under the scrutiny of elaborate socialization pressures for specific role performances. This does not mean that no expectations accompany these roles; rather, they provide room for individual agreements and improvisation.

When roles are highly structured, the issue of *person-role fit* comes into question. Under conditions of lack of fit, a role occupant experiences continual frustration at the demands for behavior that is not compatible with his or her temperament, talents, or motives. In contrast, when the fit is comfortable, a highly structured role may provide the reassurance and support that come from knowing the expectations for behavior. Under conditions of person-role compatibility, a highly structured role may offer opportunities for the development of new competences that will contribute to a person's maturation and growth.

When there is less consensus about a role, the occupant generally has more opportunities to shape it to reflect personal predispositions. However, privately defined roles can generate considerable conflict if the people in reciprocal role positions cannot agree about how a role should be played. For example, although the roles of husband and wife offer considerable latitude for expressing personal preferences and values, if the partners cannot agree about the expectations that accompany these roles, the marriage will suffer from continual conflict and uncertainty.

Implications for Human Development

All cultures offer new roles that await individuals as they move from one stage of life to another. These roles may be directly associated with age, such as the role of "elder" or the role of high school student. Other roles may be accessible only to those of a certain age who demonstrate other relevant skills, traits, or personal preferences. The role of baby-sitter generally does not begin until adolescence; the role of dentist does not become available until young adulthood; the role of full professor is usually not possible until middle adulthood. The culture itself harbors an implicit theory of development that determines the positions open to each age group.

Some of the most important life roles persist through several stages. For example, we are someone's child from infancy until death, and we may be a partner in an intimate sexual relationship from adolescence through later adulthood. In each of these roles there is both continuity and change (Feldman & Feldman, 1975). The expectations for the role performance remain the same in some respects but change in others. We can begin to see how social roles provide a thread of consistency to life experience and how they prompt new learning.

In the following chapters, we describe a number of life roles, including kinship roles, sex roles, age roles, and occupational roles. As the number of roles that people fill simultaneously increases, individuals must learn some of the skills of role playing, role differentiation, and role integration. The developmental crisis of later adolescence (individual identity versus identity confusion) emphasizes the significance of being able to integrate several diverse roles so that one may maintain a sense of personal

Box 3.3   Role Strain and Parenthood

A recurring theme in the literature on parenthood is the experience of role strain. *Role strain* can be defined as a sense of overload that results when too many expectations are associated with a role (Biddle, 1986). Each of the four dimensions of social roles may contribute to strain in the role of parent. When parenting is added to other adult roles, especially those of worker and spouse, the demands of the new role may seem overwhelming. Because the parent role has great intensity, the sense of involvement in all the behaviors associated with the role intensifies, and so does anxiety about failure to meet the expectations of the role. First-time parents especially may have little confidence in their ability to fulfill their roles, and the level of worry associated with the role rises accordingly.

The parent role does indeed take a lot of time. Most first-time parents underestimate how much time infants and toddlers require. When new parents, especially mothers, reflect on the time they spend in a variety of social roles, they point to the parent role as more time-consuming than any other, and more time-consuming than any role they have played in the past.

Role strain linked with parenting is related to the structure of the role. Some adults have a very clear set of ideas about how they should enact their parent role; but many are unsure. Husbands and wives are likely to differ in their views on child-rearing techniques. These differences require time to resolve. Because of the hardships or distress they recall from their own childhoods, many adults do not want to raise their children the way they were raised. They have to learn a new script for this role.

There are at least four ways to minimize the role strain associated with the parent role (Rollins & Galligan, 1978; Bahr, Chappell & Leigh, 1983; Cowan & Cowan, 1988):

1. When the rewards for role enactment are frequent, the demands of the role seem less onerous. Adults who have a lot of encouragement from family, friends, and community for their active involvement in parenting will probably feel less stressed about the amount of time and effort they invest in it.

2. The ability to delegate role responsibilities can reduce role strain. Adults who can hire others to help with some of the parenting responsibilities or who can turn to family members for help will experience less role strain than those who are solely responsible for the parenting role. Couples who can flexibly alter and share household responsibilities in response to the demands of parenting will experience more satisfaction and less strain in the parent role.

3. The ability to integrate several aspects of the role in one activity can reduce role strain. Some parents become quite inventive about ways to maintain contact with their infant and still carry out their household and other work and have time with each other.

4. Role strain is reduced when marriage partners reach consensus about their parent roles. New parents who have resolved their differences in regard to child-rearing philosophy, child-care activities, and the division of household responsibilities experience less role strain and a higher level of marital satisfaction than those who continue to have opposing views on these issues.

continuity. With each new role, one's self-definition changes and the potential for influencing the world increases.

Over the life span we also lose roles. The most dramatic instance comes with the death of a reciprocal role partner. When a parent, sibling, or spouse dies, we lose an important role. Graduation from school, divorce, loss of employment, and retirement are other transitions that result in role loss. Social role theory helps us to understand the stressful nature of these changes by taking into account the time, emotional intensity, structure, and culturally shared meaning that are bound up in a single life role and the subsequent disorientation that is likely to follow its loss.

Systems

Up to this point, we have been shifting from one way of viewing individual behavior to another. Whether the behaviors we scrutinize are associated with the survival of the species or with the survival of the social organization, our attention is repeatedly drawn to the ongoing interaction of the individual and the environment. We cannot make sense of individual elements of thought or behavior without relating them to one another and to the context in which they occur. In its own way, each of the theories we have surveyed draws our attention to the fact that individuals develop within complex systems.

Systems theories attempt to describe and account for the characteristics of systems and view individuals as interconnected elements (Sameroff, 1982). To a large degree, these theories highlight *differences in perspective*. Systems theories take the position that the whole is more than the sum of its parts. Any system, whether it is a cell, an organ, an individual, a family, or a corporation, is composed of *interdependent elements* that share some common goals, interrelated functions, boundaries, and an identity. The system cannot be wholly understood by identifying each of the component parts. The processes and relationships of those parts make for a larger coherent entity. The language system, for example, is more than the capacity to make vocal utterances, to use grammar, and to acquire vocabulary. It is the coordination of these elements in a useful way within a context of shared meaning. Similarly, a family system is more than the sum of the characteristics and competences of the individual family members. Families are a composite of a sense of common destiny and the genetic heritage of the two spouses and then of their developing children. As spouses develop or create their own composite heritage, this "we-ness" of communication patterns and reciprocal role relationships identifies the family. An open or permeable family boundary is responsive to stimulation and information from within and outside the family. This openness allows the family to use input for healthy adaptive growth and change. A closed family boundary does not allow for interchange and adaptive responses to the environment. Common destiny, genetic heritage, patterns of communication, and reciprocal role relationships may be modified and elaborated as a family attempts to survive and undergo transformations.

A system cannot violate laws that govern the functioning of the parts, but at the same time it cannot be explained solely by those laws. Biological functioning cannot violate the laws of physics and chemistry, but the laws of physics and chemistry cannot fully explain biological functioning. Similarly, children's capacities for cognitive growth cannot violate the laws of biological functioning, but biological growth does not fully explain quality of thought.

As we think about individuals, families, communities, schools, and societies, we are dealing with *open systems*. Ludwig von Bertalanffy (1950, 1968) defined open systems as structures that maintain their organization even though their parts constantly change. Just as the water in a river is constantly changing while the river itself retains its boundaries and course, so the molecules of human cells are constantly changing while the various biological systems retain their coordinated functions.

Open systems share certain properties. They take in energy from the environment, they transform this energy into some type of product that is characteristic of the system, they export the product into the environment, and they draw upon new sources of energy from the environment to continue to thrive (Katz & Kahn, 1966). As we have noted, this process requires an open boundary. The more open the boundary, the more vigorously the process operates. Each specific system has a unique set of processes that are appropriate to the particular forms of energy, product, and transformations relevant to that system. In the analysis of systems, one focuses more on the processes and relationships among the parts that permit a system to survive and grow than on the characteristics of the parts themselves.

Systems move in the direction of adjusting to or incorporating more and more of the environment into themselves in order to prevent disorganization as a result of environmental fluctuations (Sameroff, 1982). Adaptation, whether the concept is articulated by Darwin, Piaget, Skinner, or Bandura, seems to be a fundamental process. Ervin Laszlo (1972) described this property of an open system as *adaptive self-regulation*. A system uses *feedback mechanisms* to identify and respond to environmental changes. The more information about the environment the system is capable of detecting, the more complex these feedback mechanisms must be. When the oxygen level of the environment is reduced, for example, you tend to grow sleepy. While you sleep, your breathing slows and you use less oxygen. Some of these adjustments are managed unconsciously by the organization of biological systems. Others are managed more deliberately by efforts to minimize the effects of environmental changes. Most systems have a capacity for storing or saving resources so that temporary shortages do not disrupt their operations.

When open systems are confronted by new and constant environmental conditions, they have the capacity for *adaptive self-organization*. The system retains its essential identity by creating new substructures, by revising the relationships among components, or by creating new, higher levels of organization that coordinate existing substructures.

From the systems perspective, the components and the whole are always in tension. What one understands and observes depends on where one stands in this complex set of interrelationships. All living entities are parts and wholes. A person is a part of a family, a classroom or workgroup, a friendship group, and a society. A person is also a whole—a coordinated complex system composed of physical, cognitive, emotional, social, and self subsystems. Part of the story of human development is told in an analysis of the adaptive regulation and organization of those subsystems. Simultaneously, the story is told in the way larger systems fluctuate and impinge on individuals, forcing adaptive regulation and reorganization as a means of achieving stability at higher levels of system organization.

Implications for
Human Development

The relevance of systems theory for human development can be most readily appreciated in its application to families. Family system theories focus on how families establish and maintain stable patterns of functioning. Families are viewed as emotional

These relatives demonstrate the concept of the family system as they plant their garden. Each family member plays a distinct but interrelated part. Together, they accomplish their goal; each person's efforts gain meaning from what the others are doing.

units identifiable by certain *boundaries* and *rules* (Kantor & Lehr, 1975; Giles-Sims, 1983). The boundaries of the family determine who is considered to be a family member and who is an outsider. They influence the way information, support, and validation of the family unit are sought and the way new members are admitted into the family. Some families have very strict rules that maintain a narrow boundary around the family. Few sources of information or contact are admitted. Other families extend the sense of belonging to a wide range of people who bring ideas and resources to the family system.

Family systems are maintained by patterns of communication. *Positive* and *negative feedback loops* operate to stabilize, diminish, or increase certain types of interactions. A feedback loop is positive when a child offers a suggestion and a parent recognizes and compliments the child on that suggestion. In such a pattern, the child is encouraged to continue to offer suggestions, and the parent comes to view the child as someone who has valuable suggestions to offer. A feedback loop is negative if a parent ignores the child's suggestion or scolds the child for making it. The child is less likely to make further suggestions, and the parent is likely to view the child as someone who has no valuable ideas to offer. Many positive and negative feedback loops operate in all families to sustain certain underlying qualities of the system, such as the power hierarchy, the level of conflict, and the balance between autonomy and dependency among the members.

One of the most commonly noted characteristics of family systems is the interdependence of the family members. Changes in one family member are accompanied by changes in the others. Imagine for a moment that family members are standing in a circle and holding a rope. Each person is trying to exert enough tension on the rope to keep it tight and preserve the circular shape. The amount of tension each person must exert depends on what every other person is doing. Now imagine that one member of the family lets go of the rope and steps away. In order to retain the shape and tension of the rope, everyone else has to adjust his or her grip. Letting go of the rope is an analogy for many kinds of changes that can occur in a family. A parent becomes ill, a child goes off to college, or a parent takes on a demanding job outside of the home. The system adjusts by redefining relationships, modifying patterns of communication, and adjusting its boundaries. The members and their interdependencies change. Similar adjustments must be made if a member is added to the family system, or when the system undergoes some other major transition.

The system's perspective offers an especially productive approach to clinical problems. A person who has been identified as dysfunctional is treated not as a lone individual but as part of a family system. The assumption is that the person's problems occur as a result of the way the person—whether a child, a parent, or a grandparent—is treated by other family members. The only way to bring about changes in the person's functioning is to alter the functioning of the other members of the system as well. If the person is "underfunctioning"—that is, acting irresponsibly, not communicating, not performing at his or her level of capability, withdrawing, or acting impulsively—one assumes that others in the family are "overfunctioning"—that is, assuming many of the person's roles and responsibilities in order to "take up the slack." The dysfunctional behavior is maintained because it is a component of an emotional unit. In other words, the dysfunction belongs neither to the person nor to the other family members but to the particular interdependence among the family members that appears to be necessary to preserve the viability of the family system as a whole (Bowen, 1978).

By definition, family systems are also interdependent with adjacent systems. Thus the understanding of families requires an analysis of the resources and demands of other social systems that impinge on families, and the opportunities families have for influencing adjoining systems. A woman who is experiencing an extremely demanding, stressful, and sexist work environment, for example, may be constantly tired, tense, and irritable in her behavior toward her family members. She may bring home the resentments from work in the way she treats and expects to be treated by males and females in her family. If the job is important to her and to her family, no one may be willing to acknowledge the bizarre impact the work setting is having on family life. Family violence, the effects of unemployment on families, participation of mothers in the labor force, day care, and the role of parents in their children's schooling are all being examined from a systems perspective.

☐ Chapter Summary

The seven theoretical perspectives we have reviewed take distinct approaches to continuity and change across the life span.

Evolutionary theory provides an overall temporal framework within which to understand individual development. Although a life span of 85 or 90 years may seem long, it is but a flicker in the 1 to 2 million years of human biological adaptation.

Evolutionary theory highlights the biologically and especially the genetically governed aspects of growth and development. This perspective does not ignore the environment; rather, it proposes that the environment provides the specific conditions that require adaptation. However, adaptive change can occur only if it is supported by the genetically based characteristics of the organism. The tempo and pattern of human development are governed by a genetic plan.

Cultural theory takes almost the opposite view. Within this framework, the significance of biological maturation depends on the way it is treated by the culture. The possibilities for cultural variation in the life span are enormous. What we understand to be the normal or natural pattern and tempo of change in competences, roles, and status depends heavily on the way our society recognizes individuals of different ages, gender, and degree of kinship.

Psychosexual theory links the evolutionary and cultural perspectives. Human development is seen as following a biologically determined path along which changing patterns of social relationships follow the unfolding of sexual impulses and the sexualization of body zones. Culture plays a major role in establishing the taboos and acceptable patterns of sexual gratification that lead to conflicts, fixations, and strategies for sublimation. Sexual impulses, wishes, and fears, many of which are unconscious, guide behavior and give it meaning. Psychosexual theory emphasizes the years of infancy and childhood as those in which basic personality patterns are established. It also establishes family relationships, especially the parent-child relationship, as the primary context within which conflicts related to the socialization of sexual impulses are resolved.

Like psychosexual theory, cognitive theory views development as a product of a biologically guided plan for growth and change. The elements that make cognitive growth possible are all present in the genetic information that governs the growth of the brain and nervous system. However, the process of intellectual growth requires interaction with a diverse and responsive environment. Cognitive development is fostered by recognition of discrepancies between existing schemes and new experiences. Through the reciprocal processes of assimilation and accommodation, schemes are modified and integrated to form the basis for organizing and explaining experience.

While psychosexual theory and cognitive theory highlight many of the similarities among individuals at each stage of development, the learning theories account for the wide range of individual differences. Learning theories focus on the mechanisms that permit individuals to respond to their diverse environments. Behavior can be shaped and modified by systematic changes in environmental conditions. According to learning theorists, human beings have an especially flexible behavioral system. No assumptions are made about universal stages of growth. As conditions in the environment change, response patterns also change. Similarity among individuals at a particular period of life is explained by the fact that they are exposed to similar environmental conditions, patterns of reinforcement, and models.

Instead of looking at the environment at the microscopic level of the learning theories, considering every unique stimulus and its corresponding response, social role theory suggests that learning is organized around key social functions called roles. As people attempt to enact roles, they integrate their behavior into meaningful units. Meaning is provided by the definition of the role and the expectations of those in reciprocal roles. Human development is a product of entry into an increasing number of complex roles over the life span. As people acquire and lose roles, they change their self-definitions and their relationships with social groups. Most societies define roles that are linked with gender, age, marital status, and kinship. These roles provide patterning to the life course. However, the patterns are understood to be products of the structures and functions of the society rather than of genetic information.

Systems theory takes a unique scientific perspective. Rather than seeking to analyze causal relationships, systems theory emphasizes the multidimensional sources of influence on individuals, and the simultaneous influence of individuals on the systems of which they are a part. Each person is at once a component of one or more larger systems and a system unto itself. One must approach the study of human development from many angles, identifying the critical resources, the flow of resources, and the transformation of resources that underlie a continuous process of adaptive reorganization and growth.

References

Alpert, J. L. (1986). *Psychoanalysis and women: Contemporary reappraisals.* Hillsdale, N.J.: Analytic Press.

Bahr, S. J., Chappell, C. K., & Leigh, G. K. (1983). Age at marriage, role enactment, role consensus, and marital satisfaction. *Journal of Marriage and the Family, 45,* 795–804.

Bandura, A. (ed.) (1971). *Psychological modeling.* Chicago: Aldine-Atherton.

Bandura, A. (1977). *Social learning theory.* Englewood Cliffs, N.J.: Prentice-Hall.

Bandura, A. (1982). Self-efficacy mechanism in human agency. *American Psychologist, 37,* 122–147.

Bandura, A. (1986). *Social foundations of thought and action: A social cognitive theory.* Englewood Cliffs, N.J.: Prentice-Hall.

Bandura, A. (1989). Regulation of cognitive processes through perceived self-efficacy. *Developmental Psychology, 25,* 729–735.

Bandura, A., & Walters, R. H. (1963). *Social learning and personality development.* New York: Holt, Rinehart & Winston.

Bem, S. L. (1989). Genital knowledge and gender constancy in preschool children. *Child Development, 60,* 649–662.

Benedict, R. (1934/1950). *Patterns of culture.* New York: New American Library.

Bertalanffy, L. von (1950). The theory of open systems in physics and biology. *Science, 111,* 23–28.

Bertalanffy, L. von (1968). *General systems theory* (rev. ed.). New York: Braziller.

Biddle, B. J. (1979). *Role theory: Expectations, identities, and behaviors.* New York: Academic Press.

Biddle, B. J. (1986). Recent developments in role theory. In R. H. Turner & S. F. Short, Jr. (eds.), *Annual Review of Sociology, 12,* 67–92.

Biddle, B. J., & Thomas, E. J. (1966). *Role theory: Concepts and research.* New York: Wiley.

Blurton-Jones, N. (1972). *Ethological studies of child behavior.* Cambridge: Cambridge University Press.

Bowen, M. (1978). *Family therapy and clinical practice.* New York: Jason Aronson.

Bowlby, J. (1958). The nature of the child's tie to his mother. *International Journal of Psychoanalysis, 39,* 350–373.

Bowlby, J. (1988). *A secure base: Parent-child attachment and healthy human development.* New York: Basic Books.

Breuer, J., & Freud, S. (1895/1955). Studies on hysteria. In J. Strachey (ed.), *The standard edition of the complete psychological works of Sigmund Freud* (vol. 2). London: Hogarth Press.

Brim, O. G., Jr. (1966). Socialization through the life cycle. In O. G. Brim, Jr., & S. Wheeler (eds.), *Socialization after childhood.* New York: Wiley.

Brown, R. (1965). *Social psychology.* New York: Free Press.

Case, R. (1985). *Intellectual development: Birth to adulthood.* Orlando, Fla.: Academic Press.

Case, R., Hayward, S., Lewis, M., & Hurst, P. (1988). Toward a neo-Piagetian theory of cognitive and emotional development. *Developmental Review, 8,* 1–51.

Charlesworth, W. (1988). Resources and resource acquisition during ontogeny. In K. B. McDonald (ed.), *Sociobiological perspectives on human behavior.* New York: Springer-Verlag.

Chomsky, N. (1972). *Language and mind.* New York: Harcourt Brace Jovanovich.

Cole, M., & Means, B. (1986). *Comparative studies of how people think.* Cambridge, Mass.: Harvard University Press.

Cornelius, S. W., & Caspi, A. (1987). Everyday problem solving in adulthood and old age. *Psychology and Aging, 2,* 144–153.

Cowan, C. P., & Cowan, P. A. (1988). Who does what when partners become parents: Implications for men, women, and marriage. In R. Palkovitz & M. B. Sussman (eds.), *Transitions to parenthood* (pp. 105–132). New York: Hawthorn Press.

Darwin, C. (1859/1979). *The illustrated "Origin of species."* Abridged and introduced by Richard E. Leakey. New York: Hill & Wang.

Darwin, C. (1872/1965). *The expression of the emotions in man and animals* (2nd authorized ed.). Chicago: University of Chicago Press.

Davey, G. (1987). *Cognitive processes and Pavlovian conditioning in humans.* New York: Wiley.

Davey, G., & Cullen, C. (1988). *Human operant conditioning and behavior modification.* New York: Wiley.

Denney, N. W. (1982). Aging and cognitive changes. In B. B. Wolman (ed.), *Handbook of developmental psychology* (pp. 807–827). Englewood Cliffs, N.J.: Prentice-Hall.

Eibl-Eibesfeldt, I. (1975). *Ethology: The biology of behavior* (2nd ed.). New York: Holt, Rinehart & Winston.

Einstein, A., & Freud, S. (1933/1964). Why war? In J. Strachey (ed.), *The standard edition of the complete psychological works of Sigmund Freud* (vol. 22, pp. 195–218). London: Hogarth Press.

Erikson, E. H. (1963). *Childhood and society* (2nd ed.) New York: Norton.

Fagot, B. I., & Leinbach, M. D. (1989). The young child's gender schema: Environmental input, internal organization. *Child Development, 60,* 663–672.

Fast, I. (1984). *Gender identity: A differentiation model.* Hillsdale, N.J.: Analytic Press.

Feldman, H., & Feldman, M. (1975). The family life cycle: Some suggestions for recycling. *Journal of Marriage and the Family, 37,* 277–284.

Ferster, C. B., & Culbertson, S. A. (1982). *Behavior principles* (3rd ed.). Englewood Cliffs, N.J.: Prentice-Hall.

Ferster, C. B., & Skinner, B. F. (1957). *Schedules of reinforcement.* New York: Appleton-Century-Crofts.

Fischer, K. W. (1980). A theory of cognitive development: The control and construction of hierarchies of skills. *Psychological Review, 87,* 477–531.

Fischer, K. W., & Silvern, L. (1985). Stages and individual differences in cognitive development. In M. R. Rosenzweig & L. W. Porter (eds.), *Annual Review of Psychology, 36,* 613–648.

Flavell, J. H., Green, F. L., & Flavell, E. R. (1989). Young children's ability to differentiate appearance-reality and level 2 perspectives in the tactile modality. *Child Development, 60,* 201–213.

Freud, S. (1933/1964). New introductory lectures on psychoanalysis. In J. Strachey (ed.), *The standard edition of the complete psychological works of Sigmund Freud* (vol. 22). London: Hogarth Press.

Freud, S. (1963). *The cocaine papers.* Vienna and Zurich: Dunquin Press.

Gardner, M. R. (1983). *Self inquiry.* Hillsdale, N.J.: Analytic Press.

Gazzaniga, M. S. (1989). Organization of the human brain. *Science, 245,* 947–952.

Giles-Sims, J. (1983). *Wife battering: A systems theory approach.* New York: Guilford Press.

Goffman, E. (1959). *The presentation of self in everyday life.* Garden City, N.Y.: Doubleday.

Goldberg, A. (1988). *A fresh look at psychoanalysis: The view from self psychology.* Hillsdale, N.J.: Analytic Press.

Greenspan, S. I., & Pollack, G. H. (1980). *The course of life,* vol. 3: *Adulthood and the aging process: Psychoanalytic contributions toward understanding personality development.* DHHS Publication no. ADM 81-1000. Washington, D.C.: U.S. Government Printing Office.

Haan, N., Weiss, R., & Johnson, V. (1982). The role of logic in moral reasoning and development. *Developmental Psychology, 18,* 245–256.

Horowitz, D. (1985). *Ethnic groups in conflict.* Berkeley: University of California Press.

Kantor, D., & Lehr, W. (1975). *Inside the family.* San Francisco: Jossey-Bass.

Katz, D., & Kahn, R. L. (1966). *The social psychology of organizations.* New York: Wiley.

Kihlstrom, J. F. (1987). The cognitive unconscious. *Science, 237,* 1445–1452.

Kohlberg, L. (1978). Revision in the theory and practice of moral development. *New Directions for Child Development, 2,* 83–87.

Kohlberg, L. (1984). *Essays on moral development,* vol 2., *The psychology of moral development.* San Francisco: Harper & Row.

Kosslyn, S. M. (1986). *Image and mind.* Cambridge, Mass.: Harvard University Press.

Labouvie-Vief, G. (1980). Beyond formal operations: Uses and limits of pure logic in life-span development. *Human Development, 23,* 141–161.

Laszlo, E. (1972). *Introduction to systems philosophy: Toward a new paradigm of contemporary thought.* New York: Harper & Row.

Lerner, I. M., & Libby, W. J. (1976). *Heredity, evolution, and society* (2nd ed.). San Francisco: W. H. Freeman.

Levy, G. D., & Carter, D. B. (1989). Gender schema, gender constancy, and gender-role knowledge: The roles of cognitive factors in preschoolers' gender-role stereotype attributions. *Developmental Psychology, 25,* 444–449.

Lewin, R. (1987). Africa: Cradle of modern humans. *Science, 237,* 1292–1295.

Lorenz, K. Z. (1935/1981). *The foundations of ethology* (trans. K. Z. Lorenz and R. W. Kickert). New York: Springer-Verlag.

Lorenz, K. Z. (1943). Die angeborenen Formen möglicher Erfahrung. *Zeitschrift für Tierpsychologie, 5,* 235–409.

Lyell, C. (1830/1833). *Principles of geology* (3 vols.). London: J. Murray.

McClelland, J. L., & Rumelhart, D. E. (1986). *Parallel distributed processing* (vol. 2). Cambridge, Mass.: MIT Press.

Mead, M. (1928/1950). *Coming of age in Samoa.* New York: New American Library.

Mead, M. (1949/1955). *Male and female: A study of the sexes in a changing world.* New York: Mentor.

Miller, P. H. (1989). *Theories of developmental psychology* (2nd ed.). New York: W. H. Freeman.

Mischel, W. (1973). Toward a cognitive social learning reconceptualization of personality. *Psychological Review, 80,* 252–283.

Mischel, W. (1979). On the interface of cognition and personality: Beyond the person-situation debate. *American Psychologist, 34,* 740–754.

Moore, C., Bryant, D., & Furrow, D. (1989). Mental terms and the development of certainty. *Child Development, 60,* 167–171.

Neisser, U. (1987). *Concepts and conceptual development: Ecological and intellectual factors in categorization.* New York: Cambridge University Press.

Parkes, C. M. (1987). *Bereavement: Studies of grief in adult life* (2nd ed.). Madison, Conn.: International Universities Press.

Parsons, T., & Bales, R. F. (eds.). (1955). *Family socialization and interaction process.* New York: Free Press.

Pavlov, I. P. (1927/1960). *Conditioned reflexes.* New York: Dover Press.

Piaget, J. (1924/1952). *Judgment and reasoning in the child.* New York: Humanities Press.

Piaget, J. (1926/1951). *The child's conception of the world.* New York: International Universities Press.

Piaget, J. (1936/1952). *The origins of intelligence in children.* New York: Humanities Press.

Piaget, J. (1941/1952). *The child's conception of number.* New York: Humanities Press.

Piaget, J. (1950). *The psychology of intelligence.* New York: Harcourt, Brace; London: Routledge & Kegan Paul.

Piaget, J. (1954). *The construction of reality in the child.* New York: Basic Books.

Piaget, J. (1978/1985). *The equilibration of cognitive structures.* Chicago: University of Chicago Press.

Piaget, J., & Inhelder, B. (1969). *The psychology of the child.* New York: Basic Books.

Rescorla, R. A. (1988). Pavlovian conditioning: It's not what you think it is. *American Psychologist, 43,* 151–160.

Resnick, L. B. (1989). Developing mathematical knowledge. *American Psychologist, 44,* 162–169.

Rollins, B. C., & Galligan, R. (1978). The developing child and marital satisfaction of parents. In R. M. Lerner & G. B. Spanier (eds.), *Child influences on marital and family interaction: A life-span perspective.* New York: Academic Press.

Ruffman, R. K., & Olson, D. R. (1989). Children's ascriptions of knowledge to others. *Developmental Psychology, 25,* 601–606.

Rumelhart, D. E., & McClelland, J. L. (1986). *Parallel distributed processing* (vol. 1). Cambridge, Mass.: MIT Press.

Sameroff, A. J. (1982). Development and the dialectic: The need for a systems approach. In W. A. Collins (ed.), *The concept of development: The Minnesota Symposia on Child Psychology* (vol. 15). Hillsdale, N.J.: Erlbaum.

Sarbin, T. R., & Allen, V. L. (1968). Role theory. In G. Lindzey & E. Aronson (eds.), *The Handbook of Social Psychology* (2nd ed., vol. 1). Reading, Mass.: Addison-Wesley.

Schermerhorn, R. A. (1978). *Comparative ethnic relations: A framework for theory and research.* Chicago: University of Chicago Press.

See, K. O., & Wilson, W. J. (1988). Race and ethnicity. In N. J. Smelser (ed.), *Handbook of sociology* (pp. 223–242). Newbury Park, Calif.: Sage.

Skinner, B. F. (1935). The generic nature of the concepts of stimulus and response. *Journal of Genetic Psychology, 12,* 40–65.

Skinner, B. F. (1938). *The behavior of organisms.* New York: Appleton-Century-Crofts.

Skinner, B. F. (1948). *Walden two.* New York: Macmillan.

Skinner, B. F. (1967). Autobiography of B. F. Skinner. In E. Boring & G. Lindzey (eds.), *History of psychology in autobiography* (vol. 5, pp. 387–413). New York: Appleton-Century-Crofts.

Skinner, B. F. (1971). *Beyond freedom and dignity.* New York: Knopf.

Skinner, B. F. (1987). Whatever happened to psychology as the science of behavior? *American Psychologist, 42,* 780–786.

Smetana, J. G. (1989). Toddlers' social interactions in the context of moral and conventional transgressions in the home. *Developmental Psychology, 25,* 499–508.

Spencer, H. (1864). *Principles of biology* (vol. 1). London: William & Norgate.

Stern, R. (1987). *Theories of the unconscious and theories of the self.* Hillsdale, N.J.: Analytic Press.

Sternberg, R. J., & Smith, E. E. (1988). *The psychology of human thought.* New York: Cambridge University Press.

Sullivan, H. S. (1953). *The interpersonal theory of psychiatry.* New York: Norton.

Tattersall, I., Delson, E., & Van Couvering, J. (1988). *Encyclopedia of human evolution and prehistory* (pp. 267–274). New York: Garland.

Thorndike, E. L. (1898). Animal intelligence: An experimental study of the associative processes in animals. *Psychological Review, 2* (Monograph Suppl. 8).

Tinbergen, N. (1951). *The study of instinct.* Oxford: Clarendon Press.

Tolman, E. C. (1932/1967). *Purposive behavior in rats and men.* New York: Appleton-Century-Crofts.

Tolman, E. C. (1948). Cognitive maps in rats and men. *Psychological Review, 55,* 189–208.

Uzgiris, I. C. (1976). The organization of sensorimotor intelligence. In M. Lewis (ed.), *Origins of intelligence: Infancy and early childhood* (pp. 123–164). New York: Plenum.

Viorst, J. (1986). *Necessary losses.* New York: Simon & Schuster.

Walker, L. J. (1989). A longitudinal study of moral reasoning. *Child Development, 60,* 157–166.

Westkott, M. (1986). *The feminist legacy of Karen Horney.* New Haven, Conn.: Yale University Press.

Whiting, B. B., & Edwards, C. P. (1988). *Children of different worlds: The formation of social behavior.* Cambridge, Mass.: Harvard University Press.

Chapter Four

The fetus develops within the context of the pregnant woman's body, her family, and her culture.

Pablo Picasso, *Pregnant Woman,* Vallauris (1950). Bronze (cast 1955), 41¼″ x 7⅝″ x 6¼″. Collection, The Museum of Modern Art, New York. Gift of Mrs. Bertram Smith. © 1991, ARS, New York/SPADEM.

The Period of Pregnancy and Prenatal Development

Our analysis of psychosocial development begins with the period of pregnancy and prenatal growth. Actually, you could take your personal life story back much further than that. You might ask about how your parents met, the socialization each had for the parent role, and the cultural context of their own infancy and childhood. You might ask about the environmental factors that could have influenced your prenatal development, such as your mother's nutritional status, exposure to environmental hazards, or use of drugs during labor and delivery. You might ask those same questions regarding your grandparents, great-grandparents, and so on back through time. Each past generation has contributed in some significant ways to your life story.

In this chapter we take the perspective of both the emerging infant and the expectant parents. For the parents, the decision to have children, the experiences of pregnancy, and the events of childbirth contribute to the actualization of the parent role. For the child, the process of growth begins with the moment of fertilization.

Genetic factors guide the tempo of growth and the emergence of individual characteristics. As the human fetus grows, sensory and motor competences emerge. The psychosocial environment during the prenatal period provides resources and challenges to healthy development. Cultural attitudes toward pregnancy and childbirth, maternal nutrition and stress, and the use of obstetric drugs are among the factors that can contribute to the pattern of growth.

Genetics and Development

Genetic information provides a set of guidelines for development. It determines the nature of a person's resources and may, in some cases, place severe constraints on development. Given a certain genetically based potential, a wide range of individual variation is possible, depending on the quality of the environment, the degree of fit between the person and the environment, and the person's unique, integrative resources for coping with the world.

Genes and Chromosomes as Sources of Genetic Information

When we talk about inherited characteristics, we are really referring to two different kinds of heredity. The first kind includes all the genetic information that comes to us as members of the human species. We inherit information that is shared by all human beings, such as patterns of motor behavior (walking upright for instance), brain size, and body structure, including the relative size of head, torso, and limbs. Two of the most relevant of these species-related characteristics are the readiness to learn and the inclination to participate in social interaction. All humans share these attributes.

The second kind of heredity consists of characteristics that have been transmitted through a specific *gene pool.* Such traits as hair color, skin color, blood group, and height all result from the genetic information passed on from one generation to the next. The principles of genetics that we will be describing refer primarily to this second group of inherited characteristics, the products of a specific gene pool (Gardner &

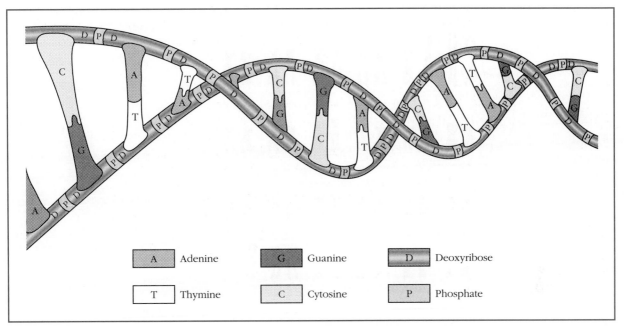

Figure 4.1   Diagram of a Small Part of a DNA Molecule

Snustad, 1984; Vogel & Motulsky, 1986). Genetic information links each new person to the human species in general and to a specific genetic ancestry.

The smallest unit of genetic information is the DNA *(deoxyribonucleic acid) molecule*. This molecule has the shape of a double helix (see Figure 4.1). The DNA molecule looks something like a twisted rope ladder. The sides of this genetic ladder are composed of alternating units of sugar (deoxyribose) and phosphate. The rungs are made up of pairs of nitrogen bases. Nitrogen bases are so named because they include the element nitrogen as well as the elements hydrogen and carbon. Four bases are involved: *adenine* (A), *guanine* (G), *cytosine* (C), and *thymine* (T). These bases are often referred to by their initial letters, and A, G, C, and T are called the genetic alphabet.

Adenine (A) and guanine (G) are *purine* bases. Cytosine (C) and thymine (T) are *pyrimidine* bases. The purine bases are smaller than the pyrimidine bases. Only combinations of adenine and thymine or guanine and cytosine are the right size to fit into the space between the sides of the genetic ladder. Thus C–G, G–C, A–T, and T–A are the only pairs of bases that are possible in DNA molecules. Figure 4.1 shows the shape and composition of DNA. The order of base pairs and the accompanying side material of sugar and phosphate determine the meaning of the genetic message.

DNA molecules form chains, which are called *chromosomes*. These chromosomes are located in the cell nucleus. Late in the 19th century, cell biologists learned how to stain the long, thin strands in the nuclei of cells. The word *chromosome* means colored body. After it was discovered that chromosomes could be stained, biologists could count and study them. They learned that the cells of the body of each species

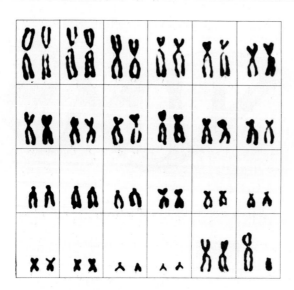

Figure 4.2   The Human Chromosome Pairs

The figure shows the 23 pairs of chromosomes in a human male. The 23rd pair determines the individual's sex. In males, one member of each pair is an X chromosome and the other a Y chromosome. In females, both are X chromosomes.

contain a specific number of chromosomes. It was not until the 1950s that Joe Hin Tjio and Albert Levan of the Institute of Genetics in Lund, Sweden, determined that human cells contained 46 chromosomes. The common fruit fly, which is used in a good deal of genetic research, has only eight chromosomes. Biologists also learned that the chromosomes in each cell occur in pairs. Humans have 23 pairs of chromosomes (Figure 4.2).

One member of each chromosome pair comes from the father and one from the mother. Of 22 pairs of chromosomes, both members are similar in shape and size. They also contain the same kinds of genes. The 23rd pair of chromosomes is a different story. Females possess two X chromosomes. Males possess one X and one Y chromosome. The X and Y notation is used because these chromosomes differ in shape and size. The X chromosome is longer than the Y chromosome. There are very few similarities in the genes present on the X and Y chromosomes.

It is important to note here that the same group of chromosomes does not appear in each *gamete* (egg or sperm cell). When the cells divide, the chromosomes separate independently. There are 2^{23} possible combinations of chromosome separation for any individual's gametes.

Additional variability in the pattern of genetic information results from *crossing over.* When the cells divide during *meiosis,* some of the material from the paternal and maternal chromosome strands may cross over and exchange places on the strand. The resulting sequence of specific genetic information on a chromosome is unlike either the original maternal or paternal code.

Through crossing over, new arrangements of genetic information may be passed on to offspring. This variation in the patterning of genetic information accounts for the diversity of offspring possible for any single individual. When one considers the fertilization process and the chance meeting of one sperm and one egg cell, the number of different individuals that might be produced by two adults is $2^{23} \times 2^{23}$, or 64 trillion, even when crossing over is not taken into account.

The laws that govern the process by which genetic information is transmitted from parent to offspring were discovered by Gregor Mendel, a monk who studied the inherited characteristics of plants, particularly garden peas (Mendel, 1866). His laws were formulated long before the discovery of the biochemical materials of which genes and chromosomes are composed.

Each element of genetic information is called a *gene*. A gene is a portion of DNA that codes for one hereditary characteristic and occupies a specific place on a chromosome. It is estimated that humans have about 100,000 functional genes. Genetic mapping involves identifying the specific location of each gene on a specific chromosome. This is an enormous task. The smallest human chromosome bands that can be recognized under the microscope contain from 2 to 5 million base pairs of DNA and many genes (Patterson, 1987). Chromosome pairs vary in size; it is estimated that some chromosomes contain over 1000 genes while others contain over 2000.

In the 22 pairs of identical chromosomes, each gene has at least two states or conditions, one on each chromosome strand in the pair. These alternative states are called *alleles*. Whatever the allelic state of the gene from one parent, the other parent's allele for that gene may be either the same or different. If both alleles are the same, the gene is said to be *homozygous*. If the alleles are different, the gene is *heterozygous*.

Genotype and Phenotype

The genetic information about a trait is called the *genotype*. The observed characteristic is called the *phenotype*. Genotype influences phenotype in three ways. Sometimes the differences in the allelic states of a gene result in a *cumulative relation,* in which more than one pair of genes influences the trait. An example of this kind of relation is the genetic contribution to height. A person who receives mostly "tall" genes will be tall; a person who receives mostly "short" genes will be short. Most people receive a mix of "tall" and "short" genes and are of average height.

In some instances, the differences between alleles can result in *codominance,* a state in which both genes are expressed in the new cell. An example of codominance is the AB blood type, which results from the joining of an A allele and a B allele. This blood type is not a mixture of A and B, nor is A subordinated to B or B to A; instead, a new blood type, AB, is formed.

The differences in the allele states of a gene can also result in a *dominance* relation. *Dominance* means that if one allele is present, its characteristic is always observed whether or not the other allele is the same. The allele that dominates is called the *dominant gene*. The allele that is present but whose characteristic is masked by the dominant gene is called the *recessive gene*.

Eye color is the result of a dominance relation. The gene for brown eyes (B) is dominant over the gene for blue eyes (b). The possible combinations of the gene

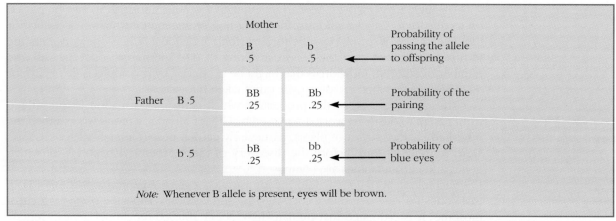

Figure 4.3   Probability of Heterozygous Parents Producing a Blue-Eyed Offspring

related to brown or blue eye color are BB, Bb, bB, and bb. Only if both parents carry the b allele and that allele is present in each of the gametes that form the offspring will the child have blue eyes. The probability of the recessive trait of blue eyes emerging in the offspring of two heterozygous parents is illustrated in Figure 4.3. As the figure shows, on the average only 25% of the offspring of heterozygous parents have blue eyes.

In the case of a dominance relation, genetic information is not always observed in some outward characteristic. For example, people with alleles BB and Bb may both have brown eyes even though they have different genetic information. For brown and blue eye color, there are two phenotypes—brown and blue—but three genotypes—BB, Bb, and bb.

Sex-Linked Characteristics

Certain genetic information is said to be sex-linked because the allele for the specific characteristic is found on the sex chromosomes. The female ova carry only X chromosomes. Half of the male sperm carry Y chromosomes, and half carry X chromosomes. Male children can be produced only when a sperm carrying a Y chromosome fertilizes an egg, resulting in an XY combination in the 23rd chromosome pair. All sperm carrying X chromosomes will produce female children.

Sex-linked traits are more likely to be observed in males even though they are present in the genotype of females. You will understand this more readily if you visualize the XY chromosome pair. When a trait is carried on the Y chromosome, it will be inherited and transmitted only by males, since only males have the Y chromosome.

Interestingly, the Y chromosome is quite small and very few Y-linked traits have been identified. However, even sex-linked traits that are carried on the X chromosome are more likely to be observed in males than in females, because males do not have a second X chromosome with which to offset the effects of an X-linked trait.

One sex-linked trait is hemophilia. Hemophiliacs lack a specific blood protein that causes blood to clot after a wound (Lawn & Vehar, 1986). The allele for hemophilia is carried on the X chromosome. If the allele is either heterozygous or homozygous for the dominant characteristic (normal clotting), a female child will have normal blood-clotting capability. Only if she is homozygous for the recessive characteristic (a very rare occurrence) will she be hemophilic. The male, on the other hand, has only one allele for the blood-clotting gene, which he inherits from his mother. If that allele is dominant, his blood will clot normally; if it is recessive, he will be hemophilic (see Figure 4.4).

There are other genes that are expressed exclusively in one sex but are not found on the sex chromosomes per se. The genes for male beard and female breast development are not located on the sex chromosomes. However, these characteristics will emerge only in the presence of the appropriate hormonal environment, which *is* directed by the sex chromosomes.

Genetic Sources of Individuality

The study of genetics reveals that individual variability is due to more than the many variations in environment and experience that confront a growing person. Variability is built into the mechanisms of heredity. Each adult couple has the potential for producing a variety of genetically distinct children. Three areas in which genetic determinants contribute to individual variability are rate of development, individual traits, and abnormal development.

Genetic Determinants of Rate of Development

Genes regulate the rate and sequence of maturation. The concept of an epigenetic plan for growth and development is based on the assumption that there is a genetically guided system that can promote or restrict the growth of cells over the life span. Genetic factors have been found to play a role in behavioral development, including the onset of various levels of reasoning, language, and social orientation.

Considerable evidence for the role of genetics in guiding the rate and sequence of development has been provided by studies of identical twins. The rates at which identical twins develop are highly correlated, even when those twins are reared apart. A number of characteristics, including the timing of the acquisition of motor skills, personality development, changes in intellectual capacity among aged twins, and the timing of physical maturation all show a strong genetic influence (Holden, 1987).

Genes can be viewed as internal regulators. They set the pace for maturation. They signal the onset of significant developmental changes across the life span, such as growth spurts, the eruption of teeth, puberty, and menopause. They also appear to set the limits of the life span. A small number of genes influence the number of times that cells from a specific organism can divide and replicate (Marx, 1988). Thus genetic information may guide the timing of decline and death as well as the unfolding of the organism.

Differences in the rate of development contribute to our understanding of psychosocial growth. These differences bring children into contact with new aspects of their environments and provide them with changing capacities at different chronological ages. Adult expectations for the accomplishment of such specific tasks as toilet

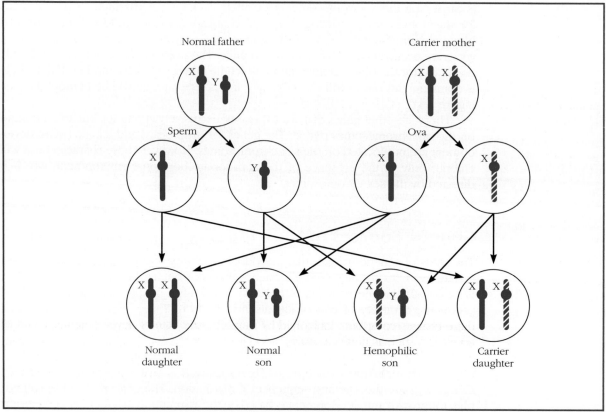

Figure 4.4   **Sex-Linked Inheritance of Hemophilia**
Sex-linked inheritance of hemophilia results from the location of the factor VIII gene on the X chromosome. A male carrying a mutant factor VIII gene lacks normal factor VIII and is hemophilic. A female carrier is protected by the normal gene on her second X chromosome, but half of her daughters will be carriers and half of her sons will be hemophilic. In the case of a hemophilic father (not shown), his sons will not be hemophilic, because they receive his Y (not his X) chromosome, but his daughters will be carriers.
Source: From "The Molecular Genetics of Hemophilia," by R. M. Lawn and G. A. Vehar, p. 50. Copyright © 1986 by SCIENTIFIC AMERICAN, Inc. All rights reserved.

training, getting dressed without help, and learning to write, interact with the child's developmental level. Disappointment may be conveyed to developmentally "late" children; pride and approval may be conveyed to developmentally "accelerated" children. Genetic processes that regulate readiness for certain kinds of growth and vulnerabilities to particular kinds of stress contribute to systematic differences among individuals.

Genetic Determinants of Individual Traits
Genes contain specific information about a wide range of human characteristics, from eye color and height to the ability to taste a particular substance called phenylthiocarbamide (which to tasters is bitter but to nontasters has no taste at all). Some of

Pablo Picasso, *Three Women, VIII* (from the suite *An Anatomy),* 1933. Individuality is in part a product of the many possible combinations of genetic information. In this drawing Picasso shows us how basic geometric shapes can be combined in a variety of ways to produce human-like figures, similar and yet each unique.

these characteristics are controlled by a single gene. However, most significant characteristics, such as height, weight, blood group, skin color, and intelligence, are controlled by the combined action of several genes. When multiple genes are involved in the regulation of a trait, the possibilities for individual differences in that trait increase. Since many characteristics are regulated by multiple genes, the variety of human genotypes is enormous.

Recent work suggests that genetic factors play a substantial role in individual differences in personality (Holden, 1987; Pedersen et al., 1988). Two basic characteristics, extroversion (a tendency to be sociable and outgoing) and neuroticism (a tendency to be anxious and emotionally sensitive), are pervasive dimensions of personality that appear to have strong genetic components. Even in rather specific areas of personality such as political attitudes, aesthetic preferences, and sense of humor, identical twins show greater similarity than fraternal twins, even when the identical twins are reared apart from each other.

Genetic Determinants of Abnormal Development

In addition to characteristics such as physical appearance, temperament, talent, and intellectual capacity, a wide variety of abnormalities or *anomalies* have a genetic cause. The most dramatic anomalies result in an abortion of the fetus early in the pregnancy. It is estimated that a majority of the spontaneous abortions that occur early in pregnancy are the results of chromosomal abnormalities in the fertilized zygotes (Clayman, 1989).

Of those infants who survive the neonatal period, an estimated 3 to 5% of newborns have one or more major recognizable anomalies (Cunningham, MacDonald & Gant, 1989). The incidence of anomalies increases to 6 or 7% as some disorders are diagnosed later in childhood. The causes of these malformations and disorders are listed in Table 4.1, along with an estimate of the incidence of each type of cause. A small percentage of birth defects are linked to a specific chromosome (6%) or single gene (8%). Similarly, a small percentage is linked solely to environmental factors, such as drugs, medications, and fetal and maternal infections. The vast majority of malformations are products of the interaction of genetic vulnerabilities in the presence of certain environmental hazards or are of unknown origin (Moore, 1988). Some genetic and chromosomal disorders are listed in Table 4.2 (Clayman, 1989):

Among genetic disorders that result from a dominant gene, about 300 have been identified; among those that result from a recessive gene, about 250 have been identified. Through the use of molecular biology techniques, it has become possible to identify the chromosomal site of a number of genetic disorders. This work will lead eventually to a clearer understanding of the molecular mechanisms that account for these disorders (Martin, 1987).

The variety of genetic abnormalities serves to broaden the range of individual variability. Many of the irregularities pose a challenge both to the adaptive capacities of the afflicted person and to the caregiving capacities of the adults involved. Even relatively mild irregularities may be significant factors in the person's psychological functioning. The presence of a shock of white hair, a birthmark, an elongated middle toe, or a long nose reminds each of us of our uniqueness. Although many of these irregularities may not be of medical concern or require treatment, they are relevant to an evolving sense of self. Sometimes the irregularities carry negative connotations or block the person's level of functioning. Such challenges to self-esteem and coping are the direct results of inheritance.

Genetic Technology and Psychosocial Evolution

The products of psychosocial evolution, including behavioral adaptations, the transfer of knowledge, new inventions, and new forms of social organization, were once considered to be carried by social mechanisms rather than incorporated in the genetic

Table 4.1 Estimated Incidence of Causes of Major Congenital Malformations

Cause	Incidence (percent)
Chromosomal aberrations	6%
Environmental factors	7
Single gene defects	8
Multifactorial inheritance*	25
Unknown	54

*Multiple genes at different loci on chromosomes interact with environmental factors to produce malformations.

Source: K. L. Moore, *The Developing Human: Clinically Oriented Embryology,* 4th ed. (Philadelphia: W. B. Saunders, 1988), p. 132.

Table 4.2   Genetic and Chromosomal Disorders

I. Genetic disorders
  A. Autosomal dominant gene
    1. *Achondroplasia (dwarfism):* Abnormal bone growth, especially in the arms and legs, results in short stature, short limbs, a well-developed trunk, and a head of normal size except for somewhat protruding forehead.
    2. *Huntington's chorea:* Rapid, jerky, involuntary movements. Deterioration of muscle coordination and mental functioning. Symptoms usually do not appear until age 35 to 50. Results from genetic defect on chromosome 4.
    3. *Marfan's syndrome:* Elongated fingers; deformed chest and spine; abnormal heart. Tendons, ligaments, and joint capsules are weak.
  B. Autosomal recessive gene
    1. *Albinism:* Hair, skin, and eyes lack the pigment melanin. Often accompanied by visual problems and a tendency to skin cancer.
    2. *Cystic fibrosis:* Certain glands do not function properly. The glands in the lining of the bronchial tubes produce excessive amounts of thick mucus, which lead to chronic lung infections. Failure of the pancreas to produce enzymes necessary for the breakdown of fats and their absorption from the intestines leads to malnutrition. Sweat glands are also affected. Often fatal by age 30. Missing base pairs on chromosome 7.
    3. *Sickle-cell anemia:* Malformation of red blood cells reduces the amount of oxygen they can carry. Results in fatigue, headaches, shortness of breath on exertion, pallor, jaundice, pain, damage to kidneys, lungs, intestine, and brain.
    4. *Tay–Sachs disease:* Absence of a certain enzyme results in the buildup of harmful chemicals in the brain. Results in death before age 3.
  C. X-linked recessive
    1. *Color blindness:* Defect of light-sensitive pigment in one or more classes of cone cells in the retina of the eye and/or an abnormality or reduced number of cone cells themselves. The two common types are reduced discrimination of light wavelengths within the middle (green) and long (red) parts of the visible spectrum.
    2. *Hemophilia:* Absence of blood protein, factor VIII, reduces effectiveness of blood clotting. Severity of disorder varies. Bleeding episodes likely to begin in toddlerhood.
    3. *Duchenne muscular dystrophy:* Progressive degeneration of muscle fibers. Most common form of childhood dystrophies. Muscle weakness early in life. Few survive teen years. Thirty percent of affected males are also mentally retarded.
II. Chromosomal disorders
  A. Autosomal abnormality
     Down's syndrome: Usually three rather than two chromosomes 21. The excess chromosome results in physical and intellectual abnormalities, including IQ in the range of 30–80; distinctive facial features, heart defects, intestinal problems, hearing defects; susceptibility to repeated ear infections. Tendency to develop narrowing of the arteries in adulthood, with attendant increase in risk of heart disease. Such people tend to be affectionate and friendly, and get along well with other family members. Most are capable of at least some learning.

(continued)

Table 4.2 *continued*
B.   Sex-chromosome abnormalities
1.   *Turner's syndrome:* Usually caused by a lack of one X chromosome in a girl; sometimes one of two X chromosomes is defective; occasionally some cells are missing on an X chromosome. These abnormalities result in defective sexual development and infertility, short stature, absence or retarded development of secondary sex characteristics, absence of menstruation, narrowing of the aorta, and a degree of mental retardation.
2.   *Klinefelter's syndrome:* One or more extra X chromosomes in a boy. This abnormality results in defective sexual development, including enlarged breasts and small testes, infertility, and often mental retardation.
3.   *Fragile X syndrome:* A small portion of the tip of the X chromosome is susceptible to breakage under certain conditions. The damage results in mental retardation, learning disabilities, and abnormalities in growth regulation, such as a big head, higher than normal birth weight, large or protruding ears, and a long face. Behavior problems include hand-flapping, hand-biting, hyperactivity, poor eye contact, autism, social withdrawal, and shyness. More boys are affected than girls, and boys' problems tend to be more severe.

structure. As a result of what has been learned scientifically, however, we are entering an era when it is possible to intervene to influence the genotype. One such intervention is *genetic counseling.* Individuals and couples whose families have a history of a genetic disease, or who for some other reason worry about the possibility of transmitting a genetic disease to their children, can have a blood test that will identify the presence of genes that might result in the inherited disorder. In the case of such abnormalities as Tay–Sachs disease, sickle-cell anemia, Duchenne muscular dystrophy, and cystic fibrosis, the location of the gene that accounts for the disease has been identified. Couples who carry genes for one of these diseases can be advised about the probability of having children who may be afflicted and can make an informed decision as to whether or not they want to reproduce. If significant numbers of carriers of genetic diseases decided not to reproduce, the incidence of these diseases in the population would decline significantly over time. Thus a psychosocial intervention would indeed modify the gene pool.

In the years ahead, genetic technology promises to take us even further than genetic counseling through the direct modification of the genetic structure of an individual. In January 1989 the National Institutes of Health launched a project to map the *human genome*—to identify and list in order all of the genome's approximately 3 billion base pairs. Once completed, this map could permit us to predict an individual's vulnerability to genetic diseases, to treat genetically caused diseases, and possibly to "enhance" a person's genetic potential through the introduction of gene modifications (Jaroff, 1989).

Toward the end of 1988 the United States government scrutinized and then approved the first transfer of a foreign gene into humans. The experiment is being conducted

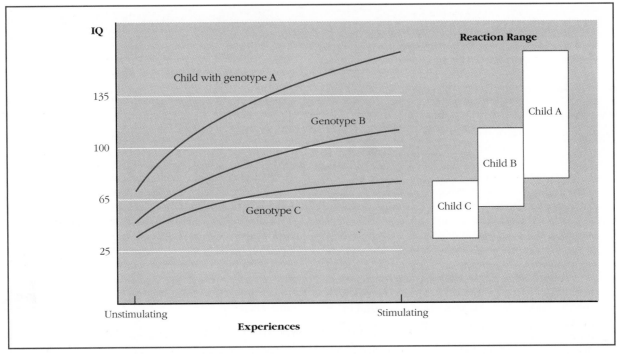

Figure 4.5   Hypothetical Reaction Ranges of Intelligence
Source: Adapted from I. Gottesman, "Genetic Aspects of Intelligent Behavior," in N. Ellis (ed.), *Handbook of Mental Deficiency* (New York: McGraw-Hill, 1963), p. 255. Reprinted by permission of the author.

at the National Institutes of Health. The initial gene-transfer experiment was limited to ten cancer patients who were not expected to live more than ninety days. In this first test, the transplanted gene served as a marker to help track the progress of an experimental cancer treatment. This experiment was not considered *gene therapy* because the transplanted gene was not expected to produce a therapeutic benefit. However, the same technique can be used to correct genetic diseases (Roberts, 1989).

Gene transfer, the patenting of new life forms created through genetic engineering, and the new technique of genetic fingerprinting, which is used to help identify criminal suspects, are just some of the topics that are raising new ethical concerns. In discussions, debates, research, observation of events, and court cases we are hammering out a set of ethics that not only deals with specific issues but sets the tone for the way we conceptualize life itself.

One way to summarize the influences of genetics on behavior is to consider the genotype as establishing a *reaction range*. In other words, a particular genotype influences the range of possible responses to environmental conditions. Figure 4.5 shows the hypothetical reaction ranges of three children with respect to intelligence. Child A has greater genetic potential for intelligence than child B, who has greater

Box 4.1   Hereditary Influences on Intelligence

A question of interest to developmental psychologists, educators, and parents is the relative contribution of genetic and environmental factors to intelligence. In fact, intelligent behavior requires the successful integration of both. It relies on the structure of the central nervous system and sense receptors, which are products of genetically guided information. However, the healthy functioning of these systems requires adequate nutrition, rest, and freedom from disease, conditions that vary with the environment. Intelligent behavior also relies on experiences with diverse stimuli, appropriate social interactions, and the cultivation of problem-solving strategies—all elements of the physical and social environment.

The influence of genetic factors on intelligence may be observed in two ways. First, we know that specific genetic irregularities can cause degrees of mental retardation. Two examples are Down's syndrome and phenylketonuria (PKU). The Down's syndrome child has 47 chromosomes rather than the normal 46. It is hypothesized that the additional chromosome leads to an overproduction of enzymes, which results in both intellectual and physical abnormalities. PKU is a condition that results from a certain recessive gene (p). When a child is homozygous for p, a specific enzyme is not produced. The outcome is that an amino acid, phenylalanine, which is normally transformed into another amino acid, does not change. Phenylalanine accumulates in the body and damages the brain. If PKU is diagnosed within the first week of life, its negative effects can be minimized through systematic control of diet to reduce the intake of phenylalanine in milk and other foods. Many other genetic diseases have some negative effect on intellectual growth. Thus genetic diseases play an indisputable role in restricting intellectual potential.

A second approach to the influence of genetics on intelligence is through the study of family relationships. Family members can be related closely or distantly. The closer the relatives, the more similar their genetic makeups. If intelligence is influenced by genetics, close relatives should be more similar in intelligence than distant relatives.

The figure opposite shows the degree of similarity found in more than 100 studies of intelligence in siblings of four degrees of relationship. Here we can see that similarity in intelligence increases with the degree of genetic relatedness. Similarity in intelligence between identical or monozygotic (MZ) twins is striking evidence for the contribution of genetics to intelligence. Fraternal or dizygotic (DZ) twins who share the same prenatal, home, and child-rearing environment show much less similarity than do identical twins and not much more than "ordinary" siblings. This comparison offers clear evidence of genetic influence on intelligence.

Many of the same studies that supply evidence of genetic contributions to intelligence highlight the role of the environment as well. For example, the Texas Adoption Project (Horn, 1983, 1985) compared IQ data on more than 400 adopted children, their adoptive mothers, and their biological mothers. Evidence of genetic influences appeared in the fact that the IQs of adopted children and their biological mothers were more highly correlated than the IQs of the children and their adoptive mothers. The brighter adopted children were the offspring of the brighter biological mothers. This pattern demonstrates that genetic factors continue to play an important role in the development of individual differences.

Evidence of environmental influences on intelligence was found in the fact that the average IQ of the adopted children as a group was significantly higher than their biological mothers', but quite similar to their adoptive mothers'. This pattern demonstrates that the adoptive environment had an enriching effect on the children, raising the IQ level of the group as a whole.

potential than child C. When all three children are in unstimulating environments, their IQs develop at the lower end of their potential ranges. When all three children are in stimulating environments, their IQs develop toward the upper end of their

Box 4.1   *(continued)*

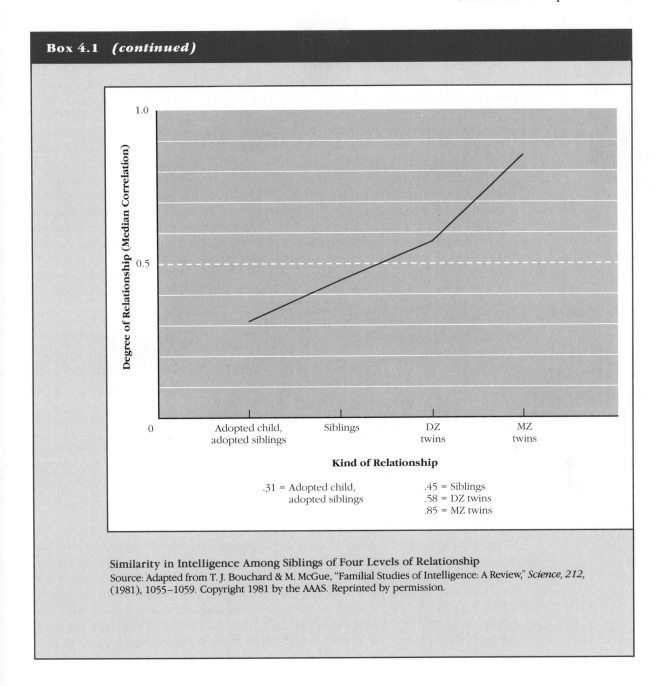

Similarity in Intelligence Among Siblings of Four Levels of Relationship
Source: Adapted from T. J. Bouchard & M. McGue, "Familial Studies of Intelligence: A Review," *Science, 212,* (1981), 1055–1059. Copyright 1981 by the AAAS. Reprinted by permission.

potential ranges. If the three children are in different environments, the differences in genetic potential may be masked by the way the environments act on this potential. If child B and child C are in stimulating environments and child A is in an unstimulating environment, child B may have the highest measured IQ, while the IQs of children C and A are lower and very similar. Each child's intellectual ability can be expressed as a range that is a product of the interaction of genetic potential and environment.

The concept of reaction range can be seen clearly in the outlook for children with Down's syndrome (Patterson, 1987). This condition, which occurs once in every 700 live births, is the most common genetic cause of mental retardation in the United States. In the early part of this century, children born with Down's syndrome had a life expectancy of nine years. Today the life expectancy of a Down's syndrome child is 30 years, and 25% of these children live to age 50. Medical care, early and constant educational intervention, physical therapy, and a nurturing home environment can have significant, positive results for children with Down's syndrome. Under optimal conditions, these children, whose IQs range from 30 to 80, are able to achieve a moderate degree of independence and to participate actively in the life of their families.

In the past few years, information gleaned from genetic research has had a major impact on the way social scientists conceptualize the role played by genetics in human development. The genetic system provides basic guidance for the direction and rate of development. Four areas have been identified as being strongly influenced by genetic information:

1. The rate of development
2. Individual traits
3. Abnormal development
4. Psychosocial evolution

Let us now explore the physical process through which genetic information is actually transmitted and see how the early phases of development unfold.

Normal Fetal Development

Fertilization

One normal ejaculation contains several hundred million sperm. This large number is necessary to ensure fertilization, because most sperm die on the path through the vagina and the uterus. Each microscopic sperm is composed of a pointed head and a tail. The head contains the genetic material necessary to reproduction. The tail moves like a whip as the sperm swims through the cervix and uterus and into the fallopian tubes. Swimming at a rate of an inch in eight minutes, sperm may reach the egg in as little as half an hour. The journey usually takes about six hours, and sperm can stay alive for up to five days in the uterus.

During most of the menstrual cycle, the plug of mucus in the cervix is thick and difficult to traverse. At the middle of the cycle, when the ovum is about ready to be released, the mucus thins out, allowing more sperm to pass through the cervix and travel farther into the uterus in search of an ovum. The change in the mucus also lessens the vagina's natural acidity, making it a more hospitable environment for sperm cells.

In contrast to the male, who produces billions of sperm in a lifetime, the female ordinarily releases just one ovum, or egg, each month, midway through the menstrual cycle. In a lifetime of approximately 40 fertile years, during which she can be expected to have two children, the average woman releases approximately 450 eggs. Each girl is born with her complete supply of eggs.

Like the sperm, the ovum is a single cell that contains genetic material. In comparison with body cells, the egg cell is quite large (0.12 millimeters)—about the size of the period at the end of this sentence. When the ovum is mature, it is encased in a sac of fluid and floats to the surface of the ovary. The sac ruptures and releases the ovum into the fallopian tube. Millions of feathery hairs in the fallopian tube sweep around the ovum and gently move it toward the uterus.

The ovum can be fertilized at any point as it moves through the fallopian tube. Usually a sperm joins the egg in the outer third of the tube, close to the uterus. Only one sperm can enter the cell. As the first sperm passes through the cell membrane, a rapid change in the membrane's chemistry effectively locks out other sperm. If the ovum is not fertilized within the first twenty-four hours of its maturity, it begins to disintegrate and is shed along with the lining of the uterus at the next menstrual period.

Inside the egg cell the sperm loses its tail and the head becomes a normal cell nucleus. The egg cell also goes through a final change in preparation for fertilization. The two nuclei meet in the egg cytoplasm, lose their nuclear membranes, and integrate their separate chromosomal material into a single set of 23 pairs of chromosomes. At this moment, all the information necessary to activate growth and produce a new, unique individual is contained in a single cell.

Infertility and Alternative Means of Reproduction

For approximately 14% of married couples of child-bearing age in the United States, the normal process of fertilization does not occur. Infertility, or the inability to conceive, can result from problems in the reproductive system of either the man or the woman, or in the systems of both. The limited research literature on the emotional impact of infertility suggests that it is a major source of stress. The discovery of infertility forces a couple to reassess the meaning and purpose of their marriage. It raises doubts about self-worth in the man and woman; it disrupts the couple's satisfaction with their sexual relationship; and it often isolates the couple because of the difficulty of discussing this very personal family problem with others (Sabatelli, Meth & Gavazzi, 1988; Jarboe, 1986).

A woman who had tried unsuccessfully to conceive for eight years put it this way:

> *"I can tell you that everyone who faces this is extremely vulnerable and will pretty much try anything . . . because we're desperate."*
> *"I felt like the fact that I couldn't do the very thing that my body was designed to do—to conceive and carry a child—must mean that I wasn't fully a woman. And all my other accomplishments seemed to fade into the background in the face of this failure."*   [Sperling, 1989]

Women who seek treatment for infertility make frequent visits to their physicians. Weight, hormone levels, temperature, blood count, and other physical indicators are monitored repeatedly.

Some remarkable alternatives are being developed for couples who are unable to conceive. With each of these alternatives come new challenges in the ways we define families and in the meanings we give to women's reproductive function (Robison, 1989; Silverman, 1989).

Artificial insemination is probably the best-developed alternative to natural fertilization. A woman who wants to conceive goes to a clinic every month and has sperm injected into her vagina. These sperm have been donated and frozen. Some sperm banks keep the donors' characteristics on file. This procedure enables the couple to select the sperm of a donor who closely resembles the husband. A single woman can select features she desires in her offspring. Other banks blend sperm so that the recipient cannot trace the donor's identity. The Office of Technology Assessment reported that approximately 172,000 women in the United States undergo artificial insemination each year, and that about 65,000 babies are conceived annually by this procedure (Byrne, 1988).

Another alternative to natural fertilization is *fertilization in vitro*. In this process, an egg is removed from the ovary and placed in a petri dish inside an incubator. A few drops of sperm are added to the dish. If the egg is fertilized and the cell begins to divide, the fertilized egg is replanted in the uterus for subsequent development. A survey of 146 clinics that perform in vitro fertilization found that the procedure is successful in about 9% of cases (Sperling, 1989).

In a third procedure, *gamete intrafallopian transfer* (GIFT), eggs and sperm are transferred into a woman's fallopian tubes. Fertilization takes place as it normally would, within the woman's reproductive system. These eggs and sperm can come from a husband and a wife or from other donors. Thus the fetus could be genetically related to the husband, to the wife, to both, or to neither.

A fourth alternative is *in vivo fertilization.* In this procedure, a husband and wife involve another woman in the conception. The other woman, who has demonstrated her fertility, is artificially inseminated with the husband's sperm. Once an embryo has formed, it is transferred to the wife's uterus, which becomes the gestational environment. The child is therefore genetically related to the husband but not to the wife.

A fifth alternative involves a *surrogate mother.* Sperm from an infertile woman's husband are injected into the surrogate mother during the time of her monthly ovulation. The surrogate bears the child and returns it to the parents at birth.

All of these alternatives have raised legal and ethical questions (Andrews, 1984). The husband of a woman who is planning to be artificially inseminated must consent to the procedure and agree to assume legal guardianship of the offspring. The lack of official guidelines for screening donors raises the issue of who should be responsible if a child resulting from artificial insemination has a severe genetic anomaly. What are the donor's rights to a relationship with his offspring? In 1983 a California man was granted weekly visitation rights to a child who had been conceived with his sperm. Finally, what limits should be placed on the production of embryos in vitro? Should we permit scientists to produce embryos from frozen sperm and egg cells for purposes other than implantation?

In the widely publicized case of Baby M., William and Elizabeth Stern paid Mary Beth Whitehead $10,000 to be a surrogate mother. After the baby was born, Mrs. Whitehead decided that she wanted to keep the baby. In ensuing court battles, the New Jersey Supreme Court decided that the contract between the couple and Mrs. Whitehead was void and that it was illegal to pay a woman to bear a child for someone else. Nonetheless, the court granted custody of the child to the Sterns, arguing that they could provide the child a more stable home environment. The court rejected the right of Elizabeth Stern to adopt the baby and supported Mrs. Whitehead's right of continued visitation. This complex pattern of decisions creates a precedent that other states may follow. Surrogate parenting may be made illegal or may be so tightly regulated that it becomes an underground practice, although it is widely endorsed by the medical community (Lacayo, 1988; Silverman, 1989).

Another troubling ethical case arose in a conflict between a couple, Risa and Steven York, and the Jones Institute for Reproductive Medicine in Norfolk, Virginia. The Yorks, who lived in New Jersey, began to participate in an in vitro fertilization program of the Jones Institute in 1986. Three implant attempts failed. Then the Yorks decided to move to California, and they asked the Jones Institute to send their frozen embryo to a comparable medical facility in Los Angeles. The institute refused. According to the Jones Institute, the Yorks must have the embryo implanted at their facility. Otherwise, the Yorks could donate it to the institute for use with another couple or for experimentation, or they could have it destroyed (Elson, 1989).

At present more than 4,000 frozen embryos are being held in various medical and laboratory facilities in the United States (Elson, 1989). State laws governing their use as well as their rights are often conflicting and confusing. Questions are raised about the right of parents to determine the fate of these embryos, the embryos' right to protection and inheritance, and the responsibility of institutes and laboratories to ensure the proper use of the embryos. The disturbing element here is the obvious detachment of the embryo from its parental origins, which tends to encourage a view of embryos as products rather than as emerging beings.

Development in the First Trimester

The nine-month period of pregnancy is often conceptualized in three three-month periods called *trimesters*. Each trimester brings changes in the status of the developing fetus and its supporting systems (Meredith, 1975; Moore, 1988). Major developments are summarized in Table 4.3. The pregnant woman also experiences changes during the trimesters. In the first trimester, many women are not certain that they are pregnant. By the last trimester, not only is the woman certain, but so is everyone else!

After fertilization, the egg begins to divide. The first series of cell divisions does not increase the mass of the cells, nor do the cells take on specialized functions; rather, the cell material is redistributed among several parts. By the sixth day after fertilization, the egg makes contact with the lining of the uterus and begins to attach itself there. Sometimes the egg does not reach the uterus but attaches itself to the fallopian tube or even some area of the intestine. The embryo may grow in these locations until the organ ruptures.

The three weeks following implantation are devoted primarily to elaboration of the supportive elements that will house the embryo. An *amniotic sac* surrounds the embryo and fills with a clear, watery fluid. This fluid acts as a cushion that buffers the embryo and permits it to move about and change position.

It is at this point, about three weeks after implantation—when the woman's menstrual period is about two weeks overdue—that the first reliable tests can determine that the woman is pregnant. Once the embryo is firmly implanted in the uterus, special cells in the placenta produce a hormone that maintains the uterine lining. This hormone is excreted through the kidneys, so a urine sample can be evaluated to determine its presence.

The *placenta* is an organ that is newly formed with each pregnancy and expelled at birth. Nutrients that are necessary for the embryo's growth pass through the placenta; the embryo's waste passes through the placenta and into the mother's blood. Thus the placenta is an exchange station at which adult material is synthesized for the embryo's use and intruders harmful to the embryo's development can be screened out. The mother's blood and the embryo's blood are contained in independent systems. The placenta permits the mother's blood and the baby's blood to come close enough so that oxygen and nutrients from the mother's blood can enter the fetal system, and waste products from the fetal system can be removed.

In the third and fourth weeks, the embryo's cells differentiate rapidly. They take on the specialized structures that will permit them to carry out unique functions in the body. Similar cells are grouped into tissues that gradually emerge as body organs. Agents that can produce malformations while the tissues and organs are forming are referred to as *teratogens*. Teratogens take a wide variety of forms—viruses, medicines that a pregnant woman ingests, alcohol and other drugs, environmental toxins. During

Table 4.3 Major Developments in Fetal Growth During the Three Trimesters		
First Trimester	*Second Trimester*	*Third Trimester*
Fertilization	Sucking and swallowing	Nervous system matures
Growth of the amniotic sac	Preference for sweet taste	Coordination of sucking and
Growth of the placenta	Skin ridges on fingers and toes	swallowing
Emergence of body parts	Hair on scalp, eyebrows, back,	Mechanisms for regulating body
Differentiation of sex organs	arms, legs	temperature
Initial formation of central nervous	Sensitivity to touch, taste, light	More efficient digestion and
system	Sucks thumb	excretion
Movement	6-month size: 10 inches,	Degeneration of the placenta toward
Grasp reflex	2 pounds	the end of the ninth month
Babinski reflex		9-month size: 20 inches,
Heartbeat		7 to $7\frac{1}{2}$ pounds
3-month size: 3 inches, about $\frac{2}{5}$ ounce		

the first trimester—especially weeks 3 through 9—the embryo is particularly sensitive to the disruptive influences of teratogens (see Figure 4.6).

The first essential changes in the embryo include the establishment of the body form as an elongated cylinder and the formation of precursors of the brain and heart. The central nervous system begins to develop very early in the prenatal period and continues to develop throughout childhood and adolescence. The *neural tube,* which is the first structural basis of the central nervous system, begins to take shape at the end of the third week after conception. By the end of the fifth week, the tube is differentiated into five bulges that are the forerunners of the major subdivisions of the brain. Most of the neurons that make up the cerebral cortex are produced by the end of the second trimester. However, regions of the cortex continue to mature over the first four years of life (Greenough, Black & Wallace, 1987; Nowakowski, 1987).

By the end of the fourth week, the head, upper trunk, lower trunk, and tail are visible. Limb buds and forerunners of the forebrain, midbrain, hindbrain, eyes, and ears can be observed. The embryo will have increased 50 times in length and 40,000 times in weight since the moment of fertilization.

By the end of the second month, the embryo looks quite human. It weighs about 2.25 grams and is about 28 millimeters (1 inch) long. Almost all the internal organs are formed and the external features of the face, limbs, fingers, and toes established. At eight weeks the embryo will respond to mild stimulation.

In the third month, the fetus grows to 3 inches and its weight increases to 14 grams. The head is about one-third of the total body length. During this month the fetus assumes the "fetal position": arms curled up toward the face and knees bent in to the stomach. The eyelids are fused.

A dramatic change takes place in the sex organs. All embryos pass through a bisexual stage during which no sex-linked characteristics can be discerned. Both females and males have a surface mass that becomes the testes in males and eventually degenerates in females. In females new sex cells grow to form the ovaries. Both males and females have two sets of sex ducts. In males the sperm ducts develop and the female

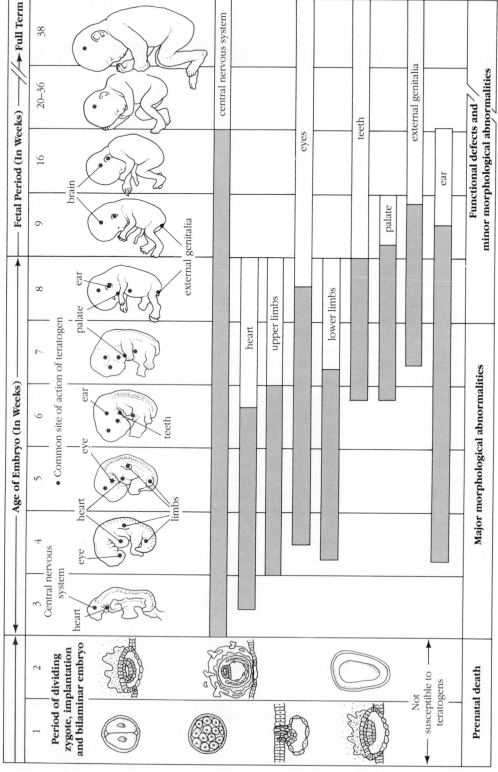

Figure 4.6

Critical Periods in Prenatal Development

During the first two weeks of development, the embryo is usually not susceptible to teratogens. During these predifferentiation stages, a substance either damages all or most of the cells of the embryo, resulting in its death, or damages only a few cells, allowing the embryo to recover without developing defects. Dark denotes highly sensitive periods; light indicates stages that are less sensitive to teratogens. Severe mental retardation may result from the exposure of the embryo/fetus to certain teratogenic agents, such as high levels of radiation, from the 8th to 16th weeks.

Source: K. L. Moore, *The Developing Human: Clinically Oriented Embryology* (Philadelphia: W. B. Saunders, 1988), p. 143. Reprinted by permission of the author.

ducts degenerate. In females the fallopian tubes, uterus, and vagina develop and the other ducts degenerate. Finally, both males and females have a conical area that is the outlet for the bladder duct. When the male testes develop, this area forms itself into the penis and scrotum. In females it remains to form the clitoris, which is surrounded by the genital swellings of the labia majora. Differentiation of the male genitalia requires the release of the hormone testosterone. If for some reason testosterone is not produced, the baby will develop the reproductive structures of a female even though the chromosomal sex is male (Stechler & Halton, 1982).

The 3-month-old fetus moves spontaneously and has both a grasp reflex and a Babinski reflex, in which the toes extend and fan out in response to a mild stroke on the sole of the foot. When an amplified stethoscope (called a *Doppler*) is applied to the mother's stomach, the fetal heartbeat can be heard through the uterine wall by the expectant parents as well as the physician. When we were expectant parents, we were unbelievably thrilled to hear those first faint heartbeats of a life still strangely remote!

Development in the Second Trimester

During the second trimester the average fetus grows to 10 inches and increases in weight to almost 2 pounds. The fetus will continue growing at the rate of about an inch every ten days from the fifth month until the end of the pregnancy. During this trimester, the uterus itself begins to stretch and grow. It rises into the mother's abdominal cavity and expands until, by the end of the ninth month, it is pushing against the ribs and diaphragm. The reality of a growing life becomes more evident to the pregnant woman during this trimester as she observes the change in her profile and experiences the early fetal movements called "quickening." These movements are first experienced as light bubbles or twitches; later they can be identified as the foot, elbow, or fist of the restless resident.

During the fourth month, the fetus begins to suck and swallow. Whenever it opens its mouth, amniotic fluid enters and cycles through the system. The amniotic fluid provides some nutrients in addition to those absorbed through the placenta. The 4-month-old fetus shows some preference for a sweet taste, evidenced by the fact that if sugar is introduced into the amniotic fluid, it will swallow fetal fluid faster (Gilbert, 1963).

In the fifth month, the skin begins to thicken and a cheesy coating of dead cells and oil, the *vernix caseosa,* covers the skin. The individuality of the fetus is marked by the pattern of skin ridges on the fingers and toes. Hair covers the scalp, eyebrows, back, arms, and legs.

The sensory receptors of the fetus are well established by the end of the sixth month. The fetus is sensitive to touch and may react to it with a muscle movement. At six months, the fetus will stick out its tongue in response to a bitter taste. Throughout the sixth month, the nostrils are plugged by skin cells. When these cells dissolve, the nose fills with amniotic fluid; thus smell is probably not possible until birth.

The external ear canal is filled with fluid, and the fetus does not tend to respond to sound until the eighth or ninth month. By the sixth month, however, the semicir-

Box 4.2   Looking In on the Fetus

Much has been written about the expanding healthy adult years. Equally great progress has been made in saving lives in the first nine months in utero. In the United States, infant mortality has been reduced from 99.9 deaths per 1000 live births in 1915 to 10 deaths per 1000 live births in 1987. Much of this progress has been due to the development of new technology that allows us to assess and monitor the development of the fetus. Four monitoring strategies are described here (Cunningham, MacDonald & Gant, 1989).

Electronic fetal heart rate monitoring: Rather than listen to the fetal heart rate periodically through a stethoscope, birth attendants can monitor it continuously, using electronic equipment that is painlessly attached to the pregnant woman's abdomen. This technique is especially useful to detect any disruption in the fetal oxygen supply during labor.

Ultrasound: Based on sonar technology used in submarine warfare during World War II, ultra-

sound uses reflected sound waves to produce a visual image of the fetus. Ultrasound can be used to date the pregnancy more precisely, diagnose multiple pregnancies, and detect certain structural defects in the fetus.

Amniocentesis: About 20 cc of amniotic fluid are withdrawn from the uterus, as in the figure below. When this procedure is carried out in the 16th week of pregnancy, fetal cells can be evaluated for chromosomal or enzyme disorders. Later in pregnancy, fetal cells can be evaluated to assess maturation of the lungs. Serious respiratory disorders can be prevented when cesarean deliveries are delayed until the lungs are adequately developed.

Fetoscopy: The fetus can be examined directly and its blood sampled through a fiberoptic lens inserted into the uterus. This technique permits diagnosis of genetic disorders, especially blood diseases that cannot be assessed with amniotic fluid, so that disorders can be treated surgically and medically before birth.

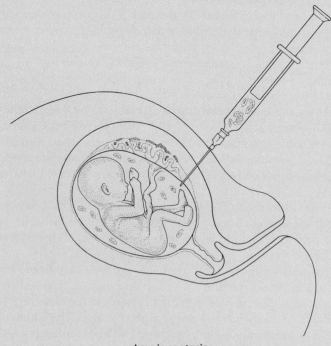

Amniocentesis

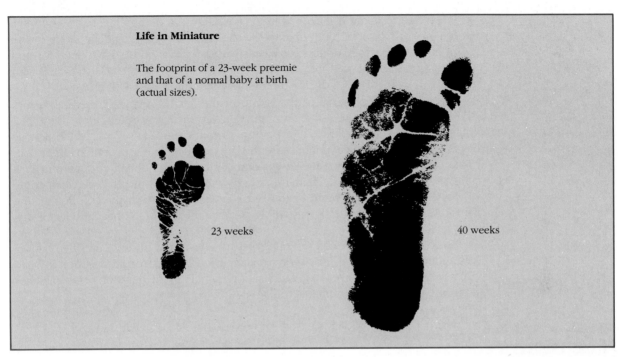

Life in Miniature

The footprint of a 23-week preemie and that of a normal baby at birth (actual sizes).

23 weeks

40 weeks

cular canals of the inner ear are sensitive to stimulation. The nerve fibers that connect the retina to the brain are developed by six months; infants born prematurely at this time respond to light.

At 24 weeks the fetus functions well within its uterine environment. It swallows, digests, excretes, moves about, sucks its thumb, rests, and grows. If it is removed from this environment, however, the fetus has almost no chance for survival. The nervous system, which begins to develop at three weeks, is still not developed enough to coordinate the many systems that must function simultaneously to ensure survival. By 30 weeks, however, survival outside the uterus is almost certain (Usher, 1987).

Development in the Third Trimester

In the last trimester, the average fetus grows from 10 to 20 inches and increases in weight from 2 to 7 or 7½ pounds. These increases in body size and weight are paralleled by a maturation of the central nervous system. Studies of infants' responses to maternal speech suggest that a fetus experiences its mother's speech sounds during the third trimester and becomes familiar with the sound of her voice (De Casper & Spence, 1986; Spence & De Casper, 1987).

The advantages that a full-term fetus has over a premature, 28-week-old fetus include (1) the ability to begin and maintain regular breathing, (2) a stronger sucking response, (3) well-coordinated swallowing movements (4) stronger peristalsis and therefore more efficient digestion and waste excretion, and (5) a more fully balanced control of body temperature.

The full-term infant has been able to take advantage of minerals in the mother's diet for the formation of tooth enamel. As the placenta begins to degenerate in the last month of pregnancy, antibodies against various diseases that have been formed in the mother's blood pass into the fetal bloodstream. They provide the fetus with immunity to many diseases during the first few months of life.

The uterus cannot serve as the home of the fetus indefinitely. Several factors necessitate the eventual termination of the fetal-uterine relationship. First, as the placenta degenerates, antibodies that form in the mother's and fetus's blood would destroy the blood of the other. Second, because the placenta does not grow much larger than 2 pounds, the fetus, as it reaches its maximum size, cannot obtain enough nutrients to sustain life. Third, the fetal head cannot grow much larger than the pelvic opening without endangering the brain in the birth process. Even with the soft connecting membranes that permit the skull plates to overlap, the size of the head is a factor that limits fetal growth.

We do not know the exact set of factors that signals the onset of uterine contractions and the birth process. The approximate period of time from conception to birth is 38 weeks. However, there is a great deal of variability in the duration of pregnancies and in the size of full-term infants.

The Birth Process

Birth is initiated by involuntary contractions of the uterine muscles referred to as *labor*. The length of time from the beginning of labor to the birth of the infant is highly variable. The average time is 14 hours for women undergoing their first labors (primiparas) and eight hours for women undergoing later labors (multiparas).

The uterine contractions serve two central functions: effacement and dilatation. *Effacement* is the shortening of the cervical canal. *Dilatation* is the gradual enlargement of the cervix from an opening only millimeters wide to one of about 10 centimeters—large enough for the baby to pass through. Effacement and dilatation occur without deliberate effort on the mother's part.

Once the cervix is fully enlarged, the mother can assist in the birth by exerting pressure on the abdominal walls of the uterus. The baby, too, helps in the birth process by squirming, turning the head, and pushing against the birth canal.

Stages of Labor

The medical profession describes three stages of labor, two of which are illustrated in Figure 4.7. The first stage begins with the onset of uterine contractions and ends with full dilatation of the cervix; this is the longest stage. The second stage involves the expulsion of the fetus. It begins at full dilatation and ends with delivery of the baby. The third stage begins with delivery and ends with the expulsion of the placenta. This stage usually lasts about five to ten minutes.

These three stages of labor do not precisely parallel the personal experience of childbirth. For example, while the birth of the placenta is considered a unique stage

Stage 1

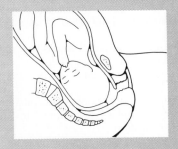
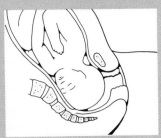

Early labor, where effacement, or thinning, has occurred and the cervix is starting to dilate.

The continuation of dilation of the cervix.

Approaching full dilation of the cervix.

Stage 2

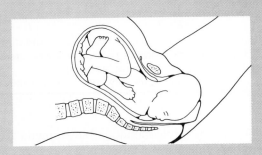
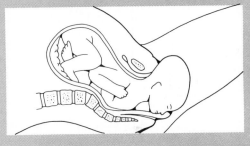

Face down, the baby's head is pressed against the perineum, which gradually stretches, widening the vaginal opening.

The baby's skull extends as it sweeps up over the perineum. First the top of the skull and then the brow emerge.

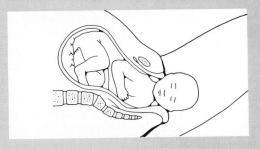
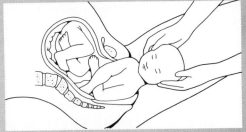

Once the head is born, the shoulders rotate in the pelvis, turning the head to left or right.

The top shoulder is born first; the rest of the body then slides out easily.

Figure 4.7   **The First Two Stages of Labor**
Source: A. Clarke-Stewart and J. B. Koch, *Children: Development through Adolescence,* Copyright ©1983 John Wiley & Sons, Inc. Reprinted by permission of John Wiley & Sons, Inc. Figure 2.3, p. 65.

Table 4.4 Significant Events of Five Psychological Stages of Labor

Phase 1: Early signs that labor is approaching
  1. Lightening (about 10 to 14 days before delivery). The baby's head drops into the pelvic area.
  2. Release of the plug that has kept the cervix closed.
  3. Discharge of amniotic fluid.
  4. False labor—irregular uterine contractions.
Phase 2: Onset of labor
  1. Transition from home to hospital or birthing center.
  2. Strong, regular contractions 3 to 5 minutes apart.
Phase 3: Transition
  1. Accelerated labor, with contractions lasting up to 90 seconds and coming 2 or 3 minutes apart.
  2. Some sense of disorientation, heightened arousal, or loss of control.
Phase 4: Birth
  1. The baby's head presses down on the bottom of the birth canal.
  2. The mother experiences a strong, reflexive urge to push to expel the baby.
  3. The mother typically is moved from a labor area to a more sterile delivery room.
Phase 5: Postpartum period
  1. Mother and infant have initial contact.
  2. Placenta is expelled.
  3. Rapid alteration of the hormone system to stimulate lactation and shrink the uterus.
  4. Mother and infant engage in early learning behaviors; infant attempts to nurse, mother explores infant and begins to interpret his or her needs.
  5. Return to the home and introduction of the newborn into the family setting.

---

of labor in the medical model, it is rarely mentioned in women's accounts of their birth experiences. On the other hand, many of the signs of impending labor that occur in the last weeks of pregnancy might well be viewed as the experiential beginning of labor.

In terms of the psychological adaptation to the birth process, labor can be viewed as having five phases: (1) early signs that labor is approaching; (2) strong, regular uterine contractions signaling that labor has begun and generally accompanied by a move from the home to the hospital; (3) the transition phase, during which contractions are strong, rest times between contractions are short, and women experience the greatest difficulty or discomfort; (4) the birth process, which allows for the mother's active participation in the delivery and is generally accompanied by a move from the labor area to the more sterile delivery room; and (5) the postpartum period, which involves the initial interactions with the newborn, physiological changes that mark a return to the prepregnant state, and a return home. The significant events of these phases are summarized in Table 4.4.

Cesarean Delivery

Sometimes a normal, spontaneous vaginal delivery is dangerous to the mother or the newborn (Cunningham, MacDonald & Gant, 1989). One alternative is to remove the baby surgically through an incision in the uterine wall. The procedure is named after the Roman emperor Julius Caesar, who, legend has it, was delivered this way. The likelihood that he actually was delivered surgically is questionable, since until as late as the 17th century the operation was usually fatal to living mothers. Most of the early cesarean deliveries were performed on dead or dying women in the hope of baptizing the unborn child (Cunningham, MacDonald & Gant, 1989).

The incidence of cesarean deliveries in the United States has increased from 5.5 percent of births in 1970 to 20.3 percent in 1988 (Burt, Vaughan & Daling, 1988). The procedure may be used if labor is severely prolonged and the fetus appears to be at risk for lack of oxygen. It may also be used when the infant is in the breech position (feet or buttocks rather than head first) or if the mother's pelvis is too small for the infant's head to pass through.

It is still standard procedure to deliver a baby by cesarean if the mother has had such an operation before. However, this practice may vary by region. With the physician's approval, some women do have vaginal deliveries following a cesarean delivery.

The cesarean delivery makes childbirth a surgical procedure, requiring anesthetics, intravenous feeding of the mother, and a prolonged recovery period. The procedure undoubtedly saves many infants and mothers who would not survive vaginal childbirth. However, there is concern as to whether the procedure is being misused for the convenience of health professionals, or busy mothers who want to be able to schedule deliveries and thus avoid waiting for the unpredictable onset of labor.

Recent research has begun to examine the impact of the cesarean delivery on both the newborn and the parents. At this point it appears that in the short term—that is, within five minutes after birth—babies delivered by cesarean are more likely to show signs of risk than babies delivered vaginally. This difference holds for babies who are delivered by repeat cesarean section, and who therefore are not at risk in other ways (Burt, Vaughan & Daling, 1988). However, long-term follow-ups of babies delivered by cesarean section find no effects on the child's IQ or standardized math and verbal test scores (Entwisle & Alexander, 1987).

The effects of cesarean delivery on parents can be seen in the findings of two studies. In the first one, mothers whose children were delivered by cesarean section expressed greater dissatisfaction with the childbirth experience itself than mothers whose children were born vaginally. However, they did not show more problems in postpartum adjustment. Their levels of anxiety, depression, perceptions of competence as mothers were about the same as those of mothers who had experienced a more normal delivery. What is more interesting is that both mothers and fathers of babies delivered by cesarean section tended to be more involved in the parent role. They viewed their children in a more positive light and had higher expectations for their children's school success than other parents did (Padawer et al., 1988). Another study found that parents' expectations for a child's academic ability and school success appear to be a long-term outcome of the birth experience, and have a significant influence on the child's own expectations of school performance in the first and second grades (Entwisle & Alexander, 1987). One explanation suggested for these findings is that the special difficulties associated with childbirth increase the commitment the parents make to their child. The child seems to benefit when both mother and father are highly involved in child rearing from infancy on. One might even speculate that the divorce rate should be lower among people who had a cesarean delivery. We must be careful not to overgeneralize the results of the research, but the implications for involvement in parenting must be studied further.

Infant Mortality

The infant mortality rate is the number of deaths per 1000 babies a year old or less. In 1987 this rate was estimated at 10 deaths per 1000 live births in the United States, a mortality rate that is equaled only by that for the 55-to-64-year-old age group and older. Although the infant mortality rate has declined for both the white and black populations, the rate for black babies was just about as high in 1986—18.8 deaths per 1000 live births—as that for white babies in 1970—17.8 deaths per 1000 (U.S. Bureau of the Census, 1989).

Infant mortality rates are influenced by many factors, including (1) the frequency of birth complications; (2) the robustness of the infants who are being born, which is influenced by their prenatal nutrition and degree of exposure to viruses or bacteria, damaging X rays, drugs and other teratogens in utero; (3) the mother's age; and (4) the facilities that are available for prenatal and newborn care. One-fourth of infant deaths result from complications associated with low birth weight. If conditions leading to prematurity could be altered, our infant mortality rate could be significantly improved (Swyer, 1987).

Infant mortality rates vary from one country and region of the world to another. One estimate of the infant mortality rate among all developing countries was 93.6 deaths for every 1000 live births (International Bank for Reconstruction and Development, 1983). Although the U.S. rate of 10 deaths per 1000 live births appears quite low against this figure, the United States in fact ranks 14th among industrialized nations, behind Australia, Canada, Denmark, France, Hong Kong, and Japan. Within the United States, regional infant mortality rates range from a low of 8.4 per 1000 in North Dakota to a high of 21.1 per 1000 in the District of Columbia (U.S. Bureau of the Census, 1989).

Density of low-income population, availability of educational materials on the impact of diet and drugs on the developing fetus, and adequacy of medical facilities for high-risk newborns all contribute to the regional variations in infant death rates among populations of different incomes. The chances that any one infant will survive the stresses of birth depend on the convergence of biological, environmental, cultural, and economic influences on his or her intrauterine growth, delivery, and postnatal care.

The Mother, the Fetus, and the Psychosocial Environment

The course and pattern of prenatal development are directly guided by genetic information. Yet we cannot ignore the psychosocial environment in which pregnant women are embedded. A woman's attitudes toward pregnancy and childbirth, her lifestyle,

A pregnant woman who can relieve her anxiety and look forward to childbirth with positive anticipation is likely to have a relatively easy labor and delivery.

the resources available to her during her pregnancy, and the behaviors demanded of her by her culture will influence her own sense of well-being. Many of these same factors may have a direct impact on the health and growth of the fetus, or on the kind of parenting environment the newborn infant will encounter.

The Impact of the Fetus on the Pregnant Woman

Consider some of the ways in which a fetus influences a pregnant woman. Being pregnant alters a woman's body image and her sense of well-being. Some women feel especially vigorous and energetic during much of their pregnancy. Other women experience distressing symptoms such as nausea, backache, swelling, headache, and irritability. In some cases, pregnancy brings on a condition known as *toxemia,* a gradual poisoning of the woman's system. As the fetus grows, the afflicted mother may experience extremely high blood pressure, kidney failure, and convulsions.

Changes in Roles and Social Status

Women who become pregnant may be treated in new ways by their boyfriends or spouses. They may be viewed in a new light by their peers. In some communities, adolescent girls who become pregnant may feel ashamed or guilty. In others, becoming pregnant during adolescence is viewed by the peer group as an accomplishment—a sign of maturity. In the world of work, women who become pregnant may be given fewer responsibilities or be passed over for promotions. In business settings, pregnancy may be viewed as an annoyance, something that is likely to interfere with productivity and is at best to be tolerated.

Within the family, a pregnant woman is likely to be treated with new levels of concern and care. Her pregnancy affects her spouse, parents, siblings, and in-laws. By giving birth to a first child, a woman will transform her husband into a father, her mother and father into grandparents, and her brothers and sisters into uncles and aunts. Being pregnant may alter the gender identity of the baby's mother and/or father: becoming pregnant may be viewed as confirmation of a woman's femininity; getting a woman pregnant can represent confirmation of a man's virility (Heitlinger, 1989).

In some societies, pregnancy and childbirth confer special status on a woman. In Japan, for example, traditional values place motherhood above all other roles a woman can play. "Only after giving birth to a child did a woman become a fully tenured person in the family" (Bankart, 1989). When they become mothers, Japanese women can begin to have an impact on government, community, and public life as the people who are specially responsible for molding and shaping the next generation.

The Mother's Emotional State

Women have emotional as well as physical reactions to pregnancy. Pregnancy is listed as the 12th most stressful life change in a list of 43 life events in the Social Readjustment Rating Scale (Holmes & Rahe, 1967). The woman's attitude toward her unborn child may be one of pride, acceptance, rejection, or—as is the case with most—ambivalence. Most normal pregnancies are associated with experiences of anxiety and depression. As a normal part of the physical changes during the gestational period, women experience symptoms that are often associated with depression, such as fatigue, sleeplessness, slowed physical movement, preoccupation with one's physical state, and moodiness (Kaplan, 1986).

Some women respond to the presence of the growing fetus with exhilaration and joy. In the traditional Chinese family, for example, the period of pregnancy has been referred to as a time when the woman has "happiness in her body" (Levy, 1968). The extent to which the child is desired by the pregnant woman depends on several factors, including the number of children she already has, her economic resources, her relationship with her husband, and her emotional maturity. American women with more than three children and few resources are less likely to hold positive attitudes about the birth of a new child than are those with fewer children and more resources (Sherman, 1971).

Women who are ambivalent about having their babies, women who are having marital difficulties, and women who do not have adequate social support during pregnancy are more likely to experience depression and anxiety during pregnancy (Fleming et al., 1988). It is possible that strong emotional reactions, such as prolonged anxiety or depression, may influence the fetal environment directly through the secretion of maternal hormones that may cross the placental barrier. However, evidence in this regard is mixed (Sameroff & Chandler, 1975; Vaughn et al., 1987). The evidence is much clearer that the mother's emotional state during pregnancy is related to her experiences during labor and to her subsequent parenting behaviors.

A woman's feelings toward her femininity, attitudes toward the unborn child, and psychological stability are somewhat associated with difficulties experienced during pregnancy and labor. Women who have more stable personalities and a positive orientation toward pregnancy react more favorably to the stresses of labor than do

Pablo Picasso, *Woman Crying,* 1937. Women who are very anxious and who feel angry about being pregnant are likely to have a stressful labor. In this painting we sense the woman's anguish extending from the depths of her body into her hands and eyes.

anxious, irritable women. The latter are more likely to have longer labors and experience more labor or delivery room complications. They tend to request and receive more medication during delivery, which may influence the responsiveness of their newborn infants (Yang et al., 1976; Standley, Soule & Copans, 1979).

The contribution of maternal anxiety to complications during labor and delivery was studied with a group of Guatemalan women (Sosa et al., 1980). The hospital normally did not permit any visitors to remain with an expectant woman on the maternity ward. Each woman in this study, however, was assigned a companion who stayed with her until delivery. This person talked, held the woman's hand, rubbed her back, and provided emotional support during labor. These mothers had fewer complications during labor than a group of women who did not have a companion, and their babies showed fewer signs of fetal distress. The mean length of labor was over ten hours shorter for those women who had a companion than for those who were alone during labor.

Recent trends in the United States have shown a dramatic trend toward greater involvement of fathers during labor and delivery. Husbands often attend childbirth classes with their wives so that they can learn to assist them during the delivery. A Gallup poll conducted in the early 1980s found that approximately 80% of fathers attend the birth of their children, as compared to 27% in the early 1970s (Kliman & Kohl, 1984).

The father's presence is clearly a great comfort to the pregnant woman during delivery. When fathers are present, women tend to have shorter labors, they report experiencing less pain, they use less medication, and they feel more positive about themselves and their childbirth experience (Grossman et al., 1980). Fathers also describe their participation in the birth as a peak experience.

As we have indicated earlier, when babies are born through cesarean delivery, fathers tend to be more involved in their parent role and devoted to their children. However, current research does not permit us to conclude that fathers who participate in the birth experience have a more intimate relationship with their children than fathers who are not present at the birth (Palkovitz, 1985; Palm & Palkovitz, 1988).

The mother's emotional state during pregnancy has an impact beyond the events of childbirth. Women who experience notable depression during pregnancy are more likely to experience continued depressed mood states in the months after giving birth. Studies of these mothers find that they have difficulty feeling attached to their babies, they are more likely to feel out of control or incompetent in their parenting, and they exhibit fewer affectionate behaviors toward their infants (Fleming et al., 1988; Field el al., 1985).

In interaction with their mothers, infants of depressed mothers are less playful, show less activity, and express fewer signs of contentment, fewer fact-to-face interactions, and less imitation of their mothers than do babies of nondepressed mothers (Field et al., 1985). At 3 months of age, infants of depressed mothers show similar characteristics even in interaction with nondepressed adults, suggesting that a "depressed" temperamental social style has developed (Field et al., 1988). This research still leaves the causal agent in question; that is, whether the impact of maternal depression on the infant is the result of genetic influences, the presence of hormones associated with the mother's depression in the prenatal environment, the style of mothering characteristic of depressed women, or some cumulative effect of these factors.

The Impact of the Pregnant Woman on the Fetus

Among the factors that influence the fetus's development are the mother's age, her use of drugs during pregnancy and delivery, and her diet. These and other such factors are summarized in Figure 4.8.

Mother's Age

The capacity for childbearing begins about a year to one and a half years after the beginning of menarche and ends at the end of the climacteric. Thus a woman is potentially fertile for about 35 years during her lifetime. Childbirth may occur at any or many points during this period. The effects of childbirth on the physical and psychological well-being of a mother will vary with her age and her emotional commitment to the mother role. Similarly, these factors will contribute significantly to the survival and well-being of her infant.

Women between the ages of 16 and 35 tend to provide a better uterine environment and to give birth with fewer complications than do women under 16 or over 35. Particularly when it is their first pregnancy, women over 35 are likely to have longer labors than younger women, and labor is more likely to result in the death of either the infant or the mother. The two groups with the highest probability of giving birth to premature babies are women over 35 and those under 16 (Schuster, 1986).

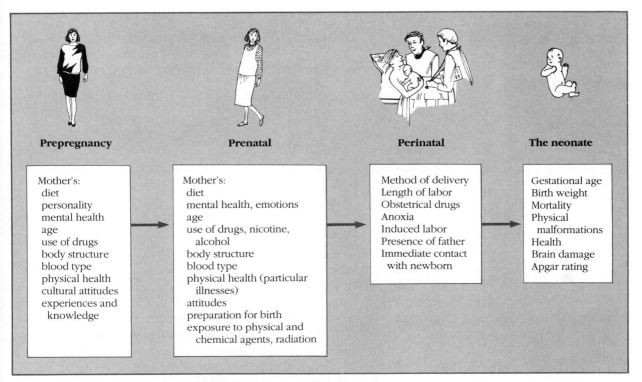

Prepregnancy	Prenatal	Perinatal	The neonate

Mother's:
  diet
  personality
  mental health
  age
  use of drugs
  body structure
  blood type
  physical health
  cultural attitudes
  experiences and
    knowledge
	Mother's:
	  diet
	  mental health, emotions
	  age
	  use of drugs, nicotine,
	    alcohol
	  body structure
	  blood type
	  physical health (particular
	    illnesses)
	  attitudes
	  preparation for birth
	  exposure to physical and
	    chemical agents, radiation
		Method of delivery
		Length of labor
		Obstetrical drugs
		Anoxia
		Induced labor
		Presence of father
		Immediate contact
		  with newborn
			Gestational age
			Birth weight
			Mortality
			Physical
			  malformations
			Health
			Brain damage
			Apgar rating

Figure 4.8   Factors That Influence Prenatal Development
Source: A. Clarke-Stewart and J. B. Koch, *Children: Development through Adolescence.* Copyright © 1983 John Wiley & Sons, Inc. Reprinted by permission of John Wiley & Sons, Inc. Figure 4.1, p. 101.

Premature children of teenage mothers are more likely than those of older mothers to have neurological defects that will influence their coping capacities. Also, mothers under 16 tend to receive less adequate prenatal care and to be less biologically mature. Consequently, adolescent mothers are more likely to experience complications during pregnancy that may endanger their infants and themselves. Evidence suggests that good medical care, nutrition, and social support can improve the childbirth experiences of adolescent mothers who are *over* 16. However, the physical immaturity of those under 16 puts the mother and infant at greater risk (Quilligan, 1983; Roosa, 1984).

A primary risk for infants of mothers who are over 40 is Down's syndrome (Moore, 1988). A woman's ova are present in a premature form from birth; the longer she lives, the older those cells become. It is hypothesized that some part of the high incidence of Down's syndrome among older women is the result of deteriorating ova. Women are increasingly sensitive to the risks of having children after age 35. Many are undergoing the procedure of amniocentesis, which permits them to detect the presence of severe fetal defects (Williams, 1987). Young adolescents, on the other hand, do not appear to be aware of the risks inherent in early childbirth. In 1983 about 183,000 babies were born to mothers age 17 and under. Over 180,000 legal

Table 4.5 Live Birth Rates by Age of Mother, 1960–1986 (births per 1000 women)							
Year	*10–14*	*15–19*	*20–24*	*25–29*	*30–34*	*35–39*	*40–44*
1960	0.8	89.1	258.1	197.4	112.7	56.2	15.5
1965	0.8	70.5	195.3	161.6	94.4	46.2	12.8
1970	1.2	68.3	167.8	145.1	73.3	31.7	8.1
1975	1.3	56.3	114.7	110.3	53.1	19.4	4.6
1980	1.1	53.0	115.1	112.9	61.9	19.8	3.9
1986	1.3	50.6	108.2	109.2	69.3	24.3	4.1

Source: U.S. Bureau of the Census, *Statistical Abstract of the United States, 1986* and *1989* (Washington, D.C.: U.S. Government Printing Office, 1985, 1989).

abortions were performed for women age 17 and under, which accounted for 11 percent of all induced abortions (Ventura, Taffel & Mosher, 1988).

Table 4.5 shows the numbers of live births for women across the age range 10 to 44 from 1960 through 1986. The pattern shows declines over the 26-year period in every age range except the youngest. Two observations about the data presented in Table 4.5 are relevant to our understanding of adult life. First, since 1960 the age periods from 20 to 24 and 25 to 29 have become equally likely times for childbearing. Second, the decline in the birth rate is also expressed in a reduction of the childbearing period: far fewer children are being born today to women 30 years and older than was the case in 1960. Since 1980 the number of children born to each 1000 women 30 years old and over has risen. However, this increase does not come close to returning to the levels of childbearing in the older age ranges that was characteristic of the early 1960s.

In the later chapters we will discuss the psychosocial consequences of childbearing for adolescents and adults. Here we want to emphasize that the pattern of fetal development, the quality of prenatal care, and the degree of risk during childbirth are all associated with the age of the mother during pregnancy.

Drugs

The range of drugs used by pregnant women is enormous. Iron, diuretics, antibiotics, hormones, tranquilizers, appetite suppressants, and other drugs are being either prescribed or taken voluntarily by pregnant women. In addition, women influence the fetal environment through their voluntary use of such drugs as alcohol, nicotine, caffeine, marijuana, cocaine, and other narcotics (Chasnoff, 1988). Studies of the effects of specific drugs on fetal growth suggest that many drugs ingested by pregnant women are in fact metabolized in the placenta and transmitted to the fetus.

Babies born to women who smoked during pregnancy weigh less than those born to nonsmoking mothers. A review of 45 studies on this relationship reported that babies born to smokers weighed an average of 200 grams less than babies born to nonsmokers (U.S. Department of Heath, Education, and Welfare, 1979). Women who smoke are at greater risk for miscarriages and stillbirths (Streissguth et al., 1989). Neurological examinations of babies exposed to nicotine during the prenatal period

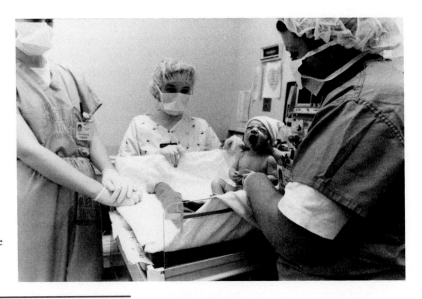

The neurological disorganization that results from having a cocaine-addicted mother can be detected in the baby's unusual high-pitched cry.

showed decreased levels of arousal and responsiveness at nine and 30 days after birth (Fried et al., 1987).

The documented evidence is strong that alcohol is a teratogen. Prenatal exposure to alcohol can influence brain development, interfere with cell development and organization, and affect the production of neurotransmitters, which are critical to the maturation of the central nervous system (West, 1986). The complex impact of alcohol on fetal development has been given the name *fetal alcohol syndrome* (Jones et al., 1973; Clarren & Smith, 1978; Abel, 1984). Fetal alcohol syndrome is associated with disorders of the central nervous system, low birth weight, and malformations of the face, eyes, ears, and mouth. The risk of fetal alcohol syndrome for infants born to women who drink heavily—that is, about 1.5 ounces or more of alcohol a day—is 30 to 50%. Even moderate daily alcohol use can produce some of these symptoms, especially if drinking is combined with malnutrition.

In a longitudinal study of the effects of prenatal exposure to alcohol, children born to mothers who consumed 1.5 ounces of alcohol (one average-strength drink) daily during pregnancy showed significantly lower IQ scores at age 4 than did children whose mothers used little or no alcohol (Streissguth et al., 1989). Alcohol use was a significant predictor of reduced IQ scores, even when many other factors—mother's educational level, child's birth order, family socioeconomic level, child's involvement in preschool, and the quality of mother-child interaction—were taken into account. In other words, the many environmental variables that are known to have a positive effect on a young child's intellectual functioning did not compensate for the insult to the central nervous system associated with exposure to alcohol during gestation. We emphasize the risks associated with prenatal exposure to alcohol because alcohol is so widely used in American society and the amount of alcohol that can have a negative effect on the fetus may well be considered a "safe" or socially acceptable level by many adults.

The use of narcotics, especially heroin and cocaine, as well as methadone (a drug used in the treatment of heroin addiction), has been linked to increased risks of birth defects and low birth weight and higher rates of infant mortality (Dinges, Davis & Glass, 1980; Zuckerman et al., 1989). During the first week of life, infants exposed to opiates, cocaine, and methadone show a pattern of extreme irritability, high-pitched crying that is evidence of neurological disorganization, fever, sleep disturbances, feeding problems, muscle spasms, and tremors (Hans, 1987). These babies are at high risk for *sudden infant death syndrome*. Longer-range studies find that children who were exposed to addictive drugs in the prenatal period continue to show problems in fine motor coordination, they have difficulty focusing and sustaining attention, and, perhaps as a result, they have more school adjustment problems. Of course, it is difficult to separate the direct prenatal effects of these drugs on the nervous system from effects after birth associated with being parented by a drug-using mother or the effects on parenting of the social and educational environment in which the mother herself may have developed.

With the widespread abuse of cocaine, law-enforcement officials are taking actions to arrest and charge women who have exposed their unborn infants to these harmful and illegal substances (Sachs, 1989). A woman who gave birth to her second cocaine-addicted infant in Hollywood, Florida, was arrested and charged with child abuse. Her baby was placed in foster care. Prosecutors want to hold pregnant women responsible for behaviors that jeopardize their infants' health. Those who oppose such actions argue that alcohol use, smoking, and other forms of maternal behavior may also have a negative effect on the developing fetus. Should all these women be charged for child abuse?

A relatively recent concern associated with intravenous drug use is the associated spread of the human immunodeficiency virus (HIV) and the acquired immunodeficiency syndrome (AIDS) from pregnant women to their unborn children. About 70% of women with HIV infection have been infected through their own drug use or that of a sex partner. The relationship of cocaine use, prostitution, and sexually transmitted diseases, including AIDS, is posing a growing health risk to unborn children, especially among poor urban minorities (Judson, 1989; Darney et al., 1989). Children born to mothers who have the HIV virus have about a 50% chance of developing the disease, and 95% of those infected die within the first three years of life. At present there is no way to treat babies infected with AIDS. Because their immune system is deficient or inoperative, they cannot fight off the many infections that babies typically encounter (Seabrook, 1987).

Other drugs have been administered to women during pregnancy as part of the treatment for a medical condition. The tragic outcome of the use of thalidomide for the treatment of morning sickness in the 1960s alerted us to the potential danger of certain chemicals for the fetus, particularly during the period of fetal differentiation and growth in the first trimester. Thalidomide taken during the 21st to 36th day after conception can cause gross deformities of the baby's limbs.

Some drugs are administered to help sustain the pregnancy. In one case, a group of boys whose mothers had been treated with estrogen and progesterone during pregnancy were studied when they were 6 and 16 years old. At both ages the boys showed lower ratings on aggressiveness and athletic ability than a matched sample of boys whose mothers had not been treated with these female hormones (Yalom, Green & Fisk, 1973). In another case, a sample of 119 women were treated with prednisone, first to alleviate infertility and then to maintain their pregnancies. The birth weight of their babies was significantly lower than that of the babies of a control group (Reinisch & Karow, 1977).

On the positive side, a group of children whose mothers had been treated with progesterone during pregnancy appeared to be developmentally advanced at 1 year and had better records of elementary school achievement than did a comparison group (Dalton, 1976). The implication is that the effects of some kinds of drugs can persist for a long time after birth. This effect may be direct, as by altering the central nervous system, or indirect, as by influencing the pattern of caregiver-infant interactions.

Environmental Toxins

As more and more women enter the work force and assume nontraditional work roles, concerns about the hazards of work settings for fetal development continue to grow. In an Allied Chemical plant, fear that fluorocarbon 22 might cause fetal damage led to the layoffs of five women workers. Two of those women chose to be sterilized in order to hold their jobs (Bronson, 1979). Wives of men who are employed in hazardous environments also may experience higher rates of miscarriages, sterility, and birth defects in their babies (Howes & Krakow, 1977).

The workplace is not the only setting in which pregnant women can come in contact with environmental toxins. Women who regularly ate a large amount of polluted Lake Michigan fish for six years before their pregnancies had infants who showed certain memory deficits at 7 months of age (Jacobson et al., 1985). Although the level of these toxins—industrial waste products found in air, water, and soil—had no measurable effect on the mothers, it was high enough to influence central nervous system functioning in the fetuses. This finding makes it clear that all communities must be sensitive to the quality of their water, air, and soil. Each unborn generation depends on its predecessor to protect itself from these environmental hazards.

Research must continue on the effects of substances that are potentially toxic to fetuses. The danger of exposure to lead for young children is well documented. However, the effects of various levels of exposure on infants and young children are still ill defined (Schroeder, 1987). The potential of herbicides and pesticides used in forests and farmlands to harm developing fetuses is arousing concern (Morris, 1987). Many of these products are discovered to be teratogens only after abnormal reproductive outcomes have been systematically documented.

Obstetric Anesthetics

The study of the effects on the newborn of drugs used during delivery provides further evidence of the infant's dependence on the immediate environment. For the most part, pain-relieving drugs have been used for the benefit and convenience of mother and physician. Until recently, their effect on the newborn had gone unnoticed. However, evidence suggests that the kind, amount, and timing of anesthetic used in delivery are all factors that can induce neonatal depression and affect the coping capacities of newborns (Stechler & Halton, 1982; Naulty, 1987). When babies whose mothers had received medication during labor were compared with babies whose mothers had not, the first group was observed to perform less well on measures of perception, motor skills, and attentiveness (Brackbill et al., 1974).

There appear to be two points of view about the seriousness of this problem. Research has shown that a range of drugs, including tranquilizers, local anesthetics, and general anesthetics administered by inhalation, can interfere with the baby's behavior. The use of anesthetic drugs during delivery has been found to interfere with the infant's ability to habituate to a stimulus (stop responding after repeated demonstrations); reduce the infant's smiling and cuddliness; and reduce alert responses to new stimuli. Further, the relationship between drug use and some infant behaviors has been observed to last as long as 28 days (Aleksandrowicz & Aleksandrowicz, 1974; Brackbill, 1977; Murray et al., 1981).

Some researchers, on the other hand, view the relationship between drug use in delivery and newborn behavior as minimal. In one study, three aspects of the pregnancy experience—maternal attitudes about pregnancy, length of labor, and use of medication—were related to infant behaviors (Yang et al., 1976). The more irritable or depressed the mother was, the more drugs she used. The more drugs that were used and the earlier they were used, the longer the first stage of labor, and the greater their influence on the newborn's behavior. The pattern of relationship between drugs and newborn behaviors did not show strong or long-lasting effects. It may not be the drugs themselves that have a lasting impact on the newborn; rather, the behavioral effects of the drugs may influence parental perceptions of the newborn. These perceptions may alter the quality of the early infant-caregiver relationship (Lester, Als & Brazelton, 1982).

Research on the susceptibility of newborns to drugs alerts us to the potential impact of a wide range of substances on an immature and rapidly changing infant. Evidence on the effects of food additives on newborns and of chemical pollutants on both fetuses and newborns warn us that infants may have some unique sensitivities to the environment that may not be observed in older children or adults (World Health Organization, 1972; Miller, 1974; Giacoia & Yaffe, 1987).

Mother's Diet

The notion that no matter what the pregnant woman eats the fetus will get what it needs for growth is simply not true. Providing adequate nutrition for fetal development requires both a balanced diet and the capacity to transform nutrients into a form that the fetus can ingest. The placenta takes care of the latter process. The mother must take care of the former (Lindblad, 1987).

Experimental research on the effects of maternal malnutrition on fetal development has been conducted primarily with rats. Fetal rats exposed to a low-protein diet were born with lower body and brain weights, fewer cerebral cells, and less cerebral protein than rats whose mothers received a normal diet. In most of these experimental studies, few of the offspring survived birth or lived to adulthood. The reproductive behavior of those that did survive was greatly reduced. Thus the experimental evidence suggests that severe malnutrition interferes with normal fetal and postnatal development (Coursin, 1974).

The effects of maternal malnutrition on the developing human fetus remain a topic of scientific controversy. Some experts suggest that birth weight is affected only when the mother experiences starvation or dramatically inadequate nutrition during the last trimester of pregnancy (Cassady & Strange, 1987). Others argue that malnutrition during the phase of cell division will result in smaller organ size that cannot be reversed by later dietary supplements (Brazelton, 1987).

Most of the data on the effects of malnutrition on human fetal growth have come from the impact of disasters and crises, such as famines, wars, and extreme poverty, that prevent access to adequate diets. Malnutrition is inferred from the baby's low birth weight in comparison with his or her *gestational age*. Babies who are small for their gestational age have a higher mortality rate, more complications during postdelivery care, and a higher risk of mental or motor impairment than do babies who are of average weight for their gestational age (Cassady & Strange, 1987). The relative contribution of malnutrition to these outcomes is difficult to assess. Women who experience these conditions encounter other stresses—increased exposure to disease, anxiety, exposure to environmental toxins—that could also affect fetal growth.

A child can be malnourished during pregnancy, after birth, or both. Although some degree of growth retardation is hypothesized to occur if a fetus is malnourished, the most severe impact on growth occurs when resources are inadequate both before and after the child is born (Brasel, 1974). This is the case in many poverty-stricken areas of the world. When prenatal malnutrition is followed by postnatal malnutrition and disease, it is impossible to study the effects of prenatal malnutrition alone.

Studies that have been designed to intervene by supplementing diet during pregnancy have provided mixed evidence that a pregnant woman's diet can be successfully modified to increase the newborn's weight. When Guatemalan mothers were able to consume 20,000 additional calories during the nine months of pregnancy, their babies were an average of 0.2 kilograms (7 ounces) heavier than the babies born to mothers whose diets had not been supplemented (Habicht et al., 1974). However, controlled studies involving samples in the United States have not found meaningful improvement in the birth weights of babies born to mothers who were receiving dietary supplements (Cassady & Strange, 1987).

Some effects of malnutrition can be offset after birth. Infants' growth potential allows those who have access to food to make up for their slowed prenatal growth (Tanner, 1978). With access to an adequate diet after birth, infants who were malnourished at birth show increased activity, make greater demands on the environment, and prompt more active caregiving responses (Brazelton, 1987). This pattern of interaction can offset initial deficits brought about by an inadequate prenatal nutritional environment.

The Impact of Culture

In order to appreciate the events surrounding the birth of a child, one must understand some of the idiosyncrasies with which our culture approaches birth. The decision to have a child, the social experience of pregnancy, the particular style of help that is available for delivery of the child, and the care and attitudes toward both mother and baby after delivery can all be viewed as components of a cultural attitude toward birth. Mead and Newton (1967) compared cultural patterns associated with pregnancy and childbirth. Much of the following discussion is derived from their work.

Two points serve as a beginning. First, although we call a particular method of training *natural childbirth,* the method is not natural in the strict sense—it requires a great deal of training. In moving away from the view of childbirth as illness to the view of childbirth as natural, we must not be misled into believing that in most traditional cultures, childbirth is an easy, unpatterned, "natural" occurrence. On the contrary, childbirth is a matter of attention, ritual, superstition, and tradition in most societies. Cultures may vary widely in the ways they treat the details of birth, but all see childbirth as a special event.

The second point is that a fundamental distinction exists between the technological, medical orientation toward birth and the orientation of many traditional societies. The medical model is committed to saving all the babies and mothers possible by altering as necessary the techniques of prenatal care and delivery in order to counteract naturally occurring difficulties. Traditional societies, on the other hand, cling to methods of prenatal care and delivery that foster the survival of some mother-infant pairs and hinder the survival of others. Some fetal abnormalities are feared, some kinds of obstetric abnormalities require technology that is unavailable, and some cultural techniques work to the disadvantage of some mother-infant dyads.

Data on methods of approaching pregnancy and childbirth in traditional cultures are drawn primarily from the Human Relations Areas Files and from Ford's (1945) comparison of reproductive behavior in 64 cultures. In many traditional societies, men and nontribal women are not allowed to observe delivery. Further, many of the events related to conception and delivery are considered too personal or private to discuss with outsiders. Thus the data on childbearing practices are not systematic. Comparisons across cultures can serve only to place the American system in a cultural context.

Reactions to Pregnancy

Many cultures share a strong assumption that the behavior of expectant parents will influence the developing fetus and the ease or difficulty of childbirth. Of the 64 cultures studied by Ford (1945), 42 prescribed certain behaviors for expectant parents and prohibited others.

Many such restrictions are dietary:

> *Among the Pomeroon Arawaks, though the killing and eating of a snake during the woman's pregnancy is forbidden to both father and mother, the husband is allowed to kill and eat any other animal. The cause assigned for the taboo of the snake is that the little infant might be similar, that is, able neither to talk nor to walk.*   [Roth, 1953, p. 122]

Attitudes toward pregnant women can be characterized along two dimensions: (1) solicitude versus shame and (2) adequacy versus vulnerability.

Solicitude versus shame   Solicitude toward the pregnant woman is shown in the care, interest, and help of others. For example,

> *It is said among Jordon villagers that "as people are careful of a chicken in the egg, all the more so should they be of a child in its mother's womb."*   [Grandquist, 1950]

Prenatal Period and Birth

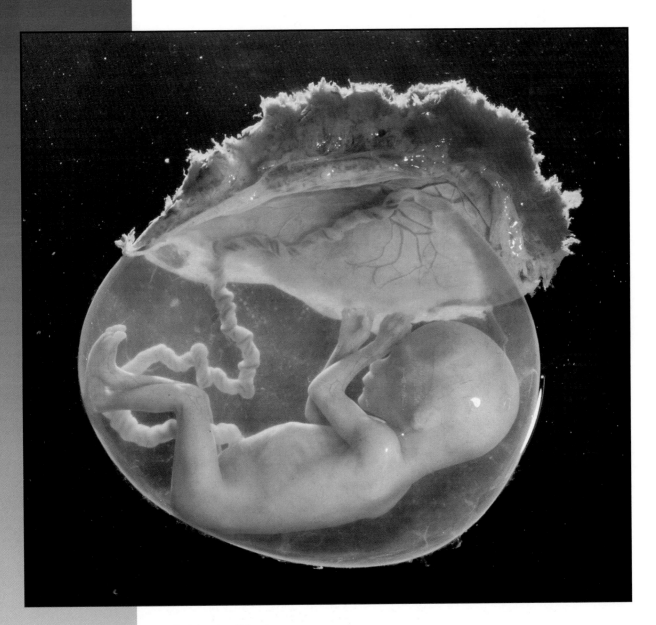

At only 6.4 inches (16 cm) long, a 16-week-old fetus is clearly recognizable as a human child.

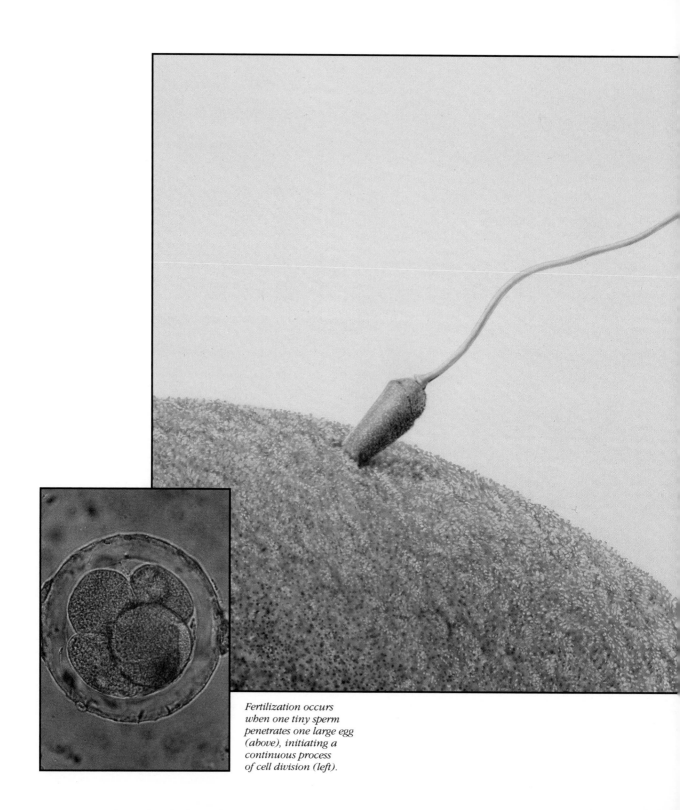

*Fertilization occurs
when one tiny sperm
penetrates one large egg
(above), initiating a
continuous process
of cell division (left).*

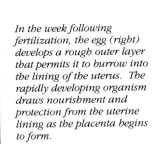

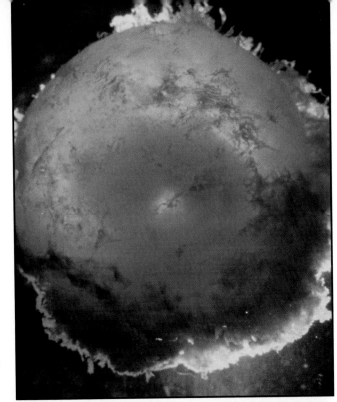

In the week following fertilization, the egg (right) develops a rough outer layer that permits it to burrow into the lining of the uterus. The rapidly developing organism draws nourishment and protection from the uterine lining as the placenta begins to form.

At 5 1/2 weeks (below), cell differentiation has resulted in an embryo that is 0.4 inch (1 cm) long. You can identify the emerging shapes of the head, arm, and fingers. At this stage, the human embryo is similar in many ways to other embryonic vertebrates.

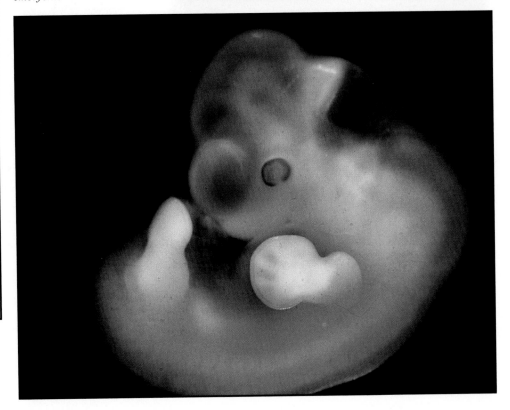

At 8 weeks (left), the fingers are clearly differentiated and the hand is distinct from the forearm. Reflexes sometimes guide the hand toward the face.

By 4 1/4 months (below), the thumb may come in contact with the mouth, stimulating the sucking reflex.

At 5 1/2 months (opposite), the fetus is about 12 inches (30 cm) long. As any pregnant woman will tell you, the fetus is active at this stage, kicking, grasping, waving its arms, and turning over.

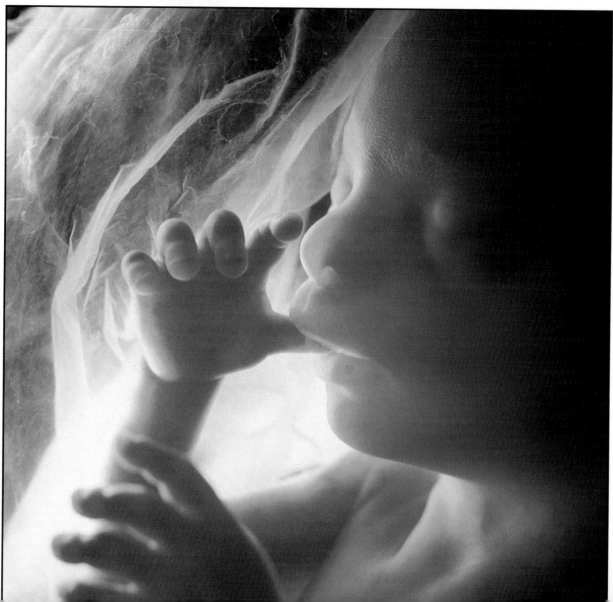

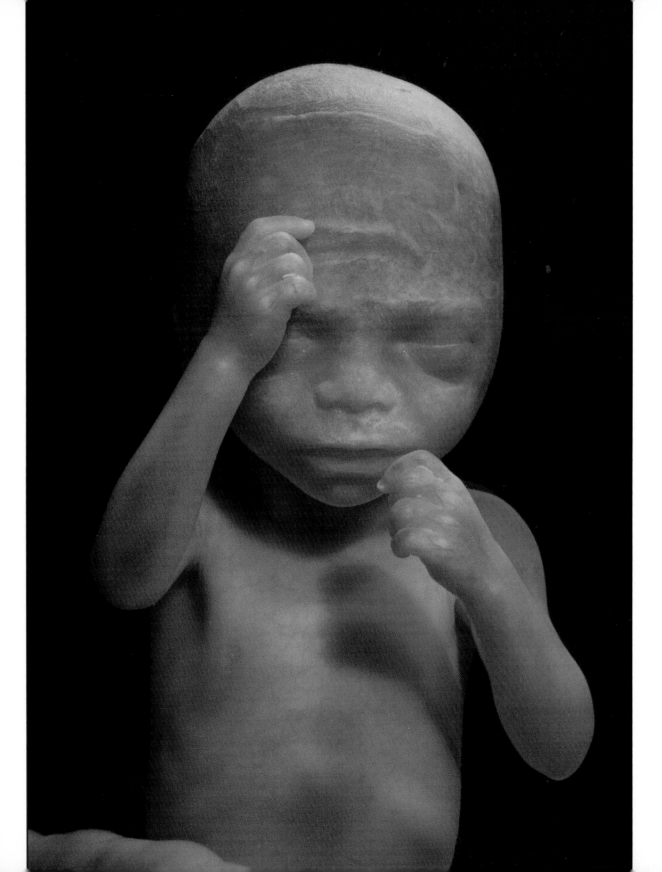

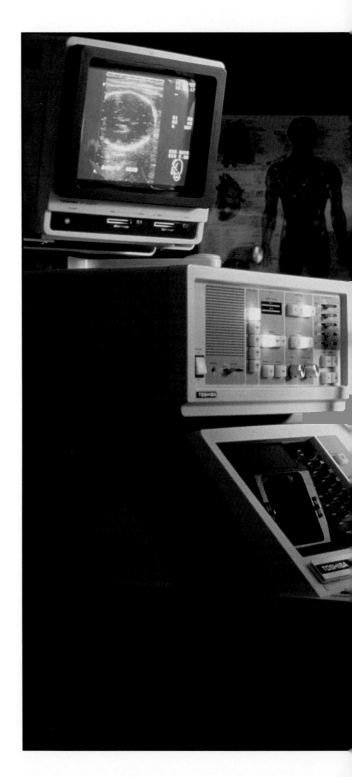

Ultrasound can provide answers to a variety of questions about the baby's development. This painless technique uses sound waves to create an image of the fetus. One can determine the size of the fetus, its position, visually apparent abnormalities, and the presence of multiple infants. The two screens at the right show the ultrasound image.

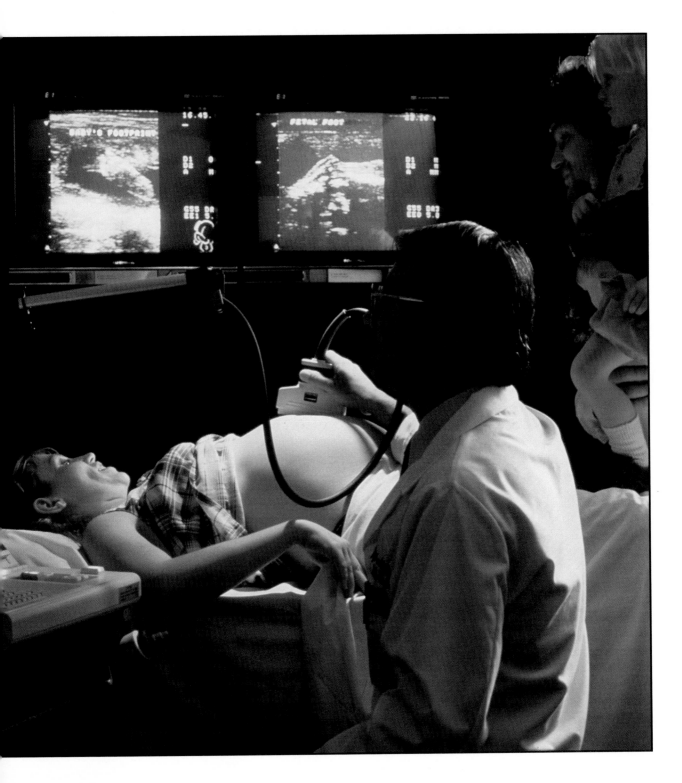

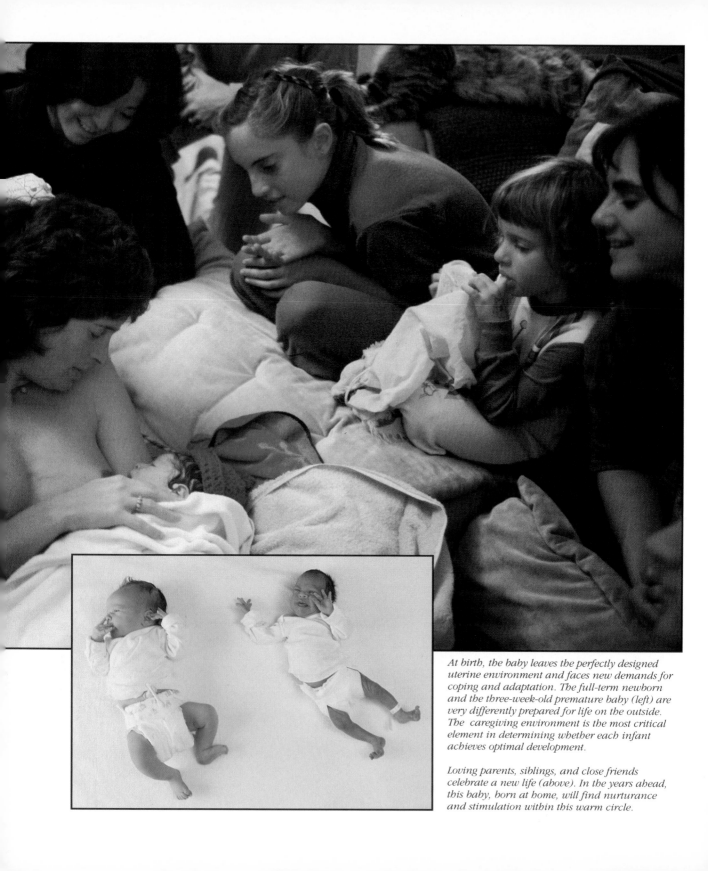

At birth, the baby leaves the perfectly designed uterine environment and faces new demands for coping and adaptation. The full-term newborn and the three-week-old premature baby (left) are very differently prepared for life on the outside. The caregiving environment is the most critical element in determining whether each infant achieves optimal development.

Loving parents, siblings, and close friends celebrate a new life (above). In the years ahead, this baby, born at home, will find nurturance and stimulation within this warm circle.

As the Chagga in Africa say, "Pay attention to the pregnant woman! There is no one more important than she."   [Guttmann, 1932]

At the other end of this dimension are the cultures that keep pregnancy a secret as long as possible. This custom may stem from a fear that damage will come to the fetus through supernatural demons or from shyness about the sexual implications of pregnancy.

Societies that demonstrate solicitude increase the care given to the pregnant woman and fetus. These attitudes emphasize the importance of birth as a mechanism for replenishing the group. Societies that instill a sense of shame in the woman do not promote the health of the mother or fetus and do not encourage a desire to have children.

Adequacy versus vulnerability   In many societies, pregnancy is a sign of sexual prowess and a means of entrance into social status. Some cultures do not arrange a wedding until after the woman has become pregnant. In a polygamous family, the pregnant wife receives the bulk of her husband's attention and may prevent her husband from taking an additional wife (Grandquist, 1950). In some cultures, women are considered more attractive after they have borne children. "Thus, the Aymara widow of South America with many children is regarded as a desirable bride" (Tichauer, 1963); "Lepcha men consider that copulation with women who have borne more than one child is more enjoyable and less exhausting than with other adult women" (Gorer, 1938).

The other end of this continuum is the view that the childmaking is exhausting, that pregnant women are vulnerable, and that women grow more frail with each pregnancy. Among the Arapesh of New Guinea (Mead, 1935), pregnancy is tiring for both men and women! Once menstruation stops, the husband and wife believe that they must copulate repeatedly in order to provide the building materials for the fetus's semen and blood.

During pregnancy the woman and the fetus may be more readily exposed to evil spirits. According to several records, the forces of life and death are engaged in particularly intense competition for the mother and the fetus around the time of delivery:

> *Half an hour previous to delivery, one of the doctresses made an examination by inserting her hand. Apparently discouraged and alarmed, she notified the mother-in-law of her intention to call upon the officers of the Great Fire fraternity to come and sing their songs. This fraternity has four songs addressed to the Beast Gods for hastening delayed delivery.*   [Stevenson, 1953, p. 115]

Pregnancy can be viewed as a time of great rejoicing or extreme shame, of feeling sexually powerful or extremely vulnerable. One might expect that the view taken toward pregnancy in the culture as a whole will determine the kinds and severity of symptoms associated with pregnancy, the types of treatment or medical assistance sought during pregnancy, and the degree to which pregnancy itself will be responded to as a life stress. The culture's attitude toward pregnancy and birth also influences parenting attitudes and behaviors. For example, embedded in attitudes of solicitude or shame are notions of the value of children and fears about whether the child will be a good or evil force in the family or community. Embedded in attitudes of adequacy versus vulnerability are ideas about whether children bring resources or drain the family of resources; whether children are an extension of the family's power or a new source of vulnerability and risk.

Reactions to Childbirth

Childbirth is an important event in primitive cultures. The delivery is usually attended by two or more assistants with specific assigned roles. Many cultures provide a special hut or other site for delivery. In no primitive culture discussed by Mead and Newton (1967) is the delivering mother asked to move from one location to another in the midst of labor. That appears to be a ritual reserved for modern, industrialized societies.

Views about the birth itself range from an extreme negative pole, at which birth is seen as dirty and defiling, to an extreme positive pole, at which it is seen as a personal achievement. The view of childbirth as a normal physical event would be the midpoint on this continuum.

When birth is viewed as dirty, as it is by the Arapesh of New Guinea and the Kadu Gollas of India, the woman must go to an area away from the village to deliver her child. Many cultures, such as that of the ancient Hebrews, employ extensive purification rituals after childbirth. Vietnamese villagers believe that mothers should not bathe or shampoo their hair for a month after giving birth so that the baby will not "fall apart." The new mother must not have sexual intercourse for 100 days (Stringfellow, 1978).

A slightly more positive orientation toward childbirth is to identify it as a sickness. This view takes the pregnant Cuna Indian woman to her medicine man for daily medication.

The midpoint of this spectrum—what we might most appropriately describe as "natural childbirth"—finds the mother delivering her baby in the presence of many members of the community, without much expression of pain and little magic or obstetric mechanics.

Clark and Howland (1978) described childbirth for Samoan women:

> *The process of labor is viewed by Samoan women as a necessary part of their role and a part of the life experience. Since the baby she is producing is highly valued by her culture, the mother's delivery is also commendable and therefore ego-satisfying.*
>
> *Pain relief for labor may well present the patient with a conflict. She obviously experiences pain as demonstrated by skeletal muscle response, tossing and turning, and fixed body positions, but her culture tells her that she does not need medication. It is the "spoiled" palagi [Caucasian] woman who needs pain-relieving drugs. Moreover, the culture clearly dictates that control is expected of a Samoan woman, and no overt expressions of pain are permissible.* [p. 166]

At the most positive end of the scale, birth is seen as a proud achievement. Among the Ila of Northern Zimbabwe, *women attending at birth were observed to shout praises of the woman who had had a baby. They all thanked her, saying, "I give thanks to you today that you have given birth to a child."*   [Mead & Newton, 1967, p. 174]

A similar sentiment is expressed in Marjorie Karmel's (1983) description of the Lamaze method of childbirth:

From the moment I began to push, the atmosphere of the delivery room underwent a radical transformation. Where previously everyone had spoken in soft and moderate tones in deference to my state of concentration, now there was a wild encouraging cheering section, dedicated to spurring me on. I felt like a football star, headed for a touchdown.   [pp. 93–94]

The American view of childbirth seems to be evolving toward an emphasis on safety for mother and child rather than illness, with a growing respect for building a sense of competence in the mother and father as they approach the care of their newborn (Sameroff, 1987). In comparison with medical practices of the 1940s and 1950s, we are seeing less use of obstetrical medication during childbirth, greater involvement of fathers during labor and delivery, more immediate contact between infants and their parents, more opportunities for the baby to spend much of the day with the mother, opportunities for siblings to visit, and shorter hospital stays.

At the same time, women are urged to take responsibility for the healthy development and safe delivery of their child. They are advised to make early and regular visits to their obstetrician during the prenatal period, and to observe restrictions in diet, the use of drugs, and exposure to certain environmental hazards that may harm the fetus. Midwifery and birthing centers have been slow to develop in the United States, and most physicians strongly urge their patients to deliver their children in a hospital. What is more, the steady increase in the use of cesarean deliveries contradicts the view of childbirth as a natural event that is well within the control and competence of mothers and their family support systems.

We might speculate that events at the time of the birth influence the mother's feelings about herself and her ability to enact her parenting role. Efforts on the part of the community, especially family members, close friends, and health-care professionals, to emphasize a woman's competence and control of the situation, as well as to express caring and support for her, seem to promote a woman's positive orientation toward herself and her mothering role. Messages of social rejection, doubts about a woman's competence, attempts to take away control or to isolate the mother from her infant or her social support system may undermine the woman's self-esteem and interfere with her effectiveness as she approaches the demanding and exhausting task at hand.

The Impact of Poverty

Perhaps the most powerful psychosocial factor that influences the life chances of the developing fetus is poverty. Poor women are likely to experience the cumulative effects of many of the factors associated with infant mortality and developmental vulnerabilities (Swyer, 1987). Poverty is linked to poor prenatal care. Poor women are likely to begin having babies at an earlier age and to have repeated pregnancies into their later adult years, both practices that are associated with low-birth-weight infants. Women who have had little education are less likely to be aware of the risks of smoking, alcohol, and drug use for their babies, and are more likely to use or abuse these substances. Poor women are less likely to have been vaccinated against some of the infectious diseases, such as rubella, that can harm the developing fetus. Poverty is linked with malnutrition, higher instances of infection, and higher rates of diabetes and cardiovascular disease, which are all linked to low birth weight and physical vulnerability (Cassady & Strange, 1987).

Many of the risks that face infants born to poor women are preventable. A well-organized, accessible system of regional medical-care facilities combined with an effective educational program on pregnancy and nutritional support could improve significantly the health and vigor of babies born to poor women (Swyer, 1987). Improvement of the life chances of these infants must be a concern of all citizens. Resources must be provided to care for, educate, and support children whose intellectual, physical, and emotional capabilities have been restricted before birth by their mothers' poverty. The life chances and quality of survival of the infants born to the poor are really a testament to the social justice of the society as a whole.

☐ **Applied Topic: Abortion**

Abortion is the termination of pregnancy before the fetus is able to live outside the uterus. With our current technology, this means before about 24 weeks from conception. Before 12 weeks, the pregnancy can be aborted by dilating the cervix and then either suctioning out the contents of the uterus with a vacuum aspirator or scraping out the uterus. After 12 weeks, abortion can be induced by an injection of a saline solution or prostaglandin. The fetus can be also be removed surgically by means of a procedure similar to that used in cesarean section (Cunningham, MacDonald & Gant, 1989).

Research in France has resulted in the development of a drug, RU 486, which interrupts pregnancy by interfering with the synthesis and circulation of progesterone (Baulieu, 1989). The drug is most effective if it is taken within the first seven to nine weeks after the last menstrual period. It results in a shedding of the lining of the uterus, so there is no need for vacuum aspiration or surgical intervention. From January through September 1989 it was used by more than 2,000 Frenchwomen per month with a success rate of over 95% when it was used within the seventh week of pregnancy. At present the drug is not available in the United States. Should it become legalized, it would bring the decision about abortion once again more directly under a woman's personal control.

In 1920, after the Russian Revolution, the U.S.S.R. was one of the first countries to permit abortion at the mother's request. Although the legalization of abortion is a modern phenomenon, abortion itself is a strategy of birth control that has been practiced, along with infanticide, throughout history and across cultures (Krannich, 1980). Both the Aranda of central Australia and the Hopi of Arizona, for example, have been noted to induce abortions by tying a belt very tightly around the mother's abdomen (Murdock, 1934).

A main point requiring definition in the abortion controversy is the developmental age at which the embryo is so far individualized as to be entitled to protection by the state. In 1973, in the case of *Roe* v. *Wade*, the U.S. Supreme Court proposed a developmental model to address that issue. The Court supported the idea that pregnancy could be divided into three trimesters. The justices considered abortion to be a woman's right in the first trimester, guarded by the Constitution's protection of privacy. They said that some restrictions could be placed on access to abortion in the second trimester, on the basis of the risk posed by abortion to the mother. The fetus's rights were still not at issue. In the final trimester, when the fetus was considered to have a good chance of surviving outside the uterus, states could choose not to permit abortion.

For some years since that decision, the Supreme Court ruled state laws that tried to regulate abortions unconstitutional. But in July 1989 the Supreme Court upheld a Missouri law that makes it illegal for any public institution or any public employee to perform an abortion. In addition, the Missouri law defines life as beginning at conception, implying the state's responsibility to protect the fetus from the earliest weeks of pregnancy. Finally, the law requires physicians who perform abortions after 20 weeks of pregnancy to test first to determine whether the fetus is capable of independent survival. If it is, abortion is illegal *(Economist,* 1989). The upholding of the Missouri law did not overturn *Roe* v. *Wade,* but it gave the states new freedom to impose restrictions on the accessibility of abortions.

What do we know about the impact of abortions on women? Are abortions medically risky? How do women cope emotionally with the experience of abortion?

In 1965, 20% of all deaths associated with pregnancy and childbirth were linked to abortion. Since the legalization of abortion, related deaths have decreased by over 50%. Currently maternal deaths associated with legal abortions are 0.8 per 100,000. Legal abortion is therefore about ten times safer for women than childbirth. Abortion, especially before 12 weeks, is at present much safer physically than carrying an unwanted pregnancy to term. In 1989, after an extensive evaluation of existing research, the then surgeon general, C. Everett Koop, reported that "the scientific studies do not provide conclusive data about the health effects of abortion on women" (Holden, 1989). President Reagan had requested the study in the hopes of using the evidence provided by the scientific literature to build a case against abortion on the grounds of its health risks. Most of the evidence that Koop reviewed focused on the psychological effects of abortion. He found that these studies were so seriously flawed methodologically that their results could not be used to support either side of the abortion debate.

The typical psychological experience of women who experience abortion is relief (Lemkau, 1988). Especially when abortion has been performed within the first 12 weeks, women generally resolve any negative feelings and thoughts they may have had soon after it is completed (Shusterman, 1976; Olson, 1980). However, many women do experience some ambivalence during the decision-making period.

Two psychological factors are associated with a positive abortion outcome (Alter, 1984). One is having an androgynous gender identity; that is, having flexible access to both masculine and feminine characteristics. Androgynous women report less sense of loss, less anxiety, fewer physical symptoms, and fewer thoughts about death than other women. (Androgyny is discussed further in Chapter 10.) The second factor is congruence between self and career. Women who view themselves as very similar to those with a strong commitment to a career tend to have more positive reactions after

What stance will society take in protecting the rights of women and their unborn children? The debate over abortion reflects a major psychosocial controversy.

an abortion. These findings suggest that the meaning a woman finds in the abortion experience is closely related to her orientation to gender and her lifestyle.

In some instances abortion is associated with lingering negative feelings. Lemkau (1988) presents some clinical cases in which abortion produced strong, unresolved negative emotions. Sometimes, when a genetic anomaly is discovered in the fetus, abortion is performed late in pregnancy. A woman who has already become attached to the fetus grieves for her loss. In other second-trimester abortions the ambivalence that caused the delay in the decision to have an abortion is exaggerated by the physical discomfort associated with a later abortion. Finally, some women discover that they are unable to conceive after an abortion. At that point, feelings of guilt, anger, and regret surface. Even though most abortions are associated with positive feelings of having taken control over one's destiny, we should not dismiss the emotional risks that some women face.

The current conservative views of the president and the Supreme Court in regard to abortion do not reflect the views of most Americans. In a Gallup poll conducted for *Newsweek* in July 1989, 58% of respondents did not want to see *Roe* v. *Wade* overturned; 31% did. In a comparison of current opinions with those of 1975, the poll found that a greater proportion of the current respondents thought that abortions should be legal under any circumstances (29%) than was the case in 1975 (21%) (*Newsweek,* 1989). As a reflection of this popular sentiment, a bill was introduced into the Congress late in 1989 called the Freedom of Choice Act. The bill would establish that women have a right to choose to terminate a pregnancy and would block states from banning abortions before the fetus can survive outside the womb.

Women and their unborn babies are not the only persons affected by the abortion decision. In 1976 the Supreme Court ruled that a woman did not need the consent of her husband or the child's father in order to have an abortion, overruling a requirement for the father's consent that had been legislated in 12 states, including Missouri, Florida, Massachusetts, and Pennsylvania (Etzioni, 1976). This ruling confirmed the 1973 decision not to interfere with the woman's authority in this matter. However, it raised the question of the legal rights of fathers to determine the fates of their unborn children.

Shostak and McLouth (1985) interviewed 1000 men who had accompanied women to abortion clinics across the United States. Of these men, 93% said they would alter their birth-control methods as a result of the experience; 83% believed that abortion was a desirable way of resolving the pregnancy problem. Many of these men expressed anxiety, frustration, and guilt in relation to the unwanted pregnancy and the abortion. This issue clearly will continue to be debated as fathers become increasingly committed to their participation in parenting.

The debate surrounding the legalization and availability of abortion services is an excellent example of a psychosocial controversy. On one side are those who insist on a woman's right to privacy and her absolute right to choose or reject motherhood. On the other side are those who seek to protect the rights of the unborn fetus, which is incapable of protecting its own interests (Allgeier, Allgeier & Rywick, 1981). Embedded in this controversy are key human development issues. When does human life begin? When is a fetus viable—that is, capable of life outside the uterus? What is the impact on a woman's physical health and psychological well-being of having an abortion? What is the impact on a woman's physical health and psychological well-being of bearing and rearing an unwanted child? What is the impact of being an unwanted child? What are the rights of fathers with respect to a woman's decision to have an abortion? What are the rights and responsibilities of parents in regard to an adolescent's decision about abortion? In much the same way that the society is struggling to define death and to resolve the ethical issues surrounding the technological interventions that prolong the lives of people who have been severely brain-damaged or who are terminally ill, the society is struggling to define the beginnings of life and to resolve the ethical issues surrounding society's responsibilities to adult women and their unborn children.

◻ Chapter Summary

A fetus develops in a psychosocial context. Genetic inheritance links each new infant to both a specific ancestry and the evolutionary history of the species. Genetic factors contribute to the rate of development as well as to the pattern of individual characteristics. Many personal competencies and abnormalities have their origins in the pattern of genetic information provided at fertilization. Our understanding of the biochemical basis of genetics is leading to the development of new technologies that may one day result in the ability to correct genetic abnormalities or to modify the genotype. These advances pose new psychosocial dilemmas and call for a public well educated in science, human development, and ethics.

The nine months of fetal development involve rapid differentiation of body organs and gradual integration of survival functions, especially the ability to suck and swallow, the regulation of breathing and body temperature, and the maturation of the digestive system. Sense receptors are prepared to respond to stimulation long before they are put into use. The central nervous system, which begins to take shape in the third and fourth weeks after conception, continues to develop and change throughout the prenatal period and into childhood and adolescence.

The birth process itself has five phases. The early signs that birth is approaching orient the parents and indicate the readying of the birth canal for the baby's passage. Labor and delivery involve involuntary uterine contractions. The length of labor is quite variable, although it is usually shorter for women who have already had a child. The most difficult phase of delivery is the transition to full labor, when the contractions become strongest and last the longest time.

The mother and fetus are interdependent. Pregnancy affects a woman's social roles and social status. It influences the way people treat her and the resources that become available to her. Pregnancy also influences a woman's physical well-being and her emotional state. A mother's attitude toward her pregnancy and the developing attachment to her unborn child set the stage for the quality of her parenting after the child is born.

Characteristics of the mother, her lifestyle, and her physical and cultural environment all influence fetal development. Of special note are the mother's age, any drugs she takes during her pregnancy, her exposure to certain diseases and environmental toxins, the use of anesthetic drugs during delivery, and her diet. Of specific social concern is the impact of poverty on fetal development. Infants conceived by very poor women are exposed to the cumulative effects of many of the environmental hazards that are known to result in low birth weight and congenital abnormalities.

Several factors involved in the prenatal period converge in the issue of abortion. The decision to abort reflects the mother's attitude toward childbirth; her criteria for a healthy, normal child; her age and economic resources; and her access to a safe means of ending the pregnancy. The decision about abortion also reflects the cultural attitudes about the moral implications of ending a life after conception. The decision as to when the fetus itself has a right to society's protection is of course highly culture-bound. Finally, the decision to abort is related to the safety, ease, and expense of the procedure. In this regard, the medical profession and the development of medical technology have contributed to the increasing use of abortion to end unwanted pregnancies.

The stage is now set to consider the remaining life stages in a psychosocial context. We have a sense of a child emerging into an existing family, community, and cultural network. The challenges to growth at every life stage reflect the balance between the unique talents and resources that a person offers and the barriers, expectations, and resources that he or she confronts in the environment. The events of birth—including the effort, the stress, the risk, the sense of achievement, and the exhilaration—are all to be experienced repeatedly throughout life as a person meets the challenges of development.

References

Abel, E. L. (1984). *Fetal alcohol syndrome and fetal alcohol effects*. New York: Plenum.

Aleksandrowicz, M. K., & Aleksandrowicz, D. R. (1974). Obstetrical pain-relieving drugs as predictors of infant behavior variability. *Child Development, 45,* 935–945.

Allgeier, A. R., Allgeier, E. R., & Rywick, T. (1981). Orientations toward abortion: Guilt or knowledge? *Adolescence, 16,* 273–288.

Alter, R. C. (1984). Abortion outcome as a function of sex-role identification. *Psychology of Women Quarterly, 8,* 211–233.

Andrews, L. B. (1984). Yours, mine and theirs. *Psychology Today, 18,* 20–29.

Bankart, B. (1989). Japanese perceptions of motherhood. *Psychology of Women Quarterly, 13,* 59–76.

Baulieu, E. (1989). Contragestion and other clinical applications of RU 486, an antiprogesterone at the receptor. *Science, 245,* 1351–1357.

Brackbill, Y. (1977). Long-term effects of obstetrical anesthesia on infant autonomic function. *Developmental Psychology, 10,* 529–535.

Brackbill, Y., Kane, J., Manniello, R. L., & Abramson, D. (1974). Obstetric premedication and infant outcome. *American Journal of Obstetrics and Gynecology, 118,* 377–384.

Brasel, J. (1974). Cellular changes in intrauterine malnutrition. In M. Winick (ed.), *Nutrition and fetal development.* New York: Wiley.

Brazelton, T. B. (1987). Behavioral competence of the newborn infant. In G. B. Avery (ed.), *Neonatology: Pathophysiology and management of the newborn* (pp. 379–399). Philadelphia: Lippincott.

Bronson, G. (1979). Issue of fetal damage stirs women workers at chemical plants. *Wall Street Journal,* February 9.

Burt, R. D., Vaughan, T. L., & Daling, J. R. (1988). Evaluating the risks of cesarean section: Low Apgar score in repeat C-section and vaginal deliveries. *American Journal of Public Health, 78,* 1312–1314.

Byrne, G. (1988). Artificial insemination report prompts call for regulation. *Science, 241,* 895.

Cassady, G., & Strange, M. (1987). The small-for-gestational-age (SGA) infant. In G. B. Avery (ed.), *Neonatology: Pathophysiology and management of the newborn* (pp. 299–331). Philadelphia: Lippincott.

Chasnoff, I. J. (1988). *Drugs, alcohol, pregnancy, and parenting.* Hingham, Mass.: Kluwer.

Clark, A. L., & Howland, R. I. (1978). The American Samoan. In A. L. Clark (ed.), *Culture childbearing health professionals* (pp. 154–172). Philadelphia: F. A. Davis.

Clarren, S. K., & Smith, D. W. (1978). The fetal alcohol syndrome. *New England Journal of Medicine, 298,* 1063–1067.

Clayman, C. B. (1989). *The American Medical Association encyclopedia of medicine.* New York: Random House.

Coursin, D. B. (1974). Overview of the problem. In M. Winick (ed.), *Nutrition and fetal development.* New York: Wiley.

Cunningham, F. G., MacDonald, P. C., & Gant, N. F. (1989). *Williams' obstetrics* (18th ed.). Norwalk, Conn.: Appleton & Lange.

Dalton, K. (1976). Prenatal progesterone and educational attainment. *British Journal of Psychiatry, 129,* 438–442.

Darney, P. D., Myhra, W., Atkinson, E. S., & Meier, J. (1989). Sero survey of human immunodeficiency virus infection in women at a family planning clinic: Absence of infection in an indigent population in San Francisco. *American Journal of Public Health, 79,* 883–885.

De Casper, A. J., & Spence, M. J. (1986). Prenatal maternal speech influences newborns' perceptions of speech sounds. *Infant Behavior and Development, 9,* 133–150.

Dinges, D. F., Davis, M. M., & Glass, P. (1980). Fetal exposure to narcotics: Neonatal sleep as a measure of nervous system disturbance. *Science, 209,* 619–621.

Economist (1989). The fearful politics of abortion. July 8, pp. 21–23.

Elson, J. (1989). The rights of frozen embryos. *Time,* July 24, p. 63.

Entwisle, D. R., & Alexander, K. L. (1987). Long-term effects of cesarean delivery on parents' beliefs and children's schooling. *Developmental Psychology, 23,* 676–682.

Etzioni, A. (1976). The husband's rights in abortion. *Trial,* November.

Field, R., Healy, B., Goldstein, S., Perry, S., Bendell, D., Schanberg, S., Zimmerman, E. A., & Kuhn, C. (1988). Infants of depressed mothers show "depressed" behavior even with nondepressed adults. *Child Development, 59,* 1569–1579.

Field, R., Sandberg, D., Garcia, R., Vega-Lahr, N., Goldstein, S., & Guy, L. (1985). Pregnancy problems, postpartum depression, and early mother-infant interactions. *Developmental Psychology, 21,* 1152–1156.

Fleming, A. S., Ruble, D. N., Flett, G. L., & Shaul, D. L. (1988). Postpartum adjustment in first-time mothers: Relations between mood, maternal attitudes, and mother-infant interactions. *Developmental Psychology, 24,* 71–81.

Ford, C. S. (1945). *A comparative study of human reproduction.* New Haven, Conn.: Yale University Publications in Anthropology, no. 32.

Fried, P. A., Watkinson, B., Dillon, R. F., & Dulberg, C. S. (1987). Neonatal neurological status in a low-risk population after prenatal exposure to cigarettes, marijuana, and alcohol. *Journal of Developmental and Behavioral Pediatrics, 8,* 318–326.

Gardner, E. J., & Snustad, D. P. (1984). *Principles of genetics* (7th ed.). New York: Wiley.

Giacoia, G. P., & Yaffe, S. J. (1987). Drugs and the perinatal patient. In G. B. Avery (ed.), *Neonatology: Pathophysiology and management of the newborn* (pp. 1317–1348). Philadelphia: Lippincott.

Gilbert, M. S. (1963). *Biography of the unborn.* New York: Hafner.

Gorer, G. (1938). *Himalayan village: An account of the Lepchas of Sikkim.* London: Michael Joseph.

Gottesman, I. (1963). Genetic aspects of intelligent behavior. In N. Ellis (ed.), *Handbook of Mental deficiency.* New York: McGraw-Hill.

Grandquist, H. (1950). *Child problems among the Arabs.* Helsinki: Söderström.

Greenough, W. T., Black, J. E., & Wallace, C. S. (1987). Experience and brain development. *Child development, 58,* 539–559.

Grossman, F. K., Eichler, L. S., Winickoff, S. A., et al. (1980). *Pregnancy, birth, and parenthood.* San Francisco: Jossey-Bass.

Guttmann, B. (1932). *Die Stammeslehvender des Chagga* (vol. 1). Munich: C. H. Beck.

Habicht, J. P., Yarbrough, C., Lechtig, A., & Klein, R. E., (1974). Relation of maternal supplementary feeding during pregnancy to birth weight and other sociological factors. In M. Winick (ed.), *Nutrition and fetal development.* New York: Wiley.

Hans, S. L. (1987). Maternal drug addiction and young children. *Division of Child, Youth, and Family Services Newsletter, 10,* 5, 15.

Heitlinger, A. (1989). Current medical, legal, and demographic perspectives on artificial reproduction in Czechoslovakia. *American Journal of Public Health, 79,* 57–61.

Holden, C. (1987). The genetics of personality. *Science, 237,* 598–601.

Holden, C. (1989). Koop finds abortion evidence "inconclusive". *Science, 243,* 730–731.

Holmes, T. H., & Rahe, R. H. (1967). The social readjustment rating scale. *Journal of Psychosomatic Research, 11,* 213–218.

Horn, J. M. (1983). The Texas Adoption Project: Adopted children and their intellectual resemblance to biological and adoptive parents. *Child Development, 54,* 268–275.

Horn, J. M. (1985). Bias? Indeed! *Child Development, 56,* 779–780.

Howes, C., & Krakow, J. (1977). Effects of inevitable environmental pollutants. In F. Rebelsky (chair), *Pollution of the fetus.* Symposium conducted at the annual convention of the American Psychological Association, San Francisco.

International Bank for Reconstruction and Development (1983). *World Tables,* vol. 2, *Social Data* (3rd ed.) (pp. 144, 148–149). Washington, D.C.

Jacobson, S. W., Fein, G. G., Jacobson, J. L., Schwartz, P. M., & Dowler, J. K. (1985). The effect of intrauterine PCB exposure on visual recognition memory. *Child Development, 56,* 853–860.

Jarboe, P. J. (1986). A comparison study of distress and marital adjustment in infertile and expectant couples. Ph.D. dissertation, Ohio State University.

Jaroff, L. (1989). The gene hunt. *Time,* Mar. 20, pp. 62–67.

Jones, K. L., Smith, D. W., Ulleland, C. N., & Streissguth, A. P. (1973). Patterns of malformation in offspring of chronic alcoholic mothers. *Lancet, 1,* 1267–1271.

Judson, F. N. (1989). What do we really know about AIDS control? *American Journal of Public Health, 79,* 878–882.

Kaplan, B. J. (1986). A psychobiological review of depression during pregnancy. *Psychology of Women Quarterly, 10,* 35–48.

Karmel, M. (1983). *Thank you, Dr. Lamaze.* Philadelphia: Lippincott.

Kliman, D. G., & Kohl, R. (1984). *Fatherhood USA.* New York: Garland Press.

Krannich, R. S. (1980). Abortion in the United States: Past, present, and future trends. *Family Relations, 29,* 365–374.

Lacayo, R. (1988). Baby M. meets Solomon's sword. *Time,* Feb. 15, p. 97.

Lawn, R. M., & Vehar, G. A. (1986). The molecular genetics of hemophilia. *Scientific American, 254,* 48–56.

Lemkau, J. R. (1988). Emotional sequelae of abortion: Implications for clinical practice. *Psychology of Women Quarterly, 12,* 461–472.

Lester, B. M., Als, H., & Brazelton, T. B. (1982). Regional obstetric anesthesia and newborn behavior: A reanalysis toward synergistic effects. *Child Development, 53,* 687–692.

Levy, M. J., Jr. (1968). *The family revolution in modern China.* Cambridge, Mass.: Harvard University Press.

Lindblad, B. S. (1987). *Perinatal nutrition.* San Diego: Academic Press.

Martin, J. B. (1987). Molecular genetics: Applications to the clinical neurosciences. *Science, 238,* 765–772.

Marx, J. (1988). Are aging and death programmed in our genes? *Science, 242,* 33.

Mead, M. (1935). *Sex and temperament in three primitive societies.* New York: William Morrow.

Mead, M., & Newton, N. (1967). Cultural patterning of perinatal behavior. In S. A. Richardson & A. F. Guttmacher (eds.), *Childbearing—its social and psychological aspects.* Baltimore: Williams & Wilkins.

Mendel, G. (1866). Experiments with plant hybrids. *Proceedings of the Brunn Natural History Society.*

Meredith, H. V. (1975). Somatic changes during human prenatal life. *Child Development, 46,* 603–610.

Miller, R. W. (1974). Susceptibility of the fetus and child to chemical pollutants. *Science, 184,* 812–814.

Moore, K. L. (1988). *The developing human: Clinically oriented embryology* (4th ed.). Philadelphia: W. B. Saunders.

Morris, R. A. (1987). The use of legislatively mandated birth registries in conducting research on behavioral teratology/toxicology. *Division of Child, Youth, and Family Services Newsletter, 10*(4), 12.

Murdock, G. P. (1934). *Our primitive contemporaries.* New York: Macmillan.

Murray, A. D., Dolby, R. M., Nation, R. L., & Thomas, D. B. (1981). Effects of epidural anesthesia on newborns and their mothers. *Child Development, 52,* 71–82.

Naulty, J. S. (1987). Obstetric anesthesia. In G. B. Avery (ed.), *Neonatology: Pathophysiology and management of the newborn.* Philadelphia: Lippincott.

Newsweek (1989). The future of abortion. July 17, pp. 14–26.

Nilsson, L. (1977). *A child is born.* New York: Delacorte Press/F. Lawrence.

Nowakowski, R. S. (1987). Basic concepts of CNS development. *Child Development, 58,* 568–595.

Olson, J. (1980). Social and psychological correlates of pregnancy resolution among adolescent women: A review. *American Journal of Orthopsychiatry, 50,* 432–445.

Padawer, J. A., Fagan, C., Janoff-Bulman, R., Strickland, B. R., & Chorowski, M. (1988). Women's psychological adjustment following emergency cesarean versus vaginal delivery. *Psychology of Women Quarterly, 12,* 25–34.

Palkovitz, R. (1985). Fathers' attendance, early contact, and

extended care with their newborns: A critical review. *Child Development, 56,* 392–406.

Palm, G. F., & Palkovitz, R. (1988). The challenge of working with new fathers: Implications for support providers. In R. Palkovitz & M. B. Sussman (eds.), *Transitions to parenthood* (pp. 357–376). New York: Haworth.

Patterson, D. (1987). The causes of Down's syndrome. *Scientific American, 257*(2), 52–61.

Pedersen, N. L., Plomin, R., McClearn, G. E., & Friberg, L. (1988). Neuroticism, extraversion, and related traits in adult twins reared apart and reared together. *Journal of Personality and Social Psychology, 55,* 950–957.

Quilligan, E. J. (1983). *Pregnancy, birth, and the infant.* NIH publication no. 82-2304. U.S. Department of Health and Human Services. Washington, D.C.: U.S. Government Printing Office.

Reinisch, J. M., & Karow, W. G. (1977). Prenatal exposure to synthetic progestins and estrogens: Effects on human development. *Archives of Sexual Behavior, 6,* 257–288.

Roberts, L. (1989). Human gene transfer approved. *Science, 243,* 473.

Robison, J. T. (1989). Noncoital reproduction. *Psychology of Women: Newsletter of Division 35, American Psychological Association, 16*(1), 3–5.

Roosa, M. W. (1984). Maternal age, social class, and the obstetric performance of teenagers. *Journal of Youth and Adolescence, 13,* 365–374.

Roth, W. E. (1953). Precautions during pregnancy in New Guinea. In M. Mead & N. Calas (eds.), *Primitive heritage.* New York: Random House.

Sabatelli, R. M., Meth, R. L., & Gavazzi, S. M. (1988). Factors mediating the adjustment to involuntary childlessness. *Family Relations, 37,* 338–343.

Sachs, A. (1989). Here come the pregnancy police. *Time,* May 22, 104–105.

Sameroff, A. J. (1987). Psychologic needs of the parent in infant development. In G. B. Avery (ed.), *Neonatology: Pathophysiology and management of the newborn* (pp. 358–378). Philadelphia: Lippincott.

Sameroff, A. J., & Chandler, M. J. (1975). Reproductive risk and the continuum of caretaking casualty. In F. D. Horowitz, M. Hetherington, S. Scarr-Salapatek, & G. Siegel (eds.), *Review of child development research* (vol. 4). Chicago: University of Chicago Press.

Schroeder, S. R. (1987). Behavioral toxicology: Assessment technology for neurotoxic effects of lead exposure in humans. *Division of Child, Youth, and Family Services Newsletter, 10*(1), 14–15.

Schuster, C. S. (1986). Intrauterine development. In C. S. Schuster & S. S. Ashburn (eds.), *The process of human development* (pp. 67–94). Boston: Little, Brown.

Seabrook, C. (1987). Children—"third wave" of AIDS victims. *Atlanta Journal,* February 19, 1A, 12A.

Sherman, J. A. (1971). *On the psychology of women: A survey of empirical studies.* Springfield, Ill.: Charles C Thomas.

Shostak, A., & McLouth, G. (1985). *Men and abortion.* New York: Praeger.

Shusterman, L. R. (1976). The psychosocial factors of the abortion experience: A critical review. *Psychology of Women Quarterly, 1,* 79–106.

Silverman, P. R. (1989). Deconstructing motherhood. *Readings: A Journal of Reviews and Commentary in Mental Health, 4,* 14–18.

Sosa, R., Kennell, J., Klaus, M., Robertson, S., & Urrutia, J. (1980). The effect of a supportive companion on perinatal problems, length of labor, and mother-infant interaction. *New England Journal of Medicine, 303,* 597–600.

Spence, M. J., & De Casper, A. J. (1987). Prenatal experience with low-frequency maternal-voice sounds influence neonatal perception of maternal voice samples. *Infant Behavior and Development, 10,* 133–142.

Sperling, D. (Mar. 10, 1989). Success rate for in vitro is only 9%. *USA Today,* p. 1D.

Standley, K., Soule, B., & Copans, S. A. (1979). Dimensions of prenatal anxiety and their influence on pregnancy outcome. *American Journal of Obstetrics and Gynecology, 135,* 22–26.

Stechler, G., & Halton, A. (1982). Prenatal influences on human development. In B. B. Wolman (ed.), *Handbook of developmental psychology* (pp. 175–189). Englewood Cliffs, N.J.: Prentice-Hall.

Stevenson, M. (1953). Childbirth ceremonies of the Sia Pueblo. In M. Mead & N. Calas (eds.), *Primitive heritage.* New York: Random House.

Streissguth, A. P., Barr, H. M., Sampson, P. D., Darby, B. L., & Martin, D. C. (1989). IQ at age 4 in relation to maternal alcohol use and smoking during pregnancy. *Developmental Psychology, 25,* 3–11.

Stringfellow, L. (1978). The Vietnamese. In A. L. Clark (ed.), *Culture childbearing health professionals* (pp. 174–182). Philadelphia: F. A. Davis.

Swyer, P. R. (1987). The organization of perinatal care with particular reference to the newborn. In G. B. Avery (ed.), *Neonatology: Pathophysiology and management of the newborn* (pp. 13–44). Philadelphia: Lippincott.

Tanner, J. M. (1978). *Foetus into man: Physical growth from conception to maturity.* Cambridge, Mass.: Harvard University Press.

Thomas, A., & Chess, S. (1977). *Temperament and development.* New York: Bruner/Mazel.

Tichauer, R. (1963). The Aymara children of Bolivia. *Journal of Pediatrics, 62,* 399–412.

U.S. Bureau of the Census. (1985). *Statistical abstract of the United States: 1986* (103rd ed.). Washington, D.C.: U.S. Government Printing Office.

U.S. Bureau of the Census (1989). *Statistical abstract of the United States, 1989* (109th ed.). Washington, D.C.: U.S. Government Printing Office.

U.S. Department of Health, Education, and Welfare (1979). *Smoking and health: A report of the surgeon general.* Washington, D.C.: U.S. Government Printing Office.

Usher, R. (1987). Extreme prematurity. In G. B. Avery (ed.), *Neonatology: Pathophysiology and management of the newborn* (3rd ed.) (pp. 264–298). Philadelphia: Lippincott.

Vaughn, B. E., Bradley, C. F., Joffe, L. S., Seifer, R., & Barglow, P. (1987). Maternal characteristics measured prenatally are predictive of ratings of temperamental "difficulty" on the Carey Infant Temperament Questionnaire. *Developmental Psychology, 23,* 152–161.

Ventura, S. J., Taffel, S. M., & Mosher, W. D. (1988). Estimates of pregnancies and pregnancy rates for the United States, 1976–85. *American Journal of Public Health, 78,* 506–511.

Vogel, F., & Motulsky, A. G. (1986). *Human genetics: Problems and approaches* (2nd ed.). New York: Springer-Verlag.

West, J. R. (1986). *Alcohol and brain development.* London: Oxford University Press.

Williams, J. H. (1987). *Psychology of women: Behavior in a biosocial context.* (2nd ed.). New York: Norton.

World Health Organization (1972). Vulnerability of young infants to food additives. World Health Organization Technical Report Series, no. 488.

Yalom, I. D., Green, R., & Fisk, N. (1973). Prenatal exposure to female hormones. *Archives of General Psychiatry, 28,* 554–561.

Yang, R. K., Zweig, A. R., Douthitt, T. C., & Federman, E. J. (1976). Successive relationships between maternal attitudes during pregnancy, analgesic medication during labor and delivery, and newborn behavior. *Developmental Psychology, 12,* 6–14.

Zuckerman, B., et al. (1989). Effects of maternal marijuana and cocaine use on fetal growth. *New England Journal of Medicine, 320,* 762–768.

Chapter Five

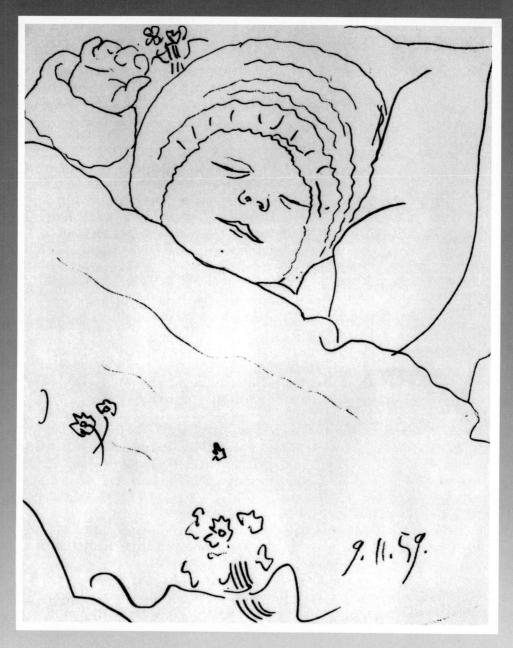

The complexity, competences, and resilience of human infants are being recognized, described, and understood.

Infancy
(Birth to 2 Years)

Infants participate in a complex social environment from the very first weeks of life. Parents who are nurturant and responsive make an enormous contribution to their children's optimal development.

Infancy is a period of dramatically rapid growth. During the first year of life the infant's birth weight almost triples. By the age of 2 the fundamentals of movement, language, and concept formation can be observed. Global behaviors of early infancy become well differentiated requests for the satisfaction of specific needs. The outstanding feature of infancy is the integration of simple responses into coordinated, meaningful patterns of behavior.

Infants are far more competent than they were once believed to be. A burgeoning literature documents many perceptual, cognitive, and social capacities that appear to be guided by genetic information. Individual differences in temperament and intellectual ability can be systematically observed, even within the first six months of life (Mandler, 1990). The role of genetics in guiding the course of infant development is becoming increasingly well documented as methods of studying infant behavior reach new levels of sophistication (Plomin, 1990).

At the same time, longitudinal studies and cross-cultural studies reveal the significant impact of the child's early environment on the developmental outcome. The mother's personality, the father's involvement in child care, the cultural beliefs surrounding child-rearing practices, and poverty are all factors that can add to a child's vulnerability or resilience.

In recent years, as American families have become smaller, we have seen a change in the emphasis society places on infancy. Each child is taken much more seriously. The medical community is devising complex technologies for saving the lives of babies born at 1200 grams (39 oz.) or 1000 grams (32 oz.). The psychological community is giving attention to infant temperament and the early origins of personality, focusing on individual differences among infants from the very first weeks of life. There is a growing baby industry, made up of special equipment, foods, toys, books, and other paraphernalia. Parents take classes, read books and magazines, and join support groups so that they can "get it right the first time."

The impact of birth cohort on the lives of individual children is just beginning to be documented. Children born in the same historical period experience certain common patterns of opportunities and challenges. We have begun to get a sense of the way the baby-boom generation has collided with the social institutions of our society, including schools, the labor market, marriage, and housing. Now we face a baby bust, and we are beginning to appreciate the special attention that these precious new lives attract.

Developmental Tasks

Five areas of development are of heightened importance during infancy: (1) social attachment; (2) sensory and motor functions (seeing, hearing, eye-hand coordination, reaching, crawling, walking); (3) understanding the relationship between actions and their consequences at a behavioral rather than a conceptual level; (4) understanding the nature of objects and creating categories that link objects, people, and events in groups; and (5) emotional development (happiness, sadness, anger). We now appreciate the degree to which infants actively select and organize information and contribute to their own care (Belsky & Tolan, 1981; Osofsky, 1987; Bower, 1989).

Social Attachment

Social attachment is the process through which people develop specific, positive emotional bonds with others. As we saw in Chapter 3, John Bowlby introduced a conceptualization of the attachment behavior system as an organized pattern of infant signals and adult responses that lead to a protective, trusting relationship during the very earliest stage of development. Recent work has begun to consider the formation of attachments at later points in the life span, but the original interest in this behavioral system focused on its relevance for keeping the infant close to the caregiver, thereby ensuring the infant's protection against possible harm. The nurturing responses of the caregiver constitute a complementary behavioral system that we often refer to as parenting or caregiving (Bowlby, 1988; Ainsworth, 1985).

Evidence that an attachment has been formed is seen in at least three behaviors. First, infants try to maintain contact with the object of attachment (Ainsworth, 1973). Second, infants show distress when the object of attachment is absent (Schaffer & Emerson, 1964). Third, infants are more relaxed and comfortable with the object of attachment and more fretful with other people (Bronson, 1973).

Stages of Attachment
Ainsworth (1973, 1985) described five sequential stages in the development of social attachment (see Table 5.1). In the first stage, during the first three months of life,

Table 5.1   Five Sequential Stages in the Development of Social Attachment

Stage	Age	Characteristics
1	Birth to 3 months	Infant uses sucking, rooting, grasping, smiling, gazing, cuddling, and visual tracking to maintain closeness with caregivers.
2	3 to 6 months	Infant is more responsive to familiar figures than to strangers.
3	6 to 9 months	Infant seeks physical proximity and contact with object(s) of attachment.
4	9 to 12 months	Infant forms internal mental representation of object of attachment, including expectations about the caregiver's typical responses to signals of distress.
5	12 months and beyond	Child uses a variety of behaviors to influence the behavior of the objects of attachment in ways that will satisfy needs for safety and closeness.

infants engage in a variety of behaviors, including sucking, rooting, grasping, smiling, gazing, cuddling, and visual tracking, which serve to maintain closeness with a caregiver or bring the caregiver to the infant. However, these behaviors do not appear to be aimed at a specific person. Through these contacts, babies learn about the unique features of their caregivers.

In the second stage, from about 3 months until about 6 months of age, an infant's attachment is expressed through preferential responsiveness to a few familiar figures. Infants smile more at the familiar person than at a stranger, show more excitement at that person's arrival, and appear to be upset when he or she leaves.

In the third stage, from about 6 to 9 months, babies actively seek physical proximity with the objects of attachment. The ability to crawl and the ability to coordinate reaching and grasping contribute to greater control over the outcomes of their actions.

In the fourth stage, from about 9 to 12 months, babies form the first internal representation of their caregivers. This internal representation provides the first robust working model of an attachment relationship. Specific characteristics of a caregiver and patterns of expectations about how a caregiver will respond to the infant's actions are organized into a complex attachment scheme, the internal, mental representations of the anticipated responses of a caregiver.

In the fifth stage, in toddlerhood and later, young children use a variety of behaviors to influence the behavior of their parents and other objects of attachment in order to satisfy their own needs for closeness. Children may ask to be read to, cuddled at bedtime, and taken along on errands. These are strategies that they develop to produce caregiver behaviors that will satisfy their continuing needs for physical contact, closeness, and love.

As children mature from toddlerhood to the early and middle school years, they begin to conceptualize new risks and threats to their security. They may initiate new strategies for maintaining closeness to the objects of their attachment. Especially when they are undergoing unusual stress, as in times of illness, divorce, or rejection, children of any age who have a secure attachment may try to activate the attachment system by sending signals that will result in comforting and closeness.

During the second half of the first year, two signs of the child's growing attachment to a specific other person are observed: stranger anxiety and separation anxiety.

Through active exploration, this baby is developing a detailed scheme of his mother.

Stranger anxiety is the baby's discomfort or tension in the presence of unfamiliar adults. Babies vary in how they express their protest to strangers and in how intensely they react. They may cling to their parents, refuse to be held, stiffen at the stranger's touch, or merely avert their eyes from the stranger's face.

The baby's response to a stranger will depend on some very specific dimensions of the situation, including how close the mother is, how the stranger approaches the baby, and how the mother responds to the stranger (Keltenbach, Weinraub & Fullard, 1980). For example, if a mother speaks in a positive tone of voice to her baby about a stranger, the baby's response to the stranger is likely to be positive (Feinman & Lewis, 1983). The baby's response will also be influenced by the amount of prior experience with unfamiliar adults. Normally we take wariness of strangers as a positive sign—that is, that babies are able to detect the differences between their parents and adults they do not know. Of course, wariness of strangers continues to be expressed throughout life. In fact, we often see more distinct expressions of suspiciousness or fear among adults encountering strangers than we do among babies.

At about 9 months, infants give another indication of the intensity of their attachment to their parents by expressing rage and despair when the parents leave. This reaction is called *separation anxiety.* Separation can evoke two different kinds of behavior. Under some conditions, separation from the caregiver will stimulate attachment behaviors, especially efforts to find the caregiver and regain physical contact (Ainsworth, Bell & Stayton, 1971). Separation can also evoke protest, despair, or detachment, depending on the length of the separation (Bowlby, 1960; Robertson & Robertson, 1989).

The baby's response to separation also depends on the conditions of separation. Infants are less distressed about separation when mothers leave them alone in a room at home than when they do so in a laboratory (Ross et al., 1975). They are less likely to protest if the mother leaves the door to the room open than if she closes the door as she leaves. The protest response to separation seems to be tied to the baby's strong desire to maintain contact with the object of attachment. The importance of contact may be to (1) meet physical needs, (2) help the child overcome physical barriers, (3) provide protection or comfort, or (4) provide novel and stimulating interactions (Hay, 1980). When there are high levels of responsiveness and warmth in the parent-infant relationship, the infant has many reasons to want to maintain access to the caregiver.

We expect babies to become more flexible over time about parents' temporary departures. Young children learn to tolerate brief separations. At 2 years of age, children are able to use a photograph of their mothers to help sustain their adaptation to a new setting in the mothers' absence (Passman & Longeway, 1982). By the age of 3, children may even look forward to a night with a baby-sitter or an afternoon at Grandfather's house. Once the attachment is fully established, children can comfort themselves by creating mental images of their parents and by remembering their parents' love for them. During infancy, however, the parents' physical presence remains a focal point of attention and concern. Parents who, for one reason or another, are forced to leave their children for a prolonged period may return to discover that the children are temporarily withdrawn and cold to them. They may find that previously loving and affectionate children will express sudden outbursts of rage. Since infants have no adequate language, such behaviors are a means of communicating anger and frustration at their experience of abandonment.

Objects of Attachment

An infant may establish an early, positive emotional relationship with both the mother and the father, and with any other person who is performing a large portion of the child-care activities and who expresses warmth and affection for the child, such as an older sibling or a childcare professional. However, the quality of attachment is not necessarily identical in each of these situations (Bretherton, 1985; Bridges, Connell & Belsky, 1988). When Lamb (1976) investigated the attachment that infants showed to their mothers and fathers, he found that the babies tended to have playful interactions with their fathers—smiling, laughing, and looking—and comforting, stress-reducing interactions with their mothers. When only one parents was present, the babies showed evidence of attachment to that parent. When both parents were present, the babies demonstrated a different pattern of interaction with each.

In a study conducted in Israel (Sagi et al., 1985), kibbutz-reared infants showed great similarity between their attachment to their fathers and that to their specially trained caregivers (called *metapelets*). However, there was no consistent pattern of similarity in the quality of their attachments to mother and father and to mother and metapelet. In subsequent research, when these kibbutz children had reached the age of 5, the quality of their infant attachment to the metapelet was a significant predictor of their socioemotional development as observed in school and at free play in their children's house (Oppenheim, Sagi & Lamb, 1988). This research suggests that infants are able to have a variety of attachment relationships. Exactly how the infant synthesizes the internal representations of various attachments is not well understood. Possibly the distinct relationships have relevance for different interpersonal domains, or become central as individuals assume a variety of social roles.

Quality of Attachment

The quality of attachment varies from family to family and from one parent-child dyad to another. The adults' acceptance of the infant and their ability to respond to the infant's varying communications are important to a secure attachment. The parents' patterns of expressing affection and rejection will influence how well babies can meet their strong needs for reassurance and comfort (Tracy & Ainsworth, 1981).

Differences in the quality of attachment have been highlighted by observations of babies and their caregivers in a standard laboratory procedure called the "strange situation" (Ainsworth et al., 1978; Bretherton, 1990). In a twenty-minute period the child is exposed to a sequence of events that are likely to stimulate the attachment system (see Table 5.2). The infant and caregiver enter an unfamiliar laboratory environment, a stranger enters, the caregiver leaves briefly, and the caregiver and infant experience opportunities for reunion. During this situation, researchers have the opportunity to make systematic observations of the child's behaviors, the caregiver's behaviors, and characteristics of their interactions as well as to compare these behaviors across segments of the situation.

Three major patterns of attachment behavior have been distinguished by means of this methodology: (1) secure attachment, (2) anxious-avoidant attachment, and (3) anxious-resistant attachment. In American samples, about two-thirds of the children tested have been characterized as securely attached. Of the remainder, more children fall into the anxious-avoidant category than into the anxious-resistant category (Ainsworth et al., 1978).

Infants who have a *secure attachment* actively explore their environment and interact with strangers while their mothers are present. After a brief separation, the mothers' return reduces their distress and permits them to return to exploration of the environment. Infants who show an *anxious-avoidant attachment* avoid contact with their mothers after separation or ignore their efforts to interact. They show less distress at being alone than other babies. Infants who show an *anxious-resistant attachment* are very cautious in the presence of the stranger. Their exploratory behavior is noticeably disrupted by the caregiver's departure. When the caregiver returns, the infants appear to want to be close to the caregiver, but they are also angry, so that they are very hard to comfort or soothe.

Within the home environment, babies who have a secure attachment are observed to cry less than other babies (Tracy & Ainsworth, 1981; Ainsworth, 1985). They greet their mothers more positively upon reunion after everyday separations, and appear to respond more cooperatively to their mothers' requests. One can sense that securely

Table 5.2   The Strange Situation Procedure

Episode	Duration	Participants*	Events
1	30 sec.	M, B, O	O shows M and B into the room, instructs M on where to put B down and where to sit. O leaves.
2	3 min.	M, B	M puts B down close to her chair, at a distance from the toys. She responds to B's social bids but does not initiate interaction. B is free to explore. If B does not move after 2 minutes, M may take B to the toy area.
3	3 min.	M, B, S	This episode has three parts. S enters, greets M and B, and sits down opposite M without talking for 1 minute. During the 2nd minute, S engages M in conversation. S then joins B on the floor, attempting to engage B in play for 1 minute. At the end of this episode, M leaves "unobtrusively" (B usually notices).
4	3 min.	B, S	S sits on her chair. She responds to B's social bids but does not initiate social interaction. If B becomes distressed, S attempts to comfort B. If this is not effective, M returns before 3 minutes are up.
5	3 min.	M, B	M calls B's name outside the door and enters (S leaves unobtrusively). If B is distressed, M comforts B and tries to reengage B in play. If B is not distressed, M goes to sit on her chair, taking a responsive, noninitiating role. At the end of the episode M leaves, saying "Bye-bye; I'll be back."
6	3 min.	B	B remains alone. If B becomes distressed, the episode is curtailed and S enters.
7	3 min.	B, S	S enters, comforting B if required. If she cannot comfort B, the episode is curtailed. If B calms down or is not distressed, S sits on her chair, taking a responsive role as before.
8	3 min.	M, B	M returns (S leaves unobtrusively). M behaves as in episode 5.

*O = observer; M = mother; B = baby; S = stranger.

Source: I. Bretherton, "Open Communication and Internal Working Models: Their Role in the Development of Attachment Relationships," in R. Dienstbier and R. A. Thompson (eds.) *Nebraska Symposium on Motivation 1988: Socioemotional Development, 36,* 60–61. Lincoln, Neb.: University of Nebraska Press. Reprinted from 1988 NEBRASKA SYMPOSIUM ON MOTIVATION, by permission of University of Nebraska Press. Copyright © 1990 by the University of Nebraska Press.

attached babies have a working model of attachment in which they expect their caregiver to be accessible and responsive. This confidence permits the securely attached infant to explore the environment and to accept brief separations with little protest.

Mothers of babies who were characterized as anxious-avoidant seem to reject their babies. It is almost as if they were angry at their babies. They spend less time holding and cuddling their babies than other mothers, and more of their interactions appear to be unpleasant or even hurtful. At home these babies cry a lot, they are not readily soothed by contact with the caregiver, and yet they appear to be quite distressed by separations. These babies have strong needs for security, but it appears that they have established an internal representation of the caregiver that predicts that their requests for comfort will be rejected. Thus they do not seek to make contact with the caregiver in the laboratory situation, defending themselves against rejection.

The third group, infants who are characterized as anxious-resistant, have mothers who are inconsistent in their responsiveness. Sometimes these mothers ignore clear signals of distress. At other times they interfere with their infants in order to make contact. Although these mothers appear to be able to enjoy close physical contact with

Anxious–resistant babies want to be close to their mothers, but they are difficult to cuddle or soothe.

their babies, they do not necessarily do so in ways appropriate to the baby's needs. The result is the formation of an internal representation of attachment that is highly unpredictable. These babies try to maintain proximity and to avoid any unfamiliar situation that will heighten the uncertainty of their accessibility to their caregiver. Their responses reflect frustration at their inability to predict or control the responsiveness of their caregiver.

Questions have been raised about the validity of the strange situation as a method for assessing attachment across cultures. Is it reasonable to expect that patterns of child rearing in different societies will produce the same patterns of attachment that are found in the United States? In an analysis of 32 studies of attachment in eight countries—the United States, Germany, Great Britain, the Netherlands, Sweden, Israel, Japan, and China—secure attachment was found to be the modal pattern (van Ijzendoorn & Kroonenberg, 1988). What is more, the proportions of children categorized as anxious-avoidant and anxious-resistant varied more in studies carried out within countries than in those that compared children of different countries. One of two studies conducted in Japan, for example, found that 32% of the children were anxiousresistant; the other study found only 19% in this category. Similarly, studies carried out with different populations of children in the United States found very different patterns of attachment. Two conclusions can be drawn from this cross-cultural analysis. First, the strange situation does appear to be a valid way to explore the attachment system in a variety of countries and ethnic populations. Second, the differences that are linked to subcultural or socioeconomic status within a country appear to be greater than the differences among countries, especially when one considers the United States and the Western European countries.

How can we account for these differences in the quality of the attachment system? Attempts to address this question have taken three paths. First, one may ask about the

Box 5.1   Is There a Critical Period for Attachment?

A *critical period* is a time of maximal sensitivity or readiness for the development of certain skills or behavior patterns. The particular skill or behavior pattern is not likely to emerge before the onset of the critical period, and it is extremely difficult, if not impossible, to establish once the critical period has passed. The successful emergence of any behavior that has a critical period for development depends on the coordination of the biological readiness of the organism and environmental supports (Scott, 1987).

The earliest work to suggest a critical period for development was done in the field of embryology. Stockard (1907, 1921) found that when certain chemicals were added to the water where fish eggs were developing, the eggs produced deformed embryos. This effect depended on the timing with which the chemicals were introduced. Exposure of a human embryo to the rubella virus during the first trimester of gestation can cause massive disruption in the formation of body organs. The third month of gestation is a critical period for sexual development. In the presence of the hormone testosterone, the bisexual fetus becomes an anatomical male. In the absence of that hormone, the fetus becomes an anatomical female.

Konrad Lorenz (1935, 1937/1961) was one of the first ethologists to compare the critical periods in physical development and those in behavioral development. Lorenz described a process of social attachment among birds that he called *imprinting*. In this process, the young bird establishes a comparatively permanent bond with its mother. In her absence the young bird will imprint on other available targets, including a model of its mother or a human being. For birds, the onset of the critical period coincides with the time at which they are able to walk. The critical period ends when they begin to fear strangers. After this point, no new model or species can be substituted as a target for imprinting. The long-lasting results of imprinting include not only the maintenance of contact with the mother bird during childhood but the focus of courting and mating behaviors toward other members of the species during the reproductive period.

The question raised with regard to a critical period for attachment is whether there is a specific time during infancy in which the child develops a strong, well-differentiated preference for one person. It is fairly obvious that soon after a child's birth the parent's attachment to the child becomes quite specific—that is, the parent would not be willing to replace his or her own child with any other child of similar age. At what point does the child make this kind of commitment to the parent?

caregiver's ability to serve as a secure base for a child. What does the caregiver bring to the relationship that supports sensitivity and responsiveness? What mental representation of a caring, parental person does the caregiver bring to this role? Adults who recall their own parents as accepting, responsive, and available are more likely to be able to transmit those qualities as they enact the caregiver role. Adults who have experienced early loss or disruption of an attachment relationship themselves have more difficulty providing a secure base for their offspring (Ricks, 1985).

Second, contemporary factors can influence the ability of an adult to provide a secure base for attachment. Among them are the caregiver's self-esteem, the degree of control the caregiver believes he or she should have over the infant's behavior, the quality of the marital relationship both before and after the child is born, the presence of a supportive social network that validates the person's caregiving efforts, and the person's involvement in the labor market (Chase-Lansdale & Owen, 1987; Donovan & Leavitt, 1989; Howes & Markman, 1989). All these factors can influence the caregiver's sensitivity to the infant's signals. *Sensitivity* is generally defined as attentiveness to the

Box 5.1   *(continued)*

Yarrow (1963, 1964, 1970) observed 100 infants who were shifted from foster mothers to adoptive mothers. The infants who were separated from their foster mothers at 6 months or earlier showed minimal distress. They did not tend to express prolonged anger or depression over separation if their physical and emotional needs continued to be met. If one recalls that separation anxiety is not usually observed before about 9 months, it is not surprising that these infants adapted so well to longer separations before this age.

All the infants who were transferred from foster mothers to adoptive mothers at 8 months or older showed strong negative reactions, including angry protest and withdrawal. These infants found the disruption of their earlier relationships very stressful. One cannot, however, infer from these observations that new attachments to the adoptive parents would not eventually form.

We can say that the onset of a critical period for attachment must begin some time after about 6 months of age. This does not mean that the first six months play no role in the establishment of a strong bond between the child and the caregiver. On the contrary, these early months provide the background experiences of consistency, warmth, and familiarity upon which the specific attachment is built.

If the critical period for attachment begins at about 6 months of age, when might this period be over? Yarrow (1964) suggested that the period of sensitivity may end at about 2 years of age:

The most sensitive time may be the period during which the infant is in the process of establishing stable affectional relationships, approximately between six months and two years. A break in relationship with a mother-figure during this period would presumably be most traumatic. [p.122]

The quality of the attachment relationship may be established well before 24 months. Longitudinal studies have reported consistency in the quality of attachment from 12 to 18 months, from 12 to 20 months, and from 12 months to 6 years. Barring prolonged separation, it appears that the mental representation of the attachment is shaped by the end of the first year of life (Main, Kaplan & Cassidy, 1985). The question that remains to be answered is whether there really is a closing-off point—a time after which a secure attachment can no longer be established.

infant's state, accurate interpretation of the infant's signals, and well-timed responses that promote mutually rewarding interactions (Isabella, Belsky & von Eye, 1989).

Third, the quality of the attachment can be influenced by characteristics of the infant. Certain aspects of the infant's temperament, especially fearfulness, sociability, and the intensity of negative emotions, will influence the way the attachment relationship is established. In the strange situation these temperamental characteristics can be identified as children are observed in the exploratory phase, in their response to the stranger, and in the intensity of their distress both when the caregiver leaves and at the point of reunion. Most studies have shown, however, that temperament per se does not determine whether or not a secure attachment can be established. Rather, it influences the kinds of responses that will create for the infant an internal representation of a secure base (Thompson, Connell & Bridges, 1988; Vaughn et al., 1989). Similarity in the quality of attachment among siblings speaks to the importance of stability in the adult's sensitivity and consistency in the adult's internal representation of the caregiver role. These qualities endure across the range of individual differences

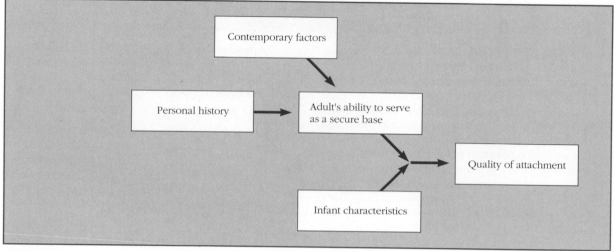

Figure 5.1   Factors That Influence the Quality of Attachment

in infant temperament that are likely to be observed among brothers and sisters (Ward, Vaughn & Robb, 1988).

Figure 5.1 indicates the elements that are considered to be important in the establishment of a secure attachment relationship. They include experiences in the adult's family of origin and early life, experiences in the adult's contemporary situation, and characteristics of the infant.

The Relevance of Attachment for Later Development.

An attachment is more than the expression of behaviors; it is an internal representation of the characteristics of a specific relationship (Main, Kaplan & Cassidy, 1985). This representation provides the infant with a set of rules with which to organize information and interpret experiences related to the attachment relationship. The representation takes shape as a product of the infant's efforts to maintain contact with the caregiver and the caregiver's customary responses to these attempts. A secure attachment is a representation based on the infant's confidence that his or her attempts to make contact with the caregiver will be accepted.

During the period from 12 to 18 months, the quality of infant-mother attachment appears to remain quite stable. Secure attachments in infancy have been associated with positive adaptive capacities when the child is 3½ to 5 years old. Securely attached infants become preschoolers who show greater resilience, self-control, and curiosity (Vaughn et al., 1979).

During childhood the characteristics of the central attachment relationship remain stable unless the caregiver significantly modifies his or her responses. In adolescence and adulthood, however, it is possible to reflect on the nature of these early attachments and reinterpret their meaning. For example, a boy who had viewed his mother

When young people fall in love they show many of the behaviors that characterize the mother–infant attachment system.

as rejecting because she was often unavailable for comfort and contact during his infancy and toddler years might, as an adolescent, realize that his mother was often away because she was working. He might understand that his mother was doing everything she could to provide for her family and that she was really too exhausted to respond to him when she was at home. This insight might modify the nature of the attachment representation and allow the young man to approach new relationships in a more confident, sociable manner.

From a life-span perspective, the quality of the attachment formed in infancy has implications for the formation of later relationships (Ainsworth, 1989). Children who have formed secure attachments are likely to be able to find more enjoyment in close peer friendships during their preschool years (Park & Waters, 1989). It makes sense to think that the cognitive representation one forms of an attachment relationship would influence one's expectations about an intimate partner. Adult love relationships can be characterized along many of the same dimensions as infant attachments, including the desire to maintain physical contact with the loved one, increased disclosure and responsiveness to the loved one, the effectiveness of the loved one in providing comfort and reassurance that reduce distress, and an element of exclusiveness or preferential response in comparison with friends, other relatives, and acquaintances.

The parenting relationship can also be understood as an elaboration of the attachment representation. Adults who have experienced a secure attachment in their own infancy are more likely to be able to supply comfort and responsiveness to their children. Adults whose childhood attachments were unpredictable or even hostile may have more difficulty coping with the intensity of their young infants' needs (Ricks, 1985).

We do not mean to imply that the quality of adult love relationships or parental behavior is determined solely by the quality of childhood attachments. Many experiences and concepts intervene to modify the attachment representation and to expand

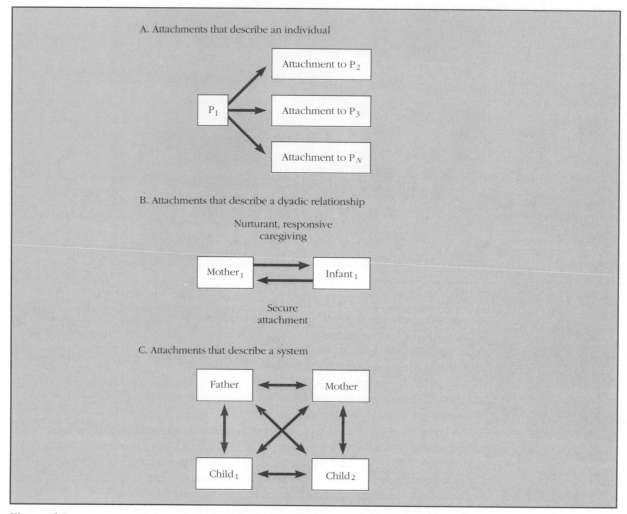

Figure 5.2   Three Levels of Attachment

Source: P. R. Newman and B. M. Newman, "Parenthood and Development," in R. Palkovitz & M. B. Sussman (eds.), *Transitions to Parenthood*, special issue of *Marriage and Family Review, 12,* 316.

one's capacity to love another person after infancy. However, we find that throughout life it makes sense to apply the attachment construct as a way of describing an individual, a dyadic relationship, and an intimate system (see Figure 5.2).

Maturation of Sensory/Perceptual and Motor Functions

The average full-term baby born in the United States weighs 3,300 grams (7 to 7.5 pounds) and is 51 centimeters (20 inches) long. Boys are slightly heavier and longer than girls. At birth, girls' nervous systems and bones are about two weeks more mature than boys'.

Babies vary a great deal in their degree of physical maturity at birth. These differences have clear consequences for their capacity to regulate such survival functions as breathing, digesting, waking, and sleeping. Infants who weigh less than 2,500 grams (about 5 pounds, 8 ounces) are called *low-birth-weight babies*. Low birth weight may be a result of being born before the full period of gestation. It may also result from the mother's inadequate diet, smoking, or use of drugs, and from genetic disorders. These factors tend to lower the fetus's weight for a given gestational age. Babies who are light for their gestational age are at greater *risk*. They are more likely to experience problems at birth and afterward than those who are born prematurely but are of average weight for their gestational age (Cassady & Strange, 1987). Box 5.2 discusses some of what is known about the development of very small babies.

At birth the genetic program that has been carried out during the gestation period provides most newborn infants with intact sensory organs and a well-formed brain. The infant brain contains about 100 billion neurons, or nerve cells, which are already linked in pathways that are designed to perform specific functions. Experience appears to place its own imprint on the finer structure of the brain, however, before the developing brain can attain the full power to process and analyze sensory experience. The basic organization of the brain does not change after birth, but details of its structure seem to demonstrate *plasticity* for some time, particularly in the cerebral cortex (the tissue that forms the folded ridges on the brain's surface). Sights, smells, sounds, tastes, touches, and posture activate and, with time, strengthen specific neural pathways, while others fall into disuse. A childhood imbalance in the use of the two eyes, for example, will cause permanent deficits in the visual perception of the underused eye. It appears that in the neural network of the brain less used pathways may be abandoned, well-used pathways broadened, and new pathways added where they are needed (Aoki & Siekevitz, 1988).

During the first months of life the sensory/perceptual system—vision, hearing, taste, smell, touch, motion sensitivity, and responsiveness to internal cues (proprioception)—is developing rapidly and appears to function at a more advanced level than the motor system. Since voluntary muscle movements are not yet under the infant's control in the early days and months of life, researchers have had to apply considerable ingenuity to study infants' sensory/perceptual competences. Current work uses behaviors such as gazing time, changes in heart rate, sucking, facial action, and head turning as indicators of infants' responses. Infants appear to be quite sensitive to internal and environmental stimuli rather early. In the first months of life, genetic programs and experience combine to construct neural networks, and before very long, sensations appear to be organized and represented as meaningful perceptions in the infant's brain. One thing is becoming increasingly clear: an infant's sensory/perceptual capabilities provide the basis for establishing effective interactive relationships with caregivers.

Infants respond to a variety of visual dimensions, including movement, color, brightness, complexity, light/dark contrast, contours, depth, and distance (Hickey & Peduzzi, 1987; Banks & Dannemiller, 1987). Four-month old infants respond to wavelengths of light as though they perceive distinct hues of blue, green, yellow, and red

Box 5.2   Very Small Babies

In our culture we count our age from the date of our birth. But today many babies are born before they are fully developed. Modern technology has pushed back the limits of fetal viability to about 24 weeks of gestational age, or a weight of about 500 grams (slightly over one pound). These tiny babies, not much bigger than the palm of your hand, go through weeks of round-the-clock care in a struggle to survive. About 17,000 infants who weigh less than two pounds are cared for in the nation's intensive care nurseries. These babies have about a 70% chance of survival; the smallest babies have only a 20% chance (Kantrowitz, 1988).

What do we know about the developmental progress of these very small babies? What is the quality of their relationship with their parents, modified by their prolonged hospitalization and their obvious vulnerability and risk? How do parents cope with the anxieties and frustrations of caring for their very tiny baby? What is the outcome with respect to the child's cognitive capacities and later intellectual development? Because this is really a very new population, a group that has survived in appreciable numbers only in recent decades, many of these questions are still being addressed. But we are beginning to have a picture of the psychosocial development of very small babies.

When we think about the formation of an attachment between a parent and an infant, we have to realize that very-low-birth-weight preterm babies are clearly different from full-term babies. They are less physically attractive; they have higher-pitched, unpleasant cries; they are more easily overstimulated and more difficult to soothe; and they are less able to establish rhythmic patterns of social interaction. What is more, the early weeks and months of parental contact with these babies takes place in the intimidating environment of the hospital, where the babies are usually hooked up to monitors, have one or more tubes in their bodies, and are going through periodic physical crises in the struggle for survival. In this situation it's a wonder that any kind of attachment relationship can develop at all.

But with opportunities to interact with and care for their very small babies during the hospital stay, an almost irresistible tendency to become absorbed in their child appears to unfold in the parents of these very small babies, just as it does in parents of full-term babies. The process of attachment, however, appears to face greater challenges. Parents find that it is harder to synchronize their parenting activities with the activities of their babies. They perceive their babies as difficult, and find that they receive few cues of satisfaction or responsiveness from them. In other words, the establishment of a sense of reciprocity between parent and infant is more difficult to establish in the early months of life (Levy-Shiff et al., 1989). Nonetheless, in assessments of the quality of attachment at age 2, very-low-birth-weight babies and full-term babies did not differ in the quality of their attachments with their mothers or their fathers (Easterbrooks, 1989). Preterm infants were just as likely to form secure attachments with both their mothers and their fathers as were full-

(Bornstein, Kessen & Weiskopf, 1976; Teller & Bornstein, 1987). Infants one to two days old are able to discriminate and imitate the happy, sad, and surprised expressions of a live model (Field et al., 1982). Some two-day-old infants discriminate between the mother's face and the face of a stranger (Field et al., 1984). By 3 months, almost all infants distinguish a parent's face from that of a stranger (Zucker, 1985). Infants in the first few months are able to discriminate specific facial features. Sometime between 4 and 7 months, infants are able to classify some expressions. For example, they are able to look at an expression posed by a variety of people of both sexes and maintain recognition of that expression (Caron et al., 1982; Nelson, 1987; Nelson & Dolgin, 1985).

There is evidence that human infants are sensitive and responsive to auditory stimuli in utero (De Casper and Spence, 1986). Newborns can distinguish their moth-

Box 5.2 *(continued)*

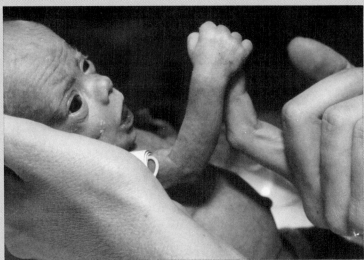

term babies. Depending on the health and robustness of the infants, and with the appropriate parental support, parents and low-birth-weight babies are able to establish a framework of secure, trusting interactions by the end of the child's infancy.

Extreme low-birth-weight infants appear to be at risk for problems in subsequent cognitive development. Infants who are born weighing less than 1500 grams are likely to suffer serious brain hemorrhages. In addition, their undeveloped lungs cannot deliver an adequate supply of oxygen to the brain. Severe respiratory distress experienced during the early months of life is associated with cognitive deficits that can be observed in the first year of life, and with learning and language deficits during the preschool years (Rose et al., 1988; Field, Dempsey & Shuman, 1983). Those at greatest risk for cognitive delays are the babies born before 30 weeks to parents who have very limited educational and financial resources.

er's voice from another female voice (De Casper & Fifer, 1980). Young infants can distinguish changes in loudness, pitch, duration, and location of sounds (Kuhl, 1987). One of the earliest stimuli to evoke a smile is the sound of the human voice. Infants appear to be capable of making most basic sound distinctions used in human speech throughout the world. Sound sensitivity becomes more focused as infants become more reliant on language-specific sounds, indicating a reorganization of sensory capabilities as the child learns to listen to people speaking a particular language (Werker, 1989). Here we see a possible example of the fine-tuning of a neural network as a result of experience.

There is evidence that the sense of taste is at least partially functional in utero (Mistretta & Bradley, 1977). Newborns can differentiate sweet, sour, bitter, and salty tastes. Two hours after birth, an infant's facial responses to a sweet taste (sucrose) are

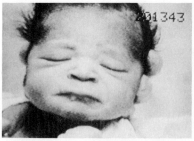
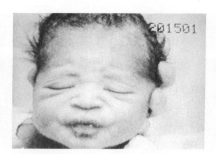
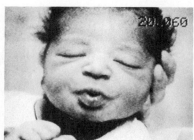

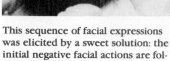
This sequence of facial expressions was elicited by a sweet solution: the initial negative facial actions are followed by relaxation and sucking.

characterized primarily by relaxation and sucking. Facial responses to salty, sour, and bitter solutions share the same hedonically negative upper- and mid-face responses but differ in the accompanying lower-face actions: the lips purse in response to a sour taste, the mouth gapes in response to a bitter taste, and no distinctive lower facial reaction is seen in response to a salty taste. Adults seem to be able to identify the infant's response to sweet tastes (Rosenstein & Oster, 1988).

Breast-fed infants are particularly sensitive to their mothers' body odors (Cernoch & Porter, 1985). One study found that seven-day-old babies could use the sense of smell to distinguish their own mothers' nursing pads from those of other mothers (MacFarlane, 1975). The mother's odor may play an important role in stimulating early mother-infant interactions (Porter, Balogh & Makin, 1988).

Infants respond to and process much of the sensory stimulation that confronts them. They are not adrift in a buzz of sensory confusion. It appears that from birth sensory/perceptual capacities are vital resources that help infants to establish affective links with their caregivers.

At birth an infant's voluntary muscle responses are poorly coordinated. Motor responses include several behaviors that appear to be reflexive. This means that a specific stimulus will evoke a particular motor response without any voluntary control or direction. Many of these built-in responses help infants survive and lead them on the road to developing more necessary, more complicated sequences of voluntary behavior. The sucking reflex is a good example of this. At birth, inserting something in an infant's mouth produces a sucking reflex. This helps infants gain nourishment relatively easily before sucking behavior is under their control. Before very long, infants become very skillful at controlling the strength and sensitivity of sucking behavior. They become rather accomplished at exploring their hands and other objects with their mouths as well as efficiently ingesting nourishment. In Table 3.1 in Chapter 3 you saw several common infant reflexes, the evoking stimulus, and the response. Infant reflexes include sucking, grasping, rooting (turning the head in the direction of the cheek that is stroked), coughing, and stepping. With time, many of these behaviors make a transition from an involuntary to a voluntary behavior. In the process, infants first gain control over simple movements. Then they blend several of these new voluntary movements into increasingly coordinated and complex patterns of behavior (Fentress & McLeod, 1986). For example, very young infants can support their full weight through the strength of their grasping reflex. When propped in an infant seat, they will reach and grasp reflexively at an object—and reach their target about 40% of the time. At 4 weeks of age this reflexive reaching behavior seems to disappear, but by 5 months it is replaced by voluntary reaching, accurate grasping, clutching, and letting go (Bower, 1987).

The transition from involuntary to voluntary reaching and grasping appears to result from a process of repeated discovery, exploration, and practice of controlled, coordinated muscle movements. Here a 2½-month-old girl learns that she can voluntarily control her hands and fingers.

> *She has discovered her hands, stares at them many times a day for three or four minutes at a time, watches them as she wiggles fingers, extends and flexes them, rotates wrists. She also clasps her hands together and stares at them out in front of her at arm's length.* [Church, 1966, p. 7]

Motor skills also develop as a result of physical growth, maturation of bones and muscles, and maturation of the nervous system. Figure 5.3 shows the normal sequence of development of motor and movement skills during the first year of life. Babies vary in the sequence and rate at which they acquire these skills. Usually, however, during the first 12 months babies begin to hold their heads up and to roll over by themselves; they learn to reach for things and grasp them; they sit, crawl, stand, and walk. Each of these accomplishments requires practice, refinement, struggle, and, finally, mastery.

Consider Brad's efforts to crawl. He is placed face down in the middle of a gaily colored blanket. His mother kneels at the edge of the blanket and dangles a favorite stuffed bear. She smiles and says encouragingly, "Come on, Brad, come get Teddy." Brad looks intently, reaches toward the bear, and, by kicking and squirming, manages to move forward. This snakelike movement is Brad's first accomplishment en route to well-organized crawling. Before he masters crawling, however, he must learn to raise himself on his knees, coordinate hand and leg movements, and propel himself forward rather than backward. Thus the crawling behavior that tends to be regarded as natural and easily performed in infancy is in fact achieved by long and patient effort.

The achievement of competence in each of the sensory/perceptual and motor tasks depends on a child's maturational level and environmental conditions, and on the strength of the child's desire for mastery. Each advance in motor coordination brings an infant into a new type of contact with the environment. Increases in motor control permit children to experience more varied stimulation, explore objects more deliberately, and voluntarily pursue their goals.

Infants advance socially, intellectually, and emotionally as they achieve sensory/perceptual and motor skills. Such accomplishments allow infants to gain access to and awareness of their surroundings. They also help bring important aspects of the environment under control. Changes in the process of social attachment, for example, reflect changes in sensory/perceptual and motor skills. The achievements of creeping, crawling, and walking allow children to increase their control over making and maintaining contact with caregivers, thereby enhancing their feelings of effectiveness, security, and well-being.

Box 5.3   Temperament

In a child's temperament we can see how genetic determinants of individuality can influence the process of adaptation to the family group. *Temperament* is a theoretical construct that refers to relatively stable characteristics of response to the environment that can be observed during the first months of life (Thomas & Chess, 1980; Hubert et al., 1982; Lerner & Lerner, 1983). There is considerable evidence that some aspects of temperament, including activity level, sociability, and emotionality, are heavily influenced by a person's genetic makeup (Thomas & Chess, 1977, 1986; Buss & Plomin, 1984, 1986; Goldsmith et al., 1987; Goldsmith & Campos, 1986; Wilson & Matheney, 1986).

A child's temperament has consequences for the tone of interactions, the frequency with which interactions take place, the way others react to the child, and the way the child reacts to the reactions of others. Highly active, social children are likely to initiate interactions and to respond positively to the attentions of others. More passive, introverted children will be less likely to initiate interactions and may withdraw when other children or adults direct attention to them. Here we can see that a single home environment may not actually be the same for two temperamentally distinct children. These two children have the potential to call forth different patterns of response from parents, siblings, and other caregivers.

The fit between the parents' temperaments and the child's temperament plays an important part in the quality of the parent-child relationship (Plomin, 1990). An active, socially responsive parent may feel some disappointment with a baby who does not respond eagerly to social interaction. The home environment, including the quality of parent-child interactions and the resources that are made available to children, is to a degree the product of certain inherited characteristics of parents and children. An adult's warmth, sociability, intelligence, and activity level, which are genetically guided, will be expressed in parenting behaviors. Similarly, infants' characteristics, such as physical appearance, sensitivity to stimulation, sociability, and intelligence, which are genetically guided, will call forth certain parental responses and shape the direction of parenting. One can expect that siblings in the same family will experience some important differences in parenting, not only because of the commonly recognized factor of sibling order but because of each child's own genetically guided individuality.

Sensorimotor Intelligence and Primitive Causality

How do infants organize their experiences? Jean Piaget (1970) suggested that the primary mechanism underlying the growth of intelligence during infancy is a process of sensorimotor adaptation. In this process infants actively engage the environment. They alter their instinctive responses to take into account the unique properties of objects around them and at the same time they use those instinctive responses to explore their world. Infants do not make use of the conventional symbolic system of language to organize experience. Rather, they form concepts through perception and direct investigation of the environment. The notion of sensorimotor intelligence, then, encompasses the elaboration of patterns of movement and sensory experiences that the child comes to recognize in association with specific environmental events.

Think for a moment of a familiar experience such as tying a shoelace. The pattern of tying the shoelace unfolds with little, if any, language involved. In fact, the task of explaining to a young child how to tie a shoelace is particularly difficult because very few words or concepts are part of the process. This kind of motor routine is an instance of sensorimotor intelligence at the adult level. When infants begin to adapt their sucking reflex to make it more effective, or when they use different techniques of

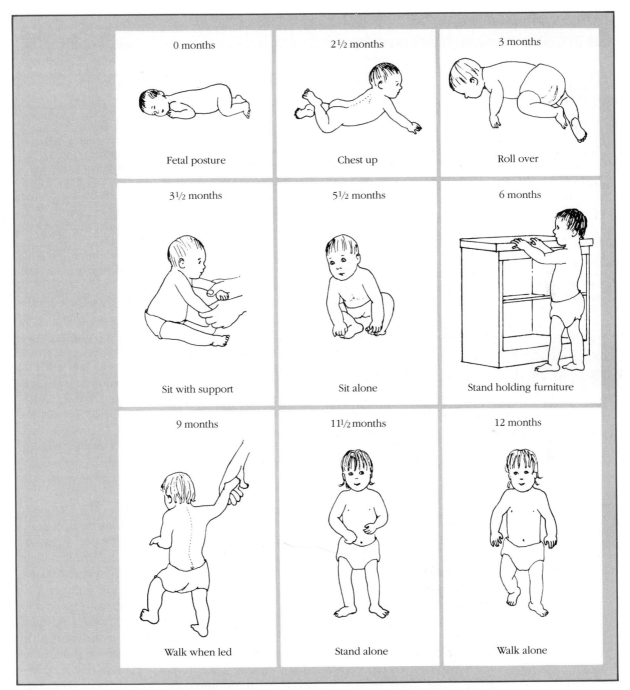

Figure 5.3

Sequence of Motor Development and Locomotion in Infants
Note: The age at which 50% of babies mastered each skill is indicated. These norms were established in the 1960s by means of the Denver Developmental Screening Test.
Source: Adapted from W. K. Frankenberg and J. B. Dodds, "The Denver Developmental Screening Test," *Journal of Pediatrics, 71* (1967), 181–191.

Period	Approximate Age	Characteristic
Table 5.3 Six Phases in the Development of Sensorimotor Causality		
1. Reflexes	From birth	Reflexive responses to specific stimuli
2. First habits	From 2nd week	Use of reflexive responses to explore new stimuli
3. Circular reactions	From 4th month	Use of familiar actions to achieve familiar results
4. Coordination of means and ends	From 8th month	Deliberate use of actions to achieve new goals
5. Experimentation with new means	From 11th month	Modification of actions to reach goals
6. Insight	From 18 months	Mental recombination of means and ends

Source: Adapted from J. Piaget and B. Inhelder, *The Psychology of the Child* (New York: Basic Books, 1969).

sucking for the breast and the bottle, they are demonstrating sensorimotor intelligence. The familiar scheme for sucking is modified so that it takes into account the special properties of the breast and the bottle.

One of the most important components of sensorimotor intelligence is the capacity to anticipate that certain actions will have specific effects on objects in the environment. In other words, infants develop an understanding of *causality* based solely on sensory and motor experience. Babies discover that if they cry, Mama will come to them; if they kick a chair, it will move; and if they let go of a spoon, it will fall to the floor. These predictable sequences are learned through repetition and experimentation. The predictability of the events depends on the consistency with which objects in the world respond as well as on the child's initiation of the action. Babies learn to associate specific actions with regularly occurring outcomes. They also experiment with their own actions to determine the variety of events that a single behavior may cause (Keil, 1975; Rovee & Rovee, 1969). Eventually they are able to work backward: they can select a desirable outcome and then perform the behavior that will produce it.

In an intriguing analysis, researchers made videotapes of infants over a six-month period to document the emergence of the use of a spoon as a tool for eating (Connolly & Dalgleish, 1989). At first actions involving the spoon appeared to focus on exploration of the spoon itself: the infants banged the spoon, sucked it, or rubbed it in their hair. Then the babies showed an understanding of the purpose of the spoon as a tool by repeating the action sequence of dipping the spoon in the dish and bringing it to the mouth. However, no food was on the spoon. In the third phase, babies began to incorporate the function and the action by loading the spoon with food and then bringing it to the mouth. During this phase, they made so many errors that very little food actually got to the mouth via the spoon. Finally, babies were able to coordinate the action and the function by using the other hand to steady the bowl, altering the angle of the spoon, picking up food they had dropped, and devising other strategies to enhance the function, depending on the type of food involved. Here we see a demonstration of how one rather complex motor behavior becomes part of a problem-solving action sequence during the sensorimotor period of development.

The achievement of complex, purposeful causal behaviors develops gradually during the first two years of life. This achievement requires that infants have an understanding of the properties of objects in their environment. They must also have a variety of strategies for manipulating objects. Finally, they must be able to select the most effective strategies for coordinating actions to achieve specific goals. One does not use the same behaviors to reach a ball that has rolled under the couch that one uses to tape a new drawing on the wall.

Six Phases in the Development
of Causal Schemes

Piaget and Inhelder (1966/1969) described the development of causal schemes in six phases (see Table 5.3) Subsequent research and related theoretical revisions confirm these levels of cognitive development (Fischer & Silvern, 1985). In the first phase, *reflexes*, cause and effect are linked through the involuntary reflexive responses. Babies suck, grasp, and root in response to specific types of stimulation. These built-in responses are the genetic origins of intelligence.

In the second phase, *first habits*, the reflexive responses are used to explore a wider range of stimuli. Babies explore toys, fingers, parents' noses, and blankets by sucking on them. Gradually they discover the unique properties of objects and modify their responses according to the demands of those objects. The fact that a baby can satisfy his or her own need to suck by bringing an object to the mouth is a very early form of purposive causal behavior.

The third and fourth phases involve coordination of means and ends, at first with familiar situations and then with new ones. In the third phase, *circular reactions*, babies connect an action with an expected outcome. They shake a rattle and expect to hear a noise; they drop a spoon and expect to hear a crash; they pull Daddy's beard and expect to hear an "ouch." They do not yet understand why the specific action leads to the expected outcome, but they will signal surprise when the expected outcomes does not follow.

In the fourth phase, *coordination of means and ends*, infants use familiar actions or means to achieve new outcomes. They may shake a rattle to startle Mommy or pull Daddy's beard to force him to look away from the television set. The means and the outcomes have become quite distinct. There can be no question about the purposiveness of behavior at this point.

The fifth phase, *experimentation with new means*, begins with experimentation with familiar means to achieve new goals. When familiar strategies do not work, children will modify them in light of the situation. One can think of this stage as one of sensorimotor problem solving. Children will try to reach a drawer by standing on a box, to fix a broken toy with a string, or to make a gift by wrapping a toy in a piece of tissue.

The last phase in the development of sensorimotor causality, *insight*, involves mental manipulations of means-end relationships. Children carry out trial-and-error problem-solving activities and planning in their minds. Instead of actually going through a variety of physical manipulations, they anticipate the outcomes of some actions in their minds. They can sort out possible solutions and reject some without having to

Pablo Picasso, *Paloma Playing*, 1950.
In the fourth phase of developing a scheme for causality, infants use familiar actions to achieve new outcomes. Here Paloma combines reaching and crawling to grab hold of her toy car.

try them out. The result is insight. Mental experimentation brings the child to the best solution, which is the only one necessary to enact.

The capacity to perceive oneself as a causal agent and to predict the outcome of one's actions is essential to all subsequent experiences of mastery. This capacity is the cornerstone of the development of a sense of competence. It involves investigation of the environment, directed problem solving, and persistence toward a goal (Yarrow et al., 1983; MacTurk et al., 1987). The adults' abilities to formulate a plan, execute it, and evaluate its outcome depend on this skill.

Understanding the Nature of Objects and Creating Categories

When infants are given freedom to explore, they show a remarkable propensity for such behavior. From birth they try to make direct, sensory contact with objects in their environment. They reach for, grasp, and mouth objects. They track objects visually and alter their gaze to maintain visual contact with them. Rather than being passive spectators, babies are active explorers of their environment (Rochat, 1989). As products of this active engagement with the object world, two related but independent aspects of infant intelligence develop, an understanding of the nature of objects and the ability to categorize similar objects.

The Nature of Objects

Through repeated manipulation and experimentation, infants establish that objects have basic properties. Objects have boundaries, size, weight, color, malleability, texture, the capacity to contain something else or not, and the capacity to occupy space. All of these properties can influence the types of actions infants use to explore the object and the ways the objects are eventually woven into other actions or causal schemes (Sera, Troyer & Smith, 1988; MacLean & Schuler, 1989; Palmer, 1989; Spelke, von Hofsten & Kestenbaum, 1989).

One of the most carefully documented of these properties is *object permanence* (Wellman, Cross & Bartsch, 1986). During the ninth or tenth month of life, infants develop the concept that objects in the environment are permanent and do not cease to exist when they are out of reach or view. This notion is elaborated by Piaget (1970) in a description of sensorimotor intelligence.

Initially the infant is aware of only those objects that are in the immediate perceptual field. If a 6-month-old girl is playing with a rattle, it exists for her. If the rattle drops out of her hand or is taken away, she may show some immediate distress, but she will not pursue the object. In a very real sense, out of sight is out of mind. Progress in developing the concept of object permanence can be traced through a child's reactions when objects are removed from the perceptual field or displaced from one location to another (Harris, 1975; Bertenthal & Fischer, 1983; Sophian & Yengo, 1985). Babies as young as 9 months can understand that an object has been moved from one location to another. However, even 2-year-olds can get confused if the object is displaced more than two or three times.

As an experiment, we can remove a rattle from a baby's grasp and hide it under a cushion. If the baby makes no effort to pursue the rattle, we can assume that he or she has no sense of its continued existence. If the baby pursues the rattle and looks for it under the cushion, we take our experiment one step further. Again we take the rattle from the baby and place it under the cushion. Then we remove it from beneath that cushion and place it under a second one. This transition from cushion 1 to cushion 2 takes place in the child's full view. The normal adult would go directly to the second cushion and retrieve the rattle. The child who has developed a sense of object permanence will also do this. Some children, however, will look for the rattle beneath the first cushion and, not finding it, cease their search. Slightly older children will trace the movement of the rattle exactly by looking first under cushion 1 and then under cushion 2. The last two groups of children have learned some of the steps in pursuing an object but have not yet attained the concept of object permanence.

As a final test of the child's certainty about object permanence, we can once again transfer the rattle from cushion 1 to cushion 2 in the child's view and then stealthily hide it in a third place. The child who has attained the concept of object permanence will look beneath cushion 2 and, failing to find the beloved rattle, continue to search, fully convinced that it is somewhere. The child who earlier followed the path of the rattle from cushion 1 to cushion 2 will do the same thing this time. Not finding the rattle beneath cushion 2, this child will cease searching.

The concept of object permanence can be easily understood by anyone who has observed the excitement and delight of a young boy engaged in a game of peek-a-boo. When he covers his eyes, what he has been looking at no longer exists. When he uncovers his eyes, he is thrilled and somewhat surprised to see the object again. The game is most fun for those children who have not developed the concept of object permanence, as the object's reappearance is not totally predictable.

Certain experiences appear to help build the scheme for object permanence. Babies who are adept at crawling or who have mobility through the use of an infant walker seem to be more effective in their search strategies when objects are hidden from view (Benson & Uzgiris, 1985; Kermoian & Campos, 1988). As babies gain greater control over their movement through the environment, they are better able to use landmarks other than their own body to locate objects. They can also experiment with the notion of leaving and retrieving objects, and discovering familiar objects in novel locations.

Even at very early ages, before infants can search for and retrieve objects, they appear to have a memory of the locations of objects and can anticipate that objects take up space (Baillargeon, 1987; Baillargeon & Graber, 1988). If babies of 8 or 9 months are permitted to search for an object immediately after it is hidden, they are very effective in finding it. However, if they have to wait for 5 or 10 seconds before they can search, or if the object has been moved from one container to a very similar container, they may become confused. By the age of about 17 months, infants can solve even the most complex object permanence tasks in which objects are moved from one hiding place to the next in such a way that the infant cannot follow the path of the object (Uzgiris & Hunt, 1975; Gopnik & Meltzoff, 1987).

The attainment of the concept of the permanent object frees children from total reliance on what they can see. The ability to hold the image of an object in the mind is the first step in the emergence of complex representational thinking (Ramsay & Campos, 1978).

We can also appreciate the interrelatedness of object permanence and the process of social attachment. One reason why babies experience separation anxiety is that they do not have the certainty that a person to whom they are attached will continue to exist when that person is out of sight or inaccessible. The scheme for the permanent object is applied to both humans and inanimate objects. Once the infant has a clear understanding of object permanence, the fear that a loved caregiver may vanish when he or she leaves the house is reduced. Interestingly, some qualities of maternal care are associated with the emergence of object permanence during the first seven months of life. The babies of mothers who communicate with them frequently, who express positive feelings toward them, and who actively stimulate their achievements are more likely to apply the scheme of permanence to people as well as things (Chazen, 1981). The growth of social attachment and the achievement of object permanence may thus be mutually enhancing.

Babies react differently to people and to inanimate objects. It appears that the button and not the other child has captured this baby's attention.

The Categorization of Objects

Objects have not only properties but functions. As infants explore and experiment with objects, they begin to devise schemes for grouping objects together. They modify these schemes to add new items to the category and to differentiate one category from another. Categories can consist of the physical properties of objects, such as "smooth" and "rough"; they can consist of the functions of objects, as in "something to sit on" and "something to dig with."

We have known for some time that infants were capable of forming categories at a visual level. Early work on preference for "faceness" in a visual presentation suggested that very young infants were able to see regularity in certain stimuli, and to differentiate those stimuli from others that may be just as complex but have no resemblance to a face. Recent studies find that infants 3 to 5 months old can differentiate abstract stimuli, such as patterns of dots, and detect those that fit the category from those that do not (Hayne, Rovee-Collier & Perris, 1987; Younger & Gotlieb, 1988). One may wonder, however, whether these observations reflect more of a capacity for visual memory than a capacity to create an internal representation of a kind of object or event.

By 18 months of age, children can perform what are considered more typical categorization tasks. They can, for example, sort eight objects, such as four brightly colored yellow rectangles and four human-shaped plastic figures, into two distinct groups (Gopnik & Meltzoff, 1987). This kind of sorting does not require the ability to give names to the objects. However, shortly after children demonstrate the capacity to manage two-group sorting, they often show a rapid acceleration in the acquisition of names for objects. Thus categorizing and naming appear to be closely linked. By the close of the second year of life, babies know that objects have certain stable properties, that some objects "belong" with others, and that objects have names. With these achievements, infants impose a new degree of order and predictability on their daily experiences.

Emotional Development

Emotions provide an organizing framework for the communication system during infancy (Campos & Barrett, 1984). An infant has the capacity to produce a range of emotional expressions, including fear, distress, disgust, surprise, excitement, interest, joy, anger, and sadness, although they are not fully developed. Parents and other caregivers rely on the facial, vocal, and behavioral cues related to these emotions as ways of determining an infant's inner states and goals (Malatesta & Izard, 1984). In cycles of interaction, responsive caregivers monitor changes in a baby's affect as a way of determining whether their interventions are effective. When interactions go astray and an adult cannot understand what a baby needs, the adult tries to repair or revise the communication (Tronick, 1989).

Think of a 6-month-old baby who wants a toy that is out of reach. The baby waves her arms in the direction of the toy, makes fussy noises, and looks distressed. As the father tries to figure out what the baby wants, he watches the baby's expressions in order to discover whether he is on the right track. Parents who are attuned to this form of communication are more likely to help babies achieve their goals, and babies are more likely to persist in attempts to communicate because they have experienced success in such interactions.

Babies can also detect and differentiate the affective expressions of others. Very young infants can differentiate facial expressions of fear, anger, happiness, sadness, and surprise (Walker-Andrews, 1986; Hornik, Risenhoover & Gunnar, 1987; Caron, Caron & MacLean, 1988; Ludemann & Nelson, 1988). They tend to use visual and auditory information to make these distinctions.

Under certain circumstances, infants make use of the emotional responses of another person to guide their own behavior. Infants often use their mothers as a *social reference*, but other adults can serve this function as well (Klinnert et al., 1986; Hornik & Gunnar, 1988; Walden & Ogan, 1988). As infants approach an unfamiliar adult or an ambiguous situation, they look to their mother and use her facial and/or verbal expressions as a source of information about the situation. If the mother expresses wariness or a negative emotion, the infant is more likely to withdraw or to explore with caution. If the mother expresses a positive emotion, the infant is more likely to approach the situation or the unfamiliar person with confidence.

The domain of emotions is a two-way channel through which infants and their caregivers can establish *intersubjectivity*. From the very earliest months, infants interact differently with people than they do with objects (Brazelton, Koslowski & Main,

Expressions of pleasure and joy establish powerful communication between this mother and her baby.

1974; Trevarthen, 1989). Babies and caregivers are able to engage in reciprocal, rhythmic interactions, to appreciate state changes in one another, and to modify their actions in order to take into account information being sent by the other. Through a shared repertoire of emotions, babies and their caregivers are able to understand one another and to create shared meanings. Thus emotional expression becomes a building block of trust.

Emotional development during infancy can be understood along three dimensions. First, new emotions emerge and emotions are differentiated along dimensions of intensity. Second, with cognitive maturation, a child interprets events differently. New emotions may be attached to familiar situations. An experience that may once have been cause for wariness, such as a new toy or a loud noise, becomes a source of excitement or joy as the child gains mastery over the situation. Third, children develop strategies for regulating their emotions so that they are not overwhelmed by emotional intensity.

Emotional Differentiation

Emotions gradually become differentiated during the first two years of life. Peter Wolff (1966) described seven states of arousal in newborn infants. Each is characterized by a distinctive pattern of respiration, muscle tone, motor activity, and alertness (see Table 5.4). In these states we see the earliest differentiation among distress (crying), interest (alert inactivity), and excitement (waking activity). The earliest smiles are found during rapid eye movement (irregular sleep). A newborn's state of arousal will influence his or her capacity to respond to the environment. Changes in state also serve to cue responses from caregivers. Crying usually brings some effort to comfort

Table 5.4 States of Arousal in Newborns	
Regular sleep (RS)	Full rest; low muscle tonus; low motor activity; eyelids firmly closed and still; even, regular respiratory rhythm, about 36 breaths per minute.
Irregular sleep (IS)	Slightly greater muscle tonus; gentle motor activity; frequent facial grimaces and smiles; occasional rapid eye movement; irregular respiration, about 48 breaths per minute.
Periodic sleep (PS)	Intermediate between RS and IS; bursts of rapid, shallow breathing alternate with bursts of deep, slow breathing.
Drowsiness (D)	More active than RS but less active than IS or PS; eyes open and close; eyes, when open, are dull and glazed and may roll upward; respiration variable but of higher frequency than during RS.
Alert inactivity (AI)	Slight activity; face relaxed; eyes open and "bright"; respiration constant and more rapid than in RS.
Waking activity (WA)	Frequent, diffuse motor activity; vocalizations; skin flushed when active; irregular respiration.
Crying (C)	Vigorous, diffuse motor activity; facial grimaces; skin red; eyes open or partially closed; crying vocalization.

Source: Adapted from P. H. Wolff, "Causes, Controls, and Organization of Behavior in the Neonate," *Psychological Issues,* 5 (1, whole no. 17) (1966).

or soothe. Visual alertness is likely to prompt social interactions. Parents try to interact with their infants, achieve eye contact, and initiate nonverbal exchanges during the alert phases (Tronick, Als & Brazelton, 1979).

The differentiation of emotions follows a regular pattern, as Table 5.5 suggests. This table describes age-related changes on three dimensions of emotion: pleasure-joy, wariness-fear, and rage-anger. Emotional responses during the first month are closely tied to the internal state of an infant. Physical discomfort, arousal, pain, and changing tension in the central nervous system are the major sources of emotions. During the period from 1 to 6 months, emotions begin to be tied more to a separation of self and environment. Babies smile at familiar faces. They show interest in and curiosity about novel stimuli. They show rage when nursing is disrupted or when they are prevented from viewing an activity that they have been intently watching.

The period from 6 to 12 months reflects a greater awareness of the context of events. Emotions of joy, anger, and fear are tied to a baby's ability to recall previous experiences and to compare them with an ongoing event. These emotions also reflect a baby's ability to exercise some control over the environment and frustration when goals are blocked.

Emotions that are observed during the second year of life—especially anxiety, pride, defiance, and shame—suggest an emerging sense of self. Infants recognize that they can operate as causal agents. They also begin to respond to the emotions of others. They can give love to others through hugs, kisses, and tender pats. They can share toys, comfort another distressed infant, and imitate another person's excitement. In becoming a more distinct being, an infant achieves a new level of awareness of the capacity to give and receive pleasure as well as of the vulnerability of self and others.

Emotional Interpretation

Observations of the facial expressions of emotions provide a key to the meaning of significant events. In one study, when babies were videotaped after an inoculation at

Table 5.5 Ontogenesis of Some Basic Human Emotions

Month	Pleasure-Joy	Wariness-Fear	Rage-Anger
0–3	Endogenous smile; turning toward	Startle/pain; obligatory attention	Distress due to covering the face, physical restraint, extreme discomfort
3	Pleasure		Rage (disappointment)
4–5	Delight; active laughter	Wariness	
7	Joy		Anger
9		Fear (stranger aversion)	
12	Elation	Anxiety; immediate fear	Angry mood, petulance
18	Positive valuation of self	Shame	Defiance
24	Affection		Intentional hurting
36	Pride, love		Guilt

Note: The age specified is neither the first appearance of the affect in question nor its peak occurrence; it is the age at which the literature suggests the reaction is common.

Source: L. A. Sroufe, "Socioemotional Development," in J. D. Osofsky (ed.), *Handbook of Infant Development,* pp. 462–516 (New York: Wiley, 1979). Copyright © 1979 John Wiley & Sons, Inc. Reprinted by permission of John Wiley & Sons, Inc.

2 and 4 months of age, their emotional reactions included closed-eye expressions of physical distress and anger. However, when they were filmed at 19 months, their expressions involved more open-eyed anger, suggesting greater awareness of the source of their discomfort (Izard et al., 1983).

Emotional expression following brief separation from the mother gives another clue to the development of attachment as well as to the quality of attachment in mother-infant pairs (Hyson & Izard, 1985). Table 5.6 shows the number of children who used specific emotional expressions during separation from their mothers at 13 and 18 months of age. Interest, anger, and sadness, as well as blends of these emotions, could all be observed in the babies being studied.

Some emotions were highly stable from one age to the next. Infants who reacted to separation with expressions of interest at 13 months were likely to show the same emotion at 18 months. Infants who reacted with anger at 13 months were also likely to show anger at 18 months. Expressions of sadness, however, did not show continuity. Over time there was an increase in the expression of sadness, either alone or blended with other emotions. This change suggests that many babies give a new level of meaning to the separation experience during the second year of life—a meaning that reflects greater capacity to separate self and other, and therefore a more complex appreciation of loss.

Emotional Regulation

Infants develop strategies for coping with intense emotions, both positive and negative. Most of the research in this area has focused on the ways children deal with distress (Dodge, 1989). Even newborns have some strategies for reducing the intensity of distress, such as turning the head away, sucking on the hands, or closing the eyes. As infants gain new motor coordination and control, they can move away, distract themselves with other objects, or soothe themselves by rocking, stroking themselves, or thumb-sucking (Kopp, 1989).

Box 5.4   What Is in a Smile?

The infant's smile is a social treasure. Parents and grandparents may go to great lengths to bring out this sweet expression. Yet researchers have discovered that an infant's smile can have a wide variety of meanings and can be produced in response to many stimuli.

The very earliest smiles, observed during the first month of life, may occur spontaneously during sleep or in response to a high-pitched human voice. Gentle tactile stimulation—touching, tickling, and rocking—can produce these early smiles. A baby's first smiles are not a true form of social communication, although they are likely to produce positive feelings in the adult caregiver (Wolff, 1963, 1987).

Social smiles begin to be observed at about 5 weeks of age. These smiles are first produced in response to a wide range of stimuli—familiar faces and voices (especially the mother's), strangers, and nonhuman objects. After about 20 weeks the smiling response becomes differentiated. Infants continue to smile broadly and frequently at familiar people and objects, but they no longer smile readily at strangers or unfamiliar objects. The social smile conveys both a recognition of familiarity and an invitation to further communication or interaction (Ambrose, 1963; Sroufe et al., 1984).

The cognitive smile seems to develop alongside the social smile. Infants smile in response to their own behaviors, as if they were expressing satisfaction with their accomplishments (Papousek & Bernstein, 1969; Watson, 1970). At 3 months babies smile in response to events that are moderately familiar, as if expressing pleasure in understanding the situation (Kagan, 1984). Infants smile elaborately when they are able to make something happen, as when they wiggle a mobile or hear a bell jangle when they kick their feet (Cicchetti & Schneider-Rosen, 1984). These "mastery" smiles do not appear to have a social intention. By 8 months, infants smile when they are able to resolve uncertainty or when they are able to grasp a new concept (Kagan, 1984). In the second year of life, smiling is associated with a primitive form of humor. Babies smile when they recognize incongruity, such as a picture of a mother drinking from a baby bottle or crawling on her hands and knees. These smiles suggest that the baby appreciates something about the discrepancy between what is being presented and what is normally observed (Cicchetti & Schneider-Rosen, 1984).

Babies smile in a variety of contexts. The conditions that evoke smiles change as the baby matures. Thus smiles, like other emotional expressions, should be interpreted in relation to the infants' existing schemes and goals.

The mastery smile!

Table 5.6   Number of Children Using Specific Emotional Expressions in Response to Separation from Mother at 13 and 18 Months

Emotion Variables	13 Months	18 Months
Interest	16	16
Anger	14	15
Sadness	7	11
Sadness-anger blend	7	12
Interest-anger blend	4	11
Interest-sadness blend	3	10

Source: M. C. Hyson and C. E. Izard, "Continuities and Changes in Emotion Expressions during Brief Separation at 13 and 18 Months," *Developmental Psychology, 21* (1985), 1168. Copyright © 1985 by the American Psychological Association. Reprinted by permission of the author.

One of the most important elements in the development of emotional regulation is the way caregivers assist infants in this effort (Kopp, 1989; Tronick, 1989). Caregivers can provide direct support when they observe that a child is distressed. They may cuddle, hug, rock, or swaddle a baby. They may offer food, a pacifier, or some other form of comfort. Through words and actions, they may help a child interpret the source of the stress or suggest ways to reduce the distress.

Caregivers' approaches to the issue of emotional regulation vary with the culture. Some cultures regulate emotions by preventing a child from being exposed to certain arousing situations. Japanese mothers, for example, try hard to prevent their children from being exposed to anger. They avoid frustrating young children so that they will not experience anger. Parents rarely express anger to their young children, especially in public. Thus Japanese parents try to regulate anger by minimizing the child's experiences with it (Miyake et al., 1986).

Emotions also come to be regulated through experiences with emotions themselves (Campos, Campos & Barrett, 1989). Children observe anger, pride, shame, or sadness in their parents in response to their own emotional expressions. Parents can interrupt their child's anger by expressing their own disapproval. Children can be distracted from their sadness by seeing laughter and joy in someone else. Through empathy, children can reduce their angry feelings toward someone else by seeing how sad or frightened the other person is.

As children understand the consequences or implications of a situation, they have new motives for regulating or failing to regulate their emotions. Children may extend or expand their signals of distress if they think these signals will help them achieve their goals, such as special attention or nurturing. Children may try to disguise their distress if they think that signals of distress will provoke additional pain. Emotional regulation, just like emotional signaling, takes place within an interpersonal context. The degree to which an infant devises effective strategies for reducing distress depends on how signals of distress are treated by others, on the child's goals in the situation, and on the child's ability to synchronize the cognitive, physical, and affective elements of the situation.

Summary

Infants are born with complex sensory/perceptual competences that permit them to participate in social interactions from the first days of life. During the first year, voluntary motor functions mature rapidly. Social attachment has been viewed as the cornerstone of the individual's ability to establish interpersonal relationships. The development of sensorimotor intelligence leads to the use of sensory/perceptual and motor skills to establish a sense of causality. Two related developments on the road to logical thinking are understanding the nature of objects and forming categories for grouping similar objects together. These aspects of intellectual development permit infants to impose a greater degree of order and predictability on their experiences. Emotions provide a central mode for infant-adult communication. We depend on the capacity for emotional expression to help us understand infants' needs and goals.

The tasks of infancy are intricately interconnected. It is difficult to discuss intelligence without considering sensory/perceptual and motor skills. It is difficult to discuss attachment without considering object permanence and emotional expression. In childhood we see a gradual clarification and an increasing distinctiveness of competences. It seems that in adulthood we strive once again to unify these themes in order to achieve a sense of integrity.

The Psychosocial Crisis:
Trust versus Mistrust

The term *psychosocial crisis* refers to a state of tension that occurs as a result of the developmental needs of the individual and the social expectations of the culture. In infancy, the specific nature of this crisis is described in terms of the developing trust that infants experience in relation to their caregivers. Infants seek warmth, nurturance, comfort, and stimulation from their parents (Erikson, 1950, 1963). In adult relationships, *trust* refers to an appraisal of the predictability, dependability, and genuineness of another person (Rempel, Holmes & Zanna, 1985). Trust emerges in the course of a relationship as one person discovers that another is honest, understanding, and dependable. As the level of trust grows, the partners may take some risks by disclosing information or feelings that may lead to rejection. Relationships that endure through periods of risk grow in feelings of trust. However, trust is more than a summary of the past: it is a faith that the relationship will survive the uncertainties of an unpredictable future. A trusting relationship links confidence about the past with faith about the future.

For infants, trust is an emotion, an experiential state of confidence that their needs will be met and that they are valued. Trust is inferred from the infant's increasing capacity to delay gratification and from the warmth and delight that are evident in interactions with family members. The infant's sense of trust is an emotional state that provides an undifferentiated sense of oneness with the world.

Erikson (1978) has tied the capacity for trust with the basic human strength of hope: "Hope is the enduring belief in the attainability of primal wishes, in spite of the

Pablo Picasso, *Maternity*, 1905. The crisis of trust versus mistrust is resolved as the child and the caregiver establish a feeling of mutuality. The angle of the mother's face, the placement of her hands, and the tiny infant hand touching the mother's breast convey the tenderness of this early relationship.

dark urges and rages which mark the beginnings of existence and leave a lasting residue of threatening estrangement" (p. 26). The hope that is born during infancy provides optimism in the face of risk. Throughout life, the capacity for trust and a sense of trustworthiness give one the energy to seek new solutions and the hope of resolving difficult challenges.

Experiences of mistrust during infancy can arise from two sources. First, babies can lack confidence in the good intentions of others. If the caregiver is unable to differentiate the infant's needs and respond appropriately to them, or if the caregiver is unusually harsh while meeting the infant's needs, seeds of doubt about the trustworthiness of the environment may be planted within the infant. Second, babies experience the power of their own rage. Inner feelings of anger provide an early understanding of evil. Babies can doubt their own lovableness as they encounter the violence of their own capacity for anger.

Parents play a central role in helping infants resolve the conflict between trust and mistrust. Most parents make some mistakes in responding to their infant's signs of distress, particularly when the baby is very small. They try the bottle and, if crying continues, may change diapers, give water, move the child to another room, or put the child to bed, until something "works." Over time, however, they learn to interpret their child's signals correctly and to respond appropriately (Kropp & Haynes, 1987).

It appears that feelings of doubt or anxiety about the bond of trust are more common than one may have expected. About one-third of American infant-mother pairs that have been systematically observed show evidence of an insecure attachment. Cross-cultural research provides further evidence that a significant proportion of infants have difficulty deriving emotional comfort and security from their attachment relationships. In extreme cases, parents grossly neglect their infant. They leave the baby alone without anyone to care for his or her needs. They refuse to change or bathe the baby. They do not treat the baby's wounds or protect the child from danger. They may consistently express hostility to the infant, or provide almost no communication at all (Lyons-Ruth et al., 1987). Under these circumstances, infants discover that their parents are physically and psychologically unavailable (Egeland & Sroufe, 1981). The growth of mistrust stems from their inability to gain physical or psychological comfort. The sense of mistrust may manifest itself in withdrawal from interaction and in symptoms of depression and grief, which may include sobbing, lack of emotion, lethargy, and loss of appetite (Field et al., 1988).

In infancy, as in each of the other life stages, the energy expended to resolve the psychosocial conflict serves as an integrating force in the individual's efforts to succeed in the developmental tasks of the stage. A positive resolution of the crisis of trust versus mistrust will facilitate psychological growth. Children who experience a basic security and sense of trust are able to benefit from relationships with other adults. They are in a strong position to explore their environment and to encounter novelty with curiosity and self-confidence (Aber & Allen, 1987).

The Central Process: Mutuality with the Caregiver

Underlying the resolution of the crisis of trust versus mistrust is the process whereby a child and a caregiver establish a feeling of mutuality. Initially this mutuality is built on the consistency with which the caregiver responds appropriately to the child's needs. When a child cries because of thirst, the caregiver becomes able to interpret that cry and gives the child water rather than changing the child's diaper. The caregiver comes to appreciate the variety of needs expressed by a child, and the child learns to expect that personal needs will be met.

An infant influences the responses of a caregiver in many ways. Infants' irritability and soothability contribute to the kinds of responses that adults make to them. Infants can reject or end an interaction by fussing, becoming tense, crying, or falling asleep. They can maintain an interaction by smiling, cooing, snuggling comfortably, or maintaining eye contact. Techniques of comforting do not call forth the same responses from all babies (Campos, 1989). A pacifier helps comfort some babies, others respond to being wrapped snugly in a warm blanket. Bringing an infant to the shoulder is more effective in reducing crying than cradling from side to side or comforting while the baby remains lying down. These differential responses are evidence of the infant's active role in the establishment of the bond of mutuality.

An infant and a caregiver learn to regulate the amount of time that passes between the expression of a need and its satisfaction. In a study of mother-infant interactions, Bell and Ainsworth (1972) observed mothers' responses to infant crying during the first year of life. Over the course of the year, the infants' crying decreased and mothers tended to respond more quickly to their cries. This finding suggests a process of mutual adaptation by mothers and infants. The mothers were more consistent in their strategy of responses than were the infants. Some mothers came quickly and ignored few cries. Other mothers waited a long time and ignored much of the crying. A striking finding was that the longer mothers delayed in responding to their infants' cries, the more crying the infants did in later months. Babies whose mothers responded promptly in the first six months of life cried less often in the second six months.

The study of mutuality with the caregiver has focused in some detail on the coordination of social interaction. Infants and their caregivers develop a cycle of interaction (Brazelton, Koslowski & Main, 1974; Tronick & Cohn, 1989). *Coordination* refers to two related characteristics of interaction, matching and synchrony. *Matching* means that the infant and the caregiver are involved in similar behaviors or states at the same time. They may be playing together with an object, cooing and smiling at each other, or fussing and angry at each other. *Synchrony* means that the infant and the caregiver move from one state to the next in a fluid pattern. When infants are paying attention to their caregivers, the caregivers attempt to stimulate them. As they withdraw attention, the caregivers learn to reduce stimulation and wait until the infants are ready to engage again.

In the normal pattern of development, mother-infant interactions become increasingly coordinated (Tronick & Cohn, 1989; Bernieri, Reznick & Rosenthal, 1988). This does not mean that most of the interactions are coordinated. In fact, especially when babies are very young, matched interactions appear to become mismatched rather quickly. The explanation may lie partly in the infant's inability to sustain coordinated communication, partly in a rapid shift of need states, and partly in the inability of adults to sustain nonverbal communication for lengthy periods. In normal dyads, however, periods of mismatch are usually followed by *communication repairs*, so that infants and mothers cycle again through points of coordination in their interactions.

At a theoretical level, we can view this process of coordination, mismatch, and repair as a fundamental building block of mutuality. Infants and caregivers gain confidence in their ability to communicate. Infants have many opportunities to experience the satisfaction of shared communication and the sense of being embedded in a responsive social environment. They also experience frequent recovery from a mismatched state to a state of effective communication, so that they can be hopeful about the ability to make these repairs in the future.

The importance of reciprocal interactions in building trust and hope during infancy is highlighted by studies of parents with psychological problems. Sensitivity to an infant's emotional states, the ability to respond appropriately to an infant's needs, and the quality of common, daily interactions can all be impaired by *family risk factors*. Studies of parents who are experiencing marital discord, who have been victims of child abuse or neglect, who are depressed, or who are mentally ill suggest that the interactional cycles of these parents and their children lack synchrony (Rutter, 1990).

When depressed and nondepressed mothers and their 3-month-old infants were filmed in face-to-face interactions, depressed mothers and their infants were found to spend less time in matched behavior states than the nondepressed mothers and their

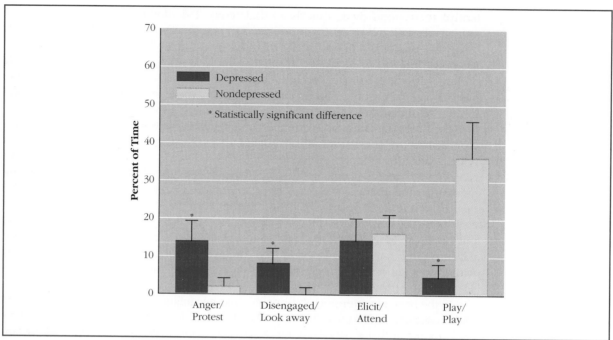

Figure 5.4   Percentage of Time Depressed and Nondepressed Mothers and Infants Matched Four Behavioral States

Source: T. Field, B. Healy, S. Goldstein, and M. Guthertz, "Behavior-State Matching and Synchrony in Mother-Infant Interactions of Nondepressed versus Depressed Dyads," *Developmental Psychology, 26* (1990), 11. Copyright 1990 by the American Psychological Association. Reprinted by permission of the author.

infants (Field et al., 1990). What is more, the quality of those interactions was different. As Figure 5.4 indicates, depressed mothers and their infants spent more of their matched time in states of anger/protest or disengaged/looking away. Nondepressed mothers and their infants spent more of their matched time in play.

We cannot be certain of the influence of this pattern of interaction on the long-term psychosocial development of the infants. For some, the effect seems to be depression and a sense of mistrust. If the mothers recover from their depression, or if the infants have opportunities to interact with other, nondepressed adults, the dyad may establish more positive social interaction patterns. This study, as well as others, suggests that even at very early ages infants are sensitive and responsive to the content and mood of their mothers' interactive style.

The initial formation of mutuality seems to rely heavily on the parents' ability to respond appropriately and in the "right" amount of time to a child's behaviors. Soon children are expected to wait until the caregiver is ready to attend to them. They are expected to remain calm and preoccupied while a parent leaves the room for a short time, trusting that the parent will return. In our culture they are also expected to modify their schedule of needs so that by the end of the first year of life they sleep when the rest of the family sleeps, play when the rest of the family is awake, and eat three or at most four times a day, generally when the other family members eat.

The match or mismatch between an infant's rhythms and the family's rhythms is an important factor in the overall adjustment of a family to a new baby (Sprunger, Boyce & Gaines, 1985). Some babies are quite predictable; the timing of their sleeping, eating, playtime, and even fussy periods follows a clear pattern. Other babies are much less regular. Families also vary in the regularity of their daily schedules. Some families have consistent mealtime hours, rather strict bedtime and waking hours, and a predictable pattern of work and leisure activities. Other families are more erratic. When the degrees of rhythmicity in an infant and family are similar, little additional adjustment may be required to integrate the new family member. However, when there is a mismatch in rhythmicity, the parents and the infant must undergo a process of mutual regulation in order to achieve a comfortable balance. The essential spirit of mutuality depends on confidence that basic needs will be met. Because of this confidence, both the child and the parents become willing to modify their behavior. The consequence is a rhythmic interdependent system (Osofsky & Connors, 1979).

Summary

Trust has been defined as an emotional feeling of well-being and confidence that one's needs will be met. Trust evolves from repeated interactions with responsive caregivers. Infants play an active role in stimulating the behavior of their caregivers. A negative resolution of the crisis of infancy leads to the development of a sense of mistrust, characterized by lethargic, withdrawn, and grief-stricken behaviors. The crisis of trust versus mistrust is resolved through a process of mutuality as both infant and caregiver learn to modify their behavior and adjust to each other's needs and capabilities.

☐ Applied Topic: The Role of Parents

As we consider the need to integrate the psychosocial crisis of trust versus mistrust with the tasks of development during infancy, we are impressed by the responsibility that parents have for maintaining and promoting the psychological growth of their children. We have portrayed infants as active, adaptive, and eager to master the environment. At the same time, we have pointed to a number of examples that demonstrate the need for environmental support to facilitate growth. The immaturity of human infants at birth necessitates a long period of dependence on adults. The lack of instinctive behaviors in human infants in comparison with the infants of other species is compensated for by an enormous capacity to learn. For this potential to be realized, infants must rely on their parents to maintain their health, provide stimulation, and protect them from danger (Fraiberg, 1977). During the long period of dependence, infants become entwined in complex social systems and develop strong emotional bonds with those who have been caring for them.

In considering the parents' role during infancy, we would like to concentrate on the interplay between their ability to facilitate emotional development and their ability to promote cognitive development. As we see it, many of the behaviors that appear to be important for the development of strong emotional bonds between infants and parents are also central to the fostering of intellectual growth.

Let us look at some examples. Social attachment and object permanence were discussed earlier as two developmental tasks of infancy. What do parents do to encourage attachment? They respond consistently and appropriately to their infants' needs. They maintain contact with their infants by holding, cuddling, looking at, and speaking to them. They smile at their infants, and they expend energy to make the infants smile. All of these behaviors help infants achieve a well-differentiated image of the parents, to which positive feelings of warmth and a wish to stay close to them are added.

The vividness of the parental image is enhanced through a variety of sensory experiences and through repeated contact. We get clues about the richness of infants' images of their parents from their preferential smiling at them and from their distress at being left in the care of strangers.

Once specific attachments have been formed, children will pursue their parents all around the house. When parents leave the room, infants will cry out to them, crawl after them, or gaze intently in the direction in which they left. All of these behaviors are evidence of attachment, but they are also signs of the emergence of a concept of the permanent object. The fact that children will pursue the parents when the parents are out of sight means that they have an image of them in their minds that is more permanent than their visual perception of them. Here we have an exciting example of the parents' dual function: in maintaining a close bond with the child, the parents nurture emotional attachment and provide a basis for conceptual growth (Jackson, Campos & Fischer, 1978).

If you have ever observed a child and parent in a novel environment, such as a doctor's office, you may have seen another example of this dual function. The parent serves as an island of safety and reassurance from which the child can explore (Ainsworth, 1979; Bowlby, 1988). The child moves out into the environment and returns to the parent. The next time the child may wander a bit farther, poking at magazines, couches, or other children before once again returning to the parent. One may even see the child leave the room and wander into the hallway or into an empty examining room, eventually to return (if not retrieved by a watchful nurse) to the parent's side. Parents can use the trust and confidence they have built with their infants to encourage exploration, to bring their infants into contact with new and unfamiliar objects, and to support the infants' efforts to master difficult motor tasks. The image comes to mind of a smiling mother with outstretched arms bending toward her child and saying, "Walk to Mommy." Trust in a human relationship serves to generate trust in the environment as a whole. Once children trust the bond between themselves and their parents, parents can use that confidence to encourage an open, exploring attitude toward the unfamiliar (Zahn-Waxler, Radke-Yarrow & King, 1977; Heckhausen, 1987).

Another way that parents foster both emotional and intellectual growth is by structuring the stimulus environment to suit the developmental level of the infant (Yarrow & Goodwin, 1965; Bornstein, 1985; Stevens & Bakeman, 1985; Bradley, Caldwell & Rock, 1988). The central idea is that parents should take the infant's perspective

Fathers tend to underestimate babies' competence and often interact inappropriately.

into account in providing toys, sounds, and visual stimulation. Part of the parents' function is to initiate interactions and not just to respond to infants' demands for attention. Parents need to create what they perceive to be a suitable environment: one that allows a variety of experiences, a reasonable amount of frustration, and adequate opportunities to experience success. Furthermore, parents should be attuned to infants' developing skills and alter the environment appropriately. As children mature, parents must add more complex stimuli and provide more opportunities for autonomy and more encouragement for tolerating frustration.

In one interesting study that demonstrated this process, mothers and fathers were videotaped as they played with their 7-, 10-, and 13-month old babies. Toy play changed to reflect the developmental competences of the infants. Parents of older babies were more likely to encourage turn-taking, pretend play, and play involving the coordination of several toys. Parents of younger babies were more likely to demonstrate or direct their infants' play. Parents of older babies were more likely to use verbal rather than physical techniques. Their babies showed greater competence at exploring the toys, and the parents demonstrated developmentally appropriate strategies as play companions (Power, 1985).

Some questions have been raised about the roles of father and mother in the child-rearing process. We noted earlier that babies form strong attachments to their fathers as well as to their mothers. Fathers may be just as involved and sensitive to their babies' needs as mothers. However, the daily interactions between mothers and babies and those between fathers and babies are distinct (Belsky, Gilstrap & Rovine, 1984; Power, 1985). A greater proportion of the time mothers spend with their babies is devoted to caregiving. Fathers, who spend less time overall with their babies, tend to focus more on play, especially physical play. When mothers play with their babies, the play tends to be verbal or with toys as opposed to rough-and-tumble activity (Power, 1985).

Mothers more frequently respond to their babies, express affection, and follow up on behaviors their babies are initiating. Fathers are more likely to disregard babies' cues and direct their attention to new targets. At home fathers are more likely to continue their leisure activity, such as reading or watching television, in the presence of their babies, whereas mothers are more likely to interact with their babies.

One implication of these differences is that fathers and mothers probably view their parental roles differently. American mothers tend to emphasize the *process* of development: they use parenting techniques that focus on enhancing their children's sense of comfort, trust, and curiosity. American fathers tend to emphasize *product:* they use parenting techniques to strengthen their children's bodies and to direct their behavior toward correct solutions to problems.

Evidence also suggests that mothers and fathers view their infants differently. Fathers tend to consider infants as less cognitively and socially competent than mothers do. The more involved a father is in infant care, however, the less difference there is between his conception of the infant's competence and his wife's (Ninio & Rinott, 1988). These differences in perception may help explain why fathers pay less attention to infants, engage them in rough-and-tumble play, and disregard babies' cues in playful interchanges. This style of play may tend to underestimate the infant's needs for and capabilities for engaging in more demanding and stimulating activities. One might argue that fathers may learn to be more effective parents if they are helped to understand the complexity and sophistication of infant competences. They then may see their efforts with their children as more valuable and may learn to interact with their infants in more appropriate ways.

In addition to providing care, more and more parents are becoming responsible for arranging alternative care arrangements for their infants. In this case the parent becomes an advocate for the child. Parents must review the alternatives available to them and select a setting that will meet their infant's needs as well as fit within the constraints posed by work and economic resources. Family day care, in-home babysitting, and day care at a center are three common alternatives for the single-parent or two-earner family.

In order to function as advocates for their children, parents may have to engage in an unfamiliar kind of thinking. They may even feel unqualified to make the kinds of judgments that are required. For example, parents must evaluate the competence of the adults who will care for their children. They must estimate how successful a caregiver will be in meeting their child's needs for security and stimulation. They must assess the caregiver's motivation. They must consider the degree to which alternative caregivers will reflect their own parental philosophy and how the caregiver's philosophy will influence their child.

Even when pressures to continue with a caregiving arrangement are very strong, parents must be able to assess its impact on their children. They must try to judge whether their children are continuing to experience the kind of responsive, stimulating environment that will enhance development. In the best situations, alternative care settings can actually complement a parent-infant relationship. In the worst settings, infants can be neglected and abused. The parents' role is critical in maintaining communication with alternative caregivers, in assessing the quality of the care, and in promptly intervening when necessary to ensure their infant's well-being.

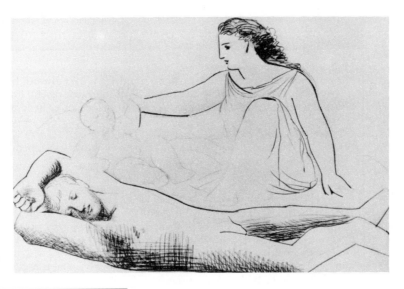

Pablo Picasso, *The Family*, 1923. Picasso observed in 1923 what researchers in the 1990s have verified. Mothers are more likely to interact with their babies, while fathers continue in their own leisure activities.

A variety of contextual factors play their parts in parents' ability to promote their child's optimal development. Adults who themselves have had difficult experiences with a caregiver come to the parent role with special challenges. They may not have experienced the comfort, responsiveness, or appropriate stimulation that we have learned are essential for effective parenting. Some factors, however, can help to make up for these deficits. The quality of one's marriage and the emotional support one receives from one's spouse play important roles in sustaining positive parent-child relationships (Cox, et al., 1989; Dickstein & Parke, 1988; Egeland, Jacobvitz & Sroufe, 1988). Couples who experience mutuality and trust in their own relationship are better able to create a predictable, supportive, and caring family environment for their children.

Sources of social support beyond the marriage partner can enhance one's effectiveness as a parent. Support can come from the child's grandparents and other family members, from health and mental health professionals, and from friends (Levitt, Weber & Clark, 1986; Stevens, 1988). The effective use of a social support network ensures that the adults are not isolated as they enact the parenting role, and that other people are available to help the parent identify and interpret child-rearing problems. Often the help is of a very direct kind—child care or sharing of clothes, playthings, and furniture. Support may also come in the form of companionship and validation of the importance of the parenting role.

A third contextual factor that influences effective parenting is the adult's prior experience with child rearing. Adults who have had previous child rearing experiences are likely to be more efficient and accurate in solving child-rearing problems (Holden, 1988). They are more likely to recognize and differentiate infants' signals as meaningful, and they are more likely to consider the infant's developmental level as a relevant factor in interpreting the child's behavior (Adamson et al., 1987).

In reviewing the material in this chapter, you can begin to appreciate the demanding nature of the parents' role in promoting optimal development during infancy. The

Table 5.7   Optimizing an Infant's Development

Provide stimulation.

Provide warmth and affection; express positive feelings toward the baby in many ways, verbally, through touching and hugging, and through playful interactions.

Encourage the child's active engagement and exploration of the environment; encourage the child's mobility.

Try not to control the child's behavior too much.

Help the child understand that he or she causes things to happen.

Help the child engage in directed problem solving.

Encourage the child to persist in efforts to reach a goal.

Keep things predictable, especially when the infant is very young.

Spend time with the child; be available when the child needs you.

Communicate often directly with the child; engage the child in verbal interaction.

Guide language development by using words to name, sort, and categorize objects and events.

Accept the child's efforts to achieve closeness.

Be responsive; be sensitive to the child's state; learn to interpret the child's signals accurately; time responses appropriately.

Find effective ways to soothe and comfort the child in times of distress.

Help the child interpret sources of distress and find ways to regulate distress.

To the extent possible, prevent the child from being exposed to intensely negative, hostile, and frightening events.

Be aware of the visual and auditory cues you send when you interact with the child.

Pay attention to ways the child is changing over time.

Monitor the child's emotional expressions to evaluate the success of specific actions and interventions.

elements of effective parenting that we have identified or implied are listed in Table 5.7. As a parent, one must rely heavily on one's own psychological well-being and on the loving support of caring friends and family to sustain the ego strengths and emotional resources necessary to the task.

The way parents conceive their roles has major implications for the direction and rate of infants' development. Parenting also provides adults with opportunities for creative problem solving, empathy, physical closeness, and self-insight. The role of parent makes considerable cognitive and emotional demands, but attachment to a child also provides opportunities for the parent's own psychological development. These contributions to adult development will be described further in Chapters 11 and 12.

☐ Chapter Summary

During infancy a child rapidly develops sensory and motor skills, social relationships, and conceptual skills. Infants are born with the capacity to perceive their environment and to evoke responses from their caregivers. In this sense, they are not helpless.

The establishment of trust between the infant and the caregiver is significant for both intellectual and social development. Through repeated interaction with the caregiver, the infant develops a concept of the adult as both separate and permanent. The process of social attachment is closely tied to the infant's recognition of parents as separate beings. Once established, the trusting relationship between the infant and the caregiver serves as a source of security for his or her further explorations of the environment.

Infants are skilled at adapting to their environment, but they cannot bring about gross changes in that environment. Parents and other caregivers are ultimately responsible for structuring the environment so that it is maximally suited to the infant. They are also the sources of the responsiveness and warmth that create an atmosphere conducive to the establishment of trust.

References

Aber, J. L., & Allen, J. P. (1987). Effects of maltreatment on young children's socioemotional development: An attachment theory perspective. *Developmental Psychology, 23*, 406–414.

Adamson, L. B., Bakeman, R., Smith, C. B., & Walters, A. S. (1987). Adults' interpretation of infants' acts. *Developmental Psychology, 23*, 383–387.

Ainsworth, M. D. S. (1973). The development of infant-mother attachment. In B. M. Caldwell & H. N. Ricciuti (eds.), *Review of child development research* (vol. 3). Chicago: University of Chicago Press.

Ainsworth, M. D. S. (1979) Infant-mother attachment. *American Psychologist, 34*, 932–937.

Ainsworth, M. D. S. (1985). Patterns of infant-mother attachments: Antecedents and effects on development. *Bulletin of the New York Academy of Medicine, 61*, 771–791.

Ainsworth, M. D. S. (1989). Attachments beyond infancy. *American Psychologist, 44*, 709–716.

Ainsworth, M. D. S., Bell, S. M. V., & Stayton, D. J. (1971). Individual differences in strange-situational behavior of one-year-olds. In H. A. Schaffer (ed.), *The origins of human social relations.* London: Academic Press.

Ainsworth, M. D. S., Blehar, M. C., Waters, E., & Wall, S. (1978). *Patterns of attachment: A psychological study of the strange situation.* Hillsdale, NJ: Erlbaum.

Ambrose, J. A. (1963). The concept of a critical period in the development of social responsiveness. In B. M. Foss (ed.), *Determinants of infant behavior* (vol. 2). New York: Wiley.

Aoki, C., & Siekevitz, P. (1988). Plasticity in brain development. *Scientific American, 259*, 56–64.

Baillargeon, R. (1987). Object permanence in 3½ and 4½-month-old infants. *Developmental Psychology, 23*, 655–664.

Baillargeon, R., & Graber, M. (1988). Evidence of location memory in 8-month-old infants in a nonsearch AB task. *Developmental Psychology, 24*, 502–511.

Banks, M. S., & Dannemiller, J. L. (1987). Infant visual psychophysics. In P. Salapatek & L. Cohen (eds.), *Handbook of infant perception* (vol. 1). Orlando, Fla.: Academic Press.

Bell, S. M., & Ainsworth, M. D. S. (1972). Infant crying and maternal responsiveness. *Child Development, 43*, 1171–1190.

Belsky, J., Gilstrap, B., & Rovine, M. (1984). The Pennsylvania infant and family development project, vol. 1: Stability and change in mother-infant and father-infant interaction in a family setting at one, three, and nine months. *Child Development 55*, 692–705.

Belsky, J., & Tolan, W. (1981). The infant as producer of his development: An ecological analysis. In R. Lerner & N. Busch-Rossnagel (eds.), *The child as producer of its own development: A life-span perspective.* New York: Academic Press.

Benson, J. B., & Uzgiris, I. C. (1985). Effect of self-initiated locomotion on infant search activity. *Developmental Psychology, 21*, 923–931.

Bernieri, F. J., Reznick, J. S., & Rosenthal, R. (1988). Synchrony, pseudosynchrony, and dissynchrony: Measuring the entrainment process in mother-infant interactions. *Journal of Personality and Social Psychology, 54*, 243–253.

Bertenthal, B. I., & Fischer, K. W. (1983). The development of representation in search: A social-cognitive analysis. *Child Development, 54*, 846–857.

Bornstein, M. H. (1985). How infant and mother jointly contribute to developing cognitive competence in the child. *Proceedings of the National Academy of Science, USA, 82*, 7470–7473.

Bornstein, M. H., Kessen, W., & Weiskopf, S. (1976). The categories of hue in infancy. *Science, 191,* 201–202.

Bower, T. G. R. (1987). *Development in infancy* (2nd ed.) New York: W. H. Freeman.

Bower, T. G. R. (1989). *The rational infant: Learning in infancy.* New York: W. H. Freeman.

Bowlby, J. (1960). Separation anxiety. *International Journal of Psychoanalysis, 41,* 69–113.

Bowlby, J. (1988). *A secure base: Parent-child attachment and healthy human development.* New York: Basic Books.

Bradley, R. H., Caldwell, B. M., & Rock, S. L. (1988). Home environment and school performance: A ten-year follow-up and examination of three models of environmental action. *Child Development, 59,* 852–867.

Brazelton, R. B., Koslowski, B., & Main, M. (1974). The origins of reciprocity: The early mother-infant interaction. In M. Lewis & L. A. Rosenblum (eds.), *The effect of the infant on its caregiver* (pp. 49–76). New York: Wiley-Interscience.

Bretherton, I. (1985). Attachment theory: Retrospect and prospect. In I. Bretherton & E. Everett (eds.), *Growing points of attachment theory and research* (pp. 3–35). Monographs of the Society for Research in Child Development, *50* (1-2 serial no. 209).

Bretherton, I. (1990). Open communication and internal working models: Their role in the development of attachment relationships. In R. Dienstbier & R. A. Thompson (eds.), *Nebraska Symposium on Motivation 1988: Socioemotional Development, 36,* Lincoln, Neb.: University of Nebraska Press, 57–113.

Bridges, L. J., Connell, J. P., & Belsky, J. (1988). Similarities and differences in infant-mother and infant-father interaction in the strange situation: A component process analysis. *Developmental Psychology, 24,* 92–100.

Bronson, G. W. (1973). Infants' reactions to an unfamiliar person. In L. J. Stone, H. T. Smith & L. B. Murphy (eds.), *The competent infant.* New York: Basic Books.

Buss, A. H., & Plomin, R. (1984). *Temperament: Early developing personality traits.* Hillsdale, N.J.: Erlbaum.

Buss, A. H., & Plomin, R. (1986). The EAS approach to temperament. In R. Plomin & J. Dunn (eds.), *The study of temperament: Changes, continuities, and challenges.* Hillsdale, N.J.: Erlbaum.

Campos, J. J., & Barrett, K. C. (1984). Toward a new understanding of emotions and their development. In C. E. Izard, J. Kagan, & R. B. Zajonc (eds.), *Emotions, cognition, and behavior* (pp. 229–263). Cambridge: Cambridge University Press.

Campos, J. J., Campos, R. G., & Barrett, K. C. (1989). Emergent themes in the study of emotional development and emotion regulation. *Developmental Psychology, 25,* 394–402.

Campos, R. G. (1989). Soothing pain-elicited distress in infants with swaddling and pacifiers. *Child Development, 60,* 781–792.

Caron, A. J., Caron, R. F., & MacLean, D. J. (1988). Infant discrimination of naturalistic emotional expressions: The role of face and voice. *Child Development, 59,* 604–616.

Caron, R. F., Caron, A. J., & Myers, R. S. (1982). Abstraction of invariant face expressions in infancy. *Child Development, 53,* 1008–1015.

Cassady, G., & Strange, M. (1987). The small-for-gestational-age (SGA) infant. In G. B. Avery (ed.), *Neonatology: Pathophysiology and management of the newborn* (pp. 299–331). Philadelphia: Lippincott.

Cernoch, J. M., & Porter, R. H. (1985). Recognition of maternal axillary odors by infants. *Child Development, 56,* 1593–1598.

Chase-Lansdale, P. L., & Owen, M. T. (1987). Maternal employment in a family context: Effects on infant-mother and infant-father attachments. *Child Development, 58,* 1505–1512.

Chazan, S. E. (1981). Development of object permanence as a correlate of dimensions of maternal care. *Developmental Psychology, 17,* 79–81.

Church, J. (1966). *Three babies: Biographies of cognitive development.* New York: Random House.

Cicchetti, D., & Schneider-Rosen, K. (1984). Theoretical and empirical considerations in the investigation of the relationship between affect and cognition in atypical populations of infants. In C. E. Izard, J. Kagan, & R. B. Zajonc (eds.), *Emotions, cognition, and behavior* (pp. 366–408). Cambridge: Cambridge University Press.

Connolly, K., & Dalgleish, M. (1989). The emergence of a tool-using skill in infancy. *Developmental Psychology, 25,* 894–912.

Cox, M. J., Owen, M. T., Lewis, J. M., & Henderson, V. K. (1989). Marriage, adult adjustment, and early parenting. *Child Development, 60,* 1015–1024.

De Casper, A., & Fifer, W. (1980). Of human bonding: Newborns prefer their mothers' voices. *Science, 208,* 1174–1176.

De Casper, A. J., & Spence, M. J. (1986). Prenatal maternal speech influences newborns' perception of speech sounds. *Infant Behavior and Development, 9,* 133–150.

Dickstein, S., & Parke, R. D. (1988). Social referencing in

infancy: A glance at fathers and marriage. *Child Development, 59,* 506–511.

Dodge, K. A. (1989). Coordinating responses to aversive stimuli: Introduction to a special section on the development of emotion regulation. *Developmental Psychology, 25,* 339–342.

Donovan, W. L., & Leavitt, L. A. (1989). Maternal self-efficacy and infant attachment: Integrating physiology, perceptions, and behavior. *Child Development, 60,* 460–472.

Easterbrooks, M. A. (1989). Quality of attachment to mother and to father: Effects of perinatal risk status. *Child Development, 60,* 825–830.

Egeland, B., Jacobvitz, D., & Sroufe, L. A. (1988). Breaking the cycle of abuse. *Child Development, 59,* 1080–1088.

Egeland, B., & Sroufe, L. A. (1981). Attachment and early maltreatment. *Child Development, 52,* 44–52.

Erikson, E. H. (1950). *Childhood and society.* New York: Norton.

Erikson, E. H. (1963). *Childhood and society* (rev. ed.). New York: Norton.

Erikson, E. H. (1978). Reflections on Dr. Borg's life cycle. In E. H. Erikson (ed.), *Adulthood* (pp. 1–31). New York: Norton.

Feinman, S., & Lewis, M. (1983). Social referencing at ten months: A second-order effect on infants' responses to strangers. *Child Development, 54,* 878–887.

Fentress, J. C., & McLeod, P. J. (1986). Motor patterns in development. In E. M. Blass (ed.), *Handbook of behavioral neurobiology,* vol. 8, *Developmental psychobiology and developmental neurobiology.* New York: Plenum.

Field, R. M., Cohen, D., Garcia, R., & Greenberg, R. (1984). Mother-stranger face discrimination by the newborn. *Infant Behavior and Development, 7,* 19–25.

Field, R. M., Woodson, R. W., Greenberg, R., & Cohen, C. (1982). Discrimination and imitation of facial expressions by neonates. *Science, 218,* 179–181.

Field, T., Dempsey, J., & Shuman, H. H. (1983). Five-year follow-up of preterm respiratory distress syndrome and postterm postmaturity syndrome in infants. In T. Field & A. Sostek (eds.), *Infants born at risk: Physiological, perceptual, and cognitive processes* (pp. 317–335). New York: Grune & Stratton.

Field, T., Healy, B., Goldstein, S., & Guthertz, M. (1990). Behavior-state matching and synchrony in mother-infant interactions of nondepressed versus depressed dyads. *Developmental Psychology, 26,* 7–14.

Field, T., Healy, B., Goldstein, S., Perry, S., Bendell, D., Schanberg, S., Zimmerman, E. A., & Kuhn C. (1988).

Infants of depressed mothers show "depressed" behavior even with nondepressed adults. *Child Development, 59,* 1569–1579.

Fischer, K. W., & Silvern, L. (1985). Stages and individual differences in cognitive development. *Annual Review of Psychology, 36,* 613–648.

Fraiberg, S. (1977). *Every child's birthright: In defense of mothering.* New York: Basic Books.

Goldsmith, H. H., Buss, A. H., Plomin, R., Rothbart, M. K., Thomas, A., Chess, S., Hinde, R. A., & McCall, R. B. (1987) Roundtable: What is temperament? Four approaches. *Child Development, 58,* 505–529.

Goldsmith, H. H., & Campos, J. J. (1986). Fundamental issues in the study of early development: The Denver twin temperament study. In M. E. Lamb & A. Brown (eds.), *Advances in developmental psychology.* Hillsdale, N.J.: Erlbaum, 231–283.

Gopnik, A., & Meltzoff, A. (1987). The development of categorization in the second year and its relation to other cognitive and linguistic developments. *Child Development, 58,* 1523–1531.

Harris, P. (1975). Development of search and object permanence during infancy. *Psychological Bulletin, 82,* 332–334.

Hay, D. F. (1980). Multiple functions of proximity seeking in infancy. *Child Development, 52,* 636–645.

Hayne, H., Rovee-Collier, C., & Perris, E. E. (1987). Categorization and memory retrieval by three-month-olds. *Child Development, 58,* 750–767.

Heckhausen, J. (1987). Balancing for weaknesses and challenging developmental potential: A longitudinal study of mother-infant dyads in apprenticeship interactions. *Developmental Psychology, 23,* 762–770.

Hickey, T. L., & Peduzzi, J. D. (1987). Structure and development of the visual system. In P. Salapatek & L. Cohen (eds.), *Handbook of infant perception* (vol. 1). Orlando, Fla; Academic Press.

Holden, G. W. (1988). Adults' thinking about a child-rearing problem: Effects of experience, parental status, and gender. *Child Development, 59,* 1623–1632.

Hornik, R., & Gunnar, M. R. (1988). A descriptive analysis of infant social referencing. *Child Development, 59,* 626–634.

Hornik, R., Risenhoover, N., & Gunnar, M. (1987). The effects of maternal positive, neutral, and negative affective communications on infant responses to new toys. *Child Development, 58,* 937–944.

Howes, P., & Markman, H. J. (1989). Marital quality and child functioning: A longitudinal investigation. *Child Development, 60,* 1044–1051.

Hubert, N. C., Wachs, T. D., Peters-Martin, P., & Gandour, M. J. (1982). The study of early temperament: Measurement and conceptual issues. *Child Development, 53,* 571–600.

Hyson, M. C., & Izard, C. E. (1985). Continuities and changes in emotion expressions during brief separation at 13 and 18 months. *Developmental Psychology, 21,* 1165–1170.

Isabella, R. A., Belsky, J., & von Eye, A. (1989). Origins of infant-mother attachment: An examination of interactional synchrony during the infant's first year. *Developmental Psychology, 25,* 12–21.

Izard, C. E., Hembree, E., Dougherty, L., & Spizziri, C. (1983). Changes in two-to-nineteen-month-old infants' facial expression following acute pain. *Developmental Psychology, 19,* 418–426.

Jackson, E., Campos, J. J., & Fischer, K. W. (1978). The question of decalage between object permanence and person permanence. *Developmental Psychology, 14,* 1–10.

Kagan, J. (1984). The idea of emotion in human development. In C. E. Izard, J. Kagan, & R. B. Zajonc (eds.), *Emotions, cognition, and behavior* (pp. 38–72). Cambridge: Cambridge University Press.

Kantrowitz, B. (1988) Preemies. *Newsweek,* May 16, 62–70.

Keil, P. F. (1975). The development of the young child's ability to anticipate the outcome of simple causal events. Paper presented at the meeting of the Society for Research in Child Development, Denver.

Keltenbach, K., Weinraub, M., & Fullard, W. (1980). Infant wariness toward strangers reconsidered: Infants' and mothers' reactions to unfamiliar persons. *Child Development, 51,* 1197–1202.

Kermoian, R., & Campos, J. J. (1988). Locomotor experience: A facilitator of spatial cognitive development. *Child Development, 59,* 908–917.

Klinnert, M. D., Emde, R. N., Butterfield, P., & Campos, J. J. (1986). Social referencing: The infant's use of emotional signals from a friendly adult with mother present. *Developmental Psychology, 22,* 427–432.

Kopp, C. B. (1989). Regulation of distress and negative emotions: A developmental view. *Developmental Psychology, 25,* 343–354.

Kropp, J. P., & Haynes, O. M. (1987). Abusive and nonabusive mothers' ability to identify general and specific emotion signals of infants. *Child Development, 58,* 187–190.

Kuhl, P. K. (1987). Perception of speech and sound in early infancy. In P. Salapatek & L. Cohen (eds.), *Handbook of infant perception* (vol. 1). Orlando, Fla.: Academic Press.

Lamb, M. E. (1976). Twelve-month-olds and their parents: Interaction in a laboratory playroom. *Developmental Psychology, 12,* 237–244.

Lerner, J. V., & Lerner, R. M. (1983). Temperament and adaptation across life: Theoretical and empirical issues. In P. B. Baltes & O. G. Brini (eds.), *Life span development and behavior, 5,* New York: Academic Press, 197–231.

Levitt, M. J., Weber, R. A., & Clark, M. C. (1986). Social network relationships as sources of maternal support and well-being. *Developmental Psychology, 22,* 310–316.

Levy-Shiff, R., Sharir, H., & Mogilner, M. B. (1989). Mother- and father–preterm infant relationship in the hospital preterm nursery. *Child Development, 60,* 93–102.

Lorenz, K. (1935). Der Kumpan in der Urwelt des Vogels. *Journal Ornithologie, 83,* 137.

Lorenz, K. F. (1937/1961). Imprinting. In R. C. Birney & R. C. Teevan (eds.), *Instinct.* Princeton, N.J.: Van Nostrand.

Ludemann, P. M., & Nelson, C. A. (1988). Categorical representation of facial expressions by 7-month-old infants. *Developmental Psychology, 24,* 492–501.

Lyons-Ruth, K., Connell, D. B., Zoll, D., & Stahl, J. (1987). Infants at social risk: Relations among infant maltreatment, maternal behavior, and infant attachment behavior. *Developmental Psychology, 23,* 223–232.

MacFarlane, J. A. (1975). Olfaction in the development of social preferences in the human neonate. In *Parent-infant interaction.* Ciba Foundation Symposium 33, 103–113.

MacLean, D. J., & Schuler, M. (1989). Conceptual development in infancy: The understanding of containment. *Child Development, 60,* 1126–1137.

MacTurk, R. H., McCarthy, M. E., Vietze, P. M., & Yarrow, L. J. (1987). Sequential analysis of mastery behavior in 6- and 12-month-old infants. *Developmental Psychology, 23,* 199–203.

Main, M., Kaplan, N., & Cassidy, J. (1985). Security in infancy, childhood, and adulthood: A move to the level of representation. In I. Bretherton & E. Everett (eds.), *Growing points of attachment theory and research* (pp. 66–104). Monographs of the Society for Research in Child Development, *50* (1-2, serial no. 209).

Malatesta, C. A., & Izard, C. E. (1984). The ontogenesis of human social signals: From biological imperative to symbol utilization. In N. A. Fox & R. J. Davidson (eds.), *The psychobiology of affective development* (pp. 161–206). Hillsdale, N.J.: Erlbaum.

Mandler, J. (1990). A new perspective on cognitive development in infancy. *American Scientist, 28,* 236–243.

Mistretta, C. M., & Bradley, R. M. (1977). Taste in utero: Theoretical considerations. In J. M. Weiffenbach (ed.), *Taste and development* (pp. 279–291). DHEW Publication no. NIH 77–1068. Bethesda, Md.: U.S. Department of Health, Education, and Welfare.

Miyake, K., Campos, J., Kagan, J., & Bradshaw, D. (1986). Issues in socioemotional development in Japan. In H. Azuma, I. Hakuta, & H. Stevenson (eds.), *Kodomo: Child development and education in Japan* (pp. 239–261). New York: W. H. Freeman.

Nelson, C. A. (1987). The recognition of facial expressions in the first two years of life: Mechanisms of development. *Child Development, 58,* 889–909.

Nelson, C. A., & Dolgin, K. (1985). The generalized discrimination of facial expression by 7-month-old infants. *Child Development, 56,* 58–61.

Ninio, A., & Rinott, N. (1988). Fathers' involvement in the care of their infants and their attributions of cognitive competence to infants. *Child Development, 59,* 652–663.

Oppenheim, D., Sagi, A., & Lamb, M. E. (1988). Infant-adult attachments on the kibbutz and their relation to socioemotional development four years later. *Developmental Psychology, 24,* 427–433.

Osofsky, J. D. (1987). *Handbook of infant development* (2nd ed.). New York: Wiley.

Osofsky, J. D., & Connors, K. (1979). Mother-infant interaction: An integrative view of a complex system. In J. D. Osofsky (ed.), *Handbook of infant development* (pp. 519–548). New York: Wiley.

Palmer, C. F. (1989). The discriminating nature of infants' exploratory actions. *Developmental Psychology, 25,* 885–893.

Papousek, H., & Bernstein, P. (1969). The functioning of conditioning stimulation in human neonates and infants. In A. Ambrose (ed.), *Stimulation in early infancy.* London: Academic Press.

Parle, K. A., & Waters, E. (1989). Security of attachment and preschool friendships. *Child Development, 60* 1076–1081.

Passman, R. H., & Longeway, K. P. (1982). The role of vision in maternal attachment: Giving 2-year-olds a photograph of their mother during separation. *Developmental Psychology, 18,* 530–533.

Piaget, J. (1970). Piaget's theory. In P. H. Mussen (ed.), *Carmichael's manual of child psychology* (3rd ed.). New York: Wiley.

Piaget, J., & Inhelder, B. (1966/1969). *The psychology of the child.* New York: Basic Books.

Plomin, R. (1990). *Nature and nurture: An introduction to human behavioral genetics.* Pacific Grove, Calif.: Brooks/Cole.

Porter, R. H., Balogh, R. D., & Makin, J. W. (1988). Olfactory influences on mother-infant interactions. In C. Rovee-Collier & L. Lipsitt (eds.), *Advances in infancy research* (vol. 5, pp. 39–68). Norwood, N.J.: Ablex.

Power, T. G. (1985). Mother- and father-infant play: A developmental analysis. *Child Development, 56,* 1514–1524.

Ramsay, D. S., & Campos, J. J. (1978). The onset of representation and entry into stage six of object permanence development. *Developmental Psychology, 14,* 79–86.

Rempel, J. K., Holmes, J. G., & Zanna, M. P. (1985). Trust in close relationships. *Journal of Personality and Social Psychology, 49,* 95–112.

Ricks, M. H. (1985). The social transmission of parental behavior: Attachment across generations. In I. Bretherton & E. Waters (eds.), *Growing points of attachment: Theory and research* (pp. 211–227). Monographs of the Society for Research in Child Development, *50,* (1-2, serial no. 209).

Robertson, J., & Robertson, J. (1989). *Separation and the very young.* New York: Free Association Books.

Rochat, P. (1989). Object manipulation and exploration in 2- to 5-month-old infants. *Developmental Psychology, 25,* 871–884.

Rose, S. A., Feldman, J. F., McCarton, C. M., & Wolfson, J. (1988). Information processing in seven-month-old infants as a function of risk status. *Child Development, 59,* 589–603.

Rosenstein, D., & Oster, H. (1988). Differential facial responses to four basic tastes in newborns. *Child Development, 59,* 1555–1568.

Ross, G., Kagan, J., Zelazo, P., & Kotelchuck, M. (1975). Separation protest in infants in home and laboratory. *Developmental Psychology, 11,* 256–257.

Rovee, C. K., & Rovee, D. T. (1969). Conjugate reinforcement of infant exploratory behavior. *Journal of Experimental Child Psychology, 8,* 33–39.

Rutter, M. (1990. Commentary: Some focus and process considerations regarding effects of parental depression on children. *Developmental Psychology, 26,* 60–67,

Sagi, A., Lamb, M. E., Lewkowicz, K. S., Shoham, R., Dvir, R., & Estes, D. (1985). Security of infant-mother, -father, and -metapelet attachments among kibbutz-reared Israeli children. In I. Bretherton & E. Everett (eds.), *Growing points of attachment theory and research* (pp. 257–275). Monographs of the Society for Research in Child Development, *50* (1–2, serial no. 209).

Schaffer, H. R., & Emerson, P. E. (1964). *The development of social attachments in infancy.* Monographs of the Society for Research in Child Development, *29* (whole no. 94).

Scott, J. P. (1987). Critical periods in processes of social organization. In M. H. Bornstein (ed.), *Sensitive periods in development: Interdisciplinary perspectives* (pp. 247–268). Hillsdale, N.J.: Erlbaum.

Sera, M. D., Troyer, D., & Smith, L. B. (1988). What do two-year-olds know about the sizes of things? *Child Development, 59,* 1489–1496.

Sophian, C., & Yengo, L. (1985). Infants' understanding of visible displacements. *Developmental Psychology, 21,* 932–941.

Spelke, E. S., von Hofsten, C., & Kestenbaum, R. (1989). Object perception in infancy: Interaction of spatial and kinetic information for object boundaries. *Developmental Psychology, 25,* 185–186.

Sprunger, L. W., Boyce, W. T., & Gaines, J. A. (1985). Family-infant congruence: Routines and rhythmicity in family adaptations to a young infant. *Child Development, 56,* 564–572.

Sroufe, L. A., Schork, E., Motti, F., Lawroski, N., & La Freniere, P. (1984). The role of affect in social competence. In C. E. Izard, J. Kagan, & R. B. Zajonc (eds.), *Emotions, cognition, and behavior* (pp. 38–72). Cambridge: Cambridge University Press.

Stevens, J. H., Jr. (1988). Social support, locus of control, and parenting in three low-income groups of mothers: Black teenagers, black adults, and white adults. *Child Development, 59,* 635–642.

Stevens, J. H., Jr., & Bakeman, R. (1985). A factor analytic study of the HOME scale for infants. *Developmental Psychology, 21,* 1196–1203.

Stockard, C. R. (1907). The artificial production of a single median cyclopian eye in the frog embryo by means of sea water solutions of magnesium chloride. *Archiv für Entwicklungs mechanik der Organismen, 23,* 249.

Stockard, C. R. (1921). Developmental rate and structural expression. *American Journal of Anatomy, 28,* 115.

Teller, D. Y., & Bornstein, J. H. (1987). Infant color vision and color perception. In P. Salapatek & L. Cohen (eds.), *Handbook of infant perception* (vol. 1). Orlando, Fla.: Academic Press.

Thomas, A., & Chess, S. (1977). *Temperament and development.* New York: Bruner/Mazel.

Thomas, A., & Chess, S. (1980). *The dynamics of psychological development.* New York: Bruner/Mazel.

Thomas, A., & Chess, S. (1986). The New York longitudinal study: From infancy to early adult life. In R. Plomin & J. Dunn (eds.), *The study of temperament: Changes, continuities, and challenges.* Hillsdale, N.J.: Erlbaum.

Thompson, R. A., Connell, J. P., & Bridges, L. J. (1988). Temperament, emotion, and social interactive behavior in the strange situation: A component process analysis of attachment system functioning. *Child Development, 59,* 1102–1110.

Tracy, R. L., & Ainsworth, M. D. S. (1981). Maternal affectionate behavior and infant-mother attachment patterns. *Child Development, 52,* 1341–1343.

Trevarthen, C. (1989). Origins and directions for the concept of infant intersubjectivity. *Newsletter of the Society for Research in Child Development,* Autumn, 1–4.

Tronick, E. Z. (1989). Emotions and emotional communication in infants. *American Psychologist, 44,* 112–119.

Tronick, E. Z., Als, H., & Brazelton, R. B. (1979). Early development of neonatal and infant behavior. In F. Falkner & J. M. Tanner (eds.), *Human growth,* vol. 3, *Neurobiology and nutrition* (pp. 305–328). New York: Plenum.

Tronick, E. Z., & Cohn, J. F. (1989). Infant-mother face-to-face interaction: Age and gender differences in coordination and the occurrence of miscoordination. *Child Development, 60,* 85–92.

Uzgiris, I. C., & Hunt, J. M. V. (1975). *Assessment in infancy: Ordinal scales of psychological development.* Urbana: University of Illinois Press.

van Ijzendoorn, M. H., & Kroonenberg, P. M. (1988). Cross-cultural patterns of attachment: A meta-analysis of the strange situation *Child development, 59,* 147–156.

Vaughn, B., Egeland, B., Sroufe, L.A., & Waters, E. (1979). Individual differences in infant-mother attachment at twelve and eighteen months: Stability and change in families under stress. *Child Development, 50,* 971–975.

Vaughn, B. E., Lefever, G. B., Seifer, R., & Barglow, P. (1989). Attachment behavior, attachment security, and temperament during infancy. *Child Development, 60,* 728–737.

Walden, T. A., & Ogan, T. A. (1988). The development of social referencing. *Child Development, 59,* 1230–1240.

Walker-Andrews, A. S. (1986). Intermodal perception of expressive behaviors: Relation of eye and voice?

Developmental Psychology, 22, 373–377.

Ward, M. J., Vaughn, B. E., & Robb, M. D. (1988). Social-emotional adaptation and infant-mother attachment in siblings: Role of the mother in cross-sibling consistency. *Child Development, 59,* 643–651.

Watson, J. S. (1970). Smiling, cooing, and "the game." Paper presented at the annual meeting of the American Psychological Association, Miami Beach.

Wellman, H. M., Cross, D., & Bartsch, K. (1986). *Infant search and object permanence: A meta-analysis of the A-not-B error.* Monographs of the Society for Research in Child Development, *51* (3, serial no. 214 whole).

Werker, J. F. (1989). Becoming a native listener. *American Scientist, 77,* 54–59.

Wilson, R. S., & Matheny, A. P., Jr. (1986). Behavior genetics research in infant temperament: The Louisville twin study. In R. Plomin & J. Dunn (eds.), *The study of temperament: Changes, continuities, and challenges.* Hillsdale, N.J.: Erlbaum.

Wolff, P. H. (1963). Observations on the early development of smiling. In B. M. Foss (ed.), *Determinants of infant behavior* (vol. 2). New York: Wiley.

Wolff, P. H. (1966). Causes, controls, and organization of behavior in the neonate. *Psychological Issues, 5* (1, whole no. 17).

Wolff, P. H. (1987). *The development of behavioral states and the expression of emotions in early infancy.* Chicago: University of Chicago Press.

Yarrow, L. J. (1963). Research in dimensions of early maternal care. *Merrill-Palmer Quarterly, 9,* 101-114.

Yarrow, L. J. (1964). Separation from parents in early childhood. In M. L. Hoffman & L. W. Hoffman (eds.), *Review of child development research* (vol. 1). New York: Russell Sage Foundation.

Yarrow, L. J. (1970). The development of focused relationships during infancy. In J. Hellmuth (ed.), *Exceptional infant* (vol. 1.) New York: Brunner/Mazel.

Yarrow, L. J., & Goodwin, M. S. (1965). Some conceptual issues in the study of mother-infant interaction. *American Journal of Orthopsychiatry, 35.*

Yarrow, L. J., McQuiston, S., MacTurk, R. H., McCarthy, M. E., Klein, R. P., & Vietze, P. M. (1983). The assessment of mastery motivation during the first year of life. *Developmental Psychology, 19,* 159–171.

Younger, B., & Gotlieb, S. (1988). Development of categorization skills: Changes in the nature or structure of infant form categories? *Developmental Psychology, 24,* 611–619.

Zahn-Waxler, C., Radke-Yarrow, M., & Kling, R. A. (1977). The impact of the affective environment on young children. Paper presented at the biennial meeting of the Society for Research in Child Development, New Orleans.

Zucker, K. J. (1985). The infant's construction of his parents in the first six months of life. In T. M. Field & N. A. Fox (eds.), *Social perception in infants.* Norwood, N.J.: Ablex.

Chapter Six

Pablo Picasso, *Paulo as Harlequin*, 1924. Picasso painted his first son, Paulo, as Harlequin when Paulo was three. The Harlequin role was one that both father and son enjoyed—a fantasy linked to the magic and mystery of circus life that Picasso had detailed so carefully 20 years earlier.

Toddlerhood
(2 to 4 Years)

The dominant characteristic of the stage of life called *toddlerhood* is activity. The toddler is extremely busy—talking, moving, fantasizing, and planning all the time. The outpouring of physical activity—its vigor, constancy, and complexity—is remarkable. Equally impressive is the flood of cognitive accomplishments, especially language production and unique forms of playful fantasy. Toddlers seem to bubble with unpredictable, startling thoughts and actions that keep adults in a state of puzzled amazement.

The motivation for this abundance of activity appears to be a need for self-assertion and mastery. During the years from 2 through 4, children grow increasingly aware of their individuality and are driven to test it out. The familiar negativism of the 2-year-old, which evolves into a more mature willfulness by 3, is evidence of this powerful need to define and assert the self.

New motor and cognitive capacities give children new abilities to move around freely in their environment and to accept the challenges of a wide variety of exploratory activities. The delight of stacking colored circles on a post changes to the glee of stacking pots and pans in the kitchen, and further to stacking boxes or blocks for a fantasy spacecraft. Each new accomplishment is accompanied by the pride and pleasure of having mastered an activity at a new level of complexity.

Another characteristic of this life stage is a readiness to learn to limit and regulate one's actions. Once children learn to run, they may take great pleasure in chasing madly around the room pretending to be a wild stallion or a racing car. This new skill is a delight to them, and they eagerly try it out. Before long, however, one also has to control one's running behavior in order to avoid injury or the wrath of parents or other caregivers. The control of action requires considerable responsiveness to one's physical and social environment, and makes use of such cognitive skills as information processing and decision making (Pick, 1989). Toddlers must learn to take the needs of others and their own needs into account in the process of their self-discovery.

Between the ages of 2 and 4 the toddler changes dramatically from an egocentric child who is unaware of interdependence with others to a more self-conscious person. At the beginning of the stage, toddlers assert themselves in what appear to be very independent ways. By the end of the stage, this pseudo independence is transformed into a more realistic assessment of ways in which they are dependent on others and ways in which they are independent. In sum, toddlerhood is a period of activity and mastery, self-regulation, and increasing awareness of dependence and independence.

Developmental Tasks

Elaboration of Locomotion

The use of the word *toddler* to describe the life stage from 2 to 4 is in itself a clue to the important part that locomotion plays. In fact, it is only during the first year of this stage that the child actually toddles. By age 3, the child's walk has changed from the precarious, determined, half-humorous waddle known as the toddle to a more graceful, continuous, effective stride. Removal of diapers plays an important role in the progress of the child's walk. When toddlers no longer have a large wad of padding

Pablo Picasso, *First Steps*, 1943. A child's first steps are a major symbol of the movement toward autonomy. In this painting, the child relies on the mother for stability and guidance but with the clear purpose of taking leave of her.

between their legs, it is easier for them to make the transition from ugly duckling to swan. As walking becomes a more comfortable form of locomotion, new skills are added to the child's repertoire. Running and jumping are the first to emerge. By the age of 4, children are likely to leap from stairways, tables, porch railings, or ladders. They have begun to imagine what it might be like to fly. Jumping is their closest approximation to flying. Evidence suggests that the underlying structure of the jumping pattern remains stable throughout childhood and into adulthood (Clark, Phillips & Peterson, 1989). The child's delight in exploring jumping behavior may be the result of the acquisition of a fundamental movement pattern that fills the child with a basic sense of mastery as well as a sense of lifelong possibilities.

Children's running abilities become more elaborated all through toddlerhood. At first, youngsters may run for the sake of running. They practice the art over and over again for a long time. Later in toddlerhood, children find the skill of running to be valuable in games of chase. For most children, running changes from a kind of game in itself to a valuable component of many other games. The absolute speed of toddlers is limited by somewhat precarious balance and short legs. This does not discourage them, however, from devoting a great deal of time and energy to running. The goals of mastery and getting to new places for exploration are too strong to dampen their enthusiasm.

Toddlers are often exposed to a wide variety of other forms of locomotion, such as swimming, skiing, skating, sledding, and dancing. Children seem eager to use their bodies in a variety of ways, and they learn quickly (Ridenour, 1978). One of the vehicles of locomotion that has special meaning for the American toddler is the tricycle. The tricycle provides enormous pleasure because of its potential speed, reversibility, turning capability, and horn. It is also an object through which the toddler can identify with other children and adults. The connection among tricycle, bicycle, and car is quickly and easily made by the toddler. The tricycle combines the joys of physical movement, the thrill of danger and independence, and the social significance of mechanized transportation. A tricycle (or comparable pedal toy) usually has a great deal of psychological significance for the child. It is the first in a chain of objects that will symbolize the child's increased independence from the family and heightened identification with the peer group.

One might conclude that when taken literally, *toddler* is a poor word to apply to these youngsters. Children actually leave toddling early in this stage of life and acquire a range of locomotive skills that they can use with speed and precision. Large-muscle movement and control are great sources of pleasure to a child, confirming feelings of competence and selfhood. All the same, the connotations of the word *toddler*—a short, cherubic, smiling, uncertain little person with an overhanging belly and a bulging behind who lurches on tiptoe from place to place—are too accurate in the figurative sense to be abandoned.

Still, it is important not to underestimate the amazing complexity of the locomotor skills acquired by infants and toddlers. Difficulties encountered by engineers and inventors in trying to duplicate human locomotor skills with robots have demonstrated just how intricate and exquisite the toddler's accomplishments are (Pick, 1989). The possibility that lifelong movement patterns are acquired during these two years extends our appreciation of toddlers' locomotor accomplishments.

Fantasy Play

Jean Piaget (1970) described the years from about 2 to 5 or 6 as the stage of *preoperational thought*. This is a transitional period during which the schemes that were developed during infancy are represented internally. The most significant achievement of this new stage of cognitive development is the capacity for *semiotic* thinking, the understanding that one thing can stand for another (Miller, 1989). Children learn to recognize and use symbols and signs. *Symbols* are usually related in some way to the object for which they stand. The cross, for example, is a symbol of Christianity. In

Locomotor mastery is accelerated when a toddler gets behind the wheel of a tricycle.

pretend play, a scarf or a blanket can be a symbol for a pillow or a dress. *Signs* stand for things in a more abstract, arbitrary way. Words are signs. There is no direct relation between the word *dog* and the animal to which the word refers, yet the word stands for the object.

Children acquire five representational skills that allow them to manipulate objects mentally rather than by actual behavior. These representational skills are imitation in the absence of the model, mental images, symbolic drawing, symbolic play, and language. Each of these skills frees children from real events. They can express relationships they may have known in the past by imitating them, drawing them, or acting them out in fantasy. They can also portray events and relationships that they wish would occur or that they wish to alter in some way from the original form.

The capacity for pretense, whether through symbolic play, symbolic drawing, or telling make-believe stories, requires that children understand the difference between pretend and real. Sometimes adults wonder whether children can in fact distinguish between what is real and what is pretend. The line between make-believe and reality can become blurred for all of us. We encounter such confusion frequently when we watch television. Which of the things we see on television are pretend and which are real? Are commercials advertising products real or pretend? Is a television news story real or pretend? Are dramatic reenactments of historical events real or pretend?

In very simplified situations, children as young as 3 can tell the difference between what an object really is and what someone is pretending that it is (Flavell, Flavell & Green, 1987). Three-year-olds understand that a sponge is really a sponge, for example, but that you can pretend it is a boat floating in the water or a car driving along the road. Before the period of preoperational thought, children do not really pretend because they cannot let one thing stand for something else. Once the capacity for symbolic thought emerges, children become increasingly flexible in allowing an object to take on a wide variety of pretend identities.

Fantasy play and language are contrasting forms of representation. In acquiring language, children learn to translate their thoughts into a commonly shared system of signs and rules. For language to be effective, children must use the same words and grammar as the older members of the family. To engage in verbal communication, children must translate their thoughts into existing words and categories. Fantasy serves almost the opposite function. In fantasy, children create characters and situations that may have very private meanings. There is no need to make the fantasy comprehensible to an audience. There are probably many times when children have strong feelings but lack the words to express them. They may be frustrated by their helplessness or angry at being overlooked. They can express and soothe these feelings in the world of imagination even though such feelings may never become part of a shared conversation.

During infancy, play consists primarily of the repetition of motor activity. Infants delight in sucking their toes or dropping a spoon from the high chair. These are typical sensorimotor play activities. Toward the end of infancy, sensorimotor play includes deliberate imitation of parental acts. Children who see their mothers washing the dishes may enjoy climbing up on a chair and getting their hands wet too. At first these imitations occur only when they are stimulated by the sight of the parent's activity. As children enter toddlerhood, they begin to imitate parental activities when they are alone. A vivid mental image of an action permits them to copy what they recall instead of what they see. This is the beginning of symbolic play. Children are able to direct their play in responses to mental images that they have generated by themselves. Toddlers' symbolic play is characterized by the simple repetition of very familiar activities. Pretending to sweep the floor, to be asleep, to be a dog or cat, and to drive a car are some of the early play activities of toddlers.

Fantasy play changes along four dimensions during toddlerhood (Lucariello, 1987):

1. The action component becomes more complex as the child integrates a sequence of actions.
2. The child's focus shifts from the self to fantasies that involve others and the creation of multiple roles.
3. The play involves the use of substitute objects, including objects the child only pretends to have, and eventually the invention of complex characters and situations.
4. The play becomes more organized and planned, and play leaders emerge.

First, children include a number of actions into a play sequence. From pretending to sweep the floor or pretending to take a nap, children devise strings of activities that are part of a complex play sequence. While playing fireman, the child may pretend to be the fire truck, the hose, the ladder, the engine, the siren, the people being rescued, and the firefighters. All the elements of the situation are brought under the child's control through this fantasy enactment.

Second, children become increasingly able to include others in their play and to shift the focus of the play from the self to the others (Howes, 1987; Howes, Unger & Seidner, 1989). One can see a distinction here between solitary pretense, social play, and social pretend play. Children engaged in solitary pretense are involved in their own fantasy activities. They may be pretending that they are driving a car or giving a baby a bath. Children engaged in social play join with other children in some activity. They may dig together in the sand, build with blocks, or imitate each other's silly noises. Children engaged in social pretend play have to coordinate their pretense. They establish a fantasy structure, take roles, agree on the make-believe meaning of props, and solve pretend problems. The fact that 2- and 3-year-olds can participate in this type of coordinated fantasy play is quite remarkable, especially given their very limited use of language to establish and sustain coordination.

Fantasy play changes along a third dimension as children become more flexible in their ability to use substitute objects in their play. Fantasy play begins in areas closest to a child's daily experience. Children use real objects or play versions of those objects as props in their pretense. They pick up a toy telephone and pretend to make a call to Grandma, or pretend to have a picnic with toy cups, plates, and plastic foods. But as they develop their fantasy skills, these props are no longer essential. Children can invent objects, create novel uses for common objects, and sometimes pretend to have an object when they have nothing.

The play moves away from common, daily experiences to invented worlds based on stories, on television programs, or on purely imagined characters and situations. Children may take the roles of characters with extraordinary powers. They may pretend to fly, become invisible, or transform themselves into other shapes with the aid of a few secret words or gestures. Identification with a particular fantasy hero or heroine may last for days or even weeks as the child involves the characters of the story in a variety of fantasy situations.

Fourth, fantasy play becomes more planned and organized. The planning element is in part a product of the desire to coordinate play among several players. It is also a product of a new realization of what makes pretend play most fun, and the desire to make sure that those components are included in the play. In a preschool or day-care group, certain children are likely to take the lead in organizing the direction of fantasy play. They may set the play in motion, or give it direction by suggesting the use of certain props, assigning roles, or working out the context of the play. Here we see a child demonstrating this kind of leadership:

Stuart (climbing up on a tractor tire): This will be our shark ship, OK? Get on quick, Jeremy! The sharks will eat you!

Jeremy: No! This is my police helicopter!

Stuart: Well, OK. We're police. But we need to chase the sharks, OK? I see the sharks way down there! Come on!

Jeremy: OK. Let's get 'em! (They both make helicopter noises and swat at make-believe sharks with plastic garden tools.)   [Trawick-Smith, 1988, p. 53]

Dramatic role playing, in which a child takes on the role of another person or creates a fantasy situation, increases steadily from the ages of 3 through 5. By the age of 6, however, children become involved in games with rules. They tend to use their fantasy skills during play by making up new games or new rules rather than by engaging in pretend play. If you are looking for the experts in diversified, elaborated fantasy, observe 4- and 5-year-olds (Cole & La Voie, 1985).

Fantasy play is not simply a diversion. Children use fantasy to experiment with and understand their social and physical environments, and to expand their thinking (Piers & Landau, 1980; Hutt et al., 1988). Views of the importance or value of fantasy play vary widely. Piaget (1962) emphasized the assimilative value of play. Through fantasy and symbolic play, he believed, children are able to make meaning of experiences and events that are beyond their full comprehension. Fantasy play is a private world in which the rules of social convention and the logic of the physical world do not necessarily apply. From this perspective, fantasy play frees the child from the immediacy of reality, permitting mental manipulations and modifications of objects and events.

Researchers who have studied children who do not engage in much pretend play and others who have tried to increase the level of pretend play among toddlers find that pretend play actually fosters cognitive and social development (Rubin, 1980; Saltz & Saltz, 1986). Children who have well-developed pretending skills tend to be well liked by their peers and to be viewed as peer leaders (Ladd, Price & Hart, 1988). This is the result of their advanced communication skills, their greater ability to take the point of view of others, and their ability to reason about social situations. Children who have experiences that encourage a playful, imaginative approach to the manipulation and exploration of materials and objects through fantasy show evidence of more complex language use and more flexible approaches to problem solving (Burke, 1987). Clearly the importance of fantasy play in the full social, intellectual, and emotional development of young children cannot be underestimated. Some parents and teachers want to define a young child's cognitive growth in terms of the acquisition of words and concepts that seem relevant to the "real world." They emphasize the importance of learning numbers and letters, memorizing facts, and learning to read. However, research on cognitive development suggests that gains in the capacity for symbolic thought will provide the essential underpinnings for subsequent intellectual abilities such as abstract reasoning and inventive problem solving.

The Role of Play Companions

Cognitive developmental theory emphasizes the normal emergence of representational thought and symbolic play as natural outcomes of cognitive maturation during toddlerhood. However, the quality of that play as well as its content depend in part on the behavior of a child's play companions. Consider the following incident. In a university preschool, where college students were having their first supervised experience as teachers of young children, a child of 3 made a bid for some pretend play with a student teacher. The child picked up the toy telephone and made ringing noises. The student teacher picked up another phone and said, "Hello." The child asked, "Is Milly there?" The student teacher said "no" and hung up the phone. In this interaction, the student teacher had not yet learned how to help expand the child's play or to help the child build the initial symbolic play of the telephone call into a more elaborate social pretend situation.

As play companions, parents, siblings, peers, and child-care professionals can enrich significantly a child's capacity for fantasy play. Play companions can elaborate a child's capacity for fantasy, legitimize fantasy play, and help the child to explore new domains of fantasy. Research has shown that when mothers are available as play companions, the symbolic play of their 2-year-old children is more complex and lasts for a longer time (Slade, 1987). When adults are trained to engage in and encourage pretend play with toddlers, the toddlers show an increasing capacity to coordinate their responses with those of an adult. Over the period from 16 to 32 months, toddlers become increasingly skillful at directing an adult's behavior and negotiating changes in kinds of play (Eckerman & Didow, 1989).

Within child-care settings, the availability of a stable group of agemates results in more complex, coordinated play. Children who have had many changes in their child-care arrangements are less likely to engage in complex social pretend play with other children (Howes & Stewart, 1987). Since toddlers rely so heavily on imitation and nonverbal signals to initiate and develop their social pretend play, the more time they have together, the more complex their fantasy play can be.

Imaginary Companions

Probably the most sophisticated form of symbolic play involves the creation of an imaginary friend (Singer, 1975). An imaginary friend springs, complete in concept, from the mind of a child. It may be an animal, child, or some other creature. It has its own personality, which is consistent from day to day. It has its own likes and dislikes, which are not necessarily the same as those of its creator. It occupies space. For adults, it is very difficult, perhaps impossible, to get to know this friend.

Several functions are served by the imaginary friend. It takes the place of other children when there are none around. It serves as a confidant for children's private expressions. It is often involved in their efforts to differentiate between right and wrong. Sometimes toddlers may do things they know are wrong because they cannot stop themselves. Under these circumstances, they find it difficult to accept responsibility for their misdeeds. They did not wish to be bad. They do not want to displease their parents. The imaginary friend becomes a convenient scapegoat. Toddlers report that although they tried very hard to stop their friend, it went right ahead and did the "bad" thing anyway. When children use an excuse of this kind, they are communicating that they understand the difference between right and wrong but are unwilling or unable to assume total responsibility for their misconduct. In general, imaginary friends can be seen as evidence of toddlers' ability to differentiate themselves from others and of their attempts to gain control over their impulses.

Language Development

In the process of language development, children acquire *communicative competence:* they become adept at using all the aspects of language that a child must master (Hymes, 1972). They learn the sound system (phonology), the system of meanings (semantics), the rules of word formation (morphology), the rules of sentence formation (syntax), and the adjustments to the social setting that are necessary to produce and interpret communication (pragmatics).

Prelinguistic Accomplishments

Thought and language seem to travel independent courses that intersect during the second year of life (Anglin, 1977; Molfese, Molfese & Carrell, 1982). Before that time, we observe vocalization without meaning; that is, cooing (mostly vowel sounds noticeable at 1 to 2 months) and babbling (consonant-vowel sounds repeated over and over, which begin at about 4 months). We also observe thoughtful action patterns without verbal labels—reaching and grasping, for example, or retrieving a toy that has rolled under a table. (This is the type of behavior we referred to as sensorimotor intelligence in Chapter 5.)

In addition, we observe language perception. Infants are able to recognize sounds and differentiate between sound combinations before they understand the meanings of the sounds (Eimas, 1975; Trehub, 1973). By approximately 10 to 12 months, infants produce the sounds of their native language, as distinct from the full range of sounds of human language, which had been evident in their earlier cooing and babbling (Best, McRoberts & Sithole, 1988; Werker & Lalonde, 1988). Babbling, initially characterized by sounds used in many languages, begins to reflect the sounds and intonation infants are most likely to hear. Sounds they do not hear drop out of their babbling.

Infants of this age also use sounds, like grunting and whining, in combination with gestures to achieve a goal such as getting their mother to reach something for them. Sounds may also be used to express emotion or to get someone's attention (Dore, 1978; Bates, O'Connell & Shore, 1987). These vocalizations before language are early forms of purposeful communication. Around this time it becomes clear that infants understand the meanings of some individual words (Huttenlocher, 1974; Oviatt, 1980). This ability to understand words, called *receptive language*, precedes the ability to produce spoken words and phrases.

Words with Meaning

One of the first significant events in the development of language production is the naming of objects. With repetition, a sound or word becomes associated with a specific object or a set of related objects. For example, a child may say *ba* whenever she sees her bottle. If she is thirsty and wants her bottle, she may try saying *ba* in order to influence her mother to produce the bottle. Gestures, actions, and facial expressions often accompany the "word" and help establish its meaning in the caregiver's mind. If the baby's "word" has meaning to the mother and serves to satisfy the baby's needs, it will probably be retained as a meaningful sign. *Ba* may come to mean "bottle" and other liquids the child wishes to drink, such as juice, water, or soda.

The important characteristic of first words is their shared meaning. Even though *ba* is not a real word, it functions in the same way that any noun does: it names a person, place, or thing (Greenfield & Smith, 1976). These single-word utterances accompanied by gestures, actions, vocal intonation, and emotion are called *holophrases*. They convey the meaning of an entire sentence. For example, saying *ba, ba* in a pleading tone while pointing to the refrigerator and jumping up and down conveys the meaning "I need a bottle" or "Get me the bottle." Gradually the child discovers that every object, action, and relationship has a name.

Young children first talk about what they know and what they are interested in. Common first words include important people *(Mamma, Dadda,* names of siblings), foods, pets, toys, body parts *(eye, nose),* clothes *(shoe, sock),* vehicles *(car),* favorite objects *(bottle, blanket)*, other objects in the environment *(keys, trees)*, actions *(up, bye-bye)*, *yes, no, please, down, more*, pronouns *(you, me)*, and states *(hot, hungry)*. During the period from 15 to 18 months, the infant makes significant progress in learning the names of objects and applying those names to pictures or real examples of them (Oviatt, 1982). During the second year, the child's vocabulary increases from about 10 words to almost 300.

Sometime around 18 months the child quickly acquires a large number of new words, and the rapid rate at which the vocabulary grows continues throughout the toddler and early school years (Rice, 1989). One researcher found that during this period children learn about 14,000 new words (Templin, 1957). In order to accomplish this feat, children seem to "fast-map" new meanings as they experience words in conversation. To fast-map is to form an initial, partial understanding of a word's meaning quickly. A child fast-maps by relating the word to the known vocabulary and restructuring the known-word storage space and its related conceptual categories (Carey, 1978). The child has to hear the new word only once or a very few times in a context that makes its meaning clear (Rice & Woodsmall, 1988). Thus, without direct word-by-word tutoring, children accumulate numerous samples of their culture's language from the speech they hear and attach a minimally satisfactory definition to each word or phrase. During the early and middle school years, children devote considerable time and attention to exploring vocabulary, correcting some meanings that were incorrectly learned, and expanding the full range of meanings and underlying concepts that are linked to the many words they acquired so rapidly.

Two-Word Sentences

The second year is marked by the second important stage of language development: the formation of two-word sentences. These two-word sentences are referred to as *telegraphic speech*. Children link two words that are essential to communicate what they intend to say. Just as in a telegram, however, other words—verbs, articles, prepositions, pronouns, conjunctions—are left out. A child will say: "Big ball," "More juice," "All gone." Before this point, children tend to utter single words accompanied by gestures and actions. When they string two words together, they convey more meaning, and they rely less heavily on gestures and actions to communicate their intensions. The acquisition of telegraphic speech allows a child to make fuller use of the symbolism inherent in language to communicate meaning.

Children are quite innovative in using two-word sentences. They continue to understand more than they are able to say, but they appear to use their limited number of words and the newfound ability to combine them to get their point across. Children may convey different meanings with the same sentence. "Daddy go," for example, may be used to tell someone that Daddy has left, or it may be used to tell Daddy to leave. Children often indicate their meanings by tone of voice or by the words they stress. The use of two-word sentences is characteristic of toddler-age language learners in many cultures (Slobin, 1985).

Braine (1976) analyzed the first word combinations spoken by children in English, Samoan, Finnish, Hebrew, and Swedish. His goal was to identify the kinds of rules or patterns that governed these early combinations. Ten patterns of word combination were embedded in those early language samples:

1. Making reference to something: See + X (see Mother)
2. Describing something: Hot + X (hot coffee)
3. Possession: X had a Y (Billy had a bottle)
4. Plurality: Two + X (two dogs)
5. Repetition or other examples: More + X (more Coke)
6. Disappearance: All gone + X (all gone milk)
7. Negation: No + X (no sleep)
8. Actor-action relations: Person + X (Daddy sleep)
9. Location: X + here (Grandma here)
10. Requests: Have + X (Have it, ball)

Braine concluded that the word combinations were not guided by the grammatical categories of the spoken language but were related to the meanings that the child wished to express and to the variety of objects, people, and interactions in the immediate environment. He found considerable variability in the word combinations used by children within a culture. The patterns of word combinations used by some children did not overlap at all with the patterns used by other children. This observation of pattern variability has been confirmed by subsequent research. The objects and actions children talk about may be similar but the word patterns they use to talk about them are their own (Bloom et al., 1975). Children also vary widely in the rate at which they acquire language, in the way they master specific aspects of language, and in their patterns of combining words (Ferguson, 1989). They vary in their preference for the use of nounlike words (Nelson, 1973). Children who prefer to use nounlike words and then extend their use of language to verbs and other words begin to master grammar earlier and more effectively than children who begin with another pattern of usage (Bates, Bretherton & Snyder, 1988).

Early language appears to be closely tied to the representation of sensorimotor schemes. It expresses the properties and relationships of objects and people that are important in a child's life. Language use emerges within a larger communication system and reflects a child's cognitive capacities. At the same time, it reflects the perceptual and functional characteristics of the environment. The kinds of objects and relationships that are central to daily life influence the content and complexity of a child's early language (Nelson, 1981).

Grammatical Transformations

The grammar of a particular language provides a set of rules that permit the complexity and variety of one person's thinking to be readily understood by someone else. Consider the difference in meaning between "The boy hit the ball" and "The ball hit the boy." The simple matter of word order in a sentence is critical for preserving meaning. The basic format of an English sentence, noun phrase followed by verb phrase, is a central part of its grammar. In order to ask a question or to produce a negative sentence, the speaker transforms this word order according to a specific set of rules. The addition of certain inflections and modifiers conveys complexities of time, pos-

Table 6.1   Basic Sequence in Adding Grammatical Inflections

Inflection	*Example*
-ing	Puppy is runn*ing*.
in	*In* the pot.
on	I am *on* the bed.
Plural: -*s*	Apple*s*
Past irregular	*Fell, hit, ran*
Possessive: -*'s*	Baby*'s* toy.
Use of *to be* as main verb without contraction	The boys *are* home.
Articles	I want *a* bottle.
Past regular	You walk*ed* too fast.
Third person regular	He walk*s*
Third person irregular	She *has,* he *does*
Uncontractible progressive auxiliary	This *is* going fast.
Use of *to be* as main verb with contraction	That*'s* Bill.
Contractible progressive auxiliary	I*'m* talk*ing*.

session, number, and relation. As children learn the grammatical transformations of their language, they become much more effective in conveying exactly what they have in mind.

When Brown (1973) analyzed the development of grammar in three children, he found that although the rate of acquiring inflections varied among the children, the order was surprisingly constant. The typical order in which children learn basic grammatical inflections is listed in Table 6.1.

A surprising observation is that children use correct transformations for the past tenses of irregular verbs *(went, gave, ran)* before they use correct inflections of regular verbs *(talked, walked, jumped).* It appears that at first children learn the past tenses of irregular verbs through rote memory. Once they learn the rule for expressing the past tense by adding *-ed,* they *overgeneralize* this rule and begin making errors in the use of the past tense. So while a 2-year-old is likely to say "I ran fast," a 3-year-old may say "I runned fast."

The errors young children make alert us to the fact that they are working to figure out a system of rules with which to communicate meaning. It is unlikely that these errors result from imitation of adult speech. Children say such things as "What dat feeled like?" or "Dose are mines." They have certainly not copied those expressions from adults; rather, these errors suggest the beginning of a grammar that becomes more specialized and accurate as children acquire the opportunity to match their speech to that of others (Schatz, 1983).

Milestones and Limitations

The milestones in language development during the first four years of life, as described by Eric Lenneberg (1967) are seen in Table 6.2. During the first year of life babies are highly sensitive to spoken language. They use vocalization in a playful way as a source of sensory stimulation. Gradually babies produce vocalizations that imitate spoken

Table 6.2	**Milestones in Language Development**
At the Completion of:	*Vocalization and Language*
12 weeks	Markedly less crying than at 8 weeks; when talked to and nodded at, smiles, followed by squealing-gurgling sounds usually called cooing, that is, vowel-like in character and pitch-modulated; sustains cooing for 15–20 seconds.
16 weeks	Responds to human sounds more definitely; turns head; eyes seem to search for speaker; occasionally some chuckling sounds.
20 weeks	The vowel-like cooing sounds begin to be interspersed with more consonantal sounds; acoustically, all vocalizations are very different from the sounds of the mature language of the environment.
6 months	Cooing changing into babbling resembling one-syllable utterances; neither vowels nor consonants have very fixed recurrences; most common utterances sound somewhat like *ma, mu, da,* or *di.*
8 months	Reduplication (or more continuous repetition) becomes frequent; intonation patterns become distinct; utterances can signal emphasis and emotions.
10 months	Vocalizations are mixed with sound play such as gurgling or bubble-blowing; appears to wish to imitate sounds, but the imitations are never quite successful; beginning to differentiate between words heard by making differential adjustment.
12 months	Identical sound sequences are replicated with higher relative frequency of occurrence and words (*mama* or *dadda*) are emerging; definite signs of understanding some words and simple commands ("Show me your eyes").
18 months	Has a definite repertoire of words—more than 3 but fewer than 50; still much babbling but now of several syllables with intricate intonation pattern; no attempt at communicating information and no frustration at not being understood; words may include items such as *thank you* and *come here,* but there is little ability to join any of the lexical items into spontaneous two-item phrases; understanding is progressing rapidly.
24 months	Vocabulary of more than 50 items (some children seem to be able to name everything in environment); begins spontaneously to join vocabulary items into two-word phrases; all phrases appear to be own creations; definite increase in communicative behavior and interest in language.
30 months	Fastest increase in vocabulary with many new additions every day; no babbling at all; utterances have communicative intent; frustrated if not understood by adults; utterances consist of at least two words, many have three or even five words; sentences and phrases have characteristic child grammar, that is, they are rarely verbatim repetitions of an adult utterance; intelligibility is not very good yet, though there is great variation among children; some seem to understand everything that is said to them.
3 years	Vocabulary of some 1,000 words; about 80% of utterances are intelligible even to strangers; grammatical complexity of utterances is roughly that of colloquial adult language, although mistakes still occur.
4 years	Language is well established; deviations from the adult norm tend to be more in style than in grammar.

Source: E. H. Lenneberg, *Biological Foundations of Language* (New York: Wiley, 1967). Copyright © 1967 John Wiley & Sons, Inc. Reprinted by permission of John Wiley & Sons, Inc.

language. In the second year, babies understand words and phrases. They develop a vocabulary and begin to form two-word phrases. During the third year, language is definitely used to communicate ideas, observations, and needs. Comprehension of spoken language seems almost complete. Some of their speech may not be easily understood by people outside the family, partly because they are unable to produce clear phonetic sounds and partly because their knowledge of adult grammar is limited. During the fourth year, most children acquire an extensive vocabulary. They can create sentences that reflect most of the basic rules of grammar. Their language is a vehicle for communicating complex thoughts that are usually understood by children and adults outside the family.

Although the fundamentals of language are well established by age 4, there are still some things that toddlers cannot achieve with language. For example, you might ask a 4-year-old boy to go upstairs and find an orange towel. He may be able to repeat your instructions exactly and still not be able to follow them. He will go upstairs and forget what it is that he is looking for, or he may return with a pillow instead of a towel. You might find him trying to wheel the TV set to the stairs. Verbal instructions do not necessarily have the desired impact on the toddler's behavior. The child is not deliberately trying to violate your instructions. He is merely unable to use verbal instructions effectively to guide his own behavior (Tinsley & Waters, 1982). Mary may raise a fuss about wanting the biggest piece of cake. If you allow her to make a choice, she selects a piece with lots of frosting. Clearly, the word *biggest* is not being used correctly. Even though Mary is able to memorize and repeat the words *big, bigger,* and *biggest,* she does not yet understand the concept to which they refer.

Both of these examples demonstrate that toddlers' language development can be somewhat misleading. One may assume that children fully understand the more abstract meanings of the words they use, but in fact their language continues to be very idiosyncratic throughout toddlerhood. The skills of language are being developed, but children are directing their efforts toward acquiring the building blocks. Fancy, subtle, complex verbal skills come only after they have learned the fundamentals.

Interaction and Language Development

Probably the most important factor that caregivers contribute to cognitive growth is the opportunity for interactions. An interactive human being can respond to a child's questions, provide information, react in unexpected ways to surprise the child, explain plans or strategies, or offer praise.

Burton White compared the child-rearing practices of mothers whose children were judged to be socially and intellectually competent with those of mothers whose children were judged to be below average (White & Watts, 1973; White, Kaban & Attanucci, 1979). The mothers of the competent children spent more time in interaction with them than did the mothers of the below-average children. This was true at every age period from 12 to 33 months. "The amount of live language directed to a child was perhaps the strongest single indicator of later intellectual and linguistic and social achievement" (White, Kaban & Attanucci, 1979). This does not mean that it is necessary to be with a child continuously. One implication is that children may benefit from frequent opportunities for interaction. Another is that competent children may generate more interaction than below-average children.

Certain characteristics of a language partner have been shown to facilitate a child's language acquisition and communication skills (Snow, 1984). When talking to toddlers, adults tend to modify their speech so that they are more likely to be understood. They use simplified, redundant speech that corresponds to the child's level of comprehension and interest. It is interesting that a caregiver will speak to an infant in long, complex sentences, but as soon as the baby begins to speak, the caregiver's speech becomes exaggerated and simplified (Moskowitz, 1978).

This style of speaking to a child who is learning language has been called "motherese." When speaking to toddlers, adults and other children adjust their spoken language in the following ways (Rice, 1989):

1. They simplify utterances to correspond with the toddler's interests and comprehension level.
2. They emphasize the here and now.
3. They use a more restricted vocabulary.
4. They do a lot of paraphrasing.
5. They use simple, well-formed sentences.
6. They use frequent repetitions.
7. They use a slow rate of speech with pauses between utterances and after the major content words.

These characteristics of caregiver speech are not universal. They seem to reflect cultural norms for addressing toddlers (Pye, 1986). Motherese is most typically observed in white, middle-class Western societies. Black adults in the rural south, by contrast, do not simplify or censor their speech for young children (Heath, 1989). They may not address children directly, but expect the children to hear what they say and to interrupt if they have something to add. Adults ask children real questions, questions they want answered. Adults and children direct one another's behavior with specific commands. It is just as acceptable for a toddler to command an adult as the other way around. Adults tease children, especially in the presence of others, in order to give the children a chance to show off their quick wit and to practice assertiveness. As active listeners, children have the opportunity to hear a variety of opinions, to gather information that extends their direct experience, and to observe shifts in language tone and style that accompany changes in the topic or purpose of the conversation.

The process of language learning involves a pattern of mutual regulation and upward "scaffolding." Nelson (1973) observed that children try to match the verbal expressions used by adults, both in pronunciation and in selection of words. Sometimes a child may be misunderstood because the child's pronunciation is so discrepant from the real word (*ambiance* for *ambulance, snuffin' cake* for *stomach ache*). At the same time, adults may use motherese or some other strategy to make sure they are being understood. Through frequent interactions, adults encourage language development by establishing a good balance between modifying their own speech somewhat and modeling more elaborated, accurate expressions for their children.

Adults make some hypotheses about the relationship between the verbal expression and the cognitive meaning associated with it. They may make use of several strategies to clarify a child's meaning. One is *expansion*, or the elaboration of the child's expression:

Child: Doggie wag.
Parent: Yes, the dog is wagging her tail.

As parents and toddlers explore books together, young children come to think of themselves as readers.

Another strategy is *prompting,* often in the form of a question. Here the parent urges the child to say more:

Child: More crackel.
Parent: You want more what?

In both of these interactions, the adult is helping the child to communicate more effectively by expanding on or asking the child to elaborate on something of interest to the child. The immediate matching of the adult utterance to the content or topic of the child's verbalization is called *semantic contingency*. This style is effective in facilitating language acquisition. The kinds of sentences parents use help children to see how they can produce new sentences that are more grammatically correct and therefore more meaningful to others.

Socially interactive rituals such as telling stories, playing word games, verbal joking and teasing, and reading books together also seem to enhance language development, especially by building vocabulary and preparing children to use language comfortably in social situations. Reading aloud has been identified as an especially important language activity in preparation for literacy. In the toddler period, an adult reads and the child asks questions and engages the adult in conversation. Some books are read aloud so often that the toddler begins to "read" them from memory or by retelling the story from the pictures. As children enter early school age, this type of ritualized reading activity provides a framework for the child's concept of what it means to be a reader.

Children and parents often engage in language games that expand the child's use of words and phrases. These games are usually part of ongoing family life. They are introduced not as a separate activity but as an extension of a related activity. Hoffman (1985) described one of her 3½-year-old son David's spontaneous games that began to build the bridge from speech to literacy. As the game developed, the object was for David to point to road signs as he rode with his mother to nursery school and for her to read as many of the signs as possible while they were driving along. David had created this game, and his mother played along willingly:

> *On the way to nursery school, David said, "Let's talk about signs! What does that sign say?"*
> *I answered, "Right turn signal."*
> *David proceeded with, "And what does that yellow and red shell say?"*
> *I answered him, "It says 'Shell'—that's a gasoline station."*
> *He asked, "Does it have seashells in it?"*
> *I answered, "No."*
> *We proceeded to read signs. I read the majority as he requested. However, David read "Speed Limit 35," "Bike Route," "No Parking Any Time." When we came to "No Parking This Side of Street," he thought it was "No Parking Any Time."*
> *These were the signs that I was able to read as he requested while I was driving. They were not the only ones on the route.*

SPEED LIMIT 40	NO TURN ON RED (3 times)
SPEED LIMIT 35 (12 times)	WATCH CHILDREN
NO PARKING ANY TIME (20 times)	SIGNAL AHEAD (3 times)
SCHOOL SPEED LIMIT (2 times)	NO LITTERING
NO PARKING THIS SIDE OF STREET (7 times)	DRIVEWAY
BIKE ROUTE (2 times)	

> *In this example we can see where patience was needed in order to communicate with a young child while I was driving the car.* [p. 90]

We have evidence that mothers differ in their verbal interactions and that these differences have implications for children's problem-solving abilities. But what about fathers and siblings? Can their interactions also influence language development? In a study of low-income black families, the contributions of siblings to the toddlers' language skills were observed (Norman-Jackson, 1982). Preschoolers whose older siblings were successful readers showed greater language competence. The older siblings were a significant source of verbal stimulation for their younger brothers and sisters. These differences suggest that parents and siblings make distinct contributions to the child's language environment. What is more, children may learn to interact in different ways with their mothers, fathers, and siblings.

The Language Environment
Parents do not interact with their infants and toddlers for the sole purpose of teaching language skills. In fact, direct language instruction plays a very minimal role in the verbal exchanges that take place within families. Language is a cultural tool, a means for socializing and educating young children; it is one of many inventions for creating

a sense of group identity and for passing the mythology, wisdom, and values of the culture from one generation to the next. Language is a part of the psychosocial environment. Competence in the use of language solidifies the young child's membership in the immediate family and in the larger cultural group (Rogoff & Morelli, 1989).

Of course, children grow up in a wide range of language environments. Subgroups and families vary not only in the language or dialect they speak but in their reliance on verbal as opposed to nonverbal expression, their typical patterns of communication, and the importance they place on language as a means to help children achieve competence in various domains (Bernstein, 1972; Hess & Shipman, 1965; Wertsch, 1978).

At the present time, the United States faces critical challenges with respect to the education of young children. Many of these challenges are related to the quality of the young child's language environment, its correspondence with the language environment of the schools, and the relevance of the school's approach to the requirements of the workplace for oral and written communication. The concept of multicultural education suggests that we must begin to recognize and value differences in the context and style of language use in various subcultures as one component of intellectual development, and introduce opportunities for children with different language competences to build on their strengths in the educational environment.

There is considerable evidence that children develop problem-solving strategies and verbal responses in specific social environments (Miller-Jones, 1989). Language proficiency has at least two components (Snow, 1987). One is the use of language in face-to-face interactions—language used specifically for social situations. The other is language removed from any specific context—language knowledge as it is usually measured by tests of vocabulary, verbal reasoning, and writing. Proficiency in one area may not predict proficiency in another.

Take *bilingualism*. Bilingualism is a social as well as a linguistic characteristic. Children who are proficient in two or more languages are also embedded in a complex sociocultural environment (Hakuta & Garcia, 1989). Research has found that the learning of two languages generally does not hamper children's cognitive development, especially if being a native speaker of one language rather than another has no stigmatizing consequences (Diaz, 1983). It appears that young bilingual children are adept at switching from one language to another as the conversational situation demands. In fact, children may use their two languages as a way to impose boundaries on social interactions and to add a degree of clarity to social relationships.

In the United States, however, the schools assign high priority to proficiency in English. Even at a time when educators bemoan American schoolchildren's ignorance of foreign languages, the criteria for success in bilingual education is proficiency in the abstract, academic English-language skills. Thus the school may impose a conflict between proficiency in English and proficiency in the native language, a conflict that challenges the child's language competence as well as the child's social identification with the non-English-language environment (Olsen, 1988).

The development of language skills is by no means complete at the close of toddlerhood. Important language functions develop more fully during early and middle school age. Older children can use language to help them plan a problem-solving strategy, guide a complex series of motor activities, or identify the relationships among

Parents are important to the development of bilingualism in children. This Hispanic mother encourages her daughter in switching playfully from Spanish to English and back again.

objects. Vocabulary expands, and words are used more and more in the ways they are used in adult speech. Sentences become more complex, including conditional and descriptive clauses. The irregular verbs and nouns are learned and used correctly (Moskowitz, 1978). As children attend school, they learn to conceptualize the grammatical structure of their language. Beyond the formal elements of vocabulary, grammar, reading, and writing, language development plays a critical role in subsequent psychosocial crises, especially the establishment of group identity, intimacy, and generativity. It is primarily through the quality of one's spoken language that one achieves the levels of disclosure that sustain significant personal relationships. Language also serves as a mechanism for resolving conflicts and for building a sense of cohesiveness within groups, whether of friends, co-workers, or family members.

Self-Control

Self-control has been defined as the ability to comply with a request, modify behavior according to the situation, postpone action, and behave in a socially acceptable way without having to be guided or directed by someone else (Kopp, 1982). These abilities reflect a growing sense of selfhood. They also reflect the cognitive ability to assess a situation and to compare it with previously learned guidelines on how to behave. Finally, they reflect the ability to express or redirect impulses in order to reduce their intensity.

Early in infancy, babies can increase or reduce their level of arousal (Kopp, 1982). By sucking or rocking, for example, babies can soothe themselves. Babies can resist overstimulation by turning away, crying, or going to sleep. From about 3 to 9 months, motor development permits increasing control over objects and behavior. Reaching and crawling give babies experience in directing action and experimenting with the consequences of action. From 9 to 18 months, infants show the ability to comply with a request. They can give a hug, pass a toy to another child, or draw back a hand if a parent says "No." They also begin to inhibit their own behavior. A child may reach for a knife on the counter, shake her head, say "Don't touch," and pull back her hand.

Control of Impulses

During toddlerhood, self-control develops in two directions: control of impulses and self-regulated goal attainment. First, children improve their ability to modify and control their impulses. The case of Colin illustrates how toddlers can fall prey to their impulses. Sometimes they simply cannot interrupt an ongoing action, even one they know is inappropriate. Colin, aged 2 years, 9 months, is just starting nursery school:

> *In his relations with children, Colin progressed quickly from a quiet, friendly, watching relationship on the first few days to actively hugging the other children. The hugging seemed to be in an excess of friendliness and was only mildly aggressive. Having started hugging he didn't know how to stop, and usually just held on until he pulled the child down to the floor. This was followed very closely by hair pulling. He didn't pull viciously, but still held on long enough to get a good resistance from the child. He grabbed toys from others. When stopped by an adult from any of these acts, he was very responsive to reason, would say, smiling, "I won't do it any more," would tear around the room in disorganized activity, and then return to hugging or pulling hair.* [Murphy, 1956, pp. 11–12]

During the years from 2 to 4, children develop the ability to withstand delays in the gratification of impulses. On the one hand, children experience far less frustration than they did previously; on the other, they develop successful ways of managing the frustrations that they experience (Vaughn, Kopp & Krakow, 1984).

One reason children experience less frustration is that they begin to develop a rudimentary sense of time, which involves some appreciation of the future. Toddlers repeatedly discover that although what they want is not available to them at the moment, it is often available after a brief delay. Their sense of trust helps children appreciate this. As they become aware that after a period of delay their needs will very likely be met, the delay itself generates less frustration. This sequence depends heavily on the caregivers' responsiveness and on their ability to provide the gratifications that they have asked the children to delay.

Of course, some events challenge even the most patient child's limits. Children must learn techniques for managing their emotions when they are aroused. One of the first tactics toddlers use to inhibit an impulse is to divert their attention from a forbidden object. In a study of the ability to delay behavior, an adult showed 2-year-olds an unusual telephone and asked them not to touch it, then stepped out of the room for a few moments. In the experimenter's absence, the children's behaviors were observed and the time that elapsed before they touched the phone was measured. The experimenter returned as soon as a child touched the phone, or within 2½ minutes. Behaviors associated with an ability to delay touching the phone were

Pablo Picasso, *Paulo on a Donkey,* 1923. Self-control is expressed in Paulo's poise, his trusting expression, and his confident mastery of the burro.

looking away from the phone, playing with their hands or covering their faces with their hands, and talking about something other than the telephone. In the course of this study it became clear that some rudiments of delay strategies become more focused and effective by ages 3 and 4 (Vaughn et al., 1986).

Language and fantasy are the most useful tools that children have for managing their impulses. The more articulate children can be in expressing their wishes, the better the chances that their needs will be met. When their needs cannot be met, they can use language to express how they feel. Feelings that are expressed are easier for children to control than those that are not. Children can also learn to use language in order to interrupt an impulsive act. For example, when young children were exposed to a clown box, they were able to resist the distraction and return to their work by saying such things as "I'm not going to look at Mr. Clown Box" or "Don't bother me" (Mischel & Patterson, 1976; Patterson & Mischel, 1976).

When children are asked to resist temptation, they use a variety of verbal strategies, including talking quietly to themselves and singing songs to distract themselves (Mischel, Shoda & Rodriguez, 1989). Toddlers who can talk to themselves may be able to control their fears, modify their anger, and soften their disappointments. They may repeat comforting words that their parents have spoken to them, or they may develop their own verbal strategies for reducing pain and suffering. When a boy who feels bad about something tells you that "superheroes don't cry," you realize that he is making an effort to control his emotional state.

The development of symbolic imagery allows children to create imaginary situations in which disturbing problems can be expressed and resolved. Through fantasy play, toddlers can control situations that are far beyond their real-world capacities (Singer, 1973, 1975). They can punish and forgive, harm and heal, fear and conquer fear, all within the boundaries of their own imaginations.

Children can dissipate some of the intensity of their impulses by talking about them and weaving them into fantasy situations. They gradually become more masters than slaves of their emotional needs. Children enter the stage of toddlerhood on the tail end of the whip of emotional impulses. They seem easily frustrated, impatient, and demanding. Their feelings may quickly gain momentum until they are beyond control. By the end of toddlerhood, children move into the pivot position in the whip. They are better able to control the speed with which emotions build up and the manner in which emotions are expressed. Just as the pivot person in the whip is occasionally pulled off stride, so may children lose control from time to time. In general, however, toddlers begin to regulate their own impulses effectively as an understanding of time, the use of language, and the capacity for fantasy expression develop.

For 30 years Walter Mischel and his colleagues have investigated the process by which children delay gratification. One of their consistent findings is that the ability to delay gratification varies with the individual. At age 4, children who tend to delay gratification longer tend to be more intelligent, to be more likely to resist temptation, to demonstrate greater social responsibility, and to have higher achievement strivings (Mischel, Shoda & Rodriguez, 1989).

A 4-year-old's ability to use self-regulatory strategies to delay gratification seems to have enduring effects. More than ten years later, children who had waited longer in the experimental situation that required self-imposed delay of gratification at age 4 were described by their parents as socially and academically more competent than their peers. Parents rated these children as more verbally fluent and able to express ideas; they used and responded to reason, and they were more competent and skillful. They were more attentive and able to concentrate, to plan, and to think ahead. They were also seen as better able to cope with frustration and to resist temptation.

As Freud hypothesized, the ability to delay gratification seems to be an important component of ego development. The work of Mischel and his colleagues suggests that toddlers who are able to delay gratification make greater strides in ego development throughout childhood. Even though most children acquire the skills needed for more successful delay as they get older, the ones who demonstrate these skills earliest seem to gain an advantage by elaborating the growing network of ego skills more effectively.

Box 6.1   The Control of Angry Feelings

The expression of anger, which is important to the child's development of a sense of autonomy, constantly generates tension between parents and children (Wenar, 1982). A toddler gets angry for many reasons, including inability to perform a task, parental restrictions on behavior, and peer or sibling rivalry. As toddlers become increasingly involved in directing the outcomes of their activities, they get angry when someone interrupts them or offers unrequested assistance (Bullock & Lutkenhaus, 1988). In addition, it appears that some children are temperamentally more aggressive than others (Olweus, 1979; Parke & Slaby, 1983). Although the expression of anger is inevitable and understandable, it is never pleasant. Parents who have encouraged their children to be independent, to try new things, and to express their feelings may still find it difficult to accept the hostility that accompanies growing selfhood. Parents are faced with the tasks of providing acceptable mechanisms for the expression of anger and of teaching children how to control angry feelings.

Children rely heavily on parents as models for learning how to control anger. The times when parents are angry are very important. Children learn as much or more about the expression of anger from watching their parents when they are angry as they do from verbal explanations or punishment (Bandura, 1977). Children are sensitive to anger when it is expressed between their parents, even when it is not directed to them. Parents' hostility to each other, expressed through quarrels, sarcasm, and physical abuse, increases a child's sensitivity to anger and is closely related to distur-

bances in development (Cummings, Pellegrini, Notarius & Cummings, 1989).

The child who can express anger and not lose control makes tremendous gains in the development of autonomy. Anger and conflict with parents give toddlers evidence that they are indeed very separate from their parents and that the separateness, although painful, is legitimate. Children who are severely punished or ridiculed for their anger are left in a state of doubt. They see models for the expression of anger in the way their parents respond to them and yet are told that anger is not appropriate for them.

Several strategies help young children to manage or reduce the intensity of their anger. These include ignoring aggression; providing brief "timeout" periods in a nearby quiet area until the emotion has subsided; arousing feelings that are incompatible with the anger, especially empathy for the victim; minimizing exposure to stimuli that arouse aggressive impulses; explaining the consequences of aggressive actions for the other person; and explaining the circumstances that may have led to the initial feelings of anger or frustration (Berkowitz, 1973). For the sake of the child's emerging self-concept, angry feelings must be allowed some form of legitimate expression. In the process of expressing angry feelings, children learn to control themselves and to channel these emotions into constructive rather than destructive activity. Over the period between ages 2 and 5, the frequency of angry, aggressive behaviors declines as children develop effective strategies for self-control (Cummings, Iannotti & Zahn-Waxler, 1989).

Self-Regulated Goal Attainment

The second sense in which self-control develops has to do with toddlers' feelings that they can direct their behavior and the behavior of others to achieve intended outcomes (Messer et al., 1987). During infancy, children become increasingly aware of themselves as causal agents. They make things happen. In toddlerhood, children become much more assertive about their desire to initiate actions, to persist in activities, and to determine when these activities should stop. Their sense of *agency*—their view of

Dish washing is a wonderful task for toddlers. It is something adults do every day; it involves many kinds of motor coordination; and if the dishes are metal or plastic, it's a safe activity.

themselves as the originators of action—expands to include a broad array of behaviors. Children make efforts to participate in decisions about bedtime, the clothes they wear, the kinds of foods they eat, and family activities. They want to do things they see their parents and older siblings doing. Their confidence in their own ability to handle very difficult tasks is not modified by a realistic assessment of their skills. According to toddlers, "Anything you can do, I can do better." When they have opportunities to do some of these new and complex things and succeed, they gain confidence in themselves and their abilities. They feel themselves to be valuable members of the family as they contribute to routine household tasks. Their feelings of confidence and value are matched by the acquisition of a wide variety of complex, coordinated skills.

A number of abilities must come together before the toddler can engage in these self-regulated, goal-directed behaviors.

First, the actor must be able to anticipate a not yet attained goal state and must understand that this goal can be reached through some specific activity. Second, the actor must represent the means-end relation between activities and their outcomes. . . . Beyond such representational abilities, however, additional skills, that we will label volitional skills, are necessary for translating knowledge into successful action. Generally, volitional skills involve remaining task oriented, that is keeping the anticipated goal in mind, and monitoring progress toward an anticipated goal state. This includes waiting or searching for appropriate opportunities to act, resisting distractions, overcoming obstacles, correcting actions, and stopping acting when a goal is reached." [Bullock & Lutkenhaus, 1988, p. 664]

Sometimes toddlers' enthusiasm and self-confidence go beyond their potential for performance. They watch parents who are easily managing a task and think they can do it just as easily. If left to try the task on their own, they fail. They become discouraged and frustrated because they did not expect an unsuccessful outcome. If parents tell them not to try, they are also frustrated, because they are certain that they would do a good job. Probably the best solution to this problem is to cooperate with toddlers, allowing them to do what they can but giving assistance when they need it. As children engage in tasks that are somewhat beyond their capacity, they learn to evaluate their strength and skill more realistically without feeling humiliated by failure. By the end of toddlerhood, children are better able to evaluate the requirements of a wide variety of tasks. They can judge whether or not they can accomplish a task by themselves.

We have considered two rather different phenomena under the development task of self-control. Children's ability to control their impulses is closely linked to the psychoanalytic concept of delay of gratification as Freud (1953), used it to describe development during the oral and anal stages. Mastery is a general motivation that accounts for children's efforts to increase their competence through persistent investigation and skillful problem solving (White, 1960; Harter, 1982). Both abilities foster toddlers' growing awareness of themselves. To function effectively as family members, toddlers must feel confident in their ability to control the inner world of their feelings and the outer world of decisions and tasks. As toddlers discover that they can tolerate stress, express or withhold their anger as appropriate and approach difficult tasks and succeed at them, they also lay claim to a growing definition of selfhood. Toddlerhood is an important time in the development of a person's sense of self-efficacy, the confidence that one can perform the behaviors demanded by a specific situation (Bandura, 1989). The more toddlers can do by themselves, the more confidence they will have in their ability to control the outcomes of their actions and to achieve their goals.

Summary

We have discussed four developmental tasks of toddlerhood: the elaboration of loco-motive skills, fantasy play, language development, and self-control. During infancy the developmental tasks focus on the emergence of boundaries and awareness of the connections between the self and other objects and people in the environment. Once the separateness of the self is well established, the emphasis shifts to concern over control—control of the self and of the environment. Thus the tasks of toddlerhood can be seen as serving to improve children's ability to bring some order and consistency to their world. Through self-control they feel more confident about managing their impulses. With language they can begin to influence others to respond to their needs and to give them more information about the world. Increased agility and speed bring them into contact with more of the environment. These locomotive skills also heighten their personal sense of mastery. In areas in which control is very difficult or perhaps impossible, fantasy allows a pseudo-mastery in which barriers are overcome and the limitations of reality are less critical. Success in these tasks should enhance children's feelings of competence and effectiveness.

The Psychosocial Crisis: Autonomy versus Shame and Doubt

During toddlerhood, children become aware of their separateness. Through a variety of experiences they discover that their parents do not always know what they want and do not always understand their feelings. In the early phases of toddlerhood, children use rather primitive devices to explore their independence. They may say no to everything offered to them whether they want it or not. This is the period that people often refer to as the "terrible twos." Toddlers seem very demanding and insist on having things done their own way. It is difficult to reason with 2-year-olds.

Children may develop certain well-ordered rituals for doing such things as going to bed, getting dressed, and leaving the house (Albert et al., 1977). They insist that these rituals be followed precisely and threaten to become extremely angry if the rituals are violated. Rituals represent efforts to bring control and order to the environment. They also help provide a feeling of sameness and continuity during changes in setting or state that may threaten children's feelings of selfhood. In day-to-day activities, toddlers encounter a wide range of situations for which they have no explanation. In their efforts to bring some predictability to these events, they design their own rituals. The rituals usually do not repeat adult ways of doing things. Toddlers' rituals, however, like those of adults, serve an important psychological function.

In the development of autonomy, toddlers shift from a somewhat rigid naysaying, ritualized, unreasonable style to an independent, energetic, persistent one (Erikson, 1963). The behavior of older toddlers is characterized by the phrase "I can do it myself." They are less concerned with doing things their own way and more concerned with doing them on their own. Toddlers demonstrate an increasing variety of skills. Each new accomplishment gives them great pride. When doing things independently leads to positive results, the sense of autonomy grows. Toddlers begin to create an image of themselves as people who can manage situations competently and satisfy many of their own needs. Children who have been allowed to experience autonomy should, by the end of toddlerhood, have a strong foundation of self-confidence and feelings of delight in behaving independently.

The unique characteristics of growth toward autonomy are its energy and persistence. Children do not just prefer to do most things on their own; they *insist* on doing so. Once children begin to work on a task such as putting on pajamas or tying shoes, they will struggle along time after time until they have mastered it. They may reject help adamantly and insist that they can manage on their own. They will allow someone else to help them only when they are sure that they can progress no further by themselves.

The establishment of a sense of autonomy requires not only tremendous effort by the child but extreme patience and support from parents. Toddlers' demands for autonomy often are exasperating. They challenge the parents' good sense, goodwill, and good intentions. Parents must learn to teach, cajole, absorb insults, wait, and praise. Sometimes they must allow children to try things that the children may not be able to do. By encouraging children to engage in new tasks, parents hope to promote their sense of competence.

Some children fail to emerge from toddlerhood with a sense of mastery. Because of failure at most attempted tasks or continual discouragement and criticism from parents—or, most likely, because of both—some children develop an overwhelming sense of shame and self-doubt. This is the negative resolution of the psychosocial crisis of toddlerhood (Erikson, 1963). *Shame* is an intense emotion that can result from two different types of experiences (Morrison, 1989). One source of shame is social ridicule or criticism. You can probably reconstruct feelings of shame by imagining being scolded for having spilled your milk or for having lost your jacket. When you are shamed, you feel small, ridiculous, humiliated. Some cultures rely heavily on public humiliation as a means of social control. Adults in those cultures grow up with a strong concern about "saving face." One of their greatest fears is to be publicly accused of immoral or dishonorable actions. In some instances, such shame can lead to suicide.

The other source of shame is internal conflict. As children construct an understanding of what it means to be a good, decent, capable person, they build a mental image of an ideal person, the *ego ideal*. Children feel shame when they recognize that their behavior is not meeting the standards of their ideal. Even though they have not broken a rule or done something naughty, they may feel shame when they fail to live up to their own private idea of how they think they should behave.

The experience of shame is extremely unpleasant. In order to avoid it, children may refrain from all kinds of new activities. These children lack confidence in their abilities; they expect to fail at what they do. The acquisition of new skills thus becomes slow and painful. Feelings of self-confidence and worth are replaced by constant doubt. Children who have a pervasive sense of *doubt* feel comfortable only in highly structured and familiar situations in which the risk of failure is minimal. This is the extreme negative resolution of the conflict of autonomy versus shame and doubt.

Under normal conditions, all children experience some failures amid their many successes. Even the most patient parent may occasionally shame a child for making a mess or disturbing others. Such occurrences help children make a more realistic assessment of their independence and skills. Children who resolve the crisis in favor of autonomy will still question whether they can succeed, and they may still experience shame when they fail, but they will usually be predisposed toward trying many activities. The few children who resolve the crisis in favor of shame and doubt will avoid new activities and cling to what they already know.

Toilet Training

The classic psychological conflict between individual autonomy and social demands for conformity is toilet training. As Robert White (1960) points out, in this particular conflict children are destined to lose. They must subordinate their autonomy to expectations for a specific routine for elimination. Toddlers must master a number of skills in order to succeed at toilet training. They must have some word or signal that they can use to communicate to their parents their need to go to the bathroom. They must be able to get to the bathroom either by finding their own way there or by finding someone to direct them there. They must be able to delay elimination until they have arrived at the bathroom and removed their clothes.

Children cannot control elimination until their musculature is sufficiently developed. This is an obvious but extremely important point. The sphincter muscles, which control the ability to hold on to and let go of fecal material, do not become fully mature and workable until the average child is between 1½ and 2 years old. The implication of this fact of physical development is that a child will be unable to control bowel movements before the sphincters have attained this maturation.

For the child to experience a sense of competence during the toilet-training period, a number of things must occur: (1) The body must be ready; (2) the child must be able to give a signal when it is time to go; and (3) the child must be able to respond to an internal cue and anticipate necessary action. There is some evidence that girls achieve bladder control earlier than boys. More boys than girls are enuretic into adolescence. This difference in bladder control probably reflects a difference in muscle development rather than a difference in motivation, frustration, or activity level.

If parents wait to begin toilet training until children show signs of readiness in all areas, children are likely to see this task as a source of pride and accomplishment rather than as a struggle of wills. They will be happy to be able to accomplish something that is so important to their parents. Their success will increase their self-confidence.

Classic psychoanalytic theory (Freud, 1905/1953, 1913/1958) considers the ages of 2 through 4 to be a period of obsessive-compulsive characteristics and neuroses. *Obsessions* are persistent, repetitive thoughts that serve as mechanisms for binding anxiety. *Compulsions* are repetitive, ritualized actions that serve the same function. The sources of anxiety that motivate obsessive and compulsive behavior, according to psychoanalytic theory, are unconscious conflicts related to the anal region of the body and the process of bowel control. Obsessive-compulsive behaviors are observable in the normal person's concern with order, cleanliness, and planning. They are usually under the person's control and can be useful tools for personal organization. In the neurotic individual, however, such thoughts and behaviors are beyond personal control and often impede effectiveness.

Although toilet training is an interesting paradigm that highlights issues of willfulness, body control, and parental authority, the concept of autonomy encompasses a much broader spectrum of behavior. The historical emphasis on toilet training in the development of personality seems to have been too narrow and restrictive. Bowel control is only one of a variety of skills that develop during toddlerhood. The experiences that the healthy child gains in mastering skills of many kinds are channeled into the development of autonomy and competence.

The Central Process: Imitation

The primary mechanism by which toddlers emerge as autonomous individuals is *imitation*. Although imitation requires the presence of active models, its outcome is a shift of the action from the model to the imitator. In other words, once toddlers succeed in imitating a certain skill, that skill belongs to them, and they can use it for any purpose they like. Toddlers seem driven to imitate almost everything they observe, including parents' positions at the toilet. Toddlers' vocabularies expand markedly

Imitation makes a connection that helps older and younger siblings play together.

through the imitation of words heard in adult conversations, on television, and in stories. Their interest in dancing, music, and other activities stems from imitation of parents and peers. As soon as one child in a play group makes a funny noise or performs a daring act, the other children appear to be compelled to recreate this novel behavior.

The imitative behavior of the toddler is very different from the socially induced conformity observed in older children. The toddler is not aware of a great many social norms and therefore feels little pressure to conform to them. Imitative behavior is really a vehicle for learning (Bandura, 1977; Parton, 1976). Every act becomes one's own, even if it has been inspired by others. The primary motivation for imitation during toddlerhood is the drive for mastery and competence.

In studies of imitation in the home environment, toddlers show an impressive pattern of imitating parents' household, self-care, and caretaking activities. They show increasing interest in imitating behaviors that are socially meaningful and valued. These observations lead researchers to suggest that imitation serves a critical function in satisfying the toddler's need for social competence (Kuczynski, Zahn-Waxler & Radke-Yarrow, 1987). Through imitation, children may also derive pleasure from the similarity they perceive between themselves and the model. This perceived similarity is a secondary benefit of the imitative process (Kagan, 1958).

Imitation is also a means of participating in and sustaining social interactions (Grusec & Abramovitch, 1982). Within a peer setting, imitation emerges as a dominant strategy whereby children coordinate their behaviors with those of other toddlers. Before verbal communication becomes much of a useful tool for establishing or maintaining social contact, toddlers imitate one another. Through imitation, toddlers can feel connected to one another and begin to invent coordinated games (Eckerman,

Davis & Didow, 1989). With increasing cognitive maturity, children select for imitation behaviors that have relevance to their own needs for mastery, for nurturance, and for social interaction.

We pointed out earlier the importance of imitation to the development of vocabulary. Learning rules of grammar, however, appears to require originality and problem-solving skills. In language learning, imitation provides a means for accumulating words as building blocks, but in order to use language autonomously, children must figure out the form through which their thoughts can be translated into words. The relationship between imitation of words and autonomy of language also holds for imitation of activities and autonomy of personality. The wide range of actions that children learn through imitation is gradually ordered to suit their individual preferences. Children rely on imitation to acquire many skills, but the unique use of those skills soon comes under the management of their own will.

Summary

The psychosocial crisis of autonomy versus shame and doubt builds up and is resolved during the years from 2 through 4. This period is dominated by the child's persistent needs for self-expression and mastery. Self-doubt results from repeated experiences of failure and inadequacy. The mechanism for achieving a strong sense of autonomy is the development of competence at a variety of skills. Imitation is the primary vehicle for skill learning during toddlerhood. Through imitation, children develop a repertoire of language and skills that enable them to express their own needs and to coordinate their behavior with that of others.

☐ Applied Topics: Discipline and Day Care

Discipline

Discipline is a tool for shaping the child to the parents' expectations of what is culturally acceptable or valued. The content of the discipline (the kinds of acts that are prohibited) and the techniques (the methods of control) bring the range of the child's behavior within culturally shared norms. Discipline also gives children some techniques for controlling their own behavior. A continuing tension for humans in their efforts to create a moral society is the conflict among self-gratification, the assertion of ego, and the satisfaction of others' needs. Only by helping their children to grasp the consequences of their acts can parents successfully challenge their children's egocentrism.

Toddlers' naive egocentrism and physical exuberance frequently bring them into conflict with parents, siblings, and peers. Negativism, or the clear refusal to comply with the requests of others, is a hallmark of toddlerhood (Wenar, 1982; Haswell, Hock & Wenar, 1981). Eventually the child's refusal to comply will conflict with a parent's insistence on a particular behavior. Thus we can expect occasions for discipline to be an inevitable element of parent-child interactions during toddlerhood. As we suggested in the discussion of the psychosocial crisis of toddlerhood, the ideal result of parental discipline is toddlers' confidence in their own ability to impose limits on their behavior without feeling extremely inhibited by fears of their parents' scorn.

Discipline practices have been described in three general categories (Hoffman, 1977):

1. *Power assertion:* Physical punishment, shouting, attempts to physically move a child or inhibit behavior, taking away privileges or resources, or threatening any of these things.
2. *Love withdrawal:* Expressing anger, disappointment, or disapproval; refusing to communicate; walking out or turning away.
3. *Inductions:* Explaining why the behavior was wrong; pointing out the consequences of behavior to others; redirecting behavior by appealing to the child's sense of mastery, fair play, or love of another person.

In addition to these three general categories of discipline techniques, parental modeling and reinforcement of acceptable behaviors are significant in the development of internal control (Mussen & Eisenberg-Berg, 1977). If children are to correct their behavior, they must know what acts would be considered appropriate as well as how to inhibit their inappropriate acts. Modeling and reinforcement aid children in directing their behavior, while discipline serves to inhibit or redirect it.

Early research on parental discipline focused on its impact on the internalization of moral prohibitions. To what extent do children raised with one primary mode of discipline succeed in exerting control over their own behavior and in confessing when they fail? Hoffman (1970) summarized the findings as follows:

> *The frequent use of power assertion by the mother is associated with weak moral development to a highly consistent degree. Induction discipline and affection, on the other hand, are associated with advanced moral development, although these relationships are not quite as strong and consistent across the various age levels as the negative ones for power assertion. . . . In contrast to induction, love withdrawal relates infrequently to the moral indices and the few significant findings obtained do not fit any apparent pattern.*   [p. 292]

Studies have consistently reported that children of parents who frequently use power-assertive techniques tend to show high levels of aggression themselves (Anthony, 1970; Chwast, 1972). Several hypotheses have been raised to explain this relationship. First, physical punishment may serve to frustrate the child and create further aggressive impulses. Second, parents who discipline a child with physical punishment may provide a model for aggressive behavior. Third, parents who punish aggression toward themselves may also encourage or reward aggressiveness toward others, and this may cause the child to be aggressive. Finally, aggressive children may provoke parents into using power-assertive strategies. For example, Buss (1981) reported that there was more conflict in parent-child interactions when the child had a very high activity level. Parents of more active children were more likely to use physical control and become involved in power struggles with their children than were parents of less active children.

The toddler's naive exuberance and willfulness are often in conflict with parents' wishes, which creates occasions for discipline. Luckily, the child's appealing looks and winning ways usually soften the adult's anger.

Some laboratory studies, however, suggest that physical punishment may succeed in inhibiting undesirable behavior if it is used just at the onset of the undesired behavior (Aronfreed & Reber, 1965; Walters, Parke & Cane, 1965). This use of punishment might be more appropriately described as *avoidance conditioning*. In these situations, children were prevented from touching a preferred toy just before they were going to handle it. When left alone with the toy, children who were thus punished directed their attention to another toy. We suggest that when punishment is used in a natural setting, it is probably used after the misdeed has occurred. Under these conditions, physical punishment tends to heighten rather than inhibit aggressive impulses.

Love withdrawal has little, if any, positive effect on the internalization of moral prohibitions. It may be effective in bringing about compliance with adult expectations (Forehand et al., 1976). The effect of love withdrawal is to stimulate the child's need for approval and increase his or her anxiety about the expression of hostility. The child whose parents use love withdrawal as a primary discipline technique tends to be anxious about the expression of impulses and willing to conform to adult authorities (Hoffman, 1980). These characteristics are differentiated from morality because they have a minimal conceptual component (children do not know why they should refrain from some activity) and a high level of anxiety about external consequences (parents may withdraw love).

Inductions succeed when the other two techniques fail because they provide children with a conceptual framework to guide their behavior. They arouse children's empathy by pointing out the consequences of their behavior for others (Leizer &

Table 6.3   Discipline Techniques and Their Consequences for Personality and Moral Development

Discipline Technique	Personality Correlates	Moral Behaviors
Power assertion	Aggressive behavior and fantasy	Minimal internalization of moral prohibitions
Love withdrawal	Anxiety and dependence	No clear relationship to moral behavior
Inductions	Autonomy and concern for others	Advanced moral development

Rogers, 1974). Families who use inductions as the primary discipline technique may be described as democratic rather than authoritarian. Such families are characterized by a warm, accepting atmosphere, a high degree of communication among family members, and an orientation of concern and tolerance for others (Odom, Seeman & Newbrough, 1971). Children of parents who set firm, age-appropriate standards for behavior are generally sociable, responsible, self-confident, and considerate of others (Baumrind, 1971). In addition to their effectiveness in producing compliance with parental wishes, inductions involve more elaborate parent-child communication than do the other techniques. Thus inductions have the effect of promoting verbal skills as well as "good" behavior (Lytton, 1976).

Table 6.3 summarizes the three discipline techniques that we have discussed. Each technique is associated with specific consequences for moral behavior and for various dimensions of personality development.

The Discipline Context

More recent research has considered some of the immediate contextual dimensions that influence a parent's approach to discipline. Three elements seem relevant to a comprehensive picture of discipline.

First, an adult's personal theory about the appropriate role of parents in guiding the behavior of children at various ages will influence the way that person interprets and reacts to a child's actions. This theory is shaped by a person's own level of psychosocial maturity, by cultural assumptions regarding children and how they should be treated, and by the person's earlier experiences in observing and interacting with young children. When Mondell and Tyler (1981) investigated the relationship between parents' psychosocial maturity and parent-child interactions, they found that parents with a high degree of competence and trust were more likely to perceive their children as capable and resourceful than were parents low in these qualities. Such parents were also more likely to approach a joint problem-solving task with warm, positive, and helpful interactions.

An adult's approach to discipline is guided by a subjective assessment of a child's actions. Parents are likely to be less stern about punishing an action if they think the child did not understand that what he or she did was wrong. Parents' views of a child's competence and sense of responsibility or intention in respect to the misconduct will influence the type and severity of the discipline they apply (Dix, Ruble & Zambarano, 1989). Parents tend to take a child's age and relevant skills into account as they assess the seriousness of a misdeed. They also feel angrier and tend to be more stern when they conclude that a child was in fact deliberately responsible for the misdeed.

Another element in a parent's assessment of misconduct is whether the parent believes a child's behavior is a product of a personal trait or a product of the situation (Mills & Rubin, 1990). A parent who concludes that a child is "naturally" aggressive and boisterous may react calmly to an aggressive outburst. The parent who believes the child is being purposefully defiant may react with greater force. This pattern depends heavily on the parent's cultural outlook and values.

Another parent may believe that it is important to be very firm with a child who is temperamentally aggressive in order to help the child develop self-control. This adult might be more understanding and calm in reaction to a child who is usually very easy going but suddenly becomes aggressive. Culture and child-rearing values influence an adult's interpretation of a child's behavior and thus the course of action (Kochanska, Kuczynski & Radke-Yarrow, 1989).

Second, the situation may influence both whether and how a child is disciplined. We all know that a behavior such as loud singing or asking Mom to play house may be acceptable when everyone is relaxed. The same behavior may not be acceptable, however, when Mom is trying to pay the bills or get dinner ready. In a laboratory simulation of this phenomenon, parents were in a room with their two children, one in the 3-to-5-year range and one under 3 (Zussman, 1980). Parental behavior toward the children was observed under two conditions: when the parents could play with the children and when they were preoccupied with a task that competed with the children for attention. When the parents were involved in the competing task, they had fewer positive interactions with their older child and more frequent critical or punishing interactions with their younger one. Here we see that the circumstances that lead to discipline may reflect the parents' agenda as well as the child's.

Third, the child's response to a parent's initial request for compliance may influence subsequent actions. A discipline situation is interactive. With very young children, a parent's request or command is often followed by compliance. The father says: "No, don't touch!" and the baby withdraws her hand. In other instances, an adult can redirect a young child's misbehavior by distracting the child and offering some alternative activity or object. As children reach the age of 3 or 4, however, they become more active advocates for their own wishes. They may resist a command by negotiating: "I do it later"; "I already tried some"; or "Just a little more." When parents point out a mistake or a misdeed, a 3-year-old can offer a justification and try to avoid punishment: "Baby did it"; "I'm tired"; "I need it"; "It is mines." These justifications can lead to new negotiations. In some instances, parents may change their minds upon hearing a child's reasoning and allow the child to continue the behavior. In general, toddlers are more effective in offering reasonable justifications and negotiating alternative behaviors when their parents engage in these types of interactions than when parents issue stern commands and apply physical punishment (Dunn & Munn, 1987; Kuczynski, Kochanska, Radke-Yarrow & Girnius-Brown, 1987).

Generally toddlers are very sensitive to expressions of parental disapproval. As they move through toddlerhood, they begin to appreciate the extent of their dependence on parents. Most of children's behavior can be regulated with minimal adult intensity. Often children know immediately after a misdeed that they have done the wrong thing. Extensive punishment or shaming at that point serves only to generate anxiety rather than to reinforce the child's internal recognition of an inappropriate act.

When parents decide on a strategy for discipline, they must be sensitive to the child's changing motives, aspirations, competence, and fears. If a discipline technique does not succeed in inhibiting a specific behavior and if the same threat or punishment has to be used over and over, it must be concluded that, from the child's point of view, the technique is not meaningful. Consider a boy who becomes very boisterous, over-active, and rude whenever company is present. The parent consistently sends him out of the room as a punishment. If this pattern is repeated a number of times, one would assume that the boy knows the consequence of his behavior and does not see it as negative. Perhaps he is made very anxious by the presence of so many strangers and is glad to be removed from them without having to ask. Perhaps the special attention that his mother gives him as she removes him from the room is exactly what he wants in the midst of all the adult-centered activity. A punishment is a punishment only if it succeeds in reducing the likelihood of a particular behavior.

Each of the three orientations toward control of the child—power assertion, love withdrawal, and induction—has implications for the child's capacity to internalize moral controls. These discipline techniques reflect more global orientations toward child rearing that convey parents' attitudes toward intimacy, impulsiveness, and respect for authority. Discipline techniques must be evaluated in terms of the context of the behavior, the developmental abilities of the child, and the history of earlier discipline sequences.

Day Care

We have focused in some detail on discipline, especially within the framework of parent-child relations, because it is a major mechanism for socialization. Most of today's young children are actually exposed to a variety of socialization settings in which expectations for behavior vary.

As of 1987, 57% of married American women with children under the age of 6 were in the labor force. For divorced women, the rate was 70% (U.S. Bureau of the Census, 1987a, 1987b). It has become commonplace for mothers of young children to be employed outside the home. Child-care arrangements vary with the presence of a father in the family, the child's age, and whether the mother is employed full- or part-time. About 28% of the children under age 5 whose mothers are employed full-time are in organized day-care facilities, 42% are cared for in someone else's home, and 24% are cared for in their own home. Family members, especially fathers and grandparents, are responsible for about a third of the children who are cared for in their own homes or in someone else's home. More than one child-care arrangement is made for about 13% of the children. A child may be in a half-day nursery and then have a baby-sitter for the rest of the day; or a child may be in day care all day and have a relative baby-sitting in the early evening.

In quality day care the schedule is flexible enough to incorporate the children's ideas. This is a day for splashing in the pool!

Within this context of growing needs for child care and a wide range of child-care arrangements, parents, educators, and policy makers are asking critical questions: (1) What are the essential features of quality day care? (2) What is the effect of day care on the development of young children? (3) Where do we go from here to ensure quality care for children whose parents are in the labor force?

Essential Features of Quality Day Care

What constitutes quality care? For toddlers, in the age range 2 to 4, quality is based on the "three *p*'s": personnel, program, and physical plant.

The key ingredients with respect to *personnel* are the quality of training the teachers have had, a small group of children for each teacher, and low staff turnover (Phillips, McCartney & Scarr, 1987). The personnel must be trained in child development. They must have had supervised experiences working with very young children and the ability to communicate their knowledge effectively to parents. If they are properly educated for their role, they will understand the need to function as responsive, caring adults. They will know how to provide developmentally appropriate experiences and how to expand on young children's interests in order to promote cognitive and social growth. These caregivers will appreciate the young child's need to experience mastery and will provide a variety of opportunities for the exercise of autonomy. They will understand the role of symbolic activities of all types for a child's intellectual and emotional well-being, and will be able to facilitate imaginative play through a variety of media. They will expect children to have strong urges for physical activity and will encourage vigorous movement. They will also expect children to have strong needs for affection and approval, and they will be generous in their warmth.

Having interacted with a large number of young children, day-care personnel will be familiar with individual differences in temperament, learning style, emotional expressiveness, and stamina. They will design activities that permit these differences to be expressed, and they will encourage the children in their care to recognize and value differences in one another.

The *program* emphasis may vary from one center to another. However, quality programming should address the development of the total child, including physical, emotional, intellectual, and social growth. Since children need opportunities to encounter diversity, the program should provide a variety of sensory experiences, introducing novel materials and opportunities to encounter diverse aspects of the community, either by bringing guests to the children or by taking the children out into the community.

The program will be structured to provide predictability. This means following a patterned daily schedule with some routines that the children can anticipate. The program will also be flexible enough to respond to the changing interests and needs of the group. Activities will be designed to be adapted to the varying developmental levels of the children, so that children will not have to be left out if they have not achieved a certain level of skill.

Children will have opportunities to interact with each other in pairs and in small and large groups, in order to develop the range of social skills that fosters a sense of belonging and companionship. Children will also have opportunities for one-to-one interaction with adults. They will also have some time for solitude, when they are not isolated or rejected from the group, but free to remain alone.

The program will include many strategies for fostering communication and preparing children to participate in a literate world. This means that children will be encouraged to verbalize their thoughts and feelings, to describe their observations, to plan out loud, to tell stories and to react to stories, to experience expression through poetry, music, dance, drama, and art, to explore printed materials, and to learn the relationship between the spoken and written word.

The *physical plant* of a day-care center will depend to a considerable degree on its location. Day-care centers can be found in church basements, in buildings designed specifically for child care, in classrooms of an elementary school, and in the wing of a hospital. In order to be licensed, a day-care center must meet specific state laws with respect to building codes, fire and safety regulations, and minimum square footage of indoor and outdoor space for the number of children attending the program. Usually state standards establish the minimum requirements.

However, certain physical characteristics are found in all quality day-care centers. There is adequate floor space for large-muscle activity to take place safely indoors during inclement weather. Outdoor space is readily available and safe from environmental hazards and intruders. Furniture, toilets, and drinking fountains are child-size so that children can function as autonomously as possible within the setting. There are quiet areas where children can sleep and private areas where a child can withdraw from the group for a while without being out of sight of a caregiver. Lighting, heat, and ventilation are such that children can play actively without getting too overheated and can work comfortably on the floor. Materials are durable. Children's exploration should not be restricted out of fear that they will damage the setting. Children have

The day-care focus on early language development and problem solving can have a positive effect on long-term intellectual development.

opportunities to mark some space as their own by having a special cubbyhole, cot, locker, or shelf where they can keep their personal things.

In addition to these elements, quality programs actively include parents. Members of the staff work with parents to form partnerships on behalf of the children. Parents learn to extend the program's activities at home and to appreciate their children's developmental advances. Staff members encourage parents to assist in program development and evaluation. They try to be sensitive to the life conditions impinging on parents, such as poverty, illness, or divorce, which may affect a child's ability to participate successfully in the day-care program. Day-care teachers often contribute to a family's well-being by linking parents to needed health, educational, and economic resources (Schweinhart & Weikart, 1988).

The Impact of Day Care

The impact of day-care experiences on children has generally been assessed with regard to consequences for intellectual abilities, socioemotional development, and peer relations. Research has tended to focus on the impact of day care on children of very poor families, children who are especially at risk for school failure, illiteracy, and subsequent minimal employment or unemployment.

Although researchers are coming increasingly to agree on the positive impact of day care for 2- and 3-year-olds, the literature is still developing and many questions

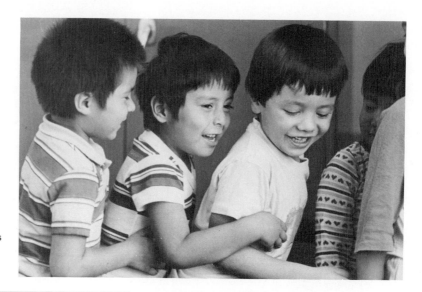

Very young children who share a day-care environment develop complex play strategies and experience the pleasures of companionship.

are still unanswered. It appears that quality day care contributes to intellectual achievement, as reflected in IQ scores, both during the preschool years and during the first grade (Burchinal, Lee & Ramey, 1989). In one long-term follow-up study, later adolescents at age 19 who earlier had experienced a quality child-care program had higher grades, fewer failing grades, a more positive attitude toward schooling, and a higher literacy rate than a comparable group of very poor young adults who had not participated in a quality child-care program (Schweinhart & Weikart, 1988).

In studies of the impact of day care on intelligence and school achievement, researchers in the United States have tended to concern themselves with the ability of quality child care to modify the negative effects of poverty. This focus leaves open the question whether early day-care experiences are enriching for children of middle-class parents, whose resources and educational backgrounds are likely to be more supportive of a child's intellectual achievement. In a study of Swedish child care, positive effects of early day-care experiences (beginning sometime after 6 or 7 months of age) on cognitive performance and teacher ratings were observed for children of parents with both low and middle income and with varying educational backgrounds (Andersson, 1989).

The socioemotional consequences of quality day care have been described as leading to higher levels of social competence, self-esteem, and empathy. Children who have positive interactions with adults in their day-care settings are more likely to continue to interact positively and comfortably with school adults and classmates in the elementary grades (Vandell, Henderson & Wilson, 1988). Some studies have found that children with day-care experience are less compliant with their parents and more aggressive with their peers than children who have not been in day care (Clarke-Stewart & Fein, 1983). This evidence of willfulness may be a result of a greater need to assert oneself in a group in order to have one's needs met. It may also reflect an advanced level of independence that results from functioning in more than one social-ization setting (Clarke-Stewart, 1989). Whether or not these qualities of noncompli-ance and aggressiveness lead to long-term problems in social adjustment has not been determined.

Quality day care also has an impact on peer relations. Children benefit from opportunities to interact with a variety of peers in settings where adults are readily available to help them make choices and resolve differences. The quality and com-plexity of social play are especially enhanced when children remain in the same child-care setting rather than move from one arrangement to another. Under conditions of stability, toddlers, whose verbal skills are limited, develop expanded strategies for coordinating their play with others and for exploring shared fantasies (Clarke-Stewart, 1989; Howes & Stewart, 1987). By the time they reached age 8, children who had experienced quality care at age 4 were more likely to engage in friendly interactions with their agemates, less likely to be playing alone, and less likely to be described as shy in comparison with children who had low-quality day-care experiences (Vandell, Henderson & Wilson, 1988).

Next Steps

We face a critical gap between the demand for affordable quality day care and its availability. Concern over the need for affordable quality day care is expressed by parents who are in the labor market as well as by those who would like to be in the labor market. We need to devise a parental leave policy so that parents can take time to care for their newborns without risking the loss of their jobs. In addition, policies and resources are needed to improve the training of child-care professionals, to pro-vide subsidies to help cover the costs of child care, and to improve the licensing regulations for people who provide day care in their homes (Buie, 1988).

Corporations are recognizing the need to address their employees' child-care needs. Worries about their children and the difficulty of making adequate child-care arrangements result in parental anxiety, missed workdays, and decrements in pro-ductivity. Companies are addressing this issue in several ways (Quinn, 1988).

Emergency care: temporary care for those days when an employee's regular arrangement fails.

Discounts: the company arranges for a 10% discount with a national child-care chain, or picks up 10% of the fee.

Vouchers: the company makes payments toward whatever child-care arrangement a parent selects. One company provides special assistance for all employees who earn less than $30,000. Another provides a subsidy during a child's first year of life.

Referral services: companies identify and list good day-care centers they can rec-ommend to their employees.

On-site day care: day-care centers are created at the workplace. The U.S. Senate and House of Representatives provide on-site day care for their members and employees.

Flexible benefits: employees arrange to have money to cover child care deducted from their salaries. This money does not count as taxable income.

The movement toward a comprehensive, national policy that places quality child care high on the list of priorities is evolving slowly. Some people are still reluctant to accept the participation of women, especially mothers of young children, in the labor force. The public tends to underestimate and devalue the training and expertise necessary to provide quality care. This attitude leads to low salaries and very difficult working conditions for child-care professionals. Furthermore, most adults, having had little or no formal training in child development and parenting, are poorly informed about the characteristics of quality care. They do not know what to look for or what questions to ask. As a result, they may end up placing their child in a setting that meets their own requirements for cost and convenience but does not contribute to their child's optimal development.

☐ Chapter Summary

Mastery and autonomy are intricately intertwined. Young children develop individuality through the exercise of skills that develop during toddlerhood. The limits of autonomy are imposed by a child's own capacities and by cultural norms for behavior.

Language is both a tool for the expression of feelings and concepts and a primary mechanism of socialization. Toddlers' use of language gives us clues to their cognitive development and to their needs. The emergence of fantasy provides children with a more internal, personal form of symbolic representation. Fantasy may be enhanced by language, but it most certainly can thrive in the absence of verbal performance.

Autonomy and individuation ordinarily emerge in the context of a parent-child relationship. It must be remembered that toddlers are avid observers, imitating and incorporating parental behaviors and values into their own routines. Parental interaction, acceptance, and discipline all contribute to a child's emerging sense of individuality.

Increasing numbers of young children are experiencing child care in group settings. The impact of those experiences depends heavily on the quality of the personnel, the nature of the program, and an appropriate physical environment. Many studies suggest that quality child care contributes to the toddler's optimal development. A major concern, however, is the availability of quality care at a cost that makes it accessible for all those families who need it.

References

Albert, S., Amgott, T., Krakow, M., & Marcus, H. (1977). Children's bedtime rituals as a prototype rite of safe passage. Paper presented at the annual convention of the American Psychological Association, San Francisco.

Andersson, B. (1989). Effects of public day care: A longitudinal study. *Child Development, 60,* 857–866.

Anglin, J. M. (1977). *Word, object, and conceptual development.* New York: Norton.

Anthony, E. J. (1970). The behavior disorders of children. In P. H. Mussen (ed.), *Carmichael's manual of child psychology* (3rd ed., vol. 2). New York: Wiley.

Aronfreed, J., & Reber, A. (1965). Internalized behavioral suppression and the timing of social punishment.

Journal of Personality and Social Psychology, 1, 3–16.

Bandura, A. (1977). *Social learning theory.* Englewood Cliffs, N.J.: Prentice-Hall.

Bandura, A. (1989). Regulation of cognitive processes through perceived self-efficacy. *Developmental Psychology, 25,* 729–735.

Bates, E., Bretherton, I., & Snyder, L. (1988). *From first words to grammar.* Cambridge: Cambridge University Press.

Bates, E., O'Connell, B., & Shore, C. (1987). Language and communication in infancy. In J. Osofsky (ed.), *Handbook of infant development* (2nd ed., pp. 149–203). New York: Wiley.

Baumrind, D. (1971). Current patterns of parental authority. *Developmental Psychology Monographs, 4,* 99–103.

Berkowitz, L. (1973). Control of aggression. In B. M. Caldwell & H. N. Ricciuti (eds.), *Review of child development research* (vol. 3). Chicago: University of Chicago Press.

Bernstein, B. (1972). Social class, language, and socialisation. In P. P. Giglioli (ed.), *Language and social context.* Harmondsworth: Penguin.

Best, C. T., McRoberts, G. W., & Sithole, N. M. (1988). Examination of perceptual reorganization for non-native speech contrasts. Zulu click discrimination by English-speaking adults and infants. *Journal of Experimental Psychology: Human Perception and Performance, 14,* 345–360.

Bloom, L., Lightbown, P., & Hood, B. (1975). *Structure and variation in child language.* Monographs of the Society for Research in Child Development, 40 (2, serial no. 160).

Braine, M. D. S. (1976). *Children's first word combinations.* Monographs of the Society for Research in Child Development, *41* (1).

Brown, R. (1973). *A first language: The early stages.* Cambridge, Mass: Harvard University Press.

Buie, J. (1988). Efforts for better child care increase. *APA Monitor, 19,* 28.

Bullock, M., & Lutkenhaus, P. (1988). The development of volitional behavior in the toddler years. *Child Development, 59,* 664–674.

Burchinal, M., Lee, M., & Ramey, C. (1989). Type of daycare and preschool intellectual development in disadvantaged children. *Child Development, 60,* 128–137.

Burke, B. (1987). The role of playfulness in developing thinking skills: A review with implementation strategies. In S. Moore & K. Kolb (eds.), *Reviews of research for practitioners and parents,* no. 3 (pp. 3–8). Min-

neapolis: Center for Early Education and Development.

Buss, D. M. (1981). Predicting parent-child interactions from children's activity level. *Developmental Psychology, 17,* 59–65.

Carey, S. (1978). The child as word learner. In M. Halle, G. Miller & J. Bresnan (eds.), *Linguistic theory and psychological reality* (pp. 264–293). Cambridge, Mass.: MIT Press.

Chwast, J. (1972). Sociopathic behavior in children. In B. B. Wolman (ed.), *Manual of child psychopathology.* New York: McGraw-Hill.

Clark, J. E., Phillips, S. J., & Petersen, R. (1989). Developmental stability in jumping. *Developmental Psychology, 25,* 929–935.

Clarke-Stewart, K. A. (1989). Infant day care: Maligned or malignant? *American Psychologist, 44,* 266–273.

Clarke-Stewart, K. A., & Fein, G. G. (1983). Early childhood programs. In P. H. Mussen (ed.), *Handbook of child psychology,* vol. 2, *Infancy and developmental psychobiology* (pp. 917–1000). New York: Wiley.

Cole, D., & La Voie, J. C. (1985). Fantasy play and related cognitive development in 2 to 6 year olds. *Developmental Psychology, 21,* 233–240.

Cummings, E. M., Iannotti, R. J., & Zahn-Waxler, C. (1989). Aggression between peers in early childhood: Individual continuity and developmental change. *Child Development, 60,* 887–895.

Cummings, J. S., Pellegrini, D. S., Notarius, C. I., & Cummings, E. M. (1989). Children's responses to angry adult behavior as a function of marital distress and history of interparent hostility. *Child Development, 60,* 1035–1043.

Diaz, R. M. (1983). Thought and two languages: The impact of bilingualism on cognitive development. *Review of Research in Education, 10,* 23–54.

Dix, T., Ruble, D. N., Zambarano, R. J. (1989). Mothers' implicit theories of discipline: Child effects, parent effects, and the attribution process. *Child Development, 60,* 1373–1391.

Dore, J. (1978). Conditions for the acquisition of speech acts. In I. Markova (ed.), *The social context of language.* New York: Wiley.

Dunn, J., & Munn, P. (1987). Development of justification in disputes with mother and sibling. *Developmental Psychology, 23,* 791–798.

Eckerman, C. O., Davis, C. C., & Didow, S. M. (1989). Toddlers' emerging ways of achieving social coordinations with a peer. *Child Development, 60,* 440–453.

Eckerman, C. O., & Didow, S. M. (1989). Toddlers' social

coordinations: Changing responses to another's invitation to play. *Developmental Psychology, 25,* 794–804.

Eimas, P. D. (1975). Auditory and phonetic coding of the cues for speech: Discrimination of the (r-l) distinction by young infants. *Perception and Psychophysics, 18,* 341–347.

Erikson, E. H. (1963). *Childhood and society* (2nd ed.). New York: Norton.

Ferguson, C. (1989). Individual differences in language learning. In M. L. Rice & R. L. Schiefelbusch (eds.), *Teachability of language.* Baltimore: Brookes.

Flavell, J. H., Flavell, E. R., & Green, F. L. (1987). Young children's knowledge about the apparent-real and pretend-real distinctions. *Developmental Psychology, 23,* 816–822.

Forehand, R., Roberts, M. W., Doleys, D.M., Hobbs, S. A., & Resick, P. A. (1976). An examination of disciplinary procedures with children. *Journal of Experimental Child Psychology, 21,* 109–120.

Freud, S. (1905/1953). Three essays on the theory of sexuality. In J. Strachey (ed.), *The standard edition of the complete psychological works of Sigmund Freud* (vol. 7). London: Hogarth Press.

Freud, S. (1913/1958). The disposition to obsessional neurosis: A contribution to the problem of choice of neurosis. In J. Strachey (ed.), *The standard edition of the complete psychological works of Sigmund Freud* (vol. 2). London: Hogarth Press.

Greenfield, P. M., & Smith, J. H. (1976). *The structure of communication in early language development.* New York: Academic Press.

Grusec, J. E., & Abramovitch, R. (1982). Imitation of peers and adults in a natural setting: A functional analysis. *Child Development, 53,* 636–642.

Hakuta, K., & Garcia, E. E. (1989). Bilingualism and education. *American Psychologist, 44,* 374–379.

Harter, S. (1982). The perceived competence scale for children. *Child Development, 53,* 87–97.

Haswell, K., Hock, E., & Wenar, C. (1981). Oppositional behavior of preschool children: Theory and intervention. *Family Relations, 30,* 440–446.

Heath, S. B. (1989). Oral and literate traditions among black Americans living in poverty. *American Psychologist, 44,* 367–372.

Hess, R. D., & Shipman, V. C. (1965). Early experiences and the socialization of cognitive modes in children. *Child Development, 36,* 869–886.

Hoffman, M. L. (1970). Moral development. In P. H. Mussen (ed.), *Carmichael's manual of child psychology* (3rd ed., vol. 2). New York: Wiley.

Hoffman, M. L. (1977). Moral internalization: Current theory and research. In L. Berkowitz (ed.), *Advances in experimental social psychology* (vol. 10). New York: Academic Press.

Hoffman, M. L. (1980). Moral development in adolescence. In J. Adelson (ed.), *Handbook of adolescent psychology.* New York: Wiley.

Hoffman, S. J. (1985). Play and the acquisition of literacy. *Quarterly Newsletter of the Laboratory of Comparative Human Cognition, 7,* 89–95.

Howes, C. (1987). *Peer interaction of young children.* Monographs of the Society for Research in Child Development, *53* (1, serial no. 217).

Howes, C., & Stewart, P. (1987). Child's play with adults, toys, and peers: An examination of family and child-care influences. *Developmental Psychology, 23,* 423–430.

Howes, C., Unger, O., & Seidner, L. B. (1989). Social pretend play in toddlers: Parallels with social play and with solitary pretend. *Child Development, 60,* 77–84.

Hutt, S. J., Tyler, S., Hutt, C., & Foy, H. (1988). *Play exploration and learning: A natural history of the preschool.* New York: Routledge.

Huttenlocher, J. (1974). The origins of language comprehension. In R. L. Solso (ed.), *Theories in cognitive psychology.* Potomac, Md.: Erlbaum.

Hymes, D. (1972). On communicative competence. In J. B. Pride & J. Holmes (eds.), *Sociolinguistics,* (pp. 269–285). Harmondsworth: Penguin.

Kagan, J. (1958). The concept of identification. *Psychological Review, 65,* 296–305.

Kochanska, G., Kuczynski, L, & Radke-Yarrow, M. (1989). Correspondence between mothers' self-reported and observed child-rearing practices. *Child Development, 60,* 56–63.

Kopp, C. B. (1982). Antecedents of self-regulation: A developmental perspective. *Developmental Psychology, 18,* 199–214.

Kuczynski, L., Kochanska, G., Radke-Yarrow, M., & Girnius-Brown, O. (1987). A developmental interpretation of young children's noncompliance. *Developmental Psychology, 23,* 799–806.

Kuczynski, L., Zahn-Waxler, C., & Radke-Yarrow, M. (1987). Development and content of imitation in the second and third years of life: A socialization perspective. *Developmental Psychology, 23,* 276–282.

Ladd, G. W., Price, J. M., & Hart, C. H. (1988). Predicting preschoolers' peer status from their playground behaviors. *Child Development, 59,* 986–992.

Leizer, J. I., & Rogers, R. W. (1974). Effects of method of discipline, timing of punishment, and timing of test on resistance to temptation. *Child Development, 45,* 790–793.

Lenneberg, E. H. (1967). *Biological foundations of language.* New York: Wiley.

Lucariello, J. (1987). Spinning fantasy: Themes, structure, and the knowledge base. *Child Development, 58,* 434–442.

Lytton, H. (1976). The socialization of two-year-old boys: Ecological findings. *Journal of Child Psychology and Psychiatry, 17,* 287–304.

Messer, D. J., Rachford, D., McCarthy, M. E., & Yarrow, L. J. (1987). Assessment of mastery behavior at 30 months: Analysis of task-directed activities. *Developmental Psychology, 23,* 771–781.

Miller, P. H. (1989). *Theories of developmental psychology* (2nd ed.). New York: W. H. Freeman.

Miller-Jones, D. (1989). Culture and testing. *American Psychologist, 44,* 360–366.

Mills, R. S. L., & Rubin, K. H. (1990). Parental beliefs about problematic social behaviors in early childhood. *Child Development, 61,* 138–151.

Mischel, W., & Patterson, C. J. (1976). Substantive and structural elements of effective plans. *Journal of Personality and Social Psychology, 34,* 942–950.

Mischel, W., Shoda, Y., & Rodriguez, M. L. (1989). Delay of gratification in children. *Science, 244,* 933–938.

Molfese, D. L., Molfese, V. J., & Carrell, P. L. (1982). Early language development. In B. B. Wolman (ed.), *Handbook of developmental psychology* (pp. 301–322). Englewood Cliffs, N.J.: Prentice-Hall.

Mondell, S., & Tyler, F. B. (1981). Parental competence and styles of problem-solving/play behavior with children. *Developmental Psychology, 17,* 73–78.

Morrison, A. P. (1989). *Shame: The underside of narcissism.* Hillsdale, N.J.: Analytic Press.

Moskowitz, B. A. (1978). The acquisition of language. *Scientific American, 239,* 92–108.

Murphy, L. (1956). *Personality in young children, vol. 2., Colin, a normal child.* New York: Basic Books.

Mussen, P. H., & Eisenberg-Berg, N. (1977). *Roots of caring, sharing, and helping.* San Francisco: W. H. Freeman.

Nelson, K. (1973). *Structure and strategy in learning to talk.* Monographs of the Society for Research in Child Development, *38* (1–2).

Nelson, K. (1981). Individual differences in language development: Implications for development and language. *Developmental Psychology, 17,* 170–187.

Norman-Jackson, J. (1982). Family interactions, language development, and primary reading achievement of black children in families of low income. *Child Development, 53,* 349–358.

Odom, L., Seeman, J., & Newbrough, J. R. (1971). A study of family communication patterns and personality integration in children. *Child Psychiatry and Human Development, 1,* 275–285.

Olsen, L. (1988). *Crossing the schoolhouse border: Immigrant students and the California public schools.* San Francisco: California Tomorrow.

Olweus, D. (1979). Stability and aggressive reaction patterns in males: A review. *Psychological Bulletin, 86,* 852–875.

Oviatt, S. L. (1980). The emerging ability to comprehend language: An experimental approach. *Child Development, 51,* 97–106.

Oviatt, S. L. (1982). Inferring what words mean: Early development in infants' comprehension of common objects' names. *Child Development, 53,* 274–277.

Parke, R. D., & Slaby, R. G. (1983). The development of aggression. In E. M. Hetherington (ed.), *Handbook of child psychology,* vol. 4, *Socialization, personality, and social development* (4th ed., pp. 547–641). New York: Wiley.

Parton, D. A. (1976). Learning to imitate in infancy. *Child Development, 47,* 14–31.

Patterson, C. J., & Mischel, W. (1976). Effects of temptation-inhibiting and task-facilitating plans on self-control. *Journal of Personality and Social Psychology, 33,* 209–217.

Phillips, D., McCartney, K., & Scarr, S. (1987). Child care quality and children's social development. *Developmental Psychology, 23,* 537–543.

Piaget, J. (1962). *Play, dreams, and imitation in childhood.* New York: Norton.

Piaget, J. (1970). Piaget's theory. In P. H. Mussen (ed.), *Carmichael's manual of child psychology* (3rd ed., vol. 1). New York: Wiley.

Pick, H. L. (1989). Motor development: The control of action. *Developmental Psychology, 25,* 867–870.

Piers, M. W., & Landau, G. M. (1980). *The gift of play.* New York: Walker.

Pye, C. (1986). Quiché Mayan speech to children. *Journal of Child Language, 13,* 85–100.

Quinn, J. B. (1988). A crisis in child care. *Newsweek,* February 15, p. 57.

Rice, M. L. (1989). Children's language acquisition. *American Psychologist, 44,* 149–156.

Rice, M. L., & Woodsmall, L. (1988). Lessons from television: Children's word learning when viewing. *Child Development, 59,* 420–429.

Ridenour, M. V. (ed.) (1978). *Motor development: Issues and applications.* Princeton, N.J.: Princeton Books.

Rogoff, B., & Morelli, G. (1989). Perspectives on children's development from cultural psychology. *American Psychologist, 44,* 343–348.

Rubin, K. H. (1980). Fantasy play: Its role in the development of social skills and social cognition. *New Directions in Child Development, 9,* 69–84.

Saltz, R., & Saltz, E. (1986). Pretend play training and its outcomes. In G. Fein & M. Rivkin (eds.), *The young child at play: Reviews of research* (vol. 4, pp. 155–173). Washington, D.C.: National Association for the Education of Young Children.

Schatz, M. (1983). Communication. In J. H. Flavell & E. M. Markman (eds.), *Handbook of child psychology* (vol. 3, pp. 841–889). New York: Wiley.

Schweinhart, L. J., & Weikart, D. P. (1988). The High/Scope Perry preschool program. In R. H. Price, E. L. Cowen, R. P. Lorion, & J. Ramos-McKay (eds.), *Fourteen ounces of prevention* (pp. 53–66). Washington, D.C.: American Psychological Association.

Singer, J. L. (1973). *The child's world of make-believe: Experimental studies of imaginative play.* New York: Academic Press.

Singer, J. L. (1975). *The inner world of daydreaming.* New York: Colophon Books.

Slade, A. (1987). A longitudinal study of maternal involvement and symbolic play during the toddler period. *Child Development, 58,* 367–375.

Slobin, D. I. (1985). *The cross-linguistic study of language acquisition* (vols. 1 & 2). Hillsdale, N.J.: Erlbaum.

Snow, C. E. (1984). Parent-child interaction and the development of communicative ability. In R. L. Schiefelbusch & J. Pickar (eds.), *Communicative competence: Acquisition and intervention* (pp. 69–108). Baltimore: University Park Press.

Snow, C. E. (1987). Beyond conversation: Second language learners' acquisition of description and explanation. In J. P. Lantolf & A. Labarca (eds.), *Research in second language learning: Focus on the classroom* (pp. 3–16) Norwood, N.J.: Ablex.

Templin, M. C. (1957). *Certain language skills in children.* Minneapolis: University of Minnesota Press.

Tinsley, V. S., & Waters, H. S. (1982). The development of verbal control over motor behavior: A replication and extension of Luria's findings. *Child Development, 53,* 746–753.

Trawick-Smith, J. (1988). "Let's say you're the baby, OK?": Play leadership and following behavior of young children. *Young Children, 43,* 51–59.

Trehub, S. E. (1973). Infants' sensitivity to vowel and tonal contrasts. *Developmental Psychology, 9,* 91–96.

U.S. Bureau of the Census (1987a). *Who's minding the kids? Childcare arrangements: Winter 1984–85.* Current Population Reports, ser. P-70, no. 9. Washington, D.C.: U.S. Government Printing Office.

U.S. Bureau of the Census (1987b). *Statistical Abstract of the United States, 1988.* (Table 624). Washington, D.C.: U.S. Government Printing Office.

Vandell, D. L., Henderson, V. K., & Wilson, K. S. (1988). A longitudinal study of children with day-care experiences of varying quality. *Child Development, 59,* 1286–1292.

Vaughn, B. E., Kopp, C. B., & Krakow, J. B. (1984). The emergence and consolidation of self-control from 18 to 30 months of age: Normative trends and individual differences. *Child Development, 55,* 990–1004.

Vaughn, B. E., Kopp, C. B., Krakow, J. B., Johnson, K., & Schwartz, S. S. (1986). Process analyses of the behavior of very young children in delay tasks. *Developmental Psychology, 22,* 752–759.

Walters, R. H., Parke, R. D., & Cane, V. A. (1965). Timing of punishment and the observation of consequences to others as determinants of response inhibition. *Journal of Experimental Child Psychology, 2,* 10–30.

Wenar, C. (1982). On negativism. *Human Development, 25,* 1–23.

Werker, J. F., & Lalonde, C. E. (1988). Cross-language speech perception: Initial capabilities and developmental change. *Developmental Psychology, 24,* 672–683.

Wertsch, J. V. (1978). Adult-child interaction and the roots of metacognition. *Quarterly Newsletter of the Institute for Comparative Human Development, 2,* 15–18.

White, B. L., Kaban, B. T., & Attanucci, J. S. (1979). *The origins of human competence.* Lexington, Mass.: D. C. Heath.

White, B. L., & Watts, J. C. (1973). *Experience and envi-*

ronment (vol. 1). Englewood Cliffs. N.J.: Prentice-Hall.

White, R. W. (1960). Competence and the psychosexual stages of development. In M. R. Jones (ed.), *Nebraska Symposium on Motivation* (vol. 8). Lincoln: University of Nebraska Press.

Zussman, J. V. (1980). Situational determinants of parental behavior: Effects of competing cognitive activity. *Child Development, 51,* 792–800.

Chapter Seven

Going to school is more than a symbol of growing up. The child's self-concept changes as he or she enters the formal role of student.

Early School Age (4 to 6 Years)

From a psychosocial perspective, the *early-school-age* period brings increasingly complex social influences on children. By the age of 6, virtually all American children are enrolled in school. Children today are encountering school or schoollike experiences at earlier ages than they have in the past. In 1986, close to 40% of 3- and 4-year-olds were enrolled in school, an increase from 20% in 1970 (U.S. Bureau of the Census, 1987). School brings external evaluation, new opportunities for success and failure, settings for peer-group formation and social evaluation, and the initiation of a set of experiences that may lead to advancement of socioeconomic status in adulthood. At a more immediate level, school introduces a new source of influence on the child beyond the family. Beliefs and practices followed at home will come under scrutiny and be challenged by community norms and values. The personal hopes and aspirations that parents have for their children will now be tempered by the reality of school performance. In addition to family and school, peer group, neighborhood, and television all make their influences felt on a child's self-concept during early school age.

To match this exposure to a diversity of social influences, most early-school-age children exhibit wide-ranging curiosity about all facets of life. Once children become aware of alternatives to their own families' philosophies and lifestyles, they act as if familiar notions are legitimate material for questioning. The rebelliousness of action that is seen in the toddler is replaced by rebelliousness of thought in the early-school-age child.

Developmental Tasks

Sex-Role Identification

During early school age, one's sex and its implications for behavior and social relationships become a central focus. Children at this age are most likely to interact with same-sex friends (Maccoby, 1988). They are aware of sex-typed expectations for dress, play, and career aspirations (Martin, 1989). In fact, many dual-career parents are rather dismayed to find that despite the egalitarian model they think they are providing for their child, the child will still say, "Women can't be doctors, only nurses."

There is currently some debate about the adaptive value of having a distinctly masculine or feminine sex-role identity. The proposition has been raised that it is more appropriate to be able to blend the best qualities of what have been described as masculinity and femininity than to be tied to one set of behaviors and reject the others (Bem, 1975; Spence, 1982). The contrasting position is that clarity of sex-role identity is a positive characteristic that is associated with competence and directness, especially in one's role as parent (Baumrind, 1982).

We do not expect a lifetime's work on sex-role identity to have been completed by early school age. During this period, however, significant conceptual and emotional changes give sex role a greater degree of clarity and highlight the relevance of one's sex in the overall self-concept. Among the major aspects of sex-role identification are an understanding of gender, sex-role standards, identification with parents, and sex-role preference.

1. Correct use of the gender labels.
2. Gender is stable.
3. Gender is constant.
4. Gender has a genital basis.

Figure 7.1   The Development of the Gender Concept

Understanding Gender

The correct use of the appropriate gender label is the earliest component of sex-role identification to be achieved. Even before the abstract categories *male* and *female* are understood, children learn through imitation of parental expressions to refer to themselves as a boy or a girl. From infancy, parents make continual reference to a child's gender in such sentences as "That's a good boy" or "That's a good girl."

During the second year of life, children begin to apply such labels as *Mommy* and *Daddy, brother* and *sister,* and *boy* and *girl* accurately (Thompson, 1975). Given these sex-related labels, children seek out other cues that will help them make these distinctions correctly. Their attention is thereby directed to differences between males and females.

The understanding of gender involves four elements that emerge in a developmental sequence from toddlerhood through early school age (see Figure 7.1). The first element is a correct use of the gender label when asked "Are you a boy or a girl?" The second element is an understanding that gender is stable: if one is a boy, one will grow up to be a man. The third element is an understanding of constancy. Even if a child plays with opposite-sex toys, wears clothes of the opposite sex, or has a hairstyle like that of the opposite sex, he or she will still remain the same sex. The fourth element is an understanding of the genital basis of gender. In research involving 3-, 4-, and 5-year-olds, the majority of children who understood the genital differences between the sexes could also tell that a child's sex was not changed simply because the child was dressed up to look like a member of the opposite sex. These young children understood that sex is a constant feature of a person, no matter how the person is dressed or whether the hair is long or short. The majority of the children who had no knowledge of genital differences were also unable to respond correctly to questions about constancy (Bem, 1989).

Sex-Role Standards

Sex-role standards are cultural and subcultural expectations about appropriate behavior for boys and girls and men and women. What are the sex-role standards? This is a very difficult question to answer because of subcultural differences in definition and changes in the conceptualization of the male and female roles that have been occurring over the past several years. Traditionally the physical characteristics of strength, largeness, short hair, heavy muscle mass, and ruggedness have been associated with the male. The female has been described as delicate, fair, soft, long-haired, and curvy. Both of these sets of characteristics have always been, and still are, only caricatures or stereotypes of the physical attributes of males and females.

The significance of sex-role standards for an early-school-age child is a result of their translation into adult and peer expectations for the child's behavior. Accompanying these expectations are conditional rewards, incentives, and sanctions. Parents not only expect things of a child in relation to the child's gender but also do things in order to produce compliance with these expectations. Some parents believe that boys should be assertive and fight for their rights. Others believe that boys should think carefully about what is right and wrong and guide their actions by reason rather than impulsive aggression. Each of these sets of parents has a conception of male attributes that is communicated to their sons by a variety of means over a long period of time. The toys parents give their children, the experiences to which they expose the children, and the activities in which they encourage their children's participation all reflect some dimensions of the parents' sex-role standards. By the time children reach school age, they have been encouraged to adopt those standards and punished for what their parents have viewed as sex-inappropriate behavior. Young girls may be shamed for their assertiveness by being told that they are acting "very bold," and young boys may be warned to "stop acting like a sissy."

Langlois and Downs (1980) compared the reactions of mothers, fathers, and peers to a child who was playing with same-sex or opposite-sex toys. Opposite-sex toy choices had different consequences for boys and girls. A girl was likely to be rewarded for playing with same-sex toys and punished for playing with opposite-sex toys, whether she was with her mother, her father, or a peer. Boys received more punishment from their peers for playing with same-sex toys than for playing with opposite-sex toys. Mothers were actually likely to *reward* boys more for opposite-sex play than for same-sex play. Fathers, however, were likely to punish opposite-sex toy choices by boys. The picture we get from this study is that girls experience more consistent sex-role socialization from parents and peers than do boys. Boys encounter more diverse and contradictory socialization pressures. In addition, fathers appear to be more consistent than mothers in guiding girls and boys toward traditional play behavior. Mothers seem to direct both boys and girls toward female-typed activities.

As a consequence of learning sex-role expectations and searching for rules that will guide behavior, young children begin to apply sex-role standards to their own behavior and to that of their peers (Eisenberg, Murray & Hite, 1982; Martin, 1989). Damon (1977) interviewed children aged 4 through 9 to determine how they applied

Pablo Picasso, *Paulo as Torero,* 1925. Every culture has its own sex-role standards. For Spanish children, the matador is one standard of masculinity.

sex-role standards to the behavior of other children. In the interview, they were told about a little boy named George who liked to play with dolls. The children were asked why people told George not to play with dolls, whether it was all right for George to play with dolls, and what might happen to George if he kept doing so. Children who were close to the age of 6 believed that it was wrong for George to play in a girlish way. Here is how Michael, aged 5 years, 11 months, explained it:

> *Well, he should only play with things that boys play with. The things that he's playing with now is girls' stuff. . . . [Can George play with Barbie dolls if he wants to?] No*

sir! [How come?] If he doesn't want to play with dolls, then he's right, but if he does want to play with dolls, he's double wrong. [Why is he double wrong?] All the time he's playing with girls' stuff. [Do you think people are right when they tell George not to play with girls' dolls?] Yes. [What should George do?] He should stop playing with the girls' dolls and start playing with G.I. Joe. [Why can a boy play with a G.I. Joe and not a Barbie doll?] Because if a boy is playing with something, like if a boy plays with a Barbie doll, then he's just going to get people teasing him, and if he tries to play more, to get girls to like him, then the girls won't like him either. [p. 255]

During the early-school-age period, children have rather strict, stereotyped ideas about sex-role behavior. Their views may be based in part on what they have been told or on behaviors that they have observed. They may also be based on an inability to conceptualize a more individual, culturally relative view of social behavior.

Acceptance of behaviors that cross gender boundaries becomes more common during the middle school years. Children in the age range of 8 to 10 are less critical of boys and girls who experiment with opposite-sex-typed behaviors, such as a boy putting on nail polish or a girl wearing a boy's suit. By adolescence, however, this cross-gender behavior is once again considered highly inappropriate (Stoddart & Turiel, 1985). Early-school-age children and early adolescents are very similar in their adherence to strict criteria of sex-role behaviors.

Identification with Parents

The third component of sex-role identification involves parental identification. *Identification* is the process through which one person incorporates the values and beliefs of another. To identify with someone is not to become exactly identical to that person but to increase one's sense of allegiance and closeness to that person. During early school age, most children admire and emulate their parents. They begin to internalize their parents' values, attitudes, and world views. We emphasize the concept as a major mechanism of socialization in childhood, but identification can occur at any point in the life span.

Identification has received a great deal of attention in the psychological literature. The most persistent question raised is why children alter their behavior in the direction of becoming more like one parent or the other. What motives are satisfied in this process? There appear to be four substantially different theories about motives for identification. (See Table 7.1.) Two of these processes are suggested by psychoanalytic theory: fear of loss of love and identification with the aggressor.

The *fear of loss of love* is a very primitive motive. It is founded on a child's initial realization of dependence on the parents. A child behaves like a parent in order to ensure a continued positive relationship. Eventually the child incorporates aspects of the loved one's personality into his or her own self-concept. The child then can feel close to the loved person even when they are not physically together (Jacobson, 1964). If a child can be like a loved parent, the parent's continuous presence is not required to reassure the child about that love.

Identification with the aggressor is described in detail by Anna Freud (1936). This motive is aroused when children experience some degree of fear of their parents. In

Table 7.1	**Four Motives for Parental Identification**
Motive	*Definition*
Fear of loss of love	A child behaves like a parent in order to ensure a continued positive love relationship.
Identification with the aggressor	A child behaves like a parent in order to protect him- or herself from the parent's anger.
Identification to satisfy needs for power	A child behaves like a parent in order to achieve a vicarious sense of the power associated with the parent.
Identification to increase perceived similarity	A child behaves like a parent in order to increase perceived similarity with the parent and thereby share in the parent's positive attributes.

order to protect themselves from harm, they perform behaviors that are similar to those they fear. This kind of identification may give children a magical feeling of power as well as decrease the parents' tendency to aggress against them. Parents who see a great deal of similarity between themselves and their children are less likely to threaten or harm them.

Social learning theory focuses attention on a third motive for identification, the need for *status and power* (Mischel, 1966; Bandura, 1977, 1986). Studies of modeling show that children are more likely to imitate the behavior of a model who controls resources in a situation than they are the behavior of a model who is rewarded. The imitative behavior is motivated by a vicarious feeling of power experienced when they behave in the same way as the powerful model. Within a family, children are likely to have personality characteristics similar to those of the more dominant parent (Hetherington, 1967).

Kagan (1958) has contributed a fourth motive for identification by suggesting that children behave like their parents in order to increase the *perceived similarity* between them. Children attribute a number of valued characteristics to their parents, including physical size, good looks, special competences, power, success, and respect. Children can more readily share these positive attributes when they perceive a degree of similarity between themselves and their parents. There are three principal ways in which children can experience this sense of similarity: (1) by perceiving actual physical and psychological similarities, (2) by adopting parental behaviors, and (3) by being told about similarities by others. Increasing perceptions of similarity promote stronger identifications.

These motives apply to the process of identification at all ages and regardless of the sex of the identifier or the model. How do these motives function with regard to the specific task of developing sex-role identification? One or another of these motives may dominate the dynamics of sex-role identification for a particular child, but all four motives are involved in the process. The most obvious motive is that of perceived similarity (Heilbrun, 1974). A child who is 5 or 6 years old recognizes the similarity in gender with the same-sex parent. This perception is often enhanced by comments like "When you're a daddy, you'll do this too" or "You have your mother's patience." A child who perceives the same-sex parent as possessing valued attributes will build on existing similarities in order to increase self-esteem. The initial content of sex-role identity is heavily weighted by those attributes of the same-sex parent that a child has deliberately tried to emulate.

The process of identification does not proceed as unidirectionally as the "perceived similarity" hypothesis would suggest. Depending on the amount of interaction that takes place between child and parents, strong bonds of attachment develop with both the mother and the father. Further, according to Freud (1929/1955), young children are bisexual. They have sexual impulses and wishes involving both male and female targets.

There is no strong evidence that boys preferentially imitate or identify with their fathers and that girls preferentially imitate or identify with their mothers (Maccoby, 1980). The sex typing of fathers and mothers does not appear to predict that of the children. In other words, the most feminine mothers do not necessarily have the most feminine daughters. This finding suggests that it is the warmth and dominance of the parent rather than his or her sex or sex typing that are most relevant to promoting identification.

Sex-Role Preference

The fourth component of sex-role identification is the development of a personal preference for the kinds of activities and attitudes that are associated with the masculine or feminine sex role. Preferences for sex-typed play activities and same-sex play companions have been observed among preschoolers as well as older children (Caldera, Huston & O'Brien, 1989; Maccoby, 1988). The attainment of these preferences is a more complex accomplishment than might be imagined. In fact, one's sex-role preference may fluctuate considerably throughout life.

Sex-role preference depends primarily on three factors. First, the more closely one's own strengths and competences approximate the sex-role standard, the more one will prefer being a member of that sex. Second, the more one likes the same-sex parent, the more one will prefer being a member of that sex. These two factors begin to have a significant impact on a child's sex-role preference as the self-concept becomes more clearly differentiated. As children enter school and are exposed to the process of evaluation, they begin to have a more realistic sense of their unique qualities. As they acquire this self-reflective ability, they are able to appreciate the similarities and discrepancies between (1) self and the sex-role standard and (2) self and the same-sex parent.

The third determinant of sex-role preference consists of environmental cues as to the value of one sex or the other. The cues can emanate from the family, ethnic and religious groups, media, social institutions (such as the schools), and other culture carriers. Many cultures traditionally have valued males more than females and have given males higher status (Huber, 1990). To the extent that such culturally determined values are communicated to children, males are likely to establish a firmer preference for their sex group and females are likely to experience some ambivalence toward, if not rejection of, their sex group. In other words, it is easier to be happy and content with oneself if one feels highly valued and more difficult if one feels less valued.

Some families develop a strong preference regarding the sex of an expected child. In a sample of over 6000 married women in the United States, 63% of those who had never had children expressed a preference that their first child be a male and their

Table 7.2 Dimensions of Sex-Role Identification

Dimension	Sex-Role Outcome
Developing an understanding of gender	I am a boy; I will grow up to be a man. I am a girl; I will grow up to be a woman.
Acquiring sex-role standards	Boys are independent; they play with trucks. Girls are interpersonal; they play with dolls.
Identifying with same-sex parent	I am a lot like Daddy. I want to be like him when I grow up. I am a lot like Mommy. I want to be like her when I grow up.
Establishing sex-role preference	I like being a boy. I'd rather be a boy than a girl. I like being a girl, I'd rather be a girl than a boy.

second a female. Women who considered an even number of children to be ideal wanted to have an equal number of boys and girls. Women who preferred an uneven number of children wanted more sons than daughters (Westoff & Rindfuss, 1974). If the wish for a child of a particular sex is not fulfilled and the parents do not shed their commitment to the "missed" sex, the family may present obstacles to sex-role preference.

Thus it is possible to know what sex one is and what behaviors are expected of members of that sex and yet wish one were a member of the opposite sex. In our own experience, if groups of men and women are asked whether they ever wished to be of the opposite sex, many more women than men will admit to having wished to be of the opposite sex. This finding may reflect some perceived advantages of the male role in our culture. It may also reflect the more serious sanctions against men who value or exhibit behaviors they perceive as feminine.

The four components of the acquisition of sex-role identification—(1) developing an understanding of gender, (2) learning sex-role standards, (3) identifying with parents, and (4) establishing a sex-role preference—are summarized in Table 7.2. The outcome of the process for an individual child depends greatly on the characteristics of his or her parents, personal capacities and preferences, and the cultural and familial values placed on one gender or the other.

**Sex-Role Identification and
the Interpretation of Experiences**

A child's sex-role identity becomes a major cognitive structure (Bem, 1981; Martin, 1989). It becomes a basic scheme that influences a child's interpretation of experiences. Children learn that people can be grouped into two sexes, males and females. In our society, this dichotomy tends to impose itself in a vast array of social situations, even in situations where one's genital sex is not necessarily relevant. Once children have this powerful category, they go about the business of figuring out how to use it. They recognize people as men and women, boys and girls. They recognize themselves as members of one of these two groups. But still further, they build expectations that certain toys, interests, and behaviors are appropriate for boys and others are appropriate for girls; certain activities, dispositions, and occupations are appropriate for men and women. These expectations are generally reinforced by the beliefs of the older boys and girls and men and women with whom they interact.

Girls and boys establish peer friendship groups with members of the same sex and may reject or compete with members of the opposite sex (Maccoby, 1988). As time goes along, the kinds of activities and dynamics of social interaction that take place within these same-sex groups become differentiated so that the quality of play that most boys experience really is different from the quality of play experienced by most girls. Older children may recognize that not all boys match their expectations of what boys ought to like and do, and not all girls match their expectations of what girls ought to like and do. But this realization does not necessarily dampen their commitment to a belief that the two sexes are very different in some basic ways and that there is great risk in acting too much like someone of the opposite sex.

Early Moral Development

During toddlerhood, a child's attention is focused on the limits of and standards for behavior. Children feel that demands for proper behavior do not come from within themselves but emanate from elements of the external world. During the early-school-age period, standards and limits become part of a child's self-concept. Specific values are acquired from parents, but they become integrated elements of a child's world view.

Early moral development involves a process of taking parental standards and values as one's own. This process is called *internalization*, and it takes place gradually over the early-school-age years.

A 3-year-old boy, for example, may take great delight in hitting his dog with a stick. In the midst of one of these attacks, his mother scolds him. She insists that he stop and explains that it is cruel to hurt the dog. If her punishment is not very harsh, she may have to remind the boy on several other occasions that hitting the dog is not permitted. As the boy internalizes this standard, he begins to experience internal control over his own behavior. He may see the dog lying calmly in the sun and, with a gleam in his eye, begin to pick up a stick. At that moment his behavior is interrupted by a feeling of tension, which is accompanied by the thought that it is wrong to hit the dog. If the standard has been successfully internalized, the emotional tension and the thought will be sufficient to inhibit the boy from hitting the dog.

For school-age children, the achievements in moral development include learning the moral code of the family and the community and then being able to guide behavior by using it. The primary question psychologists raise is "How does the process of *internalization* occur?" There are a variety of theoretical explanations (Windmiller, Lambert & Turiel, 1980).

Learning Theory

Behavioral learning theory provides explanations for the shaping of moral behavior. One can view moral behavior as a response to environmental reinforcements and punishments (Aronfreed, 1969). A behavior that is rewarded is likely to be repeated. If a child is in an unpleasant or painful environment and performs a behavior that reduces or eliminates the unpleasantness, he or she is more likely to perform this

By the time Japanese children are of early school age, the strong, consistent moral code of family, school, and community is firmly internalized.

same behavior again in similar situations. For example, if a child says, "I'm sorry, I'll try to do better next time," and this apology reduces the parent's anger or irritability, this behavior is likely to be repeated at other times when the parent is angry at the child. Internalization may result, therefore, from producing behaviors that lead to a more comfortable, less unpleasant or threatening environment. If a behavior is ignored or punished, it is less likely to occur. If a child performs a misdeed or defies an authority and suffers negative consequences, these consequences ought to reduce the likelihood that such behavior will recur. If the child contemplates performing a misdeed, a sense of tension ought to arise because of previous punishments. Avoiding or inhibiting the impulse to misbehave reduces the tension and is therefore reinforcing.

Social learning theory offers another source of moral learning—the observation of models. By observing and imitating helpful models, children can learn prosocial behavior. By observing the negative consequences that follow the misdeeds of models, children also can learn to inhibit misbehavior. Their moral behavior is not limited to the actions they have performed. It can be based on expectations formulated from observations of the way the conduct of relevant models has been rewarded or punished (Bandura, 1977). Children may even formulate abstract rules, concepts, and sets of propositions about moral behavior by extracting meaningful elements from several incidents of observational learning. In this process, a child forms a representational model in the mind by selecting and organizing observed responses and uses this mental representation to guide, compare, and modify moral behavior (Bandura, 1986).

Finally, cognitive learning theory describes how moral behavior is influenced by the interaction of situational factors and expectancies, values, and goals that have been derived from earlier learning (Mischel, 1973). For example, some people place great value on success in athletics and may be more tempted to violate norms in order to succeed in such a milieu than in an academic setting. The expectation that a misdeed will be observed and punished leads to greater resistance to temptation than does

Table 7.3   Stages of Moral Judgment

Level I: Preconventional

Stage 1	Judgments are based on whether behavior is rewarded or punished.
Stage 2	Judgments are based on whether the consequences result in benefits for self or loved ones.

Level II: Conventional

Stage 3	Judgments are based on whether authorities approve or disapprove.
Stage 4	Judgments are based on whether the behavior upholds or violates the laws of society.

Level III: Postconventional

Stage 5	Judgments are based on preserving social contracts based on cooperative collaboration.
Stage 6	Judgments are based on ethical principles that apply across time and cultures.

the expectation that a misdeed will go unnoticed. Similarly, the expectation that positive, prosocial behaviors are expected and will be noticed influences a child's generosity and helpfulness (Froming, Allen & Jensen, 1985). These factors suggest that although enduring moral qualities may be developed through consistent reinforcement of empathetic, sensitive, and just responses, the specific situation will also influence the extent to which moral behavior is displayed (Carroll & Rest, 1982).

Cognitive-Developmental Theory

Cognitive-developmental theorists have focused on the orderly sequence of development of the child's thoughts about moral issues. Piaget (1932/1948) described the major transition in moral judgment as a shift from heteronomous to autonomous morality. With *heteronomous* morality, rules are understood as fixed, unchangeable aspects of social reality. Children's moral judgments reflect a sense of subordination to authority figures. An act is judged as right or wrong depending on the letter of the law, the amount of damage that was done, and whether or not the act was punished. With *autonomous* morality, children see rules as products of cooperative agreements. Moral judgments reflect a child's participation in a variety of social roles and the egalitarian relationship among friends. Give-and-take with peers highlights the relevance of mutual respect and mutual benefit as rewards for holding to the terms of agreement or abiding by the law.

Expanding on this view, cognitive-developmental theorists have described a sequence of stages of moral thought (Kohlberg, 1976; Gibbs, 1979; Damon, 1980). Moral judgments change as children become increasingly skillful at evaluating the abstract and logical components of a moral dilemma. At the core of these changes is a transformation of the concept of justice. Kohlberg (1969, 1976) described three levels of moral thought, each characterized by two stages of moral judgment (see Table 7.3). At level I, *preconventional morality*, stage 1 judgments of justice are based on whether a behavior is rewarded or punished. Stage 2 judgments are based on an instrumental view of whether or not the consequences will be good for "me and my family." This is the level of moral thought that bears on children of early school age. Level II,

In stage 1 of moral reasoning, judgments of right and wrong are based on the results of actions. If this little boy is punished for cutting up something important, children of early school age will conclude that his behavior is wrong; if he is praised for cutting carefully, they will assume that it is right.

conventional morality, is concerned with maintaining the approval of authorities at stage 3 and upholding the social order at stage 4. Level III, *postconventional morality*, brings an acceptance of moral principles that are viewed as part of a person's own ideology rather than simply imposed by the social order. At stage 5, justice and morality are determined by a democratically derived social contract. At stage 6, a person develops a sense of universal ethical principles that apply across history and cultural context. We will consider levels II and III in greater depth in Chapter 10.

Research indicates that stage 6 reasoning is rarely achieved, and very few people function at this level consistently. One can think of a few individuals, such as Ghandi, Mother Theresa, and Martin Luther King, Jr., whose moral judgments were based on ethical principles that apply across time and culture, transcending the laws and conventions of a specific society. Kohlberg (1978) admitted the rarity of this type of thinking and argued that stage 6 reasoning was more of a hypothetical construct to which moral reasoning might progress. Most of the research has included children, adolescents, and young adults as subjects. From the point of view of our psychosocial perspective, it is reasonable to conclude that stage 6 reasoning may be most likely to be observed beginning in middle adulthood, when people become preoccupied with issues of generativity and concerns that transcend their own lifetime.

Research on movement through the stages suggests that they reflect a developmental sequence. People do not necessarily use only one level of moral reasoning at a time. Over time, however, there does appear to be a gradual shift toward the maximum use of one perspective and the decreasing use of less mature views (Carroll & Rest, 1982; Kohlberg, 1979; Rest, 1983).

This theory of moral development leads one to expect the moral reasoning of early-school-age children to be dominated by concerns about the consequences of their behavior. At stage 1, judgments of good and bad, right and wrong, are based on whether a behavior has been rewarded or punished. At stage 2, moral judgments are based on whether the behavior brings about benefits for oneself or for other people the child cares about. Thus the young child's moral outlook has a utilitarian orientation (Kohlberg, 1976). Research with first-graders confirms that this outlook is quite common, whether children are discussing hypothetical moral dilemmas or real-life moral situations (Walker, 1989).

The preoccupation with consequences highlights the significance of the home and school environments for establishing and supporting a young child's moral code. In order to build a basis for making moral judgments, children need to understand the consequences of their behaviors for others. Thus we can appreciate clearly why inductions—explanations that emphasize the effects of a child's actions on others— are such a key disciplinary method for young children. In addition, the moral climate of the home and school provide the early structure for the content of the moral code. Behaviors that are linked to moral principles, such as telling the truth, being generous, respecting the feelings of others, and being respectful of authority figures, become integrated into a child's concepts of right and wrong. The intensity of this moral code depends on the consistency with which positive examples lead to positive outcomes and negative examples lead to negative outcomes.

Not all rules or prohibitions have to do with moral concerns. There is a difference between the moral domain, which usually involves the rights, dignity, and welfare of others, and the domain of social convention, which involves socially accepted norms and regulations (Turiel, 1983). For example, in the preschool context, a moral transgression would involve stealing another child's toy; a transgression of social convention would be getting up and wandering away during large-group time. Pre-school-age children are consistently able to differentiate between moral and social-convention transgressions. They understand that moral transgressions are wrong because they affect the welfare of others but social-convention transgressions are wrong because they are disruptive or create disorder (Smetana, 1985). Social-convention transgressions depend on the situation. It might be permissible to get up from the table during dinnertime and wander off at home, whereas it is not permissible to get up from the snack table at preschool. Moral transgressions apply more consistently across settings: it is morally wrong to steal at home, at preschool, or at a friend's house. It is significant that children as young as 4 or 5 make this distinction when they evaluate transgressions. One might expect that the more settings a child had encountered, the clearer this distinction would be.

Psychoanalytic Theory

The psychoanalytic theorists suggest that a moral sense develops as a result of strong parental identifications. The focus of the psychoanalytic theory of moral development is on the internalization of values and the factors that sustain impulse control under conditions of temptation. The earlier discussion of identification with parents and the

Pablo Picasso, *Four Girls with Chimera*, 1934. The child's conscience develops out of the tension between strong impulses and the need for parental love. In this painting, the sweet innocence of the four young girls is contrasted with the terrible, ugly monster. According to the psychoanalytic perspective, that monster is actually within each of us, making demands and wanting to be satisfied.

discussion of superego development in Chapter 3 provide a good basis for understanding the psychoanalytic treatment of moral development. Psychoanalytic theory views a child's conscience, or superego, as an internalization of parental values and moral standards. It holds that the superego is formed as a result of the conflict between internal sexual and aggressive impulses and the ways in which the parents deal with the behavioral manifestations of those impulses.

According to psychoanalytic theory, the more severely a parent forces a child to inhibit impulses, the stronger the child's superego will be. Freud (1925/1961) assumed that males would develop more highly differentiated and punitive superegos than females because he believed that males' impulses are more intense. He also believed that because of the greater impulsive energy demonstrated by males, boys would be treated more harshly by their parents than girls would be. Finally, Freud suggested that males identify with the father for two reasons: fear of losing the father's love and fear of the father as an aggressor. The identification with the father is an intense one and should lead to a fully incorporated set of moral standards. According to Freud, a female identifies with her mother for a single reason: fear of loss of love. Since Freud considered this motivation for identification to be less intense than that of the male, he believed that the female's superego would be correspondingly weaker.

Research on the Development of Conscience

Research on the development of conscience has failed to support Freud's hypotheses. Studies that have investigated the ability to resist temptation or to confess after wrongdoing have found that young girls are better able to resist temptation than boys and show a pattern of decreasing moral transgressions over the toddlerhood and early school years (Mischel et al., 1989). Studies that have attempted to assess the relative contributions of mothers and fathers to children's moral behavior have found that mothers' values and attitudes are strongly related to the moral behavior of their children, whereas the values and attitudes of fathers show little relationship to their children's moral behavior (Hoffman, 1970). Finally, studies that have explored the relationship between parental discipline techniques and moral behavior have found that the children of parents who employ harsh physical punishment tend to be physically aggressive and do not control their behavior well when they are away from home (Anthony, 1970; Chwast, 1972). Parental warmth, democratic decision making, and the modeling of resistance to temptation appear to contribute to high levels of prosocial behavior and social responsibility (Baumrind, 1975; Hoffman, 1979).

These findings raise doubts about Freud's views on the formation of conscience and the relative strength of the superego in males and females. In fact, psychoanalytic theory now tends to consider that the critical time in personality development comes earlier in life, in infancy (Mahler, 1963; Kohut, 1971). Infants develop an awareness of three domains: the body and its physical experiences and needs; the existence of others; and the relations between the self and others (Beit-Hallahmi, 1987). All subsequent psychological growth must be assimilated into these three domains. Thus, according to this view, the origins of moral reasoning and behavior will have links to very early feelings about the self and its needs, especially the feelings of pleasure and pain. Morality will have a basis in the awareness of others who are valued in a young child's life, and on behaviors that strengthen or threaten the bonds between the self and others. This view suggests that some basis of early morality lies in the child's own sense of self-love, a wish to enhance and not harm or violate the self. Another basis is the extension of this self-love to the other and the wish to preserve the feelings of connection, trust, and security that have been established in the early parent-infant relationship. If we accept these assumptions, it makes sense to expect that parenting strategies that convey warmth and nurturance are closely tied to a young child's ability to delay gratification and resist moral transgressions.

Freud's work remains a significant contribution to the area of moral development because he drew attention to the powerful role of the superego and the ego ideal in motivating and inhibiting behavior. He also created interest in the origins of moral beliefs in early childhood. However, his description of the process whereby parental values are incorporated into a child's moral code appears to be faulty. Most likely, Freud underestimated the power of the need to reassure oneself about parental love. The strong affectional bonds between a parent and a child are the most effective forces in promoting positive moral behavior.

Research on Empathy and Perspective Taking

Empathy has been defined as sharing the perceived emotion of another—"feeling with another." (Eisenberg & Strayer, 1987, p. 5). This definition emphasizes one's emotional reaction to the observation of another person's emotional condition. By merely observing the facial expressions, body attitudes, and vocalizations of another person, a child can identify that person's emotion and feel it personally. The range of

This mother must foster a new level of empathy in her older daughter in order to protect the new baby.

emotions with which one can empathize depends on the clarity of the cues the other person sends and on one's own prior experiences.

The capacity for empathy changes with development. Hoffman (1987) described four levels of empathy, especially in reference to the perception of another person's distress:

Global empathy: You experience and express distress as a result of witnessing someone else in distress. Example: A baby cries upon hearing the cries of other infants.

Egocentric empathy: You recognize distress in another person and respond to it in the same way you would respond if the distress were your own. Example: A toddler offers his own cuddle blanket to another child who is crying.

Empathy for another's feelings: You show empathy for a wide range of feelings and anticipate the kinds of reactions that might really comfort someone else.

Empathy for another's life conditions: You experience empathy when you understand the life conditions or personal circumstances of a person or group.

The capacity for empathy thus begins in infancy and evolves as a child achieves new levels of understanding about the self and others, and a greater capacity to use language to describe emotions. Very young children appear to be able to recognize and interpret auditory and facial cues that suggest emotional expressions in others. In the newborn nursery, when one infant starts to wail, the other infants begin to cry

(Martin & Clark, 1982; Sagi & Hoffman, 1976). Three- and 4-year-olds can recognize what emotional reactions children might have to specific problem situations. Both American and Chinese children were able to recognize "happy" and "unhappy" reactions by age 3. The differentiation among "afraid," "sad," and "angry" developed slightly later. The specific cues for these feelings were linked to cultural patterns of expressing emotions. Nevertheless, it was clear that the youngest children in both cultural groups had the capacity to recognize emotional states in another person (Borke, 1973). In addition, early-school-age children can use the social circumstances that may have produced a child's emotional response, especially responses of anger and distress, to understand and empathize with another child's feelings (Hoffner & Badzinski, 1989; Fabes et al., 1988).

The ability to identify pleasurable and unpleasurable emotions in others and to empathize with those emotions makes the child receptive to moral teachings. Empathy can serve a proactive function by enlisting a child's efforts to help another person. It can also serve a reactive function by generating remorse for having caused an emotional state in another person. In either case, the child is able to experience how the other person feels and therefore to modify his or her own behavior (Hoffman, 1987).

Another element in the development of a conceptualization of morality is the child's appreciation of the other person (Chandler & Boyes, 1982). *Perspective taking* refers to a person's ability to consider a situation from the point of view of another person. This faculty requires a recognition that someone else's point of view may differ from one's own. It also requires the ability to analyze the factors that may account for these differences. When children can assess these factors, they can begin to transcend the personal perspective and attempt to look at a situation from the point of view of another person.

Imagine a child who wants to play with another child's toy. If the child thinks, "If I had that toy, I would be happy, and if I am happy, everyone is happy," then the child may take the toy without anticipating that the other child will be disappointed. Although empathy provides an emotional bridge that enables a child to discover the similarities between self and other, it does not teach a child about differences. This requires perspective taking. In fact, several psychologists have argued that the capacity to take the perspective of another person is achieved only gradually through peer interaction and peer conflict (Flavell, 1974; Piaget, 1932/1948; Selman, 1971).

Children of 4 and 5 frequently exhibit prosocial behavior that evidences understanding of the needs of others. The most common of these behaviors are sharing, cooperating, and helping. Two examples illustrate the nature of this kind of social perspective taking:

The path of a child with an armload of Playdough was blocked by two chairs. Another child stopped her ongoing activity and moved the chair before the approaching child reached it.

A boy saw another child spill a puzzle on the floor and assisted him in picking it up.   [Iannotti, 1985, p. 53]

Interestingly, young children who score highest in formal measures of perspective taking do not necessarily exhibit high levels of prosocial behavior in preschool settings. At this early age, an important determinant of whether children will spontaneously offer help is whether they can pinpoint the emotional states of others.

Robert Selman (1980) has studied the process of social perspective taking by analyzing children's responses to a structured interview. Children see audiovisual filmstrips that depict interpersonal conflicts. Then they are asked to describe the motivation of each actor and the relationship among the various performers. Four levels of social perspective taking are described. At level 1, the youngest children (4 to 6 years old) can recognize different emotions in the various actors, but they assume that all the actors view the situation much as they do. The children at level 4 (about 10 to 12 years old) realize that two people can take each other's perspective into account before deciding how to act. Furthermore, they realize that each of those people may view the situation differently from the way they do.

Many moral dilemmas require that a child subordinate personal needs for someone else's sake. To resolve such situations, a child must be able to separate personal wants from the other person's. Selman's research suggests that children under the age of 10 are rarely able to approach interpersonal conflicts with this kind of objectivity.

Research on Parental Discipline

The last contribution to a theory of moral development that we will consider comes from the research on parental discipline, which was discussed in detail in Chapter 6. In the process of disciplining a child, the parent emphasizes that certain behaviors are really misdeeds. This in itself begins to form the content of the child's moral code.

In addition, the parent uses some specific techniques of discipline. Four elements seem to be important in determining the impact of these techniques on the child's future behavior. First, the discipline should help the child interrupt or inhibit the forbidden action. Second, the discipline should point out a more acceptable form of behavior so that the child will know what is right in a future instance. Third, the discipline should provide some reason, understandable to the child, that explains why one action is inappropriate and the other more desirable. Fourth, the discipline should stimulate the child's ability to empathize with the victim of misdeeds. In other words, children are asked to put themselves in their victim's place and see how much they dislike the feelings they caused in the other person.

In considering discipline as a mechanism for teaching morality, one becomes aware of the many interacting and interrelated components of a moral act. The discipline techniques that are most effective in teaching morality to children are those that help them control their own behavior, understand the meaning of their behavior for others, and expand their feelings of empathy. Discipline techniques that do not include these characteristics may succeed in inhibiting undesired behavior but fail to achieve the long-term goal of integrating moral values into future behavior.

Summary

The child of early school age is in the process of developing an initial moral code. The six approaches to this issue are summarized in Table 7.4. Each highlights an

Table 7.4   Contributions to the Study of Moral Development

Conceptual Source	Significant Contributions	Consequences for a Particular Aspect of Moral Development
Learning theory	Relevance of an external system of rewards and punishments Imitation of models Formation of expectations about the reward structure	Moral behavior Internalization of a moral code
Cognitive theory	Conceptual development of notions of intentionality, rules, justice, and authority Stages of moral judgment	Moral judgments Distinction between moral transgression and social-convention transgressions
Psychoanalytic theory	Parental identification Formation of the superego	Internalization of parental values Experience of guilt
Research on the development of conscience	Sex differences Parenting: discipline and warmth	Impulse control Internalization of values
Research on empathy and perspective taking	Ability to experience another's feelings begins very early and changes with age Ability to recognize differences in point of view emerges slowly during the early and middle school years Peer conflict, peer interactions, and specific role-taking training can all increase perspective-taking skills	Empathy heightens concern for others; helps inhibit actions that might cause distress Perspective taking can foster helping and altruism
Research on parental discipline	Parents define moral content Parents point out the implications of a child's behavior for others Creation of a reward structure Differential impact of power, love withdrawal, warmth, and inductions	Moral behavior Moral reasoning Internalization of moral values Empathy and guilt

essential element of the larger, more complex phenomenon. Learning theory points out that an external reward structure inhibits or reinforces behavior. Cognitive theory suggests that an element of conceptual immaturity characterizes this early phase of moral development. Psychoanalytic theory is especially concerned with the relationship between parental identification and the development of conscience. Research on the development of conscience challenges some of Freud's notions about the process of superego formation. The work on empathy and perspective taking shows that moral behavior requires an emotional and cognitive understanding of the needs of others. These prosocial skills help children to appreciate how other children or adults may be experiencing reality. With this insight, children can modify their own actions so that they can benefit others. Theory and research on parental discipline suggest that moral development is promoted when parents try to increase children's understanding

Karate instruction helps develop self-esteem by increasing a child's capacity for self-discipline and building a sense of connection to an ancient code of honor.

of the implications of their behavior for others. It seems reasonable to conclude that moral behavior involves an integration of moral judgments, understanding of the reward structure, parental identifications, and empathy for others.

Self-Esteem

At every period of life, thoughts about the self and self-understanding are constructed and modified through interactions with objects and people in the environment. We can think of the self-concept as a theory that links a person's understanding about the nature of the world, the nature of the self, and the meaning of interactions between the self and the environment (Epstein, 1973). One's theory about oneself draws on such inner phenomena as dreams, emotions, thoughts, fantasies, and feelings of pleasure or pain. It is also based on the consequences of transactions with the environment. As with any set of concepts, the complexity and logic of the self-theory depend on the maturation of cognitive functions. Further, since the self-theory is based on personal experiences and observations, one would expect it to be modified by changing physical and socioemotional competences as well as by participation in new roles, all of which bring new content to the flow of experience.

The Self-Theory

At each stage, the self-theory is the result of a person's cognitive capacities and dominant motives as they come in contact with the stage-related expectations of the culture. In infancy, the self primarily consists of an awareness of one's independent existence. The infant discovers body boundaries, learns to identify recurring need states, and feels the comfort of loving contact with caregivers. These experiences are gradually integrated into a sense of the self as a permanent being existing in the context of a group of other permanent beings who either do or do not respond adequately to the infant's internal states.

In toddlerhood, the self-theory grows through an active process of self-differentiation. Children explore the limits of their capacities and the nature of their impact on others. Because of toddlers' inability to entertain abstract concepts and their tendency toward egocentrism—the perception of oneself as the center of the world—their self-theories are likely to depend on being competent and being loved. There is little concern about the perceptions of others, cultural norms, or future plans.

During early and middle school age, children become more aware of the differences in perspective among people. An understanding of logical relations contributes to an appreciation of the concept of cultural norms: if one is in a certain role, one is expected to act in a certain way. Sex-role standards are especially important in this regard. Children are very sensitive to any implication that they are not living up to expectations for how a boy or girl ought to act. Children are also aware of moral imperatives that define good and evil. All these cognitive gains make a child more sensitive to social pressure, more likely to experience feelings of guilt or failure, and more preoccupied with issues of social comparison, self-criticism, and self-evaluation. At the same time, the child remains relatively dependent on adults for material and emotional resources. For these reasons, the issue of self-esteem becomes especially salient during the early- and middle-school-age periods.

Self-Evaluation

For every component of the self—the physical self, the self as reflected in others' behavior, the array of personal aspirations and goals—a person makes an evaluation of worthiness. This self-evaluation, or *self-esteem*, is based on three essential sources: (1) messages of love, support, and approval from others; (2) specific attributes and competences; and (3) the way one regards these specific aspects of the self, both in comparison with others and in relation to one's ideal self (Pelham & Swann, 1989). Feelings of being loved, valued, admired, and successful contribute to a sense of worth. Feelings of being ignored, rejected, scorned, and inadequate contribute to a sense of worthlessness. These very early affective experiences contribute to a general sense of pride or shame, worthiness or worthlessness, which can be captured in global statements children make about themselves even as young as 3 or 4 years of age (Eder, 1989; Eder, Gerlach & Perlmutter, 1987).

Information about specific aspects of the self is accumulated through experiences of success and failure with daily tasks or when particular aspects of one's competence are challenged. A young child may develop a positive sense of self in the domain of athletics, problem solving, or social skills through the encouraging reactions of others as well as through the pleasure associated with succeeding in each of these areas.

With experience in a variety of roles and settings, each specific ability takes on a certain level of importance for a person. Not all abilities are equally valued at home, at school, and by friends. People can believe they have abilities in some areas but not in those they consider highly important. Others can believe they have only one or two areas of strength, but they may highly value those areas and believe them to be critically important to overall success. Self-esteem is influenced by the value one assigns to specific competences in relation to one's overall life goals and personal ideals. Thus it is possible to be a success in the eyes of others and still to feel a nagging sense of worthlessness. Similarly, it is possible to feel proud and confident even though others may not value the activities and traits in which one takes great satisfaction.

By adulthood, one has a pervasive sentiment about one's worth that sets a tone of either optimism or pessimism about future life events. Level of self-esteem contributes to willingness to take risks, expectations of success or failure, and expectations that one will have a meaningful impact on others.

Rosenberg (1979) has considered the impact on self-esteem of what he described as *contextual dissonance*. Children are influenced by the social groups that immediately surround them. During early school age, children emerge from the continuity of their families and neighborhoods into the more diverse context of school. This new context can complement or contrast with the major social characteristics of the family, specifically religion, race, and social class. Rosenberg cited evidence of the negative effects of a dissonant environment in all three of these areas. Catholics who had been raised in a non-Catholic neighborhood were likely to have lower self-esteem than those raised in a Catholic one. Similar findings were observed among Protestants and Jews raised in dissonant neighborhoods. Racial dissonance and economic dissonance have also been found to be related to low self-esteem. For example, black preschool-age children in an all-black Mississippi rural town reportedly had higher self-esteem than did those in a racially mixed Michigan urban area (McAdoo, 1985). The implication of these studies is that self-esteem is bolstered by a feeling of continuity and belongingness. Even qualities that are valued in the context of a child's family may generate the feeling that one is strange or wrong if they are discrepant with those that are valued in the child's immediate social context. Such feelings plant seeds of doubt about self-worth.

Feelings of self-worth provide a protective shield around the self. If a person has a positive, optimistic self-evaluation, then messages that are negative and incongruent with that self-evaluation will be deflected. A person with high self-esteem will explain a failure by examining the task, the amount of time needed for completion, the other people involved, or the criteria for evaluating success and failure. A person with low self-esteem, by contrast, will see the failure as another bit of evidence about his or her lack of worth (Wells & Marwell, 1976; Newman & Newman, 1980).

Self-Esteem and the Early-School-Age Child

At each life stage, as individuals set new goals for themselves or as discrepancies in competence become apparent, temporary periods of lowered self-esteem may be anticipated. Research on self-esteem suggests that early-school-age children may be especially vulnerable to fluctuations in feelings of self-worth (Kegan, 1982; Cicirelli, 1976; Long, Henderson & Ziller, 1967). Preschool- and kindergarten-age children assess their own competences to be significantly higher than do children in grades 1 through 4. In addition, girls in the early school grades are more critical of their abilities than boys and have lower expectations of success (Frey & Ruble, 1987; Butler, 1990).

Toddlers have been described as highly egocentric. In general, they feel good about themselves and do not differentiate between competence and social approval;

rather, they respond to all positive experiences as evidence of their ultimate importance and value. They use social comparison and imitation to build a greater sense of their own mastery (Butler, 1989).

Early-school-age children, by contrast, are increasingly aware of the discrepancy between their own competences and what they recognize as the skills of older children. They are able to view themselves as objects of the evaluations of others. They are also aware of the importance of acceptance by adults and peers outside the family, especially teachers and classmates (Weinstein et al., 1987). These newly valued others may not be as proud of their skills or as understanding about their limitations as family members are. Under conditions of peer competition, they begin to experience anxiety about their performance and about the way their abilities will be evaluated in comparison with those of others (Butler, 1989). At school, for example, young children often make critical comments about one another's work. Criticisms tend to outnumber compliments, and boys tend more than girls to be critical of their peers' work (Frey & Ruble, 1987). The combination of open peer criticism and a heightened emphasis on peer competition can make the school an environment in which one's self-esteem is frequently challenged.

Finally, early-school-age children are beginning to achieve a degree of internalization of social norms, including ideals to be attained as well as prohibitions, which they apply in a rather strict, rule-bound way. They are highly critical of rule violations, whether committed by themselves or by others. Intentions, motives, and special circumstances are less salient to early-school-age children than the overt consequences of behavior. Thus their newly formed capacity for guilt may lead to heightened anxiety over failure to live up to their moral code.

For all these reasons, the early-school-age child is likely to experience feelings of depression and worthlessness. This decrease in self-esteem can be seen as a temporary fluctuation. Young children need frequent reassurance from adults that they are competent and that they are loved. They need numerous opportunities to discover that their unique talents and abilities are useful and important. As competences increase, as thought becomes more flexible, and as the child makes meaningful friendships, we expect self-esteem to rise.

Group Play

Group Games

The early-school-age child continues to make use of vivid fantasies in play. During this period a new form of play emerges. Children show interest in group games that are more structured and somewhat more oriented to reality than play that is based primarily on imagination. Such games as ring-around-the-rosie, London Bridge, and farmer-in-the-dell are examples of early group play. Hide-and-seek and statue maker are more complex games of early school age. They involve more cognitive complexity, physical skill, and ritual. These games combine the element of fantasy with an emphasis on peer cooperation. Group play can be seen as a form of play that is transitional between the fantasy play of the toddler and the structured team sports and other games with rules of the middle-school-age child (Erikson, 1977).

Pablo Picasso, *Circle of Children*, 1952. Group games combine the element of fantasy with an emphasis on peer cooperation. Ring-Around-the-Rosie, Little Sally Saucer, and London Bridge Is Falling Down are three group games in which children dance and sing together.

Group games involve a few rules, which differentiate them from ongoing free-play activity. The rules are simple enough so that the child can use them effectively to begin a game and determine a winner without the help of an adult. Usually no team concept is involved in these games. A game is played many times so that many individual children may have an opportunity to win. The particular pleasure that children derive from these games seems to result more from peer cooperation and interaction than from the possibility of being a winner (Garvey, 1977).

Many of these games permit children to shift roles. A child is the hider and then the seeker, the catcher and then the thrower, the statue maker and then the statue. Through group play, children have a chance to experience the reciprocal nature of role relationships. Whereas many of their social roles are fixed—son or daughter, sibling, student—in play with peers children have opportunities to experience a variety of perspectives (Lee, 1975; Sutton-Smith, 1972).

Friendship Groups
Friendship relations in early school age are based on the exchange of concrete goods and the mutual enjoyment of activities. Friendships may be maintained through acts

Most children establish sex-segregated friendship groups during the early-school-age years. This is where His and Her worlds begin.

of affection, sharing, or collaboration in fantasy or constructive play. Children build a snow fort together, play space adventure with one another, or sleep over at one another's houses. Friendships can be broken by the taking of a toy, hitting, or name-calling (Damon, 1977).

Young children tend to evaluate situations on the basis of outcomes rather than intentions. Therefore, they are often harsh in assigning blame in the case of negative outcomes. For example, children were asked how much they should be blamed for a child's getting hurt. The "injury" took place in six different hypothetical situations. In the case of lowest level of responsibility, the child was accidentally hurt by some-one's toy, but the owner did not actually cause the injury. At this level, 6-year-olds were more likely than older children or adults to blame themselves for the outcome (Fincham & Jaspars, 1979). Because of this rigid approach to social responsibility, peer play is frequently disrupted by quarrels, "tattling" on others, and hard feelings about injustices. Even though children appear to be drawn into the active world of peer friendships, this is an uneven, difficult, and often extremely frustrating terrain for many early-school-age children to master.

One of the most notable characteristics of young children's friendship groups is that they are segregated by sex. When boys and girls are free to choose play compan-ions, they tend to choose others of their own sex. This pattern of same-sex social groupings among children is found not only in the United States but in most other cultures (Edwards & Whiting, 1988). In one longitudinal study, children age 4½ were found playing with same-sex friends about three times more often than with opposite-sex friends. By age 6½, they were *11* times more likely to be playing with same-sex friends (Maccoby & Jacklin, 1987).

The important implication of the formation of same-sex social groups is that boys and girls grow up in quite distinctive peer environments (Maccoby, 1988). Boys and girls tend to use different strategies to achieve dominance or leadership in their groups. Boys are more likely to use physical assertiveness and direct demands; girls are more likely to use verbal persuasiveness and polite suggestions. The verbal exchanges in all-boy groups tend to include frequent boasts, commands, interruptions, heckling, and generally playful teasing. Boys try to top one another's stories and establish dominance through verbal threats. The interactions in all-girl groups tend to include agreement with and acknowledgment of the other persons' comments, listening carefully to one another's statements, and talking about things that bind the group together in a shared sentiment or experience. In mixed-sex groups, girls are likely to find that the leadership and interpersonal skills they have developed in their all-girl groups are not very effective in controlling the behaviors of boys. As a result, their negative views of boys are reinforced and their tendency to seek all-girl peer interactions increases.

Though of course many young children do form friendships with children of the opposite sex, the general tendency to form same-sex friendship groups is an important aspect of social development that is established during the early childhood years and continues into adolescence. Even though a boy and a girl grow up in the same culture, in the same neighborhood, and even in the same family, the social milieus in which the two are embedded have some very distinctive features. Early-school-age boys and girls find same-sex play companions more compatible. The tendency to establish separate play and friendship groups fosters the development of distinctive gender-linked communication strategies and makes the achievement of mutual understanding between boys and girls difficult.

Summary

The four tasks of early school age are closely interrelated. The complex process of sex-role identification has cognitive, affective, physical, and interpersonal elements. As young children clarify the content of their sex-role identity they create a set of beliefs about their own self-worth, their relationships with other children, and their future. Because of the strict rule orientation that characterizes moral thought at this age, children are likely to assume some fundamental equivalences between sex-role standards and moral standards. They may feel a moral obligation to uphold certain sex-role standards and may feel moral guilt if they violate them. The development of conscience, with its capacity to reward and punish, brings an internalization of moral standards. Self-esteem can fluctuate as a result of the child's experiences with transgressions, guilt, or praise for prosocial behavior. The clarification of the self-concept and the development of feelings of competence and worth are also brought about through peer interactions and encounters with new social settings, especially the day-care center, preschool, and kindergarten. Moral development suggests an emerging allegiance to a cultural code that includes such basic values as honesty and fidelity.

A significant cognitive change comes about with the change in children's play behavior. As they interact with peers, they become aware of the variety of perspectives that other children bring to their games. They learn to be more sensitive to the fact that others do not always perceive events exactly as they do. The reduction in egocentrism that takes place during the early school years has implications for the development of logical thought and the maturation of morality. The synthesis of these developmental tasks contributes to the formation of a set of powerful early scripts about fundamental rules that govern one's view of the self in transactions with key social groups, especially family, teachers, classmates, and friends.

The Psychosocial Crisis: Initiative versus Guilt

As children resolve the toddlerhood crisis of autonomy versus shame and doubt in a positive way, they emerge from that stage with a very strong sense of themselves as unique individuals. During the early-school-age period, they shift the focus of their attention toward the investigation of the external environment. They attempt to discover the same kind of stability, strength, and regularity in the external world that they have discovered within themselves.

The active investigation of the environment is what Erikson (1963) described as *initiative*. The child's motivation for and skill at investigation depend on the successful development of a strong sense of autonomy. When children acquire self-control and confidence in themselves, they are able to perform a variety of actions and observe the consequences. They discover, for example, the kinds of things that make parents or teachers angry and the kinds of things that please them. They may deliberately perform a hostile act in order to evoke a hostile response. Children's curiosity about the order of the universe ranges from the physical to the metaphysical. They may ask questions about the color of the sky, the purpose of hair, the nature of God, the origin of babies, or the speed at which fingernails grow. They take things apart, explore the alleys and dark corners of their neighborhood, and invent toys and games out of odds and ends. Initiative is the active, conceptual investigation of the world in much the same sense that autonomy is the active, physical manipulation of it.

One expression of inquisitiveness is children's playful exploration of their own bodies and sometimes their friends'. It is not uncommon to find 5- and 6-year-old children intently involved in a game of "doctor" in which both "doctor" and "patient" have their pants off. Boys of this age can occasionally be observed in a game that is won by the individual who can achieve the longest urine trajectory. Girls report occasions on which they have attempted to urinate from a standing position "in the same way a boy does." Both boys and girls engage in some form of masturbation. These behaviors are evidence of children's growing curiosity about and pleasure in their bodies and their physical functioning.

Every culture imposes some limits on legitimate experimentation and investigation. Some questions may not be asked; some acts may not be performed. Adults' reactions will determine whether the child learns to view sexual play and masturbation as wrong or as acceptable. Children gradually internalize the cultural prohibitions and learn to inhibit their curiosity in the taboo areas. Guilt is the internal psychological mechanism that signals when a taboo is about to be violated. Guilt is an emotion that accompanies the sense that one has been responsible for an unacceptable thought, fantasy, or action (Izard, 1977).

One taboo shared by most cultures is the prohibition against incest (Gagnon, 1977; McCary, 1978). Most children learn that any behavior that suggests sexual intimacy between family members is absolutely forbidden. Even the thought of such a relationship comes to generate feelings of anxiety and guilt. The child's curiosity in other domains is limited to the extent that the family and the school impose restrictions on areas of legitimate inquiry or action.

Box 7.1   Childhood Phobias

Occasionally a child will experience an increasingly burdensome amount of guilt rather than the usual sense of initiative. One expression of overwhelming guilt is the development of a strong, irrational fear of some object or situation. This is called a *phobia*. Some common phobias that develop during early childhood are fear of going to school, of the dark, and of some kind of animal. These fears preoccupy the child's fantasies and limit his or her ability to explore the environment. The child tends to think a lot about the object of the fear and to experience a great deal of anxiety in connection with these thoughts.

The case of school phobia is an interesting example. An estimated 17 children per 1000 experience school phobia each year (Davison & Neale, 1990). The phobia consists of a dread of some aspect of the school situation, such as a teacher, another child, a janitor, or even eating school food. As the time to go to school arrives each morning, the child's anxiety increases. The child may complain of nausea or stomach pain and may even vomit. Once parents agree to let the child stay home, the anxiety and symptoms fade quickly—until the next morning (Coolidge, 1979).

From a psychoanalytic perspective, school phobia is seen as a conflict related more closely to separation from the parents—usually the mother—than fear of school itself. The initial fear of some event at school is echoed in the parents' reluctance to separate from the child. At a symbolic level, the child senses that his or her mother is in danger of serious illness or death. These fears are a projection of the child's unacceptable hostile feelings toward the mother. This threat to the mother can be averted only if the child stays home to protect her. Going to school thus is equated with losing mother, childhood, and safety. Since the actual fears of school are not confronted and the unconscious hostility toward the mother is not expressed, the idea of going to school becomes even more frightening.

A phobia can be understood as a means of directing anxiety and guilt over unacceptable thoughts, behaviors, or fantasies to a specific target. Rather than accept personal responsibility for inappropriate behavior, the child projects the unacceptable impulses to an element of the environment, such as a horse or

School phobia is interpreted within the psychoanalytic framework as an expression of a child's reluctance to leave the mother.

a dog. It is not the child who is doing fearful and harmful things; they are being done by something out there that evokes the child's fear.

The phobia provides a way for the child to express guilty feelings without having to take personal blame. In that sense, the phobia serves as a temporary protective device until the child can identify and control those impulses that are specifically linked to social disapproval. For the child who cannot take responsibility for socially devalued impulses or who experiences a great deal of anxiety in many areas, the range of feared objects and settings may grow rather than diminish. The extremely phobic child fears danger in most of the environment and cannot distinguish between those fears that emanate from personal impulses and those that are realistic appraisals of external danger.

The psychosocial crisis of initiative versus guilt is resolved positively through the development of a sense that an active, questioning investigation of the environment is an informative and pleasurable experience. Inquiry is tempered by a respect for personal privacy and cultural values. However, the preponderant psychological state of mind is curiosity and experimentation. The child learns that even though certain areas are off limits, efforts to understand most aspects of the world are appropriate.

Guilt, like other negative poles of the psychosocial crises, can have an adaptive function. As children grow in their sense of empathy and their ability to take responsibility for their actions, they are able to acknowledge when their actions may have caused harm or when their words may have been hurtful to someone else. Feelings of guilt generally lead to remorse and some attempt to set things right again, to restore the positive feelings in a relationship. At the extreme, however, children can suffer from an overwhelming sense of guilt. When adults severely limit experimentation and investigation, children begin to feel that every question or doubt about the world is an inappropriate intrusion. They begin to believe that their thoughts and actions are responsible for much of the misfortune or unhappiness of others. For example, young children of depressed mothers express unusually high levels of distress, concern, and feelings of responsibility about someone else's unhappiness. Mothers who are consistently sad set an example of blaming themselves for most of the bad things that happen. In addition, depressed mothers are likely to withdraw love when the child has misbehaved, a discipline technique associated with high levels of guilt and anxiety (Zahn-Waxler et al., 1990). In this kind of environment, a child learns to severely restrict new behaviors out of fear that they may cause harm or unhappiness to someone else. In effect, the child comes to feel that curiosity itself is taboo and feels guilty whenever it is aroused. The child who resolves this crisis in the direction of guilt is left to rely almost totally on parents or other authorities for directions on how to operate in the world.

The psychosocial crisis of initiative versus guilt highlights the intimate relationship between intellectual curiosity and emotional development. During this stage, the parents and the school transmit the cultural attitudes toward experimentation, curiosity, and investigation. They also make demands that direct the child's curiosity away from familial, subgroup, and cultural taboo areas. Children are expected to develop the ability to control their own questions and behavior. Whereas violations may bring shame and punishment, successful self-control may attract no notice whatsoever. Children must develop a strong internal moral code that will help them avoid punishment. They must also develop the ability to reward themselves for correct behavior. The more areas of restriction that are imposed on children's thinking, the more difficult it will be for children to distinguish between legitimate and inappropriate areas of investigation. The only way that children have of coping with this problem is to develop a rigid moral code that restricts many aspects of thought and action.

The Central Process: Identification

The discussion of the developmental tasks during early school age points directly to identification as the central process in the resolution of the conflict between initiative and guilt. Children at this age actively strive to enhance their self-concepts by incorporating into their own behavior some of the valued characteristics that their parents exhibit. Identification is one mechanism that children use to maintain connectedness with parents. Children identify even with parents who are extremely brutal. Since most of the behaviors that these children incorporate are aggressive ones, the children of aggressive parents often tend to be aggressive toward others. Parental identification allows children to feel that their parents are with them even when they are not physically present. This feeling of connectedness with parents provides an underlying sense of security for children in a wide variety of situations.

Viewed from another perspective, identification allows the child a growing sense of independence from parents (Jacobson, 1964). Children who know how their parents would respond in a given situation no longer need the parents' physical presence to direct their behavior. Children who can praise or punish themselves for their actions are less dependent on their parents to perform these functions.

Parental identification figures in the child's development in two rather different ways. On the one hand, the closeness with parents provides the basis for the incorporation of parental sanctions and prohibitions. Once children have integrated these guidelines for behavior, they are bound to feel guilty any time they anticipate abandoning them. On the other hand, the security that results from strong parental identification allows children increased freedom when they are away from their parents. The child whose parental identifications are strong is more likely to question the environment, take risks, and initiate action.

Identification with parents results in a strengthening of the child's personality. An important outcome of early-school-age identifications is the formation of an ideal self-image. Psychoanalytic theorists sometimes referred to it as the *ego ideal* (Freud, 1929/1955; Sandler et al., 1963). The conscience functions not only to punish misdeeds but also to reward actions that bring the child closer to some aspect of the ideal self-image. The ideal self is a complex view of the self as it may be in the future, including skills, profession, values, and personal relationships. The ideal self is a fantasy, a goal that is unlikely to be attained even in adulthood. Nonetheless, the discrepancy between the real self and the ideal self is a strong motivating factor. As children strive to achieve their ideal, they attempt new activities, plan things that strain the limits of their abilities, take risks, and resist temptations that might interfere with their desired goals.

The ego ideal is more unrealistic during early school age than it is at later stages. Children can fantasize anything they wish about themselves in the future. They take their parents' values very literally and use them to project an ideal person of mythical proportions. The ideal self might include the strength of Hercules, the wealth of Queen Elizabeth, the wisdom of Confucius, and the compassion of Jesus. The lack of realistic constraints on the ego ideal allows the child to investigate and experience vicariously certain human qualities that may always be beyond reach. As people grow older, it is important that the fantasy of the ideal self-image become increasingly attainable, albeit still beyond what has been attained. People who find it difficult to modify their ideal self-images become vulnerable to personal frustration and psychological despair because they are unable to be what they wish. Many 6-year-old children may wish to become

Pablo Picasso, *Mother and Daughter*, 1904. Parental identification provides the child both security and freedom. By becoming more like her mother, the young girl can feel close to her even when they are apart.

president of the United States. This largely unrealistic fantasy is very exciting and, for some, ennobling. However, very few people actually achieve this position. By the time one reaches early adulthood, it is important to have developed an occupational ideal that is closer to what is actually attainable.

Identification with parents is the process by which the ideal self-image and moral prescriptions are blended into the child's personality. To the extent that children are unable to control their behavior so that it corresponds to the sanctions and ideals that they have internalized, they will experience guilt. To the extent that children's behavior approaches their ideals and conforms to internalized sanctions, they will experience feelings of self-confidence that will allow them to take initiative. The balance between guilt and self-confidence determines the eventual resolution of the psychosocial crisis of initiative versus guilt.

Summary

The crisis of initiative versus guilt captures the child's need to question existing norms and the emerging feelings of moral concern when norms are violated. This crisis does not focus specifically on intellectual development; rather, one must assume that the level of questioning that takes place during this stage is possible only because of an increase in cognitive complexity. The process of positive parental identification promotes the incorporation of cultural norms and strengthens the child's sense of competence. Socialization during this stage can foster a creative openness or an anxious dread of novelty.

▣ Applied Topic: The Impact of Television

Television is a significant socialization agent in the lives of young children. If you were to look around the homes of American families in the early 1940s, you would find that only a few of the most wealthy families had televisions. Today over 90% of American families have at least one TV set, and many families have more than one. College students have television sets in their dormitory rooms, hospitals provide television in the rooms, motels and hotels have televisions with additional pay channels for viewing movies, there are televisions that can be plugged into the cigarette lighter of the car for "on-the-road viewing," and there are hand-held televisions that children can carry with them just like small radios and tape players. The centrality of television as a force in daily life is vividly seen in the movie *Rain Man*, in which the main character becomes intensely anxious if he thinks he is going to miss his regular daytime television programs.

Televisions are operated an average of about seven hours per day in American homes (Steinberg, 1985). Studies of the viewing time of individuals of different ages suggest that even infants are exposed to about half an hour of television daily. The pattern of hours of viewing is shown in Figure 7.2. On average, children in the age range 4 to 6 watch about two and a half hours of television daily (Liebert & Sprafkin, 1988). This average of course gives no indication of the wide variation in practices observed among children in this age range. Some children watch as much as six or eight hours of television a day on the weekends. A study of first-graders found that about one-third watched four or more hours of television daily and about 10% watched none (Lyle & Hoffman, 1972).

Since television is so pervasive in our lives, it makes sense to ask about its impact on development. How do the amount of time spent watching television and the content of the programs that are watched influence the cognitive and socioemotional development of young children? To what extent can television be a stimulus for optimal development? Can we draw any implications that might be useful to parents and teachers who have responsibility for guiding young children's choices in regard to television viewing?

Cognitive Consequences

Many parents and educators worry that television is turning our children into a generation of couch potatoes who are lulled into a life of mental and physical passivity.

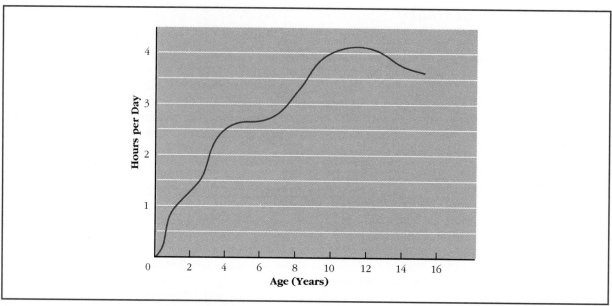

Figure 7.2   Estimated Average Hours of TV Viewing by Age, United States, 1987
Source: R. M. Liebert and J. Sprafkin, *The Early Window: Effects of Television on Children and Youth*, 3rd
ed. (New York: Pergamon), Fig. 1.2, p. 5. Reprinted by permission.

A review of over 200 studies of the impact of television on children's cognitive development found that researchers have described a mixed picture of television's impact
(Landers, 1989a). Television viewing does appear to replace certain other activities
that children might be involved in, such as going to the movies, reading comic books,
listening to the radio, and participating in organized sports. In a natural experiment,
Williams and Handford (1986) compared the daily activities of adults and children in
three Canadian towns: one that had no television (NOTEL), one that had only one
television channel (UNITEL), and one that had four channels (MULTITEL). Data were
collected before television came to NOTEL and then again four years later. Before
television, the children and youths in NOTEL were significantly more involved in community and sports activities than youths in the other two towns. Once NOTEL had
television reception, participation in these activities dropped dramatically.

Television does not appear to replace time spent doing homework. To the distress
of many adults, children often have the television on when they do their homework
(Sheehan, 1983). Even when the television is on, however, children are not really
glued to the tube. Preschool-age children are observed to tune out frequently while
they watch television. They often ignore long portions of the audio component of
programs (Hayes & Birnbaum, 1980). They are especially distracted by the presence
of toys, by aspects of programs that seem lifeless or boring, and by the mere fact of
having already watched television for a while (Anderson, 1977). A study of 5-year-old
children in their own homes found that the children were looking at the television
only 67% of the time they were in the room while it was on (Anderson et al., 1985).

When parents watch television with their children, they can help interpret what the children are perceiving.

In any attempt to assess the impact of television, it is important to determine whether heavy viewers are actually focusing their attention on the television or treating it as background for other activities.

Research on cognitive development suggests that social interaction is an important stimulus for cognitive growth. Children benefit by interacting with others who express ideas and opinions that differ from their own. Day-to-day exchanges with adults and peers force children to examine their own point of view and to "decenter" as they seek solutions to problems or make plans as members of a group. From this perspective, television can have a negative effect on cognitive development insofar as it reduces social interaction. We have already seen that the mere presence of television in a community reduces participation in community activities. Even within the family, when the television is on, conversation dwindles. An observational study of family television viewing found that children interacted less both with each other and with their fathers during viewing than during nonviewing periods (Brody, Stoneman & Sanders, 1980). The need for peer-group interaction is certainly not met during the hours when the child watches television (Gadberry, 1974). For many young children, watching television is a solitary activity. This is a time when they are interacting neither with peers nor with adults. The noninteractive aspect of television does not serve to reduce the young child's egocentrism. Without interaction, children cannot discover whether their interpretation of what they are viewing is the same as or different from what was intended.

One aspect of watching television that has received attention is the impact of televised advertising on the attitudes and buying preferences of children (Liebert & Sprafkin, 1988; Comstock, 1977). Children as young as 3 and 4 can usually tell the difference between programs and commercials. Under the age of 8, however, children are not clearly aware of the marketing intention of the advertisement. Young children tend to trust that what is said or shown about a product during a commercial is accurate and true. They do not understand disclaimers ("some assembly required"), and they do not understand the company's motivation for presenting the commercial. From age 8 up to age 12, there is a marked increase in children's understanding of the profit motive associated with advertising and an accompanying decline in trust in commercial messages.

Advertisements aimed at young viewers have at least two negative consequences. First, children are likely to have conflicts with their parents when they want to buy products that they have seen advertised on television. Since young children are more gullible than adults, they find it hard to accept their parents' judgment about the actual worth of the advertised product. Parents and children are very likely to differ as to whether the product will really be as much fun as the child has been led to believe. The only way some children can learn to be more discerning is to buy something and be disappointed.

The second negative consequence applies specifically to highly sugared food products—candies, sweet fruit-flavored drinks, sugared cereals. Advertisements for these products make up about 80% of children's television advertising (Liebert & Sprafkin, 1988). Exposure to these advertisements is likely to influence a young child's beliefs about nutrition as well as the selection of foods and snacks. Young children do not understand that eating these heavily sugared foods produces cavities in their teeth or that children who eat a lot of heavily sugared foods are likely to gain weight. When children are exposed to commercials for these sugary snacks, they are likely to select them when they have a choice even when they know that fruits and vegetables are healthier snacks than candies (Gorn & Goldberg, 1982).

Socioemotional Consequences

The dominant focus of research on the socioemotional impact of television viewing has been on the role of televised *violence* on the beliefs and behaviors of young children. Concern with television violence is particularly meaningful within the context of the child's growing moral consciousness. More than 20 years of laboratory experiments, field experiments, and analyses of naturally occurring behaviors have led to the conclusion that televised violence has definite negative consequences for young children's behaviors and beliefs.

Studies of children in the United States and in other countries support the belief that at least three processes are at work that might increase the level of aggressiveness in children who watch televised violence (see Table 7.5) (Huesmann & Eron, 1986; Huesmann & Malamuth, 1986; Josephson, 1987; Liebert & Sprafkin, 1988). First, children observe televised role models who perform aggressive actions. Especially when the hero is provoked and retaliates with aggression, the child is likely to imitate the aggressive actions. Thus the viewing of televised violence adds new violent behaviors to the child's repertoire. In addition, when the hero is rewarded or viewed as successful as a result of his or her violent actions, children's tendencies to express aggression are increased (Bandura, 1973).

The second process linked to the impact of televised violence is a heightening of arousal. The fast action that usually accompanies televised violence captures the viewer's attention. The violent incident raises the child's level of emotionality, bringing to

Table 7.5   Three Processes That May Increase the Level of Aggression in Children Who Watch Televised Violence

Process	Possible Consequence
Observing role models who engage in aggressive actions	Imitation of violent action likely when: 1. hero is provoked and retaliates with aggression 2. hero is rewarded for violent actions New violent behaviors added to repertoire
Viewing aggressive actions leads to heightened level of arousal	Brings network of aggressive thoughts, feelings, memories, and action tendencies into consciousness Repeated stimulation strengthens this network Stimulation interacts with aggressive temperament to increase the likelihood of aggressive action
Viewing aggression affects beliefs and values	Aggressive behavior is seen as acceptable way to resolve conflicts Viewers are hardened to use of aggression in peer interactions Aggression is used as a response to frustration Viewers expect others to be aggressive toward them Viewers worry about being victims of aggression Viewers see the world as a dangerous place

the fore other aggressive feelings, thoughts, memories, and action tendencies. The more frequently this network of elements is activated, the stronger will be their association. Thus young children who have seen a lot of televised violence and are temperamentally aggressive are likely to engage in overt acts of aggression because of the strength of arousal prompted by the televised stimulus (Berkowitz, 1984, 1986).

Finally, exposure to televised violence affects a young child's beliefs and values. Children who are exposed to frequent episodes of televised violence are more likely to believe that aggressive behavior is an acceptable way to resolve conflicts, and they become hardened to the use of aggression in peer interactions. They are also more accepting of the use of aggression as a response to frustration. In addition, children (and adults) who are exposed to televised violence are more likely to expect that others will be aggressive toward them; they are more likely to worry about being victims of aggression; and they are more likely to see the world as a dangerous place (Bryant, Carveth & Brown, 1981; Gerbner et al., 1980; Thomas & Drabman, 1977).

Television as a Stimulus for Optimal Development

Researchers have barely begun to scratch the surface of television's uses for promoting optimal development. There is clear evidence that children who are exposed to pro-social programming can be influenced toward more positive social behavior (Hearold, 1986). Programs such as *Mister Rogers' Neighborhood* attempt to teach socially positive messages that help children to develop feelings of self-worth, to accept their feelings, to show concern for others, and to value other members of the community. Children who have watched *Mister Rogers' Neighborhood* as part of their regular preschool curriculum have been found to demonstrate higher levels of task persistence than children who have not seen this program. They are also more willing to tolerate delays, and they are more cooperative with authority figures (Friedrich & Stein, 1973).

Many other programs, some developed for children and others intended for a broader viewing audience, convey positive ethical messages about the value of family life, the need to work hard and sacrifice in order to achieve important goals, the value of friendship, the importance of loyalty and commitment in relationships, and many other cultural values. A number of contemporary programs include characters of many races and ethnic backgrounds. Many feature women who function in positions of authority or perform acts of heroism. Through exposure to these programs, children can learn to challenge racial and gender stereotypes and develop positive images of people of other racial and cultural groups. Children who watch these kinds of programs and who have opportunities to discuss the underlying ideas with others are likely to incorporate these ideas into their beliefs and values (Liebert & Sprafkin, 1988).

Public television has been successful in developing programs that directly address the educational needs of young children. *Sesame Street* is the best known and most well documented of these efforts. It is clear that young children who consistently watch *Sesame Street* benefit in a variety of intellectual tasks, such as recognizing letters, numbers, and shapes, sorting objects into groups, and recognizing relationships among objects. When *Sesame Street* introduced a simple Spanish vocabulary, children who were consistent viewers benefited in their recognition of these words as well (Bogatz & Ball, 1972). Although the program was originally intended to reach the wide range of young children in an effort to promote the development of school-related skills, it appears that children in more affluent families who watch *Sesame Street* with their parents are more likely to demonstrate intellectual gains than children of lower socioeconomic status (Cook et al., 1975).

After the success of *Sesame Street*, other programs directed at development of literacy, science education, and mathematical skill appeared. Professionals are confident that we can introduce ideas and information to children and have the technology to produce quality public television to supplement instruction and improve literacy for a broad range of children. However, relatively few resources are directed toward this activity. Japan, Great Britain, and Australia all invest significantly more in the development of public television programming for children than the United States does. "In 1985, the British Broadcasting Corp. carried 590 hours of newly produced TV programs for children compared to 87.5 hours in the United States" (Landers, 1989b).

Advice to Parents and Teachers

Many families find that they end up arguing about the amount of television their children are watching. Withdrawal from television becomes a punishment for a wide range of misbehaviors, from telling a lie to getting in trouble in school. Parents and children may argue about which programs to watch or about turning off the television at bedtime. Children may find that their parents are so involved in television that they cannot get their attention; and parents may use the television as a substitute for companionship for their children when they are not home. Since television is a component of contemporary life, it makes sense to help children get the most out of it. Making it the focus of conflicts and battles over control does not seem to be very productive. Parents and teachers need to take a proactive stance with respect to the child's experiences with television (Tangney, 1987). They should emphasize more do's than don'ts.

1. Do watch television with young children when you can and talk about the stories and information presented. Talk about how situations that are presented on television may or may not be similar to real life.
2. As appropriate, follow up ideas and suggestions presented in educational programming with activities at home or in the classroom. Such activities give children ideas about how to become more actively involved with the information being presented on television.
3. Encourage children to sample a wide variety of television programs. Introduce them to news specials, science programs, opera, concerts, classic movies, and coverage of special events as well as children's programming.
4. Talk with children about the purpose of commercials, how they are made, how they intend to influence children's behaviors, and what children should listen for in evaluating televised commercials.
5. Limit young children's exposure to television violence. It will probably not be possible to eliminate it entirely, but special efforts should be made to reduce the early-school-age child's exposure to violent programming before bedtime, and to talk about how and why violence is used.
6. Talk about the other activities children can participate in instead of watching television. Help children choose among many uses of their time.
7. Use the VCR to select programs that are developmentally appropriate for children. This is especially important at times when children are home because of illness, or when the regular evening programming is judged to be unsuitable for a child of a certain temperament or developmental level.

☐ Chapter Summary

Early school age marks the beginning of work on developmental tasks that will persist well into adulthood. The sex-role identity of the early-school-age child will be revised and reintegrated as it becomes a core element of personal identity in adolescence. Continuous moral development is woven into a philosophy of life.

Although self-esteem is revised with entry into new roles, a positive sense of worth brings an important tone of optimism when the child faces new challenges. Competence and social acceptance are the essential antecedents of self-esteem. The increased involvement with peers in play brings about appreciation of others' perspectives, social acceptance, and delight in intimacy with friends.

The psychosocial crisis of initiative versus guilt has direct implications for such essential personality characteristics as self-esteem, creativity, curiosity, and risk taking. The child who resolves this crisis positively will be fortified with an active, exploratory approach to the environment. Little has been done to investigate this concept directly.

The impact of television on the early-school-age child highlights the interconnectedness of emotional and cognitive development. The potential for television to contribute to the optimal development of young children has only begun to be realized.

References

Anderson, D. R. (1977). Children's attention to television. Paper presented at the biennial meeting of the Society for Research in Child Development, New Orleans.

Anderson, D. R., Field, D. E., Collins, E. P. L., & Nathan, J. G. (1985). Estimates of young children's time with television: A methodological comparison of parent reports with time-lapse video home observation. *Child Development, 56,* 1345–1357.

Anthony, E. J. (1970). The behavior disorders of children. In P. H. Mussen (ed.), *Carmichael's manual of child psychology* (3rd ed., vol. 2). New York: Wiley.

Aronfreed, J. (1969). The concept of internalization. In D. A. Goslin (ed.), *Handbook of socialization theory and research.* Chicago: Rand McNally.

Bandura, A. (1973). *Aggression: A social learning analysis.* Englewood Cliffs, N.J.: Prentice-Hall.

Bandura, A. (1977). *Social learning theory.* Englewood Cliffs, N.J.: Prentice-Hall.

Bandura, A. (1986). *Social foundations of thought and action.* Englewood Cliffs, N.J.: Prentice-Hall.

Baumrind, D. (1975). *Early socialization and the discipline controversy.* Morristown, N.J.: General Learning Press.

Baumrind, D. (1982). Are androgynous individuals more effective persons and parents? *Child Development, 53,* 44–75.

Beit-Hallahmi, B. (1987). Critical periods in psychoanalytic theories of personality development. In M. H. Bornstein (ed.), *Sensitive periods in development: Interdisciplinary perspectives* (pp. 211–221). Hillsdale, N.J.: Erlbaum.

Bem, S. L. (1975). Sex-role adaptability: One consequence of psychological androgyny. *Journal of Personality and Social Psychology, 31,* 634–643.

Bem, S. L. (1981). Gender schema theory: A cognitive account of sex-typing. *Psychological Bulletin, 88,* 354–364.

Bem, S. L. (1989). Genital knowledge and gender constancy in preschool children. *Child Development, 60,* 649–662.

Berkowitz, L. (1984). Some effects of thoughts on anti- and prosocial influences of media events: A cognitive-neoassociation analysis. *Psychological Bulletin, 95,* 419–427.

Berkowitz, L. (1986). Situational influences on reactions to observed violence. *Journal of Social Issues, 42,* 93–103.

Bogatz, G. A., & Ball, S. (1972). *The second year of "Sesame Street": A continuing evaluation.* Princeton, N.J.: Educational Testing Service.

Borke, H. (1973). The development of empathy in Chinese and American children between 3 and 6 years of age: A cross-cultural study. *Developmental Psychology, 9,* 102–108.

Brody, G. H., Stoneman, Z., & Sanders, A. K. (1980). Effects of television viewing on family interactions: An observational study. *Family Relations, 29,* 216–220.

Bryant, J., Carveth, R. A., & Brown, D. (1981). Television viewing and anxiety: An experimental examination. *Journal of Communication, 31,* 106–119.

Butler, R. (1989). Mastery versus ability appraisal: A developmental study of children's observations of peers' work. *Child Development, 60,* 1350–1361.

Butler, R. (1990). The effects of mastery and competitive conditions on self-assessment at different ages. *Child Development, 61,* 201–210.

Caldera, Y. M., Huston, A. C., & O'Brien, M. (1989). Social interactions and play patterns of parents and toddlers with feminine, masculine, and neutral toys. *Child Development, 60,* 70–76.

Carroll, J. L., & Rest, J. R. (1982). Moral development. In B. B. Wolman (ed.), *Handbook of developmental psychology* (pp. 434–451). Englewood Cliffs, N.J.: Prentice-Hall.

Chandler, M., & Boyes, M. (1982). Social-cognitive development. In B. B. Wolman (ed.), *Handbook of developmental psychology* (pp. 387–402). Englewood Cliffs, N.J.: Prentice-Hall.

Chwast, J. (1972). Sociopathic behavior in children. In B. B. Wolman (ed.), *Manual of child psychopathology.* New York: McGraw-Hill.

Cicirelli, V. G. (1976). Effects of evaluating task competence on the self-concept of children from different socioeconomic status levels. *Journal of Psychology, 94,* 217–223.

Comstock, G. (1977). Priorities for action-oriented psychological studies of television and behavior. Paper presented at the annual convention of the American Psychological Association, San Francisco.

Cook, T. D., Appleton, H., Conner, R. F., Shaffer, A., Tabkin, G., & Weber, J. S. (1975). *"Sesame Street" revisited.* New York: Russell Sage.

Coolidge, J. C. (1979). School phobia. In J. D. Noshpitz (ed.), *Basic handbook of child psychiatry* (pp. 453–463). New York: Basic Books.

Damon, W. (1977). *The social world of the child.* San Francisco: Jossey-Bass.

Damon, W. (1980). Patterns of change in children's social reasoning. A two-year longitudinal study. *Child Development, 51,* 1010–1017.

Davison, G. C., & Neale, J. M. (1980). *Abnormal psychology: An experimental clinical approach* (5th ed.). New York: Wiley.

Eder, R. A. (1989). The emergent personologist: The structure and content of 3½-, 5½-, and 7½-year-olds' concepts of themselves and other persons. *Child Development, 60,* 1218–1228.

Eder, R. A., Gerlach, S. G., & Perlmutter, M. (1987). In search of children's selves: Development of the specific and general components of the self-concept. *Child Development, 58,* 1044–1050.

Edwards, C. P., & Whiting, B. B. (1988). *Children of different worlds.* Cambridge, Mass.: Harvard University Press.

Eisenberg, N., Murray, E., & Hite, T. (1982). Children's reasoning regarding sex-typed toy choice. *Child Development, 53,* 81–86.

Eisenberg, N., & Strayer, J. (1987). Critical issues in the study of empathy. In N. Eisenberg & J. Strayer (eds.), *Empathy and its development* (pp. 3–13). Cambridge: Cambridge University Press.

Epstein, S. (1973). The self-concept revisited; or, a theory of a theory. *American Psychologist, 28,* 404–416.

Erikson, E. H. (1963). *Childhood and society* (2nd ed.). New York: Norton.

Erikson, E. H. (1977). *Toys and reasons.* New York: Norton.

Fabes, R. A., Eisenberg, N., McCormick, S. E., & Wilson, M. S. (1988). Preschoolers' attributions of the situational determinants of others' naturally occurring emotions. *Developmental Psychology, 24,* 376–385.

Fincham, F., & Jaspars, J. (1979). Attribution of responsibility to the self and other in children and adults. *Journal of Personality and Social Psychology, 37,* 1589–1602.

Flavell, J. H. (1974). The development of inferences about others. In W. Mischel (ed.), *Understanding other persons.* Oxford: Blackwell, Basil & Mott.

Freud, A. (1936). *The ego and mechanisms of defense.* New York: International University Press.

Freud, S. (1925/1961). Some psychical consequences of the anatomical distinction between the sexes. In J. Strachey (ed.), *The standard edition of the complete psychological works of Sigmund Freud* (vol. 19). London: Hogarth Press.

Freud, S. (1929/1955). Three essays on the theory of sex-uality. In J. Strachey (ed.), *The standard edition of the complete psychological works of Sigmund Freud* (vol. 7). London: Hogarth Press.

Frey, K. S., & Ruble, D. N. (1987). What children say about classroom performance: Sex and grade differences in perceived competence. *Child Development, 58,* 1066–1078.

Friedrich, L. K., & Stein, A. H. (1973). *Aggressive and prosocial television programs and the natural behavior of pre-school children.* Monographs of the Society for Research in Child Development, 38 (whole no. 4).

Froming, W. J., Allen, L., & Jensen, R. (1985). Altruism, role-taking, and self-awareness: The acquisition of norms governing altruistic behavior. *Child Development, 56,* 1123–1228.

Gadberry, S. (1974). Television as baby-sitter: A field comparison of preschoolers' behavior during playtime and during television viewing. *Child Development, 45,* 1132–1136.

Gagnon, J. H. (1977). *Human sexualities.* Glenview, Ill.: Scott, Foresman.

Garvey, C. (1977). *Play.* Cambridge, Mass.: Harvard University Press.

Gerbner, G., Gross, L., Morgan, M., & Signorelli, N. (1980). The "mainstreaming" of America: Violence profile no. 11. *Journal of Communication, 30,* 10–29.

Gibbs, J. C. (1979). Kohlberg's moral stage theory: A Piagetian revision. *Human Development, 22,* 89–112.

Gorn, G. J., & Goldberg, M. E. (1982). Behavioral evidence of the effects of televised food messages on children. *Journal of Consumer Research, 9,* 200–205.

Hayes, D. S., & Birnbaum, D. W. (1980). Preschoolers' retention of televised events: Is a picture worth a thousand words? *Developmental Psychology, 16,* 410–416.

Hearold, S. (1986). A synthesis of 1043 effects of television on social behavior. In G. Comstock (ed.), *Public communications and behavior* (vol. 1, pp. 65–133). New York: Academic Press.

Heilbrun, A. B., Jr. (1974). Parent-identification and filial sex role behavior: The importance of biological context. In J. K. Cole & R. Dienstbier (eds.), *Nebraska Symposium on Motivation* (pp. 125–194). Lincoln: University of Nebraska Press.

Hetherington, E. M. (1967). The effects of familial variables on sex typing, on parent-child similarity, and on imitation in children. In J. P. Hill (ed.), *Minnesota Symposium on Child Psychology* (vol. 1, pp. 82–107). Minneapolis: University of Minnesota Press.

Hoffman, M. L. (1970). Moral development. In P. H. Mussen (ed.), *Carmichael's manual of child psychology* (3rd ed., vol. 2). New York: Wiley

Hoffman, M. L. (1979). Development of moral thought, feeling, and behavior. *American Psychologist, 34,* 958–966.

Hoffman, M. L. (1987). The contribution of empathy to justice and moral judgment. In N. Eisenberg & J. Strayer (eds.), *Empathy and its development* (pp. 47–80). Cambridge: Cambridge University Press.

Hoffner, C., & Badzinski, D. M. (1989). Children's integration of facial and situational cues to emotion. *Child Development, 60,* 411–422.

Huber, J. (1990). Macro-micro links in gender stratification. *American Sociological Review, 55,* 1–10.

Huesmann, L. R., & Eron, L. D. (1986). *Television and the aggressive child: A cross-national comparison.* Hillsdale, N.J.: Erlbaum.

Huesmann, L. R., & Malamuth, N. M. (1986). Media violence and antisocial behavior: An overview. *Journal of Social Issues, 42,* 1–6.

Iannotti, R. J. (1985). Naturalistic and structured assessments of prosocial behavior in preschool children: The influence of empathy and perspective taking. *Developmental Psychology, 21,* 46–55.

Izard, C. E. (1977). *Human emotion.* New York: Plenum.

Jacobson, E. (1964). *The self and the object world.* New York: International Universities Press.

Josephson, W. L. (1987). Television violence and children's aggression: testing the priming, social script, and disinhibition predictions. *Journal of Personality and Social Psychology, 53,* 882–890.

Kagan, J. (1958). The concept of identification, *Psychological Review, 65,* 296–305.

Kegan, R. (1982). *The evolving self: Problems and process in human development.* Cambridge, Mass.: Harvard University Press.

Kohlberg, L. (1969). Stage and sequence: The cognitive-developmental approach to socialization. In D. A. Goslin (ed.), *Handbook of socialization theory and research.* Chicago: Rand McNally.

Kohlberg, L. (1976). Moral stages and moralization: The cognitive-developmental approach. In T. Lickona (ed.), *Moral development and behavior.* New York: Holt, Rinehart & Winston.

Kohlberg, L. (1978). Revisions in the theory and practice of moral development. In W. Damon (ed.), *Moral development: New directions for child development* (vol. 2, pp. 83–88). San Francisco: Jossey-Bass.

Kohlberg, L. (1979). *The meaning and measurement of moral development.* Worcester, Mass.: Clark Lectures, Clark University.

Kohut, H. (1971). *The analysis of the self.* New York: International Universities Press.

Landers, S. (1989a). Watching TV, children *do* learn. *APA Monitor, 20*(3), 25.

Landers, S. (1989b). Big Bird, experts sing praises of kids' shows. *APA Monitor, 20*(7), 32.

Langlois, J. H., and Downs, A. C. (1980). Mothers, fathers, and peers as socialization agents of sex-typed play behaviors in young children. *Child Development, 51,* 1217–1247.

Lee, L. C. (1975). Toward a cognitive theory of interpersonal development: Importance of peers. In M. Lewis & L. A. Rosenblum (eds.), *Friendship and peer relations.* New York: Wiley.

Liebert, R. M., & Sprafkin, J. (1988). *The early window: Effects of television on children and youth* (3rd ed.). New York: Pergamon.

Long, B. H., Henderson, E. H., & Ziller, R. C. (1967). Developmental changes in the self-concept during middle childhood. *Merrill-Palmer Quarterly, 13,* 201–215.

Lyle, J., & Hoffman, H. R. (1972). Children's use of television and other media. In E. A. Rubinstein, G. A. Comstock, & J. P. Murray (eds.), *Television in day-to-day life: Patterns of use* (pp. 129–256). Washington, D.C.: U.S. Government Printing Office.

Maccoby, E. E. (1980). *Social development: Psychological growth and the parent-child relationship.* New York: Harcourt Brace Jovanovich.

Maccoby, E. E. (1988). Gender as a social category. *Developmental Psychology, 24,* 755–765.

Maccoby, E. E., & Jacklin, C. N. (1987). Gender segregation in childhood. In E. H. Reese (ed.), *Advances in child development and behavior* (vol. 20, pp. 239–287). New York: Academic Press.

Mahler, M. S. (1963). Thoughts about development and individuation. *Psychoanalytic Study of the Child, 18,* 307–324.

Martin, C. L. (1989). Children's use of gender-related information in making social judgments. *Developmental Psychology, 25,* 80–88.

Martin, G. B., & Clark, R. D., III. (1982). Distress crying in neonates: Species and peer specificity. *Developmental Psychology, 18,* 3–9.

McAdoo, H. P. (1985). Racial attitude and self-concept of young black children over time. In H. P. McAdoo & J. L. McAdoo (eds.), *Black children: Social, educational, and parental environments* (pp. 213–242). Newbury Park, Calif.: Sage.

McCary, J. L. (1978). *McCary's human sexuality* (3rd ed.). New York: Van Nostrand.

Mischel, W. (1966). Theory and research on the antecedents of self-imposed delay of reward. In B. A. Maher (ed.), *Progress in experimental personality research* (vol. 3, pp. 81–132). New York: Academic Press.

Mischel, W. (1973). Toward a cognitive social learning reconceptualization of personality. *Psychological Review, 80,* 252–283.

Mischel, W., Shoda, Y., & Rodriguez, M. L. (1989). Delay of gratification in children. *Science, 244,* 933–938.

Newman, B. M., & Newman, P. R. (1980). *Personality development through the life span.* Pacific Grove, Calif.: Brooks/Cole.

Pelham, B. W., & Swann, W. B., Jr. (1989). From self-conceptions to self-worth: On the sources and structure of global self-esteem. *Journal of Personality and Social Psychology, 57,* 672–680.

Piaget, J. (1932/1948). *The moral judgment of the child.* Glencoe, Ill.: Free Press.

Rest, J. R. (1983). Morality. In J. H. Flavell & E. M. Markman (eds.), *Handbook of child psychology: Cognitive development* (vol. 3). New York: Wiley.

Rosenberg, M. (1979). *Conceiving the self.* New York: Basic Books.

Sagi, A., & Hoffman, M. L. (1976). Empathic distress in the newborn. *Developmental Psychology, 12,* 175–176.

Sandler, J., et al. (1963). The ego ideal and the ideal self. *Psychoanalytic Study of the Child, 18,* 139–158.

Selman, R. (1980). *The growth of interpersonal understanding: Developmental and clinical analysis.* New York: Academic Press.

Selman, R. L. (1971). Taking another's perspective: Role-taking development in early childhood. *Child Development, 42,* 1721–1734.

Sheehan, P. W. (1983). Age trends and the correlates of children's television viewing. *Australian Journal of Psychology, 35,* 417–431.

Smetana, J. G. (1985). Preschool children's conceptions of transgressions: Effects of varying moral and conventional domain-related attributes. *Developmental Psychology, 21,* 18–29.

Spence, J. T. (1982). Comments on Baumrind's "Are androgynous individuals more effective persons and parents?" *Child Development, 53,* 76–80.

Steinberg, C. (1985). *TV facts.* New York: Facts on File.

Stoddart, T., & Turiel, E. (1985). Children's concepts of cross-gender activities. *Child Development, 56,* 1241–1252.

Sutton-Smith, B. A. (1972). Syntax for play and games. In R. E. Herron & B. Sutton-Smith (eds.), *Child's play.* New York: Wiley.

Tangney, J. P. (1987). TV in the family. *Bryn Mawr Now, 14,* 1, 14.

Thomas, M. H., & Drabman, R. S. (1977). Effects of television violence on expectations of others' aggression. Paper presented at the annual convention of the American Psychological Association, San Francisco.

Thompson, S. K. (1975). Gender labels and early sex role development. *Child Development, 46,* 339–347.

Turiel, E. (1983). *The development of social knowledge: Morality and convention.* Cambridge, Mass.: Cambridge University Press.

U.S. Bureau of the Census (1987). *Statistical Abstract of the United States, 1988.* Washington, D.C.: U.S. Government Printing Office.

Walker, L. J. (1989). A longitudinal study of moral reasoning. *Child Development, 60,* 157–166.

Weinstein, R. S., Marshall, H. H., Sharp, L., & Botkin, M. (1987). Pygmalion and the student: Age and classroom differences in children's awareness of teacher expectations. *Child Development, 58,* 1079–1093.

Wells, L. E., & Marwell, G. (1976). *Self-esteem: Its conceptualization and measurement.* Newbury Park, Calif.: Sage.

Westoff, C. F., & Rindfuss, R. R. (1974). Sex preselection in the United States: Some implications. *Science, 184,* 633–636.

Williams, T. H., & Handford, A. G. (1986). Television and other leisure activities. In T. H. Williams (ed.), *The impact of television: A natural experiment in three communities* (pp. 143–213). Orlando, Fla.: Academic Press.

Windmiller, M., Lambert, N., & Turiel, E. (1980). *Moral development and socialization.* Boston: Allyn & Bacon.

Zahn-Waxler, C., Kochanska, G., Krupnick, J., & McKnew, D. (1990). Patterns of guilt in children of depressed and well mothers. *Developmental Psychology, 26,* 51–59.

Chapter Eight

Children struggle to increase their competence in the shadow of the large figure of mother, teacher, or culture, who urges, compliments, and criticizes.

Middle School Age (6 to 12 Years)

Historically, the *middle-school-age* period was not considered to be of major importance for an understanding of development. Sigmund Freud's psychoanalytic theory treated the years following the resolution of the Oedipal conflict as a time when sexual and aggressive impulses are repressed and active only in the unconscious. He called this period the *latency stage,* a term that suggested that no significant contributions to personality formation could be traced to it. For a long time, psychologists tended not to study psychological development during the middle-school-age years.

More recent interest in the theories of Erik Erikson and Jean Piaget has stimulated developmental research focusing on children who are between the ages of 6 and 12. Their theories emphasize intellectual growth, competence, and a growing investment in work. During this time, children are learning the fundamental skills of their culture. They spend a great deal of their day-to-day time learning the skills that are valued by their society, whether these skills be reading, writing, and arithmetic or hunting, fishing, and weaving. As children gain confidence in their skills, they begin to have more realistic images of their potential contributions to the larger community.

The competence that develops during the middle school years applies to social as well as work-related skills. This is a time when parent-child relationships, peer friendships, and participation in meaningful interpersonal communication can provide children with the social skills they will need if they are later to cope with the challenges of adolescence. Children's cognitive accomplishments appear to develop in conjunction with achievements in the social and emotional domains.

For many middle-school-age children, this is a joyful, vigorous time. The fears and vulnerabilities of their early school days are behind them. Energized by ego qualities of hope, will, and purpose, most middle-school-age children are able to enjoy many of the resources and opportunities of their communities. Even as the presence of their family members continues to be a comfort to them, they begin to explore more complex social relationships with peers and other significant adults (Galbo, 1983).

In those children who develop core pathologies, we notice withdrawal, a compulsion to perform repetitive behaviors, and inhibition of thought, expression, and activity. These children often come to the attention of school officials as they begin to demonstrate a paralysis of action and thought that prevents productive work in all aspects of life.

Developmental Tasks

Friendship

Can you remember some things about a friend you had when you were ten years old? Friendships of the middle school years are not likely to be as enduring as attachment relationships. Yet some of these friendships are quite memorable; they can have many of the elements of a close affectional bond. At this age, children describe close friends as people who like the same activities, share common interests, enjoy each other's company, and can count on each other for help (Youniss, 1980; Ainsworth, 1989).

Friendships may not be as essential to survival as attachment relations, but they clearly provide social and developmental advantages (Ainsworth, 1989; Hartup, 1989). Being a member of a group has protective advantages. Group cooperation gives a selective advantage to many social species, especially in tracking and hunting for food. Therefore, skills of cooperation and sociability can prove to advance the species as a whole as well as the individual. On an individual level, children who are able to participate in positive peer friendships are embedded in an intellectually and socially stimulating environment.

Family Influences on Social Competence

Not all children enter the middle school years with the same capacity to have friends and to enjoy the benefits of close peer relations. Early family experiences contribute to a child's sociability and social competence. The process of becoming ready for friendship may begin in infancy. Children who have secure attachments in infancy are more popular in preschool and engage more freely in social interactions. They are perceived as more helpful and better able to consider the needs of others (Sroufe & Fleeson, 1986; Park & Waters, 1989).

A mother's discipline techniques, the way she speaks to her child, and her parenting values are all linked to a child's social competence and popularity. Mothers who use power-assertive discipline techniques and who believe that aggression is an acceptable way of resolving conflicts have children who expect to get their way by asserting power in peer conflicts. Children whose mothers interact with them in positive, agreeable ways and who openly express their feelings are likely to have more positive friendship relations. These patterns are observable as early as preschool and continue to be found in the elementary grades.

The family environment influences a child's social competence in at least three ways. First, children may directly imitate their parents' positive and aggressive behaviors. If parents ask a lot of questions and invite their child's opinions, for example, the child may be more likely to show interest in the ideas and opinions of others. Second, a parent's discipline technique may influence what a child expects in a social interaction. Children who have been exposed to aggressive parent techniques believe that these same strategies will work with their peers. As a result, these children are more likely to experience social rejection. Third, parents who are highly restrictive and who try to control their children's behavior are less likely to permit their young children to have much exposure to peer social interaction. These children arrive at the middle school years with less experience in peer play (Putallaz, 1987; Pettit, Dodge & Brown, 1988; Hart, Ladd & Burleson, 1990).

Three Lessons of Friendship

Children learn at least three lessons from daily interactions with peers. The first lesson teaches an increasing appreciation of the many points of view that are represented in the peer group. As children play together, they discover that there may be several versions of the same song, differing sets of rules for the same game, and different customs for the same holiday. The second lesson teaches children to be increasingly sensitive to the social norms and pressures of the peer group. The third teaches experiences of closeness with a same-sex peer.

In the familiar game of jump rope, friends learn to solve problems, make and modify rules, and take one another's point of view. Friends challenge each other to new levels of accomplishment in a spirit of friendly rivalry.

As children interact with peers who see the world differently than they do, they begin to understand the limits of their own points of view. Piaget (1932/1948) suggests that peers have an important influence in diminishing one another's self-centered outlook precisely because they interact as equals. Children are not forced to accept one another's ideas in quite the same way as they feel forced to accept the ideas of adults. They argue, bargain, and eventually compromise in order to maintain friendships. The opportunity to function in social peer groups for work and for play leads children away from the egocentrism of early childhood and closer to the eventual flexibility of adult thought. A substantial body of evidence demonstrates that the behavior of well-adjusted, competent children is maintained in part by a number of social-cognitive abilities, including social perspective taking, interpersonal problem solving, and information processing (Renshaw & Asher, 1982; Dodge, Murphy & Buchsbaum, 1984; Asarnow & Callan, 1985; Dodge et al., 1986; Elias, Beier & Gara, 1989; Downey & Walker, 1989). These cognitive abilities appear to foster a child's entry into successful peer interactions. At the same time, active participation with peers tends to promote the development of these social-cognitive abilities.

Perspective-taking ability relates to other social skills that can contribute to the quality of a child's social relationships. Such skills include the ability to analyze social problems, the ability to empathize with the emotional state of another person, and a willingness to accept individual differences (Chalmers & Townsend, 1990). Children who are sensitive to the variety of perspectives that coexist in a social situation are also likely to be more positively evaluated by their peers (Pellegrini, 1985). Rejected and withdrawn children lack the social skills that would win them acceptance by their agemates (Patterson, 1982; French, 1988).

An interactive process is set in motion. Children who have opportunities to participate in peer friendships make progress in achieving new levels of interpersonal understanding. As interpersonal understanding grows, children acquire the skills and sensitivity with which to be more effective—and usually more valued—by their peers. Rejected children come to expect negative behaviors by others. A vicious cycle develops between the rejected child and peers, each having negative expectations of the other. As this cycle continues, the rejected child's reputation becomes increasingly negative and the child has little opportunity to develop positive relationship skills (Waas, 1988).

The peer group evolves norms for acceptance and rejection. As children become aware of these social norms, they begin to experience pressures to conform. Adults, particularly teachers, lose some of their power to influence children's behavior. In the classroom, the early-school-age child focuses primarily on the teacher as a source of approval and acceptance, whereas the middle-school-age child perceives the peer group as an equally significant audience. Children often play to the class instead of responding to the teacher. The roles of class joker, class snob, and class hero or heroine emerge during the middle school years and serve as ways of gaining approval from the peer group.

The need for peer approval becomes a powerful force toward conformity (Pepitone, Loeb & Murdock, 1977). Children learn to dress, talk, and joke in ways that are acceptable to peers. From grades 3 through 9 they become increasingly willing to conform to peer behaviors that might be considered antisocial. For example, it has been reported that ninth-graders are more willing than third-graders to go along with peer cheating, stealing, and trespassing (Berndt, 1979). Heterosexual antagonism, which is very common during this stage, is perpetuated largely by the pressure toward conformity. If all the fifth-grade boys hate girls, Johnny is not very likely to admit openly that he likes to play with Mary. There are indications that perceived pressures to conform are stronger in the fifth and sixth grades than at later times, even though the importance of specific peer groups has not yet peaked (Gavin & Furman, 1989).

With the increased emphasis on peer acceptance and conformity comes the risk of peer rejection and feelings of loneliness. In a study of over 500 children between the ages of 8 and 11, more than 10% expressed feelings of loneliness and social dissatisfaction (Asher, Hymel & Renshaw, 1984). A significant proportion of the children had trouble making friends (17%), felt left out (18%), and agreed that they felt alone (14%). Not surprisingly, children who were infrequently mentioned as a best friend by others were more lonely than those who were mentioned as a best friend by three or more other children. The effect of peer rejection is especially powerful in producing feelings of loneliness.

Some children who are rejected tend to be disruptive and aggressive with peers; others tend to be socially withdrawn but do not exhibit aggressive tendencies. Both groups tend to have multiple problems. Children in the former group exhibit anxiety, poor self-control, and social withdrawal in addition to aggressive behavior. They are more likely than nonaggressive children to attribute hostile intentions to others. Thus they tend to see peer interactions as threatening (Sancilio, Plumert & Hartup, 1989). Children in the latter group tend to be inhibited, anxious, and interpersonally reserved. They experience difficulty dealing with stress. These children also exhibit inappropriate affect and display various unusual behavioral mannerisms that are likely to draw

Box 8.1   When Friends Disagree

We have argued that peer interaction fosters cognitive growth because peers are free both to share and to disagree with others' points of view. But does this really happen? Are children more open to and honest with their friends than they are with children who are not their friends? Will children change their views when friends disagree with them?

A study of boys and girls aged 8 through 10 approached the question of how friends and nonfriends handle conflict (Nelson & Aboud, 1985). Pairs of children who were friends and pairs who were not friends were asked to resolve their differences about a social/ethical problem. Among the problems they had to discuss were "What should you do if you get home and find that you accidentally picked up something at a store and forgot to pay for it?" and "What is the thing to do if a boy (girl) much smaller than you starts a fight with you?" In describing the interactions among the pairs, three differences were observed:

1. Friends offered each other more explanations than did nonfriends.
2. Friends criticized each other more than did nonfriends.
3. Friends who disagreed more readily changed their opinions following discussions than did nonfriends. Further, such changes were likely to be in the direction of a higher level of social responsibility.

Although friends may not seek out conflict and criticism in their friendship, its presence appears to play a valuable role in promoting moral reasoning and social cognition.

ridicule from peers (French, 1988). Rejected children tend to retain this status throughout elementary school. They are likely to have future adjustment problems and often require psychiatric treatment in adolescence or adulthood (Coie & Krehbiel, 1984).

The opportunity for peer-group interaction usually leads to the formation of dyadic friendships that can become quite intimate (Berndt, 1981). These are the years in which children have "best friends." In the course of these friendships, children share private jokes, develop secret codes, tell family secrets, set out on "dangerous" adventures, and help each other in times of trouble. They also fight, threaten, break up, and reunite. Sullivan (1949) pointed out the significance of these early same-sex friendships as building blocks for adult relationships. It is significant that the child experiences love and closeness for a peer rather than for an adult. The relationship is more likely to allow for mutuality of power, status, and access to resources (French, 1984). Conflicts in a relationship can be worked out in terms that the children can control rather than being escalated into dimensions having adult significance. One child cannot take away another child's allowance or send the other child out of the room when a conflict arises. The children must resolve their differences within the framework of commitment to each other.

The structure of a school or classroom influences friendship formation. Close friends often see each other during the school day in classes and extracurricular activities (Hallinan, 1979; Epstein, 1983b). Close friendships appear to be influenced by attractiveness, intelligence, classroom social status, and satisfaction with and commitment to the best friend (Clark & Ayers, 1988).

The friendship structures of boys differ somewhat from those of girls; boys' friendship networks are somewhat larger and looser (Karweit & Hansell, 1983). The number

Boys are more likely than girls to make friends outside of school and to congregate at neighborhood functions.

of reciprocated female friendships increases with age (Epstein, 1983a). Middle-school-age girls spend more time each day talking on the phone to their best friends than boys, and their time spent talking to friends increases from sixth to eighth grade (Crockett, Losoff & Petersen, 1984). Girls have more in-school contact in service clubs and student government while boys have their greatest contact with close friends in athletics (Karweit, 1983). Boys come into more contact with their best friends at nonschool functions and make more out-of-school friends than girls. Boys are more concerned than girls with status in selecting friends, and they make more unreciprocated friendship choices as a result (Karweit & Hansell, 1983; Clark & Ayers, 1988).

Children's need for the friendship of peers brings them into an increasingly complex social system. They learn that approval is conditional upon conformity to certain norms, that other children do not necessarily share their point of view about the world, and that there are opportunities for unique emotional experiences that cannot be duplicated in the home. The friendship group is a transitional allegiance between commitment to the family and commitment to the larger social community.

Concrete Operations

We have described intelligence during infancy as consisting of sensory and motor patterns that children use to explore their environment and gain specific ends. During toddlerhood children develop a variety of representational skills. These skills free them from complete reliance on their immediate physical environment. They can create novel situations and solve problems by using thought, fantasy, and language. Piaget (Piaget & Inhelder, 1969) suggested that at about age 6 or 7 a qualitatively new form of thinking develops. He described this new stage of intellectual development as *concrete operational thought*.

Before beginning our account of concrete operational thought, let us discuss the Piagetian notion of mental operations. The word *operation* suggests an action that is performed on an object or set of objects. A mental operation is a transformation that is carried out in thought rather than in action. Piaget argued that such transformations are built on some physical relationship that the younger child can perform but cannot articulate. For example, a toddler can arrange a graduated set of circles on a stick such that the largest circle is at the bottom of the stick and the smallest circle is at the top. The child does not have a verbal label for the ordering operation but can perform the action. During concrete operations, children begin to appreciate a large group of actions that can be performed on objects and can perform them mentally without having to do so behaviorally. Thus a mental operation is an internal representation of an alteration in the relationship among objects.

During the stage of concrete operations, a number of conceptual skills are gradually achieved. The ones that have received the most attention are (1) conservation skills, (2) classification skills, and (3) combinatorial skills. Each one comprises a group of interrelated operations. These skills bring children in touch with the logic and order of the physical world. They allow children to experience the predictability of physical events. As children take a new approach to problem solving through the use of the logical principles associated with concrete operational thought, they generalize these principles to their thinking about friendships, team play and other games with rules, and their own self-evaluation. As the order of the physical world becomes more apparent, children begin to seek logic and order in social and personal domains. Sometimes this search for order is frustrated by the unpredictability of the social world. At other times children find that they can use their enhanced capacities for reasoning to solve interpersonal problems and to arrange their daily life so that it better meets their interests and needs.

Conservation

The basic meaning of the *conservation* scheme is that physical matter does not magically appear or disappear despite changes in form or container. The concept of conservation can be applied to a variety of dimensions, including mass, weight, number, length, and volume. The child who conserves is able to resist perceptual cues that alter the form of an object, insisting that the quantity remains the same despite the change in form. One of the most common problems of this type that Piaget investigated involves conservation of mass. The child is presented with two clay balls and asked to tell whether or not they are equal. Once the child is satisfied that the balls are equal, one of them is flattened out into a pancake. The child is then asked "Which has more—this one [the pancake] or this one [the ball]?" Sometimes the child is also asked whether the clay pieces are still the same. The child who does not conserve says the pancake has more clay because it is a lot wider than the ball. This child is still in the preoperational stage of thought. He or she is using personal perceptions to make judgments. The child who conserves knows that the two pieces of clay are still identical and can explain why.

Three concepts that allow the child to ascertain that equality along any physical dimension has not been altered are eventually employed (see Figure 8.1). First, the

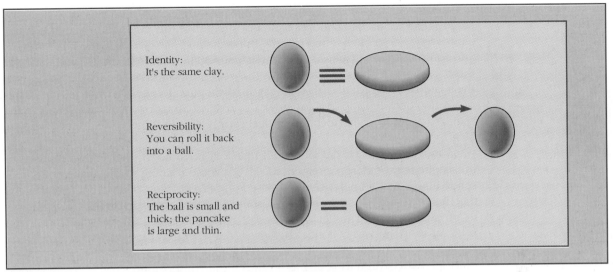

Figure 8.1   Three Concepts That Contribute to Conservation

child may explain that the pancake has the same amount of clay as the ball; no clay has been added or taken away. This is an example of the concept of *identity:* the pancake is still the *same* clay—nothing has been changed except its shape. Second, the child may point out that the experimenter can turn the pancake back into a ball. This is an example of the concept of *reversibility:* the child becomes aware that operations can be reversed, so that their effects are nullified. Third, the child may notice that although the pancake has a larger circumference, the ball is much thicker. When the child can simultaneously manipulate two dimensions such as circumference and thickness, we observe the concept of *reciprocity.* In the clay ball example, change in one dimension is compensated for by change in another; the total mass remains the same. With consolidation of the concepts of identity, reversibility, and reciprocity, the child is able to conserve along any physical dimension.

There appears to be a developmental sequence in the capacity to conserve. Children generally conserve mass and number earliest, weight later, and volume last. Piaget also noted that the development of conservation does not proceed evenly across all of the physical modes. Research has shown that children who are unable to conserve quantity with an unfamiliar object such as poker chips can do so with a more familiar substance such as M&M's (Lovell, 1961; Uzgiris, 1964; Goodnow, 1969; Gulko et al., 1988).

Questions have been raised about the meaning of conservation tasks, the timing for the emergence of conservation, and the possibility of teaching children to conserve. The way the task is presented and the kinds of questions that are asked can influence a child's responses. For example, the task can emphasize identity or equivalence.

In an identity task the child is asked to judge whether a clay ball (V) has the same amount of clay after it has been rolled into a sausage (V_1). In an equivalence task, there are two balls of clay. The child is asked to judge whether the ball that is rolled into a sausage has the same amount of clay as the standard, comparison ball. Some studies have found that children can perform the identity task earlier than the equivalence task; some have found just the opposite; and some have argued that identity and equivalence are achieved at the same time (Brainerd & Hooper, 1978; Miller, 1978; Silverstein et al., 1982). In a study of 5-to-7-year-olds, children were asked to say how the materials looked, and then to say how they really were. Giving the child this distinction between appearance and reality resulted in more correct answers than the standard procedure, in which this distinction is not made (Bijstra, Van Geert & Jackson, 1989).

Some studies have demonstrated that it is possible to train young children of preschool age to conserve (Brainerd, 1977). These training studies have both theoretical and practical implications. Theoretically, Piaget's view of development suggests that there is a period of maturational readiness for the application of logical operations to physical objects. Thus explanations of rules and relationships ought not to be relevant to a child who is not cognitively ready to understand them. The training studies suggest that it is possible to introduce such concepts as identity and reversibility so that children as young as 4 can achieve conservation. Further, conservation will be transferred from the tasks involved in training to other materials and dimensions (Field, 1981; May & Norton, 1981). The implication here is that entry into a new stage of thought may emerge earlier and be more readily influenced by the environment that Piaget's cognitive developmental theory had predicted.

Practically speaking, the implication is that preschool- and kindergarten-age children are capable of integrating and applying more abstract concepts than educators once believed they could. Early-childhood educators have found that through a systematic program of exploring, experimenting, and describing transformation of materials, young children can be guided to conceptualize the physical world in a systematic, abstract manner.

Piaget warned about a possible risk in this type of training: "Each time one prematurely teaches a child something he could have discovered for himself, that child is kept from inventing it and consequently from understanding it completely" (Piaget, 1983, p. 113). The long-term trade-offs between early strategic training in logical problem solving and a more open-ended process of exploration and insight are not really understood.

Classification Skills

One component of *classification* skills is the ability to group objects according to some dimension that they share. The other component is the ability to order subgroups hierarchically, so that each new grouping will include all previous subgroups. Vygotsky (1932/1962) suggested a method for studying classification in young children. Children are presented with a variety of wooden blocks that differ in shape, size, and color. Under each block is a nonsense syllable. The children are instructed to select one at a time all the blocks that have the same syllable. The youngest children, who would be characterized as preoperational in Piaget's stage theory, tend to select blocks by their color. Their technique for grouping is highly associative (Nelson, 1974). They choose each new block to match some characteristic of the previous selection, but they do not hold in mind a single concept that guides their choices.

Older children who have entered the stage of concrete operations tend to focus on one dimension at first, perhaps shape, and continue to select blocks until they discover that they have made an incorrect choice. They use this discovery to change their hypothesis about which characteristics of the blocks are associated with the nonsense syllable. This classification task demonstrates the concrete operational child's ability to hold a concept in mind and to make a series of decisions on the basis of that concept. It also demonstrates that during the stage of concrete operations, children can use mistakes to reorient a problem-solving strategy.

Piaget studied reasoning about class hierarchies or class inclusion by asking questions about whether a group of objects included more members of one subtype than of the group as a whole. Thus, when a set of pictures shows three ducks, six sparrows, and two robins, one might ask: "Are there more sparrows or more birds in these pictures?" This is an unusual kind of question, one that children are probably rarely asked. By the age of 8 or 9, however, many children can respond correctly because they recognize the distinction between classes and subclasses. In order to handle such problems, children have to inhibit their tendency to reinterpret the question in line with a more common comparison, such as "Are there more sparrows than ducks?"

In one study of class inclusion reasoning, an intriguing pattern was found. Children aged 3 and 4, who could not repeat the question and who clearly had not learned any rules about classes, were more likely to answer correctly than children of 5 and 6. Children aged 7 and 8 performed better than children of all the younger ages. The 5- and 6-year-olds, who answered quickly and confidently, were consistently incorrect. They seemed unable to inhibit the more obvious comparison in order to consider the actual question (McCabe et al., 1982).

Many children greatly enjoy classifying and ordering the environment. These children are preoccupied with a chain of relationships that define their family trees. They order their friends in terms of closeness: first-best friend, second-best friend, and so on. During this time, children may start collections of dolls, cars, model planes, or marbles. A great part of the pleasure in these collections is the appraising, ordering, and reordering of the parts.

Combinatorial Skills

A third characteristic of concrete operational thought is the development of *combinatorial skills*. Once they have acquired the scheme for conservation of number, children understand that certain physical transformations will not alter the number of units in a set. If ten poker chips are lined up in a row, there will still be ten chips whether they are spread out, squeezed tightly together, or stacked one on top of another. Conservation of number is achieved around age 6 or 7 (Halford & Boyle, 1985). Addition, subtraction, multiplication, and division are all learned during this stage. Children learn to apply the same operations no matter what specific objects or quantities are involved. Piaget claims that it is no coincidence that schools begin to instruct children in the basic skills of arithmetic at age 6. It is probably a strength of our schools that they meet an important aspect of intellectual readiness at the appropriate time.

The stage we have identified as early school age marks the beginnings of concrete operational thought. During this time, children's performances on tests of cognitive

Pablo Picasso, *The Gourmet,* 1901. During the stage of concrete operational thought, combinatorial skills are applied to real-world tasks, such as cooking.

maturity are likely to be inconsistent. For example, children will be able to conserve quantity but will make errors in conservation of weight, volume, or space. They may be able to perform a classification task correctly when they sort by one dimension, such as color, but may make errors when asked to sort objects that have more than one dimension in common. The conceptual awareness of the process of classifying objects or the logic of conservation is not fully integrated until sometime during middle school age and may not reach peak performance until later adolescence or adulthood (Flavell, 1982).

As concrete operational intelligence develops, the child gains insight into the regularities of the physical world and the principles that govern relationships among objects. Table 8.1 summarizes the components of concrete operational thought. Perceptions of reality become less convincing than logical understanding of how the world is organized. For example, even though it looks as if the sun sinks into the water, we know that what we see is a result of the earth's rotation on its axis. However,

Table 8.1 Components of Concrete Operational Thought°		
Component	**New Abilities**	
Conservation	Ability to perceive identity	
	Ability to perceive reversibility	
	Ability to manipulate two dimensions simultaneously in reciprocity	
Classification	Ability to group objects according to some common dimension	
	Ability to order subgroups in a hierarchy	
Combinatorial skills	Ability to manipulate numbers in addition, subtraction, multiplication, and division	

experiences in the grocery store with large, partially filled cereal boxes and attractively shaped bottles of shampoo attest to the occasional failure of the cognitive system to dominate perceptual experience.

Metacognition

As Piaget began his method of inquiry about concrete operational thought, he pointed the way to the study of metacognition. Rather than being concerned with the exact answers children gave to the questions he asked, he was concerned with how they explained their answers. How do children know what they know? What reasons can they give to justify or support their answers? *Metacognition* refers to a whole range of processes and strategies we use to assess and monitor our knowledge. It includes the "feeling of knowing" that accompanies problem solving, the ability to distinguish those answers about which we are confident from those answers about which we have doubts (Butterfield, Nelson & Peck, 1988). Metacognition includes the ability to review various strategies for approaching a problem in order to choose the one that is most likely to result in a solution (Carr et al., 1989). It includes the ability to monitor one's comprehension of the material one has just read and to select strategies for increasing comprehension (Cross & Paris, 1988).

Metacognition develops in parallel with other cognitive capacities. As children develop in their ability to attend to more variables in their approach to problems, they simultaneously increase their capacity to take an "executive" posture in relation to cognitive tasks. They can detect uncertainty and introduce strategies to reduce it. They can learn study techniques that will enhance their ability to organize and recall information. These capacities continue to develop as the child becomes a more sophisticated learner. They are also quite amenable to training, both at home and at school. Metacognition appears to be a natural component of cognitive development, but a concerned person can nurture and stimulate it by helping children respond to feelings of doubt with effective strategies for increasing feelings of knowing.

Games like checkers and chess require metacognitive abilities. Children must evaluate alternative problem-solving strategies against a variety of possible actions by the opponent.

Skill Learning

Perhaps the area in which growth is most impressive during middle school age is the acquisition of skills. As children emerge into the stage of concrete operations, they are able to direct their attention through the use of conceptual principles as well as through perceived events. The areas of science, history, and mathematics are accessible to children who can master the principles of classification and causality.

Middle-school-age children have a growing appreciation of time as a nonsubjective unit. As a result of the maturation of concrete operational thought, they are able to manipulate techniques for measurement. They are capable of entertaining an explanatory hypothesis and evaluating the evidence that supports or disproves it. All of these cognitive skills allow children to move rapidly beyond the limits of their own experience into consideration of events that happened long ago, might happen in the future, or are hypothesized to be happening all the time.

Children vary in their rate of intellectual development. One comparison of fifth- and seventh-graders found that the bright fifth-graders were able to solve more complex problems by formal operational skills than the average seventh-graders (Keating, 1975). In a longitudinal study of cognitive growth, Klausmeier (1977) reported an enormous variability in the attainment of all concepts. For example, 17% of the fourth-graders understood the notion of supraordinate-subordinate relations, a concept that 30% of the 12th-graders did not understand. By the age 11 or 12, some children were making use of strategies that included hypothesizing, inferring, organizing, and generalizing, while some slowly developing children did not attain this range of skills until age 17 or 18.

In some ways reading is the most significant intellectual skill that develops during middle school age because it opens the door to all the others. Reading provides access to new information, new uses of language, and new forms of thinking. Children are limited in their ability to learn mathematics, social studies, and science if they cannot read. Once a child can read fluently, the possibility for all manner of independent inquiry expands significantly.

Children probably begin to read in a variety of ways. David and his mother, whom we met in Chapter 6, used a game with street signs along the road to build the bridge from language to literacy. David began to "read" by memorizing words and phrases that were linked to certain shapes and patterns in the signs. Other children begin to read by learning letters and the sounds that are linked to them, and experimenting with sounding out the letters when they are strung together. At first most children are bewildered and confused by these experiences. This is a time when they require a good deal of support and encouragement for their efforts. Gradually, through a process of trial, feedback, and repetition, children learn to read simple words and simple sentences.

Early in the process of learning to read, children can understand and communicate orally a great deal more than they can read by themselves. They must learn how to use these oral communication skills in the comprehension of written language (Carroll, 1986). At some point the child begins to articulate the concept "I can read" or "I am a reader." Once a child acquires this idea as part of his or her self-concept, efforts to read increase and are energized by a confidence in one's potential for success.

Skilled readers use a variety of strategies to enhance their comprehension. Children of middle school age can expand their understanding of what they read by working together on projects and sharing their interpretations.

Reading is a complex skill and involves the acquisition of many new techniques over the middle-school-age years. Box 8.2 helps us to understand the complexity of skilled reading. Children do not have to score extremely high in intelligence tests to make substantial progress in learning to read (Share, McGee & Silva, 1989). Most children, unfortunately, spend little or no time reading books outside of school; over time those who do some book reading show the greatest gains in reading achievement between second and fifth grades (Anderson, Wilson & Fielding, 1988).

Parents' influence on children's reading achievement is consistently documented. Parents appear to affect their children's reading in at least five ways: in the value they place on literacy, in the emphasis they place on academic achievement, in the reading materials they make available in the home, in the time they spend reading with their children, and in the opportunities they provide for verbal interaction in the home (Hess & Holloway, 1984). Parents who value the ability to read, who urge their children to do well in school, who provide resources for reading, who read with them, and who talk with them produce children who are more skilled readers than parents who don't.

Parents may also have an indirect effect on how well a child learns to read by influencing the child's placement in a school reading group (Goldenberg, 1989). They may do so by helping a child understand his or her school's reading curriculum (schools differ in their approaches to teaching reading), and by encouraging good work habits, and appropriate classroom behavior. Parents who do these things may influence a teacher's perception of their child and, as a result, the child's assignment to a reading-level group. Ability grouping for reading instruction is practically universal in elementary schools (Slavin, 1987). Teachers depend on their perceptions of a child's ability, work habits, and behavior when they assign students to reading groups (Haller & Waterman, 1985). The higher the level of the children's reading group, the better they learn how to read.

Box 8.2   Characteristics of Skilled Reading

Four basic assumptions about the characteristics of skilled reading have been described (Spiro, Bruce & Brewer, 1980) and appear to have received research support (Hall, 1989):

1. Skilled reading depends on perceptual, cognitive, and linguistic processes.

2. Skilled readers obtain information from many levels simultaneously by synthesizing information derived from graphophonemes (the shapes of letters associated with sounds), morphemes (basic units that make up words), semantics (meanings), syntax (rules of grammar that dictate word order), pragmatics (cues provided by the context and past experience), schematics (construction and use of conceptual schema to account for the way information is arranged; prior knowledge about story structure), and interpretation. Thus reading may be viewed as a process of simultaneous interactions that do not proceed in strict sequence from basic perceptual units to general interpretation of text.

3. The capacity of the human information-processing system limits the amount that a person can perceive in a single fixation on a text, the speed of eye movement, the number of chunks of information that can be held in short-term memory, and the speed with which information can be retrieved from long-term memory. It appears that in the skilled reader, lower-level processes such as decoding function automatically, allowing the reader to attend to higher-order comprehension processes.

4. Reading involves the use of strategies. The skilled reader reads with a purpose and continuously monitors comprehension. Skilled readers perceive breakdowns in understanding, are selective in focusing attention on various aspects of what they are reading, and refine their interpretation of the text as they read.

Much research still remains to be done before we can explain how these processes work and identify other processes that are essential for skilled reading. Still, the characteristics that have been identified give us a sense of just how complex the reading process is. The array of skills middle-school-age children acquire as they learn to be skillful readers is marvelous indeed.

The rudiments of a wide range of other skills may also be acquired during the middle school age:

mathematics	dance
science	theater
writing	art
computer operation	cooking
sports	sewing
mechanics	crafts
music	

Using the information provided in Box 8.2 concerning characteristics of skilled reading, we can construct a somewhat more general model that helps us understand what is being accomplished in the building of complex behavioral skills.

First, the development of skill depends on a combination of sensory, motor, perceptual, cognitive, linguistic, emotional, and social processes.

Second, skills are attained through an integration of many levels of the component elements of skill behavior simultaneously. Skills are not acquired in strict sequence, from simple to complex. Simple and more complex components of skilled behavior are worked on at the same time.

Third, limits of the human system place constraints on an individual's capacity to perform skilled behavior. With practice, lower-level processes begin to function automatically, so that the person can attend to higher-order processes. A skilled writer, for example, may write or type words automatically while attending to questions about plot or character development.

Fourth, skilled behavior requires the use of strategies. Skillful people operate with purpose and continuously monitor their performance. They perceive breakdowns in performance, are selective in focusing attention on various aspects of what they are working on, and refine higher-order processes as they perform the skill.

The emphasis on skill building and the energy that middle-school-age children bring to the acquisition of new skills suggest a strong parallel to toddlerhood. At both stages, children's motives for competence and mastery are directed outward to the environment. At both stages, children appear to be delighted by the potential for learning that almost every new encounter offers. However, as a result of their cognitive capacities and their awareness of social expectations, skill learning at middle school age is embedded in a much more complex framework of continuous monitoring and self-assessment.

Self-Evaluation

The emphasis on skill building during the middle school-age years is accompanied by a new focus on self-evaluation. Children strive to match their achievements to internalized goals and external standards. Simultaneously they receive feedback from others about the quality of their performance. During the early-school-age years children begin to receive messages about how well they are managing to accomplish tasks set before them. They may be designated as "Red Group" readers, or they may see a long line of stars after their names on the bulletin board. They may be asked to sit in the left-hand row in order to receive "special" help or be told to go down the hall for tutoring. All these and many other signs serve as sources of social evaluation that children incorporate into their own self-evaluations. By the age of 11, children are able to differentiate specific areas of competence that contribute to overall self-evaluation. In particular, they perceive the domains of cognitive, physical, and social competence separately and weigh their contributions to self-satisfaction in different ways (Stigler, Smith & Mao, 1985; Harter, 1982).

During middle school age, the process of self-evaluation is further complicated because the peer group joins the adult world as a source of both criticism and approval. Pressures toward conformity, competition, and the need for approval feed into the evaluation process. The child's athletic skills, intellectual abilities, and artistic talents are no longer matters to which only teachers and parents respond. Peers also identify others' skills and begin to generate profiles of one another: "Oh, Bob is good in math, but he runs like a girl"; "Jane is kind of fat, but she writes great stories"; "I like Lisa best because she's good at everything." Depending on the resolution of the crises of toddlerhood and early school age, children approach the process of self-evaluation from a framework of either self-confidence or self-doubt. They may expect to find tasks easy to accomplish and approach them vigorously, or they may anticipate failure and approach tasks with hesitation.

Pablo Picasso, *Maya*, 1943. It is extremely difficult for children to develop independent criteria for judging their worth. This moment of solemn reflection suggests the kind of self-evaluation middle-school-age children can sustain.

Self-Efficacy

Albert Bandura (1982) has theorized that judgments of self-efficacy are crucial to understanding a person's behavior. *Self-efficacy* is defined as the person's sense of confidence that he or she can perform the behaviors demanded in a specific situation. Expectations of efficacy vary with the situation. In other words, a child may view efficacy in one way in a situation requiring mathematical ability and in another way in one requiring physical strength.

Bandura has suggested that four sources of information contribute to judgments of self-efficacy (see Figure 8.2). The first source is *enactive attainments,* or prior experiences of mastery in the kinds of tasks that are being confronted. A child's general assessment of ability in any area (mathematics, writing, gymnastics) is based on accomplishments in that area (Skaalvik & Hagtvet, 1990). Successful experiences increase perceived self-efficacy, whereas repeated failures diminish it. Failure experiences are especially detrimental when they occur early in the process of trying to master a task. Many boys and girls are diverted from mastering such sports as tennis and baseball because they have made mistakes early in their participation. They develop doubts about their abilities that prevent them from persisting at the task.

The second source is *vicarious experience.* Seeing a person similar to oneself perform a task successfully can raise one's sense of self-efficacy; seeing a person similar to oneself fail at a task can lower it (Brown & Inouye, 1978).

Verbal persuasion is the third source. Children can be encouraged to believe in themselves and to try a new task. Persuasion is likely to be most effective with children

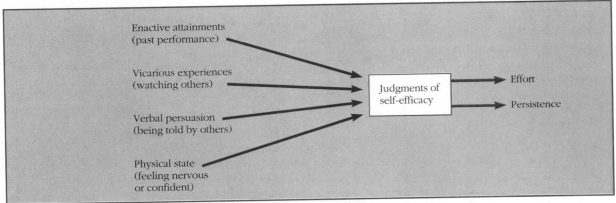

Figure 8.2   Four Components of Self-Efficacy

who already have confidence in their abilities. The persuasion helps to boost their performance level.

The fourth source is *physiological*. People monitor their body states in making judgments about whether or not they can do well. When children feel too anxious or frightened, they are likely to anticipate failure. Children who are excited and interested but not overly tense are more likely to perceive themselves as capable of succeeding.

Self-efficacy judgments are related to children's perceptions of the likelihood of success. They also determine the factors to which children attribute their success or failure (McAuley, Duncan & McElroy, 1989). In the face of difficulty or failure, children who have confidence in their abilities will work harder to master challenges. They will attribute their difficulties to failure to try hard enough, and they will redouble their efforts. Children who have a low sense of self-efficacy tend to give up in the face of difficulty because they attribute their failure to a basic lack of ability (Bandura & Schunck, 1981). The level of self-efficacy also affects how children prepare to handle new challenges. The thoughts, emotions, and preparation for action of those who are preoccupied by self-doubts differ from those who believe in themselves.

Social Expectations
In our society it is extremely difficult for children to develop independent internal criteria by which to judge their abilities. If the skills of the culture were more manual, perhaps it would be easier for children to make such judgments. In learning to plow a field, for example, one can look back over the land and see whether the furrows are deep enough and the rows straight. Many important areas of accomplishment, however, have no clear, objective standards against which a child can readily compare past performance. In learning to write an English composition, how can one judge whether one has done an adequate job? How, indeed, can a child evaluate improvement?

In attempting to assess their own abilities, children tend to rely on many external sources of evaluation, including grades, teachers' comments, parental approval, and peer approval (Crooks, 1988). If feedback from important adults suggests to children that they are cooperative, intelligent, and creative, these attributes are likely to be

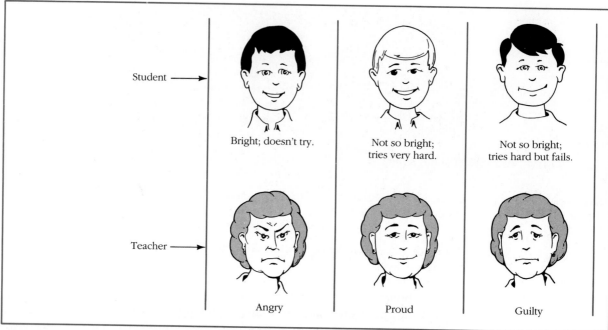

Student →

Bright; doesn't try.

Not so bright;
tries very hard.

Not so bright;
tries hard but fails.

Teacher →

Angry

Proud

Guilty

Figure 8.3   Students' Ability and Effort—Teacher's Reaction

incorporated into their self-evaluations (Jensen & Moore, 1977). Children who see themselves as cooperative and intelligent are likely to approach social and intellectual tasks with optimistic expectations about their performance. Conversely, feedback suggesting lack of competitiveness, intelligence, and creativity can produce a pessimistic or antagonistic approach to the challenges of skill development.

The feedback that students receive from their teachers is not wholly objective. It is influenced by the teachers' expectations about their abilities. In one study it was found that when teachers misperceived bright children as "average," the children's IQs dropped significantly after five months in those classes (Sutherland & Goldschmid, 1974). In an observational study of math classrooms for grades 5 through 9, teachers' expectations, student-teacher interaction, and students' abilities were examined. When teachers had high expectations for the math abilities of female students, those students received less praise than did other groups. When teachers had low expectations for the math abilities of male students, those students received more criticism than did other groups (Parsons, Kaczala & Meece, 1982).

Teachers' expectations for student performance are influenced by their assessments of both the student's ability and the student's effort. In a study of elementary school teachers, a relationship was found between the teachers' explanations for students' success and failure and the emotions they felt under the various conditions (see Figure 8.3). It was presumed that these emotional reactions were among the major cues that teachers sent to students about their performances. When teachers believed that students' poor performances were due to a lack of effort, they were likely to feel angry toward them, particularly if they believed the students were capable

Children who have high expectations of their performance in school are more likely to take risks and volunteer to answer questions than children who think of themselves as below average academically.

of very good work. When children of low ability suddenly began putting forth a great deal of effort, teachers were likely to experience pride in their own accomplishments with them. If low-ability students who were trying very hard failed, teachers felt a sense of guilt. Teachers were more willing to accept personal responsibility for certain configurations of student success and failure than for others. The students who made teachers the angriest were the bright ones who did not try hard. The research on teacher expectations illustrates how social expectations operate to influence both perceptions of other people and the quality of interpersonal communication (Prawat, Byers & Anderson, 1983).

Social expectations also contribute to children's expectations about their own abilities and behavior (Harris & Rosenthal, 1985). Evaluative feedback that is associated with intellectual ability or skill tends to feed into children's conceptualization of their own competence. Repeated failure information or remarks that imply lack of ability tend to make children less confident of success on subsequent tasks. The pattern of expectations appears to crystallize during the second and third grades. Preschoolers do not make systematic use of success or failure feedback in predicting their next success (Parsons & Ruble, 1977). Even in the first grade, children's expectations about the grades they will receive on their first report cards are not clearly related to their IQs or to parents' or teachers' expectations, nor are they closely related to their later estimates of their grades. By the end of the first grade, however, children begin to be more accurate predictors of their performance (Entwisle et al., 1987; Alexander & Entwisle, 1988). By fifth grade, children are very aware of their teachers' expectations for their performance, and they are likely to mirror those expectations in their own academic achievement (Weinstein et al., 1987). The impact of social expectations is seen in a study of parents' and children's attitudes about math aptitude (Parsons, Adler & Kaczala, 1982). Children in grades 5 through 11 and their parents were asked about their attitudes toward the children's mathematics achievement. Parents had lower expectations for their daughters' math achievement than for their sons'. They believed that mathematics is more difficult for daughters than for sons and requires more effort. Their expectations about their children's aptitude were better predictors of the children's self-assessments than were the children's own past performances in mathematics.

Other studies have examined the impact of parents' expectations on the judgments that academically capable children make about their abilities. In a phenomenon described as the "illusion of incompetence," some children who perform well on tests of academic achievement (at the 90th percentile or above) perceive themselves as below average in academic ability. These children expect lower levels of success, are less confident, attempt less challenging tasks, and say that their schoolwork is more demanding than peers of similar high ability who have more positive self-evaluations. It appears that parents play a central role in establishing these children's low assessments of themselves. Children who have an illusion of incompetence think that their parents have a low opinion of their abilities and expect little of them. They see their fathers, in particular, as holding to very rigorous standards that they are not expected to meet (Phillips, 1987, 1984). In a comparison of children aged 3½ to 11, expectations of school failure tended to gain momentum in the second and third grades and became a basis for children's predictions about their own potential during the later elementary years (Parsons & Ruble, 1977). In the 6½- to 8-year-old age group, girls showed greater drops in expectations after failure than did boys. Of all the children in this study, the eldest girls had the lowest initial expectations for success. Other research confirms that girls are more likely than boys to receive feedback that is irrelevant to or inconsistent with the quality of their work. In addition, girls become sensitive to social expectations that their public statements ought to reflect modesty. Thus, when asked, girls are likely to express concern about their lack of ability rather than self-confidence (Frey & Ruble, 1987).

The discussion of social expectations highlights children's sensitivity to their social environment. They become aware of existing roles, norms, and sanctions for norm violation. Direct experiences with success and failure are important, but they are embedded in a context of social expectations. Messages of reassurance and encouragement from parents and teachers can play a key role in establishing a positive sense of competence and in motivating children to persist in the face of difficult challenges.

Team Play

During middle school age, a new dimension is added to the quality of a child's play. Children begin to evolve a sense of team success as well as personal success. Three significant characteristics of the experience of team membership are relevant to development during this stage: (1) the subordination of personal goals to group goals; (2) the principle of the division of labor; and (3) competition.

Team sports are generally more complicated than the kinds of games described as group play in Chapter 7. The rules are so complex that they may require a referee or an umpire if they are to be followed accurately. In these sports, children join together into teams that remain together for the duration of the game. Some children join teams that play together for an entire season, such as Little League. Team mem-

Children of middle school age enter the drama of competitive sports. The jerseys, the practices, the coaching, the games, the fans (mostly parents), the trophies, and the team photos are all part of a new degree of ritualization imposed on the world of play.

bership carries with it the awareness that one's acts may affect the success or failure of the entire group. There is a definite emphasis on winning and losing. Children may be ostracized or ridiculed if they contribute to a team loss. Although team sports do provide opportunities for individual recognition, it is quite clear that team success casts a halo over even the poorest players and team failure a shadow over even the best. In this sense, participation in team sports is an early lesson about interdependence. All of the team members rely on one another, and ideally it is to everyone's advantage to assist the weaker members in improving the quality of their play. What usually happens, however, is that the poorest players are scorned and scapegoated, particularly if the team loses.

The notion of the division of labor as an effective strategy for attaining a goal is experienced through participation with peers on teams. Children learn that each position on a team has a unique function and that the team has the best chance of winning if each player performs a specific function rather than trying to do the work of all the other players. The concept of the team encompasses the variety of activities in which each of the team members actually engages. A complementary concept is cooperation. Team members learn that if the team as a whole is to do its best, the members must help one another. Rather than playing all the roles, a team member tries to help each other member play his or her role as well as possible. Cooperation can take many forms; members share resources, take time to help other team members improve their skills, plan strategies together, bring out the equipment or clean up after the game. In many sports, there is a dynamic tension between competition and cooperation. Team members may compete with each other for a more desirable position or to be considered the top player. At the same time, the team members know that they have to support each other, especially when they play against another team.

The team may well become an experiential model for approaching other complex organizations (Shears & Bower, 1974). Once children learn that certain goals can best be attained when tasks are divided among a group of people, they begin to conceptualize the principles behind the organization of social communities. A subsequent task is the recognition that some children are better suited to handle one aspect of the task and others do better at another aspect. Some children enjoy the skill development associated with team play, others enjoy learning the rules and devising strategies, others especially value the chance for peer companionship, and still others have a strong inner motive to compete and to try to win (Klint & Weiss, 1987). The distribution of roles to fit the children's individual skills and preferences is a subtle element of the learning that is acquired through team play.

Finally, team play teaches children about the nature of competition and the importance of winning (Sutton-Smith, 1971). Children are already sensitive to the pain of failure. The public embarrassment and private shame that accompany failure are powerful emotions even for the early-school-age child. Some children will go to remarkable extremes in order to avoid failing. In team sports, each game ends with a winning and a losing side. One cannot avoid the interpretation that losing is failing. Children who have a low sense of self-esteem are more likely to experience intense anxiety about losing in a competitive situation (Brustad, 1988). One can claim that losing is an important kind of learning for children, but, as Vince Lombardi has been known to say, "Show me a good loser, and I'll show you a loser." Involvement in team sports is guaranteed to bring with it the bitterness of losing and the commitment to avoid losing.

In team sports both sides cannot win; success for one side must result in failure for the other. If the team experience is a laboratory for learning lessons about the larger social community, this characteristic of team games certainly generates a perpetuation of in-group/out-group antagonism. Children learn to see social situations in competitive terms. They think of politics as winning or losing. They think of wars as bringing victory or defeat. They think of personal conflicts as resulting in success or failure. Team sports teach children to want to beat their opponents.

Team play has implications for both intellectual and social learning. Children who play team sports learn to conceptualize the game and their role in it in more relational terms. They see themselves as contributors to a larger effort and learn to anticipate the consequences of their behavior for the group. The games that involve teams are generally so complex that children are called upon to learn many rules, make judgments about those rules, plan strategies, and assess the strengths and weaknesses of the other players. All of these components of team play can be seen as potentially stimulating to children's cognitive growth and to their general sense of worth (Smith, 1986).

The social consequences of team play can be divided into in-group and out-group attitudes. With regard to the in-group, the child learns to value team goals and to contribute to them. Identification with team goals may even require a child to relinquish a personal goal, such as being first at bat, for the good of the team. The child

Table 8.2 Development of Attitudes as a Result of Team Play Experiences

In-Group Attitudes	*Out-Group Attitudes*
The child learns: 1. To value and contribute to team goals. 2. To relinquish personal goals for team goals. 3. To receive and use feedback and help from team members. 4. To value one's role as an element in a larger system and to perceive interdependence. 5. That team victories give personal satisfaction and team defeats bring frustration and depression.	The child learns: 1. That the outcome of competition is win or lose. 2. That the other team is the "enemy." 3. That one must try one's hardest to defeat the other team. 4. That there is and should be antagonism between teams. 5. That assisting the other team is unethical.

receives feedback from team members about skills and may even be helped to improve by team members. Children learn to value their roles as elements in the larger system and to see the interdependence between themselves and the other players. They learn that team victories can give them great personal satisfaction and team defeats can be a source of frustration and depression.

The child learns to see the outcome of competition as a win-or-lose situation. The other team is the "enemy," and there is no alternative to trying one's hardest to defeat it. Antagonism toward the out-group is valued in team sports, and any attempt to assist the other team is seen as highly unethical.

All human societies observe distinctions between in-group and out-group attitudes and behaviors. Feelings of cohesiveness and similarity to one group prompt behaviors supportive of that group's survival. We learn that moral principles that apply to members of the in-group do not necessarily apply to members of the out-group. In the extreme, many adults can even justify killing a member of an out-group if our government declares war on that group.

The expression of in-group and out-group boundaries was observed in a study of sharing among middle-school-age children (Dickstein, 1979). Children shared more with a friend than with a disliked peer. With friends, children always preferred a norm of equal treatment. With nonfriends, children always preferred a norm of rivalry. Even those children who were quite skillful at perspective taking were not likely to apply these abilities to disliked peers. Table 8.2 shows the in-group and out-group attitudes that result from experiences in team play.

Summary

The developmental tasks of middle school age reflect the child's expansion with respect to friendship relations, skill development, logical reasoning, commitment to the social community, and a growing sense of independence. Children become sensitive to others' evaluations of their performances. Such evaluations can teach them how to assess their own behavior and how to establish personal goals. Middle-school-age children are able to make significant contributions to the social groups to which they belong. They are also committed to seeking approval and acceptance from those groups.

Children take their sense of industry very seriously. They want to show that they can succeed at tasks that are valued by adults.

The Psychosocial Crisis:
Industry versus Inferiority

According to psychosocial theory (Erikson, 1963), the person's fundamental attitude toward work is established during the middle-school-age period. As children develop skills and acquire personal standards for evaluation, they make an initial assessment of whether or not they will be able to make a contribution to the social community. They also make an inner commitment to strive for success. Some children are keenly motivated to compete against a standard of excellence and to achieve success. Others have low expectations about the possibility of success and are not motivated by achievement situations. The strength of a child's need to achieve success is well established by the end of this stage (Atkinson & Birch, 1978).

The concept of *industry* refers to an eagerness to acquire skills and perform meaningful work. During middle school age, many aspects of work are intrinsically motivating. The skills are new. They bring the child closer to the capacities of adults. Each new skill allows the child some degree of independence and may even bring new responsibilities that heighten his or her sense of worth. In addition to the self-motivating factors associated with increased competence, external sources of reward promote skill development. Parents and teachers encourage children to "get better" at what they do through grades, material rewards, additional privileges, and praise. Peers are also sources of encouragement for the acquisition of some skills, though they may have some negative input with regard to others. Certain youth organizations, such as the Girl Scouts and Boy Scouts, make the acquisition of skills a very specific route to success and higher status.

Given the internal thrust toward skill building that is generated by motives for competence and external rewards for mastery, it might appear that there should be no real conflict at this stage. One might think that everyone would be united in a commitment to the joy and fulfillment that accrue from experiences of competence.

What experiences of middle school age, then, might generate a sense of inferiority? Feelings of worthlessness and inadequacy come from two sources: the self and the social environment. Alfred Adler (1935) has directed our attention to the central role that organ inferiority can play in shaping person ability. *Organ inferiority* is any physical or mental limitation that prevents the acquisition of certain skills. Children who are not capable of mastering certain skills will experience feelings of inferiority. Individual differences in aptitude, physical development, and prior experience will inevitably result in experiences of inadequacy in some domain. No one can do everything well. Children must discover at this time that they will not be able to master every skill they attempt. Even the child who feels quite positive toward work and finds new challenges invigorating will experience some degree of inferiority with regard to a specific skill that cannot be mastered.

If we assumed that success in one area could compensate for failure in another, we would be safe in minimizing the effect of individual areas of inadequacy on the overall resolution of they psychosocial conflict. However, the social environment does not reinforce success in all areas equally. During the middle-school-age years, success in reading is much more highly rewarded than success in tinkering with broken automobile engines. Success in team sports is more highly valued than success in operating a ham radio. It is extremely difficult for a child who does not excel in the culturally valued skills to compensate through mastery of others.

The social environment also generates feelings of inferiority through the process of social comparison. Particularly in the school setting but even in the home, children are confronted by statements suggesting that they are not as "good" as some peer, sibling, or cultural subgroup. Children are grouped, graded, and publicly criticized on the basis of how their efforts compare with someone else's. The intrinsic pleasure of engaging in a task for the challenge it presents conflicts with messages that stimulate feelings of self-consciousness, competitiveness, and doubt: "I like playing ball, but I'm not as good as Ted, so I don't think I'll play." During middle school age, children may refuse to try a new activity because they fear the possibility of being bettered by their peers (Crooks, 1988).

Finally, the social environment stimulates feelings of inferiority through the negative value it places on any kind of failure. Two types of failure messages that may contribute to feelings of inferiority have been described. One type consists of criticisms of the child's motivation. Such criticisms imply that if one had really tried, one could have avoided failure. The other type refers more specifically to a lack of ability. Here the implication is that the child just does not have the competence necessary to succeed. This type of failure message is most closely associated with a pattern of attitudes about the self that has been described as "learned helplessness." In response to even a few remarks about their lack of ability, children generate a self-definition that leads them to take a pessimistic view of future success (Phillips, 1984; Holloway, 1988).

Middle-school-age children are often shamed for failure just as toddlers are shamed when they wet their pants. Earlier themes of doubt and guilt are intimately associated with feelings of inferiority. Messages about failure usually suggest that there is an external standard of perfection, an ideal, that the child did not meet. A few failure experiences can generate such strong negative feelings that the child will avoid engaging in new tasks in order to preclude failure.

Failure in school and the public ridicule that it brings have been shown to play a central role in the establishment of a negative self-image. This is especially the case when the initial self-concept is negative (Calhoun & Morse, 1977). The school represents the voice of the larger society. Children who continually fail to meet the standards set by school adults have no alternative to incorporating a view of themselves as failures. Even efforts to compensate through peer influence or social deviance cannot alleviate the feelings of inferiority that result from school failure. Much as it may appear that children do not care about school or scorn school goals, the school remains a symbol of cultural authority. Failure in school can easily lead a child to feel locked out of the larger social community.

In extreme cases, we see the reluctance, the self-doubt, and the withdrawal of children who feel very inferior. Such resolutions of the crisis in the direction of inferiority suggest that these children cannot conceive of themselves as having the potential to contribute to the welfare of the larger community. This is a very serious consequence. It makes the gradual incorporation of the individual into a meaningful social group very difficult. The irony of the crisis at this stage is that the social environment, which theoretically depends on the individual's motives toward mastery for its survival, is itself such a powerful force in negating those motives by communicating messages of inferiority.

The Central Process: Education

Every culture must devise ways of passing on the wisdom and skills of past generations to its young. This is the meaning of education in its broadest sense. Education can be differentiated from schooling. The practice of separating formal educational experiences from the direct, intimate, hands-on activities of home and community is only about 100 years old. Before the Industrial Revolution, most children became educated by participating with their parents in the tasks of home life, farming, commerce with neighbors, and participation in religious life (Coleman, 1987).

Today, however, schools bear the primary responsibility for education. Teaching, which began as an extension of the parent role, has become a distinct profession. In our culture, education is not the kind of continuous interplay between the skilled and the unskilled that it may be in more traditional cultures. Formal learning takes place in a special building during certain hours of the day. To be sure, the success of that experience in building a child's skills and a sense of the self as a learner depends heavily on the ongoing involvement and commitment of family members (Coleman, 1987; Stevenson & Baker, 1987). For contemporary children, however, school experiences play a critical role in the formation of a personal sense of industry.

During the elementary school years, the goal of education is to help children develop the basic tools of learning. Central to this process is the introduction of students to the language of concepts, theories, and relationships that will allow them

Schooling, in which groups of children are exposed to formal instruction, has become an almost universal experience.

to organize experience (Cole & D'Andrade, 1982). The schools aim to develop verbal/analytic problem solving. Instruction focuses on rules, descriptions, and abstract concepts (Tharp, 1989). Children are exposed to a range of disciplines and to methods of inquiry for dealing with complex problems. Throughout the educational process, children are presented with problems of increasing difficulty. They are given many opportunities to practice their newly developing skills. The practice offers children continuous feedback about their level of competence. During the process of skill acquisition, most children experience a preponderance of success experiences. They learn that diligence and industry provide a meaningful route to the acquisition of valued abilities. Over time, children who are developing a sense of industry can see that they have acquired new skills. They recognize that they can master ever more demanding challenges.

Participation in a school environment results in exposure to adults who provide models for commitment to learning (Rutter, 1983). These adults generally have skills of their own that give children some sense of how much more there is to learn. Participation in school, therefore, provides opportunities not only for mastery but for developing goals and standards for development of more advanced skills.

Middle-school-age children are at a stage of cognitive development that permits them to grasp the fundamental principles of the problems that the school poses for them. The art of teaching lies in presenting problems at a level of complexity that will be meaningful to children but just a step beyond their present ability level. In this way, learning becomes a tantalizing process in which the problems themselves lure the children into expending effort to solve them.

However, not all children approach schooling with the same expectations for success or the same trust in the formal education process. Some groups view education as the means to economic security, intellectual development, and political empowerment. Other groups are skeptical of teachers, schools, and education. They expect to be alienated from the learning process through a devaluing of their basic language, heritage, and beliefs. They believe that the only way to improve their condition is through major political and economic change. In their view, education per se will not empower them or their children. Children in these groups may conclude that the only way they can retain their basic sense of self-confidence is to withdraw from school and try to establish their competence among their peers (Spencer, 1985; Ogbu, 1987).

An integral approach to providing a successful educational environment for all children is contextualization of the learning process. To *contextualize* instruction is to carry it out in ways that first draw upon a child's existing experiences, previous knowledge, and concepts, and then to expand those understandings in new directions. Contextualizing may call for recognition that the classroom may be organized in a variety of ways: children may engage in private study and small-group problem solving, for instance, as well as form a large group that listens and responds to the teacher. Contextualization may require the teacher to draw upon the heroes and heroines, stories, songs, and myths of a cultural group in order to help children feel comfortable with more abstract concepts. It may require acknowledgment of different modes of expression, patterns of social conversation, and language. Finally, contextualizing may call for parents and other important community figures to become involved in the learning process so that children are not isolated from their significant social community (Tharp, 1989; Tharp & Gallimore, 1988).

All these efforts may be particularly beneficial to groups that have been alienated from schooling or that approach schooling with a sense of mistrust. When the educational process is contextualized, children are strengthened in their own cultural identity. When their strivings for personal and cultural achievement are validated, the conflict that often develops between school professionals and members of minority cultures need not arise. Teachers and school administrators become more confident about the school abilities of children, and children become more willing to persist in order to build competence in school-related tasks (Comer, 1985).

Summary

During the day-to-day experiences of success and failure, most middle-school-age children learn that work, effort, and perseverance will bring them the rewards of competence, mastery, and approval that they desire. As children internalize these behaviors, they develop a sense of industry. When difficult problems arise, they are ready to confront them and to persevere until they are solved. Children who experience a preponderance of failure during middle school age run the risk of internalizing a sense of inferiority. When such children confront a difficult problem, they feel inadequate and unable to proceed with any solution. Education is the process through which children work on the crisis of industry versus inferiority. The school is the environment in which continuous attention is given to the child's success or failure at a variety of learning tasks. The resolution of the psychosocial crisis is the result of individual differences in ability and effort, social expectations for success, and the compatibility of the school environment with the child's cultural and family orientation toward education.

◻ Applied Topic: Sex Education

Why should sex education be considered an issue of middle childhood? No developmental theory suggests that this is a stage of heightened sexuality—in fact, most people who work with children at this stage report frequent expressions of antagonism between males and females. However, the life-span approach is encouraging about the possibility of preparing oneself during an earlier stage for events that are anticipated during a later one. We know that the next stage of development, early adolescence, is one that arouses both anxiety and excitement about sexual encounters. Many girls will be experiencing the transitions of puberty at age 11 or 12. Boys follow soon after at ages 13 to 15. The United States has one of the highest rates of births to adolescent girls of any industrialized nation. (This problem is discussed in greater detail in Chapter 10.) Entry into parenthood at an early age introduces critical developmental risks for young mothers and fathers as well as for their babies. To delay sex education until most children have already entered puberty and take the chance of engaging in sexual activity without having had the opportunity to discuss and anticipate its possible consequences seems to be a serious societal mistake.

What is more, the transition into middle school or junior high school is a very stressful event for many children. This school change is often accompanied by a drop in self-esteem and in school performance. Without appropriate support, young adolescents are likely to experience a decline in their academic aspirations and an increase in their willingness to explore sexual activity (Brooks-Gunn & Furstenberg, 1989). Therefore, it seems to us that the introduction of sex education during the middle school years will produce the benefits of reducing the rate of unwanted adolescent pregnancies and providing a new level of emotional support that will help sustain continued cognitive growth during the early adolescent years.

The usefulness of information about sexuality and the reproductive process can be measured by the extent to which such information minimizes a child's uncertainty, embarrassment, and feelings of isolation during the actual events of puberty. In addition, it can be evaluated in light of the kinds of sexual decisions young adolescents make.

How might such a program be structured so that it would be readily integrated into children's understanding of their world? The developmental tasks of the middle-school-age years are useful in designing an approach to the problem. The child's involvement in skill learning, increased capacity for logical reasoning, investment in the social group, and growing ability to set standards and evaluate personal performance all suggest that a relatively structured group learning situation would be a successful format for the discussion of sexuality.

Three themes are particularly important with regard to sex education at this age. First, sexuality must be discussed within the context of its role as a central mechanism for evolution and for the survival of the culture. With this orientation, children can approach the topic logically, as an element in a larger natural system. They can begin to ask questions about the mechanisms of reproduction as part of an investigation of the more complex matter of species survival. The facts of sexual maturation can then be presented as a natural necessity. The children can begin to appreciate that their own maturity allows them to participate in a kind of activity that has meaning at a biological, anthropological, and historical level as well as at a personal level. Sex

Pablo Picasso, *Sleeping Peasants,* Paris, 1919. Sex education is most appropriate before the intense sexual drives of adolescence are fully awakened. For these two sleeping peasants, sexuality does not seem to pose a barrier to a relaxed, uninhibited relationship. Tempera, watercolor, and pencil on paper, 12¼" x 19¼". Collection, The Museum of Modern Art, New York. Abby Aldrich Rockefeller Fund. © 1991, ARS, New York/SPADEM.

education becomes a vehicle for introducing the biological facts of sexuality and reproduction within a larger intellectual examination of such topics as the evolution of humans, the adaptive nature of social living units, the roles of males and females in a society, factors that promote reproductive success, and the contributions of males and females to the survival of children.

The presentation of facts about sexuality in this context has several consequences. It allows children to approach the matter as an intellectual problem that requires an extension of skills and information in order to solve it. It also expands children's view of their own development as an expression of a much larger evolutionary process. Children are challenged to abandon their somewhat egocentric view of their behavior by seeing the link between their own body functions and impulses and the survival of a species. Finally, children are made aware of the norms that have been established for the expression of sexual impulses in their own and other cultures. They learn to appreciate the meaning of their own cultural identity as they become acquainted with rituals, ceremonies, and practices that are carried out in other cultural groups.

Second, the child must learn to see sexual intimacy within the context of intimate personal relationships as well as in relation to human survival. Here we would emphasize the distinction between sex as a biological dimension and love as a psychological one. Knowing the facts about sexual reproduction does not help most children to accept the reality that their parents have had sexual intercourse. It does not help them to manage the expression of their impulses or to assess the emotional costs of sexuality. There is a gap between the child's ability to process information about sexual matters and the ability to apply that information to real-life events.

Teachers must help children to expand their understanding of intimacy in order to enhance their appreciation of the role of sexuality in adolescent and adult relationships. Children must understand that sexual closeness is a means of communicating love as well as making babies. This type of sex education curriculum would examine the range of human efforts to communicate feelings of love and to come to terms with the expression of sexual impulses. Painting, sculpture, drama, poetry, and song are media through which people have attempted to share their confusion, delight, and sorrow about love. Children can learn to see the beauty that has been captured in these artistic expressions and through them begin to share some of their own feelings about love. The goal is to increase children's feelings of competence in the expression of personal emotions and to aid them in valuing their emotional life as a part of their character.

The capacity to love will not become fully mature until adulthood. Nonetheless, during the middle-school-age years children can learn that the feelings they experience toward others are emotions with which people have struggled for centuries. Hidden in those feelings is the possibility of great personal joy. Children can learn that the feelings of love that they now share with friends, parents, and boyfriends or girlfriends, and that they may later share with husbands or wives and their own children, will all bring them closer to an ultimate personal fulfillment.

Third, sexuality must be studied within the interpersonal contexts that adolescents are likely to experience (Juhasz & Sonnenshein-Schneider, 1987; Boltan & Mac-Eachron, 1988; Marsiglio, 1988). Students must be helped to locate the place of sexuality in their definitions of masculinity and femininity. Family and cultural factors that shape these definitions need to be explored. Children need to raise questions about the responsibility of men and women for procreation and nurturance of infants, including cultural norms about their respective responsibilities for preventing unwanted pregnancies. This curriculum could include an exploration of family and community attitudes and values in regard to contraception, and those factors that prevent consistent use of contraceptives. Through role playing and problem solving, children could assess the consequences of early pregnancy in the light of their goals for personal freedom, academic achievement, and a career. At the interpersonal level, they need to practice assertiveness strategies as well as alternative strategies for satisfying their needs for intimacy and sexuality. Ideally, such a curriculum would help young people build a peer culture in which they supported the values of postponing entry into sexual activity and preventing unwanted pregnancy.

This description of the focus of a sex education course clearly expands the concept as it is currently approached. Sex education can be seen as an exciting invitation to teach children about their bodies, their function in the history of evolution, and their potential for creative expression. This version of a sex education program would be a legitimate school-centered function that would fulfill a spirit of what we described earlier as the process of education. Such a program could be seen as an intellectually stimulating process rather than the embarrassing, bothersome chore that is currently associated with the traditional "health class." Here is an opportunity to take a topic in which children are already intensely interested and to expand that naive curiosity into a full view of one of the most powerful themes in human history.

☐ Chapter Summary

The middle-school-age child develops work and social skills that are crucial to later life stages. In addition to acquiring school-related skills, children increase their capacity for social cooperation, self-evaluation, and peer-group participation.

Industry, as we have discussed it, focuses primarily on building competence. Nonetheless, it is quite clear that the family, peer group, and school environment all play their parts in support of feelings of mastery or failure. An understanding of skill development must combine an appreciation of the child's intellectual maturity with a sense of the significant motives that may influence his or her willingness to learn.

Although earlier psychological theories have not considered middle school age to be very influential in the process of psychological development, the events of this stage play an extremely important part in the psychology of the person. Issues of industry, mastery, achievement, success, social skills, cooperativeness, and interpersonal sensitivity are all salient to the events of middle school age. A person's orientation toward friendship and work, two essential aspects of adult life, begin to take shape during this stage.

References

Adler, A. (1935). The fundamental views of individual psychology. *International Journal of Individual Psychology, 1,* 5–8.

Ainsworth, M. D. S. (1989). Attachments beyond infancy. *American Psychologist, 44,* 709–716.

Alexander, K. L., & Entwisle, D. R. (1988). *Achievement in the first two years of school: Patterns and processes.* Monographs of the Society for Research in Child Development, 53, (2, serial no. 218).

Anderson, R. C., Wilson, P. T., & Fielding, L. G. (1988). Growth in reading and how children spend their time outside of school. *Reading Research Quarterly, 23,* 285–303.

Asarnow, J. R., & Callan, J. W. (1985). Boys with social adjustment problems: Social cognitive processes. *Journal of Consulting and Clinical Psychology, 53,* 80–87.

Asher, S. R., Hymel, S., & Renshaw, P. D. (1984). Loneliness in children. *Child Development, 55,* 1456–1464.

Atkinson, J. W., & Birch, D. (1978). *Introduction to motivation* (2nd ed.). New York: Van Nostrand.

Bandura, A. (1982). Self-efficacy mechanism in human agency. *American Psychologist, 37,* 122–147.

Bandura, A., & Schunck, D. H. (1981). Cultivating competence, self-efficacy, and intrinsic interest through proximal self-motivation. *Journal of Personality and Social Psychology, 41,* 586–598.

Berndt, T. J. (1979). Development changes in conformity to peers and parents. *Developmental Psychology, 15,* 608–616.

Berndt, T. J. (1981). Relations between social cognition, nonsocial cognition, and social behavior: The case of friendship. In J. H. Flavell & L. D. Ross (eds.), *Social cognitive development: Frontiers and possible futures.*

Cambridge: Cambridge University Press.

Bijstra, J., Van Geert, P., & Jackson, S. (1989). Conservation and the appearance-reality distinction: What do children really know and what do they answer? *British Journal of Developmental Psychology, 7,* 43–53.

Bolton, F. G., Jr., & MacEachron, A. E. (1988). Adolescent male sexuality: A developmental perspective. *Journal of Adolescent Research, 3,* 259–273.

Brainerd, C. J. (1977). Cognitive development and concept learning: An interpretive review. *Psychological Bulletin, 84,* 919–939.

Brainerd, C. J., & Hooper, F. H. (1978). More on the identity-equivalence sequence: An update and some replies to Miller. *Psychological Bulletin, 85,* 70–75.

Brooks-Gunn, J., & Furstenberg, F. F., Jr. (1989). Adolescent sexual behavior. *American Psychologist, 44,* 249–257.

Brown, I., Jr., & Inouye, D. K. (1978). Learned helplessness through modeling: The role of perceived similarity in competence. *Journal of Personality and Social Psychology, 36,* 900–908.

Brustad, R. J. (1988). Affective outcomes in competitive youth sport: The influence of intrapersonal and socialization factors. *Journal of Sport and Exercise Psychology, 10,* 307–321.

Butterfield, E. C., Nelson, T. O., & Peck, V. (1988). Developmental aspects of the feeling of knowing. *Developmental Psychology, 24,* 654–663.

Calhoun, G., Jr., & Morse, W. C. (1977). Self-concept and self-esteem: Another perspective. *Psychology in the Schools, 14,* 318–322.

Carr, M., Kurtz, B. E., Schneider, W., Turner, L. A., & Borkowski, J. G. (1989). Strategy acquisition and transfer among American and German children: Environmental influences on metacognitive development. *Developmental Psychology, 25,* 765–771.

Carroll, D. W. (1986). *Psychology of language.* Pacific Grove, Calif.: Brooks/Cole.

Chalmers, J. B., & Townsend, M. A. R. (1990). The effects of training in social perspective taking on socially maladjusted girls. *Child Development, 61,* 178–190.

Clark, M. L., & Ayers, M. (1988). The role of reciprocity and proximity in junior high school friendships. *Journal of Youth and Adolescence, 17,* 403–411.

Coie, J. D., & Krehbiel, G. (1984). Effects of academic tutoring on the social status of low-achieving, socially rejected children. *Child Development, 55,* 1465–1478.

Cole, M., & D'Andrade, R. (1982). The influence of schooling on concept formation: Some preliminary conclusions. *Quarterly Newsletter of the Laboratory of Comparative Cognition, 4,* 19–26.

Coleman, J. S. (1987). Families and schools. *Educational Researcher, 16,* 32–38.

Comer, J. P. (1985). Empowering black children's educational environments. In H. P. McAdoo & J. L. McAdoo (eds.), *Black children: Social, educational, and parental environments* (pp. 123–138). Newbury Park, Calif.: Sage.

Crockett, L., Losoff, M., & Petersen, A. (1984). Perceptions of the peer group and friendship in early adolescence. *Journal of Early Adolescence, 4,* 155–181.

Crooks, T. J. (1988). The impact of classroom evaluation practices on students. *Review of Educational Research, 58,* 438–481.

Cross, D. R., & Paris, S. G. (1988). Developmental and instructional analyses of children's metacognition and reading comprehension. *Journal of Educational Psychology, 80,* 131–142.

Dickstein, E. B. (1979). Biological and cognitive bases of moral functioning. *Human Development, 22,* 37–59.

Dodge, K. A., Murphy, R. R., & Buchsbaum, K. (1984). The assessment of intention-cue detection skills in children: Implications for developmental psychopathology. *Child Development, 55,* 163–173.

Dodge, K. A., Petit, G. S., McClaskey, C. L., & Brown, M. M. (1986). *Social competence in children.* Monographs of the Society for Research in Child Development, 51 (2, serial no. 213).

Downey, G., & Walker, E. (1989). Social cognition and adjustment in children at risk for psychopathology. *Developmental Psychology, 25,* 835–845.

Elias, M. J., Beier, J. J., & Gara, M. A. (1989). Children's responses to interpersonal obstacles as a predictor of social competence. *Journal of Youth and Adolescence, 18,* 451–465.

Entwisle, D. R., Alexander, K. L., Pallas, A. M., & Cadigan, D. (1987). The emergent academic self-image of first-graders: Its response to social structure. *Child Development, 58,* 1190–1206.

Epstein, J. (1983a). Examining theories of adolescent friendships. In J. Epstein & N. Karweit (eds.), *Friends in school: Patterns of selection and influence in secondary schools.* New York: Academic Press.

Epstein, J. (1983b). Selection of friends in differently organized schools and classrooms. In J. Epstein & N. Karweit (eds.), *Friends in school: Patterns of selection and influence in secondary schools.* New York: Academic Press.

Erikson, E. H. (1963). *Childhood and society,* (2nd ed.). New York: Norton.

Field, D. (1981). Can preschool children really learn to conserve? *Child Development, 52,* 326–334.

Flavell, J. H. (1982). On cognitive development. *Child Development, 53,* 1–10.

French, D. C. (1984). Children's knowledge of the social functions of younger, older and same-age peers. *Child Development, 55,* 1429–1433.

French, D. C. (1988). Heterogeneity of peer-rejected boys: Aggressive and nonaggressive subtypes. *Child Development, 59,* 976–985.

Frey, K. S., & Ruble, D. N. (1987). What children say about classroom performance: Sex and grade differences in perceived compliance. *Child Development, 58,* 1066–1078.

Galbo, J. J. (1983). Adolescents' perceptions of significant adults. *Adolescence, 18,* 417–428.

Gavin, L. A., & Furman, W. (1989). Age differences in adolescents' perceptions of their peer groups. *Developmental Psychology, 25,* 827–834.

Goldenberg, C. N. (1989). Parents' effects on academic grouping for reading: Three case studies. *American Educational Research Journal, 26,* 329–352.

Goodnow, J. J. (1969). Problems in research on culture and thought. In D. Elkind & J. H. Flavell (eds.), *Studies in cognitive development: Essays in honor of Jean Piaget.* New York: Oxford University Press.

Gulko, J., Doyle, A., Serbin, L. A., & White, D. R. (1988). Conservation skills: A replicated study of order of acquisition across tasks. *Journal of Genetic Psychology, 149,* 425–439.

Halford, G. S., & Boyle, F. M. (1985). Do young children understand conservation of number? *Child Development, 56,* 165–176.

Hall, W. S. (1989). Reading comprehension. *American Psychologist, 44,* 157–161.

Haller, E., & Waterman, M. (1985). The criteria of reading group assignments. *Reading Teacher, 38,* 772–782.

Hallinan, M. (1979). Structural effects on children's friendships and cliques. *Social Psychological Quarterly, 42,* 43–54.

Harris, M. J., & Rosenthal, R. (1985). Mediation of interpersonal expectancy effects: 31 meta-analyses. *Psychological Bulletin, 97,* 363–386.

Hart, C. H., Ladd, G. W., & Burleson, B. R. (1990). Children's expectations of the outcomes of social strategies: Relations with sociometric status and maternal disciplinary styles. *Child Development, 61,* 127–137.

Harter, S. (1982). The perceived competence scale for children. *Child Development, 53,* 87–97.

Hartup, W. W. (1989). Social relationships and their developmental significance. *American Psychologist, 44,* 120–126.

Hess, R., & Holloway, S. (1984). Family and school as educational institutions. *Review of Child Development Research,* vol. 7, *The Family* (pp. 179–222). University of Chicago Press.

Holloway, S. D. (1988). Concepts of ability and effort in Japan and the United States. *Review of Educational Research, 58,* 327–345.

Jensen, R. E., & Moore, S. G. (1977). The effect of attribute statements on cooperativeness and competitiveness in school-age boys. *Child Development, 48,* 305–307.

Juhasz, A. M., & Sonnenshein-Schneider, M. (1987). Adolescent sexuality: Values, morality, and decision making. *Adolescence, 22,* 579–590.

Karweit, N. (1983). Extracurricular activities and friendship selection. In J. Epstein & N. Karweit (eds.), *Friends in school: Patterns of selection and influence in secondary schools.* New York: Academic Press.

Karweit, N., & Hansell, S. (1983). Sex differences in adolescent relationships: Friendships and status. In J. Epstein & N. Karweit (eds.), *Friends in school: Patterns of selection and influence in secondary schools.* New York: Academic Press.

Keating, D. P. (1975). Precocious cognitive development at the level of formal operations. *Child Development, 46,* 276–280.

Klausmeier, H. J. (1977). Individual differences in cognitive development during the school years. Paper presented at the annual convention of the American Psychological Association, San Francisco.

Klint, K. A., & Weiss, M. R. (1987). Perceived competence and motives for participating in youth sports: A test of Harter's competence motivation theory. *Journal of Sport Psychology, 9,* 55–65.

Lovell, K. (1961). *The growth of basic mathematical and scientific concepts in children.* New York: Philosophical Library.

Marsiglio, W. (1988). Adolescent male sexuality and heterosexual masculinity: A conceptual model and review. *Journal of Adolescent Research, 3,* 285–303.

May, R. B., & Norton, J. M. (1981). Training-task orders and transfer in conservation. *Child Development, 52,* 904–913.

McAuley, E., Duncan, T. E., & McElroy, M. (1989). Self-efficacy cognitions and causal attributions for children's motor performance: An exploratory investigation. *Journal of Genetic Psychology, 150,* 65–73.

McCabe, A. E., Siegel, L. S., Spence, I., & Wilkinson, A. (1982). Class-inclusion reasoning: Patterns of performance from three to eight years. *Child Development, 53,* 780–785.

Miller, S. A. (1978). Identity conservation and equivalence conservation: A critique of Brainerd and Hooper's analysis. *Psychological Bulletin, 85,* 58–69.

Nelson, J., & Aboud, F. E. (1985). The resolution of social conflict between friends. *Child Development, 56,* 1009–1017.

Nelson, K. (1974). Variations in children's concepts by age and category. *Child Development, 45,* 577–584.

Ogbu, J. U. (1987). Variability in minority school performance: A problem in search of an explanation. *Anthropology and Education Quarterly, 18,* 312–334.

Park, K. A., & Waters, E. (1989). Security of attachment and preschool friendships. *Child Development, 60,* 1076–1081.

Parsons, J. E., Adler, T. F., & Kaczala, C. M. (1982). Socialization of achievement attitudes and beliefs: Parental influences. *Child Development, 53,* 310–321.

Parsons, J. E., Kaczala, C. M., & Meece, J. L. (1982). Socialization of achievement attitudes and beliefs: Classroom influences. *Child Development, 53,* 322–339.

Parsons, J. E., & Ruble, D. N. (1977). The development of achievement-related expectancies. *Child Development, 48,* 1075–1079.

Patterson, G. R. (1982). *Coercive family processes.* Eugene, Oreg.: Castalia.

Pellegrini, D. S. (1985). Social cognition and competence in middle childhood. *Child Development, 56,* 253–264.

Pepitone, E. A., Loeb, H. W., & Murdock, E. M. (1977). Social comparison and similarity of children's performance in competitive situations. Paper presented at the annual convention of the American Psychological Association, San Francisco.

Pettit, G. S., Dodge, K. A., & Brown, M. M. (1988). Early family experience, social problem-solving patterns, and children's social competence. *Child Develop-*

ment, 59, 107–120.

Phillips, D. A. (1984). The illusion of incompetence among academically competent children. *Child Development, 55,* 2000–2016.

Phillips, D. A. (1987). Socialization of perceived academic competence among highly competent children. *Child Development, 58,* 1308–1320.

Piaget, J. (1932/1948). *The moral judgment of the child.* Glencoe, Ill.: Free Press.

Piaget, J. (1983). Piaget's theory. In W. Kessen (ed.), *Handbook of child psychology,* vol. 1, *History, theory, and methods* (4th ed.). New York: Wiley.

Piaget, J., & Inhelder, B. (1969). *The psychology of the child.* New York: Basic Books.

Prawat, R. S., Byers, J. L., & Anderson, A. H. (1983). An attributional analysis of teachers' affective reactions to student success and failure. *American Educational Research Journal, 20,* 137–152.

Putallaz, M. (1987). Maternal behavior and children's sociometric status. *Child Development, 58,* 324–340.

Renshaw, P. D., & Asher, S. R. (1982). Social competence and peer status: The distinction between goals and strategies. In K. H. Rubin & H. S. Ross (eds.), *Peer relationships and social skills in childhood.* New York: Springer-Verlag.

Rutter, M. (1983). School effects on pupil progress: Research findings and policy implications. *Child Development, 54,* 1–29.

Sancilio, M. F. M., Plumert, J. M., & Hartup, W. W. (1989). Friendship and aggressiveness as determinants of conflict outcomes in middle childhood. *Developmental Psychology, 25,* 812–819.

Share, D. L., McGee, R., & Silva, P. A. (1989). IQ and reading progress: A test of the capacity notion of IQ. *Journal of the American Academy of Child and Adolescent Psychiatry, 28,* 97–100.

Shears, L. M., & Bower, E. M. (1974). *Games in education and development.* Springfield, Ill.: Charles C Thomas.

Silverstein, A. B., Pearson, L. B., Aguinaldo, N. E., Friedman, S. L., Tokayama, D. L., & Weiss, Z. T. (1982). Identity conservation and equivalence conservation: A question of developmental priority. *Child Development, 53,* 819–821.

Skaalvik, E. M., & Hagtvet, K. A. (1990). Academic achievement and self-concept: An analysis of causal predominance in a developmental perspective. *Journal of Personality and Social Psychology, 58,* 292–307.

Slavin, R. E. (1987). Grouping for instruction in the elementary school. *Educational Psychologist, 22,* 109–127.

Smith, T. L. (1986). Self-concepts of youth sport participants and nonparticipants in grades 3 and 6. *Perceptual and Motor Skills, 62,* 863–866.

Spencer, M. B. (1985). Racial variations in achievement prediction: The school as a conduit for macrostructural cultural tension. In H. P. McAdoo & J. L. McAdoo (eds.), *Black Children: Social, Educational, and Parental Environments* (pp. 85–111). Newbury Park, Calif.: Sage.

Spiro, R. J., Bruce, B. C., & Brewer, W. F. (eds.) (1980). *Theoretical issues in reading comprehension.* Hillsdale, N.J.: Erlbaum.

Sroufe, L. A., & Fleeson, J. (1986). Attachment and the construction of relationships. In W. W. Hartup and Z. Rubin (eds.), *Relationships and development* (pp. 51–72). Hillsdale, N.J.: Erlbaum.

Stevenson, D. L., & Baker, D. P. (1987). The family-school relation and the child's school performance. *Child Development, 58,* 1348–1357.

Stigler, J. W., Smith, S., & Mao, L. (1985). The self perception of competence by Chinese children. *Child Development, 56,* 1259–1270.

Sullivan, H. S. (1949). The collected works of Harry Stack Sullivan (vols. 1 and 2). New York: Norton.

Sutherland, A., & Goldschmid, M. L. (1974). Negative teacher expectation and IQ change in children with superior intellectual potential. *Child Development, 45,* 852–856.

Sutton-Smith, B. A. (1971). Syntax for play and games. In R. E. Herron & B. Sutton-Smith (eds.), *Child's Play* (pp. 298–310). New York: Wiley.

Tharp, R. G. (1989). Psychocultural variables and constants: Effects on teaching and learning in schools. *American Psychologist, 44,* 349–359.

Tharp, R. G., & Gallimore, R. (1988). *Rousing minds to life: Teaching, learning, and schooling in social context.* Cambridge: Cambridge University Press.

Uzgiris, I. C. (1964). Situational generality of conservation. *Child Development, 35,* 831–841.

Vygotsky, L. S. (1932/1962). *Thought and language.* Cambridge, Mass.: MIT Press; New York: Wiley.

Waas, G. A (1988). Social attributional biases of peer-rejected and aggressive children. *Child Development, 59,* 969–975.

Weinstein, R. S., Marshall, H. H., Sharp, L., & Botkin, M. (1987). Pygmalion and the student: Age and classroom differences in children's awareness of teacher expectations. *Child Development, 58,* 1079–1093.

Youniss, J. (1980). *Parents and peers in social development: A Sullivan-Piaget perspective.* Chicago: University of Chicago Press.

Chapter Nine

Physical changes, self-consciousness, and need for peer approval are characteristics of early adolescence. At age 16, Picasso showed himself as serious and manly, perhaps picturing himself as more mature than he really was.

Early Adolescence (12 to 18 Years)

Developmental Tasks

Physical Maturation
 Physical Changes in Boys
 Physical Changes in Girls
 The Secular Trend
 Individual Differences in Maturation Rate
 Summary
Formal Operations
 Egocentrism
 Factors That Promote Formal Operational Thought
Emotional Development
Membership in the Peer Group
 Parents and Peers
Sexual Relationships
 Parenthood in Early Adolescence
Summary

The Psychosocial Crisis: Group Identity versus Alienation

The Central Process: Peer Pressure
 Ethnic-Group Identity
Summary

Applied Topic: Adolescent Alcohol Use
Chapter Summary
References

At this point in our discussion of life stages, we depart once again from Erikson's conceptualization. His psychosocial theory views adolescence as a single stage unified by the resolution of the central conflict of identity versus identity confusion. This approach attempts to treat the tasks and needs of children ranging in age from approximately 11 to 21. From our own research with adolescents and our assessment of the research literature, we have come to the conclusion that two distinct periods of psychosocial development occur during these years. This chapter discusses the stage of early adolescence. Chapter 10 will discuss the stage of later adolescence.

We have identified one stage that begins with the onset of puberty and ends with graduation from high school (or roughly 18 years of age). *Early adolescence* is characterized by rapid physical changes, significant cognitive maturation, and a heightened sensitivity to peer relations. We have called the psychosocial crisis of this stage *group identity versus alienation.* The second stage, *later adolescence,* begins at approximately 18 years of age and continues for about three or four years. This stage is characterized by new advances in the establishment of autonomy from the family and the development of a personal identity. The psychosocial crisis of this period is *individual identity versus identity confusion.* The second adolescent stage closely parallels Erikson's conceptualization of the entire period of adolescence.

Although we agree that the crisis of individual identity accurately reflects the concerns of the college-age adolescent, we have found that this conceptualization is inadequate for understanding the concerns of younger adolescents. Young adolescents must resolve questions about relationships with peer groups before they can resolve questions about relationships with families or create individual identities. It seems quite crucial to us that high-school-age adolescents develop a sense of group identity as a prelude to a sense of individual identity. Of course, elements of personal identity are forged in this stage, as are elements of subsequent psychosocial orientations, including intimacy, generativity, integrity, and immortality. In addition, early adolescents may rework and synthesize earlier psychosocial orientations as they engage in a more complex and demanding sociocultural environment.

Developmental Tasks

Physical Maturation

The onset of early adolescence is marked by rapid physical change. The changes associated with puberty—a "height spurt," the maturation of the reproductive system, the appearance of secondary sex characteristics, and the redistribution of body weight—generally begin at age 11 for females and 13 for males. Variability in the rate of development is well documented (Faust, 1977; Tanner, 1978). The time from the appearance of breast buds to full maturity may range from 1½ to 6 years for girls; the male genitalia may take from 2 to 5 years to reach adult size. These individual differences in maturation suggest that during early adolescence the chronological peer group is biologically far more diverse than it was during early and middle school age.

Pubertal development can influence psychological and social development in at least three ways (Clausen, 1975). First, physical growth can alter a person's actual *ability to perform tasks.* Early adolescents are taller and stronger than younger children, and have greater coordination and endurance. Second, physical growth can alter the *ways in which one is perceived by others.* For example, early adolescents may be viewed as less cuddly or more threatening than younger children. Third, physical growth can influence the *ways in which adolescents perceive themselves.* The physical changes may make them feel more like adults, or, if the results are disappointing, may make adulthood harder to accept.

The degree to which one's body matches the desired or socially valued body build of the culture will influence social acceptance by peers and adults. This match between body shape and cultural values influences the future course of psychosocial development. In our culture, it gives some special self-esteem advantages to muscular, well-developed males and petite, shapely females. In contrast, it detracts from the self-esteem of thin, gangling boys and overweight males and females.

Physical Changes in Boys

Physical maturation poses different problems for males and females. Although both sexes must adjust to a changing body image, the culture places distinct values and taboos on the kinds of changes experienced by each.

For the boy, increased height and muscle mass are welcome changes that bring him one step closer to adult maturity. On the one hand, a mature physique usually brings well-developed physical skills that are highly valued by peers and adults alike. On the other hand, the period of rapid growth may leave a boy awkward and uncoordinated for a time. This awkwardness results because growth does not take place at the same rate in all parts of the body. One particular discrepancy is the time lag between the height spurt and the increase in muscle strength. For boys, the peak increase in muscle strength usually occurs about 12 to 14 months after the peak height spurt (Carron & Bailey, 1974). This time lag results in a temporary period during which a boy simply cannot accomplish what he might expect, given his physical size. Psychologically, this awkward period poses some strong challenges to the boy's self-esteem. He simply looks funny and out of shape. He may be easily embarrassed by this condition. He cannot fully accept his new body image at first, and he doubts whether others can.

The onset of the growth of the testes and penis also poses some important problems for early adolescent males. They are generally not well prepared by their parents for the maturation of the reproductive organs (Bolton & MacEachron, 1988). Specifically, they are not taught about spontaneous ejaculation and may be surprised, scared, or embarrassed by it. The sexual connotation of the event may make it difficult for them to seek an explanation from their parents. They are left to gain information from friends and reading material or to worry in private about its meaning. For many boys, spontaneous ejaculation provides an important clue to the way in which physical adult sexuality and reproduction are accomplished. The pleasure of the ejaculation experience and the positive value of the new information that it provides are counterbalanced by a mild anxiety (Gaddis & Brooks-Gunn, 1985; Marsiglio, 1988). This is only one of the developments that arouse ambivalence in many boys during early adolescence.

A third area of physical development that has psychological and social meaning for the boy is the development of secondary sex characteristics, particularly the growth

Pablo Picasso, *Barefoot Boys,* 1903. Because of differences in the rate of development at puberty, boys of the same age and grade level can be quite different in height and physical maturation.

of facial and body hair. The equipment and the ritual behaviors associated with shaving are closely linked to the masculine sex role. Most boys are eager to express their identification with this role through the act of shaving, and they will use the slightest evidence of hairy outgrowth as an excuse to take razor in hand. The ritual of shaving not only provides some affirmation of the boy's masculinity but allows him an acceptable outlet for his narcissism. As he shaves, it is legitimate for him to gaze at and admire his changing image. In some subcultures, a mustache is an important symbol of manliness. Thus some young men cultivate and admire their mustaches as evidence of their enhanced male status.

Physical Changes in Girls

For the girl, the onset of puberty occurs at approximately 11 years of age—almost two years sooner than the parallel experience for the boy. Initially the increase in height may be responded to with embarrassment as she finds herself towering above her male classmates. Girls often slouch in an attempt to disguise their increased height. Girls' predominant concern about their changing physique is obesity. At the onset of the growth spurt, most girls notice a plumping of their features. They do not seem to be aware of the eventual redistribution of this new body weight. In an attempt to ward off what they perceive as a tendency toward obesity, many early adolescent girls begin a process of strict and often faddish dieting. This strategy is ill timed, since their bodies require well-balanced diets and increased calorie intake during this period of rapid growth.

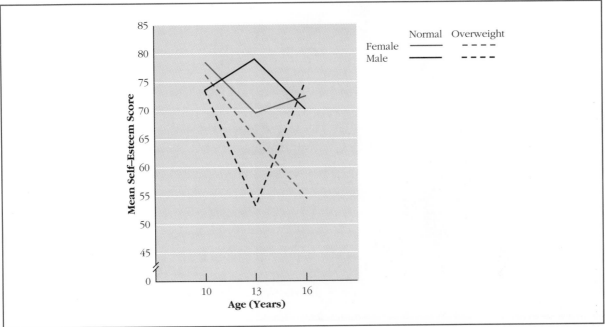

Figure 9.1   Mean Self-Esteem Score of Normal and Overweight Boys and Girls as a Function of Age
Source: B. K. Mendelson and D. R. White, "Development of Self-Body Esteem in Overweight Youngsters,"
Developmental Psychology, 21 (1985), 92. Copyright 1985 by the American Psychological Association. Reprinted
by permission of the author.

During the early adolescent years, obesity is associated with negative feelings
about one's appearance and one's body. Research suggests that being overweight has
little relation to self-esteem in middle school age but does begin to have a negative
relation to self-esteem during early adolescence (see Figure 9.1). Overweight boys
tend to have lower self-esteem than boys of normal weight at age 13 but not at younger
or older ages. Overweight girls tend to have lower self-esteem than girls of normal
weight at 16 (Mendelson & White, 1985; Martin et al., 1988). The impact of obesity on
self-esteem is an important example of the effect of physical development and body
shape on self-evaluation and acceptance during this stage.

For girls, the development of primary sex characteristics includes the maturation
of breast buds and the onset of the menstrual cycle. For the average girl, the development of breast buds is a welcome sign of her growing maturity and femininity.
Some girls begin to wear brassieres in anticipation of the onset of breast development.
Most are prepared by their mothers for the specific events associated with menstruation. However, menstruation is often handled as a matter of hygiene rather than as a
sexual or maturational transition (Logan, 1980). Many girls do not understand the
relation of menstruation to the total process of reproduction. They simply accept the
fact of monthly periods as another sign of their femininity.

At the time at which girls begin to menstruate (approximately 12 years of age),
their male peers may still be ignorant of this phenomenon. The girl is often put in a

Shopping for a bra is one of a young girl's first steps in the transition to adolescence.

position of having to explain or hide the facts of her growth from them. The discrepancy in the onset of puberty in boys and girls and the uneven dissemination of information about it may make it difficult for a girl to fully accept the changes she is experiencing. The memoirs of Simone de Beauvoir (1959) reflect this ambivalence:

> *We were staying with friends. . . . I awake horror-stricken one morning: I had soiled my nightdress. I washed it and got dressed: again I soiled my underclothes. I had forgotten Madeleine's vague prophecies, and I wondered what shameful malady I was suffering from. Worried and feeling somehow guilty, I had to take my mother into my confidence: she explained to me that I had now become "a big girl," and bundled me up in a very inconvenient manner. I felt a strong sense of relief when I learned that it had happened through no fault of my own; and as always when something important happened to me, I even felt my heart swell with a sort of pride.*

Most girls seem to react to menstruation with a mix of positive and negative feelings. The positive feelings reflect a pride in maturing and in the confirmation of their womanliness. The negative feelings reflect the inconvenience, some unpleasant symptoms, and possible embarrassment of menstruation (Ruble & Brooks-Gunn, 1982; Grief & Ulman, 1982).

The development of secondary sex characteristics, especially the growth of body hair, may be a greater burden for girls than it is for boys. The cultural preference for smooth-skinned females requires regular shaving of underarms and legs. This shaving

Pablo Picasso, *The Toilette,* 1906. Narcissism is expressed in a preoccupation with one's mirror image. Most early adolescent girls and boys take longer in grooming and are more self-conscious about their physical appearance than younger children.

ritual, however, is not filled with the same positive sex-role validation as is face shaving for the adolescent boys. The adolescent girl learns that she must make certain alterations of her physical appearance in order to meet the cultural standards for femininity.

Generally, girls are more dissatisfied than boys with their physical appearance and their overall body image. This pattern was found among Finns as well as Americans (Peterson et al., 1984; Rauste–von Wright, 1989). For girls, self-consciousness and dissatisfaction with appearance reach their peak between the ages of 13 and 15. By age 18, the more satisfied a young woman is with her body image, the more likely she is to have a positive outlook on social relationships with her family, her peers, and people in general.

The Secular Trend

Given a genetic potential for growth and sexual maturation, the environment can play an important role in the eventual attainment of one's growth potential. A *secular growth trend* is an increase or decrease in adult height or a change in the age at which physical maturation takes place (Van Wieringen, 1978). Changes in hygiene, nutrition, and health care have contributed to an earlier growth spurt over the past century. Children aged 10 to 14 increased in height by an average of 2 to 3 centimeters every decade from 1900 to 1960. Adult height is not necessarily greater; it is simply attained earlier.

Other evidence of a secular trend is provided by the shift in age at menarche. There is some controversy about the extent of this shift. Data reported by Tanner

(1978) show a decrease in average age at menarche from 13.5 to 14 in 1950 to 12.5 to 13 in 1970. At present the mean age at menarche is 12.3, but the range is from 9 to 17. Age at menarche varies among countries and even among socioeconomic groups within a country. Sources based on Roman, Islamic, and medieval writings suggest that females have matured in the age range of 12 to 14 for many centuries (Bullough, 1981). Lack of precise records and the confounding of health and social class with age at menarche make it difficult to confirm long-term historical trends. Lower age at the onset of menarche is associated with improved standard of living, including health, diet, and social class (Tanner, 1981).

Individual Differences in Maturation Rate

The rate of physical maturation varies for boys just as it does for girls. It has been noted that boys who mature later than their agemates experience considerable psychological stress and develop a negative self-image (Clausen, 1975; Mussen & Jones, 1957). Late-maturing boys are treated as if they were younger than they really are. They may become isolated from their peers and behave in a silly, childish manner in order to gain attention. Boys who mature earlier than their agemates tend to have an advantage. They are likely to be given increased responsibility by parents and teachers. They develop a positive self-image. They are generally more satisfied with their bodies; they feel more positive about being boys; and they are likely to be more involved in school activities by the tenth grade than are late-maturing boys (Blyth, Bulcroft & Simmons, 1981).

The consequences of early and late maturation differ for girls and boys (Dwyer & Mayer, 1971). Both early- and late-maturing girls experience some tension with regard to physical development. Since girls mature about two years earlier than boys, the early-maturing girl stands out among all her male and female agemates. Her stature and breast development violate the cultural equation of femininity with petiteness. Early onset of menstruation is especially stressful, resulting in heightened self-consciousness and anxiety (Hill, 1988). For a time, at least, early-maturing girls may be embarrassed by their femininity. Not only do they look very different from their peers, but they are experiencing significant physical changes that they cannot discuss readily with their agemates.

There is some evidence that early-maturing girls are less likely to earn good grades or to score well on academic achievement tests. They are more likely to be identified as behavior problems in school (Blyth, Bulcroft & Simmons, 1981). Early-maturing girls are likely to start dating earlier and to perceive themselves as more popular with boys than are late-maturing girls. Whether this is a long-term advantage or disadvantage with respect to psychological or social development is not easy to determine.

These examples of the psychological impact of the timing of physical maturation serve to highlight the interaction between the somatic and the social systems on development. Early-maturing girls and late-maturing boys may become isolated from their peers. Individuals who deviate from the normal physical growth pattern may be rejected by the group because they look different and are experiencing different psychological events than are most of the group members. In the same vein, the advantages of early maturation for boys are primarily a product of the admiration and leadership role attributed to them by their parents and peers. These differences in rate and timing of physical maturation can result in perceptions of body image and dissatisfaction with one's physical appearance that persist well beyond adolescence (Rauste–von Wright, 1989).

Summary

Both boys and girls experience parallel phases of physical maturation during early adolescence. Although girls experience these changes somewhat earlier, both sexes must adapt to increases in height and weight and to the maturation of primary and secondary sex characteristics. As a result of earlier maturation of the reproductive system, girls often introduce issues of dating, "going together," and romance into the peer culture. Biological changes in the group of girls energizes the social system to incorporate and evolve rituals to deal with reproductive and sexual topics. This is a good example of the way biological systems acting together modify the social system.

Four points have been made with respect to the psychological meaning of these body changes for males and females:

1. The physical changes enable adolescents to think of themselves as approaching adulthood.
2. The changes influence the young person's identification with the role of man or woman.
3. The person becomes more egocentric and self-involved.
4. The changes produce ambivalence about new aspects of the self. If the peer group is not supportive of these changes, negative feelings and conflicts are likely to result.

The timing of physical growth can have an impact on whether the changes of puberty are experienced as positive or negative. Acceptance of these physical changes seems to require adequate information about their meaning, a positive identification with one's sex role, and an atmosphere of family and peer support.

The concept of the secular trend alerts us to the importance of the psychosocial context of physical development. Not only are peers experiencing diverse patterns of growth; parents and grandparents may be reacting to a discrepancy between their children's development and their own timetable for growth. What is more, the fact that the period of reproductive capacity starts earlier than it did 50 years ago poses special challenges to the young people who must cope with the expression and regulation of sexual impulses.

Formal Operations

Early adolescents begin to think about the world in new ways. Their thought becomes more abstract, and they are able to generate hypotheses about events that they have never perceived. The complex conceptual capacities have been described by Jean Piaget as *formal operations* (Inhelder & Piaget, 1958; Piaget, 1970, 1972; Chapman, 1988). Piaget proposed that these thoughts are governed more by logical principles than by perceptions and experiences.

Children in the sixth
and seventh grades
begin to confront and
solve problems that
require formal opera-
tional thought.

An important feature of formal operational thought is the ability to raise hypotheses to explain an event, and then to follow the logic that a particular hypothesis implies. "Hypothetical reasoning implies the subordination of the real to the realm of the possible, and consequently the linking of all possibilities to one another by necessary implications that encompass the real, but at the same time go beyond it" (Piaget, 1972, p. 3).

One of the classic experiments that Piaget and Inhelder designed to demonstrate the development of hypothetico-deductive reasoning involves the explanation of the swing of a pendulum. The task is to find out what variable or combination of variables controls the speed of the swing. Four factors can be varied: the mass of the object; the height from which the pendulum is pushed; the force with which it is pushed; and the length of the string. To investigate this problem, it is necessary to begin by varying only one factor at a time, while keeping the others constant. As it happens, only the length of the string influences the speed of the pendulum. The challenge is to demonstrate that the length of the string accounts for the speed and that the other factors do not. Using formal operational thought, a child can test each factor separately and evaluate its contribution (Inhelder & Piaget, 1958; Flavell, 1963).

Several skills are involved in problem solving of this kind. First, one must be able to identify the separate factors and the possible effect of each factor. Second, one must be able to consider possible interactions among the factors. Third, one must be able to develop a systematic method for testing each factor in combination with each other factor. The conceptual system of possible solutions guides problem solving (Neimark, 1975; Siegler, Liebert & Liebert, 1973).

Several new conceptual skills emerge during the stage of formal operations (Neimark, 1982; Demetriou & Efklides, 1985). First, early adolescents are able to manipulate mentally more than two categories of variables at the same time; for example, they can consider the relationship of speed, distance, and time in planning a trip

---

Table 9.1   New Conceptual Skills That Emerge During the Stage of Formal Operational Thought

1. Ability to manipulate mentally more than two categories of variables simultaneously.
2. Ability to think about the changes that come with time.
3. Ability to hypothesize logical sequences of events.
4. Ability to foresee consequences of actions.
5. Ability to detect logical consistency or inconsistency in a set of statements.
6. Ability to think in relativistic ways about self, others, and the world.

(Acredolo, Adams & Schmid, 1984). Second, they are able to think about things changing in the future; they can realize, for instance, that their relationship with their parents will be very different in ten years' time. Third, they are able to hypothesize about a logical sequence of possible events; for example, they are able to predict college and occupational options that may be open to them, depending on how well they do in certain academic coursework in high school. Fourth, they are able to anticipate consequences of their actions. For instance, they realize that if they drop out of school, certain career possibilities will be closed to them. The fact they can do so enables them to achieve a prior knowledge of the possible outcomes of doing something and allows them to decide on that basis whether or not they wish to do it.

Fifth, they have the capacity to detect the logical consistency or inconsistency in a set of statements. They can test the truth of a statement by finding evidence that supports or disproves the statement. They are troubled, for example, by the apparent contradictions between statements such as "All men are equal before the law" and the possibility of a presidential pardon for certain high-status lawbreakers. Sixth, they are able to think in a relativistic way about themselves, other individuals, and their world. They can draw upon many variables to explain their behavior as well as the behavior of others. Table 9.1 gives a synopsis of the conceptual skills.

They know that they are expected to act in a particular way because of the norms of their community and culture. They also know that in other families, communities, and cultures different norms may govern the same behavior. As a result, the decision to behave in a culturally accepted manner becomes a more conscious commitment to the society. At the same time, it is easier for them to accept members of other cultures, because they realize that these people are the products of societies with different sets of rules and norms (O'Mahoney, 1989).

In general, the changes in conceptual development that occur during early adolescence result in a more flexible, critical, and abstract view of the world. The abilities to hypothesize logical sequences of action, to conceptualize change, and to anticipate consequences of actions all contribute to a more realistic sense of the future (Klineberg, 1967; Lessing, 1972). The view of the future includes both hopes, such as career goals, educational attainment, and beginning a family, and fears, such as concerns about unemployment or the possibility of war (Nurmi, 1987; Gillies, 1989).

The transition to formal thinking is neither sudden nor uniform across all problem areas. For example, Neimark (1975) followed changes in problem-solving strategies over a 3½-year period. Even the oldest subjects in her study, who were 15, did not apply formal operational strategies across all problems. In a study of formal operational thinking among 13-year-olds, other researchers found few significant correlations in performance on six different measures (Overton & Meehan, 1982). Although performance across problems was not consistent, there did appear to be a progression through levels of problem-solving approaches during the years from 11 to 15. Neimark (1982) has described these levels as (1) no rule, (2) limited rules, (3) collection of rules or unelaborated principles, and (4) general principles.

Egocentrism

The term *egocentrism* refers to the child's limited perspective at the beginning of each new phase of cognitive development (Piaget, 1926; Inhelder & Piaget, 1958). In the sensorimotor phase, egocentrism appears as an inability to separate one's actions from their effects on specific objects or people. As the scheme for causality is developed, the first process of decentering occurs. Infants recognize that certain actions have predictable consequences and that novel situations call for new, relevant behaviors— for example, one cannot turn the light on by turning the knob on the radio.

In the phase of preoperational thought, egocentrism is manifested in an inability to separate one's own perspective from that of the listener. When a 4-year-old girl tells you about something that happened to her at the zoo, she may explain events as if you had seen them too. When a 3-year-old boy is explaining something to his grandmother over the phone, he may point to objects in the room, unaware that his grandmother cannot see over the phone lines.

The third phase of heightened egocentrism occurs in the transition from concrete to formal operational thought. As children develop the capacity to formulate hypothetical systems, they begin to generate assumptions about their own and others' behavior that will fit into these abstract formulations. For example, an early adolescent boy may insist that cooperation is a more desirable mode of interaction than competition. He believes that in theory, cooperation ought to benefit each participant and provide more resources for the group as a whole. This boy may become angry or disillusioned to discover that teachers, parents, and even peers seek competitive experiences and appear to enjoy them. He may think, "If the cooperative system is so superior, why do people persist in their illogical joy in triumphing over an opponent?" This kind of egocentrism reflects an inability to recognize that others may not share one's own hypothetical system.

In early adolescence, decentering requires an ability to realize that one's ideals are not shared by all others. We live in a pluralistic society in which each person is likely to have distinct goals and aspirations. Early adolescents gradually discover that their neat, logical life plans must be constantly adapted to the expectations and needs of relevant others. As they develop the flexibility of thought that accompanies formal operational perspective taking, their egocentrism should decline. Social acceptance also reduces egocentrism. Early adolescents who are confident of their parents' emotional support are less self-conscious than those who experience parental rejection or overcontrol (Riley, Adams & Nielsen, 1984).

Early adolescent egocentrism has two characteristics that may affect social interaction as well as problem solving. First, early adolescents are preoccupied by their

Pablo Picasso, *Boy with a Pipe,* 1905. This boy has an air of detachment, almost as if his thoughts and fantasies were more real than the world around him. This is one aspect of the quality we recognize as adolescent egocentrism.

own thoughts. They may become somewhat withdrawn and isolated as the domain of their consciousness expands. Thoughts about the possible and the probable, the near and the distant future, and the logical extension of contemporary events to future consequences all flood their minds. This tendency to withdraw into their own speculations may cut off access to new information or ideas. Second, early adolescents may assume that others share their preoccupations. Instead of considering that everyone is equally wrapped up in his or her own concerns and plans, early adolescents envision their own thoughts as being the focus of other people's attention (Elkind, 1967). This subjectivity generates an uncomfortable self-consciousness that makes interaction awkward.

We begin to see early adolescence as a time in which young people's ideas of reality take on convincing intensity. Early adolescents are likely to believe that their interpretations of interactions are correct and therefore are less flexible in considering alternative possibilities. Needless to say, egocentrism is a problem not only during these years. At each new phase of expanding awareness, people tend to rely heavily on their own experiences and perceptions in order to minimize the anxiety associated with uncertainty. Part of the progress of formal thought implies a reliance on reason over experience. We have more confidence in what we know than in what we can see or hear. Thus we can find ourselves trapped in an egocentric perspective. We may interpret new experiences as examples of familiar concepts rather than as novel events. We may reject evidence for an argument because it does not support an already carefully developed explanation. The business of casting around for new evidence and new explanations is a lifelong challenge. It is much easier to rely on earlier assumptions than to continually call one's perspective into question.

Factors That Promote Formal Operational Thought

Several environmental conditions facilitate the development of formal operational thought and reduce egocentrism. First, early adolescents begin to function in a variety of role relationships that place both compatible and conflicting demands on them. Among these role relationships are son or daughter, worker, student, friend, dating partner, religious believer, and citizen. Early adolescents experience at firsthand the pressures of multiple expectations for behavior. At times, for example, expectations for the student role may be at odds with those for the child or the friend role. Ongoing interactions with parents provide a powerful stimulus for cognitive development, especially when parents encourage children to examine their assumptions, to find evidence to support their arguments, and to evaluate the sources of information as they approach problems in daily life (Dunham, Kidwell & Portes, 1988).

Early adolescents must learn to manipulate and balance these demands. In order to do so successfully, they must learn to manipulate mentally more than two variables at any one time. The experience of participating in a variety of roles also facilitates relativistic thinking by demonstrating that what is acceptable and valued in one situation may not be acceptable or valued in another (Chandler & Boyes, 1982).

The second environmental condition that facilitates the development of the cognitive skills of early adolescence is the adolescent's participation in a more heterogeneous peer group (Looft, 1971). When children move from their community elementary school to a more centralized junior high and high school, they are likely to become acquainted with other students whose family backgrounds and social class are different from their own. In working and playing with these children, they realize the extent to which their expectations for the future differ from those of their new acquaintances and the extent to which their present values are shaped by the families and neighborhood from which they come.

The third condition that fosters the development of the cognitive skills of early adolescence is the content of the high school curriculum. Courses in science, mathematics, and language formally expose the student to the logical relationships inherent in the world. The student is also formally introduced to the hypothetico-deductive style of reasoning. The fine arts and the humanities foster imaginary conceptions of ways in which the world has been or might be. In sum, the gains in conceptual skill made during early adolescence are facilitated by the person's active involvement in a more complex and differentiated academic environment (Kuhn, Amsel & O'Loughlin, 1988; Rabinowitz, 1988; Linn et al., 1989).

We do not expect to see a mature scientist or a profound philosopher by the end of early adolescence. Formal operational thought still has to be brought to bear on the reality of significant problems. There is a process of rejecting or building on strategies that have been acquired earlier. However, the opportunity for cognitive growth during this period is extensive. Adolescents are capable of generating novel solutions and applying them to current life challenges. They also are able to be objective about the problem-solving process and to gain insight into their own mental activity.

Emotional Development

Many descriptions of adolescence refer to new levels of emotional variability, moodiness, and emotional outbursts. Adolescents clearly are more aware than younger children of gradations in their emotional states and are able to attribute emotions to a wider range of causes. However, some researchers have questioned whether adolescence really brings the peaks and valleys of emotional intensity that are stereotypically linked to this time of life.

In an attempt to assess this question, researchers gave an electronic paging device to children and adolescents aged 9 through 15 and asked them to describe their emotional state every time they were paged. Over one week, each participant responded about 37 times. The variability of emotions was not found to increase with age. However, both boys and girls in the older group expressed fewer extremely positive emotions and more mildly negative emotions than did children in the younger group. This finding suggests that rather than experiencing new levels of intensity in positive and negative emotions, adolescents have fewer daily experiences of outright joy and more experiences of the mildly negative emotions that we tend to call moodiness or apathy (Larson & Lampman-Petraitis, 1989).

Adolescents are aware of a more differentiated palette of emotions. Among the more troublesome of these emotions are anxiety, shame, embarrassment, guilt, shyness, depression, and anger (Adelson & Doehrman, 1980). Adolescent girls are likely to have a heightened awareness of new levels of negative emotions that focus inward, such as shame, guilt, and depression; boys are likely to have a heightened awareness of new levels of negative emotions that focus on others, such as contempt and aggression (Stapley & Haviland, 1989; Ostrov, Offer & Howard, 1989).

Given the likelihood of a more differentiated range of emotions during adolescence, a major task is to gain a tolerance for one's emotionality. This means accepting one's feelings and not interpreting them as a sign of "going crazy" or being "strange." Adolescents who are highly sensitive to social expectations or overly controlled about expressing or accepting their feelings will probably experience a sense of shame about their emotional states. Attempts to rigidly control or defend against feelings are likely to result in social alienation or the development of maladaptive behaviors.

In a study of the coping style of adolescents, Moriarty and Toussieng (1976) summarized the basic orientation toward emotions that is achieved during this life stage. The subjects were described as either *sensers* or *censors*. The sensers were willing to be influenced by new experiences. They preferred to seek out new activities, engage people, and question inconsistencies. They accepted their emotions and sought out experiences that would modify their values. The censors preferred to limit their sensory experiences. They tried to clarify their parents' values by discovering what was acceptable in society. They had limited peer interaction and were uninvolved with school. They rejected experiences or ideas that did not confirm their traditional

Adolescents periodically feel discouraged and depressed. They have to learn coping strategies that will renew their optimism.

views. Both sensers and censors are normal, healthy adolescents whose coping styles will work in our society. However, the two orientations reflect rather distinct solutions to the challenge of integrating emotional experiences into the self-concept.

One consequence of anxiety and overcontrol of emotions is a disorder known as *anorexia nervosa* (Yates, 1989). Adolescents with this condition cannot regulate their eating behavior. They experience intense eating binges, followed by prolonged avoidance of food. During the latter phase, they are continuously nauseous and have trouble holding food down. The outcome of this condition is a potentially life-threatening loss of weight. The origins of anorexia nervosa are not fully understood. However, adolescents who suffer from this condition do tend to have difficulty accepting and expressing their emotions. As compared with adolescents who have other types of emotional disorders, anorexics show less emotional expressivity, greater timidity, and more submissiveness. Anorexics have been described as "duty bound, rigidly disciplined, and moralistic with underlying doubts and anxious hesitancy" (Strober, 1981, pp. 289–290).

In contrast to adolescents whose overcontrol of emotions can be problematic are others who are impulsive and highly reactive to any emotionally arousing environmental stimulus. They seem to be unable to modify the intensity of their reactions. A consequence of this impulsiveness for a large proportion of normal adolescents is involvement in delinquent acts. "Over 80 percent of American adolescents admit to committing one or more delinquent acts, most of these minor, in the course of a few years of adolescence" (Gold & Petronio, 1980, p. 523). The inability to exert intellectual control over their impulses may be a passing experience for most young people. The fear and guilt that follow a delinquent act are enough of a punishment to prevent further violations. For some adolescents, however, committing several delinquent acts weakens the ability to impose social constraints on such behavior, and the involvement in delinquency intensifies.

One of the emotions that is receiving considerable attention in the recent literature is depression (Garrison et al., 1989; Robertson & Simons, 1989). *Depression* refers to feelings of sadness, a loss of hope, a sense of being overwhelmed by the demands of the world, and general despair. Almost everyone experiences depression at some time or another. You may refer to it as the "blues," feeling "down in the dumps," or feeling "low." People who suffer from depression may experience other symptoms, including worrying, moodiness, crying, loss of appetite, difficulty sleeping, tiredness, loss of interest or enjoyment in activities, and difficulty concentrating. Depression can range from mild, short-lived periods of feeling sad and discouraged to severe feelings of guilt and worthlessness.

Depression is of special concern during early adolescence for several reasons (Maag, Rutherford & Parks, 1988). First, it is associated with adolescent suicide. Although depression is not always a precursor to suicide, there is some link between depression and thoughts of suicide. Second, depression is linked to alcohol and drug abuse. Adolescents who are struggling with strong feelings of depression may turn to alcohol or other drugs as a way of trying to alleviate or escape from these feelings. Third, adolescents who are depressed may be unable to participate effectively in the classroom, so that their academic performance deteriorates. Finally, depression during adolescence may be a forerunner of severe depression later in adulthood.

Experiences of parental loss or parental rejection have been found to increase an adolescent's vulnerability to depression (Robertson & Simons, 1989). In addition, adolescence is a time of life when one is likely to encounter loss, failure, and rejection. Adolescents are inexperienced at coping with these kinds of life crises. They may not have developed strategies for interrupting or reducing the feelings of grief or discouragement that are likely to accompany stressful life events. The feelings of depression may be intensified by accompanying hormonal changes. Young people may become convinced of their worthlessness, and this distortion of thought may lead them toward social withdrawal or self-destructive actions.

Membership in the Peer Group

We pointed out the importance of peer interaction for psychological development in Chapters 7 and 8. During early adolescence, the peer group tends to become more structured and organized than it was previously (Newman, 1982). The implications of the individual's relation to the peer group are more clearly defined than they were earlier. Before the adolescent period, it is important to have friends but not so important to be a member of a definable group. The child's friends are often found in the neighborhood, local clubs, community centers, or classrooms. Friendship groups are homogeneous. They are the product of informal associations, residential area, and convenience. In early adolescence, young people spend more time away from home. Talking with friends, either in person or on the telephone, becomes a dominant daily activity, especially for girls (Raffaelli & Duckett, 1989). Peer-group friendships begin to provide opportunities for emotional intimacy, support, and understanding as well

Members of a particular peer group can be identified by the way they dress, their language, and the places where they get together.

as companionship and fun. Early adolescents have the cognitive skills to consider the needs and feelings of others. The qualities of self-disclosure and intimate knowledge of the other become more central to the formation and maintenance of adolescent friendships (Berndt, 1982; Tedesco & Gaier, 1988).

In the more heterogeneous environment of the high school, there is a reordering of students according to a variety of abilities and a corresponding reordering of friendships. Friendships become more intimate and more selective. One adolescent boy whose friendship had ended described the process as follows:

> *[My friend] is trying to single out his friends now. At the beginning of the year, he was friends with almost everybody because he wanted to be friends over the school year with a lot of kids. Now he's singling out best friends.*   [Berndt & Hoyle, 1985, p. 1013]

When the "leading crowd" of a particular neighborhood elementary or middle school goes off to a more centralized high school, the members of that group find that they are, to some degree, competing with the "leading crowds" of the other neighborhood schools from which the high school draws its students. After some contact at the high school, the several "leading crowds" are reordered into a single "leading crowd." Some students find that their social positions have been maintained or enhanced, whereas others find them to have deteriorated somewhat as a result of a reevaluation of their abilities, skills, or traits.

Popularity and acceptance into a peer group at the high school level may be based on one or more of the following characteristics: good looks, athletic ability, social class, academic performance, future goals, affiliation with a religious, racial, or ethnic group, and special talents. Although the criteria for membership may not be publicly

Box 9.1 Interracial Friendships Among High School Students

One of the anticipated outcomes of the movement to desegregate America's schools was that through opportunities for daily cross-race interactions, children would form interracial friendships and thereby reduce the level of racism in the society. To what extent are black-white friendships being formed during the high school years?

Drawing upon a national sample of over 58,000 sophomores and seniors at more than 1,000 public and private high schools in the United States, researchers attempted to address this question (Hallinan & Williams, 1989). They considered the possible dyadic (two-person) groups that could be formed among students, and then asked whether a friendship existed in these dyads. In other words, of all the two-person groups in a school, how many are friendships in which person A says that person B is a friend? The results showed that cross-race friendships were quite rare. When all factors are taken into account, such as school size and

the proportion of black students in a school, same-race friendships were six times more likely than cross-race friendships. However, cross-race friendships were more likely to be reciprocated than same-race friendships. If student A named someone of another race as a friend, that person was very likely to name student A as a friend as well.

The results of this analysis are disappointing. Of more than 18,000 friendships identified by students, only about 350 involved black and white friends. There was no relationship between the proportion of black students in a school and the likelihood of identifying interracial friendships. The data do not address the possibility that racial attitudes are influenced by participation in racially diverse schools. They do, however, alert us to the fact that the natural process of friendship formation will not lead to greater levels of interracial interaction without some additional structural or curricular intervention.

articulated, the groups tend to include or exclude members according to consistent standards. Physical attractiveness continues to be a powerful force in determining popularity. Especially for very attractive and unattractive adolescents, physical appearance may be a primary determinant of social acceptance or rejection (Cavior & Dokecki, 1973; Musa & Roach, 1973). Some of the well-known peer groups present in American high schools today are affectionately called *frats* or *preppies, greasers* or *hoods, athletes* or *jocks,* and *hippies* or *druggies.* A new group, affectionately called the *mods* or the *progressives,* expressly rejects this traditional social stratification. The mods emphasize individuality and the value of forming a personal identity. In setting themselves apart from the other groups, however, they form a new one (Stevenson et al., 1987). Each of these groups can be identified within a school setting by their dress, their language, the activities in which they participate, and the school settings in which they are most likely to congregate.

Individual adolescents are faced with a variety of choices for peer-group membership. Upon entering high school, they come in contact with a number of people who may offer their friendship. This is the informal route to membership in a peer group. The adolescent learns to look beyond the initial offer of friendship and to assess the group from which the potential friend comes. The person may decide to accept the friendship or reject it on the basis of the reputation of the potential friend's peer-group association (see Box 9.1).

Peer groups have boundaries. Some students try to push their way into a certain high-status group. Others may fall out of a crowd. Dating someone of a higher status or getting involved in a high-status school activity (such as athletics or cheerleading) may be a way of moving into a new peer group. When the school population is relatively stable, however, it is very difficult to lose the group identity that has already been established (Jones, 1976). What is more likely is that through gossip, refusal to adhere to group norms, or failure in heterosexual relationships, individuals can slip outside the boundaries of their cliques and lose access to the larger social crowd.

An important skill that is learned in becoming a member of a peer group is the ability to assess the group structure and select the particular group or groups with which one would like to affiliate. As one begins to develop a focused peer-group affiliation, one becomes aware of that group's internal structure and norms (Dunphy, 1963). For adolescents, the structure may include patterns of dominance, dating, and relationships with others outside the group. Associated with each of these dimensions of social structure are sets of norms or expectations for the behavior of the peer-group members. As adolescents discover their positions in the dominance hierarchy of the group, they learn how they may advance within it and what behaviors are expected of members at various levels. On the basis of all this information, they must decide whether their personal growth is compatible with the peer-group affiliation they have made. Generally, adolescents do not abandon the initial peer group unless such a change offers the potential for a considerable gain in status. Further, adolescents quickly become bound to a peer group because of the expectations of others both within and outside it.

We suggest that membership in an adolescent peer group is a forerunner of membership in an adult social group. Adolescent peer groups are somewhat less organized than their adult counterparts, but they are considerably more structured than childhood friendship groups. Through peer-group membership, adolescents begin to learn techniques for assessing the organization of social groups and their own positions within them. They develop aspirations for advancing their own social standing. In addition, they gain some insight into the rewards and costs of extensive group identification. Although the actual friends made during adolescence may change as one grows older, the social skills learned at this time provide a long-lasting basis for functioning in a mature social group.

Parents and Peers

How does involvement with peers during early adolescence relate to closeness with family members? Do adolescents abandon family interactions and values for peer interaction and peer values? Is closeness with peers an attempt to compensate for a lack of closeness with parents, or does the intimacy achieved with parents extend outward to a circle of friends? Adolescents describe a variety of overt signs of independence from family. They may make decisions about clothes, dating, and so on; they may have cars; they may stay out late; and they may earn their own money. However, they maintain an emotional attachment to their families and to the value orientations of their families.

The attachment of adolescents to family has been confirmed by recent research. One study assessed relations between parents and boys and girls in grades 4, 7, 10, and college (Hunter & Youniss, 1982). Three dimensions of the relationship were measured: control, nurturance, and intimacy (see Figure 9.2). Children at each age

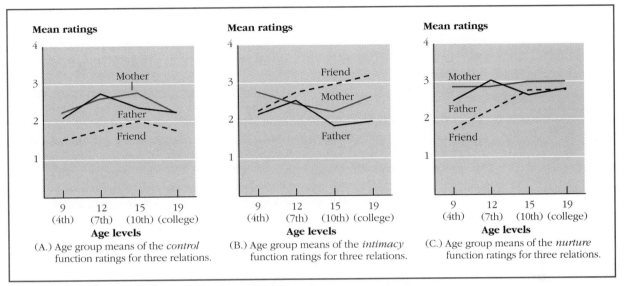

Mean ratings

(A.) Age group means of the *control* function ratings for three relations.

(B.) Age group means of the *intimacy* function ratings for three relations.

(C.) Age group means of the *nurture* function ratings for three relations.

Figure 9.2   **Changes in Functions of Three Relations During Adolescence**
Source: F. T. Hunter and J. Youniss, "Changes in Functions of Three Relations during Adolescence," *Developmental Psychology, 18,* 806–811. Copyright 1982 by the American Psychological Association. Reprinted by permission.

level perceived their parents as exerting more control over them than did their friends. Parents were perceived to be more nurturant than friends by fourth- and seventh-graders and as nurturant as friends by tenth-graders and college students. Beginning in seventh grade, adolescents perceived their relationships with friends as more intimate than those with parents. Mothers were perceived as remaining at a constant level of intimacy across all ages. Fathers were perceived as declining in intimacy from seventh to tenth grade and as remaining constant in intimacy from tenth grade through college. This trend supports a developmental pattern in the formation of close friendships. Intimacy between a child and his or her mother during the middle school years provides a basis for establishing close, affectionate relationships with adolescent friends (Gold & Yanof, 1985). With respect to three major functions of a social relationship—control, nurturance, and intimacy—parents were viewed as more prominent than peers or as prominent as peers on two dimensions across the whole age range.

What is the nature of parent-adolescent interaction? How do differences in its quality influence the adolescent's well-being? These questions have been addressed in a variety of ways. One approach has been to investigate the amount and quality of time adolescents spend with their parents. In one study, more than 400 students in grades 10 through 12 were asked to tell how many times they interacted with a variety of people during a day when they were not in school (Newman, 1979). These adolescents reported an average of 13.5 daily interactions with parents and about the same number with close friends. In another study, adolescents were given an electronic paging device. During the hours from 8 A.M. to 11 P.M., they were paged five to seven times. Each time they were paged, they were to write down what they were doing, why they were doing it, and how they were feeling. Only about 6% of the total number of observations involved interactions with adults. These adolescents reported feeling more excited when they interacted with adults but also more constrained, passive, and weak than when they interacted with peers (Czikszentmihalyi, Larson & Prescott, 1977).

Montemayor (1982) interviewed tenth-graders about how they spent time during the day. They spent most of their free time with peers, less with parents, and least alone. They spent most of their task time alone, less with parents, and least with peers. Boys spent more time with their fathers and girls more time with their mothers. Boys and girls spent about the same amount of time with both parents together. The interactions with parents were not especially conflictual. Over a three-day period, male adolescents reported an average of 0.85 conflicts with parents and females 1.21 conflicts. Conflicts between girls and their mothers were the most frequent and the most intense.

Time spent at home in positive interactions with adults appears to have positive consequences for adolescents. In a study of eighth-graders, time spent at home was positively related to perceptions of the family environment as intellectually and culturally stimulating. There was a strong relationship between time spent at home in leisure and recreational activity and a sense of well-being (McMillan & Hiltonsmith, 1982). At the opposite end of the continuum, experiences of parental rejection or neglect are closely linked to low self-esteem and depression (Robertson & Simons, 1989; Rosenberg, Schooler & Schoenbach, 1989).

Time spent in public with adults appeared to be more conflictual. Adolescents who reported a high level of parental companionship also reported feeling self-conscious about and preoccupied by the evaluations of others (Adams & Jones, 1982). Although adolescents may feel good about being affectionate and close with their parents, they are also sensitive to perceived expectations that adolescents and parents should not be too chummy. Although frequent open communication between adolescents and their parents contributes to a positive relationship, it is misleading to assume that these interactions are always positive in tone. It is hard work for parents and adolescents to keep channels of communication open.

As adolescents go through puberty, conflicts with their parents increase. Conversations are marked by new levels of assertiveness on both sides (Papini & Sebby, 1988; Papini, Datan & McClusky-Fawcett, 1988). Resolutions of these family conflicts lead to the establishment of a new balance of power or control within the family (Feldman & Gehring, 1988). This balance appears to be negotiated somewhat differently by males and females.

Steinberg (1981) described parent-child interactions among boys aged 11 to 14 and their parents. As boys proceed through puberty, the parents increasingly interrupt their sons and the boys increasingly interrupt their mothers. The parents' explanations decline, and family interactions become more rigid. After the period of rapid pubertal growth, adolescent-parent conflicts subside somewhat. Mothers interrupt their sons less, and sons become increasingly deferential to their fathers. This pattern of a hierarchical alignment in the family, with father and son dominating mother, had been observed in earlier studies of adolescent-child relationships (Jacob, 1974).

Parents and adolescent children are likely to feel secure in their relationship if they can communicate about their disagreements.

The pattern for girls is bit different (Hill, 1988). In the months following menarche, parents interrupt their daughters more during conversations. Girls are more likely to yield to the interruptions of their mothers, but they do not tend to yield to their fathers' interruptions. Daughters assert themselves with their mothers through a high frequency of interruptions and with their fathers by an unwillingness to yield the conversation when their fathers interrupt them. Over time, parents notably increase their explanations when their opinions differ from their daughter's, suggesting a new respect for the daughter's independent views and indicating a new definition of her power in the family.

A consequence of frequent, reasonable interactions is that parents can be more effective in communicating their expectations and learning about their child's point of view. Parents and adolescents are quite familiar with each other's views (LoSciuto & Karlin, 1972; Lerner, 1975). In one study, parents and adolescents completed the Offer Self-Image Questionnaire (OSIQ) (Offer, Ostrov & Howard, 1982). Out of 38 items, there were only 12 in which the parents' and the adolescents' endorsements differed by more than 10%. Parents tended to underestimate the importance of their children's having girlfriends or boyfriends. They also underestimated the extent to which their children found dirty jokes amusing. Parents thought that peers found their children more attractive than the children believed they did. Parents thought that their sons' feelings were more easily hurt than the sons thought they were. Parents thought that their daughters were more confident and more ready to enter the competition of adult life than the daughters thought they were. Parents thought that both their sons and their daughters were less able to take criticism and learn from others than the children thought they were. This discrepancy may result from the fact that children are more willing to take criticism and learn from others than they are from their parents.

This picture of parent-adolescent views is confirmed in a study describing adolescents' discussions with their parents and peers (Hunter, 1985). Over the age ranges 12 to 13 and 14 to 15, adolescents discussed academic/vocational, social/ethical, and family relations topics more often with their parents than with their friends. However, they discussed peer relations more with their friends. This finding suggests that parents really may not have as much information about their children's peer relations as about other important topics. Although adolescents generally perceive their parents as willing to explain their opinions and understanding of their points of view, in the domain of peer relations there is a noticeable contrast. In this one area, adolescents are likely to perceive low levels of understanding on the part of parents.

It is important to consider that early adolescence comes close on the heels of middle childhood. It does not make sense to assume that shortly after a period of intense socialization and dependence a child would be eager to reject most of what has been learned at home. Young adolescents are still very attached to their parents. It is unlikely that they would feel prepared to face life without their parents' emotional support and approval. Thus the parent-child conflict of early adolescence is one of achieving autonomy while preserving the bonds of affection and goodwill that have been formed earlier. There is a dynamic tension between remaining a valued, loved member of the family group and having the freedom to explore new relationships and new visions of the self.

Sexual Relationships

During adolescence, peer relationships are modified through the introduction of sexual interests and behavior. The impetus for this increased interest in sexual relationships stems from both social expectations and sexual maturation. Udry and Billy (1987) devised a model to explain the transition to coitus in early adolescence (see Figure 9.3). In that model, three basic dimensions account for the adolescent's initiation of sexual activity: motivation, social controls, and attractiveness. Motivation can be accounted for by biological factors, especially new levels of hormone production; by a new level of desire to achieve independence and to engage in adult behaviors; and by certain internalized norms and attitudes that may either encourage or reduce the motivation for sexual activity. The social controls provide the normative environment within which sexual activity is embedded. According to the model, these controls are a product of parental socialization and practices, school achievement and educational aspirations, and the attitudes and sexual experiences of friends. One might add here the influence of religious beliefs and values. The third dimension, attractiveness, will influence the availability of partners. Attractiveness is defined in part by pubertal maturation, in part by social acceptance or popularity, and in part by whether one is judged to be pretty or handsome.

In an effort to assess this model, the researchers found that the transition to sexual intercourse for white boys was most strongly predicted by hormonal levels and by popularity with the opposite sex. The norms for transition to sexual activity may be so clear for males that it is difficult to find many factors that can account for the transition. For white girls, the various social controls, including parents, school

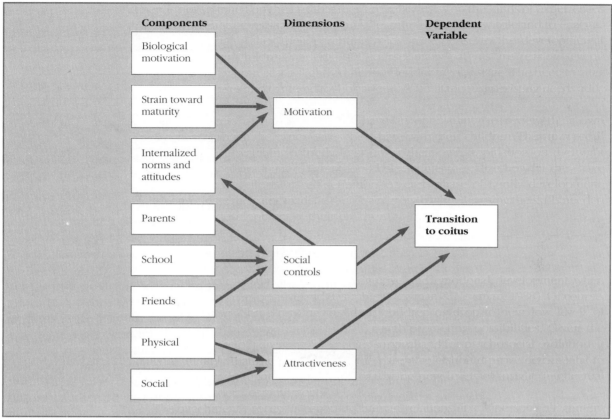

Figure 9.3   Model of Transition to Coitus in Early Adolescence

Source: J. R. Udry and J. O. Billy, "Initiation of Coitus in Early Adolescence," *American Sociological Review,* *52* (1987), 842. Reprinted by permission.

achievement, and friends' attitudes and behaviors, all played an important part in predicting sexual intercourse.

This research supports the notion that particularly for girls hormone levels alone do not account for adolescents' involvement in sexual activities. These activities are embedded in a social context. Parental values, educational expectations, the capacity of parents to exercise appropriate control over their child's social and school activities, and the norms of the peer group all play their parts in a young person's willingness to become sexually active (Brooks-Gunn & Furstenberg, 1989; Newcomer & Udry, 1987; Hanson, Myers & Ginsburg, 1987).

One of the clearest contextual influences on adolescent sexual behavior is religious participation. Adolescents who attend religious services frequently and who value religion as an important aspect of their lives have less permissive attitudes toward premarital sex. This finding applies equally to Catholic, Protestant, and Jewish young people. The relationship is accentuated for adolescents who describe themselves as fundamentalist Protestant or Baptist. However, an adolescent's attitudes toward premarital sex are shaped by many factors in addition to their religious socialization.

Table 9.2   Percentage of White High School and College Students Reporting Premarital Sexual Intercourse at Three Historical Periods

| | High School | | College | |
Period	Boys	Girls	Boys	Girls
1925–1965	25	10	55	25
1966–1973	35	35	85	65
1974–1979	56	44	74	74

Source: P. H. Dreyer, "Sexuality during Adolescence," in B. B. Wolman (ed.), *Handbook of Developmental Psychology* (p. 575). Copyright © 1982. Reprinted by permission of Prentice-Hall, Inc., Englewood Cliffs, N.J.

By the time young people are making independent decisions about religious participation, they also have opinions about whether or not they believe in premarital sex. Thus those young people who have more permissive views about sex are less likely to attend religious services and find less satisfaction in religious participation (Thornton & Camburn, 1989).

Dating relationships during early adolescence provide the initial context for sexual activity. One of the strongest predictors of early sexual activity is early age of dating. Adolescents who "go steady" are much more likely to be sexually active than are those who do not (Hanson, Myers & Ginsburg, 1987). The cultural trend has been toward earlier involvement in sexual intercourse and toward greater sexual activity among girls. Table 9.2 provides a historical review of the percentage of white high school and college students reporting premarital sexual intercourse (Dreyer, 1982). These data are a composite of information derived from studies of adolescent sexuality conducted during three periods. The percentage of boys and girls at the high school level reporting sexual intercourse increased consistently after 1925. In the period from 1974 to 1979, more than half of the boys and a bit less than half of the girls had experienced intercourse. Interestingly, at the college level there was an increase for girls at each period but a decrease for boys from 1966–1973 to 1974–1979.

Data gathered in the early 1980s describe the developmental path of initiation into sexual activity by race and gender (Hofferth & Hayes, 1987). Sixty percent of white males had intercourse by age 18, 60% of white females by age 19. Sixty percent of black males had intercourse by age 16, 60% of black females by age 18. Over 40% of black males had initiated sexual activity by age 15 or earlier. The gender differences are especially significant in that females enter puberty almost two years earlier than males, yet they lag behind males in initiation of sexual intercourse. Cultural factors clearly play a role here.

Of course, sexual relationships do not necessarily involve intercourse. Many levels of sexual activity, from handholding to heavy petting, are involved in becoming a sexual adult. What is more, initial experiences with sexual intercourse do not necessarily result in a pattern of frequent sexual activity. For example, boys who experience an early-pubertal sexual initiation may not have another sexual experience for a year or more (Brooks-Gunn & Furstenberg, 1989).

Most young people are involved in a variety of romantic relationships. Some early adolescents are sexually permissive and are regularly active in sex play, from petting to intercourse. Other early adolescents are much less physically active. Some of these people may remain relatively uninterested in sexual relationships; others think about sexual relationships a good deal. The way one thinks about sexual relationships can vary. Some early adolescents become occupied with thoughts of very romantic, beautiful relationships. Some become infatuated with rock stars, athletes, movie stars, or other sex symbols. Others manifest rather perverse obsessions with sexual material. Whatever the resulting adult sexual orientation, it can be assumed that the early-adolescent awakenings are representative of a system that is just being started up and tested out. With proper self-monitoring, social support, and socialization, most people are able to bring the sexual system under control and to integrate sexual impulses with other social needs.

The sexual system is one of the most problematic components of psychosocial development for young people in the United States. Most parents do not feel comfortable discussing sexuality with their children. In addition to private thoughts, impulses, and fantasies, which may result in feelings of guilt or confusion, the young person confronts conflicting messages about sexual behavior from peers, the mass media, and the religious community. New risks of sexually transmitted diseases, especially concerns about AIDS, introduce anxiety about the expression of sexual impulses. On television and in films young people see numerous examples of sexual intimacy that suggest that sexual gratification ought to be more immediate and more satisfying than it is likely to be in real life. What is more, the emotional closeness and understanding they may seek in a sexually intimate relationship are often not found. The sex-linked problems that many people encounter—unintended pregnancy, marital infidelity, rape, child sexual abuse, pornography, sexually transmitted diseases—are evidence that the socialization process is failing to promote mature sexuality in significant numbers of adolescents and adults in the United States.

Parenthood in Early Adolescence

One of the consequences of early entry into sexual activity can be adolescent pregnancy. To get a sense of the magnitude of this issue, consider the following data. In 1983, 500,000 live children were born to women aged 19 or younger and 427,000 legal abortions were performed on women in this age group. Close to a million adolescent girls in that year experienced pregnancy, and almost half terminated the pregnancy through abortion, a good indicator that the pregnancy was unwanted (U.S. Bureau of the Census, 1987).

Social policies advocating the prevention of early pregnancy and the role of public programs in family planning and abortion tend to emphasize the negative consequences of pregnancy for adolescent girls and their babies. However, studies of pregnant adolescents generally find that these girls do not differ much in attitudes, mental health, or cognitive abilities from those who are sexually active but have not gotten pregnant. We must be careful not to label a group of adolescents as deviant simply because they have gotten pregnant.

A critical factor in explaining the high rate of adolescent pregnancy is the ambivalence of American parents, teachers, and teens toward contraception. In comparison with adolescents in many European countries, the majority of American adolescents do not integrate contraception into their view of natural sexual activity. American adolescents are largely uninformed about the variety of methods of contraception and their relation to the biological factors that prevent pregnancy (Morrison, 1985). One study of sexually active adolescent girls reported that only 35% consistently used contraceptives, 27% never used them, and 39% were inconsistent in their use. The result of this inconsistent use or rejection of contraception was that 32% became pregnant (Zelnik & Kantner, 1980).

Use or nonuse of contraceptives is associated with religious beliefs, family attitudes and behaviors, and peer norms. For example, low-income black adolescents have more negative attitudes toward birth control than white adolescents, and they value fertility more. Thus black girls who are sexually active are less likely to use contraceptives (Edelman & Pittman, 1986; Pete & DeSantis, 1990). About 40% of adolescent girls believe contraception is the responsibility of the male, but most males are ineffective or inconsistent in their use of contraceptives (Franklin, 1988). These attitudes and values in regard to contraception, coupled with lack of concrete knowledge about how to use them, help us understand why the technology of contraception is not as successful among sexually active American youth as it might be.

The phenomenon of teenage parenthood is a complex one that touches the lives of the adolescent mother and father, the child or children born to them, their parents, and the schools, counseling services, and family planning services that have been developed to help very young parents cope with parenthood (Franklin, 1988). The consequences of teenage pregnancy and parenthood for the young mother and her infant depend on the psychosocial context within which the pregnancy occurs. The key factors appear to be the ability to retain adequate social supports through continued relationships with the baby's father and her own parents and friends and the ability to maintain sufficient financial support (Barth, Schinke & Maxwell, 1983). When these resources are lacking or when they diminish in the years after childbirth, the mental health of the adolescent mother, her educational and occupational attainment, and her subsequent ability to care for her child can very well be jeopardized.

One of the great paradoxes of adolescent parenthood is the contrast between young girls' aspirations about mothering and the actual experience of child rearing. Here are the comments of two young mothers:

Ann (14): When I got pregnant, my parents wanted me to have an abortion, but I'm an only child, and it's a lonely feeling when you're an only child. I just said, "Well, I'm going to keep the baby because now I'll have somebody I'll feel close to, instead of being lonely all the time." [Fosburgh, 1977, p. 34]

Mary (17): It was great, 'cause now I got him and nobody can take him away from me. He's mine, I made him, he's great. Something real can give me happiness. He can make me laugh and he can make me cry and he can make me mad. [Konopka, 1976, p. 39]

Many adolescents do not have the emotional, social, or financial resources to sustain the kind of caring relationship they envision with their children. They may be unable to anticipate that their own needs must often be sacrificed to their babies'

One of the greatest risks in adolescent pregnancy is that the young mother will interrupt her education and drastically reduce her chances for economic self-sufficiency.

needs. One outcome of this discrepancy between aspirations and reality is an outpouring of the young mother's hostility toward her baby. The risk of child abuse is great in families with teen parents, especially when the factors of poverty and single-parent family structure converge with early childbearing (Gelles, 1989; Zuravin, 1988).

Complications during labor and delivery can be devastating to the newborn's health. Are young mothers more likely than older ones to experience such complications? Mothers under 19 are less likely than older mothers to initiate prenatal care during the first trimester of pregnancy. Infants born to mothers under 17 are at greater risk than those born to women in their 20s and 30s. They have a higher risk of dying during the first year, of being born prematurely or at a low birth weight, and of suffering neurological damage as a result of complications associated with delivery (Held, 1981; Honig, 1978). Thus young parents are more likely to have to cope with the special needs of a developmentally handicapped child.

However, these risks may arise more from converging socioeconomic factors than from biological inadequacies. Roosa (1984) compared the labor and delivery experiences associated with more than 2,700 first births in two large urban hospitals. Table 9.3 shows the percentage of specific problems experienced by four groups of mothers: low- and middle-income teen mothers and low- and middle-income older mothers. None of the data suggest that the younger mothers were at greater risk for labor complications than the others. The younger mothers in both income groups had higher rates of spontaneous delivery than did the older mothers. Fetal distress was especially high for the older low-income mothers.

Is a pregnant adolescent who marries better off than one who does not? Adolescent pregnancy and adolescent marriage have separate consequences for future educational attainment, occupational achievement, and marital stability. Having a baby in adolescence is associated with lower educational and occupational levels, whether or not the young woman gets married. Getting married in adolescence is associated with

Table 9.3   Percentage of Mothers Having Specific Labor and Delivery Experiences by Maternal Age and Social Class

| | Teenage Mothers | | Mothers 20 to 30 Years | |
	Low Income (N = 1,188)	Middle Income (N = 199)	Low Income (N = 583)	Middle Income (N = 824)
Labor complications*	3.7	2.5	3.6	3.2
Fetopelvic disproportion†	3.7	7.2	3.8	8.4
Abnormal presentation	3.2	3.6	5.3	4.6
Fetal distress†	5.4	4.6	9.6	4.7
Spontaneous delivery†	77.9	65.6	66.6	55.4

*Including placenta previa, placenta abruption, fetal bleeding, and prolapse of cord, among others.

†Group differences are statistically significant.

Source: M. W. Roosa, "Maternal Age, Social Class, and the Obstetric Performance of Teenagers," *Journal of Youth and Adolescence, 13,* 369. Copyright 1984 by Plenum Publishing Corporation. Reprinted by permission.

a greater chance of divorce or separation than getting married at age 20 or older. Somewhat surprisingly, however, adolescent marriage without children is somewhat more likely to be associated with later marital instability than is adolescent marriage accompanied by adolescent childbirth (Teti & Lamb, 1989).

In an attempt to get a bit closer to the factors that lead to certain sexual decisions, including the decision to have a child, Pete and DeSantis (1990) conducted a case study of five black girls who were pregnant or had recently delivered a child. One must be cautious about generalizing these observations to all black adolescent mothers or to adolescent mothers as a whole. All five were 14 years old and in the eighth grade. They were from low-income families in Miami, Florida. Despite the very small sample size, the focus of this study is especially relevant because it considers the point of view of a critical group. Less than 15% of all adolescents are black, yet 47% of births to unmarried teens are to black girls. What is more, poor black adolescents are likely to have babies at a very young age, and the risks of their early childbearing contribute to the significantly higher incidence of morbidity and mortality among black babies.

Several factors that emerged from the interviews with these very young mothers challenge some of our beliefs about adolescent pregnancy and confirm others.

First, the girls all had passed up other opportunities to become sexually active. They said that they waited to become sexually active until they had established a relationship that they believed was based on trust and love. They did not delay sexual activity in order to avoid pregnancy. They assumed that the person with whom they had sex would not abandon them.

Second, they did not use contraceptives for a variety of reasons. Some believed that they could not get pregnant ("I thought I was too young to get pregnant"). Some relied on their boyfriends to use contraception, but the methods that were used were inconsistent or nonexistent. Most of the girls were confused about the use of contraceptives or lacked the means to obtain them.

Third, the girls all described a daily life that had a large amount of unsupervised free time. They all lived with adults who did not or were not able to supervise their behaviors effectively. One girl had moved out of the house when her mother became hooked on crack. Another girl lived with her grandmother, who never could talk with her about sex or her social life. Although the girls all said they felt close to their parent or guardian, the adults did not monitor these girls' social lives or talk about sexual decisions.

Fourth, the girls denied that they were pregnant as long as they could.

> *However, even though Deb had missed several periods, was sick every morning, and had fainted several times, she vehemently denied she was pregnant for seven months. . . . As Deb so clearly put it, "as long as I did not tell anyone I was pregnant, as far as I was concerned, I wasn't pregnant."*   [Pete & DeSantis, 1990, p. 151]

Finally, the girls all believed that once a person becomes pregnant, it is her responsibility to have and keep the baby. Since they waited so long to admit the pregnancy, abortion was out of the question. Adoption was also never considered. None of the parents or guardians thought the girls should get married because they were too young. All the fathers continued to maintain contact with the mother and baby, were involved in the care of the baby, and provided some financial support for the baby. Three of the fathers took their babies to their homes every other weekend. Even though the girls' parents or guardians were disappointed in the pregnancy, they did not reject these young mothers. Several even accepted some responsibility themselves for the pregnancy. The pregnancy and childbirth did not result in a deterioration of the girls' support system.

Although the focus on adolescent pregnancy has been on girls, there is growing concern about adolescent fathers. It is difficult to determine the number of teenage fathers. Many young mothers will not reveal the name of their baby's father. Many of these fathers are not adolescents but older men. National data from 1984 reported that of 479,647 infants born to teenage mothers, only 19% also had teenage fathers (Hardy & Duggan, 1988). Not much systematic research has been conducted on the attitudes, knowledge, or behaviors of adolescent fathers or the impact of fatherhood on a teenage boy's subsequent development (Robinson, 1988).

Most studies of adolescent mothers find that many of the fathers, contrary to the stereotype, remain in contact with the mother and the child. Some adolescent fathers marry the mother, others live with her for awhile. Often the couple continues to date. In many cases, the father contributes financial support to the mother and child, even when the couple do not marry. Many fathers, however, have little education and are minimally employed, so the material support they can provide is very limited (Robinson, 1988; Hardy & Duggan, 1988).

For the pregnant girl, the father is likely to remain a significant figure. In a study of the social network of adolescent mothers, Held (1981) found that each mother perceived the baby's father as the person most likely to approve of her pregnancy. The baby's father was also ranked as one of the three most significant others in the young mother's life.

Fathering a child is bound to stimulate conflicting feelings of pride, guilt, and anxiety in the adolescent boy. He must struggle with the fact that his sexual adventures have resulted in a pregnancy that may bring conflict and pain to someone for whom he cares. He must confront the choices he and his girlfriend have in coping with an unplanned pregnancy. He may have a sense of being shut out from the birth of a child he has fathered. Feelings of obligation to provide financial support for his girlfriend and child may lead him to drop out of school and enter the labor market even though he can hope to be only minimally employed (Hendricks & Fullilove, 1983).

Few adolescent pregnancy programs consider the needs of adolescent fathers. Limited evidence suggests, however, that many fathers experience stress related to the pregnancy and could benefit from some kind of counseling (Lamb & Elster, 1985). Those who have studied the problem of unwed fathers argue that much stronger emphasis ought to be placed on the father's responsibility, not only for financial support of the mother and child but for continued interaction with the baby. Efforts to include young fathers in family planning programs, parent education, and employment training initiatives would help strengthen the social context for the young mother and her child and contribute to the young man's psychosocial development.

There is no question that early entry into parenthood is problematic for both girls and boys. When adolescent pregnancy is followed by disruption of education, loss of family and peer support, and poverty, the life chances for the young girl and her child are severely reduced. However, these consequences do not necessarily have to occur. Much depends on the response of family members, schools, community agencies, and peers. Further, some young parents have greater personal resources to bring to their new parental role than others. This is an area in which educators and human service professionals can make a real difference (Olds et al., 1988).

Summary

The physical changes that occur during puberty have an impact on the adolescent's self-image and on the nature of family and peer relations. These changes in stature, body shape, sexual characteristics, and reproductive capacities serve as stimuli for new kinds of social interactions and for new levels of self-consciousness. Early adolescents are likely to begin to feel nostalgic about the days when they were less sophisticated and more carefree. As one 15-year-old girl put it, "It was like growing up overnight. I felt that I was not a little kid anymore. I couldn't ride my bicycle anymore; really I'm not kidding you" (Kagan, 1972, p. 97).

Formal operations bring a new appreciation of the complexity and relativity of the environment, as well as a growing sense of the future. The degree to which young people engage in formal reasoning depends largely on exposure to diverse models of problem solving through the school curriculum, participation in varied role relationships, and encounters with a more diverse peer group.

The combination of changing hormone levels, new cognitive capacities, and more complex social relationships results in a more differentiated range of emotions. Young people have to cope with and express their emotions in order to continue to develop cognitive problem solving and build satisfying peer relations.

There may be some tension between the task of peer-group membership and that of developing sexual relationships. Too much involvement with a dyadic relationship or "steady date" may isolate young people from more informal, less intense peer contacts. Early sexual activity can disrupt the normal developmental path and introduce significant interpersonal commitments at a very early age, especially if the girl becomes pregnant. Too much concern over peer acceptance and peer-group participation may make the possibility of a dyadic relationship remote. Adolescents must figure out which personal needs can be met by these two kinds of peer contact, and must learn to balance personal involvement appropriately.

The emphasis on the expanding role of the peer group and experimentation with sexual relationships should not overshadow the role of family members in promoting or disrupting the development of adolescents. Parents and guardians continue to foster optimal development through their nurturance, their supervision, and their willingness to engage adolescents in meaningful problem solving and communication.

The Psychosocial Crisis: Group Identity versus Alienation

We are positing an additional psychosocial conflict that confronts individuals as they make the transition from childhood to adolescence. We call this conflict *group identity versus alienation*. Early adolescents experience a search for membership, an internal questioning about the group of which they are most naturally a part. They ask themselves, "Who am I, and with whom do I belong?" Although membership in a peer group may be the most pressing concern, questions about other group identifications also arise. Adolescents may seek commitment to a religious organization; they may evaluate the nature of their ties to immediate or extended family members; and they begin to understand the unique characteristics of their racial, ethnic, or cultural identity. In the process of seeking group affiliation, the adolescent is confronted by the fit or lack of fit between personal needs and values and the values held by relevant social groups in the environment. The process of self-evaluation takes place within the context of the meaningful groups that are available for identification. Individual needs for social approval, affiliation, leadership, power, and status are expressed in the kinds of group identifications that are made and rejected during early adolescence.

A positive resolution of the conflict of group identity versus alienation is one in which adolescents perceive an existing group that meets their social needs and provides them with a sense of group belonging. It is this sense of group belonging that facilitates psychological growth and helps integrate the developmental tasks of early adolescence.

A negative resolution of the conflict leaves the adolescent with a pervasive sense of alienation from peers. The adolescent does not experience a sense of belonging to a group; rather, he or she is continually uneasy in the presence of peers. The negative outcome may be brought about if the parents press the adolescent to restrict association to a particular peer group that in turn does not offer the adolescent membership. It may result if the adolescent looks over the existing groups and does not find one that really meets his or her personal needs. In this case, the adolescent may never become a member of a peer group. A third basis for the negative outcome is the possibility that no peer group will offer acceptance or friendship, in which case the

Pablo Picasso, *A Woman's Head and Hand,* 1921. Alienation may result from irresolvable conflict between personal values and peer group expectations. In some cases, the young person is really cut off from peer acceptance by the norms of the existing groups.

adolescent is gradually shut out of all the existing groups in the social environment. For example, some young people ascribe too avidly to adult values and norms. Their peers see them as goodie-goodies or nerds and do not welcome them into the peer culture (Allen, Weissberg & Hawkins, 1989).

During early adolescence, it is common for young people to become preoccupied with their own feelings and thoughts. They may withdraw from social interactions, unwilling to share the vulnerability and confusion that accompany physical, intellectual, and social growth. In this sense, most adolescents feel some of the loneliness and isolation that are implied by the term *alienation.* Even with peers they feel they must exercise caution in sharing their most troublesome concerns for fear of rejection or ridicule. The maintenance of an interpersonal "cool"—a desire to be perceived as someone who is competent rather than vulnerable—may stand in the way of building strong bonds of commitment to social groups.

The tension between expectations for group affiliation and barriers to group commitment is a product of the self-consciousness and egocentrism of this life stage and of the potential for rejection by existing groups. The lack of peer social support that can result from a negative resolution of this crisis can have significant implications for adjustment in school, self-esteem, and subsequent psychosocial development. Chronic conflict about one's integration into a meaningful reference group can lead to lifelong difficulties in areas of personal health, work, and the formation of intimate family bonds (East, Hess & Lerner, 1987; Spencer, 1982, 1988).

The Central Process: Peer Pressure

Adolescents' circles of friends, interests, and styles of dress quickly link them to subgroups that lend continuity and meaning within the context of their neighborhoods or schools. These groups demand conformity to their norms and a demonstration of commitment and loyalty to their members. At the same time, young people outside the groups form expectations that reinforce adolescents' connections to specific peer groups and prohibit their movement to others. The peer-group social structure is usually well established in most high schools, and members of that structure exert pressure on newcomers to join one peer group or another. An individual who becomes a member of any group is more acceptable to the social system as a whole than one who tries to remain unaffiliated and aloof.

School adults both passively accept and actively encourage the organization of students into peer groupings. In the passive mode, they accept the friendship groups as they exist in the school and do little, if anything, to bring members of different peer groups into a working relationship with one another. They allow students to establish boundaries, rivalries, and areas of cooperation in their relationships. In the active mode, they reinforce some characteristics of the peer groups by selecting certain students for particular kinds of tasks. In most schools, for example, members of one peer group monitor the halls and assist in record-keeping functions, while members of another fix the teachers' cars and operate equipment.

There is an implicit acceptance by school adults of the peer group structure as it exists. They make almost no effort to alter this structure, which they may remember from their own high school days. Explicitly, school adults rely on members of specific peer groups to perform certain functions and to act along particular lines. Teachers as well as students appear to expect that individuals who dress in a certain way will be members of one peer group and that students who have a particular level of intellectual skill will belong to another. School adults often rely on the leaders of the various peer groups to convey and enforce school norms for acceptable behavior within their own groups. The peer-group structure, then, is an important vehicle for the maintenance of order and predictability in the school. Far from challenging this arrangement, school adults count on it to facilitate their jobs.

The process of affiliating with a peer group requires one to open oneself up to the pressure and social influence imposed by it. This pressure provides the context within which the crisis of group identity versus alienation is resolved. Adolescents are at the point in their intellectual development at which they are able to conceptualize themselves as objects of expectations. They may perceive these expectations as forces urging them to be more than they think they are—braver, more outgoing, more confident, and so forth. In these cases, peer pressure has a positive effect on the adolescent's self-image and serves as a motive for group identification. Those dimensions of the self that are valued by the peer group become especially salient in each young person's self-assessment (Hoge & McCarthy, 1984).

As members of peer groups, adolescents have more influence than they would have as single individuals. They begin to understand the value of collective enterprise. In offering membership, peer groups expand adolescents' feelings of self-worth and

Some adolescents become loners. They aren't accepted by a group, or they don't want to be part of one. They miss the experience of being valued and supported by their peers.

protect them from loneliness. When family conflicts develop, adolescents can seek comfort and intimacy among peers. For adolescents to benefit in these ways from affiliation with a peer group, they must be willing to suppress some of their individuality and find pleasure in focusing on those attributes that they share with peers.

Peer pressure may be exercised in a variety of areas, including involvement with peers, school, and family, drug use, engaging in misconduct, sexual activity, and conformity to patterns of preference in dress, music, or entertainment. Within a particular group, pressures may be strong in one or two areas but not in the others. For example, in a comparison of three peer groups—the jock-populars, the druggie-toughs, and the loners—the druggie-toughs perceived the strongest peer pressure toward misconduct. Jock-populars perceived greater pressure toward school involvement than the druggie-toughs. However, pressure toward peer involvement (spending free time with peers) was equally high in all three groups (Clasen & Brown, 1985).

Peer groups do not command total conformity. In fact, most peer groups depend on the unique characteristics of their members to lend definition and vigor to the roles that emerge within them. However, the peer group places considerable importance on some maximally adaptive level of conformity in order to bolster its structure and strengthen its effectiveness in satisfying members' needs—indeed, most adolescents find some security in peer-group demands to conform. The few well-defined characteristics of the group lend stability and substance to adolescents' views of themselves. In complying with group pressure, adolescents have an opportunity to state unambiguously that they are someone and that they belong somewhere.

Adolescents may also perceive some peer expectations as being in conflict with their personal values or needs. For example, they may feel that intellectual skills are devalued by the peer group, that they are expected to participate in social functions they do not enjoy, or that they are encouraged to be more independent from their

The dynamics of peer pressure are most evident during high school. Students are constantly on display, sending and receiving hundreds of small messages every day about acceptance and rejection.

families than they prefer to be. In most cases, adolescents' personal values are altered and shaped by peer-group pressure to increase their similarity with the other group members. If, however, the peer group's expectations are too distant from adolescents' own values, establishing a satisfying group identification will become much more difficult. In this case, adolescents will always be experiencing tension and conflict as they try to balance the allure of peer-group membership with the cost of abandoning personal beliefs.

This persistent conflict and the accompanying tension are painful and confusing to adolescents. If they move closer to the peer group, they find the tension increasing, perhaps to an uncomfortable level. They must, therefore, pull back from the group to a safer level of tension. As they do so, their own values dominate and they return to a level of emotional arousal that is tolerable for them. During the years from 12 to 16, adolescents become more adept at resisting peer pressure. Through encounters with peer pressure and opportunities to see how it feels to conform or resist, they develop a growing appreciation of personal values against the backdrop of peer expectations. However, if the emotional costs of approaching the peer group become too great, adolescents may not truly open themselves up to group pressures. Therefore, they will be unable to establish the sense of group identity that is so central to psychosocial growth during this period of life. An inability to reduce the tension and conflict between group pressure and personal values produces a state of alienation in which the individual is unable either to identify with social groups or to develop personal friendships.

Ethnic-Group Identity

One of the most challenging aspects of establishing group identity facing minority adolescents is the formation of an ethnic-group identity (Spencer & Markstrom-Adams,

1990). Ethnic identity is not merely knowing that one is a member of a certain racial or ethnic group, but recognizing that some aspects of one's thoughts, feelings, and actions are influenced by one's ethnic identity. One's ethnic group becomes a significant reference group whose values, outlook, and goals are taken into account as one makes important life choices.

In the United States, a history of negative imagery, violence, discrimination, and invisibility has been linked to African-Americans, Native Americans, Asian-Americans, and Hispanics. Young people in each of these groups encounter conflicting values as they consider the larger society and their own ethnic identity. They must struggle with the negative or ambivalent feelings that are linked with their own ethnic group as a result of the cultural stereotypes that have been conveyed to them through the media and the schools, and the absence of role models of their own group who are in positions of leadership and authority.

Issues of ethnic-group identity may not become salient until early adolescence. As minority children grow up, they tend to incorporate many of the ideals and values of the Anglo culture. Suddenly, in adolescence, they may find themselves excluded from it. At that time, peer groups become more structured. Sanctions against cross-race friendships and dating relationships become more intense, both within the ethnic group and from members of other groups. They may encounter more overt rejection and failure in areas of academic achievement, employment, and school leadership. Minority adolescents may find that their family and ethnic-group values are actually in conflict with the values of the majority culture. They may feel that they have to choose between their ethnic-group identity and membership in a nonminority group. In some cases, commitment to an ethnic-group identity takes the place of membership in a peer group. In other instances, minority youths are rejected by their Anglo peers. They may flounder, not having established a clear ethnic identity, and struggle through a period of bitter rejection.

Strategies are needed to help parents transmit ethnic cultural values to their children so that young people enter adolescence with a firm appreciation of their ethnic heritage. What is more, schools must introduce a multicultural curriculum so that children of all ethnic groups encounter information that emphasizes the value of ethnic identity.

Summary

Young adolescents are engaged in a process of self-evaluation within the context of their peer group. They are extremely sensitive to the opinions others hold of them and are preoccupied by the need for peer acceptance. Peer groups can bolster adolescents' self-confidence or present continuous pressures for conformity and compliance. In most cases, peers adjust to the eccentricities of their fellow members and provide an atmosphere of mutual support as they try out adult roles. In extreme situations, adolescents are unable to meet the social expectations that permit membership into any peer group. Because of either personal choice or social rejection, these adolescents are unable to identify with any of the existing groups. If they are resourceful, they may create their own new groupings. Otherwise, it is likely they will experience alienation from their peers and some decline in self-esteem.

☐ Applied Topic: Adolescent Alcohol Use

American high-school-age youths have a higher level of illicit drug use than those of any other industrialized nation. Roughly 60% of American students try an illegal drug such as marijuana, amphetamines, heroin and other opiates, cocaine, or barbiturates by their senior year in high school. However, the use of most of these drugs has been declining since 1975. In contrast, alcohol use has remained at a stable and relatively high level since then. An ongoing national study of high school seniors' drug use and related attitudes shows widespread use of alcohol from 1975 to 1986. Among high school seniors, nearly all of the students (over 90%) had tried alcohol at least once. About 30% had first used alcohol by the eighth grade or earlier. In a rural sample of seventh-graders, about 60% had used alcohol in the past year, and about 8% drank four or five times a month (Sarvela & McClendon, 1988). In the senior class of 1986, 65% had used alcohol in the past month, 37% reported at least one binge (five or more drinks in a row) during the past two weeks, and about 5% reported daily use (Johnston, O'Malley & Bachman, 1987).

Alcohol depresses the central nervous system. Although many people think that alcohol makes one "high," at its greatest levels of concentration in the body it can cause death by suppressing breathing. Although this outcome is extremely rare, it may occur after "chugging" large quantities of alcohol, a practice that is sometimes included in certain adolescent initiation rites and demonstrations of manliness. There are two other situations in which alcohol use has potentially lethal consequences. One is the use of alcohol in combination with other drugs, especially barbiturates. The other is its use in combination with driving. One study of tenth-, 11th-, and 12th-graders found that 57% had driven while intoxicated and 78% had ridden in a car while the driver was drinking (DiBlasio, 1986).

Table 9.4 shows the effects associated with various concentrations of alcohol in the blood. These effects depend on body weight and the amount of food consumed during drinking. However, it is clear that even three beers or two cocktails can alter behavior so as to produce feelings of warmth, relaxation, and some increase in sociability (Coleman, 1980).

Let us look at some of the factors associated with the use of alcohol and at the part alcohol use plays in the adolescent's life. We are especially concerned to understand the relationship between alcohol use and the major themes of early adolescence: physical development, cognitive development, peer relations, and parent-child relationships.

We have noted that the physical development accompanying puberty leads to a heightened awareness of body sensations. In small quantities, alcohol has a relaxing effect that may accentuate pleasurable bodily sensations. Adolescents may use alcohol in an attempt to increase the sense of physical arousal, reduce sexual inhibitions, and minimize the self-consciousness that is a barrier to social interactions. In larger quantities, alcohol may alter reality testing in such a way that adolescents are willing to take risks or ignore certain physical limitations. While adolescents are intoxicated, the barriers of physical appearance, height, weight, or sexual immaturity can be minimized. Thus dissatisfaction with body image may contribute to an inclination to drink heavily in social situations.

Table 9.4   Effects Associated with Various Amounts of Alcohol for a 150-Pound Person

Amount of Beverage	Alcohol Concentration in Blood (Percent)	Effects
1 highball 5½ ounces of wine 1 bottle of beer	0.03	Slight changes in feeling
2 highballs 11 ounces of wine 3 bottles of beer	0.06	Feelings of warmth, relaxation
3 highballs 16½ ounces of wine 5 bottles of beer	0.09	Exaggerated emotion and behavior—noisy, talkative, or morose
4 highballs 22 ounces of wine 7 bottles of beer	0.12	Clumsiness—unsteady in standing and walking
5 highballs 27½ ounces of wine ½ pint of whiskey	0.15	Gross intoxication

From *Abnormal Psychology and Modern Life,* 5th ed., p. 416, by J. C. Coleman. Copyright © 1976, 1972 by Scott, Foresman and Company. Reprinted by permission of HarperCollins Publishers.

Growth in cognitive development during adolescence suggests that young people are increasingly able to anticipate the consequences of their actions. They can hypothesize about events that have not yet occurred and reason about their possible outcomes. Adolescents should be able to manipulate several variables at one time in order to solve a problem or make a decision. These skills suggest that adolescents can use information about the impact or risk of alcohol to guide their drinking behavior.

Finn and Brown (1981) asked junior and senior high school students about their perceptions of the risks associated with getting drunk. Eighty percent saw getting drunk as involving risks, including driving while drunk, falling and hurting oneself, becoming "hooked" on alcohol, saying something to a friend that one might regret later, getting into a fight, getting into trouble with parents, and committing a crime. The students who were frequent and heavy drinkers (three or more drinks on a single occasion) were less likely to see a great deal of risk in drinking. The students who drank little or not at all were more likely to see a great deal of risk. This finding is consistent with the notion that adolescents can use information about the consequences of behavior to guide their actions. However, 60% of the heavy drinkers perceived that getting drunk involves some risks. This finding suggests that other factors that outweigh those risks must be associated with drinking.

The two reference groups that influence the acceptability of drinking and the manner in which alcohol is consumed are the family and the peer group (Brook, Whiteman & Gordon, 1983). There appear to be many similarities between the ways in which students and adults in a community think about and use alcohol. Barnes (1981) surveyed students and adults in the same community to assess the similarity in their respective patterns of use. Adults and students showed similar patterns of use of beer, wine, and other liquors. They described similar patterns of alcohol use in the home on special occasions or at mealtimes. Three basic reasons for drinking were described by the two groups: conforming functions (so I won't be different from my friends); social, festive functions (it's a good way to celebrate); and personal effects (it helps relieve pressure). The first reason was somewhat more important to adolescents than to adults. The second was most important to both groups. The third was somewhat more important to adolescents than to adults. Neither the first nor the third reason helps to predict whether a person will be a heavy drinker, whether a student or an adult. Barnes concluded that the drinking patterns of students and adults were extremely similar. The adult members of a community set the attitudinal and behavioral tone with regard to alcohol use, and adolescents are socialized to internalize that position.

A somewhat different view is seen if one asks adolescents about parental approval of drinking patterns. Adolescents perceive their parents as disapproving of almost any drug use. With respect to alcohol use, 92% perceive their parents to be disapproving of having one or two drinks a day, and 85% see their parents as disapproving of binge drinking (Johnston et al., 1987).

The impact of parental sanctions against alcohol use depends heavily on the quality of the parent-child relationship:

> *Compared to users, nonusers feel closer to both parents, consider it important to get along well with them, and want to be like them when they grow up. Nonusers' parents more typically provide praise and encouragement, develop feelings of interpersonal trust, and help with personal problems. Perceived as stricter, nonusers' parents more typically have rules about homework, television, curfew, and drugs and alcohol. Yet, they are not more punitive. Instead, parental control is enhanced by praise and encouragement and by an emotionally close relationship that encourages youngsters to seek parental advice and guidance. Young people who feel loved and trusted by parents want to emulate them, not bring embarrassment by inappropriate behavior.*   [Coombs & Landsverk, 1988, p. 480]

The peer group also contributes to the patterns of alcohol use in adolescence. Here we see some explanation for the potential inconsistencies in alcohol use. Over 65% of high school seniors say that they are around peers who use alcohol to get high. Fully one-third of high school seniors say that most or all of their friends get drunk once a week. Binge drinking is more frequent among boys than girls (46% vs. 28%) and more frequent among the non-college-bound than among the college-bound (41% vs. 34%). Although adolescents say they perceive greater risk with binge drinking than with taking one or two drinks every day, they are less likely to disapprove of binge drinking than of daily drinking. Further, adolescents perceive their peers' attitudes as being much more similar to their own and much less disapproving of binge drinking than the attitudes of their parents (Johnston et al., 1987).

Most adolescents do not drink every day. However, many do engage in binge drinking, which they perceive as risky, but somehow acceptable within the peer context. Alcohol is a part of the life experience of almost every adolescent. Drinking is something an adolescent can do that symbolizes celebration, adult status, and some degree of behavioral independence from parents. Since most adults also drink, adolescents may readily perceive their disapproval of adolescent drinking as hypocritical. In this way, drinking can become an avenue for testing the limits of adult authority.

From our knowledge of the central role of the peer group during this stage of life, we must assume that alcohol use is also the result of peer pressure to conform to a group norm. If the peer-group leaders approve of binge drinking, alcohol use at parties, or driving while intoxicated, they are highly influential in encouraging other group members to share this experience. The norm for alcohol use, then, may become one criterion for peer-group acceptance. If peer norms reject alcohol use, the peer group can serve to shield members from alcohol use and to deny membership to those who drink. The support of social reference groups for alcohol use during adolescence has long-term effects. In a study of collegiate drinking, those students who began drinking at an early age and who drank heavily in high school were more likely to drink heavily during the first two years of college (Friedman & Humphrey, 1985).

We have not attempted to provide detailed information about alcoholism. Most cities and towns currently support drug and alcohol information centers that supply such information. We have also not attempted to depict the characteristics and problems of the alcoholic family or the impact of parental alcoholism on adolescents. We have tried to point out how alcohol may become a part of the life of normal adolescents during the high school years. Experimentation with alcohol is relatively easy to understand in the context of the adolescent's psychosocial needs and the modeling of alcohol use in the family, and the peer group, and the community.

☐ Chapter Summary

In the use of alcohol by high school students we can see all the central themes of early adolescence. First, the physical sensations associated with a drug high point to the adolescent's general sensitivity to sensuality and preoccupation with body changes. Second, the issue of perceived risks suggests the adolescent's growing cognitive capacities. The adolescent is capable of relating to a hypothetical situation as well as to a factual one. Third, the use of alcohol suggests the significance of the peer group and identification with it. Alcohol use is only one behavior that may be motivated primarily by a need for peer acceptance and a desire to conform to peer-group norms.

The crisis of group identity versus alienation involves a potential tension between individual and family values and peer pressures toward violation of them. In many cases, no deep contradiction exists. Adolescent resistance to parental values may be more realistically interpreted as a demonstration of personal independence than as a declaration of guerrilla warfare. On the other hand, the threat of peer rejection may push those adolescents who lack confidence in their own worth to violate very essential values in the pursuit of acceptance. Teenage pregnancy, drug addiction, drunken driving, and serious delinquent behavior all suggest that the adolescent has a capacity for self-destruction that was less obvious in the earlier developmental stages. The cultural climate in which the adolescent works out peer-group relationships is of critical importance for success in this stage. Existing social expectations, stereotypic roles, and value orientations may either strengthen or undercut the adolescent's efforts to achieve personal satisfaction in the context of the peer group.

References

Acredolo, C., Adams, A., & Schmid, J. (1984). On the understanding of the relationships between speed, duration, and distance. *Child Development, 55,* 2151–2159.

Adams, G. R., & Jones, R. M. (1982). Adolescent egocentrism: Exploration into possible contributions of parent-child relations. *Journal of Youth and Adolescence, 11,* 25–31.

Adelson, J., & Doehrman, M. J. (1980). The psychodynamic approach to adolescence. In J. Adelson (ed.), *Handbook of adolescent psychology* (pp. 99–116). New York: Wiley.

Allen, J. P., Weissberg, R. P., & Hawkins, J. A. (1989). The relation between values and social competence in early adolescence. *Developmental Psychology, 25,* 458–464.

Barnes, G. M. (1981). Drinking among adolescents: A subcultural phenomenon or a model of adult behaviors? *Adolescence, 16,* 211–229.

Barth, R. P., Schinke, S. P., & Maxwell, J. S. (1983). Psychological correlates of teenage motherhood. *Journal of Youth and Adolescence, 12,* 471–487.

Beauvoir, S. de. (1969). *Memoirs of a dutiful daughter.* New York: World.

Berndt, T. J. (1982). The features and effects of friendship in early adolescence. *Child Development, 53,* 1447–1460.

Berndt, T. J., & Hoyle, S. G. (1985). Stability and change in childhood and adolescent friendships. *Developmental Psychology, 21,* 1007–1015.

Blyth, D. A., Bulcroft, R., & Simmons, R. G. (1981). The impact of puberty on adolescents: A longitudinal study. Paper presented at the annual convention of the American Psychological Association, Los Angeles.

Bolton, F. G., Jr., & MacEachron, A. E. (1988). Adolescent male sexuality: A developmental perspective. *Journal of Adolescent Research, 3,* 259–273.

Brook, J. S., Whiteman, M., & Gordon, A. S. (1983). Stages of drug use in adolescence: Personality, peer, and family correlates. *Developmental Psychology, 19,* 269–277.

Brooks-Gunn, J., & Furstenberg, F. F., Jr. (1989). Adolescent sexual behavior. *American Psychologist, 44,* 249–257.

Bullough, V. L. (1981). Age at menarche: A misunderstanding. *Science, 213,* 365–366.

Carron, A. V., & Bailey, O. A. (1974). *Strength development in boys from 10 through 16 years.* Monographs of the Society for Research in Child Development, 39 (4).

Cavior, N., & Dokecki, P. R. (1973). Physical attractiveness, perceived attitude similarity, and academic achievement as contributors to interpersonal attractions among adolescents. *Developmental Psychology, 9,* 44–54.

Chandler, M., & Boyes, M. (1982). Social cognitive development. In B. B. Wolman (ed.), *Handbook of developmental psychology* (pp. 387–402). Englewood Cliffs, N.J.: Prentice-Hall.

Chapman, M. (1988). *Constructive evolution: Origin and development of Piaget's thought.* New York: Cambridge University Press.

Clasen, D. R., & Brown, B. B. (1985). The multidimensionality of peer pressure in adolescence. *Journal of Youth and Adolescence, 14,* 451–468.

Clausen, J. A. (1975). The social meaning of differential physical and sexual maturation. In S. E. Dragastin & G. H. Elder (eds.), *Adolescence in the life cycle: Psychological change and social context.* Washington, D.C.: Hemisphere.

Coleman, J. C. (1980). *Abnormal psychology and modern life* (6th ed.). Glenview, Ill.: Scott, Foresman.

Coombs, R. H., & Landsverk, J. (1988). Parenting styles and substance use in childhood and adolescence. *Journal of Marriage and the Family, 50,* 473–482.

Csikszentmihalyi, M., Larson, R., & Prescott, S. (1977). The ecology of adolescent activity and experience. *Journal of Youth and Adolescence, 6,* 281–294.

Demetriou, A., & Efklides, A. (1985). Structure and sequence of formal and postformal thought: General patterns and individual differences. *Child Development, 56,* 1062–1091.

DiBlasio, F. A. (1986). Drinking adolescents on the roads. *Journal of Youth and Adolescence, 15,* 173–188.

Dreyer, P. H. (1982). Sexuality during adolescence. In B. B. Wolman (ed.), *Handbook of developmental psychology* (pp. 559–601). Englewood Cliffs, N.J.: Prentice-Hall.

Dunham, R. M., Kidwell, J. S., & Portes, P. R. (1988). Effects of parent-adolescent interaction on the continuity of cognitive development from early childhood to early adolescence. *Journal of Early Adolescence, 8,* 297–310.

Dunphy, D. C. (1963). The social structure of urban adolescent peer groups. *Sociometry, 26,* 230–246.

Dwyer, J., & Mayer, J. (1971). Psychological effects of variations in physical appearance during adolescence. In R. E. Muuss (ed.), *Adolescent behavior and society: A book of readings.* New York: Random House.

East, P. L., Hess, L. E., & Lerner, R. M. (1987). Peer social support and adjustment of early adolescent peer groups. *Journal of Early Adolescence, 7,* 153–163.

Edelman, M. W., & Pittman, K. J. (1986). Adolescent pregnancy: Black and white. *Journal of Community Health, 11,* 63–69.

Elkind, D. (1967). Egocentrism in adolescence. *Child Development, 38,* 1025–1034.

Faust, M. S. (1977). *Somatic development of adolescent girls.* Monographs of the Society for Research in Child Development, 42 (1, serial no. 169).

Feldman, S. S., & Gehring, T. M. (1988). Changing perceptions of family cohesion and power across adolescence. *Child Development, 59,* 1034–1045.

Finn, P., & Brown, J. (1981). Risks entailed in teenage intoxication as perceived by junior and senior high school students. *Journal of Youth and Adolescence, 10,* 61–76.

Flavell, J. H. (1963). *The developmental psychology of Jean Piaget.* Princeton, N.J.: Van Nostrand.

Fosburgh, L. (1977). The make-believe world of teen-age maturity. *New York Times Magazine,* August 7, 29–34.

Franklin, D. L. (1988). Race, class, and adolescent pregnancy: An ecological analysis. *American Journal of Orthopsychiatry, 58,* 339–355.

Friedman, J., & Humphrey, J. A. (1985). Antecedents of collegiate drinking. *Journal of Youth and Adolescence, 14,* 11–21.

Gaddis, A., & Brooks-Gunn, J. (1985). The male experience of pubertal change. *Journal of Youth and Adolescence, 14,* 61–69.

Garrison, C. Z., Schluchter, M. D., Schoenbach, V. J., & Kaplan, B. K. (1989). Epidemiology of depressive symptoms in young adolescents. *Journal of the American Academy of Child and Adolescent Psychiatry, 28,* 343–351.

Gelles, R. J. (1989). Child abuse and violence in single-parent families: Parent absence and economic deprivation. *American Journal of Orthopsychiatry, 59,* 492–501.

Gillies, P. (1989). A longitudinal study of the hopes and worries of adolescents. *Journal of Adolescence, 12,* 69–81.

Gold, M., & Petronio, R. J. (1980). Delinquent behavior in adolescence. In J. Adelson (ed.), *Handbook of adolescent psychology* (pp. 495–535). New York: Wiley.

Gold, M., & Yanof, D. S. (1985). Mothers, daughters, and girlfriends. *Journal of Personality and Social Psychology, 49,* 654–659.

Grief, E. B., & Ulman, K. J. (1982). The psychological impact of menarche on early adolescent females: A review of the literature. *Child Development, 53,* 1413–1430.

Hallinan, M. T., & Williams, R. A. (1989). Interracial friendship choices in secondary schools. *American Sociological Review, 54,* 67–78.

Hanson, S. L., Myers, D. R., & Ginsburg, A. L. (1987). The role of responsibility and knowledge in reducing teenage out-of-wedlock childbearing. *Journal of Marriage and the Family, 49,* 241–256.

Hardy, J. B., & Duggan, A. K. (1988). Teenage fathers and the fathers of infants of urban teenage mothers. *American Journal of Public Health, 78,* 919–922.

Held, L. (1981). Self-esteem and social network of the young pregnant teenager. *Adolescence, 16,* 905–912.

Hendricks, L. E., & Fullilove, R. E. (1983). Locus of control and use of contraception among unmarried black adolescent fathers and their controls: A preliminary report. *Journal of Youth and Adolescence, 12,* 225–233.

Hill, J. P. (1988). Adapting to menarche: Familial control and conflict. In M. R. Gunnar & W. A. Collins (eds.), *Development during the transition to adolescence.* Minnesota Symposium on Child Psychology, vol. 21 (pp. 43–77). Hillsdale, N.J.: Erlbaum.

Hofferth, S. L., & Hayes, C. D. (eds.) (1987). *Risking the future: Adolescent sexuality, pregnancy, and childbearing,* vol. 2, *Working papers and statistical reports.* Washington, D.C.: National Academy Press.

Hoge, D. R., & McCarthy, J. D. (1984). Influence of individual and group identity salience in the global self-esteem of youth. *Journal of Personality and Social Psychology, 47,* 403–414.

Honig, A. S. (1978). What we need to know to help the teenage parent. *Family Coordinator, 27,* 113–119.

Hunter, F. T. (1985). Adolescents' perception of discussions with parents and friends. *Developmental Psychology, 21,* 433–440.

Hunter, F. T., & Youniss, J. (1982). Changes in functions of three relations during adolescence. *Developmental Psychology, 18,* 806–811.

Inhelder, B., & Piaget, J. (1958). *The growth of logical thinking from childhood to adolescence.* New York: Basic Books.

Jacob, T. (1974). Patterns of family conflict and dominance as a function of age and social class. *Developmental Psychology, 10,* 1–12.

Johnston, L. D., O'Malley, P. M., & Bachman, J. G. (1987). *National trends in drug use and related factors among American high school students and young adults,*

1975–1986. Rockville, Md.: National Institute on Drug Abuse.

Jones, S. S. (1976). High school status as a historical process. *Adolescence, 11,* 327–333.

Kagan, J. (1972). A conception of early adolescence. In J. Kagan & R. Coles (eds.), *12 to 16: Early adolescence.* New York: Norton.

Klineberg, S. L. (1967). Changes in outlook on the future between childhood and adolescence. *Journal of Personality and Social Psychology, 7,* 185–193.

Konopka, G. (1976). *Young girls: A portrait of adolescence.* Englewood Cliffs, N.J.: Prentice-Hall.

Kuhn, D., Amsel, E., & O'Loughlin, M. (1988). *The development of scientific thinking skills.* New York: Academic Press.

Lamb, M. E., & Elster, A. B. (1985). Adolescent mother-infant-father relationships. *Developmental Psychology, 21,* 768–773.

Larson, R., & Lampman-Petraitis, C. (1989). Daily emotional states as reported by children and adolescents. *Child Development, 60,* 1250–1260.

Lerner, R. M. (1975). Showdown at generation gap: Attitudes of adolescents and their parents toward contemporary issues. In H. D. Thornburg (ed.), *Contemporary adolescence: Readings* (2nd ed, pp. 114–126). Pacific Grove, Calif.: Brooks/Cole.

Lessing, E. E. (1972). Extension of personal future time perspective, age, and life satisfaction of children and adolescents. *Developmental Psychology, 6,* 457–468.

Linn, M. C., Clement, C., Pulos, S., & Sullivan, P. (1989). Scientific reasoning during adolescence: The influence of instruction in science knowledge and reasoning strategies. *Journal of Research in Science Teaching, 26,* 171–187.

Logan, D. D. (1980). The menarche experience in 23 foreign countries. *Adolescence, 15,* 247–256.

Looft, W. R. (1971). Egocentrism and social interaction in adolescence. *Adolescence, 12,* 485–495.

LoSciuto, L. A., & Karlin, R. M. (1972). Correlates of the generation gap. *Journal of Psychology, 81,* 253–262.

Maag, J. W., Rutherford, R. B., Jr., & Parks, B. T. (1988). Secondary school professionals' ability to identify depression in adolescents. *Adolescence, 23,* 73–82.

Marsiglio, W. (1988). Adolescent male sexuality and heterosexual masculinity: A conceptual model and review. *Journal of Adolescent Research, 3,* 285–303.

Martin, S., Houseley, K., McCoy, H., Greenhouse, P., Stigger, F., Kenney, M. A., Shoffner, S., Fu, V., Korslund, M., Ercanli-Huffman, F. G., Carter, E., Chopin, L., Hegsted, M., Clark, A. J., Disney, G., Moak, S., Wake-field, T., & Stallings, S. (1988). Self-esteem of adolescent girls as related to weight. *Perceptual and Motor Skills, 67,* 879–884.

McMillan, D. W., & Hiltonsmith, R. W. (1982). Adolescents at home: An exploratory study of the relationship between perception of family social climate, general well-being, and actual behavior in the home setting. *Journal of Youth and Adolescence, 11,* 301–315.

Mendelson, B. K., & White, D. R. (1985). Development of self-body-esteem in overweight youngsters. *Developmental Psychology, 21,* 90–96.

Montemayor, R. (1982). The relationship between parent-adolescent conflict and the amount of time adolescents spend alone and with parents and peers. *Child Development, 53,* 1512–1519.

Moriarty, A. E., & Toussieng, P. W. (1976). *Adolescent coping.* New York: Grune & Stratton.

Morrison, D. M. (1985). Adolescent contraceptive behavior: A review. *Psychological Bulletin, 98,* 538–568.

Musa, K. E., & Roach, M. E. (1973). Adolescent appearance and self-concept. *Adolescence, 8,* 385–395.

Mussen, P. H., & Jones, M. C. (1957). Self-conceptions, motivations, and interpersonal attitudes of late and early maturing boys. *Child Development, 28,* 243–256.

Neimark, E. D. (1975). Longitudinal development of formal operations thought. *Genetic Psychology Monographs, 91,* 171–225.

Neimark, E. D. (1982). Adolescent thought: Transition to formal operations. In B. B. Wolman (ed.), *Handbook of developmental psychology* (pp. 486–499). Englewood Cliffs, N.J.: Prentice-Hall.

Newcomer, S., & Udry, J. R. (1987). Parental marital status effects on adolescent sexual behavior. *Journal of Marriage and the Family, 49,* 235–240.

Newman, P. R. (1979). Persons and settings: A comparative analysis of the quality and range of social interaction in two suburban high schools. In J. G. Kelly (ed.), *Adolescent boys in high school: A psychological study of coping and adaptation.* Hillsdale, N.J.: Erlbaum.

Newman, P. R. (1982). The peer group. In B. B. Wolman (ed.), *Handbook of developmental psychology* (pp. 526–535). Englewood Cliffs, N.J.: Prentice-Hall.

Nurmi, J. (1987). Age, sex, social class, and quality of family interaction as determinants of adolescents' future orientation: A developmental task interpretation. *Adolescence, 22,* 977–991.

Offer, D., Ostrov, E., & Howard, K. I. (1982). Family perceptions of adolescent self-image. *Journal of Youth and Adolescence, 11,* 281–291.

Olds, D. L., Henderson, C. R., Jr., Tatelbaum, R., & Chamberlin, R. (1988). Improving the life-course development of socially disadvantaged mothers: A randomized trial of nurse home visitation. *American Journal of Public Health, 78,* 1436–1445.

O'Mahoney, J. F. (1989). Development of thinking about things and people: Social and nonsocial cognition during adolescence. *Journal of Genetic Psychology, 150,* 217–224.

Ostrov, E., Offer, D., & Howard, K. I. (1989). Gender differences in adolescent symptomatology: A normative study. *Journal of the American Academy of Child and Adolescent Psychiatry, 28,* 394–398.

Overton, W. F., & Meehan, A. M. (1982). Individual differences in formal operational thought: Sex role and learned helplessness. *Child Development, 53,* 1536–1543.

Papini, D. R., Datan, N., & McCluskey-Fawcett, K. A. (1988). An observational study of affective and assertive family interactions during adolescence. *Journal of Youth and Adolescence, 17,* 477–492.

Papini, D. R., & Sebby, R. A. (1988). Variations in conflictual family issues by adolescent pubertal status, gender, and family member. *Journal of Early Adolescence, 8,* 1–15.

Pete, J. M., & DeSantis, L. (1990). Sexual decision making in young black adolescent females. *Adolescence, 25,* 145–154.

Petersen, A. C., Schulenberg, J. E., Abramowitz, R. H., Offer, D., & Jarcho, H. D. (1984). A self-image questionnaire for young adolescents (SIQYA): Reliability and validity studies. *Journal of Youth and Adolescence, 13,* 93–111.

Piaget, J. (1926). *The language and thought of the child.* New York: Harcourt, Brace.

Piaget, J. (1970). Piaget's Theory. In P. H. Mussen (ed.), *Carmichael's manual of child psychology* (3rd ed., vol. 1). New York: Wiley.

Piaget, J. (1972). Intellectual evolution from adolescence to adulthood. *Human Development, 15,* 1–12.

Rabinowitz, M. (1988). On teaching cognitive strategies: The influence of accessibility of conceptual knowledge. *Contemporary Educational Psychology, 13,* 229–235.

Raffaelli, M., & Duckett, E. (1989). "We were just talking . . .": Conversations in early adolescence. *Journal of Youth and Adolescence, 18,* 567–582.

Rauste–von Wright, M. (1989). Body image satisfaction in adolescent girls and boys: A longitudinal study. *Journal of Youth and Adolescence, 18,* 71–83.

Riley, T., Adams, G. R., & Nielsen, E. (1984). Adolescent egocentrism: The association among imaginary audience behavior, cognitive development, and parental support and rejection. *Journal of Youth and Adolescence, 13,* 401–417.

Robertson, J. F., & Simons, R. L. (1989). Family factors, self-esteem, and adolescent depression. *Journal of Marriage and the Family, 51,* 125–138.

Robinson, B. E. (1988). Teenage pregnancy from the father's perspective. *American Journal of Orthopsychiatry, 58,* 46–51.

Roosa, M. W. (1984). Maternal age, social class, and the obstetric performance of teenagers. *Journal of Youth and Adolescence, 13,* 365–374.

Rosenberg, M., Schooler, C., & Schoenbach, C. (1989). Self-esteem and adolescent problems: Modeling reciprocal effects. *American Sociological Review, 54,* 1004–1018.

Ruble, D. N., & Brooks-Gunn, J. (1982). The experience of menarche. *Child Development, 53,* 1557–1566.

Sarvela, P. D., & McClendon, E. J. (1988). Indicators of rural youth drug use. *Journal of Youth and Adolescence, 17,* 335–348.

Siegler, R. S., Liebert, D. E., & Liebert, R. M. (1973). Inhelder and Piaget's pendulum problem: Teaching preadolescents to act as scientists. *Developmental Psychology, 9,* 97–101.

Spencer, M. B. (1982). Personal and group identity of black children: An alternative synthesis. *Genetic Psychology Monographs, 103,* 59–84.

Spencer, M. B. (1988). Self-concept development. In D. T. Slaughter (ed.), *Black children in poverty: Developmental perspectives* (pp. 59–72). San Francisco: Jossey-Bass.

Spencer, M. B., & Markstrom-Adams, C. (1990). Identity processes among racial and ethnic minority children in America. *Child Development, 61,* 290–310.

Stapley, J. C., & Haviland, J. M. (1989). Beyond depression: Gender differences in normal adolescents' emotional experiences. *Sex Roles, 20,* 295–308.

Steinberg, L. D. (1981). Transformations in family relations at puberty. *Developmental Psychology, 17,* 833–840.

Stevenson, B. W., Roscoe, B., Brooks, R. H., II, & Kelsey, T. (1987). Profiles of mod revivalists: A case study of a reemerging adolescent group. *Adolescence, 22,* 393–404.

Strober, M. (1981). A comparative analysis of personality organization in juvenile anorexia nervosa. *Journal of Youth and Adolescence, 10,* 285–295.

Tanner, J. M. (1978). *Fetus into man: Physical growth from conception to maturity.* Cambridge, Mass.: Harvard University Press.

Tanner, J. M. (1981). A history of the study of human growth. Cambridge, England: Cambridge University Press.

Tedesco, L. A., & Gaier, E. L. (1988). Friendship bonds in adolescence. *Adolescence, 23,* 127–136.

Teti, D. M., & Lamb, M. E. (1989). Outcomes of adolescent marriage and adolescent childbirth. *Journal of Marriage and the Family, 51,* 203–212.

Thornton, A., & Camburn, D. (1989). Religious participation and adolescent sexual behavior. *Journal of Marriage and the Family, 51,* 641–654.

Udry, J. R., & Billy, J. O. G. (1987). Initiation of coitus in early adolescence. *American Sociological Review, 52,* 841–855.

U.S. Bureau of the Census (1987). *Statistical Abstract of the United States, 1988.* Washington, D.C.: U.S. Government Printing Office.

Van Wieringen, J. C. (1978). Secular growth changes. In F. Falkner & J. M. Tanner (eds.), *Human growth* (vol. 2, pp. 445–473). New York: Plenum.

Yates, A. (1989). Current perspectives on the eating disorders: I. History, psychological, and biological aspects. *Journal of the American Academy of Child and Adolescent Psychiatry, 28,* 813–828.

Zelnik, M., & Kantner, J. F. (1980). Sexual activity, contraceptive use, and pregnancy among metropolitan area teenagers: 1971–1979. *Family Planning Perspectives, 12,* 230–237.

Zuravin, S. J. (1988). Child maltreatment and teenage first births: A relationship mediated by chronic sociodemographic stress? *American Journal of Orthopsychiatry, 58,* 91–103.

Chapter Ten

The active resolution of the identity crisis means that young people begin to deliberately shape their adult psychology. In a self-portrait at 20, Picasso gives a sense of a young man with vision and intensity.

Later Adolescence (18 to 22 Years)

Erik Erikson (1959) has described adolescence as the final stage of childhood. In our conceptualization, it is *later adolescence* that is the final stage of childhood. After this life stage, individuals are compelled to make a wide variety of relatively permanent choices about their lives. They make decisions about marriage and select an occupation, a moral code, and perhaps a political ideology that will structure their social context during the adult years. Before they make these choices, individuals are engaged in a process of preparing for these critical decisions. In some cultures, these decisions are made for the child at a rather early age. In this case, adolescence may represent a single, relatively brief psychological stage of development. In such cultures, rituals and ceremonies mark the transition from childhood to adulthood. Circumcision ceremonies, hunting rituals, cleansing ceremonies, and bar mitzvahs are typical rites of passage into adulthood.

In complex societies, adolescence appears to be a two-stage process. The training necessary for adapting to the demands of industrial society requires that the person remain in a subordinate role for a comparatively long time. The student years may be over legally at age 16, but for many they continue until age 25 or older. Young people may participate in events and relationships that are considered adult activities, such as military service, marriage, and childbearing, and still view themselves as adolescents with respect to their social status and control of resources in the adult community. The period of later adolescence can eventually be brought to a close only through commitment to a personal integration of values, goals, and abilities which has been called *identity* (Erikson, 1950, 1959, 1968). The period of early adolescence draws to a close after choices are made concerning one's relations with peers.

For most individuals, the resolution of the crisis of individual identity comes as a result of both environmental demands and personal choices. The former include demands for education, marriage, work, family development, and military service. These demands are the same for many people and occur at relatively specifiable ages. Individuals in our society learn what is expected of them and at what times in life these expectations are salient. Many people in the later adolescent stage of development are prepared to accept the demands of adulthood and, along the way, to make the best choices they can about self-characteristics relating to personal identity. At the same time, there is room for new configurations of roles and relationships. There are opportunities to select some alternatives and reject others. For most later adolescents, the resolution of a sense of individual identity is a product of choices they make regarding anticipated or actual environmental demands. Individual identity results from the integration of personal choices with societal expectations.

Developmental Tasks

Autonomy from Parents

The goal of autonomy from parents must be understood as a multidimensional task that is accomplished gradually over the course of later adolescence and early adulthood. Autonomy is an ability to regulate one's behavior, to select and guide one's

Later adolescents are strongly motivated to demonstrate their independence from parents. Overly solicitous parents may face rejection or withdrawal in their children.

decisions and actions, without undue control from or dependence on parents (Steinberg & Silverberg, 1986; Ryan & Lynch, 1989). Autonomy is not the same as rejection, alienation, or physical separation from parents. It is an independent psychological status in which parents and children accept each other's individuality. Many areas of similarity between parents and children may very well provide bonds for a continued close, supportive relationship into adulthood. However, those bonds are discovered through a process of self-definition. Adolescents who achieve autonomy can recognize and accept both the similarities and the differences between themselves and their parents without feeling totally absorbed in their parents' identity or totally alienated from their parents' love.

Autonomy requires independence of thought and action. Much of the psychosocial development that has occurred before this stage can be seen as preparing the individual for independence from parents. Such skills as dressing oneself, handling money, cooking, driving a car, reading, and writing have been mastered. Although we take these skills for granted, they are essential for someone who is living independently. The physical maturation that has taken place also contributes to the possibility of autonomy. Daily survival requires a certain amount of physical strength, coordination, and endurance. These qualities finally come with the physical maturity of adolescence. The process of identification and the accompanying internalization of values allow the person to function autonomously with a sense of what is appropriate behavior. The person's ability to leave the intimacy of the family can also be promoted by a growing involvement with the peer group. As peer relations become more reciprocal, they begin to satisfy many of the needs for closeness and support that were initially satisfied only within the boundaries of the family. Finally, the young person's cognitive maturity provides a fund of information, a level of problem-solving ability, and a capacity to plan for the future that help sustain independent living.

Within the family context, identity exploration is facilitated by an open exchange of ideas and a certain level of challenge. Adolescents must have opportunities to express their separateness within the boundaries of the family. They must feel that their parents accept and understand their need to have distinct opinions and views. Separateness is achieved within a context of mutual caring and emotional support. A secure attachment to parents, based on a perception of the parents as committed to their child's well-being, is essential for growth toward independence (Hauser et al., 1984; Grotevant & Cooper, 1985; Armsden & Greenberg, 1987).

Adolescents tend to feel comfortably independent if their parents encourage them to share in decision making and provide explanations for the limits they set. Parents who are able to combine authoritative control with reason and frequent communication are likely to have assertive, responsible, and independent children. Either too restrictive or too permissive a pattern of parental demands seems to interfere with the adolescent's ability to differentiate his or her value system from the values held by parents. Although adolescents may perceive any efforts to control their behavior as intrusive or condescending, the clear communication of limits and expectations gives them a sense of stability and confidence that appears to encourage the internalization of morality and self-reliance. Adolescents whose parents proceed in this way are confident about their values, willing to discuss problems with them, and, at the same time, ready to disregard parental views that appear inappropriate (Kamptner, 1988; Adams & Jones, 1983; Enright et al., 1980).

Autonomy and Leaving Home

Many later adolescents live outside their parents' homes. Living away from one's parents has become a symbol of independence, not only in our society but in other cultures as well (Mitchell, Wister & Burch, 1989; DeVos, 1989). Whether young people leave home to go to college, join the military, get married, or take a job in another community, they and their parents see this as a critical transition to adulthood.

Before about 1960, marriage was the most traditional reason for moving to a new residence, other than leaving temporarily for college or the military. Since that time, however, it has become increasingly common for adolescents and young adults to expect to live in a separate residence for some time before marriage. A survey of high school seniors in 1980 found that three-fourths expected to live on their own before marriage (Goldscheider & Goldscheider, 1987).

There are differences of opinion about the age at which children are expected to leave home. Parents tend to expect children to leave home at an older age, more closely tied to the expected age of marriage, than do adolescent children. Parents with more resources are likely to accept an earlier age of home leaving than are low-income families. In addition, parents expect daughters to live at home longer than sons, but these differences are not reflected in the expectations of the adolescents themselves. This is a potential source of family conflict. In stepfamilies neither parents nor children are likely to expect home leaving to be related to the age of marriage. Children in these families are more likely to view leaving home as a way of becoming independent of a family environment that is not entirely comfortable (Goldscheider & Goldscheider, 1989).

Table 10.1 Definitions of Leaving Home	
Category	*Examples*
Personal control	Less parental control Make own decisions Must do things for self now Feel mature enough
Economic independence	Financial independence Have a job
Residence	Have all my belongings with me Live in a different place Moved to an apartment
Physical separation	Distance from home Physically away from home Family is not here
School affiliation	Dorm is center of life Consider school to be home
Dissociation	Won't go back each summer Have broken the ties
Emotional separation	Have feeling of being a visitor at home Have feeling of not belonging at home Don't feel close to family
Graduation	After graduation

Source: Adapted from D. Moore and D. F. Hotch, "Late Adolescents' Conceptualizations of Home-Leaving," *Journal of Youth and Adolescence, 10* (1981), 1–10.

Autonomy and the College Experience

Going away to college is an intermediate move between establishing a permanent residence before marriage and living at home. Of the freshmen who entered colleges and universities in 1989, about 30% lived with parents or other relatives. The others were living in campus housing, fraternities or sororities, or private apartments (Dodge, 1990). The mere act of going to college does not in itself bring a sense of leaving home or independence from parents. When college students in one study were asked to tell how they knew when they had left home, eight categories of explanations were generated (Moore & Hotch, 1981).

These categories (see Table 10.1) included physical separation (moved to an apartment), emotional separation (don't feel close to the family), and personal control (make own decisions). Some students viewed leaving home as a positive experience and tied it to a sense of increased personal control. Others linked leaving home to negative feelings of emotional separation or homesickness. It is likely that all the aspects of home leaving listed in Table 10.1 are confronted by each person at some time. The process of achieving a psychological sense of independence from home includes working through feelings of separation and loss, uncertainties about economic independence, and challenges of autonomous decision making.

The experience of going away to college imposes a particular context on the process of achieving autonomy. Sullivan and Sullivan (1980) studied the reactions of

Pablo Picasso, *Student with a Pipe,* Paris (winter), 1913–1914. Picasso offers this whimsical view of the French college student with his beret and his pipe. The traditional student is usually set apart from the rest of the community by a few subtle signs. Gesso, sand, pasted paper, and charcoal on canvas; 28¾″ x 23⅛″. Collection: The Museum of Modern Art, New York. Nelson A. Rockefeller Bequest. © 1991, ARS, New York/SPADEM.

boys and their parents during the boys' senior year of high school and their first year of college. Some of the boys were boarding at college. Others were commuting and living at home. More affection toward parents, better communication with parents, and greater independence from parents were reported by the boarders than by the commuters. The boarders showed increased affection toward their parents from their senior year in high school to their freshman year in college. The mothers of the boarders also expressed more affection toward their sons during this transition. It is possible that the physical separation between mother and son permitted a more open sharing of affection. Such affection might be more threatening if it were displayed within the home context. The fathers of the boarders perceived their sons as becoming less independent after going away to college. One possible explanation is that the boarders may have been less likely to be employed while at college and therefore in greater need of financial help from home.

Commuters had a more contentious relationship with parents. Parents of commuters, especially mothers, were also somewhat less positive about the affection and communication they experienced with their sons. Here is a picture of two distinct paths toward autonomy. Physical distance may foster closeness between mothers and sons, a closeness that is less likely to be achieved when sons live at home. Physical distance also permits more opportunities for decision making without creating conflict with parents. Independence may be more difficult to achieve when one lives at home. It may require displaying less affection and less interaction with parents in order to affirm one's separateness.

The developing sense of autonomy has implications for young people's relationships with authorities outside the home. As they become more confident about their independence, they are better able to evaluate the judgment of other authority figures. They may be less likely to transfer their dependent relationship with parents into situations that involve other authority figures. Previous infantile conceptualizations of the legitimacy and adequacy of people in positions of authority no longer suffice. Young people must evaluate teachers, bosses, national leaders, and other authority figures in a more mature and independent manner.

Sex-Role Identity

A person's gender—that is, whether the person is female or male—has a critical impact on the totality of life experiences. *Sex role* is a theoretical construct that refers to the "normative expectations about the division of labor between the sexes and to the gender-related rules about social interactions that exist within a particular cultural and historical context" (Spence, Deaux & Helmreich, 1985, p. 150). Sex-role expectations exist at the cultural, institutional, interpersonal, and individual levels. Yet individuals play a part in learning, accepting, and synthesizing these expectations with their own private assessments of their personal needs and goals. *Sex-role identity* refers to the formulation of a set of beliefs, attitudes, and values about oneself functioning as a man or woman in many areas of social life, including intimate relations, family, work, community, and religion (Giele, 1988).

Four critical experiences between early school age and later adolescence result in a reconceptualization and consolidation of sex-role identity (Figure 10.1) (Emmerich, 1973). First, the child engages in close same-sex peer relationships. These friendships teach children about the possibility of intimacy between equals. They also expose children to peer norms for appropriate sex-role behavior. During early adolescence, the impact of the peer group expands to communicate expectations about opposite-sex as well as same-sex relationships.

Second, early adolescence brings the onset of physical changes that must be incorporated into the sex-role identity. Adolescents must integrate an adult body into the self-concept. Notions of physical attractiveness become more salient. Adolescent boys and girls are aware that first impressions are often based on physical appearance. Physical appearance may determine an adolescent's popularity within the peer group. It may also influence the particular peers who find him or her attractive. Some research shows that one's body image during early adolescence is retained well into adulthood.

Although the body shape changes, one tends to retain a mental image of the body as it appeared during adolescence. Satisfaction with one's physical appearance provides an important basis for approaching social relations with a positive, optimistic outlook (Lerner, 1985; Rauste–von Wright, 1989).

Third, the hormonal changes of puberty bring new sexual impulses as well as the capacity for reproduction. Individual differences in hormone levels, especially of testosterone, can be linked to sex-role characteristics. In particular, high levels of testosterone production are associated with aggressiveness in males and with strong needs for achievement and independence in females. Women who have strong feminine sex-role identities have lower concentrations of testosterone than those with masculine

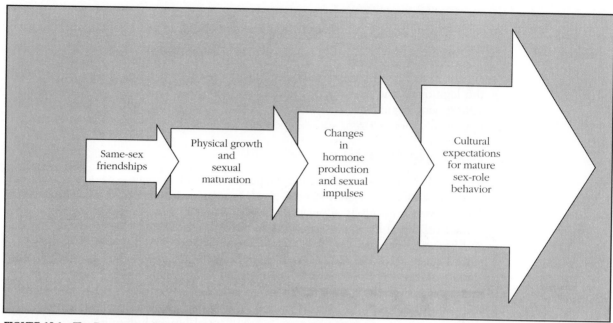

FIGURE 10.1   The Reconceptualization and Consolidation of Sex-Role Identity

or undifferentiated sex-role identities. Women who have high levels of testosterone describe themselves as robust, resourceful, impulsive, and unconventional (Baucom, Besch & Callahan, 1985). Maturation of the hormonal system accounts for some of the enduring personal characteristics that contribute to one's sex-role identity.

Fourth, as young people progress through later adolescence, they begin to encounter adult expectations for mature sex-role behavior. For males, such expectations may include holding a steady job, being able to provide for a family, or being competitive. For females, they may focus on expressing maternal, nurturant behavior; being a good homemaker; or exhibiting interpersonal skills. As in the early-school-age period, individuals are confronted with social expectations that may complement or conflict with their personal temperaments. The resolution of the mature sex-role identity will depend on whether the person can achieve some fit between these adult expectations and personal preferences (Feather, 1985; Page, 1987).

A unique challenge faces women of certain ethnic backgrounds who have been socialized to have traditional views of women's roles within a changing context of American sex-role norms. For example, Asian-American women are likely to have grown up in an environment that discouraged them from exhibiting such traits as independence and competitiveness and encouraged them to develop such traits as altruism, affiliation, and timidity. Yet in the workplace those Asian-American women who ascribe to a traditional feminine sex role have lower self-esteem and lower occupational attainment than Asian-American women who are more masculine in orientation (Chow, 1987).

Asian-American women may have to reject aspects of their sex-role socialization in order to achieve professional success.

There has been widespread publicity about changing definitions of the male and female sex roles. The women's movement, changing attitudes about sexuality and marriage relationships, and the increasing proportion of women who combine work and parenting have all influenced our concepts of masculinity and femininity. Three models of healthy sex-role development have been proposed in the psychological literature (Whitely, 1983, 1984). The *congruence model* proposes that the most positive outcome is for men to adopt strong masculine sex-role identities and for women to adopt strong feminine sex-role identities. The *androgyny model* proposes that a healthy person should be able to have access to both masculine and feminine attributes. This model suggests that the dimensions of masculinity and femininity are both associated with strengths that could be valuable under certain circumstances. An androgynous person would be able to function in either feminine or masculine style, depending on which was appropriate. The *masculinity model* emphasizes the general advantage of the masculine attributes for both sexes. From this perspective, well-being would be greater for both men and women if they had masculine sex-role orientations.

Each of the three models of sex-role orientation assumes that sex role is distinct from gender. A person of either sex may have personality characteristics that are categorized as either masculine (such as assertiveness, independence, and dominance) or feminine (such as nurturance, orderliness, and deference). The models differ in their predictions about the pattern of sex-role characteristics that is most adaptive for males and females. In a review of 35 studies that assessed the relationship between sex-role orientation and self-esteem, the strongest support was given to the masculinity model (Whitely, 1983). Masculine personality traits, especially assertiveness in social

Pablo Picasso, *Girl before a Mirror,* Boisge-loup, March 1932. An adolescent must inte-grate an adult body and sexual impulses into the self-concept. This is a process that involves a reexamination of all aspects of gender role, including sexual behav-ior, intimate relation-ships, career goals, and family values.
Oil on canvas, 64″ x 51¼″. Collection: The Museum of Modern Art, New York. Gift of Mrs. Simon Guggenheim. © 1991, ARS, New York/ SPADEM.

situations, were most closely associated with high self-esteem. Women and men who have prominent masculine traits feel more positive about their own worth than those who are either feminine or androgynous (Zedlow, Clark & Daugherty, 1985; Long, 1989).

Some ways in which masculinity is associated with effective functioning are seen in the following two studies. In one, young men and women who were classified as either masculine, feminine, or androgynous were asked to complete two sex-typed ability tests. One was a test of mechanical reasoning (a masculine-typed skill); the other was a test of speed and accuracy (a feminine-typed skill). The masculine subjects of both sexes performed better on the mechanical reasoning test than did the feminine or androgynous subjects. There was no clear advantage for the androgynous or fem-inine subject on either of the tests (Antill & Cunningham, 1982).

In the other study, women were exposed to a situation that promoted feelings of helplessness. After this experience, subjects were asked whether they wanted to assume a leadership role in a decision-making task. Women high in masculinity continued to want to take control in the new situation. Women high in femininity and androgynous women did not choose to assume control (Baucom, 1983). These studies suggest that there are clearly situations in which the masculine orientation has specific advantages over other sex-role orientations. Other work points to a general positive sense of well-being for those with a strong masculine orientation (Wells, 1980; Lubinski, Tellegen & Batcher, 1983; Nezu & Nezu, 1987).

These results are not so surprising when we think about what it means to be characterized as having a masculine sex role. Masculinity is associated with a strong sense of agency, independence, and achievement striving. Whether or not it is appropriate to think of these qualities as linked to masculinity is a separate question. In our society, both men and women tend to agree that these personality traits are part of the stereotype of masculinity. This does not mean that there are no situations in which the feminine and androgynous orientations are advantageous. It does suggest, however, that the benefits of masculine traits are more conducive to adapting to and succeeding in today's society than we may have realized.

Movement Toward a Single Standard

In addition to the evidence that a masculine sex-role orientation is linked to more positive adjustment, there is evidence that men and women are becoming more "single standard" in their views. This is clearest in the area of dating and sexuality. For example, one view of the masculine role is that men are unexpressive, restrained, and unwilling to open up to others. In a study of dating couples, however, a high proportion of both the men and the women said that they had fully disclosed their thoughts and feelings to their partners in almost all areas. Self-disclosure was less closely related to gender than to the love the partners felt for each other and to the egalitarian or traditional sex-role attitudes that the couple held (Rubin et al., 1980).

In an analysis of college students' views of sexual permissiveness, male and female students were asked to judge whether certain degrees of sexual intimacy (such as petting and intercourse) were acceptable within the context of increasing levels of commitment to the relationship (from first date to engagement) (Sprecher et al., 1988). In indicating behaviors that they considered acceptable, students made no distinctions on the basis of the sex of the person in question. In other words, they were not applying a double standard in their judgments about the sexual activities of men and women. At every level, however, men had more permissive views than women. This pattern is found also in other studies of attitudes toward sexuality. Men and women show a pattern of increasing permissiveness since the 1960s, but men continue to be more permissive than women in their acceptance of premarital sex (Thornton, 1989; Dodge, 1990).

Clearly, sex-role identity encompasses much more than one's sexual behavior. Yet the shift in the sexual script toward a more shared view of the appropriate role of sexuality in a relationship is an important element in the overall picture. It should result in a greater understanding of the need for intimacy between partners. Further,

A woman who decides
to enter a male-domi-
nated field may
encounter challenges to
her gender identity.

similarity in men's and women's views of sexuality might provide a basis for discovering similarities in other spheres of adult life.

Sex Role and Career Choice

Sexual relations is only one of the areas that has an impact on sex-role identity. Another critical area is occupation. Many jobs are conceptualized and categorized in terms of sex-role orientation. For example, the profession of surgeon is seen as very masculine, demanding strength, courage, independence, intelligence, emotional control, and an understanding of the nature of command. Many people would see this profession as appropriate for a man and inappropriate for a woman. As a result of their stereotypes of the male and female sex roles, they would find the needed traits of the surgeon to be present only in the male. Some might even see this occupation or one with similar demands (for example, construction supervisor) as leading to the development of valued masculine tendencies. The choice that an individual makes to enter the medical profession and to become a surgeon may be motivated by a concern for maintaining a masculine self-image. Similarly, the profession of nurse may be viewed as feminine, demanding nurturance, accuracy, emotional support, and interpersonal skills. Many people might see this profession as appropriate for a woman and inappropriate for a man. A person might choose to enter the field of nursing in order to maintain a feminine self-image.

The decision to enter a "sex-appropriate" career could provide the person with an environment that supports sex-role identity. The decision to enter a career that is not generally elected by members of one's own sex leads to tension because of the resulting challenges. These challenges are directed toward both the person's competence and the person's sex-role identity. In studies of career choice or career aspirations among women, it is the women with a strong sense of their own goals, an awareness of their personal needs, and an ability to cope realistically with stress who have been more likely to adopt a nontraditional sex-role definition and career choice (Nevill & Schlecker, 1988; Long, 1989).

Although adolescents are exposed to increasing efforts to reduce sex-typed thinking about careers, sex-role orientation continues to influence their career plans. One study compared occupational plans of high school seniors graduating in 1964 and 1975 (Lueptow, 1981). The students were asked about the occupation they planned to follow and the kind of work they would go into if they had absolute freedom of choice. In 1964 almost 80% of the girls intended to work in female-dominated occupations, while in 1975 only 63% planned to do so. This shift reflects the greater interest of women in white-collar work that had been dominated by men in 1964. However, there was not much change in the boys' plans. About 70% intended to work in male-dominated occupations in both 1964 and 1975. Further, in 1975 about 60% of both the boys and the girls said that their preferred occupation would be in a congruent male or female occupation. The majority of these adolescents, therefore, neither intended to enter a nontraditional field nor would have preferred to enter one if no limits were placed on their choice. One can conclude from this and similar findings that sex-role identity is a very pervasive cognitive orientation that directs life choices (Markus et al., 1982; Eccles, 1987). By the time one reaches later adolescence, one's sex-role identity acts as a filter on environmental stimuli, making some alternatives appear attractive or desirable and others unattractive or repugnant.

Sex Role and Values

Just as there is an overlap between one's occupational role and one's sex role, so too there is an overlap between one's value orientation and one's sex-role identity. The decision to conform to sex-role expectations may be seen not only as an expression of personal preference but also as an expression of moral values. Some people, for example, believe that it is immoral for a man to "allow" his wife to work in order to help support the family. The traditional status relationships between men and women have come to symbolize moral obligation. The man demonstrates his personal responsibility by caring and providing for the family. The woman demonstrates her personal fidelity and obedience by subordinating herself to her husband. For many people, the relationship between a man and a woman is an expression of their religious beliefs.

In this light, any violation of the sex-role standard becomes a moral violation as well. The sex-role standards are tenaciously maintained because of this moral overtone. Consider the Puerto Rican concept of *marianismo*. *Marianismo* is the female counterpart of *machismo*. It is a view of women based on the Catholic ideal of Mother Mary. The underlying premise is that because women are spiritually superior to men, they are able to endure greater suffering, including the suffering inflicted on them by their male partners. According to this code, Puerto Rican women place the highest value on their responsibilities to their children. They will both endure harsh treatment from their husbands and sacrifice themselves for the sake of their children. The children, in turn, have great respect and reverence for their mothers, according the mothers power and stature despite their outward passivity and submissiveness (Comas-Diaz, 1987).

The content of the sex-role identity is a product of the acceptance of one's sexuality, earlier socialization in sex-role standards and preferences, the selection of an occupation, and the nature of one's moral code. During later adolescence, one engages in the process of accepting one's sexuality in a mature way. One also wrestles with questions about occupational choice and mature morality. By the end of this stage, the young person has the potential for conceptualizing a sex-role identity that will continue through young adulthood and into middle adulthood.

Internalized Morality

The development of morality was introduced in Chapter 7, "Early School Age." At that stage, morality consists primarily of internalizing parental standards and values, recognizing the difference between right and wrong, and learning to control one's behavior in anticipation of its moral consequences. During later adolescence, the young person begins to exercise moral judgments in matters of much greater complexity than those that confront the early-school-age child. Further, later adolescents are more aware of the multiple perspectives that are possible in a moral situation. They are concerned about how principles of social responsibility, human rights, and justice can be preserved in a moral decision.

Lawrence Kohlberg (1964) has suggested that a qualitative change in a person's ability to identify moral issues and decide about moral behavior is expected from early school age to later adolescence. Kohlberg's theory of the development of moral thought includes three levels of moral reasoning, divided into six substages. (See Chapter 7, Table 7.3.)

At the preconventional level, from about ages 4 to 10, the child is concerned with the external consequences of behavior and with the power of those who represent authority. The conventional level, from about ages 10 to 18, represents a concern with the maintenance of the existing rule structure and a respect for authority. The postconventional level of moral reasoning includes an awareness of the relativism of values and a commitment to either a personal or a universal set of moral principles. The proportion of subjects who reach this level of moral reasoning is small, but it increases during early and middle adulthood.

Longitudinal data provide strong evidence for the sequential nature of these stages during childhood and adolescence. Figure 10.2 shows age trends in the use of moral reasoning among 58 male subjects who participated in a study for more than 20 years (Colby et al., 1983). Preconventional reasoning (stages 1 and 2) is dominant in the youngest subjects, but it declines sharply between ages 10 and 14. Conventional reasoning (stages 3 and 4) increases from age 10 on, becomes the dominant form of reasoning in early and later adolescence, and remains the dominant form of reasoning throughout the years of adulthood studied, with stage 4 reasoning surpassing stage 3 in the mid-20s. Postconventional reasoning (stage 5) does not appear until age 18, then increases somewhat, but remains relatively rare in the period studied. These findings support the notion that the stages are reached in the sequence predicted.

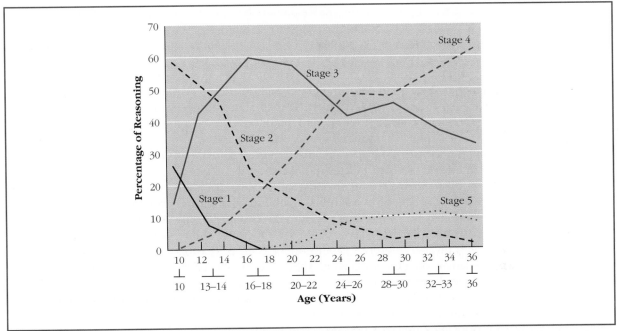

Figure 10.2   Mean Percentage of Male Subjects in Eight Age Groups Who Demonstrated Five Stages of
Moral Reasoning
Source: A. Colby, L. Kohlberg, J. Gibbs, and M. Lieberman, "A Longitudinal Study of Moral Judgment,"
Monographs of the Society for Research in Child Development, 48, (1, serial no. 200) (1983), 46. Reprinted
with permission from the Society for Research in Child Development, Inc.

Other studies confirm the order of the stages and that subjects do not skip stages
(Nisan & Kohlberg, 1982; Snarey, Reimer & Kohlberg, 1985; Colby & Kohlberg, 1987).

Individuals understand moral arguments at their own dominant level of reasoning
or below, but not more than one step higher (Walker, 1982; Walker, de Vries & Bichard,
1984). As a result of participation in thought-provoking discussions, moral reasoning
can advance to the next higher level (Berkowitz & Gibbs, 1983). Social and educational
experiences tend to promote moral reasoning when they draw upon existing constructs but also challenge those constructs by making their inadequacies clear (Gfellner, 1986).

The sequence of stages is also noted in a variety of cultures. Research has been
done in Israel, Turkey, the Bahamas, Honduras, Mexico, India, Kenya, Nigeria, and
Taiwan. The subjects in these studies used forms of reasoning similar to those used
by American samples. Adults and adolescents in every culture used levels of reasoning
that were higher than those used by the children (Nisan & Kohlberg, 1982; Rest, 1983;
Snarey, Reimer & Kohlberg, 1985; Colby & Kohlberg, 1987).

Although the sequence of stages appears to be well established, the level of moral
reasoning that any individual actually attains will depend on the kinds of moral chal-

lenges and situations the person encounters. Stage 3 reasoning seems to be the dominant mode of reasoning for adults in Turkey, while stage 4 is the more common form of reasoning among adults in the United States and Israel (Snarey, Reimer & Kohlberg, 1985). In nonindustrialized countries, people from rural villages do not use any postconventional reasoning. Tribal leaders, however, tend to reason at somewhat higher levels than other members of their tribes (Harkness, Edwards & Super, 1981; Tietjen & Walker, 1985). In the United States, high school students reason at lower levels than college students, and the differences become greater with each additional year of college completed (Rest & Thoma, 1985). In each of these comparisons, we find evidence of the principle that exposure to a diversity of information, relationships, and world views stimulates moral reasoning.

The change from conventional to postconventional morality that begins during adolescence involves a rethinking of traditional moral principles. During this period, there may be a loosening of ties to the family of origin and an increase in encounters with an expanding network of friends, students, and co-workers. Through interactions with diverse reference groups, there is an increasing recognition of the subcultural relativity of one's moral code. There may also be a degree of conflict over which moral values have personal meaning.

Turiel (1974) described a transitional stage between the conventional and postconventional levels during the late high school and early college years. At this time old principles are challenged but new, independent values have not yet taken their place. This transition in moral thought closely parallels the general process of identity formation. Older adolescents are aware of the contradictions in the existing social and value structures in which they participate. The search for identity includes a search for a moral code that will preserve the adolescent's personal integrity. The adolescent must try to reconcile notions about individual integrity and social necessity. As one 19-year-old stated:

> *It is just that I really believe you can't go into someone else's mind and tell them what is right. I can't see the world through anyone else's eyes. . . . If their vision of reality is very much different from the socially acceptable vision, then they are going to come to different conclusions as to morality.*   [Turiel, 1974, p. 21]

Later adolescents wrestle with the distinctions between moral reasoning and reasoning that applies to social convention (Windmiller, Lambert & Turiel, 1980). (This distinction was introduced in the discussion of moral development in Chapter 7.) *Social convention* refers to norms that are determined by the social system and apply to a specific social context—for example, a gentleman rising to shake the hand of a woman when they are being introduced. It might be rude to violate such a social convention, but it would not be immoral. In contrast, moral issues are not regulated by the social context but are determined by underlying principles of justice and concern for others. They should not be viewed as behaviors that are regulated solely by rules or rewards of the setting. Rules governing moral behavior do not change from one setting or situation to another. If it is morally wrong to steal, it is wrong to take chalk from a school, jewelry from a store, or ideas from a colleague. Studies of children at varying ages from preschool to later adolescence suggest that people regularly draw

College provides a context for reviewing and evaluating moral values. Students become increasingly committed to upholding basic principles of human dignity and justice.

this distinction between social convention and moral behavior. Some of the confusion about moral judgment that is seen during the later adolescent period may reflect uncertainty about social convention rather than about underlying moral principles. As young people enter new roles and participate in more complex social settings, they may be unclear about the social expectations for those situations.

Another distinction has been drawn between prohibitive moral judgments and prosocial moral judgments. *Prohibitive moral judgments* involve a decision about violating a law or breaking a promise in order to achieve some other goal. In Kohlberg's test of moral reasoning, a typical example is the case of Heinz, a man, who is placed in the dilemma of having to steal a drug from a pharmacist if he is to save his wife's life. *Prosocial moral judgments* involve a conflict between doing something helpful for someone else and meeting one's own needs. An example would be stopping to help a person whose car has stalled on the highway at the risk of being late for a very important job interview. People seem to be able to think more flexibly about a prosocial dilemma than about a prohibitive one. Moral decisions that draw on empathy and concern for the well-being of another person tend to evoke a higher level of moral reasoning than those that would require breaking a law (Kurdek, 1981; Eisenberg & Strayer, 1987).

Later adolescents must evolve an integrated, mature value system with which to guide their behavior, particularly in the face of strong pressures to violate their moral beliefs. Young people will encounter situations that they have never faced before—situations that require moral evaluation, judgment, and decisions about action. A student may be asked by a college peer to lend a paper that he has written. A young

---

Box 10.1   Morality and Gender

A controversy in the field of moral reasoning focuses on whether men and women take different approaches to ethical decisions. Carol Gilligan (1977, 1982) has presented a forceful argument that Kohlberg's description of the developmental course of reasoning about moral dilemmas is incomplete because it is based on the reasoning of male subjects in regard to hypothetical rather than real-life situations. She argues that women approach moral decisions with greater sensitivity to the context of the problem and a strong sense of caring, whereas men tend to view moral dilemmas from a more removed, abstract perspective. Their emphasis tends to be on justice and respect for individual rights. A woman, for example, might ask which outcome of a moral dilemma would result in the least harm for all concerned; a man might ask whether one person, in exercising his rights, has the right to infringe on the rights of others (Friedman, Robinson & Friedman, 1987). These differences, according to Gilligan, are the products of different socialization patterns and the resulting differences in

orientation to values and family life and in the basis of self-worth.

Several investigators have examined the claims of consistent differences in moral orientation between men and women. Two common findings begin to clarify our understanding of the matter. First, college-age women and men do not consistently differ in their use of the two types of themes, those focusing on interpersonal obligations and caring and those focusing on an abstract sense of justice. Men and women introduce both types of reasoning when they have an opportunity to do so. Second, it appears that experiential and situational issues, concerns about interpersonal obligations and caring, are more dominant in open-ended responses from both men and women than are issues of justice and individual rights. Thus Gilligan's work has had the effect of highlighting a significant set of social concerns that influence the way people construct their view of morality in a given situation (Ford & Lowery, 1986; Walker, de Vries & Trevethan, 1987; Galotti, 1989).

---

woman may be invited to spend the weekend at a male friend's apartment. A young person may be asked to engage in direct and violent political acts to demonstrate acceptance of a cause. Decisions about maintaining religious traditions and practices may confront a young person who is away from home. In each of these situations, the person may not be aware of or may not be able to assess the immediate consequences of behavior. Decisions must be based on an internalized set of moral principles that will help the person to evaluate the demands of the situation and plan a course of action that will be most congruent with personal ideals.

Continued participation in formal education has a strong relationship to advances in moral reasoning. When students were compared over the six years after they graduated from high school, those who had had two years or less of college showed no significant changes in moral reasoning. Those who had attended three or more years of college showed a pattern of increasing scores (Rest & Thoma, 1985). We do not understand exactly which aspects of continued formal education promote advanced moral reasoning. We might speculate that the individual's desire for further education and the intellectual stimulation of the college environment combine to produce a more complex analysis of moral issues. In addition, the social environment of college life presents an array of interpersonal conflicts. Students who are open to recognizing these moral dilemmas and coping successfully with them will gain insight into their own capacities for both good and bad as well as the ability to recognize these capacities in others. The terms *good* and *bad* take on a more dynamic interpersonal meaning as young people encounter conflicts in arenas in which they have made strong commitments or invested their idealism (Haan, 1985).

As young people leave their families and encounter new situations, they find that they must use the moral principles that they internalized throughout childhood to guide their behavior. They will undoubtedly discover that some of the moral principles they learned as 6- or 7-year-olds neither apply to the new situations nor provide much of a rationale for why they should behave one way and not another. Later adolescents begin to clarify the distinction between social conventions and moral issues. Behaviors that may have been viewed as moral issues during childhood may be reevaluated as social conventions. As with some aspects of identification with parents or other authorities, some aspects of childhood morality must be dissolved and restructured to meet the impending demands of adulthood.

Career Choice

The choice of occupation sets the tone for the early adult lifestyle. The world of work determines one's daily routine, including the time one wakes up, the amount of one's daily activity, expenditures of physical and mental energy, and conditions for both immediate and long-term rewards. Occupation confers social status and provides varying opportunities for advancement. Finally, occupation represents a direct or indirect expression of one's value system. In subsequent chapters we will discuss socialization in the work setting and the management of a career. Here we focus on the process of career choice and its impact on development during later adolescence.

Many adolescents hold part-time jobs while they attend high school. By the time they graduate from high school, 80% of adolescents will have had some formal work experience (Steinberg et al., 1982). However, work experiences during early adolescence are different from the socialization into a career that takes place during later adolescence and early adulthood. The kinds of work opportunities that are available to adolescents are usually minimally skilled jobs with little decision-making responsibility. For some groups of adolescents, time spent in the workplace is associated with the development of cynical attitudes toward work and greater acceptance of unethical practices by workers. Youngsters may gain a sense of personal responsibility from working, but they do not necessarily develop a great commitment to the exercise of competence in the world of work.

As Figure 10.3 suggests, the process of career decision making is influenced by six major factors: individual, psychosocial/emotional, socioeconomic, societal, familial, and situational (O'Neil, Ohlde, Barke et al., 1980). These same factors contribute to sex-role socialization. It is important to see the interrelationship of these two domains for young people in our culture. Sex-role socialization creates a powerful filter through which choices related to career development are made (Eccles, 1987).

Of the six types of factors described in Figure 10.3, high school and college students reported that it was the individual factors, such as abilities, interests, attitudes, and self-expectancies, that most strongly affected their career decision making. They perceived familial, societal, and socioeconomic factors as having little or no impact (O'Neil, Ohlde, Tollefson et al., 1980).

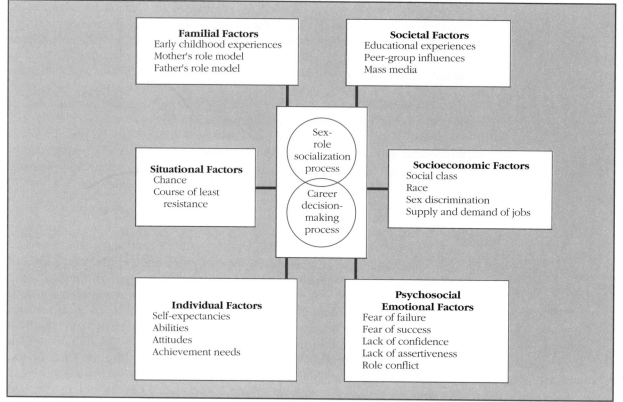

Figure 10.3   **Factors Affecting the Sex-Role Socialization and Career Decision-Making Process**
Source: J. M. O'Neil, C. Ohlde, C. Barke, B. Prosser-Gelwick, and N. Garfield, "Research on a Workshop to Reduce the Effects of Sexism and Sex-Role Socialization on Women's Career Planning," *Journal of Counseling Psychology, 27* (1980), 355–363. Reprinted by permission of the author.

Education and Career Choice

One of the major factors influencing career opportunities is education. It is a well-documented fact that career advancement and associated earnings are closely linked to levels of educational attainment. Table 10.2 shows the median earned income for men and women who were 25 years old or older in 1985 on the basis of their educational level. There is no question that continued education beyond high school is a key element in the career development process. As the data indicate, however, educational achievement does not result in the same economic advantages for men and women. Women with professional education beyond four years of college earned only slightly more than men who had a high school diploma.

For youths who leave high school or who graduate from high school but do not go on to college, the job market has several unattractive features. Most of the jobs available at this level of educational attainment are

routine, menial, temporary, more likely to be part time and to provide reduced monetary and nonmaterial rewards compared with jobs held by older workers.

Table 10.2 Median Income of Men and Women 25 Years and Older, 1985, by Educational Attainment		
	Median Income	
Education	*Men*	*Women*
No high school diploma	$18,881	$11,836
High school graduate	23,853	15,481
College graduate	32,822	21,389
Professional degree (requiring 5 or more years of college)	39,335	25,928

Source: *The Forgotten Half: Non-College Youth in America* (Washington, D.C.: William T. Grant Commission on Work, Family, and Citizenship, 1988), p. 21.

> . . . *Moreover, jobs within this sector are unusually unstable and may be supervised by rigid, autocratic employers, many of whom, particulary in the fast food industry, are not much older than the novice worker.* [Borman & Hopkins, 1987, p. 136]

The impact of school experiences on subsequent career development goes beyond whether one plans to attend college or not. Vocational coursework of a specific nature, such as agricultural training, an emphasis on math and science courses, and frequent conversations with teachers about one's work-related decisions are all associated with higher income and more stable work records after high school (Hubner-Funk, 1983; Griffin & Alexander, 1978).

For youths who do not go on to college, career development appears to have two phases (Freeman & Wise, 1982; West & Newton, 1983). Given the kinds of jobs that are available and the outlook on work that was developed during high school, many young people start out with a rather cavalier approach to work. They take whatever job is available, work without much intention of long-term commitment, and exhibit erratic work behavior. Most of these jobs do not require much training and do not lead to a career. Young people are likely to quit these jobs when they have earned enough money to pay for the things they want and then remain unemployed for a while until they need more money. During their 20s the second phase begins as young adults become more serious about their work. They try to find a good job, they become more conscientious about their work performance, and they stay with the job for a longer period. This new seriousness about work is likely to be associated with other commitments, especially marriage, and is usually seen as a positive step in the transition to adulthood.

Sex-Role Socialization and Career Choice

Sex-role socialization shapes career decisions through two significant psychological factors. First, as a result of socialization, men and women are likely to form different

The fast-food industry is a major employer of high school dropouts. Young people who take these jobs do not plan to make a long-term commitment.

expectations about their ability to succeed in various career-related skills. Second, as a result of socialization, women and men are likely to establish different value hierarchies, reflecting different views of long-range life goals and their relative importance to one another (Eccles, 1987).

Self-expectancies about the ability to fulfill the educational requirements and the job duties of specific careers are a major factor in determining career choices (Bridges, 1988; Long, 1989). In one study, college students were asked to evaluate their ability to complete the educational requirements and fulfill the job duties of ten traditionally male occupations and ten traditionally female occupations (Betz & Hackett, 1981). Males reported higher self-efficacy on five male occupations: accountant, drafter, engineer, highway patrol officer, and mathematician. Females reported higher self-efficacy on five female occupations: dental hygienist, elementary school teacher, home economist, physical therapist, and secretary. Males thought that the most difficult job duties of the 20 occupations listed were those of art teacher. Females thought the most difficult duties were those of engineer. These differences in expectations about the ability to succeed were not paralleled by differences in the students' ability tests in math or English which might have made certain career choices unrealistic. These data suggest that in the process of career decision making, strong sex-typed conceptualizations of the job demands of specific careers intervene to screen out some alternatives and highlight others.

Sex-role identity influences attitudes and values that determine one's career goals and related choices. Consider the objectives that men and women entering college

Table 10.3   Life Objectives Considered Essential or Very Important by College Freshmen

Objective	Men	Women
Becoming accomplished in a performing art	10.7%	11.5%
Becoming an authority in own field	67.8	64.1
Obtaining recognition from colleagues for contributions to field	56.1	54.0
Influencing the political structure	22.4	17.7
Influencing social values	35.2	46.1
Raising a family	68.5	69.0
Having administrative responsibility for the work of others	44.9	42.6
Being very well off financially	79.5	71.9
Helping others who are in difficulty	49.0	68.7
Making a theoretical contribution to science	20.7	14.1
Writing original works	12.2	12.7
Creating artistic work	12.4	12.6
Becoming successful in own business	50.1	40.8
Becoming involved in programs to clean up environment	28.3	24.3
Developing a meaningful philosophy of life	40.0	41.6
Participating in a community-action program	20.2	25.9
Helping to promote racial understanding	32.5	37.6
Keeping up to date with political affairs	43.4	36.0

Source: S. Dodge, "More Freshmen Willing to Work for Social Change and Environmental Issues, New Survey Finds," *Chronicle of Higher Education, 36* (January 24, 1990), A34. Data from the Higher Education Research Institute, UCLA. Reprinted by permission.

in 1989 said were essential or very important in their lives (see Table 10.3). Although men and women shared many common objectives, about 10% more women than men endorsed social values, and 20% more women emphasized helping others who were in difficulty. About 10% more men than women endorsed being well-off financially and becoming successful in their own business (Dodge, 1990). Even in areas in which men and women have very similar commitments, such as raising a family, the way the value plays out with respect to selecting a career may be very different. Women who place a high value on family life are likely to assess careers differently from women who expect to remain single or to be childless. Values are likely to direct students toward majors and future careers that will help them experience a sense of personal integrity, a balance between what they say is important and what they do.

The impact of values is demonstrated by a study of the factors that are most salient to college men and women in choosing a major (Hearn, 1980; Hearn & Olzak, 1981). In their choice of major, men are less influenced by the supportive climate and quality of instruction. They tend to choose majors that appear to be linked with high post-graduate payoff in career status or salary despite the less favorable atmosphere that may be associated with such majors. Women are more likely to consider the quality of the department's student-teacher interaction and student-centered orientation. The irony of this distinction is that internal supportiveness tends to be negatively related to high-status rewards. The decision of male students to choose high-status rewards and of female students to choose a supportive climate tends to perpetuate sex differences in career building and occupational attainment.

The life circumstances of some individuals put a career choice out of reach. High school dropouts, for example, may be forced to choose from among a very restricted set of alternatives. Without a high school diploma, the kind of jobs that can be obtained and the amount of capital that can be accumulated are restricted. Our society does provide some options, such as high school equivalency programs, military careers, military training in technical skills, and work force training programs. However, these options are not well developed. As a result, many young people enter later adolescence on a path toward lifelong poverty.

Given the constraints on occupational choice, the choice itself reflects a central component of the person's emerging identity. For some, occupational choice is a reflection of continued identification with parents. They may select the same job or career as that of one of their parents, or the parents may make the job choice for them. Little personal choice is involved for such people. For others, the choice of occupation is the result of personal experimentation, introspection, self-evaluation, fact-finding, and intuition, whether they elect a parent's career or a different one. It is this process that is important in the individual's psychological development. In order to make a career choice, people may pose very difficult questions to themselves about their skills, temperament, values, and goals. When a decision is made after this kind of personal evaluation, people are likely to see their careers as a well-integrated part of their personal identities rather than as activities from which they are alienated or by which they are dominated.

Summary

The developmental tasks of later adolescence represent continued work on some of the early tasks of childhood, particularly sex-role identity and moral development. During later adolescence, these tasks are expanded and separated from their intimate bond with the parent-child relationship.

The adolescent's emerging independence from parents requires unique energy. Although the individual is constantly involved in the process of self-differentiation, it is during later adolescence that a real departure from parental domination takes place. One may never be totally liberated from the child role with regard to one's parents, but it is primarily during this stage that one's efforts are directed toward that end.

The task of occupational choice marks the beginning of a lifelong concern with work, efficacy, productivity, and contribution to the larger social community. Although it is possible to change one's career, all but a very few must participate in some form of work. The process of choosing an occupation represents a commitment to the role of worker as well as the selection of a specific career. We see later adolescence as a truly transitional stage in our culture during which some roles are ending, others are changing, and still others are beginning.

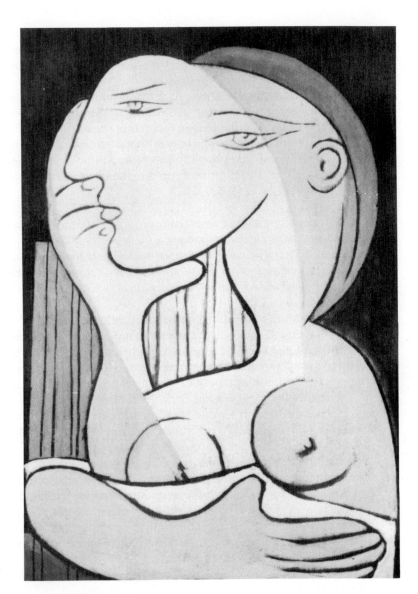

Pablo Picasso, *Seated Woman,* 1932. In this powerful painting, Picasso suggests many levels of the self, searching, questioning, and yet harmonious.

The Psychosocial Crisis: Individual Identity versus Identity Confusion

Erik Erikson has provided a comprehensive treatment of the meaning and functions of individual identity. From his inclusion of this concept in the theory of psychosocial development (1950) to his analysis of American identity (1974), Erikson has evolved a notion of identity that involves the merging of past identifications, future aspirations, and contemporary cultural issues. The major works in which he discusses identity are "The Problem of Ego Identity" (1959) and *Identity: Youth and Crisis* (1968). Our presentation of this concept is based on these works.

Later adolescents are preoccupied with questions about their essential character in much the same way that early-school-age children are preoccupied with questions about their origins. In their efforts to define themselves, later adolescents must take into account the bonds that have been built between them and others in the past as well as the direction that they hope to take in the future. The identity serves as an anchor point that allows the person an essential experience of continuity in social relationships. Erikson (1959) states:

> *The young individual must learn to be most himself where he means the most to others—those others, to be sure, who have come to mean most to him. The term identity expresses such a mutual relation in that it connotes both a persistent sameness within oneself (self-sameness) and a persistent sharing of some kind of essential character with others.*   [p. 102]

The structure of identity has two components, content and evaluation (Breakwell, 1986; Whitbourne, 1986). The *content* includes elements of the inner or private self and of the public self. The aspects of the private self—ideals, goals, personal characteristics—are often described in reference to ideological commitments, especially in the areas of religion and politics, vocational commitments, and interpersonal commitments (Marcia, 1980; Bilsker, Schiedel & Marcia, 1988). The elements of the public self include the many roles one plays and the expectations of others. As young people move through the stage of later adolescence, they find that family members, neighbors, teachers, friends, religious groups, ethnic groups, and even national leaders have expectations in regard to their behavior. A young person may be expected to work, to attend college, to marry, to serve the country in the military, to attend religious services, to vote, and to provide economic support for family members. Persistent demands by meaningful others produce certain decisions that might have been made differently or not made at all if the individual were surrounded by a different configuration of social reference groups. Thus individual identity must synthesize the characteristics that the person recognizes as the "authentic" or "true self" with the characteristics that the person derives from the many roles and relationships in which he or she is embedded.

The second structural component of identity is *evaluation*. Of all the many elements that make up the content of identity, some are viewed as more central or salient than others. Thus, even though most people play many of the same roles, their identities differ in part because they place different values on some of these roles. Some people are quite single-minded, setting great value on success in one domain, such as their vocational goals, and placing little stock in the others. Other people strive to maintain a balance of roles; they consider themselves successful if they can find enjoyment in a variety of relationships and activities.

This assessment of the importance of certain content areas in relation to others will influence the use of resources, the direction of certain decisions, and the kinds

Developing an identity requires sustained reflection and involves prolonged periods of uncertainty.

of experiences that may be perceived as most personally rewarding or personally threatening. College students, for example, may differ as to whether their academic success or their interpersonal success is most central to their sense of identity. Students who are more concerned about academic success will take quite a different approach to the college environment, become involved in different kinds of activities, and have a different reaction to academic failure than students who are more concerned about interpersonal success (Reischl & Hirsch, 1989).

Both the content and the evaluation component of identity can change over the life course. In later adolescence the focus is on integrating the various sources of content and determining which elements have the greatest salience. This is a major accomplishment that requires self-awareness, introspection, and active exploration of a variety of roles and relationships. However, the individual identity that is formulated at the end of this period is often very abstract. Later adolescents have not yet encountered many of the responsibilities, pressures, and conflicts of adult life. The ideological framework of identity has not yet been forged in the flames of reality.

Although identity provides a basic source of continuity across settings and roles, it will need to be modified when life experiences highlight inadequacies or gaps in the basic construct. Certain aspects of one's identity may become more salient if they are challenged by a life crisis, if one enters a new role that is particularly demanding, or if one experiences a change in values and goals. New content may be added, especially when the person has an opportunity to enact new roles, or evaluations may shift as some content areas receive new emphasis and others become less salient.

The basic conflict of the psychosocial crisis of later adolescence is individual identity formation versus identity confusion. This conflict results from the enormous difficulty of pulling together the many components of the self, including the diverse social demands, into a unified image that can propel the person toward positive, meaningful action. The process of identity formation is confounded by distractions of

Table 10.4 Relationship of Identity Status, Crisis, and Commitment		
	Crisis	Commitment
Identity achievement	+	+
Foreclosure	−	+
Moratorium	+	−
Identity confusion	+/−	−

all sorts. Many young people find it very hard to sort out what they want to be from what their parents have urged them to become. Others have received little encouragement to become a separate person with independent feelings and views. Some are so beleaguered by feelings of inferiority and alienation that they do not have the optimism necessary to create a positive vision of their future. Still others find many paths appealing and have difficulty making a commitment to one above the others.

Identity formation is a dynamic process that unfolds as young people assess their competences and aspirations within a changing social context of expectations, demands, and resources. A variety of potential resolutions of the psychosocial crisis of individual identity versus identity confusion have been described. At the positive pole is *identity achievement;* at the negative pole is *identity confusion.* Also discussed are a premature resolution, *identity foreclosure;* a postponement of resolution, *psychosocial moratorium;* and a *negative identity.*

One of the most widely used conceptual frameworks for assessing identity status was devised by James Marcia (Marcia, 1980; Waterman, 1982). Using Erikson's concepts, Marcia assessed identity status on the basis of two criteria: crisis and commitment. *Crisis* consists of a period of role experimentation and active decision making among alternative choices. *Commitment* consists of a demonstration of personal involvement in the areas of occupational choice, religion, and political ideology. On the basis of Marcia's questionnaire, the status of subjects' identity development is assessed (see Table 10.4). People who are classified as *identity achieved* have already experienced a crisis time and have made occupational and ideological commitments. People who are classified as *identity foreclosed* have not experienced a crisis but demonstrate strong occupational and ideological commitments. Their occupational and ideological beliefs appear to be very close to those of their parents. The foreclosed identity is deceptive. A young person of 18 or 19 who can say exactly what he or she wants in life and who has selected an occupational goal may appear to be very mature. This kind of clarity of vision may impress peers and adults as evidence of a high level of self-insight. However, if this solution has been formulated through the wholesale adoption of a script that was devised by the young person's family, it may not actually reflect much depth of self-understanding.

People who are classified as being in a state of *psychosocial moratorium* are involved in ongoing crisis. Their commitments are diffuse. People who are classified as *identity confused* may or may not have experienced a crisis and demonstrate a

Student athletes are at special risk for foreclosure. They are encouraged to focus on developing their athletic talents and have little time for the other kinds of experimentation that contribute to identity achievement.

complete lack of commitment. Marcia mentions that the identity-confused group has a rather cavalier, playboy quality that allows members to cope with the college environment. He suggests that the more seriously confused persons (such as those described by Erikson, 1959) may not appear in his sample because they are unable to cope with college.

Sometimes the cultural expectations and demands provide the young person with a clearly defined self-image that is completely contrary to the cultural values of the community. This is called a *negative identity* (Erikson, 1959). Such expressions as "failure," "good-for-nothing," "juvenile delinquent," "hood," and "loser" are labels that the adult society commonly applies to certain adolescents. In the absence of any indication of the possibilities of success or contribution to the society, the young person accepts such negative labels as a self-definition and proceeds to validate this identity by continuing to behave in ways that will strengthen it. A negative identity can also emerge as a result of a strong identification with someone who is devalued by the family or the community. A loving uncle who is an alcoholic or a clever, creative parent who commits suicide can stimulate a crystallization of the person as one who might share these undesirable characteristics.

Linda, for example, established the negative identity of a person going crazy.

Her father was an alcoholic, physically abusive man, who terrified her when she was a child. . . . Linda, herself a bright child, became by turns the standard bearer for her father's proud aspirations and the target of his jealousy. Midway through grade school she began flunking all her courses and retreating to a private world of daydreams. . . . "I always expected hallucinations, being locked up, down the road coming toward me. . . . I always resisted seeing myself as an adult. I was afraid that at the point I stopped the tape [the years of wild experimentation] I'd become my parents. . . . My father was the closest person I knew to crazy." [Ochberg, 1986, pp. 296–297]

The foreclosed identity and the negative identity both resolve the identity crisis in ways that fall short of the goal of a positive personal identity. Yet both provide the person with a concrete identity. The more psychologically acute resolution of the crisis is *identity confusion.* Young people in this state are unable to make a commitment to any single view of themselves. They are unable to integrate the various roles they play. They may be confronted by opposing value systems or by a lack of confidence in their ability to make meaningful decisions. In either case, the condition of confusion arouses anxiety, apathy, and hostility toward the existing roles, none of which they can successfully adopt.

Dolores, an unemployed college dropout, describes the feeling of meaningless drifting that is associated with identity confusion:

I have two sisters, and my father always told me I was the smartest of all, that I was smarter than he was, and that I could do anything I wanted to do . . . but somehow, I don't really know why, everything I turned to came to nothing. . . . I had every opportunity to find out what I really wanted to do. But . . . nothing I did satisfied me, and I would just stop. . . . Or turn away. . . . Or go on a trip. I worked for a big company for a while. . . . Then my parents went to Paris and I just went with them. . . . I came back . . . went to school . . . was a researcher at Time-Life . . . drifted . . . got married . . . divorced . . . drifted. [Her voice grew more halting.] I feel my life is such a waste. I'd like to write, I really would; but I don't know. I just can't get going. [Gornick, 1971]

This analysis of identity status assumes a developmental progression. Identity confusion reflects the least defined status. Movement from confusion to foreclosure, moratorium, or achievement reflects a developmental progression. Movement from any other status to confusion suggests regression. A person who has achieved identity at one period could conceivably return to a crisis period of moratorium. However, those who are in a moratorium or achieved status could never be accurately described as foreclosed, since by definition they have already experienced some degree of crisis (Waterman, 1982).

In the process of evolving an individual identity, everyone experiences temporary periods of confusion and depression. The task of bringing together the many elements of one's experience into a coordinated, clear self-definition is difficult and time-consuming. Adolescents are likely to experience moments of self-preoccupation, isolation, and discouragement as the diverse pieces of the puzzle are shifted and reordered into the total picture. Thus even the eventual positive identity formation will be the result of some degree of identity confusion. The negative outcome of identity confusion, however, suggests that the person is never able to formulate a satisfying identity that will provide for the convergence of multiple identifications, aspirations, and roles. Such individuals have the persistent fear that they are losing their hold on themselves and on their future.

Pablo Picasso, *Harlequin,* 1901. The young person experiments with roles that represent many possibilities for a mature identity. The Harlequin was Picasso's favorite masquerade, a mysterious identity that seems to blend innocence, sensuality, and creativity.

The Central Process: Role Experimentation

Later adolescents experiment with roles that represent the many possibilities for their future identities. They may think of themselves in a variety of careers in an effort to anticipate what it would be like to be members of specific occupational role groups. They may take a variety of summer jobs, change their college major, read extensively, and daydream about success in several occupations. They consider whether or not to marry. They begin to establish the ideal qualities they are looking for in a long-term intimate partner. Dating is one form of role experimentation; it allows for a different self-presentation with each new date. Friendship is another important context within which young people begin to clarify their interpersonal commitments. They may

---

Box 10.2   Attachment and Identity Formation

We tend to think of identity formation as a process that requires young people to distance themselves from the strong expectations and definitions imposed by parents and other family members. To achieve an individual identity, one must create a vision of the self that is authentic, a sense of having taken hold of one's destiny in an effort to reach goals that are personally meaningful. Yet recent research has demonstrated that the quality of family relationships contributes significantly to the young person's ability to achieve a personal identity (Kroger & Haslett, 1988; Kamptner, 1988; Papini, Sebby & Clark, 1989).

The relationship can be compared with the contribution of secure attachments in infancy to subsequent willingness to explore the environment. Later adolescents who have a secure relationship with parents and who are comfortable in loosening these ties can begin to explore the ideological, occupational, and interpersonal alternatives that will become their own identities. Later adolescents who are still emotionally dependent on parents and who require constant reassurance about their parents' affection will show a greater tendency to have a foreclosed or diffused identity.

By the time individuals reach later adolescence, those who are securely attached to their parents are confident about their parents' affection and support while at the same time they trust in their own ability to make decisions and in their own worth. A sense of family security fosters identity formation in the following ways:

- It fosters confidence in the exploration of social relationships, ideologies, and settings.
- It establishes positive expectations in regard to interpersonal experiences outside of the family.
- It fosters the formation of group identities apart from the family, thus providing a transitional context for work on individual identity.
- It provides a basic layer of self-acceptance that permits the young person to approach the process of identity formation with optimism.

---

evaluate their commitment to their religion, consider religious conversion, and experiment with different rationales for moral behavior. They may examine a variety of political theories, join groups that work for political causes, and campaign for candidates.

Later adolescence is a period in which people have few social obligations that require long-term role commitments. They are free to start and stop or join and quit without serious repercussions to their reputations. As long as no laws are broken in the process of experimenting, young people have the opportunity to play as many roles as they wish in order to prepare themselves for the resolution of the identity crisis without risking serious social censure.

The process of *role experimentation* takes many forms. Erikson (1959) used the term *psychosocial moratorium* to describe a period of free experimentation before a final identity is achieved. Under ideal conditions, the moratorium would allow individuals freedom from the daily expectations for role performance. Their experimentation with new roles, values, and belief systems would result in a personal conception of how they could fit into society so as to maximize their personal strengths and gain positive recognition from the community.

The concept of the psychosocial moratorium has been partially incorporated into those college programs that permit students to enroll in pass/fail courses before they select a major. The concern is to eliminate the problems of external evaluation during the decision-making process. Some high school students take a year for work, travel, or volunteer service before deciding about college or a career. College students often express a need for a moratorium by leaving school for a while (Ochberg, 1986). By leaving they disrupt the expected path of educational and career development. They assert their autonomy by imposing their own timetable and agenda upon a socially prescribed sequence. The time away can give students an opportunity to demonstrate their ability to provide for themselves, to express their individuality, and to break out of whatever social environment they may have felt had constrained or overshadowed their sense of self. The moratorium offers temporary relief from external demands and an opportunity to establish one's identity.

As parents observe the process of role experimentation, they may become concerned because an adolescent son or daughter appears to be abandoning the traditional family value orientation or lifestyle. The adolescent talks of changing religions, remaining single, or selecting a low-status career. The more vehemently the family responds to these propositions, the more likely the young person is to become locked into a position in order to demonstrate autonomy rather than being allowed to continue the experimentation until a more suitable personal alternative is discovered. Parents may be well advised not to take the role experimentation of the later adolescent too seriously. If anything, it might be beneficial for a loved and trusted parent to play along with the young person as he or she evaluates the characteristics of the assumed role.

Identity Formation and the College Environment

We tend to think of college as a setting that promotes role experimentation and identity formation. However, students differ in their identity status when they arrive at college. College programs also differ in the extent to which they promote role experimentation. The progress made in identity formation during the college years is a product of the interaction between student values and needs and the demands and opportunities of the college environment. The interaction between these factors is illustrated in a study that compared college males who had transferred or dropped out of college with those who had remained enrolled (Simpson, Baker & Mellinger, 1980). The students were categorized as either failing or withdrawing in good standing. Two factors were associated with all the withdrawal students: lack of social integration (feeling lonely and having few close friends) and low educational aspirations. However, there were some interesting differences between the students who withdrew in good standing and those who withdrew when they were failing. Students who were most likely to see a college degree as an occupational credential were more likely to withdraw from college when they were getting low grades. In comparison, students who held nontraditional values and who considered withdrawing even as entering freshmen were more likely to withdraw as their grade point averages rose.

The kinds of commitments students made as to the meaning of their education as they entered college influenced the way they interpreted the feedback they received about their abilities. Students who were attending college in order to achieve occupational goals interpreted low grades as a message that they did not have the ability to achieve them and thus chose to withdraw. Students who were attending college to experience a more diverse lifestyle or participate in the school's political climate interpreted good grades as evidence that they did not need the college environment in order to achieve their goals.

Here we see the filtering effect of individual identity on the college experience (Newman & Newman, 1978). Differences in career commitment and ideological commitment can direct educational choices. The choices of curriculum and college reflect the later adolescent's value orientation and have an impact on it. Students in liberal arts programs are likely to experience more support for experimentation with values, the creation of a new or interdisciplinary major, or the investigation of a variety of learning experiences outside the classroom. Within this environment, the process of identity consolidation is aided by the opportunity for experimentation. However, the postponement of closure may be accompanied by a degree of anxiety.

In a more structured, career-oriented program or college, the institutional goals are likely to be focused on preparing students to enter an already defined profession. Experimentation is less central than skill learning and the development of competence. In this situation, work toward identity resolution is aided by the clearly defined occupational identity toward which the student is striving. There is likely to be very little ambiguity about where the student is headed or the school's ability to aid the student in his or her pursuit. However, this setting allows minimal opportunity for personal experimentation or the creation of new roles. It is possible that although little change in values would be measured during the college years in such a professional program, the individual graduates may experience later periods of fluctuation in values that represent a need to resolve some aspects of individual identity not encompassed by the occupation they have chosen.

Identity Formation for Males and Females

Questions have been raised about the process of identity formation and its outcome for young men and women in our society. Some investigators have argued that the concept of identity as it has been formulated is a reflection of a male-oriented culture that focuses heavily on occupation and ideology rather than on interpersonal commitments. Others have argued that the process of identity formation is different for young women, who must resolve issues of intimacy and interpersonal commitments before they can reach closure on commitments to the world of work. Another view is that women are socialized to look to others to define their identity rather than to assume a proactive stance with respect to identity formation. All of these ideas reflect the impact of traditional distinctions in the male and female sex roles on identity formation. It might be argued, however, that the kinds of ego strengths associated with identity formation are equally important for the adaptive functioning of men and women (Ginsburg & Orlofsky, 1981). From this perspective, one might expect to find differences between males and females in the content of identity-related commitments and in the value placed on these content areas, but not in the process of crisis and commitment that leads to achieved identity.

Few sex differences in identity status have been discovered (Waterman, 1982). For both sexes, identity achievement is associated with positive ego qualities. "Identity achieved youths generally exhibit higher levels of self-esteem, greater cognitive and ego complexity, postconventional levels of moral reasoning, and a strong capacity for inner-directed behavior" (Craig-Bray, Adams & Dobson, 1988, p. 175).

In one analysis of the way older adolescents think about commitments, subjects were asked to define the concept of commitment (Galotti & Kozberg, 1987). Almost no gender differences were found in these definitions, except that women were more likely than men to mention the importance of keeping a promise or their word of honor. Other themes—mutual trust, expression of one's values, a social contract, ordering of priorities, perseverance, obligation, devotion of the self—were referred to equally often by men and women.

The uncertainty of the identity crisis is often accompanied by greater anxiety for women than for men. This anxiety may be linked to concerns over achievement strivings. Many women experience conflict between their image of femininity and their desire to set ambitious personal goals (Ginsburg & Orlofsky, 1981). Anxiety may also be a product of the general distress that women feel when they focus attention on their own agendas rather than on facilitating the agendas of others, as the society seems to expect them to do. In this context, the moratorium status, which is considered a positive interlude on the path toward achievement, has been found to be linked to higher levels of self-doubt in women than in men. This finding may result from the strong feelings of guilt women experience when they attempt to assert their self-sufficiency.

The main evidence for gender differences has been in the content of the identity. Erikson's (1968, 1982) work suggests that ideological and vocational commitments are central to identity formation. Gilligan (1982) has criticized this orientation, arguing that the interpersonal content may be more central for women, and that the clarification of interpersonal commitments opens the way for more advanced exploration in vocational and ideological contents. Research on this issue lends support to this concept (Mellor, 1989; Bilsker, Schiedel & Marcia, 1988; Schiedel & Marcia, 1985). Issues surrounding the quality of interpersonal relations and the establishment of satisfying social commitments are more relevant to the development of a woman's identity than to that of a man.

Summary

The intensity of later adolescence is both agonizing and heroic. Adolescents seek to discover those essential characteristics that will satisfy their longing for self-definition and yet not drastically alienate them from their social environment. The crisis of identity versus identity confusion suggests a fusion of earlier identifications, present values, and future goals into a consistent self-concept. This unity of self is achieved only after a period of questioning, reevaluation, and experimentation. Efforts to resolve questions of identity may take the adolescent down the path of overzealous commitment, emotional involvement, alienation, or playful wandering. Figure 10.4 demonstrates the integration of a variety of roles into a personal identity.

☐ Applied Topic: Career Decision Making

One of the primary means by which identity is expressed in our society is commitment to an occupation. Women as well as men are increasingly seeking careers. What is involved in reaching a decision about a career? How do later adolescents approach

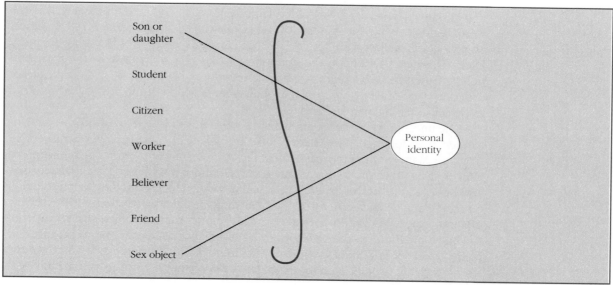

Figure 10.4   Integration of Preconflict Roles into a Personal Identity

the task of career decision making? What are some strategies that foster effective career decision making?

Studies conducted in the United States, Canada, and Australia all confirm that concerns about future educational and career decisions constitute a major source of worry for adolescents (Violato & Holden, 1988). Seventy-six percent of women and 74% of men entering college as freshmen in 1989 said that they had worried about choosing a career during the past year (Dodge, 1990). Many people assume that the younger a person is when he or she makes a career choice, the better. Perhaps that is why so many high school students worry about their career choices. Most career development professionals, however, advise that a decision about a career be delayed until later adolescence or early adulthood (Osipow, 1986). A person who delays the decision has a clearer sense of his or her adult interests and goals. Nonetheless, high schools, colleges, and various industries urge young people to make these decisions as early as possible, often for their own economic benefit. Thus some of the tension that later adolescents experience in connection with a choice of career is a product of the lack of fit between socialization pressures and their own developmental time-table. If a person is going to live to be 75 or 80 years old, there is no great rush to decide on a career by age 20.

When college students were asked to consider career commitments, they mentioned the following factors as relevant to their decisions:

working/job conditions; general appeal of the career; income/compensation; prospects for personal impact/general importance; long-term availability and job security; mesh with talents/education/abilities; nature of the co-workers; prospects for sustaining long-term interest; altruistic concerns; attitudes of/compatibility with friends,

The college curriculum can open students' eyes to work alternatives they had never considered before. As they become involved in their major, students discover many possible career applications for their new expertise.

family; concerns over future relationships with friends, family; moral concerns.   [Galotti & Kozberg, 1987]

The four most important of these items were income, how interesting the career was, availability of jobs in that career, and expected level of fulfillment.

Concerns about career choice are linked to other aspects of identity development. In particular, later adolescents worry about the extent to which commitment to a career may conflict with other commitments to family roles or to values (Kram, 1985). Some young people struggle with the idea that success in a career may require them to sacrifice intimacy in family life. A young woman summarized this conflict when she described the advice she received from her parents about her occupational future. Her mother assured her that it was possible to combine work and family life, and that there were no greater satisfactions in life than those that came from raising a family. Her father advised her that if she hoped to compete and succeed in the world of work, she would have to devote herself entirely to that goal and should give up the idea of having a family (Eccles, 1987).

The process of career decision making, then, requires a synthesis of self-concept, including an assessment of one's needs, interest, values, and abilities, with knowledge of the realities of the work environment, including the kinds of jobs and careers available, requirements for entry, and policies, regulations, and economic conditions influencing the job market. The choice of a career actually is subject to two influences at once: the education or training one chooses and the recruitment and selection policies of organizations and industries (Hall, 1976). A person has most control over the first of these factors, but the final outcome is surely influenced by the other as well.

Once a person begins to accept certain elements of the self-concept as they relate to the occupational aspect of identity, a process of career decision making begins. Tiedeman (Tiedeman & O'Hara, 1963; Miller & Tiedeman, 1972) has developed a model of phases of career decision making. The model illustrates how the making of career-related decisions helps to clarify one's occupational identity and at the same time uses the context of work to promote new learning about other aspects of the self (see Figure 10.5). A career decision depends on the outcomes of several tasks during adolescence and early adulthood. With effective problem solving, the person gains increased control over life events and is better prepared to meet the challenges of the next phase of decision making. Tiedeman posits seven phases: the first four emphasize planning and clarification; the last three emphasize implementation.

In the *exploration phase,* the person becomes aware of the fact that a decision is to be made. A need to learn more about oneself and the occupational world results. The person begins to generate alternatives for action. He or she begins to feel anxious and uncertain about the future.

In the *crystallization phase,* the person becomes more aware of alternatives for action and their consequences. Some alternatives are discarded. Conflicts among alternatives are recognized. The rewards and costs of various decisions are evaluated. The person develops a strategy for making the decision.

In the *choice phase,* the person decides which action alternative to follow. The decision is solidified in the person's mind as he or she elaborates reasons why the decision is beneficial. There is a sense of relief and optimism. The person develops a commitment to executing the decision.

In the *clarification phase,* the person more fully understands the consequences of commitment to the decision that has been made. He or she plans definite steps to take, and may actually take them in this phase or may delay them until a more appropriate time. The self-image is prepared to be modified by the decision.

During the *induction phase,* the person encounters the new environment for the first time. He or she wants to be accepted and looks to others for cues about how to behave. The person identifies with the new group and seeks recognition for his or her unique characteristics. Gradually the self-image is modified. The person learns to believe in the values and goals of the new group.

In the *reformation phase,* the person is very much involved with the new group. He or she becomes more assertive in asking that the group perform better. The person also tries to influence the group to accommodate some of his or her values. The self is strongly committed to group goals. During this phase, the group's values and goals may be modified to include the orientation of the new member.

Finally, in the *integration phase,* group members react against the new member's attempts to influence them. The new member then compromises. In the process, he or she attains a more objective understanding of self and group. A true collaboration between the new member and the group is achieved. The new member feels satisfied and is evaluated as successful by self and others.

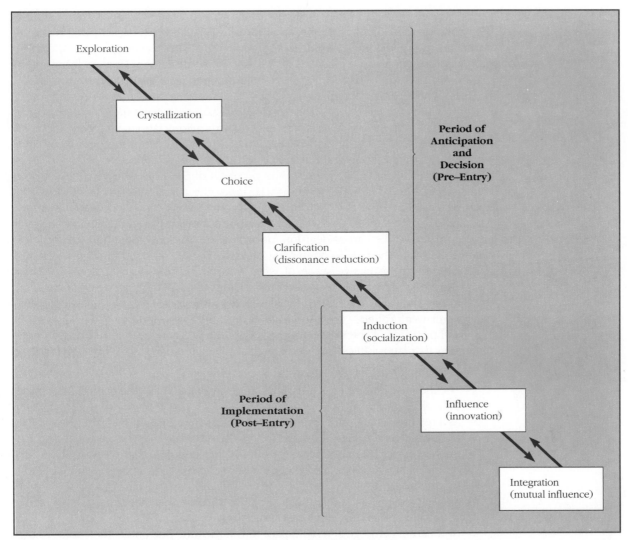

Figure 10.5   Seven Phases of Career Decision Making
Based on D. V. Tiedeman and R. P. O'Hara, *Career Development: Choice and Adjustment* (New York: College Entrance Examination Board, 1963).

This model emphasizes continuous interaction between the individual and the work context. At first interaction is necessary to clarify the person's talents and choice of career. Later it is necessary to achieve a satisfactory level of adaptation to the work environment. At each juncture, whether the decision relates to college major, occupation, job change, or career redirection, effective decision making involves all seven phases.

The seven phases of decision making are probably encountered by every person in the process of choosing a career. However, people use different decision-making styles that determine how they make use of information and how much responsibility they take for the decisions they reach. Harren (1976) has described three kinds of decision making: planning, intuitive, and dependent. The planning style is the most rational. Planners assume personal responsibility for decisions. They seek out information with which to assess both personal competences and the qualities of the situation. The intuitive style makes primary use of fantasy and emotion. A decision is reached without much information seeking. It is based on what feels right or best at the time. The dependent style is influenced by the expectations and evaluations of others. Dependent decision makers take little responsibility for their decisions. They see circumstances as forcing their choices or limiting their options.

Harren and Kass (1977) studied the progress of 578 college undergraduates in choosing a career. They focused on three tasks: the decision to go to college, the decision about a major, and the decision about a future occupation. Both academic class standing and success in decision making about major or future occupation were closely related to the career decision-making score. Students identified the intuitive style as most like their decision-making process. They responded favorably to items that reflected an instinctive sense of what would be a good career decision. They preferred this strategy to the more tedious activities of the planning style. Nevertheless, the intuitive style was not related to decisiveness, the formation of a vocational self-concept, or work values.

Characteristics of the contemporary labor market may be contributing to new difficulties that later adolescents encounter as they attempt to move through the first four phases of Tiedeman's model.

- The increasing number of jobs and careers available make the exploration phase difficult.
- As a result of changes in technology as well as in organizational structure, some skills become obsolete and some job markets dry up. With the advent of desktop publishing and computer composition, for example, jobs for typesetters are disappearing. A career can become obsolete in the time it takes a young person to prepare for it.
- As established firms lose their identities in corporate mergers, identification with a particular company ceases to be appropriate.
- New careers emerge at a rapid pace. From the time one enters the choice phase to the time one enters the reformation phase, new kinds of work roles may become possible.
- Career paths are less clear than they once were. Young people are being advised to expect three or four career changes in their lifetime. One might move from the private to the nonprofit sector, from business to education, from service provider to entrepreneur.
- The cost of living, especially the costs of housing, health care, and education, introduce concerns about the amount of money that will be needed to live comfortably. Worries about making money can interfere with effective career decision making.

As a result of the anxiety that attends career decision making, career counseling has become a significant new career. Five suggestions from career counseling literature can be of help in developing an appropriate career decision-making process in later adolescence (Hall, 1976; Eccles, 1987):

1. *Gather information about various careers.* A career decision should be approached at least as systematically as the decision to buy a car. Know enough about your own interests, abilities, and values to select a group of occupations that might be appropriate. Then find out as much as possible about the educational and training requirements, the future job market, the career ladder, and the various organizations where this kind of work is available.

2. *Engage in work-related tasks in which you experience success.* Success experiences are a critical element in judgments of self-efficacy. If you are to believe that you can succeed in a certain career, it is important to have experiences of success in demanding tasks that either approximate or are directly connected to the career in question.

3. *Recognize the needs relevant to each phase of career decision making.* A person in the crystallization phase may need more specific information about the trade-offs of certain career paths. A person in the choice phase may need to develop a more personal relationship with someone in a particular career.

4. *Seek out a variety of sources of information.* Teachers may have one view of a career, managers and supervisors quite another. Talk to people who might be co-workers as well as those who would be bosses. Parents who have their children's long-range welfare at heart are an important source of help in career decision making. Friends are another important source if they can engage in flexible fantasies about alternative futures.

5. *Build bridges between the abstract and the concrete.* Find opportunities to apply what you learn in the classroom to the work setting and to analyze observations from the work setting by reading, reflecting, and forming general principles about them. Ideally, one's career decisions will be a product of experiences and informed reflection about those experiences.

☐ Chapter Summary

At the close of later adolescence, young people are fully capable of surviving on their own in a complex culture. Those who have resolved the psychosocial crisis of this stage have an integrated identity, which includes a definition of themselves as sexual, moral, political, and career participants. Identity achievement represents a commitment to specific values that will serve as a basis for decisions later in life.

The strain of this stage can be felt in the tension between the person's quest for experimentation, questioning, and challenge and the society's expectations for closure on significant themes, particularly occupation, sex role, and political ideology. The college years expose many young people to new views that require evaluation. Experimentation during this time is an essential strategy for coping with new information and new value orientations. If young people can try out a particular stance without serious repercussions, they will have a much greater chance of discovering which poses "fit" and which are uncomfortable. Once young people know what they stand for, they can more deeply commit themselves to others.

References

Adams, G. R., & Jones, R. M. (1983). Female adolescents' identity development: Age comparisons and perceived child-rearing experience. *Developmental Psychology, 19,* 249–256.

Antill, J. K., & Cunningham, J. D. (1982). Sex differences in performance on ability tests as a function of masculinity, femininity, and androgyny. *Journal of Personality and Social Psychology, 42,* 718–728.

Armsden, G. C., & Greenberg, M. T. (1987). The inventory of parent and peer attachment: Individual differences and their relationship to psychological well-being in adolescence. *Journal of Youth and Adolescence, 16,* 427–454.

Baucom, D. H. (1983). Sex role identity and the decision to regain control among women: A learned helplessness investigation. *Journal of Personality and Social Psychology, 44,* 334–343.

Baucom, D. H., Besch, P. K., & Callahan, S. (1985). Relation between testosterone concentrations, sex-role identity, and personality among females. *Journal of Personality and Social Psychology, 48,* 1218–1226.

Berkowitz, M. W., & Gibbs, J. C. (1983). Measuring the developmental features of moral discussion. *Merrill-Palmer Quarterly, 29,* 399–410.

Betz, N. E., & Hackett, G. (1981). The relationship of career-related self-efficacy expectations to perceived career options in college women and men. *Journal of Counseling Psychology, 28,* 399–410.

Bilsker, D., Schiedel, D., & Marcia, J. (1988). Sex differences in identity status. *Sex Roles, 18,* 231–236.

Borman, K. M., & Hopkins, M. (1987). Leaving school for work. *Research in the Sociology of Education and Socialization, 7,* 131–159.

Breakwell, G. M. (1986). *Coping with threatened identities.* London: Methuen.

Bridges, J. S. (1988). Sex differences in occupational performance expectations. *Psychology of Women Quarterly, 12,* 75–90.

Chow, E. N. (1987). The influence of sex-role identity and occupational attainment on the psychological well-being of Asian-American women. *Psychology of Women Quarterly, 11,* 69–82.

Colby, A., & Kohlberg, L. (1987). *The measurement of moral judgment,* vol. 1, *Theoretical foundations and research validation.* Cambridge: Cambridge University Press.

Colby, A., Kohlberg, L., Gibbs, J., & Lieberman, M. (1983). *A longitudinal study of moral judgment.* Monographs of the Society for Research in Child Development, 48 (1, serial no. 200).

Comas-Diaz, L. (1987). Feminist therapy with mainland Puerto Rican women. *Psychology of Women Quarterly, 11,* 461–474.

Craig-Bray, L., Adams, G. R., & Dobson, W. R. (1988). Identity formation and social relations during late adolescence. *Journal of Youth and Adolescence, 17,* 173–188.

DeVos, S. (1989). Leaving the parental home in six Latin American countries. *Journal of Marriage and the Family, 51,* 615–626.

Dodge, S. (1989). More freshmen willing to work for social change and environmental issues, new survey finds. *Chronicle of Higher Education, 36,* A31–A35.

Eccles, J. S. (1987). Gender roles and women's achievement-related decisions. *Psychology of Women Quarterly, 11,* 135–171.

Eisenberg, N., & Strayer, J. (1987). *Empathy and its development* (pp. 3–13). Cambridge: Cambridge University Press.

Emmerich, W. (1973). Socialization and sex-role development. In P. Baltes & K. W. Schaie (eds.), *Life-span developmental psychology: Personality and socialization.* New York: Academic Press.

Enright, R. D., Lapsley, D. K., Drivas, A. E., & Fehr, L. A. (1980). Parental influences on the development of adolescent autonomy and identity. *Journal of Youth and Adolescence, 9,* 529–545.

Erikson, E. H. (1950). *Childhood and society.* New York: Norton.

Erikson, E. H. (1959). The problem of ego identity. *Psychological Issues, 1,* 101–164.

Erikson, E. H. (1968). *Identity: Youth and crisis.* New York: Norton.

Erikson, E. H. (1974). *Dimensions of a new identity.* New York: Norton.

Erikson, E. H. (1982). *The life cycle completed: A review.* New York: Norton.

Feather, N. T. (1985). Masculinity, femininity, self-esteem, and subclinical depression. *Sex Roles, 12,* 491–500.

Ford, M. R., & Lowery, C. R. (1986). Gender differences in moral reasoning: A comparison of the use of justice and care orientations. *Journal of Personality and Social Psychology, 50,* 777–783.

Freeman, R. B., & Wise, D. A. (1982). *The youth labor market: Problems in the United States.* Chicago: University of Chicago Press.

Friedman, W. J., Robinson, A. B., & Friedman, B. L. (1987). Sex differences in moral judgments? A test of Gilligan's theory. *Psychology of Women Quarterly, 11,* 37–46.

Galotti, K. M. (1989). Gender differences in self-reported moral reasoning: A review of new evidence. *Journal of Youth and Adolescence, 18,* 475–488.

Galotti, K. M., & Kozberg, S. F. (1987). Older adolescents' thinking about academic/vocational and interpersonal commitments. *Journal of Youth and Adolescence, 16,* 313–330.

Gfellner, B. M. (1986). Ego development and moral development in relation to age and grade level during adolescence. *Journal of Youth and Adolescence, 15,* 147–163.

Giele, J. Z. (1988). Gender and sex roles. In N. J. Smelser (ed.), *Handbook of sociology* (pp. 291–326). Newbury Park, Calif.: Sage.

Gilligan, C. (1977). In a different voice: Women's conceptions of self and morality. *Harvard Educational Review, 47,* 481–517.

Gilligan, C. (1982). *In a different voice: Psychological theory and women's development.* Cambridge, Mass.: Harvard University Press.

Ginsburg, S. D., & Orlofsky, J. L. (1981). Ego identity status, ego development, and locus of control in college women. *Journal of Youth and Adolescence, 10,* 297–307.

Goldscheider, C., & Goldscheider, F. (1987). Moving out and marriage: What do young adults expect? *American Sociological Review, 52,* 278–285.

Goldscheider, F. K., & Goldscheider, C. (1989). Family structure and conflict: Nest leaving expectations of young adults and their parents. *Journal of Marriage and the Family, 51,* 87–97.

Gornick, V. (1971). Consciousness. *New York Times Magazine,* January 10.

Griffin, L. J., & Alexander, K. L. (1978). Schooling and socioeconomic attainments: High school and college influences. *American Journal of Sociology, 84,* 319–347.

Grotevant, H. D., & Cooper, C. R. (1985). Patterns of interaction in family relationships and the development of identity exploration in adolescence. *Child Development, 56,* 415–428.

Haan, N. (1985). Processes of moral development: Cognitive or social disequilibrium. *Developmental Psychology, 21,* 996–1006.

Hall, D. T. (1976). *Careers in organizations.* Santa Monica, Calif.: Goodyear.

Harkness, S., Edwards, C. P., & Super, C. M. (1981). Social roles and moral reasoning: A case study in a rural African community. *Developmental Psychology, 17,* 595–603.

Harren, V. A. (1976). An overview of Tiedeman's theory of career decision making and summary of related research. Unpublished manuscript, Southern Illinois University, Carbondale.

Harren, V. A., & Kass, R. A. (1977). The measurement and correlates of career decision making. Paper presented at the annual convention of the American Psychological Association, San Francisco.

Hauser, S. T., Powers, S. I., Noam, G., Jacobson, A. M., Weiss, B., & Follansbee, D. J. (1984). Familial contexts of adolescent ego development. *Child Development, 55,* 195–213.

Hearn, J. C. (1980). Major choice and the well-being of college men and women: An examination from developmental, structural, and organizational perspectives. *Sociology of Education, 53,* 164–178.

Hearn, J. C., & Olzak, S. (1981). The role of college major departments in the reproduction of sexual inequality. *Sociology of Education, 54,* 195–205.

Hubner-Funk, S. (1983). Transition into occupational life: Environmental and sex differences regarding the status passage from school to work. *Adolescence, 18,* 709–723.

Kamptner, N. L. (1988). Identity development in late adolescence: Causal modeling of social and familial influences. *Journal of Youth and Adolescence, 17,* 493–514.

Kohlberg, L. (1964). Development of moral character and moral ideology. In M. L. Hoffman & L. W. Hoffman (eds.), *Review of child development research* (vol. 1). New York: Russell Sage Foundation.

Kram, K. E. (1985). *Mentoring at work: Developmental relationships in organizational life.* Glenview, Ill.: Scott, Foresman.

Kroger, J., & Haslett, S. J. (1988). Separation-individuation and ego identity status in late adolescence: A two-year longitudinal study. *Journal of Youth and Adolescence, 17,* 59–80.

Kurdek, L. A. (1981). Young adults' moral reasoning about prohibitive and prosocial dilemmas. *Journal of Youth and Adolescence, 10,* 263–272.

Lerner, R. M. (1985). Adolescent maturational changes and psychosocial development: A dynamic interactional perspective. *Journal of Youth and Adolescence, 14,* 355–372.

Long, B. C. (1989). Sex-role orientation, coping strategies, and self-efficacy of women in traditional and nontraditional occupations. *Psychology of Women Quarterly, 13,* 307–324.

Lubinski, D., Tellegen, A., & Batcher, J. N. (1983). Masculinity, femininity, and androgyny viewed and assessed as distinct concepts. *Journal of Personality and Social Psychology, 44,* 428–439.

Lueptow, L. B. (1981). Sex-typing and change in the occupational choices of high school seniors: 1964–1975. *Sociology of Education, 54,* 16–24.

Marcia, J. E. (1980). Identity in adolescence. In J. Adelson (ed.), *Handbook of adolescent psychology* (pp. 159–187). New York: Wiley.

Markus, H., Crane, M., Bernstein, S., & Siladi, M. (1982). Self-schemas and gender. *Journal of Personality and Social Psychology, 42,* 38–50.

Mellor, S. (1989). Gender differences in identity formation as a function of self-other relationships. *Journal of Youth and Adolescence, 18,* 361–375.

Miller, A. L., & Tiedeman, D. V. (1972). Decision making for the 70's: The cubing of the Tiedeman paradigm and its application in career education. *Focus on Guidance, 5.*

Mitchell, B. A., Wister, A. V., & Burch, T. K. (1989). The family environment and leaving the parental home. *Journal of Marriage and the Family, 51,* 605–614.

Moore, D., & Hotch, D. F. (1981). Late adolescents' conceptualizations of home-leaving. *Journal of Youth and Adolescence, 10,* 1–10.

Nevill, D. D., & Schlecker, D. I. (1988). The relation of self-efficacy and assertiveness to willingness to engage in traditional/nontraditional career activities. *Psychology of Women Quarterly, 12,* 91–98.

Newman, P., & Newman, B. (1978). Identity formation and the college experience. *Adolescence, 13,* 311–326.

Nezu, A. M., & Nezu, C. M. (1987). Psychological distress, problem solving, and coping reactions: Sex role differences. *Sex Roles, 16,* 205–214.

Nisan, M., & Kohlberg, L. (1982). Universality and variation in moral judgment: A longitudinal and cross-sectional study in Turkey. *Child Development, 53,* 865–876.

Ochberg, R. L. (1986). College dropouts: The developmental logic of psychosocial moratoria. *Journal of Youth and Adolescence, 15,* 287–302.

O'Neil, J. M., Ohlde, C., Barke, C., Prosser-Gelwick, B., & Garfield, N. (1980). Research on a workshop to reduce the effects of sexism and sex-role socialization on women's career planning. *Journal of Counseling Psychology, 27,* 355–363.

O'Neil, J. M., Ohlde, C., Tollefson, N., Barke, C., Piggott, T., & Watts, D. (1980). Factors, correlates, and problem areas affecting career decision making of a cross-sectional sample of students. *Journal of Counseling Psychology, 27,* 571–580.

Osipow, S. H. (1986). Career issues through the life span. In M. S. Pallack & R. Perloff (eds.), *Psychology and work: Productivity, change, and employment,* (pp. 137–168). Washington, D. C.: American Psychological Association.

Page, S. (1987). On gender roles and perception of maladjustment. *Canadian Psychology, 28,* 53–59.

Papini, D. R., Sebby, R. A., & Clark, S. (1989). Affective quality of family relations and adolescent identity exploration. *Adolescence, 24,* 457–466.

Rauste–von Wright, M. (1989). Body image satisfaction in adolescent girls and boys: A longitudinal study. *Journal of Youth and Adolescence, 18,* 71–83.

Reischl, T. M., & Hirsch, B. J. (1989). Identity commitments and coping with a difficult developmental transition. *Journal of Youth and Adolescence, 18,* 55–70.

Rest, J. R. (1983). Morality. In P. H. Mussen (general ed.), *Handbook of Child Psychology,* vol. 3, *Cognitive Development* (J. H. Flavell & E. M. Markman, eds.), New York: Wiley.

Rest, J. R., & Thoma, S. J. (1985). Relation of moral judgment development to formal education. *Developmental Psychology, 21,* 709–714.

Rubin, Z., Hill, C. T., Peplau, L. A., & Dunkel-Schetter, C. (1980). Self-disclosure in dating couples: Sex roles and the ethic of openness. *Journal of Marriage and the Family, 42,* 302–317.

Ryan, R. M., & Lynch, J. H. (1989). Emotional autonomy versus detachment: Revisiting the vicissitudes of adolescence and young adulthood. *Child Development, 60,* 340–356.

Schiedel, D. G., & Marcia, J. E. (1985). Ego identity, intimacy, sex-role orientation, and gender. *Developmental Psychology, 21,* 149–160.

Simpson, C., Baker, K., & Mellinger, G. (1980). Conventional failures and unconventional dropouts: Comparing different types of university withdrawals. *Sociology of Education, 53,* 203–214.

Snarey, J. R., Reimer, J., & Kohlberg, L. (1985). Development of social-moral reasoning among kibbutz adolescents: A longitudinal cross-sectional study. *Developmental Psychology, 21,* 3–17.

Spence, J. T., Deaux, K., & Helmreich, R. L. (1985). Sex roles in contemporary American society. In G. Lindzey & Elliot Aronson (eds.), *Handbook of Social Psy-*

chology, (vol. 1, pp. 149–178). New York: Random House.

Sprecher, S., McKinney, R., Walsh, R., & Anderson, C. (1988). A revision of the Reiss premarital sexual permissiveness scale. *Journal of Marriage and the Family, 50,* 821–828.

Steinberg, L., & Silverberg, S. (1986). The vicissitudes of autonomy in early adolescence. *Child Development, 57,* 841–851.

Steinberg, L. D., Greenberger, E., Garduque, L., Ruggiero, M., & Vaux, A. (1982). Effects of working on adolescent development. *Developmental Psychology, 18,* 385–395.

Sullivan, K., & Sullivan, A. (1980). Adolescent-parent separation. *Developmental Psychology, 16,* 93–104.

Thornton, A. (1989). Changing attitudes toward family issues in the United States. *Journal of Marriage and the Family, 51,* 873–893.

Tiedeman, D. V., & O'Hara, R. P. (1963). *Career development: Choice and adjustment.* New York: College Entrance Examination Board.

Tietjen, A. M., & Walker, L. J. (1985). Moral reasoning and leadership among men in Papua New Guinea society. *Developmental Psychology, 21,* 982–992.

Turiel, E. (1974). Conflict and change in adolescent moral development. *Child Development, 45,* 14–29.

Violato, C., & Holden, W. B. (1988). A confirmatory factor analysis of a four-factor model of adolescent concerns. *Journal of Youth and Adolescence, 17,* 101–113.

Walker, L. J. (1982). The sequentiality of Kohlberg's stages of moral development. *Child Development, 53,* 1330–1336.

Walker, L. J., de Vries, B., & Bichard, S. L. (1984). The hierarchical nature of stages of moral development. *Developmental Psychology, 20,* 960–966.

Walker, L. J., de Vries, B., & Trevethan, S. D. (1987). Moral stages and moral orientations in real-life and hypothetical dilemmas. *Child Development, 58,* 842–858.

Waterman, A. S. (1982). Identity development from adolescence to adulthood: An extension of theory and a review of research. *Developmental Psychology, 18,* 341–358.

Wells, K. (1980). Gender-role identity and psychological adjustment in adolescence. *Journal of Youth and Adolescence, 9,* 59–73.

West, M., & Newton, P. (1983). *The transition from school to work.* London: Croom Helm.

Whitbourne, S. K. (1986). *The me I know: A study of adult identity.* New York: Springer-Verlag.

Whitely, B. E. (1983). Sex role orientation and self-esteem: A critical meta-analytic review. *Journal of Personality and Social Psychology, 44,* 765–778.

Whitely, B. E. (1984). Sex role orientation and psychological well-being: Two meta-analyses. *Sex Roles, 12,* 207–225.

Windmiller, M., Lambert, N., & Turiel, E. (1980). *Moral development and socialization.* Boston: Allyn & Bacon.

Zedlow, P. B., Clark, D., & Daugherty, S. R. (1985). Masculinity, femininity, type A behavior, and psychosocial adjustment in medical schools. *Journal of Personality and Social Psychology, 48,* 481–492.

Chapter Eleven

The major themes of early adulthood—work, intimacy, marriage, and parenting—are all embedded in this image of a young circus family.

Early Adulthood
(22 to 34 Years)

Major Concepts in the Study of Adulthood

Entry into adulthood is a major transition in life. All that has gone before can be seen as preparation; all that follows can be viewed as actualization. We have considered psychosocial development through seven preparatory stages of life encompassing approximately 22 years. During these stages one undergoes rapid physical, cognitive, social, and emotional development. In the United States, life expectancy is currently about 70 to 80 years. Thus approximately 50 years of psychological development remain after the seven preparatory stages. In our conceptual scheme, four stages of development unfold during these 50 years. Let us briefly examine some of the concepts that are important to our discussion of adulthood.

Life Roles

Life role is one of the most frequently used concepts for understanding adulthood (Brim, 1966, 1968; Parsons, 1955). The major concepts of social role theory—introduced in Chapter 3—are summarized in Table 11.1. We considered this concept in Chapter 7 when we discussed sex-role identification, and again in Chapter 10 when we examined individual identity versus identity confusion. Clearly, roles are learned during childhood. In adulthood, however, people are engaged in learning and enacting multiple roles that expand the opportunities for self-expression and bring adults into contact with a great variety of social demands.

Involvement in multiple roles not only contributes to personality development but also allows adults to function as agents of socialization for younger generations (Parsons, 1955). Adulthood can be seen as a series of increasingly differentiated and complex roles that the individual plays for substantial lengths of time. Only in adulthood do individuals experience the demands of many of their roles. These experiences qualify adults to train their children for the demands of adult roles.

Social Clock

Bernice Neugarten and her colleagues (Neugarten, Moore & Lowe, 1965) proposed the concept of the *social clock* as a way of understanding adulthood. This term refers to "age norms and age expectations [that] operate as prods and brakes upon behavior, in some instances hastening behavior and in some instances delaying it" (p. 710). Neugarten and her associates suggest that social-class groups tend to agree on the appropriate age for significant life events, such as marriage, child rearing, and retirement. This consensus exerts social pressure on individuals, pushing them to assume a particular role at an expected age. Age norms also serve to suppress behaviors that are considered inappropriate for one's age. Adults not only are aware of existing norms regarding the timing of certain behaviors; they evaluate their own behaviors as being "on time" or "too soon" or "too late." The social clock is constantly being set as people confront the challenges, demands, and new structures of modern society.

Table 11.1	Major Concepts of Social Role Theory
Social role	Parts or identities a person assumes that are also social positions: kinship roles, age roles, sex roles, occupational roles
Role enactment	Patterned characteristics of social behavior generated by a social role
Role expectations	Scripts or shared expectations for behavior that are linked to each role
Role gain	Addition of roles
Role strain	Stress caused by too many expectations within a role
Role conflict	Conflict caused by competing demands of different roles
Role loss	Ending of a role; may result in stress and disorientation
Dimensions of life roles that vary from person to person	Number of roles
	Intensity of involvement in roles
	Time demands of each role
	Structure or flexibility of the role

Life Course

Life course refers to the integration and sequencing of phases of work and family life. This concept can be applied to the content of individual life histories as they are expressed in a social and historical time period (Atchley, 1975; Elder, 1975). Each person's life course can be thought of as a pattern of the adaptations that he or she has made to the configuration of cultural expectations, resources, and barriers experienced during a particular time period.

Figure 11.1 suggests one view of the age-linked changes in occupational and family careers. You can see that this is just one possible configuration of the interconnections between work and family life in the course of a life. The occupational career, for example, may look quite different for a woman who works before marriage, drops out of the labor market during the childbearing years, and then has to retrain before returning to the labor market. The family career may look very different for people who marry, have children, divorce, remarry, and have children in the new marriage.

The pattern of the life course is influenced by the historical era. The life course of a person whose life began in 1900 and ended in 1975 might have looked quite different if that person's life had run from 1920 to 1995. The person would have gone through the same chronological phases during different periods of history with different opportunities, expectations, and challenges. Differences in the occupational opportunities, educational resources, and number of people in the cohort are just three cohort factors that may affect the pattern of life events (Elder, 1981).

Although the life course is tied to the sequencing of events over time, there is still an assumption that people at different ages bring a distinct perspective to those events. People are not simply buffeted from one event to another. They make choices. Some people tend to choose more carefully and consciously than others. They accept some responsibilities and reject others. Some people accept more responsibility than others.

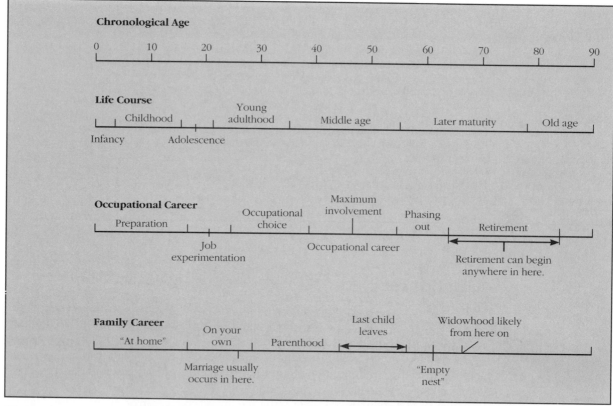

Figure 11.1   **Relationships Among Age, Life Course, Occupational Career, and Family Career**
Source: Adapted from R. C. Atchley. "The Life Course, Age Grading, and Age-Linked Demands for Decision Making," in N. Datan & L. H. Ginsberg (eds.), *Lifespan Development Psychology: Normative Life Crises,* p. 264. Copyright © 1975 by Academic Press, Inc. Reprinted by permission.

People have different profiles of role interest or salience. They view some roles as primary and others as secondary. They draw on certain past experiences to increase their effectiveness in certain roles. During early adulthood, for example, recollections of one's mother and father may have a great bearing on one's decision to marry or bear children. Memories of sibling relationships or school experiences may become more salient during middle adulthood, as one approaches the tasks of career management or leadership in community organizations (Livson, 1981).

At any time, however, each person's individual profile will determine which experiences influence current choices. In studying the life course, we are interested not only in the sequencing of events but in the psychological growth that occurs as adults strive to adjust to changing and sometimes conflicting role demands.

A total picture of the pattern of adaptations during the life course would include views of the physical process of aging as well as other biological events, including childbirth, menopause, reduction in hormone production, chronic illnesses, and death (Katchadourian, 1976). It would encompass such factors as developmental tasks and psychosocial crises and events, including phases of the occupational, marital, and child-rearing careers (Feldman & Feldman, 1975; Riegel, 1975). It would include a backdrop of normative, age-graded expectations, developmental expectations, and role expectations. It would include a broad sociohistorical backdrop of economic crises, wars, famines, political revolutions, and social movements that may have changed the interpretation of certain behaviors for a particular cohort (Erikson, 1975; Miernyk, 1975). In fact, most studies of the life course have not been quite so comprehensive. Such studies have tended to single out adaptations to psychosocial events, sometimes in the context of age-graded expectations (Brim, 1976).

Functional Autonomy of Motives

A psychosocial conceptualization of the unique aspects of growth during adulthood requires a concept that frees the mind's energy to develop new motives, skills, interests, and goals. The concept that we find most fruitful for explaining adult motivation is Gordon Allport's notion of the *functional autonomy of motives* (Allport, 1961). In this view, an individual's motive base is not fixed. A behavior is initially performed because of some need. The individual holds a job, for example, in order to earn enough money to support a family. The behavior itself becomes pleasurable and valued irrespective of its link to the original need. The person begins to enjoy work and to value it for its own sake. The valued behaviors—in this case, work behaviors— become functionally autonomous. The person will engage in work because of the satisfactions it brings. The person might refuse a higher-paying job because the current work activities are so satisfying. This situation may also be reversed. The person works because of a need for money to support a family. He or she becomes good at making money and finds the process pleasurable. The pursuit of wealth becomes a functionally autonomous motive. The work becomes less highly specific valued than opportunities to earn money. The person might readily change jobs in order to receive a higher salary. He or she might begin to ignore the family in order to direct time and energy toward this newly established goal: wealth.

The concept of the functional autonomony of motives means that the individual's motive base is flexible and open to change. Stimulated by new experiences and new roles, the individual may uncover new motives that will press behavior in directions not taken earlier. The same behavior may be perpetuated by different motives in two individuals. Similar motives may perpetuate different kinds of behavior. One implication of this concept is that adulthood must be understood in terms not only of role learning and role change but also of the variety of individual motives that direct and sustain behavior.

Tendencies Toward Growth

Robert W. White (1966, pp. 374–405) suggests five tendencies toward growth in adulthood: (1) the stabilizing of ego identity, (2) the freeing of personal relationships, (3) the deepening of interests, (4) the humanizing of values, and (5) the expansion of caring. From his work on adult personality development, White finds these to be the basic gains made during adulthood. These gains seem to be a mixture of the psycho-

Table 11.2   Tendencies for Change During Adulthood (based on Robert W. White's theory of adult maturity)

Tendency	Definition	Direction of Growth	Growth Trends	Situations That Produce Growth
Stabilizing of ego identity	The self or the person one feels oneself to be	Increase of stability, sharper, clearer, more consistent, and free from transient influences; increasing independence from the daily impact of social judgments and experiences of success and failure	Placement in social roles; preferences for emphasis in role enactment; interests and initiatives the person brings to social roles; individuality; personal integration; sense of competence.	Choices: any incident that serves to heighten the efficacy of accumulated personal experiences as against new outside judgments; fresh experiences of success and failure; new objects of possible identification
Freeing of personal relationships	Responding to people in their own right as individuals	Human relationships that are increasingly responsive to the other person's real nature.	Relationships with people who are important and with whom one has frequent and significant contact.	Situations in which the other person behaves unexpectedly, thus disrupting one's habituated way of behaving; decreasing defensiveness against anxiety, allowing the person to observe and respond to others' behavior more openly
Deepening of interests	Interest always connected with an activity that wholly engages a person; progressive mastery of knowledge and skills relevant to a sphere of interest	Increasing identification of one's own satisfaction with development of objects of interest so that the inherent nature and possibilities for development of these interests increasingly guide the person's activity and become part of the satisfaction	As we come to live and act more fully on our interests, we increase both our knowledge and our capacity to influence what pertains to those interests	Action is undertaken and favorable consequences result; discovery; encouraging the interests of an older or younger person.

Table 11.2 *(continued)*

Tendency	Definition	Direction of Growth	Growth Trends	Situations That Produce Growth
Humanizing of values	Moral judgments	The person increasingly discovers the human meaning of values and their relation to the achievement of social purposes; increasingly brings to bear his/her own experiences and motives in affirming and promoting a value system	Values, whatever their content, become increasingly a reflection of one's own experiences and purposes	Situations in which existing values become a source of conflict; sudden empathic identification with some new aspect of value conflict
Expansion of caring	Transcendence of egocentrism; such deep concern for the welfare of someone or something that the meaning of one's own life is identified with the well-being of the object of care	Increased caring for the welfare of other persons and human concerns	Falling in love; taking care of the young; caring for cultural products and institutions	Situations that evoke the caring necessary to maintain civilized institutions and an environment suitable for raising the next generation; situations which evoke nurturant feelings and which offer an opportunity for nurture to be bestowed

social crises of early and middle adulthood. They suggest movement away from preoccupation with the self and an increasing investment in meaningful social relationships. Table 11.2 summarizes these tendencies toward gains in personality development during adulthood.

Erikson (1974) describes the progression of developmental gains during adulthood in the following way. Notice the parallel to White's conceptualization.

> *In youth you find out what you* care to do *and who you* care to be—*even in changing roles. In young adulthood you learn whom you* care to be with—*at work and in private life, not only exchanging intimacies, but sharing intimacy. In adulthood, however, you learn to know what and whom you can* take care *of.* [p. 124]

In summary, we find the concepts of life roles, social clock, life course, functionally autonomous motives, and human growth tendencies to be necessary to an understanding of the psychological development of the adult. Childhood is over. One addresses one's life with great expectations and exhilaration. After the initial excitement of the period subsides, one comes to realize that there is serious work to be done. The young adult is learning to engage in intense and meaningful relationships in marriage, with friends, and with co-workers.

Developmental Tasks

The young adult establishes a style of life that will serve as a framework for the organization of experience during the rest of life. The *style of life* includes the tempo of activity, the balance of work and leisure, the establishment of a circle of friends of varying degrees of intimacy, and the selection of life activities that reflect the individual's value orientation. The most important social factors contributing to the creation of a lifestyle are whether one marries, one's marriage partner, one's children, and one's work. Each of these factors interacts with one's personality, interests, and life goals to shape a lifestyle.

Marriage

Marriage is usually the central context within which work on intimacy and mature social relationships take place. As Figure 11.2 indicates, over 90% of men and women are married by age 44.

Over the life span, fewer than 10% of men or women have never married. This pattern has remained constant from 1900 through the 1980s. Even though people today are more accepting of those who choose to remain single than they were in the 1960s, the number of young people who intend to remain single themselves has changed very little (Thornton, 1989). For most adults, happiness in life depends more on having a satisfying marriage than on any other domain of adult life, including work, friendships, hobbies, and community activities (Glenn & Weaver, 1981; Weingarten & Bryant, 1987; Broman, 1988).

The main change in the marriage pattern has been that more young adults are postponing marriage until the end of their 20s. The percentage of single women between the ages of 20 and 24 rose from 28% in 1960 to 61% in 1987. The comparable increase for single men was from 53% in 1960 to 78% in 1987 (U.S. Bureau of Census, 1976, 1989a; Stengel, 1985). The shift from fewer than 50% to more than 50% of women remaining single in their early 20s suggests a new social norm for age at first marriage. Delaying age at marriage is related to several other social trends, including having children at a later age, smaller projected family size, and therefore fewer years devoted to child rearing. Delaying age at marriage is also related to changing norms regarding sexual experimentation as a single person. Increases in rates of cohabitation and of affairs between married men and single women suggest that many young women who do not marry become involved in intimate relationships during their 20s (Richardson, 1986).

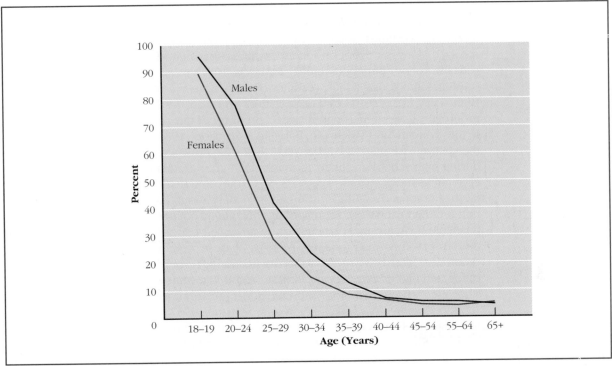

Figure 11.2   Never-Married Persons, by Age and Sex, 1987
Adapted from U.S. Bureau of the Census, *Statistical Abstract of the United States, 1989* (Washington, D.C.:
U.S. Government Printing Office, 1989), p. 43.

The decade of the 1980s brought with it the uncoupling of sexual activity, marriage, and childbearing not only for adolescent mothers but for young adult women as well. As we look to the future, it seems probable that a greater proportion of men and women will remain single than did so in the past (Glick, 1988).

Readiness to Marry
Through the dating process one meets many potential partners, some of whom may appear quite attractive on the "important" dimensions. What determines whether or not the dating relationship will end in matrimony? One very important factor is the readiness of the two individuals for a long-term commitment. Work on identity must be far enough along so that the possibility of a deep emotional involvement with another person will be regarded as exciting rather than frightening. In studies of college students, a relationship has been found between identity status and the quality of intimacy. Those students who had achieved identity reported the most genuine intimate relationships. Those who were characterized as diffuse were the least intimate and the most isolated (Orlofsky, Marcia & Lesser, 1973; Kacerguis & Adams, 1980; Craig-Bray, Adams & Dobson, 1988).

The developmental progression from identity achievement to intimacy is less clear-cut for women than it is for men. During later adolescence and early adulthood, women are likely to score higher than men on measures of intimacy. Further, it is not uncommon for some women to have high levels of intimacy even though they have foreclosed identities. Some research suggests that for women the issue of intimacy is resolved alongside work on identity, whereas for men identity resolution often precedes work on intimacy (Schiedel & Marcia, 1985).

For some young adults, readiness for marriage is a response to the social clock. Each social class has its own expectations in regard to the best age for marriage. A group's ideal age at marriage is a good predictor of the actual age at which individuals in the group marry (Teachman, Polonko & Scanzoni, 1987). For working-class groups, the ideal age for marriage is between 18 and 22. Adolescents who are dating seriously during high school are likely to marry soon after graduation. Once young working-class adults move past the age of 23 or 24, they find that the pool of eligible partners has been reduced significantly and their anxiety about finding a mate increases (Gagnon & Greenblat, 1978). Young people who attend college tend to have a slightly later timetable for marriage. Participation in advanced education tends to delay marriage more for women than for men, perhaps because women who have had more education have alternative means to secure economic resources. For men, advanced education and higher earnings are likely to result in a somewhat earlier age at marriage, since men who have a more substantial income are more confident of being able to support a family (Teachman, Polonko & Scanzoni, 1987).

Readiness for marriage may be determined by some other personal agenda, such as completing work for an advanced degree, completing military service, or earning a certain income. In each case, the person with this kind of commitment is less receptive to expressions of love than he or she will be once the goal is achieved. In our culture, individuals have a great deal of freedom to determine the time of marriage and choice of marriage partner. Expectations that one will marry are strong, but young adults can at least follow their own timetables.

Selection of a Partner

Once a person is ready to consider marriage, the choice of partner and the decision to marry are influenced by a process of deepening attraction and commitment. Figure 11.3 illustrates four phases of increasing involvement in the mate-selection process (Adams, 1986). At each phase the relationship can be terminated if the key issues of that stage produce undesirable information or evaluation. It can end if an alternative attraction becomes so strong that it reduces investment in the relationship. The alternative attraction could be another person, but it might also be a job, school, or the desire to achieve a personal goal.

In phase I, partners are selected among those who are available for interaction. Many of the choices one makes during adolescence and young adulthood, such as where to go to college, where to work, which parties to go to, and where to take a vacation, will determine whom one meets. Even one's style of interaction—for example, whether shy and withdrawn or expressive and outgoing— will influence the number and kinds of interactions that one has with others. In the most general sense, the choice of marriage partner will depend on the network of interactions in which one is involved. Among those people one encounters, some attract attention and others do not. Physical appearance is a very important element in this initial attraction. In

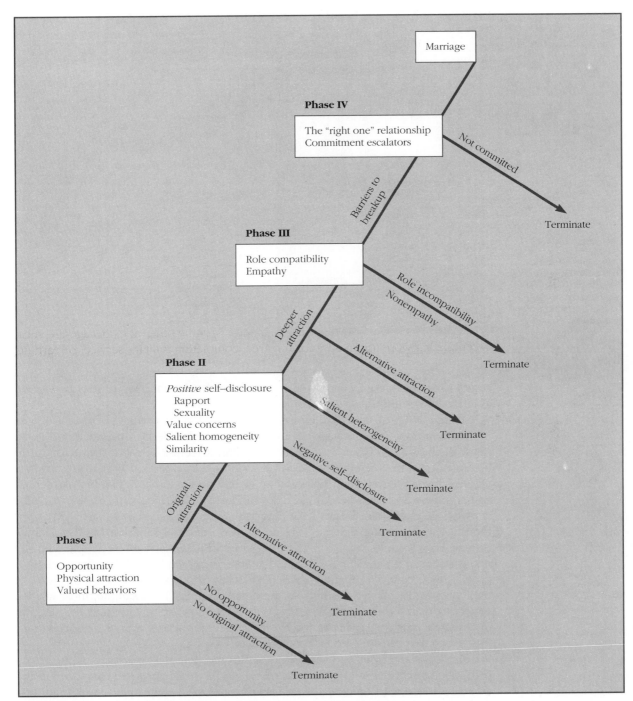

Figure 11.3   **The Mate-Selection Process in the United States**
Source: B. N. Adams, *The Family: A Sociological Interpretation,* 4th ed., p. 213. Copyright © 1986 by Harcourt, Brace and Jovanovich, Publishers. Reprinted by permission.

As couples discover basic similarities in key values and background characteristics, their mutual attraction deepens and their relationship is strengthened.

addition, people who are behaving in an admired, effective manner may be viewed as attractive or desirable.

Phase I, original attraction, moves on to phase II as the partners begin to disclose information about themselves and interact in ways that deepen the relationship. In phase II the discovery of basic similarities and a feeling of rapport are central to continuance of the relationship. Each person has key values and background characteristics that serve as a filter for assessing whether a person is an eligible partner. Of course, eligibility is defined differently by different people. For some, any person who is conscious is eligible. Others have criteria that limit the choice of marriage partner to someone of a certain age range, religion, race, educational background, and family history. For example, some adults would not consider marriage to people who did not share their religious faith. For these people, only members of their own religious group are perceived as eligible partners. Many individuals may not even be aware of their own limits on the eligibility of potential partners. For example, most women expect to marry men who are a few years older than they. Although they do not deliberately state this as a criterion for marriage, they simply do not interact with or feel drawn to a partner who is "too young" or "too old."

Similarity contributes to attractiveness. Most people seek marriage partners who will understand them and provide a sense of emotional support. They do not find attractive those who hold opposing views, come from quite different family backgrounds, or have temperamental qualities unlike their own. People of similar age and economic, religious, racial, and educational backgrounds marry each other in far greater proportions than would be expected by chance alone (Eshelman, 1985; Schoen

& Wooldredge, 1989). Of course, there are many dimensions along which two people can recognize similarities or differences. They may seem quite different on some dimensions, such as religion and social class, yet discover that they are quite similar on others, such as life goals and political ideology. The more aware individuals are of the themes that are central to their own sense of personal identity, the better they can recognize the dimensions of similarity in other people that will contribute to intimate relationships.

The relationship is likely to proceed from phase II to phase III if the partners extend the domains in which self-disclosure occurs, including sexual needs, personal fears, and fantasies. With each new risk taken, the discovery of a positive, supportive reaction in the partner deepens the level of trust in the relationship. Negative reactions following disclosure or revelation of information that is viewed as undesirable can lead to the termination of the relationship. College students of both sexes consider a person to be much more desirable as a marriage partner if that person has had only light to moderate sexual experience. In thinking about a potential marriage partner, students are especially rejecting of persons who have been involved in homosexual relationships (Williams & Jacoby, 1989). Thus disclosures regarding prior sexual experiences could very well result in the termination of a relationship during phase II.

In phase III, the discovery of role compatibility and empathy begin to give the relationship a life of its own. Role compatibility is a sense that the two partners approach a situation in ways that work well together. Whether it is a visit to a relative's home, an office party, a casual evening with friends, or running out of gas on the highway, the two people discover that they like the way each behaves and that their combined behavior is effective. Empathy builds through these observations, enabling each partner to know how the other is responding and to anticipate the other's needs.

Once the partners are enjoying role compatibility and empathy, they move on to phase IV, the "right one" relationship. In this phase, barriers to breaking up help consolidate the relationship. First, the partners have disclosed and taken risks with each other that they probably have not taken with others. Second, they have achieved comfortable feelings of predictability and empathy that make them more certain about each other than about possible alternative attractions. Third, through frequent role enactment together, they have been identified by others as a couple. There is usually social support for their remaining together. At this point, the costs of breaking up begin to be quite high, including loss of a confidant, of a companion, and of the social network in which the couple is embedded.

In contemporary society, cohabitation rather than marriage may be the outcome of this process. In 1987 there were 2.3 million unmarried couple households (U.S. Bureau of the Census, 1989a). For some couples, living together is a way of exploring phase III and determining role compatibility. For others, earlier experiences of divorce make cohabitation a safer strategy than marriage even when the commitment is very strong (Atwater, 1985). In a national study of unmarried women aged 20 to 29, about 30% had been involved in a cohabiting relationship for three months or longer at some time in their lives. A comparison of women who have cohabited with those who have not found that a significantly larger proportion of the cohabiting women want to get married. For these women, cohabitation is not a substitute for marriage but more likely an element in the courtship process (Tanfer, 1987).

Adjustment During the Early Years of Marriage

Once the choice has been made and the thrill of courtship has passed, the first few years of marriage involve a process of mutual adaptation. These years may prove to be extremely difficult, particularly because the young married couple does not anticipate the strains that are to come. The partners may be quite distressed to find their "love nest" riddled with the tensions that are part of carving out a life together. In fact, data suggest that the probability of divorce is highest during the first years of marriage and peaks somewhere between two and four years. The median duration of marriage is about seven years. This pattern has been stable for the past 20 years (U.S. Bureau of the Census, 1989a).

There are many sources of tension early in a marriage. The single factor that is most directly correlated with divorce is income. Many people seem to believe that divorce is a privilege of the rich, but the evidence suggests that the opposite is true: the divorce and separation rates are generally higher among couples with minimal education and low incomes (Reiss, 1980). Total family income is related to marital stability in some distinct ways. First, an erratic income and a high level of indebtedness are more strongly associated with marital disruption than a low but steady income. Second, a wife's income is associated with marital disruption when she earns about as much as or more than her husband, but not when she earns less than her husband (Raschke, 1987).

If the partners do not have similar religious, educational, or social-class backgrounds, they will have to compromise on many value decisions. Assuming a shared value orientation, certain lifestyle decisions will still generate tension. The couple must establish a mutually satisfying sexual relationship. They must work out an agreement about the expenditure and saving of money. They must respond to each other's sleep patterns, food preferences, work patterns, and toilet habits. The couple may find the demands of their parents and in-laws to be a source of conflict. Usually it is the number of demands rather than any single one that makes the adjustment process so difficult.

As part of the adjustment to marriage, the partners must achieve a sense of psychological commitment to each other. The marriage ceremony is intended to make the commitment public and binding. The individuals concerned probably do not fully accept the reality of those marriage vows until they have tested the relationship. There is a period of testing during which each partner is likely to put strain on the relationship just to see how strong it really is. The matter can be posed in this way: "Will you still love me even if I do . . .?" or "Am I still free to do what I did before we were married?" Every marriage relationship is different. The partners must discover the limits that their particular relationship can tolerate. Both must feel that they still have a degree of freedom. They must also believe that the limits on their freedom are worth the love they gain in return. As each test is successfully passed, the partners grow closer. They trust each other more and become increasingly sensitive to each other's feelings. The tests diminish in number as the question of trust is resolved.

In a national survey of sources of well-being, young adults were more likely to be aware of problems in their marriages and to admit to feelings of inadequacy as spouses than were middle-aged or older married adults (Veroff, Douvan & Kulka, 1981). Despite this greater sensitivity to problems in the marriage, there were no significant differences across age groups in the degree of marital happiness or in the sources of pleasure that marriage provided. The younger group may have been more willing to recognize and accept the fact that problems were a part of the early years of marriage. Of course, it is also possible that the older adults who found the problems of marriage too great to resolve had already divorced.

Communication and Marital Adjustment

It is reasonable to expect that intimacy and a high level of marital satisfaction will require effective communication and the capacity to cope effectively with conflict. Conflict may be a product of the interaction of two well-developed identities, each with a distinct temperament and a distinct set of values and goals. It may be a product of the uneven distribution of power or resources. It may be a product of the simple day-to-day need to make decisions that the couple have never made before. Finally, conflict may be a product of the failure of the partner or the relationship to meet critical expectations. Whatever the source of conflict, marital stability and satisfaction are closely tied to the quality and frequency of communication (Montgomery, 1981; Filsinger & Thoma, 1988).

Partners who have a high level of marital satisfaction are also likely to report frequent pleasurable interaction (Robinson & Price, 1980). A high degree of disclosure is associated with marital satisfaction (Jorgensen & Gaudy, 1980). Partners who are satisfied with their marriages are also likely to be good at sending and understanding messages from each other (Noller, 1980). In contrast, a decline in pleasurable interactions and an absence of communication of any kind, even conflicts, are associated with a high probability of divorce.

The idea that men and women may view the communication process differently is also supported by research. Four types of communication styles have been described: conventional, controlling, speculative, and contactful (Hawkins, Weisberg & Ray, 1980). *Conventional interactions* gloss over issues. They maintain the interaction but do not express much emotional commitment or explore the other person's views. *Controlling interactions* express the person's views quite clearly but do not take the other person's perspective into account. *Speculative interactions* are guarded, they explore the other person's point of view but do not fully reveal the person's own position. *Contactful interactions* are open to the other person's point of view and also clearly express the speaker's own position.

Husbands and wives agreed that the contactful style was most desirable and the controlling style least desirable. However, wives preferred fewer controlling interactions from their husbands than the husbands preferred for themselves. Wives also preferred more contactful interactions from their husbands than the husbands preferred for themselves. Wives perceived their husbands as being more conventional, more controlling, and less contactful than they themselves were. In other words, wives expressed the view that their husbands were less likely than they were to use the modes of interaction that they preferred. Husbands did not express the same dissatisfaction with the modes of communication used by their wives.

Even among couples who value open, direct, and accepting communication, there will be stumbling blocks to intimacy. The socialization of men and women in our culture is still sufficiently distinct to result in differences in expectations and compe-

Pablo Picasso, *The Two Saltimbanques,* 1901. To sustain a marriage, the partners must be able to interact even during periods of conflict. Withdrawal, rejection, and distancing are common reactions to conflict. These strategies may be effective during a brief cooling-down period, but they do not replace direct communication for exploring or resolving differences.

tences. Within a marriage relationship, one can anticipate conflicts and use them as a means to clarify the relationship itself as well as the problem at hand. It does seem critical that the couple be able to agree to have these conflicts and be able to establish some family rules for a "fair fight" (Blood & Blood, 1978).

Adjustment to marriage appears to be a function of identity status, desire for intimacy, open communication, closeness, parents' marital satisfaction, resources, and the way power is shared or struggled for. Several structural patterns for family composition are found in modern society. The traditional nuclear family still seems to be viewed more positively than other family structures (Ganong, Coleman & Mapes, 1990). This attitude in itself may pose challenges for adjustment, since relatively few married couples actually match the structure they view most positively.

Differences in Marital Adjustment
for Women and Men

Women experience more stress in adjusting to marriage than men (Bell, 1983). This observation can be explained in at least two ways. First, when many women enter marriage, they have completed less work on their identities than their husbands; have had little or no preparation for childbearing and child rearing; and depend on their husbands for financial security and social status (Raush et al., 1974; Rossi, 1968). The differential strength of the partners early in marriage causes women to experience more emotional strain than men. Second, women are more adequately prepared for an intimate, open relationship than men. They expect and desire a degree of closeness that is often not reciprocated. Men, on the other hand, are quite satisfied with the degree of intimacy that they find in marriage and have fewer expectations or less desire for greater closeness.

Mutual satisfaction in marriage appears to depend heavily on the husband's characteristics, including the stability of his masculine identity, the satisfaction in his own parents' marriage, his educational level, and his socioeconomic status. Barry (1970) hypothesized that "husbands with stable self-identities can supply the security their wives need and can support them emotionally in the difficult years of transition to married and parental life" (p. 50). Traditionally men have had more power in the early phases of marriage, because they have had a greater sense of their own identities and a higher status from their occupational roles; much of women's experience has depended on how men shared power in their relationships (Rodman, 1972). Today, however, the majority of people live in dual-earner families or single-parent families. Little research has been done on gender differences when a couple's identities are equally achieved and strong, or when power is shared from the outset. One can only surmise that the endurance of the marital bond and the quality of adjustment over the long haul will depend more on individual differences than on gender differences when the identities of the partners are more equally developed and one partner does not start off in a subservient position.

Adjustment in Dual-Earner Marriages

One of the greatest changes in American families in recent years has been the increase in the number of married women who are employed. The percentage of employed married women whose husbands are present rose from 30% in 1960 to 56% in 1988. The number of women with young children who work outside the house has grown substantially. In 1988, 55% of married women with children under three years old were in the labor force, compared with 33% in 1975 (U.S. Bureau of the Census, 1989a). Rather than drop out of the labor force and return to work after their children are grown, the majority of women are now remaining in the labor force throughout the early years of parenthood (Piotrkowski, Rapoport & Rapoport, 1987).

There is no question that the involvement of both husband and wife in the labor market requires a redefinition of customary family roles and the division of labor. Uncertainty about the expectations and behaviors of the husband and wife roles must be worked out between the partners. Sometimes this uncertainty helps to produce greater intimacy by generating interactions that lead to greater self-disclosure by each partner. Very personal preferences and habits must be examined if the partners are to arrive at a successful division of labor that is mutually satisfying. Sometimes this process is very threatening. The partners may not really be aware of their expectations for themselves or for the other person until they are married. It is not until some weeks have gone by and no one has done the laundry that it becomes evident that the couple must decide who will do this task or how to share it.

As the couple begins to confront the challenges posed by their lifestyle, they may discover conflicts they never expected. They may find that they do not agree about the relative importance of each person's career. If the husband feels that his work is more important than his wife's work, he may insist that she give less time to her work and more to family responsibilities. The wife may resent this expectation.

When both partners work outside the home, the chances that work-related pressures affect time together increase. Couples may not have the same vacation periods. Both partners may have to cope with unpredictable demands from the workplace. Their time at home and time at work may not coincide. While both partners are away from home, many of the tasks that are required to keep a home clean, well stocked, and conducive to relaxation cannot be completed (Rapoport, Rapoport & Bumstead, 1978). Often the wife expects and is expected to do the housework and perform other traditional "female" functions. When the couple have children, the wife is expected to care for them. These expectations often cause resentment and reduce the wife to exhaustion. A wife may pressure her husband to share the load, and the husband may resent it. These factors may make it difficult for the partners to make progress in their own sense of intimacy in their relationship.

It is not only the number of two-worker families that have increased; the number of families in which both partners pursue high-powered professional, technical, or administrative careers has risen steadily. A considerable amount of research has been done on these dual-career marriages. The main variables studied and the major findings about these marriages are summarized in Table 11.3. High quality, dual-career marriages are likely to have the following characteristics (Thomas, Albrecht & White, 1984):

- Adequate income, with husbands earning more than their wives
- Couple consensus that husband's career is preeminent
- Husband supports wife's career
- Older children
- Satisfying social life
- Husband empathic to wife's stress
- Good sexual relationship
- Discussion of work-related problems
- Role complementarity and role sharing
- Shared activities and companionship

There are indications that highly educated women who are employed in demanding work roles are less inclined to remain in a marriage relationship that is not emotionally satisfying. Economic independence allows women to choose or reject marriage, a freedom that many women of earlier historical periods did not enjoy (Cherlin, 1981).

Table 11.3   Major Findings on Aspects of Dual-Career Marriages

Variable Studied	Findings
Degree of marital satisfaction	Satisfaction related to degree of fit between husband's and wife's attitudes and aspirations. Couples with more traditional sex-role attitudes tend to experience more stress.
Early socialization experiences	Many women in dual-career marriages experienced: 1. Early adjustment to high levels of stress. 2. Little reinforcement for conventional values. 3. A close relationship with parents who supported their careers aspirations.
Effects of having husband and wife in the same career field	Wives in the same field as their husbands tend to produce more than those not married to fellow professionals, but are less productive and less professionally satisfied than their husbands.
Consequences of status differences between husbands and wives	Degree of stress is related to the extent to which the status difference is congruent with gender-role identities and expectations of the partners.
Effect of dual careers on family task sharing	Partners tend to do more sharing of traditionally female tasks than do single-career or career/earner couples.
Impact of work world on dual-career family	Negative impact of traditional business, which operates on the assumption that career takes precedence over family and that the employee has a full-time support system at home.
Effects of geographic mobility	Mobility has a negative impact on the wife's career; her needs tend not to be the determining factor in the decision to move.
Effect of particular structural variations	Couples who share less than two full-time equivalent positions favor a continuation of the arrangement, devote more time to their works and are more productive than the average full-time employee; yet employers tend to view such an arrangement with reservations.

Adapted from E. Macklin, "Non-Traditional Family Forms," in M. B. Sussman and S. K. Steinmetz (eds.), *Handbook of Marriage and the Family* (New York: Plenum, 1987), pp. 330–331.

Childbearing

During the years of young adulthood, individuals decide whether or not to have children. They often make this decision during the first few years of marriage (Brim, 1968). Here again the notion of the social clock comes into play. Couples who wait a long time to begin their families may be pressured by parents who are eager to become grandparents or by friends who have already experienced the lifestyle changes that accompany the birth of the first child. In recent years couples have begun to postpone having children until after the first years of their marriage. The decision to postpone childbearing is related to several other aspects of adult life. Couples who have a dual-earner marriage have to think about the effect of children on their family income. They may also need to anticipate the best timing for childbearing in relation to their job security or career advancement. Some couples set certain material goals for themselves as a prerequisite to having children. For example, they may decide to wait until they can buy a home, purchase some furniture, or travel together before they have

Women can be quite deliberate in deciding whether they wish to conceive and if so, when, because effective methods of birth control are available to them.

children. Given the high divorce rate, couples are likely to want to feel confident that their relationships are strong before deciding to have children.

The relationship between fertility and the value of having children was studied in a national sample of married women under 40 and their husbands (Hoffman & Manis, 1979). By far the most frequently mentioned advantages of having children were that children provide love and companionship and help protect adults from loneliness. Men and women, blacks and whites, parents and nonparents were about equally likely to recognize these advantages. Here we see an extension of the need to achieve a sense of intimacy expressed in the decision to have children—a need that is appropriately tied to the psychosocial stage of early adulthood.

In contrast to the elation that is experienced in the anticipation of and preparation for the newborn, the arrival of the first child often brings a period of stress to the marriage (Feldman, 1971, 1981). On the average, the presence of children in the family is associated with lower marital satisfaction and less marital happiness (Glenn & McLanahan, 1982; Belsky & Pensky, 1988). Ratings of marital satisfaction do not usually drop from very satisfied to very unsatisfied. Couples continue to be satisfied with marriage after their children are born, but the level of satisfaction is somewhat lower.

Looking more closely at this pattern, Belsky and Rovine (1990) found clear evidence of individual differences among couples. In their longitudinal study of 128 families, they observed four patterns of change in the assessment of marital quality. Some couples showed rapid decline in marital quality after the baby was born. Some

Parents usually include their young children in their leisure time. Even a casual walk after dinner becomes a family outing.

showed a slow, steady decline. A third group showed no significant change, and a fourth group showed slight increases in marital quality. These findings caution us not to overgeneralize group trends to individual cases.

The decline in marital satisfaction that can accompany the transition to parenthood can be accounted for in several ways. For the first months after a child is born, both parents are exhausted from lack of sleep. They are generally unskilled in the care of a newborn baby. They have new responsibilities and a new schedule. Many parents feel inadequate to care for their babies, and they turn to their parents, neighbors, pediatricians, and books for advice on how to do it. This lack of self-confidence creates tension between the marriage partners.

The baby's presence brings out areas of potential conflict between the partners about philosophies of child rearing or beliefs regarding appropriate child-care practices. Feelings of jealousy, competition, and abandonment may arise in the first months after the child is born. The exclusiveness of the husband-wife relationship is interrupted by the repeated demands of the new baby and there is less time for the couple to be together without the baby. Feelings of resentment may be stronger when a couple's sex-role attitudes conflict with the actual activities they end up carrying out after a child is born (Belsky, Lang & Huston, 1986).

It is not surprising that one's experiences as a child influence the way one reacts to the parent role. It might be a bit more surprising to realize that recollections of one's child-rearing environment are related to the level of marital satisfaction experienced after the birth of the first child. One study reported a more pronounced decline in marital adjustment after the birth of the first child when either the husband or wife recalled their own parents as cold, rejecting, and involved in a conflictual marriage. In addition, negative child-rearing experiences were related to greater discrepancies between husbands' and wives' assessments of the quality of their marriage after their children were born (Belsky & Isabella, 1985). One interpretation of these observations is that memories of negative childhood experiences are reawakened with the child's birth and stimulate increased defensiveness. Another interpretation may be that adults whose parents were cold and rejecting may not have developed adequate parenting skills. They encounter increased conflict with their spouses when they become parents because they are less competent in this new role.

In an attempt to clarify the effects of many of these factors on marital satisfaction during the transition to parenthood, researchers compared marital activities and evaluations of the marriage by parents and nonparents who had been married the same number of years (MacDermid, Huston & McHale, 1990). They found that over the first three years of marriage, couples' ratings of love and satisfaction in their marriage declined somewhat. There were no differences in the magnitude of the decline for parents and nonparents. Having children did not account for some greater drop in love or satisfaction than appears to occur as a result of adjusting to marriage in general. This is an important observation that provides new insight into much of the earlier research on marital satisfaction and the transition to parenthood.

However, having children did have a clear impact on marital companionship. The percentage of leisure activities shared by the husband and the wife dropped sharply after the baby was born, but declined only slightly for the couples without children. During the third year of marriage parents had a greater number of shared activities per day than nonparents, but very few when the child was not present. Figure 11.4 shows the number of minutes of joint leisure per day without the child for two groups of parents in comparison with joint leisure for nonparents in the first, second, and third years of marriage. After the birth of their child, couples have only about one-third as many minutes together alone as they had when they were childless. The nature of companionship in marriage clearly changes to incorporate a baby, and therefore may take on a less intimate character.

Surviving the early months of child rearing may serve to strengthen the bond between the man and woman. The partners begin to respect each other's competence in caring for their child. They also begin to conceptualize their roles as parents and to view the increasing complexity of their family structure as a challenge rather than a burden. The new child adds a degree of energy to the family through the expression of satisfaction, pleasure, and eventual loving.

As the roles of mother and father are added to the adults' repertoire of role relationships, their own expectations as well as those of others concerning the raising of a child are aroused. The daily demands that the child places on the parents help them to define their own roles more realistically. Instead of wondering what parents should do, they are preoccupied with the concrete events of parenting. Through this experiential learning, young adults actually formulate their own definitions of parental roles.

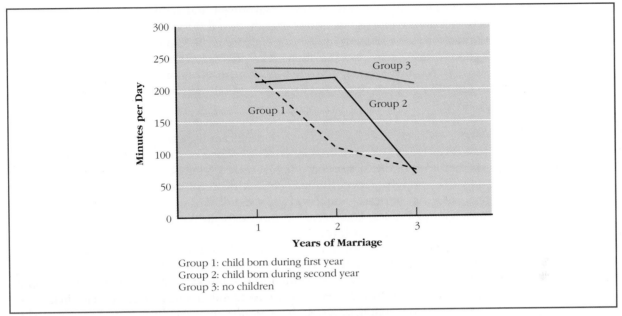

Figure 11.4   Duration of Joint Husband–Wife Leisure Without Child, by Parents and Nonparents
Source: S. M. MacDermid, T. L. Huston, and S. M. McHale, "Changes in Marriage Associated with Transition to Parenthood," *Journal of Marriage and the Family, 52* (1990), 475–486.

The process of social attachment and its impact on the infant was discussed in Chapter 5. The theme of mutuality as the central process for the establishment of trust was stressed. Here we can focus on the impact of this mutuality on parents. Infants actively engage parents, evoke unique responses, and through their differential behaviors, begin to shape adults' parenting behaviors (Brazelton et al., 1979; Bell & Harper, 1977; Lewis & Rosenblum, 1974). Mutuality is important in increasing the parents' capacity to experience intimacy. Successful child care results in the ability to anticipate children's needs, stimulate their interests, and delight their senses. Infants respond through shrieks of delight, elaborate smiles, and active pursuit of loved ones. Infants are unrestrained in their loving. They mouth, bite, grab, laugh, smile, squeal, and coo in response to pleasure. Through their open demonstrations of affection, they teach adults about the expression of love and increase the adults' ability to demonstrate love.

Parenting is a unique experience of adulthood. There may be some developmental antecedents to parenting, such as baby-sitting, caring for younger siblings, or working with children as a camp counselor or teacher. However, none of these roles involves the emotional investment and total responsibility of parenthood. As a parent, an adult has an opportunity to discover new aspects of his or her personality. The parent role brings demands that are quite distinct from the role of spouse. One must respond to a person who cannot really reciprocate one's generosity or caring. In this role, one discovers the qualities of nurturance, playfulness, and authoritativeness. As one interacts with one's children, memories of one's own childhood are revived and reviewed. Conflicts in one's relationship with one's parents, feelings of sibling jealousy, recollections of schooldays, peer relations, fears, and secret dreams are all reviewed as one strives to respond to and guide one's children. In all of this, there is a new opportunity to put old ghosts to rest, reinterpret past events, and achieve a new sense of adult maturity.

Little has been written about the psychological growth stimulated by the decision to bear children. This is a unique and significant life choice that is made in various ways. Even babies who are unplanned are products of some kind of decision making, whether it was a decision to have sexual relations knowing that pregnancy was possible, to avoid using effective means of birth control, or not to abort an unplanned pregnancy. During early adulthood the issue of reproduction is confronted not just once but many times. Adults make choices to delay parenting, to have another child, to wait awhile longer before having another child, or to stop having children altogether. In all of these decisions, many powerful themes are reflected. These themes may be linked to one's sense of fulfilling a masculine or feminine life purpose by having children. They may be linked to one's childhood socialization and identification with parental figures. They may be linked to some very intense religious beliefs about sexuality, contraception, or abortion. Reproduction is the means by which the species perpetuates itself. Regardless of the decisions one reaches, this issue cannot help but heighten one's sense of being and one's belief that the decisions of adulthood make a difference.

Childlessness

Not all married couples choose to have children. In 1987 about 5% of married women aged 18 to 34 expected to have no children. The percentage was lower for black (3.5%) and Hispanic (1.9%) women (U.S. Bureau of the Census, 1989a). Much like attitudes toward remaining single, attitudes toward childlessness have become somewhat more accepting; yet the number of young adults who intend to remain childless has not increased significantly (Thornton, 1989).

Voluntarily childless couples continue to experience social pressures to have children, and are aware of negative stereotypes attributed to them. Childless couples may be viewed as selfish, less well adjusted, less nurturant, and as likely to have a less fulfilling life than couples with children. Resisting social expectations that married women ought to bear children requires a high level of personal autonomy and less need for social support from a wide range of reference groups. Voluntarily childless men have been described as more independent, less tied to tradition, and more flexible than men who are fathers. Voluntarily childless women have been described as more self-reliant, assertive, and concerned with personal freedom than women who are mothers (Silka & Kiesler, 1977). In general, couples who are voluntarily childless are able to disregard the negative pressures, but they tend to find support from one another and from a small number of significant family members or close friends (Houseknecht, 1987).

In the workplace, adults are exposed to a variety of risks. Protective apparel will not reduce the impact of psychological hazards.

Work

Work is a complex concept. The following analysis provides a framework for the consideration of work as a psychological variable. This type of analysis is necessary because the variety of occupational roles in our society is so wide. Each job role places the individual in a somewhat different psychological context and therefore can be seen as exerting different psychological demands.

The first important distinction to be made concerning occupations has to do with the training and posttraining periods. Because of the wide variety of possible occupational choices, opportunities to prepare a young person for a specific occupational role during childhood and adolescence are slim (Brim, 1968). Most jobs require a period of training for the novice employee. The training period may vary from a few weeks in the case of an assembly-line worker to ten years in the case of a physician. For some people, the stage of young adulthood is over before the training experience is completed.

In addition to involving the transmission of information about specific skills, the training period often involves the socialization of the worker. Through this socialization process, the novice learns about the technical skills, interpersonal behaviors, work-related attitudes, and authority relations that are valued by the work group. The training period also acquaints the novice with the specific demands and hazards of the particular occupation. During the occupational search and training periods, the individual must evaluate the match between personal characteristics and the four central components of the work situation: (1) technical skills, (2) authority relations, (3) unique demands and hazards, and (4) interpersonal relations with co-workers.

Technical Skills

Most jobs require a certain degree of technical expertise. The amount required varies a great deal from one occupation to another. Individuals must evaluate whether the particular skills that are demanded of them are within their range of competence. They must determine whether they have the potential to improve their skills, and they must evaluate whether they derive pleasure and satisfaction from demonstrating their abilities. The job-training phase involves the learning of new skills. The success of individuals in this learning will determine to some extent whether they remain in the occupation.

Authority Relations

Each job role specifies status and decision-making relationships among people. One aspect of job training is learning which people evaluate one's work, which criteria they use for evaluation, and the limits of one's autonomy in the job. New workers must respond to both the authority structure and the people who occupy positions of authority. With respect to the authority structure, they must assess the channels for decision making and the ways in which they can influence decisions. With respect to the people who occupy positions of authority, new workers must be able to deal with a variety of personalities in positions of higher and lower status.

Demands and Hazards

Each job has unique occupational demands, including norms for self-preservation, productivity, and availability. In some work settings, there are expectations for a very high level of personal commitment. Leisure time, family activities, and political or community roles are all influenced by one's participation in the work role. In other work settings, workers may become quite alienated. Such workers feel little sense of personal contribution to their employers' overall objectives. The norms vary greatly from one occupation to another. It is the task of individuals to assess how well they fit and how strongly they wish to maintain a fit with the unique characteristics of a particular occupational role.

Occupational hazards include a broad range of potential physical and psychological risks associated with the workplace. In a 1978 survey on quality of employment, 78% of the respondents said that they were exposed to at least one health or safety hazard, such as air pollution, electric shock, or dangerous chemicals (Quinn & Staines, 1979). Among other occupational hazards are the effects of working the night shift (Levi, 1978); exposure to contagious diseases and personal attack reported by school-teachers (Materka, 1980); and the risk of burnout reported by social workers, police, and others who have intense emotional contact with clients (Maslach, 1978).

Settings differ in the kinds of pressures or hazards that they inflict on workers.

Interpersonal skills are required in most work settings. Workers in every kind of job must develop communication skills, to maintain an appropriate level of cooperation and to solve problems.

Similarly, individuals differ in their vulnerability to these pressures and hazards, their willingness to risk certain potential dangers, and their evaluation of the payoff for sustaining some degree of stress (Gardell, 1977). The individual ultimately must decide whether the particular vulnerabilities are tolerable in light of the rewards.

Interpersonal Relationships with Peers

The final area of learning during the period of occupational search and training involves one's interpersonal relationships with co-workers. The potential for friendship relations in the work setting is usually not advertised as a central component of job satisfaction. Yet such relations are clearly a dominant feature of the decision to be committed to a particular work setting. The need for friends and the need to share with peers the anxieties of the new job learning provide strong motives for seeking comradeship on the job. The presence of congenial co-workers who can relax together and share feelings of accomplishment can greatly enhance any work setting. In fact, the spirit of friendship on the job may compensate for many stressful situational demands.

Some work settings stress competition among co-workers. Incentives are arranged to stimulate competition rather than cooperation. In such settings, new workers must shoulder the strains of their new learning independently. They must learn the game of one-upmanship, always taking credit for successes and foisting the blame for failures onto others. The competitive setting may intrigue some individuals, whereas the affiliative setting would attract others. New workers must assess the quality of interpersonal relationships and determine whether or not they meet their social needs.

A number of factors limit the range of occupations open to a given person during the work search phase. Among the most obvious limiting factors are educational attainment, talent, and location. O'Reilly and Caldwell (1980) studied the impact of the kinds of factors that influence job choice and subsequent job satisfaction. The subjects were graduates of a master's program in business administration. Two groups of factors influenced job choice: intrinsic factors and extrinsic factors. The intrinsic

Table 11.4 New Learning in the Work Setting	
Job Component	*Dimensions of New Learning*
Technical skills	Individuals must determine whether skills: 1. Are within their range of competence 2. Can be learned through training 3. Provide pleasure and satisfaction
Authority relations	Individuals must discover: 1. Who evaluates their work and the criteria for evaluation 2. The limits of their own autonomy 3. The decision-making structure in their work setting and how they can influence this structure 4. How to deal with a variety of personalities in positions of greater or lesser authority
Unique demands and hazards	Individuals must learn: 1. Norms for self-presentation 2. Norms for productivity 3. Norms for availability 4. How their personalities fit the unique demands of the setting 5. Their degree of vulnerability to work-related hazards

Interpersonal relations with peers	Individuals must assess:
	1. The quality of social relationships in the work setting
	2. The norms for relationship
	    a. Cooperative
	    b. Competitive

factors included interest in the job, personal feelings about the job, responsibility on the job, and opportunities for advancement. The extrinsic factors included family or financial pressures, advice of others, job location, and salary. Job satisfaction and commitment to remaining in the job six months after the job was taken were positively related to the strength of the intrinsic factors that influenced job choice. Two extrinsic factors—salary and job location—were also related to job satisfaction and job commitment. Strong pressure to take a job because of family or financial need was associated with lower job satisfaction and less commitment to remain in the job.

In summary, we see the period of early adulthood as the experimental, training phase of work. Table 11.4 summarizes the kinds of new learning that occur during the training phase. Through involvement in several work settings, individuals must learn to assess the technical requirements, authority relations, job demands, and quality of interpersonal relationships that characterize specific occupational environments. They must also begin to project images of themselves moving into the future through a particular work role. In this context, they begin to assess the potential costs and gains of their occupations.

In an attempt to synthesize career development and individual development, Kathy Kram (1985) proposed a developmental model of career issues (see Table 11.5). Careers are delineated in three phases: early career, middle career, and late career, which correspond roughly to the phases of career exploration, career establishment

Table 11.5 Characteristic Developmental Tasks at Successive Career Stages

	Early Career	Middle Career	Late Career
Concerns about self	*Competence:* Can I be effective in the managerial/professional role? Can I be effective in the role of spouse and/or parent? *Identity:* Who am I as a manager/professional? What are my skills and aspirations?	*Competence:* How do I compare with my peers, with my subordinates, and with my own standards and expectations? *Identity:* Who am I now that I am no longer a novice? What does it mean to be a "senior" adult?	*Competence:* Can I be effective in a more consultative and less central role, still having influence as the time to leave the organization gets closer? *Identity:* What will I leave behind of value that will symbolize my contributions during my career? Who am I apart from a manager/professional and how will it feel to be without that role?
Concerns about career	*Commitment:* How involved and committed to the organization do I want to become? Or do I want to seriously explore other options?	*Commitment:* Do I still want to invest as heavily in my career as I did in previous years? What can I commit myself to if the goal of advancement no longer exists?	*Commitment:* What can I commit myself to outside of my career that will provide meaning and a sense of involvement? How can I let go of my involvement in my work role after so many years?
	Advancement: Do I want to advance? Can I advance without compromising important values?	*Advancement:* Will I have the opportunity to advance? How can I feel productive if I am going to advance no further?	*Advancement:* Given that my next move is likely to be out of the organization, how do I feel about my final level of advancement? Am I satisfied with what I have achieved?
	Relationships: How can I establish effective relationships with peers and supervisors? As I advance, how can I prove my competence and worth to others?	*Relationships:* How can I work effectively with peers with whom I am in direct competition? How can I work effectively with subordinates who may surpass me?	*Relationships:* How can I maintain positive relationships with my boss, peers, and subordinates as I get ready to disengage from this setting? Can I continue to mentor and sponsor as my career comes to an end? What will happen to significant work relationships when I leave?
Concerns about family	*Family role definition:* How can I establish a satisfying personal life? What kind of lifestyle do I want to establish?	*Family role definition:* What is my role in the family now that my children are grown?	*Family role definition:* What will my role in the family be when I am no longer involved in a career? How will my significant relationships with spouse and/or children change?
	Work/family conflict: How can I effectively balance work and family commitments? How can I spend time with my family without jeopardizing my career advancement?	*Work/family conflict:* How can I make up for the time away from my family when I was launching my career as a novice?	*Work/family conflict:* Will family and leisure activities suffice, or will I want to begin a new career?

Source: E. K. Kram, *Mentoring at Work: Developmental Relationships in Organizational Life,* pp. 72–73. Copyright © 1988 by University Press of America. Reprinted by permission.

and advancement, and career maintenance and disengagement (Hall, 1976; Osipow, 1986). In each phase, career development reflects *concerns about self,* including questions of competence and identity; *concerns about the career,* including questions of occupational commitment, advancement, and the quality of relationships in the work setting; and *concerns about family,* especially family role definition and possible conflicts between work and family life. Typical issues facing the person at each phase are suggested in Table 11.5. The issues of greatest concern during the early career phase reflect the need to demonstrate competence and the need to establish a satisfying lifestyle.

Lifestyle

The early years of marriage, childbearing, and work lead to a relatively permanent style of life. It is during the course of young adulthood that the experimentation with and evolution of a lifestyle occur. Central components of the lifestyle include the tempo or pace of activities, the balance between work and leisure, the focus of time and energy in specific arenas, and the establishment of social relationships at varying degrees of intimacy. One can think of lifestyle as the first enactment of the abstract construction of individual identity. Through the devotion of time and energy to certain tasks and relationships and the development of certain domains of competence, a young adult transforms values and commitments into actions. Let us consider some of the ways in which marriage, children, and career interact to dictate some characteristics of the lifestyle.

Marriage partners must develop a tempo that will reflect the activities and preferences of both. Most couples find that the presence of children requires somewhat more planning and less freedom for spontaneous activities. The work setting largely determines the structure of time, including when one goes to work and returns, what one feels energetic enough to do after work, how much time to allot for vacations, and what kinds of preparation must be made during nonworking hours for one's daily occupation (Small & Riley, 1990). To some extent, activity level is also influenced by the climate and the community. In northern climates, for example, there may be fewer social events away from home during the winter, and life may therefore revolve primarily around the home. In the summer, neighborhood activities may become a more important stimulus for interaction.

The balance of work and leisure is a result of one's disposition toward these two alternatives and the demands of the work setting. For some people, time with the family is more important than time at work. These people value highly the time they have at home with their families and make such time a priority when they choose a career. For other people, advancement in work through the expenditure of large amounts of time supersedes commitments to home and leisure. In these circumstances, the lifestyles of husband and wife may evolve somewhat separately, since the amount of leisure time they share may be rather limited. Couples who are able to enjoy together leisure activities that provide opportunities for relaxed, open conversation find that this contributes substantially to the strength and satisfaction in their marriage (Holman & Jacquart, 1988).

Pablo Picasso, *Circus Family,* 1905. Each family evolves a unique lifestyle in which the demands of work, leisure, intimacy, parenting, and friendship are delicately balanced.

The more involved one is with the competitive demands of work, the less likely one is to feel comfortable about spending time away from it. The more engrossed one is in a variety of activities away from work, including hobbies and family events, the more time one will find for leisure. In some occupations, of course, the time schedule leaves little room for personal choice. In others, the income from a single job may not suffice to support the family. Time that might be spent in leisure will then be spent in earning additional income through extra work. During later adulthood, when one experiences retirement, the balance of work and leisure time has to be revised. Young adults who have spent the better part of their time at work may then find themselves poorly prepared for a successful adjustment to the increased leisure of retirement.

During early adulthood, the husband and wife become acquainted with individuals and other couples. They form friendships in the neighborhood and at work. The orientation of the nuclear family toward outsiders is developed during this stage. In some families work-related friendships remain tied to the work role, whereas in others friends made at work become integrated into social events that involve all the family members.

An important factor in the establishment of adult friendships is the distance or degree of intimacy that is shared with nonfamily members. Some couples have only a few close friends and others have a large circle of relatively distant acquaintances. This difference in orientation toward friendship will determine one's involvement in social activities, one's reputation in the community, and the extent of one's dependence on the family to meet needs for intimacy, approval, and companionship. One source of tension in marriage can be a difference between a husband and wife regarding the orientation toward friendships. If one partner seeks intimate friendship with other adults and the other partner prefers only distant acquaintances, they may be in continuing conflict about involvement in social activities. Another source of tension in early adulthood is the competition of role demands. One part of role learning involves a widening of competences and relationships. Another part involves balancing the conflicting expectations of simultaneous role responsibilities. Adults struggle with the tension between demands from the work setting and demands for time to build an intimate relationship with one's spouse or the tension between the desire to have children and the desire for achievement in work (Voydanoff, 1988; Jones & Butler, 1980). For both men and women, the world of work is likely to provide the most rigorous test of commitment and the greatest pressures for productivity during the early adult years. Pressure from the work setting competes directly with needs for intimacy and with time and energy needed for parenting. Particularly in a dual-career family, the desires of the individual partners for occupational success may cause them to limit each other's freedom both at work and at home.

The Single Lifestyle

In addition to those young adults who are creating lifestyles within the framework of marriage, there are many who remain single during their 20s. In 1988, 32% of white men and 20% of white women aged 25 to 34 had never married. Among blacks, 49% of the men and 43% of the women had never married (U.S. Bureau of the Census, 1989b). Several stereotypes of the single lifestyle have been examined empirically. One is that singles are very lonely. Another is that singles experience a greater variety of sexual partners and have a more exciting sex life.

Comparisons of single and married adults suggest that neither of these stereotypes is totally accurate. First, many singles do not live alone; they live with family members or with roommates. It is those singles who have already been married and divorced who are most likely to suffer loneliness because of the absence of companions or confidants. The most isolated unmarried people are women who are single parents living with their children. They have the most restricted opportunities for social interaction. Many unmarried adults who live completely alone actually have compensated for their limited contacts at home by having a large number of relationships at work or in the community. Living alone is not associated with lower life satisfaction; in fact, it is often a preferred arrangement (Alwin, 1984). Second, singles who have never been married are not likely to have a great many sexual partners and are somewhat less likely than married couples to experience frequent sexual intercourse; that is, three or more times per week (Cargan, 1981).

Table 11.6 Typology of Singlehood		
	Voluntary	*Involuntary*
Temporary	*Ambivalents:* those not seeking mates but open to the idea of marriage	*Wishfuls:* those actively seeking mates but currently unsuccessful
Stable	*Resolved:* those who consciously prefer singlehood or choose it for religious reasons	*Regretfuls:* those who would rather marry but are resigned to singlehood

Source: A. B. Shostak, "Singlehood," in M. B. Sussman and S. K. Steinmetz (eds.), *Handbook of Marriage and the Family*, p. 357. Copyright © 1987 by Plenum Publishing Corporation. Reprinted by permission.

The profile of the single lifestyle is also rather different for men and women. Highly educated women who value self-determination and career achievement are likely to see distinct advantages to the single lifestyle. Women who remain single experience more rapid advancement in both educational and occupational attainment (Houseknecht, Vaughan & Statham, 1987). Men have never been subjected to great social pressure to choose between career and marriage. Single men are likely to be less educated, less successful in the world of work, and therefore less desirable as partners.

Relatively little systematic research has been done on the psychosocial development of adults who remain single. Especially critical to this picture is the path along which singlehood is established. Table 11.6 suggests a typology of singlehood along two dimensions: stability of the single status and choice of the single status. Within this framework, one might expect that the *resolved singles* might be quite satisfied about the quality of their lifestyle and effective in forming the kinds of relationships that support their choice. In contrast, the *wishful singles* and the *regretful singles* may be more depressed about their situation and more dissatisfied with the quality of their lifestyle. Generalizations about adjustment or well-being among singles often fail to consider these kinds of distinctions (Shostak, 1987; Stein, 1981).

Summary

Lifestyle is an umbrella concept for the variety of patterns of activities, commitments, and satisfactions that make up adult experience. Lifestyles are enormously diverse. Brothers and sisters may share a household. Adult children may live with their parents. Same-sex peers may live together in an intimate, loving relationship. Individuals may live alone. Couples may cohabit without any plans to marry. In all of these arrangements, a sense of intimacy may flourish or a feeling of isolation may grow. Nevertheless, the cultural expectations for marriage, childbearing, and work will be confronted, evaluated, and accepted or rejected during these early adult years. In the process of deciding about each of these life tasks, the person will begin to crystallize a life pattern that will reflect his or her personal response to the array of cultural and historical expectations.

The Psychosocial Crisis:
Intimacy versus Isolation

The establishment of intimacy is an active process. *Intimacy* is defined as the ability to experience an open, supportive, tender relationship with another person without fear of losing one's own identity in the process. Intimacy in a relationship supports independent judgments by each member of the dyad (Stone, 1973). An intimate relationship has both cognitive and affective components. The partners in such a relationship are able to understand each other's point of view. They usually experience a sense of confidence and mutual regard that reflects their respect as well as their affection for each other. An intimate relationship permits the disclosure of personal feelings as well as the sharing and developing of ideas and plans. Recent research on the dimensions of love helps clarify the structure of intimate relationships (see Box 11.1).

There is a sense of mutual enrichment in intimate interactions. Each person perceives enhancement of his or her well-being through affectionate or intellectually stimulating interactions with the other (Erikson, 1963, 1980). Coming as it does after the establishment of personal identity, the possibility of establishing intimacy depends on individuals' perceptions of themselves as valuable, competent, and meaningful people.

It is not difficult to understand that a person would be on intimate terms with parents and siblings. The family is clearly the appropriate context for sharing confidences, expressing love, and revealing weaknesses and areas of dependence. The unique task of young adulthood is to establish an intimate relationship with someone who is not a member of one's own family. In fact, two people who eventually establish intimacy may begin as complete strangers who have very few, if any, common cultural bonds. Although an extreme degree of difference is unusual, it illustrates the greatest challenge that could confront two people.

Intimacy implies the capacity for mutual empathy and mutual regulation of needs. One must be able to give and receive pleasure within the intimate context. Although intimacy is generally established within the context of the marriage relationship, marriage itself does not automatically produce intimacy. Our discussion of the early years of marriage, in fact, indicated several forces potentially disruptive to the establishment of intimacy: (1) the early period of mutual adjustment, (2) the birth of the first child, and (3) the social expectations of members of the extended family. It might be hypothesized that an intimate relationship does not develop until the couple has been married for several years.

Another common context for the establishment of intimacy is the work setting. Affiliation and close friendship are likely to develop among co-workers. Workers may express devotion to an older leader or teacher. Through conversations, correspondence, conferences, or informal interaction on the golf course or at the bowling alley, co-workers can achieve an affectionate, playful, and enriching relationship. This kind of intimacy can be seen in a conversation reported by Kram (1985):

Box 11.1   Measuring Love

For thousands of years the nature of love and qualities of a loving relationship have been described in the songs and stories of Western culture. Now love has become the focus of social science research (Hendrick & Hendrick, 1989). Robert Sternberg (1986, 1987) found that love could be described as a set of feelings, thoughts, and motives that contribute to communication, sharing, and support. According to his theory, almost all types of love can be viewed as a combination of three dimensions: *intimacy*, which is the emotional investment in the relationship; *passion*, which is the physical and psychological motivation for the relationship; and *commitment*, which is the cognitive decision to remain in the relationship.

Ten components of a loving relationship have been identified:

1. Promoting the welfare of the loved one
2. Experiencing happiness with the loved one
3. High regard for the loved one
4. Being able to count on the loved one in time of need
5. Mutual understanding of the loved one
6. Sharing oneself and one's possessions with the loved one
7. Receiving emotional support from the loved one
8. Giving emotional support to the loved one
9. Intimate communication with the loved one
10. Valuing the loved one in one's own life

These qualities are very close to Erikson's concept of intimacy. They reflect high levels of mutuality and openness as well as a deep commitment.

The nature of love is much the same in our relationships with our parents, siblings, friends, and lovers. The weighting of these factors, however, may vary. In addition, some love relationship include a dimension of sexual attraction and others do not.

The intensity of love is captured in studies by Keith Davis (1985) on the differences between love and friendship. Lovers describe their relationships as characterized by *fascination, exclusiveness,* and *sexual desire:* "I would go to bed thinking about what we would do together, dream about it, and wake up ready to be with him again." They also express more intense caring for their loved ones than for friends. This caring includes giving their utmost, even to the point of self-sacrifice. The intensity of these characteristics accounts for some of the specialness and unsettling euphoria associated with being in love. It may also explain the relative instability of love relationships. Intense emotion is difficult to sustain.

Alan was very influential. I respected him as being pretty sharp and pretty astute. He had a lot of guts to tackle the problems that existed in the area and that was the union-management business. I was really identifying with him in terms of what and how you run something, how you manage something. You would sit down and talk about or debate how you do certain things, what should we do in this kind of situation. We would be right in line. I think it was the way I came at a problem; it might be similar to the way he would come at a problem. [p. 33]

Intimate relationships are often characterized by an atmosphere of romantic illusions: "Together we can conquer the world." The romance of an intimate relationship is a reflection of the energy and sense of well-being that come from the support and understanding that are shared within it. There may also be a degree of jealousy in the relationship. The devotion and commitment of intimate partners are vulnerable to threats of competing alliances. There is a deep sense that intimate relationships are not replaceable.

The negative pole of the crisis of young adulthood is *isolation*. As with the other negative poles, most people experience some periods of this extreme. The more fully developed the ego becomes, the more it is characterized by clear boundaries. A by-product of the cultural values of individuality and independence is a heightened sense of separateness from others.

An estimated 25% of the adult population feel extremely lonely during a given month (Weiss, 1974). Feelings of loneliness can be separated into three categories: transient, situational, and chronic (Meer, 1985). Transient loneliness lasts a short time and passes, as when you hear a song or an expression that reminds you of someone you love who is far away. Situational loneliness accompanies a sudden loss or a move to a new city. Chronic loneliness lasts a long time and cannot be linked to a specific stressor. Chronically lonely people may have an average number of social contacts, but they do not achieve the desired level of intimacy in these interactions (Berg & Peplau, 1982). Many chronically lonely people are very anxious about all types of social activities. They believe that success in social relationships is very important, but they expect social encounters to be difficult and to end poorly. People who have high levels of social anxiety tend to use interpersonal strategies that place barriers in the way of intimacy. They are likely to be self-deprecating, they are obsessed by the possibilities of negative outcomes of social interactions, and they tend to let others establish the direction and purpose of interpersonal activities (Langston & Cantor, 1989).

There appears to be a strong relationship between social skills and loneliness. People who have higher levels of social skill, including friendliness, communication skills, appropriate nonverbal behavior, and appropriate responses to others, have more adequate social support systems and lower levels of loneliness (Sarason et al., 1985).

There is consistent evidence that men interact in a less intimate manner than women (Reis, Senchak & Soloman, 1985; Carli, 1989). Men generally demonstrate more competitiveness, less agreement, and lower levels of self-disclosure than women. However, levels of self-disclosure do not relate to loneliness for men as they do for women. It appears that men have the same capacity for intimate interaction as women, but they do not choose to exercise it in same-sex interactions. Whereas women consider intimacy appropriate for both same-sex and opposite-sex relationships, men tend to restrict their intimate interactions to women.

When men's and women's intimate relations were compared, men scored lower than women on intimacy, and relationships involving men were described as less intimate than those involving women. Relationships between two women were found to have the highest intimacy scores of the three possible combinations and relationships between two men the lowest. This does not mean that the relationships involving men were not intimate but that they were not as intimate as those involving women (Fischer & Narus, 1981). In general, it has been observed that husbands are more likely than wives to be satisfied with the amount of empathy and companionship in their mar-

Pablo Picasso, *The Siesta,* 1919. The support and understanding that are present in an intimate relationship produce a pervasive sense of well-being.

riages (Scanzoni & Scanzoni, 1981). There are several explanations for this finding. Perhaps men expect less in the way of empathic understanding in marriage than women do. Perhaps the socialization of little girls really makes women better than men at providing empathy and understanding.

The possibility of closeness with another person seriously threatens the sense of self of some young people. They imagine intimacy to be a blurring of the boundaries of their own identities and thus cannot let themselves engage in intimate relationships. People who experience isolation must continually erect barriers between themselves and others in order to keep their sense of self intact. Their fragile sense of self results from accumulated experiences of childhood that have fostered the development of personal identities that are rigid and brittle or else totally confused. A tenuous sense of identity requires that individuals constantly remind themselves who they are. They may not allow their identities to stand on their own strength while they lose themselves, even momentarily, in others. They are so busy maintaining their identities or struggling to make sense out of confusion that they cannot attain a sense of intimacy.

Isolation may also result from situational factors. The young man who goes off to war and returns to find that the "eligible" women in his town are married and the young woman who rejects marriage in order to attend medical school may find themselves in situations in which desires for intimacy cannot be met. Although we may say that the lonely person should try harder to meet new people or develop new social skills, it is possible that the sense of isolation interferes with more active coping strategies (Peplau, Russell & Heim, 1977).

Isolation may also be a product of diverging spheres of interest and activity. In a traditional marriage, for example, the man and the woman may participate in quite distinct roles and activities. Marriages characterized by such a division of life spheres are sometimes referred to as "his and her" marriages (Bernard, 1972). The wife stays home most of the day, interacting with the children and the other wives in the neighborhood. The husband is away from home all day, interacting with co-workers. When the partners have leisure time, they pursue different interests: the woman likes to play cards and the man likes to hunt. Over the years, the partners have less and less in common. Isolation is reflected in their lack of mutual understanding and lack of support for each other's life goals and needs.

The Central Process: Mutuality Among Peers

The central process through which a sense of intimacy is acquired is *mutuality* among peers. The two young adults must bring equal strengths and resources to the relationship. Their intimacy is built on their ability to meet each other's needs and accept each other's weaknesses. When one partner needs to be dependent, the other can be strong and supportive; at another time, the roles may be reversed. Each partner understands that the other is capable of many kinds of relationships. Commitment serves to facilitate the couple's ability to meet each other's needs in different ways over time rather than to produce a static, unitary relationship. In fact, mutuality should enhance both partners. In the process of supporting each other, both perform in ways that they might not have adopted had they been alone.

We have used the concept of mutuality to describe the development of a sense of basic trust during infancy. In that context, the distribution of resources, experience, and strength is quite uneven. Mutuality is possible only because the caregiver is committed to the infant's well-being. Through the consistent efforts of caregivers, children eventually learn to regulate their needs to fit the family pattern. However, children at this stage are not expected to be sophisticated enough to assess and meet caregivers' needs. In young adulthood, the partners are responsible for filling each other's needs. In most cases, there is no benevolent, superordinate caregiver. Just as the infant learns to trust the caregiver's ability to meet personal needs, each adult partner learns to trust the other's ability to anticipate and satisfy his or her needs. The partners may also realize that they depend on each other to solve certain problems that are posed to them as a couple. They begin to see each other as essential to their problem-solving strategy, with each partner managing separate aspects of the task. Mutuality is strengthened as the two individuals learn to rely on each other and as they discover that their combined efforts are more effective than their individual efforts would be. Mutuality, like attachment, is a characteristic of the dyadic relationship rather than of the individual members of the dyad (Barnhill, 1979). It is formed as two individuals, each of whom has a well-defined identity, discover that they can have open, direct communication, hold each other in high regard, and respond effectively to each other.

Summary

The crisis of intimacy versus isolation suggests a new level of ego development in which the individual's personal needs can be met only through satisfaction of another's needs. Experiences of loving and attachment in the family context are transformed into a new form of affection that combines sexual maturity, cognitive perspective, personal identity, and mature moral thought.

The obstacles to attainment of an intimate relationship are many. Some arise from childhood experiences of shame, guilt, inferiority, or alienation, which undermine the achievement of personal identity. Some are the result of incompatibility between partners. The number of adjustments that intimacy requires may overwhelm some young adults. Finally, obstacles to intimacy derive from environmental circumstances that may erode the person's feelings of self-worth or interfere with the evolution of a sense of mutuality.

☐ Applied Topic: Divorce

Americans have one of the highest rates of marriage among modern industrial societies. Almost everyone wants to get married, and does. However, our divorce rate is also rising rapidly. You may have read that the divorce rate is one out of every three or every two marriages. However, this rate is really not a very accurate measurement of the frequency of divorce. It is based on the number of divorces decreed and the number of marriages performed in a given year. Most divorces are not an outcome of marriages performed in the same year. There are many more marriages that could end in divorce during a single year than there are people planning to marry. The divorce-to-marriage ratio inflates our picture of the frequency of divorce.

A more stable index of the frequency of divorce is the ratio of the total number of divorces to the number of married couples in the population. This ratio is plotted in Figure 11.5 for the 124-year period from 1860 to 1984. The divorce rate peaked rapidly after World War II and then fell, after which it rose over the years from 1965 to 1980 (Raschke, 1987). About 46% of all marriages performed during 1985 involved at least one previously married partner. The lack of change in the divorce ratio from 1982 to 1985 suggests that the divorce rate may be leveling off (U.S. Bureau of the Census, 1989a).

Factors Contributing to Divorce

A large number of variables have been examined as correlates or predictors of divorce. The scope of these analyses encompasses cross-national studies, historical cohort analyses, multicounty comparisons, and cross-sectional comparisons of couples. At the societal level, countries that have fewer women than men and where women marry at a later age have lower divorce rates. Two other societal factors show a curvilinear relationship: socioeconomic development of the country and women's participation in the labor force. With respect to both of these variables, the divorce rate is lower in the mid-range than at either extreme (Trent & South, 1989).

In a comparison of divorce rates across more than 3,000 counties in the United States, another important construct was identified: *social integration,* or the degree to which "people are tied or connected to one another, shared values being an important element in such integration" (Breault & Kposowa, 1987, p. 556). Characteristics of a community influence this sense of connectedness. Among the most significant of these characteristics are *population change,* the number of people who move in or

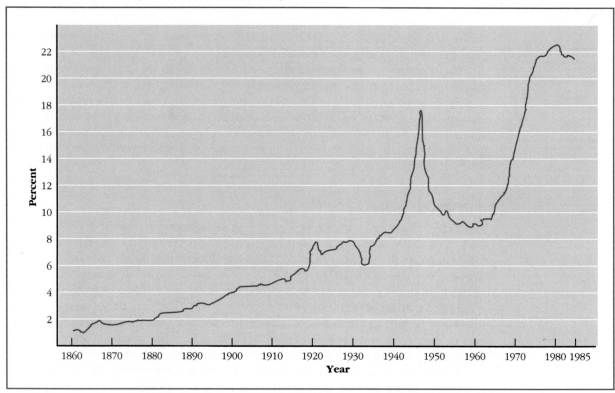

Figure 11.5   Number of Divorces as Percentage of Number of Married Couples, United States, 1860–1984
Source: H. J. Raschke, "Divorce," in M. B. Sussman & S. K. Steinmetz (eds.), *Handbook of Marriage and the Family*, p. 598. Copyright © 1987 by Plenum Publishing Corporation. Reprinted by permission.

out of a community each year; *religious integration,* the percentage of the population that belongs to a religious organization; and *urbanity,* the percentage of people within each county who live in an urban area. Divorce rates are significantly linked to each of these characteristics. They are higher in counties with high population change, low religious integration, and high urbanity. These findings suggest that the difficulties individual couples experience in their marriages can be aggravated by the community context. Or, on the positive side, marriages can be buffered and supported by a critical sense of community identity and shared destiny.

At the level of couple-to-couple comparisons, four variables have been associated with the likelihood of divorce: age at marriage, socioeconomic level, differences in socioemotional development, and the family's history of divorce. In the United States, the incidence of divorce is especially high for couples who marry under the age of 20. These couples are about twice as likely to divorce as couples who marry in their early or mid-20s. Marital instability is also greater for couples who marry in their late 20s or later than for those who marry in their early to mid-20s (Booth & Edwards, 1985). Such couples may have been single for a long time. Having coped successfully with single life, they may be less willing to remain in an unsatisfying marriage. They

Pablo Picasso, *Bust of a Woman with Self-Portrait,* 1929. Tension in the relationship with his wife, Olga, is reflected in this painting in which a woman with gaping jaw and large teeth dominates the artist's profile. At this time, Picasso was already involved with another woman who later gave birth to his daughter Maya.

may also be more firmly entrenched in behaviors and habits that are not readily modifiable.

Both for couples who marry young and for those who marry at an older age, dissatisfaction with role performance is a significant factor in marital instability. For young couples, dissatisfaction centers around sexual infidelity and jealousy. For older couples, it focuses on interpersonal conflict, a domineering style, and lack of companionship. Age at marriage is associated with different developmental needs and varying threats to marital stability. Of course, age at marriage is not a single explanatory dimension. For those who marry young, there is also a greater incidence of premarital pregnancy, dropping out of school, and lower-paying employment, all of which contribute to the likelihood of divorce.

The concept of *socioeconomic level* is complex. It can be thought of as a combination of education, occupation, and income. Each of these components is related to the divorce rate in a unique manner (Glenn & Supancic, 1984). Men with more education have lower divorce rates. Women with more education also have lower divorce rates, except that those with five or more years of college are somewhat more likely to divorce than those who have only four years (that is, graduated from college). Within this overall pattern, there is also evidence of the *Glick effect*. Both men and women who have dropped out of high school or college have higher divorce rates than those who completed high school or college. Further, those who have graduated from high school have a lower divorce rate than those who have had one to three years of college. Glick (1957) explained this pattern as evidence of lack of persistence. Those who are not committed to complete a unit of schooling may also lack the commitment to work at resolving the problems they encounter in marriage.

The relationship between income and marital instability is different for men and women. For men, higher income is associated with low divorce rates. For women, there is no clear relationship between income and marital instability. A critical factor appears to be whether a woman is earning more or less than her husband. Divorces are more likely among the former than the latter (Raschke, 1987).

Socioemotional development is reflected in such dimensions as the partners' self-acceptance, autonomy, and expressiveness. Problems in communication are frequently cited by men and women as a major cause of divorce (Cleek & Pearson, 1985; Burns, 1984). In the past, women have experienced more stress and reported more problems in adjusting to marriage than have men (Veroff et al., 1981). We examined these factors earlier in our discussion of adjustment to marriage. Because of the differences in power early in marriage, women often experience more emotional strain than men do. Mutual satisfaction in marriage depends heavily on the husband's qualities. The stability of the husband's masculine identity, the happiness of his parents' marriage, his educational level, and his social status all affect marital happiness. Many husbands, however, come to their marriages with a deep need to be nurtured and to continue the pattern of care that they received in childhood. The stability of a marriage depends on both partners' achieving a sense of their own identities. This achievement will prevent the imbalance in power or respect that seems to interfere with a real emotional and intellectual intimacy.

The family's history of divorce is still another factor that contributes to marital instability. There is some evidence that children of divorced parents are more likely to get divorced themselves than are children of intact marriages (Glenn & Kramer, 1987; Keith & Finlay, 1988). One interpretation of this finding that has received some empirical support is that children of divorce hold more favorable attitudes toward divorce as a reasonable strategy for resolving marital conflict (Greenberg & Nay, 1982). Another explanation is that children of divorce are likely to marry younger than children of intact marriages (Keith & Finlay, 1988). Generally the available evidence suggests that the attitudes of children of divorced parents toward marriage and family life are as positive as those of children of intact families. As young adults, however, they may have more reservations and ambivalence about getting married, and they may have a less idealized view of marriage than young adults from intact families. As a result, they may enter marriage with strong expectations of a negative outcome. This expectation may stand in the way of achieving the level of commitment and self-disclosure that are characteristic of a mutually intimate relationship (Glenn & Kramer, 1987; Amato, 1988; Wallerstein & Corbin, 1989).

Coping with Divorce

It is an understatement to say that divorce is stressful. Divorce can be associated with loss of resources, of emotional support, of one's role, and of social support. Studies have highlighted the dramatic income loss associated with divorce. In an analysis of over 2,500 court records dating from 1970, Weitzman (1985) found that the divorced

Divorce often brings women a dramatically reduced income, role loss, and social isolation.

woman's standard of living decreased by 73% while her husband's increased by 42%. The pattern of income loss depends on pre-divorce income. The incomes of women who were in higher income brackets before divorce (average income of $17,000) dropped to less than 50% of their former incomes in the first year after divorce. After five years, they were still at 50% of their predivorce incomes. The incomes of lower-income women (average income of $5,600) dropped to 77% of their predivorce incomes. However, most women in this group depended on public assistance for their continued incomes (Weiss, 1984).

Divorce may bring role loss and social isolation as well as financial loss. Even when a divorce is viewed as a desirable solution, the period from the suggestion of divorce to its conclusion involves a variety of decisions and conflicts that may be very painful (Melichar & Chiriboga, 1985). Many people who experience divorce go through a time of intense self-analysis. They must try to integrate the failure of their marriage with their personal definition of masculinity or femininity, their competence as loving people, and their long-held aspirations to enact the role of husband or wife, father or mother. When children are involved in a divorce, there is the additional challenge of trying to work out the continuity of parental relationships established before the dissolution.

The stress-related correlates of divorce are seen in the increased health problems of the divorced, the higher incidence of suicide among the divorced, and the over-representation of divorced adults in all forms of psychiatric settings (Stack, 1990). More than 40% of divorced adults are in some form of psychotherapy or pastoral counseling (Bloom, Fisher & White, 1978). One analysis of 80 divorced adults who had children identified six specific stressors: contacts with the former spouse, parent-child interactions, interpersonal relations, loneliness, practical problems such as cooking and cleaning, and financial problems. Of these stressors, problems involving interpersonal relations with peers were most closely tied to lower life satisfaction and a depressed, anxious mood (Berman & Turk, 1981).

Evidence of the impact of divorce on adjustment is provided in a comparison of divorced adults with those who are remarried and those who are in first marriages and have never experienced divorce (Weingarten, 1985). Divorced people have lower morale than those who have remarried. They recall the past as having been much happier than the present and are more likely to say they are not too happy at present. However, they do not have lower self-esteem, more anxiety, or more physical symptoms of stress than do remarried adults. In comparison with married people who have never divorced, the divorced have lower feelings of satisfaction, less zest for life, and greater anxiety. Even after remarriage, the experience of divorce has some lingering influence on adjustment. Remarried people say they have experienced a lot of difficult life events, are more likely to have used professional help in dealing with personal problems, and are more likely to suffer from stress-related physical symptoms than married people who have never divorced. The remarried are no different from the never-divorced in personal happiness, self-esteem, or optimism about the future. Reentering the marital state appears to boost morale, but it does not remove the strains of having encountered divorce.

One problem in coping with divorce is that many divorced people retain a strong attachment to former spouses. Grief in divorce has been compared to bereavement in widowhood. In both cases, there is a loss and a need to adjust to it. Although the loss due to death may be more intense, especially if the death was sudden, the loss due to divorce may be more bitter. If an affectionate bond has been established, there is certain to be ambivalence about losing that bond even when the divorce is desired. Attachment to a former spouse can be positive or negative (one may wish for a reconciliation or blame the spouse) or both.

In a study of over 200 divorced persons, 42% expressed moderate or strong attachment to former spouses. Some people wondered what their former spouses were doing, spent a lot of time thinking about them, expressed disbelief that divorce had really taken place, and felt that they would never get over it. The attachment was stronger for those who had not initiated the divorce. The lingering feelings of attachment were associated with greater difficulties in adjustment to divorce, especially problems of loneliness and doubt about being able to cope with single life (Kitson, 1982). The stronger the positive or negative postdivorce attachment, the more difficult the adjustment in the years following the divorce (Tschann, Johnston & Wallerstein, 1989).

The fact that divorce is stressful does not mean that it is undesirable. Even among the attached spouses described by Kitson, many said that they felt a sense of relief about the divorce. Many divorced parents report that despite the difficulties of single parenting, life is more manageable than it was in the midst of the continuing arguments and hostility that preceded divorce.

Most people who experience divorce are very determined to cope with the stresses it brings. Unfortunately, many adults may not anticipate the specific kinds of stressors that they will encounter. Of course, adults have different coping strategies, some of which may not be effective for the special demands of divorce. Berman and Turk (1981) asked divorced adults to judge the efficacy of 53 strategies for coping with their own stress. Six groups of coping strategies were identified: (1) *social activities,* such as dating or developing new friendships; (2) *learning,* including going back to school or talking to a counselor; (3) *personal understanding,* such as understanding what went wrong; (4) *expressing feelings;* (5) *autonomy;* for example, becoming more independent or taking a job; and (6) *home and family activities,* especially taking care of the house and doing more things with the children. Of these six strategies, social activities, autonomy, and home and family activities were most strongly related to postdivorce life satisfaction. Social activities and autonomy were also linked to few perceived problems in the areas of loneliness and interpersonal relations.

The process of coping with divorce requires strategies devised to deal with the aspects of divorce that are perceived as most troublesome. Further, each of these coping strategies is an area that lends itself to intervention. It seems quite possible that human service professionals could be very effective in helping adults develop coping skills with which to resolve some of the stresses of divorce.

☐ Chapter Summary

In early adulthood, individuals begin to apply to themselves all the information they have acquired about adult roles. They may marry, have children, and choose work roles. Gradually they evolve a style of life. In this process, their commitment to social institutions and to significant others expands. Their world view becomes more diverse, and their appreciation of the interdependence of systems increases. One of the major sources of stress in this life stage is competition among roles.

The crisis of intimacy versus isolation emphasizes the evolution of adult sexuality into an interpersonal commitment. This crisis requires that needs for personal gratification be subordinated to needs for mutual satisfaction. Success is comparatively difficult to achieve in our culture because of the basic tension between the norm of independence and the desire for closeness. The research on marriage suggests that willingness to make a personal commitment to another adult is no guarantee of success. One of the important elements in a marriage relationship is the ability to engage in and resolve conflict.

The theme of intimacy tends to highlight the management of emotion during adulthood. In our treatment of occupational training, however, we have suggested that many new areas of intellectual awareness are stimulated during the apprenticeship period. Coping with the challenges of early adulthood requires the integration of cognitive capacities, emotional openness, and effective interpersonal relationships. In the process of coping with divorce, we see the very clear need for day-to-day problem solving and emotional expression to manage the grief that accompanies this event.

References

Adams, B. N. (1986). *The family: A sociological interpretation* (4th ed.). San Diego: Harcourt, Brace, Jovanovich.

Allport, G. (1961). *Pattern and growth in personality.* New York: Holt, Rinehart & Winston.

Alwin, D. (1984). Living alone. *ISR Newsletter, 12,* 3–4.

Amato, P. R. (1988). Parental divorce and attitudes toward marriage and family. *Journal of Marriage and the Family, 50,* 453–462.

Atchley, R. C. (1975). The life course, age grading, and

age-linked demands for decision making. In N. Datan & L. H. Ginsberg (eds.), *Life-span developmental psychology: Normative life crises.* New York: Academic Press.

Atwater, L. (1985). Long-term cohabitation without a legal ceremony is equally valid and desirable. In H. Feldman & M. Feldman (eds.), *Current controversies in marriage and family* (pp. 243–252). Newbury Park, Calif.: Sage.

Barnhill, L. R. (1979). Healthy family systems. *Family Coordinator, 28,* 94–100.

Barry, W. A. (1970). Marriage research and conflict: An integrative review. *Psychological Bulletin, 73,* 41–54.

Bell, R. Q., & Harper, L. V. (1977). *Child effects on adults.* Hillsdale, N.J.: Earlbaum.

Bell, R. R. (1983). *Marriage and family interaction* (5th ed.). Homewood, Ill.: Dorsey.

Belsky, J., & Isabella, R. A. (1985). Marital and parent-child relationships in family of origin and marital change following the birth of a baby: A retrospective analysis. *Child Development, 56,* 342–349.

Belsky, J., Lang, M., & Huston, T. L. (1986). Sex typing and division of labor as determinants of marital change across the transition to parenthood. *Journal of Personality and Social Psychology, 50,* 517–522.

Belsky, J., & Pensky, E. (1988). Marital change across the transition to parenthood. *Marriage and the Family Review, 12,* 133–156.

Belsky, J., & Rovine, M. (1990). Patterns of marital change across the transition to parenthood. *Journal of Marriage and the Family, 52,* 5–20.

Berg, J. H., & Peplau, L. A. (1982). Loneliness: The relationship of self-disclosure and androgyny. *Personality and Social Psychology Bulletin, 8,* 624–630.

Berman, W. H., & Turk, D. C. (1981). Adaptation to divorce: Problems and coping strategies. *Journal of Marriage and the Family, 43,* 179–189.

Bernard, J. (1972). *The future of marriage.* New York: World.

Blood, R. O., & Blood, M. (1978) *Marriage.* New York: Free Press.

Bloom, B. L., Fisher, S. J., & White, S. W. (1978). Marital disruption as a stressor: A review and analysis. *Psychological Bulletin, 85,* 867–894.

Booth, A., & Edwards, J. N. (1985). Age at marriage and marital instability. *Journal of Marriage and the Family, 47,* 67–75.

Brazelton, T. B., Yogman, M. W., Als, H., & Tronick, E. (1979). The infant as a focus for family reciprocity.

In M. Lewis & L. A. Rosenblum (eds.), *The child and its family* (pp. 29–45). New York: Plenum.

Breault, K. D., & Kposowa, A. J. (1987). Explaining divorce in the United States, 1980. *Journal of Marriage and the Family, 49,* 549–558.

Brim, O. G., Jr. (1966). Socialization through the life cycle. In O. G. Brim & S. Wheeler (eds.), *Socialization after childhood: Two essays.* New York: Wiley.

Brim, O. G., Jr. (1968). Adult socialization. In J. Clausen (ed.), *Socialization and society.* Boston: Little, Brown.

Brim, O. G., Jr. (1976). Theories of the male mid-life crisis. *Counseling Adults, 6,* 2–9.

Broman, C. L. (1988). Significance of marriage and parenthood for satisfaction among blacks. *Journal of Marriage and the Family, 50,* 45–51.

Burns, A. (1984). Perceived causes of marriage breakdown and conditions of life. *Journal of Marriage and the Family, 46,* 551–562.

Cargan, L. (1981). Singles: An examination of two stereotypes. *Family Relations, 30,* 377–385.

Carli, L. L. (1989). Gender differences in interaction style and influence. *Journal of Personality and Social Psychology, 56,* 565–576.

Cherlin, A. J. (1981). *Marriage, divorce, remarriage.* Cambridge, Mass.: Harvard University Press.

Cleek, M. G., & Pearson, T. A. (1985). Perceived causes of divorce: An analysis of interrelationships. *Journal of Marriage and the Family, 47,* 179–183.

Craig-Bray, L., Adams, G. R., & Dobson, W. R. (1988). Identity formation and social relations during late adolescence. *Journal of Youth and Adolescence, 17,* 173–188.

Davis, K. E. (1985, February). Near and dear: Friendship and love compared. *Psychology Today, 19,* 22–30.

Elder, G. H. (1975). Age differentiation and the life course. *Annual Review of Sociology, 1,* 165–190.

Elder, G. H. (1981). Social history and life experience. In D. H. Eichorn, J. A. Clausen, N. Haan, M. P. Honzik, & P. H. Mussen (eds.), *Present and past in middle life* (pp. 3–31). New York: Academic Press.

Erikson, E. H. (1963). *Childhood and society* (2nd ed.). New York: Norton.

Erikson, E. H. (1974). *Dimensions of a new identity.* New York: Norton.

Erikson, E. H. (1975). *Life history and the historical moment.* New York: Norton.

Erikson, E. H. (1980). Themes of adulthood in the Freud-Jung correspondence. In N. J. Smelser & E. H. Erikson (eds.), *Themes of work and love in adulthood* (pp.

43–74). Cambridge, Mass.: Harvard University Press.

Eshelman, J. R. (1985). One should marry a person of the same religion, race, ethnicity, and social class. In H. Feldman & M. Feldman (eds.), *Current controversies in marriage and family* (pp. 57–66). Newbury Park, Calif.: Sage.

Feldman, H. (1971). The effects of children on the family. In A. Michel (ed.), *Family issues of employed women in Europe and America*. Leiden: E. F. Brill.

Feldman, H. (1981). A comparison of intentional parents and intentionally childless couples. *Journal of Marriage and the Family, 43,* 593–600.

Feldman, H., & Feldman, M. (1975). The family life cycle: Some suggestions for recycling. *Journal of Marriage and the Family,* 277–284.

Filsinger, E. E., & Thoma, S. J. (1988). Behavioral antecedents of relationship stability and adjustment. *Journal of Marriage and the Family, 50,* 785–795.

Fischer, J. L., & Narus, L. R. (1981). Sex roles and intimacy in same-sex and other-sex relationships. *Psychology of Women Quarterly, 5,* 444–455.

Gagnon, J. H., & Greenblat, C. S. (1978). *Life designs: Individuals, marriages, and families.* Glenview, Ill.: Scott, Foresman.

Ganong, L. H., Coleman, M., & Mapes, D. (1990). A meta-analytic review of family structure stereotypes. *Journal of Marriage and the Family, 52,* 287–297.

Gardell, B. (1977). Psychosocial aspects of the working environment. *Working life in Sweden, 1.*

Glenn, N. D., & Kramer, K. B. (1987). Marriages and divorces of children of divorce. *Journal of Marriage and the Family, 49,* 811–826.

Glenn, N. D., & McLanahan, S. (1982). Children and marital happiness: A further specification of the relationship. *Journal of Marriage and the Family, 44,* 63–72.

Glenn, N. D., & Supancic, M. (1984). The social and demographic correlates of divorce and separation in the United States: An update and reconsideration. *Journal of Marriage and the Family, 46,* 563–575.

Glenn, N. D., & Weaver, C. N. (1981). The contribution of marital happiness to global happiness. *Journal of Marriage and the Family, 43,* 161–168.

Glick, P. C. (1957). *American families.* New York: Wiley.

Glick, P. C. (1988). Fifty years of family demography. *Journal of Marriage and the Family, 50,* 861–874.

Greenberg, E. F., & Nay, W. R. (1982). The intergenerational transmission of marital instability reconsidered. *Journal of Marriage and the Family, 44,* 335–347.

Hall, D. T. (1976). *Careers in organizations.* Santa Monica, Calif.: Goodyear.

Hawkins, J. L., Weisberg, C., & Ray, D. W. (1980). Spouse differences in communication style preference, perception, behavior. *Journal of Marriage and the Family, 42,* 585–593.

Hendrick, C., & Hendrick, S. S. (1989). Research on love: Does it measure up? *Journal of Personality and Social Psychology, 56,* 784–794.

Hoffman, L. W., & Manis, J. D. (1979). The value of children in the United States: A new approach to the study of fertility. *Journal of Marriage and the Family, 41,* 583–596.

Holman, T. B., & Jacquart, M. (1988). Leisure-activity patterns and marital satisfaction. *Journal of Marriage and the Family, 50,* 69–78.

Houseknecht, S. K. (1987). Voluntary childlessness. In M. B. Sussman & S. K. Steinmetz (eds.), *Handbook of marriage and the family* (pp. 369–396). New York: Plenum.

Houseknecht, S. K., Vaughan, S., & Statham, A. (1987). Singlehood and the careers of professional women. *Journal of Marriage and the Family, 49,* 353–366.

Jones, A. P., & Butler, M. C. (1980). A role transition approach to the stresses of organizationally induced family role disruption. *Journal of Marriage and the Family, 42,* 367–376.

Jorgensen, S. R., & Gaudy, J. C. (1980). Self-disclosure and satisfaction in marriage: The relation examined. *Family Relations, 29,* 281–287.

Kacerguis, M. A., & Adams, G. R. (1980). Erikson stage resolution: The relationship between identity and intimacy. *Journal of Youth and Adolescence, 9,* 117–126.

Katchadourian, H. A. (1976). Medical perspectives on adulthood. *Daedalus* (Spring).

Keith, V. M., & Finlay, B. (1988). Parental divorce and children's education, marriage, and divorce. *Journal of Marriage and the Family, 50,* 797–810.

Kitson, G. C. (1982). Attachment to the spouse in divorce: A scale and its application. *Journal of Marriage and the Family, 44,* 379–393.

Kram, K. E. (1985). *Mentoring at work: Developmental relationships in organizational life.* Glenview, Ill.: Scott, Foresman.

Langston, C. A., & Cantor, N. (1989). Social anxiety and social constraint: When making friends is hard. *Journal of Personality and Social Psychology, 56,* 649–661.

Levi, L. (1978). Quality of the working environment: Protection and promotion of occupational mental health. *Working Life in Sweden,* no. 8 (November).

Lewis, M., & Rosenblum, L. A. (1974). *The effect of the infant on its caregiver.* New York: Wiley.

Livson, F. B . (1981). Paths to psychological health in the middle years: Sex differences. In D. H. Eichorn, J. A. Clausen, N. Haan, M. P. Honzik, & P. H. Mussen (eds.), *Present and past in middle life* (pp. 195–221). New York: Academic Press.

MacDermid, S. M., Huston, T. L., & McHale, S. M. (1990). Changes in marriage associated with transition to parenthood. *Journal of Marriage and the Family, 52,* 475–486.

Macklin, E. (1987). Non-traditional family forms. In M. B. Sussman & S. K. Steinmetz (eds.) *Handbook of Marriage and the Family* (pp. 317–353). New York: Plenum.

Maslach, C. (1978). Burnout: A social psychological analysis. Paper presented at the annual convention of the American Psychological Association, Toronto.

Materka, P. (1980). Teachers and stress: An unsatisfactory duo. *Rackham Reports, 6,* 5–6.

Meer, J. (1985, July) Loneliness. *Psychology Today, 19,* 28–33.

Melichar, J., & Chiriboga, D. A. (1985). Timetables in the divorce process. *Journal of Marriage and the Family, 47,* 701–715.

Miernyk, W. H. (1975). The changing life cycle of work. In N. Datan & L. H. Ginsberg (eds.), *Life-span developmental psychology: Normative life crises.* New York: Academic Press.

Montgomery, B. M. (1981). The form and function of quality communication in marriage. *Family Relations, 30,* 21–30.

Neugarten, B. L., Moore, J. W., & Lowe, J. C. (1965). Age norms, age constraints, and adult socialization. *American Journal of Sociology, 70,* 710–717.

Noller, P. (1980). Misunderstandings in marital communication: A study of couples' nonverbal communication. *Journal of Personality and Social Psychology, 39,* 1135–1148.

O'Reilly, C. A., & Caldwell, D. F. (1980). Job choice: The impact of intrinsic and extrinsic factors on subsequent satisfaction and commitment. *Journal of Applied Psychology, 65,* 559–565.

Orlofsky, J. L., Marcia, J. E., & Lesser, I. M. (1973). Ego identity status and intimacy versus isolation crisis of young adulthood. *Journal of Personality and Social Psychology, 27,* 211–219.

Osipow, S. H. (1986). Career issues through the life span. In M. S. Pallak & R. Perloff (eds.), *Psychology and work: Productivity, change, and employment* (pp. 137–168). Washington, D.C.: American Psychological Association.

Parsons, T. (1955). Family structure and the socialization of the child. In T. Parsons & R. F. Bales (eds.), *Family, socialization, and interaction process.* Glencoe, Ill.: Free Press.

Peplau, L. A., Russell, D., & Heim, M. (1977). An attributional analysis of loneliness. In I. Frieze, D. Bar-Tal, & J. Carroll (eds.), *Attribution theory: Applications to social problems.* San Francisco: Jossey-Bass.

Piotrkowski, C. S., Rapoport, R. N., & Rapoport, R. (1987). Families and work. In M. B. Sussman & S. K. Steinmetz (eds.), *Handbook of marriage and the family* (pp. 251–284). New York: Plenum.

Quinn, R. P., & Staines, G. L. (1979). *The 1977 quality of employment survey.* Ann Arbor, Mich.: Institute of Social Research.

Rapoport, R., Rapoport, R. N., & Bumstead, J. M. (1978). *Working couples.* New York: Harper & Row.

Raschke, H. J. (1987). Divorce. In M. B. Sussman & S. K. Steinmetz (eds.), *Handbook of marriage and the family* (pp. 597–624). New York: Plenum.

Raush, H. L., Barry, W. A., Hertel, R. K, & Swain, M. A. (1974). *Communication, conflict, and marriage.* San Francisco: Jossey-Bass.

Reis, H. T., Senchak, M., & Solomon, B. (1985). Sex differences in the intimacy of social interaction: Further examination of potential explanations. *Journal of Personality and Social Psychology, 48,* 1204–1217.

Reiss, I. L. (1980). *Family systems in America* (3rd ed.). New York: Holt, Rinehart & Winston.

Richardson, L. (1986, February). Another world. *Psychology Today, 20,* 22–27.

Riegel, K. F. (1975). Adult life crises: A dialectic interpretation of development. In N. Datan & L. H. Ginsberg (eds.), *Life-span developmental psychology: Normative life crises.* New York: Academic Press.

Robinson, E. A., & Price, M. G. (1980). Pleasurable behavior in marital interaction: An observational study. *Journal of Consulting and Clinical Psychology, 48,* 117–118.

Rodman, H. (1972). Marital power and the theory of resources in cultural context. *Journal of Comparative Family Studies, 3,* 51–69.

Rossi, A. S. (1968). Transition to parenthood. *Journal of Marriage and the Family, 30,* 26–39.

Sarason, B. R., Sarason, I. G., Hacker, T. A., & Basham, R. B. (1985). Concomitants of social support: Social skills, physical attractiveness, and gender. *Journal of Personality and Social Psychology, 49,* 469–480.

Scanzoni, L. D., & Scanzoni, J. (1981). *Men, women, and change: A sociology of marriage and family* (2nd ed.). New York: McGraw-Hill.

Schiedel, D. G., & Marcia, J. E. (1985). Ego identity, intimacy, sex role orientation, and gender. *Developmental Psychology, 21,* 149–160.

Schoen, R., & Wooldredge, J. (1989). Marriage choices in North Carolina and Virginia, 1969–71 and 1979–81. *Journal of Marriage and the Family, 51,* 465–482.

Shostak, A. B. (1987). Singlehood. In M. B. Sussman & S. K. Steinmetz (eds.), *Handbook of marriage and the family* (pp. 355–368). New York: Plenum.

Silka, L., & Kiesler, S. (1977). Couples who choose to remain childless. *Family Planning Perspectives, 9,* 16–25.

Small, S. A., & Riley, D. (1990). Assessment of work spillover into family life. *Journal of Marriage and the Family, 52,* 51–62.

Stack. S. (1990). The impact of divorce on suicide, 1959–1980. *Journal of Marriage and the Family, 52,* 119–128.

Stein, P. J. (1981). Understanding single adulthood. In P. J. Stein (ed.), *Single life: Unmarried adults in social context.* New York: St. Martin's Press.

Stengel, R. S. (1985). Snapshot of a changing America. *Time,* September 2, pp. 16–18.

Sternberg, R. J. (1986). A triangular theory of love. *Psychological Review, 93,* 119–135.

Sternberg, R. J. (1987). Liking versus loving: A comparative evaluation of theories. *Psychological Bulletin, 102,* 331–345.

Stone, W. F. (1973). Patterns of conformity in couples varying in intimacy. *Journal of Personality and Social Psychology, 27,* 413–419.

Tanfer, K. (1987). Premarital cohabitation among never-married women. *Journal of Marriage and the Family, 49,* 483–497.

Teachman, J. D., Polonko, K. A., & Scanzoni, J. (1987). Demography of the family. In M. B. Sussman & S. K. Steinmetz (eds)., *Handbook of marriage and the family* (pp. 3–57). New York: Plenum.

Thomas, S., Albrecht, K., & White, P. (1984). Determinants of marital quality in dual-career couples. *Family Relations, 33,* 513–521.

Thornton, A. (1989). Changing attitudes toward family issues in the United States. *Journal of Marriage and the Family, 51,* 873–893.

Trent, K., & South, S. J. (1989). Structural determinants of the divorce rate. *Journal of Marriage and the Family, 51,* 391–404.

Tschann, J. M., Johnston, J. R., & Wallerstein, J. S. (1989). Factors in adults' adjustment after divorce. *Journal of Marriage and the Family, 51,* 1033–1046.

U.S. Bureau of the Census (1976). *Population Profile of the United States, 1975.* Current Population Reports (ser. P-20, no. 292). Washington, D.C.: U.S. Government Printing Office.

U.S. Bureau of the Census (1989a). *Statistical abstract of the United States, 1989.* Washington, D.C.: U.S. Government Printing Office.

U.S. Bureau of the Census (1989b). *The black population in the United States, March, 1988.* Current Population Reports (ser. P-20, no. 442). Washington, D.C.: U.S. Government Printing Office.

Veroff, J., Douvan, E., & Kulka, R. A. (1981). *The inner American: A self-portrait from 1957 to 1976.* New York: Basic Books.

Voydanoff, P. (1988). Work roles, family structure, and work/family conflict. *Journal of Marriage and the Family, 50,* 749–762.

Wallerstein, J. S., & Corbin, S. B. (1989). Daughters of divorce: Report from a ten-year follow-up. *American Journal of Orthopsychiatry, 59,* 593–604.

Weingarten, H. R. (1985). Marital status and well-being: A national study comparing first-married, currently divorced, and remarried adults. *Journal of Marriage and the Family, 47,* 653–662.

Weingarten, H. R., & Bryant, F. B. (1987). Marital status and subjective well-being. *Journal of Marriage and the Family, 49,* 883–892.

Weiss, R. S. (1974). The provisions of social relationships. In Z. Rubin, (ed.), *Doing unto others* (pp. 17–26). Englewood Cliffs, N.J.: Prentice-Hall.

Weiss, R. S. (1984). The impact of marital dissolution on income and consumption in single-parent households. *Journal of Marriage and the Family, 46,* 115–127.

Weitzman, L. J. (1985). *The divorce revolution.* New York: Free Press.

White, R. W. (1966). *Lives in progress* (2nd ed.). New York: Holt, Rinehart & Winston.

Williams, J. D., & Jacoby, A. P. (1989). Effects of premarital sexual experience on desirability. *Journal of Marriage and the Family, 51,* 489–497.

Chapter Twelve

Just as the sculptor evaluates his works, adults ask questions about the value of what they have contributed to the quality of life for future generations.

Middle Adulthood
(34 to 60 Years)

Middle adulthood lasts from about age 34 to age 60. Many people have questioned whether any development really occurs during this period of life. Does it make sense to talk about regular sequences of change over such a long period of time? The patterning of life choices and life events is very diverse during adulthood. Although one might describe an average course, the average might not really represent the actual life history or orientation of any real person. The strict developmental perspective suggests that development occurs in a fixed sequence, with each new stage being built on the achievements of prior stages. It further suggests a direction of change toward some more highly integrated or organized system at each new stage. The question is not whether change occurs during adulthood but whether it is patterned and orderly in any describable dimensions.

If we are to consider the process of development during middle adulthood, we must take another look at the tempo of change. It may be much more difficult to describe patterns of change that occur gradually over ten or 15 years than it is to describe the rapid changes of infancy or toddlerhood or the dramatic growth of adolescence. Moreover, the kinds of changes that take place during adulthood are primarily social and psychological. They include changes in one's sense of time, self-awareness, and investment of energy in people, institutions, and communities.

From the point of view of psychosocial theory, there is a new reorganization of personality during middle adulthood that focuses on the achievement of a sense of generativity. This new stage integrates the skills and perspectives of the preceding life stages toward a commitment of energy to the future. We would expect to find evidence of a greater emphasis on intellectual achievement, a greater openness about oneself, and a greater sense of nurturance during middle adulthood (Haan, 1981). These qualities will be expressed in unique ways for each person. They will be reflected in the quality of the person's work and family life. Each culture and each historical period provides particular avenues for the expression of generativity. In order for any society to survive, its adults must achieve a sense of generativity—a commitment to the quality of life for the larger community and for future generations.

Developmental Tasks

Nurturing the Marriage Relationship

Marriage is a dynamic relationship. It changes as the partners mature, as the family constellation changes, and in response to changing events, including family crises and historical events. It takes focused effort to keep marriages healthy and vital.

What is a vital marriage? Hof and Miller (1981) describe it as an intentional, companionship marriage,

a relationship in which there is a strong commitment to an enduring marital dyad in which each person experiences increases in fulfillment and satisfaction. There is a strong emphasis on developing effective interpersonal relationships and on establishing and maintaining an open communication system. The ability to give and receive affection in an unconditional way, to accept the full range of feelings toward each other, to appreciate common interests and differences and accept and affirm each other's uniqueness, and to see the other as having equal status in the relationship.   [p. 9]

There are at least three requirements for maintaining a vital marriage (Mace, 1982). First, the partners must be committed to growth both as individuals and as a couple. This means they must accept the idea that they will change in important ways and that the relationship too will change. Holding on to a view of the marriage as it was in the first year or two will not promote vitality. Caring and acceptance of each other must deepen. Each person must also be willing to permit changes in attitudes, needs, and interests in the other (Levinger, 1983; Marks, 1989). In Table 11.2 we summarized the tendencies that Robert White associated with maturity. Looking back to this table, we see that in addition to the expansion of caring, the freeing of personal relationships, and the deepening of interests, we may expect the partners in a vital marriage to experience the stabilizing of ego identities and humanizing of values. Within any enduring marriage, each person experiences a dynamic tension between pressures and desires for personal growth on the one hand and pressures and demands of the social context on the other. Both of these forces have the potential to overwhelm or dominate the sense of mutuality. A vital marriage requires both partners to be open to the needs of the two of them to be themselves (as they continue to discover new things) and an energizing interpersonal chemistry that is resilient even in the face of the harshest challenges.

Second, the couple must develop an effective communication system. This means there must be opportunities for interaction. If competing life roles, including work and parenting, dramatically reduce opportunities for interaction, the couple will risk drifting apart. They will have fewer and fewer shared experiences and be less readily influenced by each other's observations and reactions. For many couples who do not have an effective communication system, resentments accumulate with no opportunity to resolve them. A common experience is that the wife wants to talk things over, but the husband does not see what good this will do (Rubin, 1976). *Harmonious, satisfied couples* listen to and consider each other's problems. They validate each other's concerns by expressing understanding, even if they cannot offer solutions. *Dissatisfied couples* meet the expression of a problem with either avoidance or counterattack. Instead of validating the concern, the partner raises his or her own complaints and criticisms. Over the years, levels of complaining and negativism escalate, and each partner becomes increasingly disenchanted with the other (Rands, Levinger & Mellinger, 1981). One way of thinking about the differences between these couples is to see them as differing in their ability to employ positive feedback loops (see Chapter Three). The harmonious couples develop and redevelop the needed feedback loops to maintain communication. The dissatisfied couples may not have had effective feedback loops to begin with, and the interaction pattern tends to be disruptive. The lack of internal feedback loops reduces the capacity of the system to achieve equilibrium and to adjust to changes in the partners or to changing conditions that affect the marriage. Marriages that have effective communication tend to thrive because of the centrality of communication as a mechanism for system development.

Pablo Picasso, *The Kiss*, 1969. It is challenging to nurture vitality in a marriage over a long time. Couples must be committed to individual as well as joint growth; they must develop effective communication; and they must be able to make creative use of conflict.

The third requirement for maintaining a vital marriage is the ability to make creative use of conflict. In a vital marriage in which the partners have equal status and appreciate each other's individuality, there are bound to be conflicts. The partners must understand conflict, concur that it is acceptable to disagree, and develop strategies for resolving conflict (Cole & Cole, 1985). Satisfied couples cannot always resolve their conflicts. Many times their disagreements are left at a stalemate (Vuchinich, 1987). However, these couples tend not to escalate negative reactions. If one partner expresses a complaint or acts unpleasantly, the other does not retaliate with another negative action. Rather, such behavior is likely to provoke the partner's sympathy or acceptance (Jacobson, Waldron & Moore, 1980; Roberts & Krokoff, 1990; Halford, Hahlweg & Dunne, 1990). When couples are distressed, a negative comment is often met with an equally negative response. We know that levels of conflict and hostility are greater within the family than they are at work or in the community. Among satisfied couples, however, the impact of anger is minimized and the goal remains understanding.

Nurturing vitality in a marriage is a long-term task. Change may be slow. Couples may endure long periods of minimal contact because of work, illness, or education and still preserve the quality of their relationship. It is not surprising that over 20 or 30 years a marriage may become predictable, even boring and empty. The challenge is for the partners to create continued interest, nurturance, and appreciation for each other even after they have achieved high levels of security, trust, and empathy, so that the components of a loving relationship (Box 11.1) may be operating continuously in the relationship.

Relationships Between Partners of the Same Sex

The research on gay and lesbian couples is quite incomplete. What we present here is derived from research based on self-selected, volunteer samples. Gay men and lesbians who would not volunteer to participate in research may be quite different in their outlook or adjustment from those who are comfortable enough to discuss the quality of their relationships. In addition, much of the literature is based on white, middle-class participants. Gay men and lesbians are quite a diverse group with respect to their interests, talents, educational backgrounds, family backgrounds, careers, and other important aspects of adult roles. The description of gay and lesbian relationships that can be derived from the existing research misses much of the diversity that one would expect to uncover as this form of intimate relationship is studied in greater detail (Macklin, 1987).

Lesbians are somewhat more likely to be able to establish long-term relationships than gay men. Most lesbians describe their relationships as stable, sexually exclusive, and extremely close. Greater levels of satisfaction in the relationship are associated with greater levels of equality. Equality in the relationship is dependent upon equal resources and equal commitment to the relationship (Eldridge & Gilbert, 1990). Lesbians are likely to have had sexual relationships with men, and about 25% were married at one time (Peplau & Amaro, 1982). In comparison with heterosexual wives, women in lesbian relationships are more likely to describe greater satisfaction in their sexual activity, and greater dissatisfaction about inequalities in the relationship. Lesbian women place a strong value on companionship and confiding in one another, but they also expect to experience high levels of autonomy within their relationships.

Gay men are also interested in long-term relationships. However, they are less likely than lesbians to be sexually exclusive and there is less consensus among gay men about the importance of sexual exclusiveness (Harry, 1983). Among couples who have a long-term relationship, there are few other differences between male and female couples with respect to the values they place on their relationship (Lewis et al., 1981). In view of the social conflicts that gay men and lesbians are likely to encounter and the lack of social support for their lifestyle, it is remarkable that they are able to establish enduring partnerships that provide the level of intimacy and personal satisfaction evidenced in the research literature.

Management of the Household

The household has the potential for providing an environment that will facilitate human growth and mental health. Learning to create such an environment is a task of the middle adult years. Success in the formation of a positive home environment depends on the adult's ability to anticipate the needs of all the people living there and to organize both resources and time so as to meet those needs. Effective household management requires administrative skills. The adult's skill as an administrator will affect the nature of the psychological living environment and determine whether it will enhance the growth of each family member.

Assessing Needs and Abilities

Most family households consist of more than one generation. The person who is in the stage of middle adulthood must be able to understand that each member has his or her own needs, preferences, skills, and talents. Differences among family members may be the result of variations in developmental level. The early-school-age child has needs that are quite different from those of the late adolescent. Additional reasons why people's needs differ include sex, temperament, physical prowess, intellectual

Through effective household management, adults create a home environment that promotes each family member's optimal development and peace of mind.

ability, type of work, emotional stability, birth order, and exposure to stress, to name just a few. What is important for those who are concerned with household management is that they be aware of the differences among the people in their families and be willing to respond to the diverse needs of each. Such openness to needs requires that adults learn how to help others. Their behavior is motivated not only by their own need structures but also by an awareness of the needs and demands of others.

In addition to fulfilling needs, adults learn to be responsive to the skills and talents of family members. This requires judgment, observation, and a willingness to experiment with the assignment of responsibility. The goal here is to allow each person the opportunity to experience competence in daily contributions to family life. The skill and creativity of the household manager are expressed not only in the assignment of people to tasks but also in the ability to permit the emergence of tasks that will cultivate the skills or talents of particular family members. A family may not need a garden, for example, but if a family member shows some interest and talent in gardening, it may be to everyone's benefit to have one.

In this sense, the family has the potential for much greater variety and flexibility than most work settings. Beyond a given number of tasks that must be done each day, the family may designate any kind of work as an appropriate family task. The adult's challenge is to create an environment that will enhance the potential of each family member and so benefit the entire family unit. Two areas of new learning that are stimulated through management of the household during the adult years encompass the understanding of people and the creation of opportunities and environmental conditions that will enhance the members' growth.

Making Decisions

Effective household management requires the ability to make decisions about every aspect of living. Decision making requires the ability to identify alternatives, to evaluate those possibilities, and to select a course of action. Household decisions range from daily ones, such as what meals to serve, to long-term ones that may have far-reaching consequences, such as whether or not to have a child or buy a house. Areas of household decision making that most adults have to consider include: (1) finances, (2) shelter, (3) education, (4) daily activities, (5) vacations and other recreation, (6) social life, and (7) child-rearing practices.

Many people find it difficult to make decisions. The responsibility for a household places these adults in a position in which they cannot avoid exercising their preferences. Adults take actions that will affect all those living in the household. The necessity of making decisions may put some strain on adults. Many decisions are unpopular with other family members. Sometimes one is forced to choose between two or more unpleasant alternatives. However, the active process of making decisions also serves to clarify one's value orientation and to direct the course of life closer to one's life goals.

Each family evolves a procedure for decision making. Usually those who have the most control over resources are perceived as having the most power in the family unit. However, power and responsibility can be allocated in many ways. Each pattern may have unique implications for the psychological development of family members.

We can describe four family decision-making patterns: (1) the male executive, (2) the female executive, (3) the adult executive, and (4) the family executive. The term *executive* has been chosen here to differentiate our discussion of family decision making from a more anthropological treatment of the family power structure in which the word *matriarchy* or *patriarchy* is used. These terms refer more specifically to the line of inheritance and the kinship patterns of the family than to the actual process of household management. Although inheritance or social status may influence which of the adults has more power in the family, we prefer to separate this notion from the discussion of constellations of family decision making.

The single executive   In the father-executive and mother-executive patterns, one adult assigns responsibility to all other family members and reserves the right of final approval on most decisions. This pattern may be the result of several facts: (1) one adult controls the family resources; (2) one adult perceives himself or herself as the superior decision maker; (3) one adult is absent, and all decisions are left in the hands of the other; or (4) one adult abdicates decision-making responsibility and is willing to accept the decisions of the other. In this family structure, the *single executive* decides which tasks must be done and who should do them. The single executive is likely to be the primary source of rewards and punishments in the family and therefore the central figure for identification among the children.

The role of the other spouse in this pattern depends on the activities that the executive assigns to him or her. For some people this subordinate role may be quite agreeable, particularly if the single executive is successful in creating an effective home environment. For others, the subordinate role may be experienced as stressful because it results in a limitation and misuse of their talents. If they are not able directly to influence the executive to redefine their roles, they may engage in subtler attempts to challenge the executive's authority or may even leave their marriages. In the single-executive model, the family may be subjected to some of the executive's idiosyncrasies.

If for some reason the executive thinks that six o'clock is the time to eat dinner, dinner will be served at six o'clock no matter what anyone else in the family is doing.

One-parent families   One-parent families provide a special case of the single-executive decision-making pattern. In 1987 about 27% of all family groups with children under the age of 18 were one-parent families (U.S. Bureau of the Census, 1989). Among black families, the proportion of female-headed families with children under 18 rose from 31% in 1970 to 55% in 1987. Among white families, the proportion of such families rose from 8% in 1970 to almost 18% in 1987. Among Hispanic families, about 30% are headed by a mother only. Only about 3 to 4% of families had a male head with no female adult living in the home.

The greatest stress on the single mother is the lack of financial resources. Figure 12.1 compares the poverty rate of female-headed families with the poverty rates of persons over the age of 65 and two-parent families with children (McLanahan & Booth, 1989). Poverty in these families is a result of a number of factors. Single mothers tend to have a lower earning capacity, they work fewer hours, and even when they receive some child support they bear a substantial portion of the costs of their children's expenses.

Single parents may suffer from social isolation and from continuous pressure to meet the needs of their children (Alwin, 1984). Social isolation may result from the need to move to a new residence or to change jobs frequently. Multiple demands on a single parent's time may leave little opportunity for participation in the social network of the community. The burdens of economic hardship and social isolation often result in high levels of stress and feelings of being chronically on the edge of crisis (McLanahan & Adams, 1987).

A study of decision making in female-headed families described some of the difficulties that arise in this family structure (Blechman, 1977). First, in discussions about problems, parents tended to focus on tasks while children tended to express more of the emotions, especially in large families. This means that there may be fewer opportunities to learn the interpersonal skills of listening, supporting, and conflict resolution in one-parent families. Second, when parents were task-oriented, children tended to be positive and friendly. When parents were less task-oriented, children expressed more hostility. This suggests that children have learned how to function cooperatively in a decision-making situation by acting supportive and not interfering with the task. However, when there is no clear decision at hand, hostility is likely to burst forth. Third, as families continued to talk over three sessions, the sessions grew more hostile and less task-oriented. In these families, the single parent who led most of the task-oriented conversation became the object of increasingly angry feelings as the conflicts were repeatedly raised.

Some studies find that single parents spend less time helping their children with homework, monitoring social activities, and advising them about daily decisions. Other studies find that children feel closer to their mothers in single-parent families than in two-parent families. The parent-child relationship tends to be less authoritative and more egalitarian. Before these finding are generalized too broadly, however, they need to be replicated in single-parent families of varying ethnic, racial, and educational levels (McLanahan & Booth, 1989).

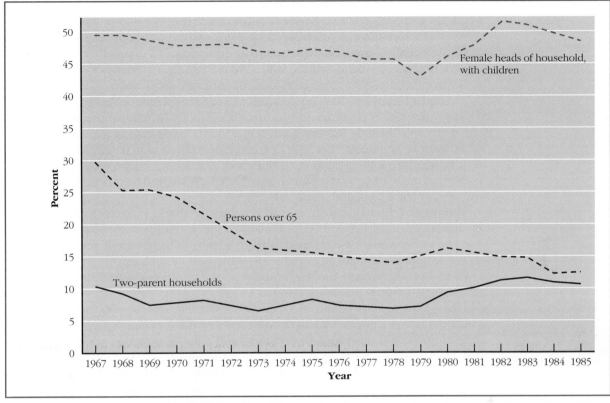

Figure 12.1   Poverty Rates for Mother-Only Families, the Aged, and Two-Parent Families, 1967–1985
Source: S. McLanahan and K. Booth, "Mother-Only Families: Problems, Prospects, and Politics," *Journal of Marriage and the Family, 51,* p. 558. Copyright © 1989 by the National Council on Family Relations, 3989 Central Ave. N.E., Suite 550, Minneapolis, MN 55421. Reprinted by permission.

The adult executive   In the *adult-executive* pattern, the adults of the household assign responsibility for household tasks. The children are subordinate and are seen as incapable of making decisions. In most cases, the adult executive is really a husband-wife executive. In some households containing grandparents, however, the adult-executive pattern may include more than the two spouses. In either case, assigning responsibilities and allocating resources become group decisions in which adults are involved. Group decisions require discussion, compromise, open conflict, consensus, and mutual respect. Occasionally decisions will be made that do not exactly reflect the opinion of one of the adult executives. The adults come to place more value on the process of joint decision making than on the feeling of being right every time.

The adult-executive pattern is probably the one most characteristic of the American family pattern (Adams, 1986). An equitable sharing of power and influence is an important component of marital satisfaction. Even in cultures in which the women and men have traditionally had very distinct spousal roles, as in Puerto Rican families, shared decision making in marriage is a highly valued characteristic (Sexton & Perlman, 1989; Rogler & Procidano, 1989). The nature of this "egalitarian" decision-making system is quite a bit more complex than one might assume. First, egalitarian attitudes do not always result in equal sharing of behaviors or responsibilities (Araji, 1977; Nye, 1976). For example, in many families the husband and the wife believe that housework should be equally shared, but in fact the wife does most of it. Similarly, many couples feel that both the husband and the wife should share the responsibility of providing income for the family, but men tend to be the primary providers.

Second, in many families decision making is tied to specific behaviors or activities. Not every decision is shared; rather, actual decisions are divided among the adults in such a way that the wife has her domain and the husband has his (Douglas & Wind, 1978). Even in families with a high degree of joint decision making, the husband is likely to be more influential in decisions about purchasing liquor, tending the lawn, or choosing and using credit cards, whereas the wife is likely to be concerned primarily with shopping for food and doing the dishes.

Attitudes in regard to the value of shared decision making and reaching consensus are difficult to translate into behavior. Many factors including traditional perceptions of sex-typed behaviors, discrepancies in the resources of the partners, and the number of people who are actually involved in or influenced by the decision will determine how a decision is reached and who ends up having primary responsibility for related behaviors (Godwin & Scanzoni, 1989).

The adult-executive pattern is somewhat slower in its functioning than the single-executive pattern. Decisions are likely to be less impulsive and less idiosyncratic. More diverse opinions, suggestions, hypotheses, and courses of action are aired in the process of assigning responsibility. There is opportunity for one of the decision makers to rest from time to time without fear of the family's malfunctioning. The exclusion of children from the spheres of responsibility may elicit some dissident response from them, including requests for participation. The psychological impact of these demands is shared rather than resting on a single individual.

The family executive   In the *family-executive* pattern, all members of the family share, insofar as they are able, in the assignment of responsibility for family tasks. The problems are posed to the entire family—children included—and each person has an opportunity to offer opinions, suggestions, or solutions. When the children are very young, they may be asked to participate in the decisions about which they are likely to have an opinion—where to go to dinner, whom to use as a baby-sitter, and what to do on a Sunday afternoon. Although the adults may initially feel that they are extending executive responsibility to the children at their own discretion, the children quickly come to believe that they should be legitimate participants in all family decisions.

The family-executive decision-making process is probably the most cumbersome of all the decision-making models, because it requires consensus among people at varying levels of cognitive and emotional development and experience. However, such a process provides the family with the benefit of children's unique points of view. Occasionally a child's solution to a family problem is better than any of the adults'. In most cases, the family executive is highly influenced by the adults' opinions, but the presence of the children in the executive group ensures that decisions are made with maximum attention paid to everyone's needs. In the family-executive pattern, the adults may need a great deal of patience and commitment to the format. The children

Table 12.1 Patterns of Decision Making in the Family		
	Advantages	*Disadvantages*
Single executive	Expediency Clear source of responsibility Personal sense of competence	Resentment of the executive's power May become easy target for blame Leadership may be idiosyncratic and impulsive Lack of participation in decision making by other adults and children
Adult executive	Decisions reached through discussion may be less idiosyncratic and impulsive Diversity of ideas and opinions Marriage relationship strengthened	Slow decision making Lack of children's participation in decision making
Family executive	Learning experience for all family members Diversity of ideas and opinions Participation in decision making strengthens family unit	Slow and cumbersome decision-making process

have the lifelong advantage of learning about issues of decision making, assigning and accepting responsibility, planning, goal setting, and evaluation.

Each of these decision-making patterns provides the executive with a significant area of learning during the adult years. The single executive learns to make decisions, shoulder the responsibility for them, and feel the personal satisfaction that comes from providing one's family with a good home. The adult-executive pattern requires mutual decision making and compromise. It makes equal use of the skills of both partners in the marriage. Success in the adult-executive pattern of decision making strengthens the bond between the marriage partners as they grow more confident in their efforts. Satisfactions and responsibilities are shared in this arrangement. The family-executive pattern requires that the adults learn to be teachers as well as decision makers. They must learn to think out loud so that the children can begin to appreciate the complexity of the decisions as they are being made. The adults must also be ready for unexpected solutions to problems and be able to admit when those alternatives are better than their own. The family-executive model probably makes for some short-term losses in efficiency, but it also provides the greatest long-term gains in group cooperation and mutual enhancement. Table 12.1 summarizes the advantages and disadvantages of each pattern of decision making.

Organizing Time

Another characteristic of successful household management is the ability to organize time effectively for the family. To some extent, the way one's day is organized depends on one's job. Some jobs set a leisurely pace and allow individuals in a family a considerable amount of time with one another in their homes, when they desire to be together. Many jobs require that people be away from home between roughly 8 A.M. and 5 P.M. A fair number of other jobs require people to work during the evening or late-night hours. Hospitals, computer centers, and some factories are in operation all night and all day and therefore require workers at all times. Some jobs require people

Pablo Picasso, *The Family Supper,* 1903. Some families spend a great deal of time preparing and enjoying meals together; others rarely eat together. As children get older, planning occasions when the entire family can be together becomes more difficult.

to be on call at all hours, even when they are not actually at work. As children enter adolescence, their involvement in school, work, and extracurricular activities, as well as their own social lives, influence the pattern and pace of a family's time. The waking, sleeping, eating, and socializing patterns of one's life are heavily influenced by factors outside the household.

Effective household management requires that a wide variety of activities, including paying the bills, maintaining the home, preparing and eating meals, relaxing, socializing, planning, and playing, be allotted enough time for each to be adequately accomplished. Families differ in how much time they want or need to spend at each of these activities. The apartment dweller may spend far less time in home maintenance than the homeowner. Homeowners themselves differ in the amount of time they invest in activities related to the upkeep of their homes. Some families spend a great deal of time preparing and enjoying group meals, while others rarely eat together. These examples illustrate the ways in which the family lifestyle is expressed through the allocation of time to various activities.

Time has more than one dimension. In addition to the organization of the day, adults must also be able to think in terms of the week, the month, the year, the stage, and the lifetime. Each of these time periods raises different planning issues that must be confronted and met. Planning for a year, for example, requires the anticipation of cycles of activity, from rather hectic to slow-paced. It requires the anticipation of periods for task activity, social activity, and vacations. Adults learn to anticipate the times when the family will need additional stimulation and times when all members will be exhausted. In most climates the weather must also be anticipated and prepared for. We do not mean to imply here that adults must plan out every day in great detail (although that may occasionally be necessary) but that they must be able to anticipate shifts in the patterns of activity level, opportunities for certain seasonal activities, and the incorporation of some special occasions or events into the family's year.

Planning for a life stage requires a *psychotemporal perspective*. This means that adults begin to expect changing needs and resources as they and their children move through each stage of development. As adults anticipate the time when their children will leave home, for example, they may have to consider new demands from them, new needs for themselves, and new patterns of daily activity. They must also anticipate that the event will require some degree of psychological reorientation (see Chapter 13). Planning for this stage, then, may include saving for college expenses, developing interests that can fill spare time when it is available, or just beginning to talk together about the changes in the family grouping that will take place at that time. Planning at a life-stage level allows adults to anticipate their parents' needs, their own needs, and the needs of their children. This is a very important quality of parenting that begins to be learned during the early months of parenthood. A parent does not usually wait until a child is screaming with hunger to prepare a bottle. Responsive parents anticipate and intervene in order to prepare the child for future events.

As adults develop skills in organizing and allocating time, they also become aware of the unpredictableness of life (Brim & Ryff, 1980). One of the major realities of middle adulthood is the likelihood that one will be expected to cope with unforeseen events. A parent becomes ill and requires continuous care. A teenage daughter becomes pregnant. An economic recession brings prolonged unemployment. A fire or flood destroys one's home. These are but a few of the unpredictable life events that can fall on the shoulders of middle adults. As middle adults strive to impose order and priorities on their lives, they must also recognize the probabilistic nature of their futures.

Setting Goals

The management of a household fosters a conceptualization of future as well as present time. In addition to requiring the ability to organize time, a conception of the future requires the ability to do three things:

- Set realistic life goals for the family.
- Develop operational steps that will lead to the attainment of the family's goals.
- Evaluate progress being made toward life goals.

The process of goal setting is rather complex. The adult identifies short-term, intermediate, and long-term goals. This goal setting depends on one's sense of where one would like to be in two, five, or 20 years.

As one thinks about goals, one begins to evaluate which things in life are really worth striving for. For some people the life goal is wealth; for others, fame; for still others, peace of mind. The formulation of life goals during middle adulthood will determine the degree of satisfaction that the individual is able to experience in later adulthood. To some extent, setting realistic life goals for the family unit requires the reevaluation and reconceptualization of life goals that were developed during childhood and adolescence. Individuals may eventually drop some fantasized goals that may still be quite attractive but are no longer appropriate to their life situations.

As people develop sets of realistic life goals during middle adulthood, they also develop a serious personal commitment to the attainment of those goals. In a sense, they must believe that what they wish to accomplish is worth accomplishing and can, in fact, be attained. The degree of involvement with life goals becomes most salient during middle adulthood, when parents begin to be confronted by their own adolescent children. At the same time that adults are approaching some sense of personal fulfillment in having achieved certain long-range goals, they are challenged by their children's process of value experimentation. The tension at this stage in the family's development results from the children's questioning of roughly 20 years of adult planning, working, and dreaming.

The second phase of goal setting involves a set of operational steps that will lead to the attainment of a goal. If one hopes to have a certain degree of financial independence during later adulthood, one must save money, invest it, and calculate its potential growth in relation to needs anticipated 30 to 40 years in the future. The same principles apply to the attainment of any long-range goal. The adult must invest resources and anticipate their capacity to change over time. The setting of a goal involves some projection of what one *hopes* things will be like in the future, whereas planning for the attainment of a goal involves some prediction of what things will really be like in the future.

The final stage in the psychological process of goal setting involves the continuous evaluation of the progress being made toward those goals. As people set goals, make plans to attain them, and carry out those plans, they become aware of how well they are progressing toward their goals. They may discover that they can make use of certain skills to reach their goals more quickly. They may find that some goals are far more difficult to attain than they had anticipated and will require increased energy. Some goals may be judged to be unattainable, and others may prove to be more easily attainable than had been expected. Throughout the process of evaluating progress toward their goals, adults are learning to adjust their goals and their efforts so that they will result in the greatest personal satisfaction.

Establishing Relationships with Other Social Structures

A final component of household management is the establishment of bonds between the family unit and other social groupings. These other groupings may include (1) individuals, (2) members of the extended family (for example, a brother's family), (3) other families, (4) business or work-related associations, (5) religious groups, (6) educational groups, and (7) community groups. The family exists in a social context that serves to expand its resources. Contact with social groups must include the maintenance of goodwill and some evidence of family commitment. Social groups also generate norms that may make demands on the family. The household executive must be able to protect the family from excessive external demands while retaining valuable and satisfying external relationships.

One of the most difficult and subtle kinds of new learning that occurs during middle adulthood is the development of an understanding of how the structures of other organizations affect one's life and the lives of family members. Most of us are not very astute at recognizing how we are influenced by the institutions in which we participate. How do hiring practices at one's workplace influence the kinds of co-workers we are likely to meet? How do hospital policies influence the way we are treated when we are patients or when we seek medical advice for a family member? How do the voting policies of our city or state influence how funds are allocated to schools, social welfare programs, or transportation resources that directly influence the quality of family life? Each of these questions suggests a possible contact between an organizational structure and an adult's efforts to maintain a feeling of control over life events (Sarason, 1980).

Families differ in their investment in relationships outside the family unit (Salamon, 1977). In some households, the nuclear family is more important than any other group. Such households expend very little energy outside the family boundaries. At the other extreme are families who are highly involved in a great many community groups and who incorporate their extended families into frequent family activities.

In some families, each person is encouraged to establish his or her own group of close friends. In others, each person's friends are screened or evaluated by the other family members. The adult's task is to define the family's preferred stance toward other social groups and to create opportunities for the establishment of relationships when these are desired.

The family's relations with the *extended family* are a most delicate matter. This is the realm of family politics. Courtesies, obligations, insults, and slights within the boundaries of family units are among the most stressful and challenging experiences with which most individuals have to deal. Fischer (1983) described one aspect of family politics in her comparison of the mother-daughter and mother-in-law–daughter-in-law relationship after the birth of the first child. The birth increased the new mother's interactions with both her mother and her mother-in-law. Interactions with the mother tended to become clarified, and there was increased convergence in views within this relationship. However, interactions with the mother-in-law became more strained after the child's birth. Ties with the husband's and wife's kin seem to become less parallel after the birth of the first child. This development may be due to the fact that the new mother shares her own mother's child-rearing experiences and therefore feels a new closeness to her. It may result from the fact that mothers-in-law are concerned for the well-being of their sons as their daughters-in-law become involved in the new mothering relationship. Regardless of the type of kinship relation, feelings of affection are a strong predictor of whether adults will maintain contact with their relatives (Leigh, 1982).

People Who Live Alone

In our discussion of household management, we have assumed that the household consists of two or more people whose lives are intertwined. Questions about decision making, consensus, and shared responsibilities are all raised in the context of a group of people living together. A large number of people, however, live alone. In 1987,

Box 12.1   Homelessness

The household provides a basic life structure for most people in all cultures. The demands and tasks of household management call forth responses that stimulate cognitive, social, and personal development during adulthood. The household is not only a physical setting, but the shared setting for a group of people. In nomadic tribal groups, for example, the continuity of the household is preserved by the group of people and their shared belongings even though the location of the household changes.

The homeless are people who live on the streets or in public shelters. Many of the people who fall into this category are mentally ill persons who have been released from mental institutions. Many are drug and alcohol abusers. Some are runaway youths. Others are families—parents and children. These people have no permanent resting place, no private space (Landers, 1989a, 1989b).

What is the psychology of these people like? For one thing, it is diverse. Some of these people are homeless by choice and some are homeless because of the cruel blows of circumstance. This is most definitely an alternative lifestyle. Some of these people are singularly alone, unable to develop minimal social relationships. This is a very unusual phenomenon, as most human beings have some ability to have meaningful social relationships. Some individuals in homeless families are bound by cruelty and coercion while others are bound by love, affection, and respect. Some homeless people are so badly beaten and bruised physically and psychologically that they can no longer protect themselves from further battering.

The number of homeless has grown. Their visibility in every major city in America is presenting a

new ethical dilemma to the nation (Gibbs, 1988). In homelessness we confront the gross failure of the socialization process—the inability of mature adults to meet their basic needs for shelter, food, and clothing. And in the face of the cultural value placed on independence, self-sufficiency, and hard work, we have difficulty making effective societal responses. The sight of homeless persons on our city streets may provoke a response of caring or of rejection. Homelessness is an especially powerful condition for highlighting the basic stability that most adults derive from the structure, familiarity, and comfort of whatever place they call home.

about 24% of households included only one person. These one-person households more frequently consist of men in the younger age groups (under 35) and women in the older age groups (55 and over) (U.S. Bureau of the Census, 1989). Single-person households include people who have never married, those who are divorced or separated, and those who are widowed. The reasons for living alone and the backgrounds for this life pattern vary considerably among these groups.

We really know little about the differences in psychosocial development between adults who live alone and those who live with others. Some of the aspects of household management, including organizing time, planning for the future, making decisions, and establishing relationships with other social groups, still pose challenges to the person living alone. On the other hand, assigning responsibility and establishing a system of group decision making clearly is not required. People who live alone may not feel the need to engage in elaborate planning and evaluation when they are the only ones who will be immediately affected by their choices. They can be freer to decide spontaneously as each opportunity presents itself.

Most people who live alone compensate for the few contacts they have within their household by maintaining a relatively large number of outside friends. They may spend less time overall in the company of others, but they are more deliberate in identifying confidants who can meet their social needs. Particularly in the area of establishing relationships with other social structures, the situation of living alone appears to promote social integration (Alwin, Converse & Martin, 1985).

In summary, the developmental task of household management is a process of skill building and conceptual learning in five areas: assessing needs and abilities, making decisions, organizing time, setting goals, and establishing relationships with other social groupings. The realm of the household is unique because it allows adults to perform with maximum flexibility, creativity, and adaptability in response to the daily needs and long-terms goals of the household members.

Parenting

Being a parent is a difficult and demanding task that requires a great deal of learning. Because children are constantly changing and often unpredictable, the adult must be sensitive and flexible in new situations in order to cope successfully with their demands. The child-rearing experience is different with each child, and the changing family constellation brings new demands for flexibility and learning (Zeits & Prince, 1982; Knox & Wilson, 1978). With each successive child, however, there does seem to be less anxiety about parenting skills. Children help adults learn about parenting through their responses to the adults' efforts and their own persistence in following the path of development.

Developmental Stages of the Family

As children grow older, the demands on parents change. Infants require constant care and attention. Preschoolers require toys and peers. They can spend a great deal of time in independent play. They may, however, also require parental reassurance about their skills, talents, and fears. The early adolescent requires little in the way of constant care but a great deal of consideration in such matters as driving a car, dating, and being away from home overnight or for a summer.

Several models of family development have been proposed by students of the family. These schemes, especially the ones described by Duvall (1977), Hill (1965), and Spanier, Sauer, and Larzelere (1979), emphasize changes in the family that are tied to changes in the developmental levels of children. The implication is that the changing needs, competence, and social interactions of the children stimulate changing interactions, activities, and values among family members.

There are a number of problems with this view of family development. First, the length of the marriage and the ages of the parents are confounded with the ages or stages of the children. It is possible that the parents' ages as much as the children's ages or some combination of the two account for changes in family emphasis (Nock, 1979; Spanier, Sauer & Larzelere, 1979). Second, this view does not help us to understand the growth of families who do not have children or families who are a product of remarriage in which the marital relationship has a shorter history than the parental one. Third, from a psychosocial perspective we regard the influence of parents and children as reciprocal. Changes in the developmental level of children have the potential to influence the quality of their interactions with parents. Changes in the developmental level of parents also have this potential. Further, each family member can prompt conflict, change, or growth in every other. The affectional bonds that family members share, as well as the need to protect one another from external threats, contribute to a dynamic interdependence. To some degree, each family member is vulnerable to the influence of every other.

For purposes of this discussion of parenting, we have chosen to consider the potential influences of phases of family development on adult development. This approach has the advantage of showing the reciprocity of psychosocial themes across the generations. It gives us some ways in which to consider the processes through which development may prompt new growth among parents. The six periods of family development that are discussed are:

1. The childbearing and postnatal years
2. The years when children are toddlers
3. The years when children are of elementary and middle school age
4. The years when children are adolescents
5. The years when no children are living at home
6. The grandparental years

The childbearing and postnatal years   The period when a child is in utero and immediately after birth is often very strenuous for both parents. The family is somewhat anxious about the health of the mother and the infant. These concerns may also be reflected in sympathetic symptoms experienced by the father. After childbirth, both adults are likely to be tense and exhausted. Many young adults are discouraged by the inadequacy of their preparation for this major adult role. With the first child, the anxieties about the infant's physical health and the uncertainties about how to handle daily events are at their most extreme. (That may be why books on child care have been such great successes.) With successive children, parents may be more tired but less anxious.

Perhaps the major change for parents during this period is the attachment that forms for each new child. Parents discover their capacity to become deeply—even irrationally—committed to protecting and nurturing their offspring. Mothers often comment that they had no idea how totally absorbing the demands of the mother role would be (Coady, 1982; Newman & Coady, 1982). Fathers as well as mothers are increasingly absorbed by the unique qualities and demands of newborns.

Parents must learn to anticipate an infant's needs on the basis of minimal or undifferentiated cues; to structure the environment so that it will permit safe, stimulating opportunities for exploration; and to convey love through warm, gentle, close

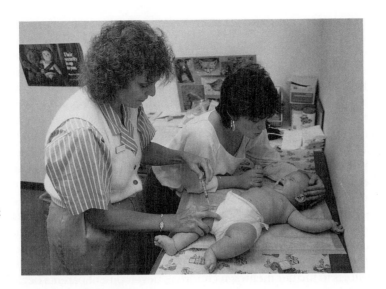

This mother has to put aside her own feelings about having an injection in order to reassure and comfort her baby.

handling. A major challenge to adults at this stage is to learn to convey calm reassurance when they are really anxious and uncertain. Parents learn that their own fears are not necessarily the fears of their children. They must learn to mask some of their personal concerns in order to foster their children's sense of trust. Of course, not all parents of infants are sensitive and skillful in the way they treat their children, as the incidence of infant abuse attests. Positive parenting techniques were recommended in Table 5.6.

The years when children are toddlers   The parents of toddlers are truly tested with regard to the issue of autonomy. Toddlers, in their efforts to gain control, challenge their parents' limits. Parents, no matter how patient, almost inevitably get pushed too far. In order for parents to be successful during this stage, they must learn a new level of self-control. They rediscover language, fantasy, and the wonders of the natural world. They also learn that they have needs for personal privacy that must be conveyed to children but nevertheless are frequently violated.

During this period, adults also begin to formulate family rules and to employ certain forms of discipline when these rules are violated. The creation of rules, rewards, and punishments is generally the result of some degree of ideology as to what is right and wrong and some degree of personal tolerance. Discipline requires full acceptance of the responsibilities of authority that come with parenthood. It also creates a new distance between adults and their children. Parents learn that they will not always be liked for doing what they believe is right.

The years when children are of early and middle school age   School-age children tap parents' resources for ideas about things to do, places to go, and friends to meet. Children seek new experiences in order to expand their competence and investigate the larger world outside the home. Parents become active as chauffeurs, secretaries, and buffers between their children and the rest of the community. Parents have many opportunities to function as educators for their children. Parents make active contributions to their children's academic success through such activities as reading with their children, helping them with homework, praising them for school success, and talking with teachers, visiting school, and participating in school projects. Research on the academic success of black children makes it very clear that parents' aspirations for their children, their overall parenting skills, and their involvement in their children's education make a substantial contribution to their children's progress (Jenkins, 1989).

Parenting during this period has the potential for boosting an adult's sense of pride in skills and knowledge already accumulated. Parents are gatekeepers to the resources of the community. They come to see themselves through their children's eyes, as people who know about the world—its rewards, treasures, secrets, and dangers.

During this phase of parenthood, adults are likely to be active in school-related organizations. They find themselves reacting to events that occur in school, planning activities to take place at school, or working with other parents to provide some service, opportunity, or facility for their children that does not currently exist. Through efforts to further their own children's development parents begin to evolve an attitude toward—even a philosophy of—education that will have implications for a whole community of children. When parents are forced to protect, defend, or reprimand their own children with regard to events that have taken place in school, they develop a stance toward that institution and its function in the community. For some parents, school seems like a hostile place. They did not do well in school themselves and do not have much confidence in their academic abilities. These parents may find it very difficult to retain a sense of self-worth if their children become too involved in school. They may even introduce barriers to their children's academic success out of their own defensiveness.

The years when children are adolescents   Parents tend to see the years of their children's adolescence as extremely trying. Adolescents are likely to have a great deal of behavioral independence. They spend most of the day away from home and apart from adult supervision. As adolescents gain in physical stature and cognitive skills, they are likely to challenge parental authority.

During this time, the principles that parents have emphasized as important for responsible, moral behavior are frequently tested. On the one hand, parents must allow their children freedom in order to permit them to exercise their judgment. On the other, they must be ready to give support when the children fail to meet adult expectations or when they show poor judgment. Parents must be able to maintain a degree of authority about standards or limits that continue to operate for young adolescents. Parents of adolescents, therefore, must attempt to balance freedom, support, and limit setting in the needed proportions so that their children can grow increasingly independent while still being able to rely on an atmosphere of family reassurance (Newman, 1989; Ryan & Lynch, 1989).

In a national survey of parents' concerns about their children, parents of teengers expressed concern that their children were more vulnerable to peer influence and out of their sphere of control. Concerns about drugs, sex, and staying out late increased during this phase of parenting. Parents were also likely to be concerned about whether there was adequate communication and understanding with their adolescent children (Hoffman & Manis, 1978). Rossi (1980) asked mothers in the age range of 36 to 51 to rate the difficulty of child rearing and the child's difficulty in growing up from the ages of infancy through adolescence. Mothers viewed the task of parenting as more difficult than that of growing up during childhood. However, they saw both growing up and parenting as becoming increasingly difficult in adolescence.

Adolescent children are the front line of each new generation. The questions they raise and the choices they make reflect not only what they have learned but also what they are experiencing in the present and what they anticipate in the future. Parents of adolescents are likely to feel persistent pressure to reevaluate their own socialization as well as their effectiveness as parents. Questions are raised about their preparation for their own futures as well as their children's. The ego boost that resulted from being viewed as wise and resourceful is likely to be replaced by doubts as both parents and children face an uncertain future. Parents who can respond to their adolescents in an open, supportive way can benefit by finding an opportunity to clarify their own values. They can begin building new parent-child relationships that will carry them and their emerging adult children into later adulthood.

The years when no children are living at home   Sometime during most parents' 40s or early 50s, children leave home to go to college, join the service, or take jobs and live in their own households. In the 1970s, the median age of mothers when the last child married was 52.3. The median age at the death of the spouse was 65.2. Thus couples with children have an average of almost 13 years when they may be together without active, daily responsibilities for parenting. This compares to approximately 1.5 years without children for couples in the 1900s (Glick, 1977, 1979). Today couples are planning for even smaller families than they were ten years ago. As the period of the healthy adult years expands, couples will have an even longer time of family life without the active responsibilities of parenting.

The period during which children leave home has been designated developmentally as the *launching period* (Mattessich & Hill, 1987). For families with only a few children, this period may last only a few years. With larger families, the transition may take ten to 15 years. Alternative patterns are clearly evident in current U.S. families. Thirty percent of parents with children in their 20s have one or more of these adult children living at home (Aquilino, 1990). By the time adult children marry they are almost always ready to leave the parental home. It is also during this phase that women experience menopause, signaling the end of childbearing for the couple.

There is no doubt that roles change during this time. The relationship between the husband and wife changes as parenting activities diminish. Some couples become closer—closer than they have been since they first fell in love. Divorces also occur when the children are gone. Parents are likely to begin a review and evaluation of their performance as parents as they see the kinds of lives their children establish for themselves. Erikson finds that many parents continue to build their identities on the accomplishments of their children (Erikson, Erikson & Kivnick, 1986). Parents must also begin to find new targets for energy and commitment that they had previously directed toward the care of their children (Rubin, 1980).

Box 12.2   Menopause

At some time during their late 40s or 50s, most women experience the climacteric, or the involution and atrophy of the reproductive organs. Many physiological changes accompany this loss of fertility, including the cessation of menstruation (menopause), gradual diminution in the production of estrogen, atrophy of the breasts and genital tissues, and shrinkage of the uterus (Morokoff, 1988). There is some controversy as to whether the menopause affects women at a psychological level because of either its symbolic meaning or the physiological changes it brings. Let us consider the research on menopause—and the entire experience of the climacteric—within the context of its meaning for the woman who is engaged in the task of developing a sense of generativity.

The most commonly reported symptom is a frequent "hot flash"—a sudden onset of warmth in the face and neck that lasts several minutes. Sometimes it is accompanied by dizziness, nausea, sweating, or headaches. About 75 to 85% of women going through natural menopause report this symptom. Other symptoms are related to the reduction of vaginal fluid and loss of elasticity (Bates, 1981; Hammond & Maxson, 1986). The symptoms appear to be closely related to a drastic drop in the production of estrogen. Postmenopausal women produce only one-sixth as much estrogen as regularly menstruating women do. Several studies on the use of estrogen treatment have found that the administration of this hormone to menopausal women alleviates or even prevents menopausal symptoms.

It is fairly well established, then, that the menopause brings about recognizable physical changes that the adult woman may or may not view as unpleasant. The severity of symptoms is determined in part by the attitude of the culture toward the infertile older woman. In cultures that reward women for reaching the end of the fertile period, menopause is associated with few physiological symptoms (Flint, 1976). Similarly, a woman's own attitudes toward aging and her involvement in adult roles will influence the ease or difficulty with which she experiences menopause. In our society, for example, a woman who is going through menopause at age 50 may also be experiencing the severe illness or death of her parents and the marriage of her youngest child. Menopausal status is not a good predictor of a woman's health or her psychological well-being. Role strain and prior health are much more accurate predictors (McKinlay, McKinlay & Brambilla, 1987).

A woman's anxiety about menopause depends on her feelings about no longer being able to bear children, on the amount of information she has about the symptoms accompanying menopause, and on the degree of her anxiety about growing old. For example, Neugarten and her colleagues (1963) found that attitudes toward menopause were more positive among their sample of postmenopausal women 45 and older than among younger women. The older group realized that the menopausal symptoms were temporary and that after menopause would come the potential for feelings of well-being and vigor. In contrast to the younger group, they were aware that menopause might bring an upsurge in sexual impulses and activity.

The younger woman tends to confuse menopause with growing old. Physical beauty may be heavily weighted in her definition of femininity. Further, the younger woman may still be quite invested in her role as mother and fearful of a potential end to her years of childbearing. The older woman, on the other hand, is likely to be glad to have reached the end of the childbearing years and may be eagerly awaiting a future of new roles and freedoms.

Menopause may serve as a significant symbolic event for women in the stage of middle adulthood. For the woman who has successfully developed a sense of personal achievement in child rearing or other work, menopause signifies the end of the child-rearing years and the beginning of a period in which new energy can be directed to broader, community-oriented tasks. For the woman who has failed to develop a sense of generativity, who continues to view her children as a path to self-fulfillment, or who is frightened by the prospect of growing old, menopause may highlight a sense of stagnation.

The transitional period during which children leave home does not seem to be a negative time for adults. A woman who was anticipating her children's leaving home described her feelings this way:

> *From the day the kids are born, if it's not one thing, it's another. After all these years of being responsible for them, you finally get to the point where you want to scream, "Fall out of the nest already, you guys, will you? It's time." It's as if I want to take myself back after all these years—to give me back to me, if you know what I mean. Of course, that's providing there's any "me" left.* [Rubin, 1980, p. 313]

There is evidence of greater cohesiveness and affection in the marriage relationship after the children leave home, especially in marriages that had been satisfactory before (Houseknecht & Macke, 1981; Mullan, 1981). Parents are usually pleased as they trace their children's accomplishments. Further, children's independence may permit parents to use their financial resources to enhance their own lifestyles. One factor that does seem to be associated with a negative view of this transition is the age of the child. Parents who view their child as too young to be leaving home are more likely to experience the transition as stressful (Mullan, 1983).

It is important to recognize that adults maintain certain parental functions during this stage. As long as the children are financially dependent on parents, the parents' work efforts must be continued on a maximally productive level. Children who have left home may not have resolved decisions about occupation and marriage. Parents remain a source of advice and support as late adolescents and young adults go through periods of identity and intimacy formation and consolidation. Parents begin to feel the pressure of challenges to their value orientation as their children experiment with new roles and new lifestyles. During this stage, parents may serve as sounding boards, as sources of stability, or as jousting partners in young people's attempts to conceptualize their own lifestyles. Because middle adults may begin to feel free to alter their roles and redirect their energies at this point in their lives, some parents may also experience resistance from their children, who expect that their parents will remain the same as they themselves change and grow.

One of the major events that occurs during this period is the child's decision to marry. Parents may be expected to accept a new person into their family as their child's husband or wife. Along with this new relationship comes a connection to an entirely new, and often totally unknown, group of in-laws. Parents are usually at the mercy of their child's decision in this matter. They may find themselves associated through marriage with a family who differs significantly from their own or who shares many of their own family's idiosyncrasies.

The first few years of marriage, as we mentioned in Chapter 11, are somewhat precarious. It may be necessary for parents to reintegrate an adult child into the family at this stage if his or her marriage is not successful. It can be assumed that a child who leaves a marriage needs some temporary parental reassurance and support in order to regain confidence in his or her ability to form an intimate relationship. Thus, at times of crisis, middle adults may be called upon to practice earlier skills of parenting

Pablo Picasso, *Study for the Ballet Quadro Flamenco,* 1921. Once children leave home, parents may find a new cohesiveness and affection in their relationship. They may rediscover one another as mature companions.

that they have not used for quite a while and to develop new skills in helping their children deal with new challenges.

Grandparenthood   Each time an adult witnesses the birth of a new generation might be considered an additional stage in family development. With grandparenthood, adults begin to observe their children as parents. As people reflect on their own roles 20 to 30 years earlier, they may attribute some of their children's successes to their own parenting techniques and take responsibility for some of the failures (Erikson, Erikson & Kivnick, 1986). In the next chapter, we will consider the role of grandparenthood and its significance for the adult in greater detail. Here, suffice it to say that as grandparents, adults have the opportunity to relate to small children as an expression of the continuity of their lives into the future. Of course, not all grandparents relate to grandchildren from this philosophical point of view. However, the attainment of the grandparent role has the potential for bringing with it a new perspective on time, purpose, and the meaning of life that can serve as a source of reassurance during later adulthood.

With regard to practical matters, adults differ in how they define the role of grandparent. They may see themselves as carriers of the family traditions and wisdom, as needed experts in child care, as convenient and trusted baby-sitters, or as admirers from afar. As grandparents, adults are asked to reinvest energy in small children. The quality of the relationship that develops between grandparents and grandchildren depends not so much on the fact that they are relatives as on the kinds of experiences that the two generations share. Adults must learn to define a new role and to enact it.

Parents learn to alter their parenting roles in response to the developmental changes that their children undergo. Of course, many parents are rearing several children, each of whom is at a slightly different developmental stage. The need to alter their own responses and to attend to the variety of simultaneously existing needs adds to the challenge.

In the process of parenting, adults have an opportunity to review their own development through the experiences they share with their children. They may recall their own thrill at watching a firefly light up or their own trepidation on the night before high school graduation. Parenthood helps adults to realize how far they have come in their own efforts at self-definition. At each phase of family development, adults consolidate the gains made in their own growth while learning the skills needed to facilitate the development of their children.

A Psychosocial Analysis of Contributions of Parenting to Adult Development

The parent role can stimulate further cognitive and emotional development when adults view the role as positive and desirable (Newman & Newman, 1988). Of course, not all parents do. Some turn against their children or drop to new, low levels of functioning. Yet this important role has growth-promoting possibilities. Given the critical importance of parenting for species survival and for psychosocial evolution, it is highly unlikely that the enactment of the parent role should prove detrimental to most adults. On the contrary, parenting can bring new levels of insight, intellectual flexibility, and social commitment.

The attachment process is central to human relationships. A person's attachment structure can change over the life course. In some respects the bond that ties children to their parents is the same as the bond that ties parents to their children. But in some ways, the attachment of parents to their children is unique. It is normally characterized by a strong sense of responsibility and an uneven distribution of resources and authority. Evidence suggests that most parents find their attachment to their children deeply satisfying. As a consequence of this deep and enduring attachment, parents are likely to be highly receptive to the new information, new experiences, and new thoughts that are evoked as they observe their children and interact with them.

Discrepancies between the competences and expectations an adult has and the realities the adult encounters with the child provide a stimulus for cognitive growth. The parent role incorporates many discrepancies and usually a strong motivation to resolve them. Parenting can be viewed as having potential influence on six aspects of cognitive development during adulthood. First, parenting requires a more probabilistic view of the future and an accompanying contingency approach to planning. Second, parenting promotes the formulation of a philosophy of life in which the rules and limits parents impose on their children are related to central values and goals.

Third, parenting supports greater appreciation for individual differences and a more highly differentiated view of individual strengths, weaknesses, and potential. Fourth, parenting requires and promotes the capacity to hold two or more opposing ideas in the mind at the same time. Fifth, the need to protect and nurture children

Parenting brings an expansion of caring. Impossible as it seems, parents discover new feelings of love and deep commitment for each child.

requires the development of greater skill at anticipating the future. Finally, parenting has the potential consequence of expanding the realm of consciousness. One becomes increasingly aware of self and others, increasingly capable of conceptualizing past, present, and future, and able to function at varying levels of abstraction in order to be effective with children at different developmental levels.

Parenting contributes to the expansion of caring. Seven aspects of emotional development can be identified as potential consequences of parenting. First, parenting brings a depth of commitment that is tied to the responsibility one feels for the survival of a child. The depth of commitment is strengthened through the reinforcing nature of the child's responses to attempts to meet his or her needs.

Second, parenting brings adults into contact with new channels for expressing affection. Third, parenting requires that adults achieve a balance between meeting their own needs and meeting the needs of others. Fourth, parenting enhances an adult's feelings of value and well-being through the significant role the adult plays in the child's life.

Fifth, parents achieve a degree of empathy for their child that widens the array of their emotional experiences. Sixth, parents may experience new levels of emotional intensity in reaction to their child's behavior. Seventh, many parents learn to help their children express and understand emotions. By playing a therapeutic role for their children, parents may become more effective in accepting and expressing their own emotions.

We realize that parenting is stressful. It is full of conflicts and challenges that demand time that a couple might otherwise spend with each other. We want to argue, however, that parenting generates the kind of conflict that promises an enormous potential for personal growth. By providing a meaningful, responsive context for children, parents have the opportunity to articulate their own value systems and to see the consequences of their efforts in the continuous development of their children.

Millions of people go to work every day. Employment provides a basic structure for adaptation in adulthood.

Psychosocial growth requires a willingness to engage in tasks that may increase stress, uncertainty, and complexity. Growth does not always mean turning away from or minimizing tension. Frequently it means choosing the challenge that is most imposing or intriguingly complex in the hope of growing while struggling to meet it.

Management of a Career

Work is a major context for adult development. Every person who enters the labor market has an occupational career. This career may not appear orderly and progressive as the term *career* has sometimes been defined (Wilensky, 1961). However, as long as the person is involved in an effort to make use of skills and talents, we can argue that there will be significant transactions between the world of work and his or her individual development.

There is clearly a reciprocity between work experiences and individual growth. We expect that people with certain kinds of experiences and abilities will enter certain kinds of work roles (Holland, 1985). Once those roles have been entered, however, the work environment and the kinds of activities that the person performs also influence intellectual, social, and value orientation. The lifelong occupational career is a fluid structure of changing activities, goals, and sources of satisfaction. As people move through middle adulthood, the management of their occupational careers becomes a task of central importance to their sense of personal effectiveness and social integration. Three aspects of work are discussed for their contribution to adaptation and individual development: interpersonal relationships, authority relationships, and skill demands.

Interpersonal Relationships

Most occupations place a great deal of emphasis on the development and use of interpersonal skills. Success in career management may require the ability to influence others, appear credible, develop a fluent conversational style, or learn to work effectively in groups or teams. Adults must devote some thought to their social presentation and work at acquiring the interpersonal skills that will increase their value in their work settings.

People use a variety of interpersonal tactics to influence their bosses, co-workers, and subordinates. In one study, subjects were asked to describe the extent to which they used specific interpersonal strategies to influence others in the work setting. Eight dimensions of influence were identified: assertiveness, ingratiation, rationality, sanctions, exchange, upward appeals, blocking, and coalitions. A variety of organizational factors influenced the kinds of strategies employed: the size of the organization, whether workers were unionized, the relationship between the person trying to use influence and the target of influence, and the event to which the target was resisting influence (Kipnis, Schmidt & Wilkinson, 1980). This analysis emphasized the complexity of interpersonal skills and the need to have access to a wide repertoire of interpersonal strategies in order to be effective in the workplace. It also suggested that the organizational structure may have a significant impact on the kinds of interpersonal strategies that adults become accustomed to using.

Individuals must also be able to understand the demands that are made on them for interpersonal behavior in their work setting. They must be able to identify and distinguish between a competitive and cooperative situation. In a highly competitive situation, some of the interpersonal demands may be gamesmanship plays designed to demonstrate one person's weaknesses and promote another person's advantages. In order to succeed in this type of situation, workers must learn to ignore some of these demands and retain their productivity. In a highly affiliative situation, workers must be very tactful so as not to appear to be in competition with peers. They may also find it necessary to comply with certain interpersonal requests even though these demands slow their performance. In most work settings, work norms are developed that may enhance or limit the productivity of the entire staff (Katz & Kahn, 1978). Once individuals are accepted into the work setting by virtue of their ability to comply with work norms and to get along with co-workers, they may be able to influence the norms. At that point, they may alter their work environment so as to more fully meet their own needs for stimulation, productivity, and interpersonal relationships.

The interpersonal values held by the leaders in a work group influence the way they shape the work environment. Leaders who place a high priority on task performance tend to have a negative attitude toward workers whom they perceive as interfering with successful task accomplishment. They try to establish an ordered, highly structured work environment in which they can exercise their authority. Leaders who give high priority to interpersonal relationships are more accepting of workers who may interfere with task accomplishment. They try to establish an environment that will foster full participation of the workers. Most work settings require some blend of competitive and cooperative behaviors. The task for the individual in such settings is

Family Life Across Cultures

Culture wraps around each child like a blanket, encompassing simple everyday activities, such as eating and sleeping, and special rituals and ceremonies. In Thailand (top), children bring an offering of food to a shrine. In Ecuador (left), a child travels wrapped on his mother's back. In Korea (right), a toddler is fed rice, with chopsticks. For each child these events are meaningfully embedded in a cultural context.

Breastfeeding is a universal behavior that is culturally defined.

All healthy human mothers have the capacity to breastfeed. However, attitudes about this form of nurturance differ from one culture to the next. The Japanese mother and her infant (opposite) are clothed in a way that prevents much direct physical contact between them. In Thailand (right), a mother nurses in the open. Because her milk is a safe and inexpensive food, she may nurse her son for several years. In the United States (below), breastfeeding is an opportunity for physical intimacy and privacy between this mother and infant. The baby will probably be weaned at eight to ten months of age.

Fathers' roles are highly varied. A father in northern Thailand (above) prepares to hunt while the children watch from a distance. In Japan (below), a father carries his infant under a good-luck umbrella. In the United States (right), a father encourages his son's involvement in drawing. Each father is contributing to his child's wellbeing in a culturally acceptable manner.

In most cultures, family life includes a strong bond among siblings. Like the Japanese toddlers (above), siblings are often each other's first playmates. In the Pueblo Indian family (left), an older girl helps her younger sister read a magazine.

Children are strongly influenced by the common bond of their family's ancestry. During the early years, brothers and sisters work and play together. But many cultures separate boys from girls by early adolescence, teaching them different skills, encouraging different behavior patterns, and guiding them toward distinct adult roles.

Grandparents often contribute significantly, nurturing and teaching the young. How cultures define the role and status of grandparents varies widely. In some societies a clear line of authority extends from the oldest kin to the youngest; for critical decisions, the most senior family member has primary authority.

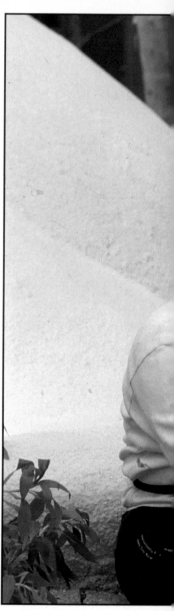

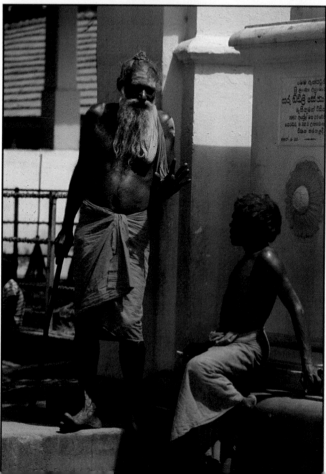

A Costa Rican grandfather (opposite, top) and a Japanese grandmother (above) are comfortable in roles quite similar to those assumed by many grandparents in the United States: They enjoy having fun with their grandchildren. In Sri Lanka (opposite, below), an elder advises a younger man in the same religious order. The two are linked socially as "grandfather" and "grandson" by their common sense of community.

Family life extends
beyond the home into
the community.
Children join their
mothers and fathers in
the marketplace, selling
potatoes in Kenya
(above) and rugs in the
mountains of Ecuador
(below). Infants stay
near their mothers.
Older children help with
the business. Adults
and children work side
by side, providing for
the family.

In most industrial
societies children are
excluded from the
world of paid work.
For children in many
traditional cultures, the
world of work is
simply an extension
of family life.

The authority structure has to be clear, to eliminate bickering about who is in charge. At the same time, managers must be able to promote teamwork and a sense of shared responsibility.

to be able to assess individual interpersonal demands as competitive or cooperative and to respond appropriately. In the process of establishing interpersonal relations, individuals will probably form temporary alliances, some lasting friendships, and some enduring animosities (Argyle, 1972).

Authority Relationships

In addition to interpersonal relationships with colleagues, there are a wide variety of authority relations in the world of work. Initially the individual must identify the authority structure operating in the work setting and begin to establish a position in that structure. Advancement in a career inevitably involves some increase in responsibility and power to make decisions. One cannot hope to advance without assuming some increased authority. Thus career management eventually involves the ability to assume authority as well as to respond to higher authorities.

Occupations vary in the patterns of advancement they offer. Some careers begin with a long period of subordination, which gradually gives way to increased authority. Other careers place new employees in positions of authority quite early and continue to move them up a ladder of authority relations at a fairly steady pace. Still others find the new worker initially established in a position of authority that never really changes much. The adult's task is to identify the authority pattern and assess which skills will be needed for advancement in the hierarchy.

Some people do not choose to advance beyond a given point in the authority structure. They find a position in which the degrees of responsibility and subordination are comfortable and choose to remain at that level. Others find that if they do not choose to advance, their careers suffer. Still others discover that advancement is not possible and that they have attained some peak in status beyond which they cannot rise.

New competitive pressures on corporations are leading to a more flexible, less hierarchical authority structure (Kanter, 1989). With a reduction in the size of many bureaucracies, companies are asking workers to relate to one another in new ways. Managers are less likely to have ultimate control over chains of communication, work strategies, and project priorities. Managers must learn to facilitate the formation of effective teams of workers and to motivate groups by helping them identify with the importance of their mission within the organization. There are new freedoms to initiate new projects, to make deals, to build partnerships across departments within an organization, and to build alliances with external services and related companies.

> *The old bases of managerial authority are eroding, and new tools of leadership are taking their place. Managers whose power derived from hierarchy and who were accustomed to a limited area of personal control are learning to shift their perspectives and widen their horizons. The new managerial work consists of looking outside a defined area of responsibility to sense opportunities and of forming project teams drawn from any relevant sphere to address them. It involves communication and collaboration across functions, across divisions, and across companies whose activities and resources overlap. Thus rank, title, or official charter will be less important factors in success at the new managerial work than having the knowledge, skills, and sensitivity to mobilize people and motivate them to do their best.* [Kanter, 1989, p. 92]

Skills

The characteristics of the occupation and the work setting will determine what kinds of work-related skills will dominate the adult's energies. It makes sense to expect that the actual tasks a person does from day to day will influence his or her intellectual development. The *Dictionary of Occupational Titles* uses 44 characteristics to describe the unique blend of aptitudes and temperament required for each type of work. These variables have been condensed to six basic factors: substantive complexity, motor skills, physical demands, management, interpersonal skills, and undesirable working conditions (Cain & Treiman, 1981). Each of these dimensions has the potential for contributing to workers' adaptation to their work life. Further, it is likely that in the process of adapting to these dimensions, the adult will carry over aspects of work-related competence to family and community roles.

Melvin Kohn (Kohn, 1980; Miller et al., 1979) has examined the relationship between occupational demands and psychological development. One of the strongest relationships identified is that between the substantive complexity of the job and intellectual flexibility. *Substantive complexity* means the degree to which the work requires thought, independent judgment, and frequent decision making. *Intellectual flexibility* refers to the person's ability to handle conflicting information, to take several perspectives on a problem, and to reflect on his or her own values and solutions.

The substantive complexity of a person's job is highly related to his or her intellectual flexibility. This is true even when one takes into account the level of intellectual flexibility that was shown at the time of job entry. In a ten-year longitudinal study, it was found that the level of intellectual flexibility shown ten years earlier was strongly related to the degree of substantive complexity present in the job ten years later. There appears to be a reciprocal effect between these two dimensions. Being in a substantively complex work setting promotes intellectual flexibility. At the same time, a high level of intellectual flexibility appears to lead one to increasingly challenging, complex work.

Midlife Career Change

Management of a career does not necessarily mean remaining within the same occupational structure throughout adult life. Work activities or work-related goals may change for at least four reasons.

First, some careers end during middle adulthood. One example is the career of the professional athlete, whose strength, speed of reaction time, and endurance decline to the point where he or she can no longer compete.

Second, some adults cannot resolve conflicts between job demands and personal goals. We read about successful business executives who turn to farming or about public relations experts who withdraw to rural areas to sell real estate. During middle adulthood, some workers recognize that the kinds of contributions they thought they could make are simply not possible within their chosen work structures. Others find that they do not have the temperament to be successful in their first careers.

A third explanation for midlife career change is the realization that one has succeeded as much as will be possible within a given career. Adults may realize that they will not be promoted further or that changing technology has made their expertise obsolete. They may decide to retrain for new kinds of work or return to school so that they can move in new career directions.

Fourth, some women decide to make a greater commitment to career once their children are in high school or college. They have chosen to withdraw from the labor market for a time in order to fulfill parenting roles. As they return to work, they may continue to expect to combine responsibilities as homemakers with career goals. However, their life course has an anticipated midlife career change built in as they shift primary involvement from the home to the labor market.

There is some question about how prevalent midlife career change really is in today's labor market. This is not to say that a reevaluation of one's career goals and one's personal sense of satisfaction is not desirable. However, the opportunities for flexibility of work roles may be limited by many conditions, including slowed industrial growth, an aging population of workers, and a baby-boom crush on the middle management positions. Table 12.2 suggests some conditions that might facilitate and others that would limit midlife career change.

The Impact of Joblessness

Some people are alienated from work. They find little satisfaction in the work setting and little opportunity for meaningful labor. If they do work, they are not very involved in their work settings and may not learn much about the interpersonal relations, authority relations, or skill-related tasks that are sources of challenge to career management. They may have little opportunity to develop competence within the context

Table 12.2 **Conditions Influencing Midlife Career Change**	
Facilitators of Change	*Inhibitors of Change*
Full employment (more job openings, greater overall job and occupational mobility)	A society that is predominantly middle-aged (workers over 35 have the lowest job and career mobility)
A high proportion of workers in categories with strong career mobility (farmers, clerical workers, laborers have highest rates)	A work force with a high proportion of white-collar and professional employees (careers in which a high level of education and certification is required have a low turnover rate)
Underemployment of workers (trained people working in lower-skill jobs are more likely to be job- and career-mobile)	Slow industrial and business growth (a stable economy has lower rates of career and job transition)
A younger work force (workers in their 20s are the most highly mobile)	A high proportion of workers with an investment in pension plans (the importance of retirement plans in financial planning discourages job change)
A high proportion of women in the work force (women are newer to the work force and even in middle age display the career traits of younger workers)	A high proportion of workers fearful of job discrimination

Source: S. Arbeiter, "Mid-life Career Change: A Concept in Search of Reality," *AAHE Bulletin, 32* (1979), no. 1. Reprinted by permission of the author.

of work. Because of the cultural emphasis on productive work, these people are likely to experience some degree of guilt about being unable to work. They may also find it hard to direct their energy toward creative solutions of life problems. The inability to work can be expected to become a serious block in the resolution of the psychosocial conflict of generativity versus stagnation.

The relationship between psychosocial development and the ability to perform meaningful work is illustrated in a study of the experiences of unemployment (Braginsky & Braginsky, 1975). A group of jobless men who had held managerial or engineering positions were compared with a group of employed men. Most of the jobless men were experiencing their first encounter with unemployment in 20 years of work. They felt unwanted, insignificant, and bitter. They were experiencing a profound reevaluation of long-held values. They expressed feelings that their college years had been wasted, that hard work and skill were less important than "brownnosing the boss," and that their friends shunned them after they had lost their jobs. Because of the importance of their previous work to their sense of worth, these men were left with deep feelings of worthlessness and low self-esteem that persisted even after they were reemployed.

Job loss has been associated with both physical and psychological consequences. In addition to the withdrawal and self-doubt that can occur, job loss can introduce family strains that lead to new levels of conflict and family violence. In some instances, adjustments that families make to a husband's unemployment can result in a further reduction of his sense of importance and accentuate the decline in his self-respect (Piotrkowski, Rapoport & Rapoport, 1987).

Work and Family Life

Clearly no married person manages a career independently of commitments to spouse and children. A decision to assume more authority, work longer hours, accept an offer with another company, quit one's job, or accept a transfer to a new location will touch the lives of other family members. One of the most draining aspects of career management is the effort to meet conflicting expectations of one's marital, parental, and work roles (Pines & Kafry, 1977; Pleck, Staines & Lang, 1980).

Family and work life are interconnected whether one or both adults are employed. In the following example, the same work-family conflict is viewed from two points of view:

Work: *The atmosphere in the office is somber as three department heads meet to discuss the complaints they have been receiving from one important work team. The focus of the complaints is the employees' travel schedules. Heavy travel during the summer season is a project necessity, but the complaints this year have been particularly bad and the number of sick days and postponed travel schedules have been increasing.*

Family: *In one of the families in which heavy travel was the issue, the wife makes a demand upon her husband. "The teacher told me today it's very important for you to spend more time with our son. She thinks a lot of his disruptive behavior can be traced to wanting more attention from his father, since he told her you're never home." The husband's response is, "But you know I have to finish up this assignment. Things will be better in the fall."* [Renshaw, 1976, p. 250]

Conflict between work and family results when the demands of work and family roles make participation in one or both of these roles more difficult or inadequate (Tiedje et al., 1990; Voydanoff, 1988). This conflict is usually a result of competing demands on time or the psychological spillover of one role to the other. Some of the characteristics of the work setting that contribute to this conflict are:

- Long work hours
- Shift work, especially on evenings or weekends
- Role ambiguity or role conflict at work
- Rapid change
- Work overload

Some of the characteristics of family life that contribute to this conflict are:

- Number of hours spent in child care and housework
- Number and ages of children
- Perceptions of husband and wife regarding appropriate role enactment

There are also some factors that can buffer or minimize potential conflict. Two of the most critical of these buffers are:

- Perceived control over the scheduling of work hours and work demands
- Perceived enhancement or enrichment of work and family roles; a view that multiple roles add to a sense of purpose and personal worth

The degree to which work and family roles conflict depends in part on how the partners view each other's participation in the world of work. Some women are heavily invested in their husbands' achievements and experience vicarious satisfaction from their successes. Women who are very concerned that their husbands provide income and prestige for their families are likely to have fewer expectations about the husbands' contributions to childrearing and household tasks (Clark, Nye & Gecas, 1978). From the other perspective, the husband may feel threatened if his wife shows excitement and involvement in her career at the very time that his own work is beginning to lose its excitement or promise. The degree to which the couple copes with these work-family conflicts depends on the husband's success in his work, his income level, and the wife's expectations regarding the kinds of commitments her husband should make to household or child rearing activities. For example, many men who work long hours also earn high salaries, which may cause their absence from home to be viewed with less resentment than it might be if they were earning less.

The conflict between work and family roles is even more complex when both husband and wife are working. Most couples tend to see child care and certain household maintenance tasks as primarily the wife's domain. This outlook is as common in other countries—Canada, Sweden, Norway—as it is in the United States (Kalleberg & Rosenfeld, 1990). When both husband and wife are working, the wife may experience considerable strain in trying to meet her work commitments while allowing adequate time for nurturance and recreational activities with her children. In a study of 200 professional couples, it was found that wives were more likely then husbands to assume greater responsibility for the home and family and to put their spouses' careers ahead of their own (Heckman, Bryson & Bryson, 1977). Thus some women resolve the conflict between career aspirations and family commitment by limiting their competitive, achievement-oriented strivings.

Other women find that the work setting limits achievement through sex-typed assumptions about the woman's commitment to her family role. Women do not tend to be promoted to high-level administrative or managerial positions in which work demands would begin to invade family commitments. Companies are reluctant to put women in positions in which they may have to be transferred for fear that husbands will refuse to make the move. In some instances, women who request flexible or part-time work schedules are labeled as not really serious about their career (Rodgers & Rodgers, 1989).

Despite many difficulties encountered in combining work and family roles, women who enter today's labor market do so in a context of cultural acceptance. Questions have been raised about the impact of employment status on the self-esteem and personality adjustment of women in middle adulthood. Earlier work found that homemakers—that is, married women who were not in the labor market—had lower self-esteem than career women (Birnbaum, 1975). However, recent work finds no differences in self-esteem between homemakers and women who have both family and career roles (Erdwins & Mellinger, 1984). According to these comparisons, homemakers tend to have higher levels of affiliation and responsibility than do career women. Career women perceive that they have greater personal control over their environment than do homemakers. From the available data, it is difficult to judge whether these personality differences contributed to the selection of one life path over the other or involvement in the two different role configurations contributed to these variations.

What is the impact of the dual-career arrangement on men? A wife's success in the world of work may reduce a husband's sense of power. Men are especially uncomfortable if their wives are earning more money than they are. Some men find themselves ill prepared to assume the more direct responsibilities of child rearing in order to support their wives' involvement in the labor market. Men may very well miss the emotional support that traditionally has been provided by wives who were committed primarily to facilitating their husbands' careers (Douvan, 1982; Bell, 1983).

The picture of adaptation to the dual-career marriage is not a simple one. We cannot say that the women always benefit or that the men always suffer. In fact, there are many dual-career arrangements, each involving the negotiation of roles and responsibilities to meet the convergence of work and family needs. However, a major issue in coping with the dual-career pattern does seem to be the partners' capacity to revise some very basic sex-role expectations in regard to their own and their spouses' behavior. This is not a simple task. It touches on very deep emotional commitments to one's view of oneself as a man or a woman, a husband or a wife, and a mother or a father. It touches on the reality of one's commitments to work-related achievements and to fostering a loving, supportive marital relationship. There are dynamic tensions among the spouse, parent, and worker roles that are not readily integrated. At the same time, the dual-career lifestyle provides new opportunities for extending one's competence across many domains. It also provides opportunities for a new understanding of gender and gender relations within the family system.

The conflicts that are created by competing demands of work and family life highlight a central experience of middle adulthood. As a result of one's sense of responsibility and the interdependence of one's multiple roles, middle adults are under pressure to seek a productive balance among their various interests, relationships, and commitments. Conflict can be between multiple roles, as when a person is torn between using time to help a child with a school project and using that time to complete a project for the work setting. Conflict can be internal, as when a person has doubts about the value or purpose of the time being spent on a particular work-related task. Both at work and in the family, conflict and its resolution or nonresolution play a key role in stimulating individual and group development. In particular, the conflicts of middle adulthood provide the context for the expression of *caring*. How conflicts are handled—whether they are avoided, denied, resolved, escalated, or transformed—determines the extent to which one's intention to function as a caring person has its desired impact.

Summary

The developmental tasks of middle adulthood are extremely complex and require long-term persistence. Each task calls for a new level of conceptualization. The similarity among the marriage, household management, child-rearing, and career-management tasks lies in their investment in a social system. During middle adulthood, people gauge their self-worth in relation to their contributions to complex social units. The tasks of middle adulthood demand an expanded conceptual analysis of social systems and an ability to balance individual needs with system goals. Adults not only learn how to function effectively within larger groups; they also invest energy in the groups with whom they can most readily identify.

The Psychosocial Crisis: Generativity versus Stagnation

A new capacity for directing the course of action in one's own life and in the lives of others emerges during middle adulthood. The skills associated with the developmental tasks of middle adulthood, including the ability to make decisions, plan for the future, anticipate the needs of others, and conceptualize the developmental phases of the life span, allow adults to make a deliberate impact on the future. Adults begin to conceptualize the long-term consequences of their behavior. The psychosocial crisis of *generativity* versus *stagnation* can be understood as a pressure on the adult to be committed to improving the life conditions of future generations (Erikson, 1963). "Generativity . . . encompasses *procreativity, productivity,* and *creativity,* and thus the generation of new beings, as well as of new products and new ideas, including a kind of self-generation concerned with further identity development" (Erikson, 1982, p. 67). According to Erikson's observations, generativity is formed as a result of experiences of maintaining the world, nurturing and being concerned, and caring (Erikson & Kivnick, 1986).

The ego strength associated with the achievement of generativity is *care.* Care is a widening commitment to *take care of* the persons, the products, and the ideas one has learned *to care for.* All the strengths arising from earlier developments in the ascending order from infancy to young adulthood (hope and will, purpose and skill, fidelity and love) now prove, on closer study, to be essential for the generational task of cultivating strength in the next generation. For this is indeed the "store of human life" (Erikson, 1982, p. 67).

Generativity is a critical capacity for the survival of any society. At some point, adult members of the society must begin to feel an obligation to contribute their resources, skills, and creativity to improving the quality of life for the young. To some degree, this motive is aroused as one recognizes the inevitability of mortality. One will not always be around to direct the course of events. Therefore, one must make contributions to the society, on both personal and public levels, that will stand some chance of continuing after one's death.

The contributions may be monumental, as were Picasso's to the world of art and Freud's to the understanding of human psychology. However, they may also be more modest or less widely known, as are the many ways in which volunteers help maintain human service organizations. Adults are often asked to donate time, money, or skills to charitable groups. They serve as advisers, government leaders, religious leaders, and educators. In each of these roles, individuals have opportunities to extend the impact of their values and goals to others. Through their loving responses to their children, the care they take to perform their work at a high standard of excellence, and their expression of respect for the diverse people they encounter, adults model

The survival of every culture depends on the ability of adults to widen their circle of caring, by teaching and cultivating the next generation.

a capacity for generativity that promotes optimism and perseverance among younger generations. In Erikson's study of older adults, he and his co-workers found that "among most of our subjects, concern for their children dominates both their reflections on earlier life's guidance and nurturance and their current involvements in caring" (Erikson, Erikson & Kivnick, 1986, p. 75).

In contrast to generativity, the failure to meet the demands of middle adulthood results in stagnation. *Stagnation* suggests a lack of psychological movement or growth. Adults who devote their energy and skills to the sole end of self-aggrandizement and personal satisfaction are likely to have difficulty looking beyond their own needs or experiencing satisfaction in taking care of others. Adults who are unable to cope with the management of a household, the raising of children, or the management of a career are likely to feel a psychological sense of stagnation at the end of middle adulthood.

The experience of stagnation may differ for the narcissistic adult and the depressed adult. *Narcissistic* people may expend energy in accumulating wealth and material possessions. They relate to others in terms of how others can serve them. They may exist quite happily until the physical and psychological consequences of aging begin to make their impact. At that point, and continuing on toward old age, self-satisfaction is easily undermined by anxieties related to death. It is not uncommon for such persons to undergo some form of "conversion" after a serious illness or emotional crisis forces them to acknowledge the limitations of a totally self-involved lifestyle.

Depressed people who do not feel a sense of accomplishment during middle adulthood are unable to perceive themselves as having sufficient resources to make any contribution to their society. These people are likely to be very low in self-esteem, very doubtful about any opportunities for future improvement, and therefore unwilling to invest any energy in conceptualizing about future progress.

In an analysis of men at midlife, Farrell & Rosenberg (1981) provide some insight into stagnation. The case of Tony Williams illustrates how a life of unresolved stresses and disappointments coupled with a defensive denial result in a picture of increasing bankruptcy of personal and interpersonal meaning.

> *A number of midlife stresses have hit Tony in the past five years. They began with the death of his mother when Tony was 40. Tony tells of the death with the same apparent stoicism he showed throughout the evening. "When your time is up, you gotta go," he says. But he says that his father went into a prolonged depression, moping around watching television, having no energy for family activities.*
>
> *Then two friends from childhood died within a year. Tony says, "Better them than me." He doesn't seem to overtly mourn their loss, but he does appear to exaggerate his fatalistic willingness to accept fate as he reports on this period, insisting that he does not fear death.*
>
> *Over the years Tony had become active in the Knights of Columbus. He helped organize an annual Christmas party for retarded children, and told of how good it felt to stand by as the kids came up to sit on Santa's knee and receive their gifts. But during the past few years he has pulled away from this activity, claiming that younger men coming in are "messing up" what he helped to build. His final break with them came last year, when he ruptured a disc in his back while lifting a heavy barrel at work. He had to spend three weeks in the hospital and none of his friends came to visit him.*
>
> *This back injury marked a sharp turning point, evoking all the bitterness and depressive symptomatology kept in check after earlier life reversals and his mother's death. His medical treatment required that he stay home a month after returning from the hospital, but that was seven months ago. Tony's doctor tells him he is fine, but Tony has not returned to work because he ostensibly is trying to obtain workman's compensation for the injury and lost work time. His lawyer is still working on the case, and Tony fears that if he goes back to work he'll lose his case. So he stays at home, takes occasional walks, listens to police calls on a police radio, and watches television. His children have grown increasingly annoyed with him. "All he does is pick," says Mary. "He won't let Mom sit down to do a crossword puzzle. He won't let me sew because it interferes with his radio. And if you stay around the house, he starts reading stories out of the newspaper to you. So me and my brother, we leave the house."**

Middle adulthood extends over many years. During this stage, people encounter many complex challenges for which they may not be fully prepared. Promotion to an administrative position, the need to care for an aging parent, and the negotiation of a divorce are examples. At many points adults doubt their ability to move ahead, achieve their goals, or make meaningful contributions. Feelings of stagnation surge temporarily into dominance. People may recognize that unless they redefine their situations or take some new risks, the quality of their lives will deteriorate. They face the possibility of feeling outdated by new technology, outmoded by new lifestyles,

---

*Excerpted from *Men at Midlife,* Michael P. Farrell and Stanley D. Rosenberg (Auburn House Pub. Co., an imprint of Greenwood Publishing Group, Inc., Westport, CT, 1981), pp. 102–103. Copyright © 1981 by Auburn House Publishing Company. Reproduced with permission.

Pablo Picasso, *Guernica*, 1937. Without a sense of generativity, no society can survive. Guernica is an expression of Picasso's outrage at Franco and fascism. Everything in this painting cries out in pain.

overburdened by role demands, or alienated from meaningful social contacts. At these moments of crisis, adults can become entangled in a process of self-protection and withdrawal that results in permanent stagnation. However, they can also muster new resources and a new perspective that will permit continuing growth and the expansion of generativity.

The Central Process: Person-Environment Interaction and Creativity

We have identified two aspects of the central process that lead to the development of generativity in middle adulthood. The first is the facilitative interaction between the individual and the social environment. The social environment includes the family, the work setting, the neighborhood, and the larger political community. To a great extent, this environment provides a person's basis of experience. Day-to-day interactions, the expectations for behavior, the available resources, and the social supports that are necessary for the growth of self-confidence are elements of the social environment.

Person-Environment Interaction

Social environments vary in their organization. Families differ not only in the styles of their organization but in size, relationships with other social groups, and internal dynamics. The dual-career family faces issues that make it distinct from the single-earner family in many important respects. Work organizations differ markedly in their demands on the individual, the nature of the work, the degree of competitiveness, the amount of stress, the rationality of the decision makers, the political orientation, and the content of the reward structure (financial compensation, prestige, fringe benefits, and so on). Neighborhoods differ in the quality of the informal social norms, in ethnic, political, or religious orientation, in the age stratification of residents, and in residents' income levels. Communities differ in their politics, services, ideals, and values and in their degree of openness toward newcomers or members of nondominant groups. Many more examples of differences in each of these environmental social structures could certainly be generated. An enormous array of environmental demands impinge on an individual throughout adult life.

Successful personality growth depends upon the interaction between a person's needs, skills, and interpersonal style and the demands of the environments to which the person responds. The concept of interaction suggests a potential for reciprocal influence between individuals and settings. The structure and demands of settings can alter a person's behavior, values, goals, and sense of self-worth. People also have an impact on the settings in which they participate. Adults do more than maintain or respond to their environment; they shape it (Endler, 1983). People play their roles to allow for the expression of their individual styles. They define their roles for themselves as well as having their roles defined by others. Parents as well as office workers live within structures of expectations. In their own ways of interpreting, denying, or otherwise responding to these expectations, adults present an increasingly more independent and authentic "me" if they are moving toward the stabilization of ego identity. If not, they may be more responsive to the expectations of others than is healthy for continued emergence of a stable identity.

The particular achievement of middle adulthood is to identify those domains in which one has opportunities to influence the quality of the social environment so that it becomes more hospitable, humane, nurturant, or supportive of one's own visions for the future. Caring will expand in different domains for different people, but the pressures always lead to having the welfare of people and enduring things (including ideas) deeply at heart. There is an action component to this caring, in that people work to care for what they can. When there is a good fit between personal needs and the expression of caring and the environment's needs and ability to increase in nurturance, a person will be able, over the years, to develop a sense of generativity.

Individuals have some degree of choice in their selection of social environment. They can, for example, decide whom they will marry, whether or not to have children, which occupation they will follow, and where they will live. To the degree that they have a choice in these matters, they will be able to influence the kinds of transactions that occur between their personality and their social milieu. This requires that they understand themselves and that they be able to conceptualize the nature of the other people and the social institutions that are part of their social environment.

The latter type of thinking is rather difficult for most people. It requires a complex understanding of social settings and some idea of the types of demands that such environments are likely to make. It also requires the ability to speculate about the future. It is one thing to fall in love with someone and decide to marry. It is quite another to try to foresee what it would be like to live with that person for 20 or more years. It is also possible to select a particular occupation and work setting only to discover that a change of boss or a particular fluctuation in the business cycle makes that decision an uncomfortable one.

Although some settings are a matter of choice, many others are the result of chance. Some settings can be abandoned or altered if they do not meet the individual's needs. Other settings are permanent and difficult to alter. If one is in an unsuitable setting, one must be willing to leave it, if that is possible, or to discover some way to influence the setting so that it will meet one's needs more adequately. Some people, however, find themselves in social settings that can be neither abandoned nor altered. For example, a group of workers in Michigan were trained for employment in an automotive plant. When the economy slumped, they were laid off. They did not have enough money saved to move to another town; there were no new jobs; and they did not have the resources or the incentive needed to retrain for other types of employment. When one is forced to remain in social settings that are contrary to one's needs, the possibility of developing generativity is seriously diminished. If one is unable to experience a personal sense of effectiveness in home, work, or community, then one is unlikely to feel capable of contributing to future growth in these spheres.

Fortunately, the social environment is so multifaceted that individuals are likely to experience satisfaction in their participation in at least one special setting even if they feel dissatisfaction in others. Under these conditions, individuals can compensate for their inability to be creative in some settings by placing increased effort and investment in those in which they can more easily attain satisfaction. This may require that individuals reorder their priorities so that frustration in one setting will in fact be less of a thorn in light of accomplishments made in another. If one has little opportunity to find satisfaction in work, for example, one must begin to reevaluate the importance of contributions to one's family, religion, or community.

Creativity

The second part of the central process in the establishment of generativity is personal creativity. Although creativity has been defined in many ways, for our purposes we will consider it as the willingness to abandon old forms or patterns of doing things in favor of new ways. This requires the generation, evaluation, and implementation of new ideas. Within this definition we can include great creative acts that touch the lives of many people as well as a kind of individual creative activity that touches the lives of a few. The importance of a creative response, no matter how small, is that it redefines the world and opens the door to new possibilities (Taylor, 1975; Arieti, 1976). Creativity provides an outlet for caring for something that has not yet been defined or experienced.

Through creative effort, adults impose a new perspective on the organization, expression, or formulation of ideas. Creative adults are no longer dominated by social forces but are able to direct the course of events themselves. These individuals are at a point in their development at which their own creative responses can become a source of influence on a great many others. Through the process of creative problem solving, adults can plan to reshape the social environment in order to meet both personal and social needs more satisfactorily. Throughout middle adulthood, adults

Table 12.3 Conditions That Foster Creativity	
Aloneness	Being alone allows the person to make contact with the self and be open to new kinds of inspiration.
Inactivity	Periods of time are needed to focus on inner resources and to be removed from the constraints of routine activities.
Daydreaming	Allows exploration of one's fantasy life and venturing into new avenues for growth.
Free thinking	Allows the mind to wander in any direction without restriction and permits the similarities among remote topics or concepts to emerge.
State of readiness to catch similarities	One must practice recognizing similarities and resemblances across perceptual or cognitive domains.
Gullibility	A willingness to suspend judgment allows one to be open to possibilities without treating them as nonsense.
Remembering and replaying past traumatic conflicts	Conflict can be transformed into more stable creative products.
Alertness	A state of awareness that permits the person to grasp the relevance of seemingly insignificant similarities.
Discipline	A devotion to the techniques, logic, and repetition that permit creative ideas to be realized.

Source: Adapted from S. Arieti, *Creativity: The Magic Synthesis* (New York: Basic Books, 1976), pp. 372–379.

are faced with situations in family, child rearing, and work settings that provide stimuli for creative problem solving. In their efforts to take into account the requirements of the social setting and to be productive in it, people must develop creative plans. They must also attempt to carry out those plans, a task that itself may require further creativity. The essence of creative problem solving is the formulation of a new plan and the ability to translate it into reality.

Fostering creativity during middle adulthood requires some deliberate attention. Given one's embeddedness in many demanding social roles, it is often difficult to step aside and view one's situation from a fresh perspective. Arieti (1976) has recommended nine conditions that foster creativity. They are listed in Table 12.3. In this list you will notice a need to engage in somewhat opposing processes, such as inactivity and alertness. One must strive to be open to the flood of inner and outer experiences and step away from trying to maintain control over all aspects of the environment. At the same time, one must be alert to insights into the relevance of certain experiences and willing to transform those insights into action.

From the outset, the creative process involves some risk. People must give up some old ways of doing things that may have been certain to work in order to try new forms. In this process, people must anticipate the possibility that their efforts will fail. For some people, the fear of failure may be so great that creative solutions are never realized. For them, the sense of generativity will be blocked by a fear of the unknown or by an inability to violate conventional norms for behavior.

For those who are not inhibited by the fear of failure, the repeated efforts to generate creative solutions eventually result in the formulation of a philosophy of life. This philosophy conceptualizes the psychological needs of people, the ideals toward

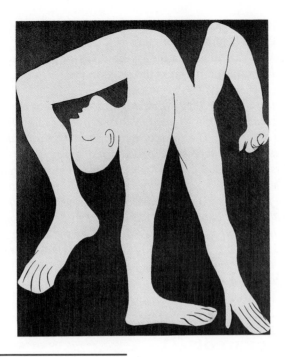

Pablo Picasso, *Acrobat,* 1930. Creative acts redefine the world and open the door to new possibilities. This provocative, graceful, yet fantastical rendering of the human form is an example of such a redefinition.

which individuals and groups strive, and the impact of social settings on the functioning of individuals as well as the direction of human development into the future. Through risk taking, occasional failure, and a predominance of successful creative efforts, adults achieve a sense of what they believe in and of what gives meaning to life. With this remarkable integration of experience and information, people enter later adulthood.

Summary

The crisis of generativity versus stagnation is a crisis in meaningfulness. What can one do during the middle adult years that will make a difference? How can a person in this institutionalized, bureaucratized, compartmentalized society have an impact on the quality of life? These questions highlight both the pressing desire to serve the community and the potentially overwhelming sense that no act can really alter the course of events.

We have stressed the themes of person-environment interaction and creativity as the means for successful resolution of this crisis. There is an old story about three men who were observed laying bricks for the wall of a church. When asked what they were doing, the first man said he was laying bricks, the second said he was building a wall, and the third said he was building a church. During middle adulthood, one must arrive at a philosophy of life that will impart significance to daily activities. One part of generativity lies in the actual attainment of creative goals. The other part lies in the perspective one brings to one's lifework.

Erikson suggests that the outcome of the crisis of generativity versus stagnation has implications for adults at the next life stage in the form of *grand-generativity:*

> *The reconciling of generativity and stagnation involves the elder in expressing a "grand-generativity" that is somehow beyond middle age's direct responsibility for maintaining the world. The roles of aging parent, grandparent, old friend, consultant, adviser, and mentor all provide the aging adult with essential social opportunities to experience grand-generativity in current relationships with people of all ages. In these relationships, the individual seeks to integrate outward-looking care for others with inward-looking concern for self. As a complement to caring for others, the elder is also challenged to accept from others that caring which is required, and to do so in a way that is itself caring. In the context of the generational cycle, it is incumbent upon the aged to enhance feelings of generativity in their care givers from the younger generations.*   [Erikson, Erikson & Kivnick, 1986, pp. 74–75]

☐ Applied Topic: Adults and Their Aging Parents

We tend to think about generativity in middle adulthood as a commitment to future generations. Another test of one's capacity for caring, however, comes in the form of commitment to one's aging parents. As one ages from 30 to 50, one's parents may age from 60 to 80. The number of noninstitutionalized adults over the age of 65 increased from 19 million in 1970 to almost 30 million in 1987. The number of adults over the age of 85 was close to 3 million, an increase of 100% since 1970 (U.S. Bureau of the Census, 1989). It is becoming increasingly likely that middle adults will confront the challenge of meeting the needs of their own aging parents. It is also increasingly possible that their aging parents will survive through a period of vigorous and independent later adulthood into a period of frail and vulnerable old age.

What is the nature of filial obligation as it is viewed from the perspectives of adult children and of their aging parents? Who provides what kinds of help? What characterizes optimal parent-child relationships during this phase of life?

What Is Filial Obligation?

What can aging parents expect of their adult children? How do adult children define their responsibilities for their parents? In an analysis of three generations of women, it was clear that each cohort perceived a strong sense of filial obligation. Both sons and daughters endorse a responsibility to care for their aging parents (Brody, Johnsen & Fulcomer, 1984; Roff & Klemmack, 1986). In one study of filial obligation, 144 elderly parents and their adult children were asked to respond to 16 items that could be viewed as elements of filial obligation. The items are listed in Table 12.4, along with the percentage of each group that endorsed them. Parents and adult children clearly

Table 12.4 Perceptions of Filial Responsibility by Adult Children and Their Parents (percent)

Item	Children	Parents
Help understand resources	99.3%	97.2%
Give emotional support	97.2	95.7
Talk over matters of importance	96.5	98.6
Make room in home in emergency*	94.4	73.0
Sacrifice personal freedom*	93.7	81.0
Care when sick*	92.4	64.3
Be together on special occasions	86.0	86.7
Give financial help*	84.6	41.1
Give parents advice	84.0	88.7
Adjust family schedule to help*	80.6	57.4
Feel responsible for parent**	78.2	66.4
Adjust work schedule to help*	63.2	42.1
Parent should live with child*	60.8	36.7
Visit once a week	51.4	55.6
Live close to parent	32.2	25.7
Write once a week	30.8	39.4

Note: Ranking reflects percent of respondents who "strongly agreed" or "agreed" with each item.

*Fisher's Exact Test indicated significant differences in proportion of endorsement for children and parents at *$p < .001$ or **$p < .05$.

Source: R. R. Harmon and R. Blieszner, "Filial Responsibility Expectations Among Adult Child–Older Parent Pairs," *Journal of Gerontology: Psychological Sciences, 45* (1990), p. 111. Reprinted by permission of the publisher.

agree on the top three items: helping to understand resources, giving emotional support, and talking over matters of importance. They also agree that children ought not to be expected to live near the parent, write weekly, or visit weekly. Items that are starred indicate a significant difference in endorsement by the two groups. In general, children have a greater sense of obligation than their parents expect of them. Parents do not seem to be comfortable with some forms of help, such as accepting financial assistance, having their children revise their work schedules in order to provide help, and living in their child's home (Hamon & Blieszner, 1990).

Who Provides Help?

The evidence suggests that daughters assume much more of the responsibility for their aging parents than sons (Finley, 1989). This involvement is one more element of the basic "kinkeeping" tasks that have been a traditional element in women's socialization. Daughters are more likely than sons to provide care for their aging parents even when the women are employed. Women are more likely to provide the direct care, such as bathing, dressing, and walking with a parent, as well as emotional support, such as listening, helping the parent deal with depression, and helping the parent feel important and loved. Sons and daughters are about equally likely to assist in some of the tasks involving relations with health and human service organizations, scheduling medical checkups, and reviewing insurance and other financial matters.

What Factors Promote an Optimal Relationship Between Adults and Their Aging Parents?

The norms of independence and self-sufficiency are very strong among the current aging population. Many older adults state that they do not need assistance from their adult children. The need for assistance increases as the parents' health fails and their financial resources dwindle. Adult children view themselves as the people who are primarily responsible for meeting their parents' needs. Most, however, do not expect to have to meet a great variety of such needs (Cicirelli, 1981). There is some evidence that when obligation to help and need for assistance are both great, older people derive less satisfaction from the parent-child relationship. Morale seems to be highest among older adults who do not need to rely on their children (Wood & Robertson, 1978). There appears to be a strong cultural norm that makes a parent's neediness difficult to express and respond to.

In adulthood, the parent-child relationship is one of choice. Children feel a moral obligation to reciprocate the care and devotion that their parents extended to them when they were young. In addition, a moral obligation to "honor thy father and thy mother" may have been incorporated into the children's religious training. However, the goal of child rearing in this society generally includes the value of promoting the offspring's independence. This means that children are encouraged to leave home, establish residences of their own, and be economically self-sufficient. After children leave home, many adult parents experience a positive sense of role transition. They enjoy focusing their time and attention on each other or on new activities and relationships. The task of reestablishing a close parent-child relationship—one that may involve sharing a household or maintaining frequent contact and interdependence—does not come easily to either the children or the parents. Success in this relationship is closely related to the affection that children continue to hold for their parents during the years in which they have lived relatively independent adult lives (Quinn, 1983).

As adult children struggle to work out the nature of their responsibilities to their parents and the means for meeting those obligations effectively, they must weigh them against their commitments to their parental, marital, and work roles. They must also resist tendencies to treat their parents like children. They may have feelings of sadness and loss from having watched a loved one lose his or her vitality in the last years of life. In some cases, the adult children are not young themselves. They may be experiencing chronic illness, reduced strength or endurance, or diminished financial resources. A woman of 60 who works full-time may not have the strength or the financial resources to meet all the needs of her frail 85-year-old mother.

One of the major transitions that evokes requests for help from children is widowhood. Providing help and emotional support to the surviving parent during this period of bereavement gives adult children an avenue for working through their own grief. Helping the widowed parent is a way of identifying with the deceased parent. Spending time with the surviving parent enables adult children to reduce their own sense of loss while meeting that parent's need for comfort (Lopata, 1979; O'Bryant, 1987).

Pablo Picasso, *Woman with a Mirror,* 1950. It is not unusual for an adult daughter to have primary responsibility for the care of her aging, widowed mother. The affection the two held for each other during earlier years will influence the quality of their parent-child relationship in adulthood.

Adult children are often in a position to help their parents by coordinating services and interacting with various agencies. Many adults feel unprepared for this aspect of the caring relationship (Sarason, 1980). They are not comfortable dealing with hospitals, insurance agencies, social service agencies, or residential treatment facilities. However, many aging adults depend on the services of these structured organizations. Middle adults who know the individual needs of their parents are among the best people to interpret those needs for service providers. In addition, through such contacts middle adults have the opportunity to modify agencies in order to make them more effective for future generations of aging adults.

Despite the difficulties in achieving a satisfying adult child–aging parent relationship, there is no question that such a relationship will continue to be encountered by many middle adults. There are some important possibilities for expressing generativity in this relationship. The manner in which adults respond to their parents provides a model for their own children. By dealing in a sensitive and caring way with their aging parents, adult children provide a pattern of responsiveness that can be a guide to their own children as the latter reach later adulthood.

Caring for aging parents brings middle adults face to face with the eventuality of their own aging and death. For many adults, this may be very anxiety provoking. Middle adults are generally not ready to die. They are in the midst of complex role demands. Many others depend on their strength and competence. However, through interaction with their aging parents they can perceive a time in life when they will be more prepared to accept death. By making a commitment to their aging parents, they may have less fear about feeling abandoned or despised in their own later years.

☐ Chapter Summary

During the middle adult years, people have an opportunity to make significant contributions to their culture. Through work, home, and child rearing, people express their own value orientations, moral codes, temperaments, and skills. They grow more sensitive to the multiple needs of those around them. They also grow more skillful at influencing the social environment.

The psychological crisis of the middle adult years is really a moral crisis of commitment to a better way of life. The society must encourage adults to care for others besides themselves. The egocentrism of toddlerhood, early school age, and adolescence must eventually come to an end if the social group is to survive. In the same way that intimacy (giving oneself to another) requires identity, generativity (giving oneself to the next generation) requires love of specific others. The interpersonal sources of satisfaction that exist during middle adulthood are the primary forces propelling people toward a generative approach to society as a whole.

References

Adams, B. (1986). *The family: A sociological interpretation* (4th ed.). San Diego: Harcourt Brace Jovanovich.

Alwin, D. F. (1984). Living alone. *ISR Newsletter, 12,* 3–4.

Alwin, D. F., Converse, P. E., & Martin, S. S. (1985). Living arrangements and social integration. *Journal of Marriage and the Family, 47,* 319–334.

Aquilino, W. S. (1990). Likelihood of parent-adult child coresidence. *Journal of Marriage and the Family, 52,* 405–419.

Araji, S. K. (1977). Husbands' and wives' attitude-behavior congruence on family roles. *Journal of Marriage and the Family, 39,* 309–320.

Arbeiter, S. (1979). Mid-life career change: A concept in search of reality. *AAHE Bulletin, 32, 1,* 11–13, 16.

Argyle, M. (1972). *The social psychology of work.* Harmondsworth: Penguin.

Arieti, S. (1976). *Creativity: The magic synthesis.* New York: Basic Books.

Bates, G. W. (1981). On the nature of the hot flash. *Clinical Obstetrics and Gynecology, 24,* 231.

Bell, R. R. (1983). *Marriage and family interaction* (6th ed.). Homewood, Ill.: Dorsey.

Birnbaum, L. A. (1975). Life patterns and self-esteem in gifted family-oriented and career-committed women. In M. T. S. Mednick, S. S. Tangri, & L. W. Hoffman (eds.), *Women and achievement: Social and motivational analyses.* New York: Halsted.

Blechman, E. A. (1977). Behavior specialization and conflict in one-parent families. Paper presented at the annual convention of the American Psychological Association, San Francisco.

Braginsky, D. D., & Braginsky, B. M. (1975). Surplus people: Their lost faith in self and system. *Psychology Today,* August, 68–72.

Brim, O. G., & Ryff, C. D. (1980). On the properties of life events. In P. B. Baltes & O. G. Brim (eds.), *Life-span development and behavior* (vol. 3, pp. 368–388). New York: Academic Press.

Brody, E. M., Johnsen, P. T., & Fulcomer, M. C. (1984). What should adult children do for elderly parents? Opinions and preferences of three generations of women. *Journal of Gerontology, 39,* 736–746.

Cain, P. S., & Treiman, D. J. (1981). The DOT as a source of occupational data. *American Sociological Review, 46,* 253–278.

Cicirelli, V. G. (1981). *Helping elderly parents: The role of adult children.* Boston: Auburn House.

Clark, R. A., Nye, F. I., & Gecas, V. (1978). Husbands' work involvement and marital role performance. *Journal of Marriage and the Family, 40,* 9–21.

Coady, S. S. (1982). Correlates of maternal satisfaction among older first time mothers. Ph.D. dissertation, Ohio State University, Columbus.

Cole, C. L., & Cole, A. L. (1985). Husbands and wives should have an equal share in making the marriage work. In H. Feldman & M. Feldman (eds.), *Current controversies in marriage and family* (pp. 131–141). Newbury Park, Calif.: Sage.

Douglas, S. P., & Wind, Y. (1978). Examining family role and authority patterns: Two methodological issues. *Journal of Marriage and the Family, 40,* 35–47.

Douvan, E. (1982). Changing roles: Work, marriage, and parenthood. *Michigan Alumnus,* October, 4–7.

Duvall, E. M. (1977). *Family development* (5th ed.). Philadelphia: Lippincott.

Eldridge, N. S., & Gilbert, L. A. (1990). Correlates of relationship satisfaction in lesbian couples. *Psychology of Women Quarterly, 14,* 43–62.

Endler, N. S. (1983). Interactionism: A personality model but not yet a theory. In M. M. Page (ed.), *Nebraska Symposium on Motivation, 1982* (pp. 155–200). Lincoln: University of Nebraska Press.

Erdwins, C. J., & Mellinger, J. C. (1984). Midlife women: Relation of age and role to personality. *Journal of Personality and Social Psychology, 47,* 390–395.

Erikson, E. H. (1963). *Childhood and society* (2nd ed.). New York: Norton.

Erikson, E. H. (1982). *The life cycle completed.* New York: Norton.

Erikson, E. H., Erikson, J. M., & Kivnick, H. Q. (1986). *Vital involvement in old age.* New York: Norton.

Farrell, M. P., & Rosenberg, S. D. (1981). *Men at midlife.* Boston: Auburn House.

Finley, N. J. (1989). Gender differences in caregiving for elderly parents. *Journal of Marriage and the Family, 51,* 79–86.

Fischer, L. R. (1983). Mothers and mothers-in-law. *Journal of Marriage and the Family, 45,* 187–192.

Flint, M. (1976). Cross-cultural factors that affect age of menopause. In P. A. Van Keep, R. B. Greenblatt, & M. Albeaux-Fernet (eds.), *Consensus on menopause research.* Baltimore: University Park Press.

Gibbs, N. R. (1988). Begging: To give or not to give. *Time,* September 5, pp. 68–74.

Glick, P. C. (1977). Updating the life cycle of the family. *Journal of Marriage and the Family, 39,* 5–13.

Glick, P. C. (1979). Future American families. *Washington COFO Memo, 2,* 2–5.

Godwin, D. D., & Scanzoni, J. (1989). Couple consensus during marital joint decision-making. *Journal of Marriage and the Family, 51,* 943–956.

Haan, N. (1981). Common dimensions of personality development: Early adolescence to mid-life. In D. H. Eichorn, J. A. Clausen, N. Haan, M. P. Hanzik, & P. H. Mussen (eds.), *Present and past in middle life* (pp. 117–151). New York: Academic Press.

Halford, W. K., Hahlweg, K., & Dunne, M. (1990). Cross-cultural study of marital communication and marital distress. *Journal of Marriage and the Family, 52,* 487–500.

Hammond, C. B., & Maxson, W. S. (1986). Estrogen replacement therapy. *Clinical Obstetrics and Gynecology, 29,* 407–430.

Hamon, R. R., & Blieszner, R. (1990). Filial responsibility expectations among adult child–older parent pairs. *Journal of Gerontology: Psychological Sciences, 45,* P110–P112.

Harry, J. (1983). Gay male and lesbian relationships. In E. D. Macklin & R. Rubin (eds.), *Contemporary family forms and alternative lifestyles: Handbook on research and theory.* Newbury Park, Calif.: Sage.

Heckman, N. A., Bryson, R., & Bryson, J. B. (1977). Problems of professional couples: A content analysis. *Journal of Marriage and the Family, 39,* 323–330.

Hill, R. (1965). Decision making and the family life cycle. In E. Shanas & G. Streib (eds.), *Social structure and the family: Generational relations.* Englewood Cliffs, N.J.: Prentice-Hall.

Hof, L., & Miller, W. R. (1981). *Marriage enrichment: Philosophy, process, and program.* Bowie, Md.: R. J. Brady.

Hoffman, L. W., & Manis, J. D. (1978). Influences of children on marital interaction and parental satisfactions and dissatisfactions. In R. M. Lerner & G. B. Spanier (eds.), *Child influences on marital and family interaction.* New York: Academic Press.

Holland, J. L. (1985). *Making vocational choices* (2nd ed.). Englewood Cliffs, N.J.: Prentice-Hall.

Houseknecht, S. K., & Macke, A. S. (1981). Combining marriage and career: The marital adjustment of professional women. *Journal of Marriage and the Family, 43,* 651–661.

Jacobson, N. S., Waldron, H., & Moore, D. (1980). Toward a behavioral profile of marital distress. *Journal of Consulting and Clinical Psychology, 48,* 696–703.

Jenkins, L. E. (1989). The black family and academic achievement. In G. L. Berry & J. K. Asamen (eds.), *Black students* (pp. 138–152). Newbury Park, Calif.: Sage.

Kalleberg, A. L., & Rosenfeld, R. A. (1990). Work in the family and in the labor market. *Journal of Marriage and the Family, 52,* 331–346.

Kanter, R. M. (1989). The new managerial work. *Harvard Business Review, 67,* 85–92.

Katz, D., & Kahn, R. L. (1978). *The social psychology of organizations* (2nd ed.). New York: Wiley.

Kipnis, D., Schmidt, S. M., & Wilkinson, I. (1980). Intraorganizational influence tactics: Explorations in getting one's way. *Journal of Applied Psychology, 65,* 440–452.

Knox, D., & Wilson, K. (1978). The differences between having one and two children. *Family Coordinator, 27,* 23–25.

Kohn, M. L. (1980). Job complexity and adult personality. In N. J. Smelser & E. H. Erikson (eds.), *Themes of work and love in adulthood* (pp. 193–210). Cambridge, Mass.: Harvard University Press.

Landers, S. (1989a). Homeless mentally ill gain research push. *American Psychological Association Monitor, 20,* (April), 33.

Landers, S. (1989b). Homeless children lose childhood. *American Psychological Association Monitor, 20,* (December), 1.

Leigh, G. K. (1982). Kinship interaction over the family life span. *Journal of Marriage and the Family, 44,* 197–208.

Levinger, G. (1983). Development and change. In H. H. Kelley et al. (eds.), *Close relationships* (pp. 315–359). New York: W. H. Freeman.

Lewis, R. A., Kozac, E. B., Milardo, R. M., & Grosnick, W. A. (1981). Commitment in same-sex love relationships. *Alternative Lifestyles, 4,* 22–42.

Lopata, Helena Z. (1979). *Women as widows: Support systems.* New York: Elsevier.

Mace, D. R. (1982). *Close companions.* New York: Continuum.

Macklin, E. D. (1987). Nontraditional family forms. In M. B. Sussman and S. K. Steinmetz (eds.), *Handbook of marriage and the family* (pp. 317–353). New York: Plenum.

Marks, S. R. (1989). Toward a systems theory of marital quality. *Journal of Marriage and the Family, 51,* 15–26.

Mattessich, P., & Hill, R. (1987). Life cycle and family development. In M. B. Sussman and S. K. Steinmetz (eds.), *Handbook of marriage and the family* (pp. 437–469). New York: Plenum.

McKinlay, J. B., McKinlay, S. M., & Brambilla, D. J. (1987). Health status and utilization behavior associated with menopause. *American Journal of Epidemiology, 125,* 110–121.

McLanahan, S., & Adams, J. (1987). Parenthood and psychological well-being. In R. Turner and J. Short (eds.), *Annual Review of Sociology* (vol. 13). Palo Alto, Calif.: Annual Reviews.

McLanahan, S., & Booth, K. (1989). Mother-only families: Problems, prospects, and politics. *Journal of Marriage and the Family, 51,* 557–580.

Miller, J., Schooler, C., Kohn, M. L., & Miller, K. A. (1979). Women and work: The psychological effects of occupational conditions. *American Journal of Sociology, 85,* 66–94.

Morokoff, P. J. (1988). Sexuality in perimenopausal and postmenopausal women. *Psychology of Women Quarterly, 12,* 489–511.

Mullan, J. (1981). Parental distress and marital happiness: The transition to the empty nest. Ph.D. dissertation, University of Chicago.

Mullan, J. (1983). The timing of the transition to the empty nest and changes in family role distress. Paper presented at the annual meeting of the Gerontological Society of America.

Neugarten, B. L., Wood, V., Kraines, R. J., & Loomis, B. (1963). Women's attitudes toward the menopause. *Vita Humana, 6,* 140–151.

Newman, B. M. (1989). The changing nature of the parent-adolescent relationship from early to late adolescence. *Adolescence, 24,* 916–924.

Newman, B. M., & Coady, S. S. (1982). Perceptions of the mother role among first-time mothers of different ages. Paper presented at the annual Michigan Women's Studies Conference, Ann Arbor.

Newman, P. R., & Newman, B. M. (1988). Parenthood and adult development. In R. Palkovitz & M. B. Sussman (eds.), *Transitions to Parenthood, Marriage and Family Review, 12,* 313–337.

Nock, S. L. (1979). The family life cycle: Empirical or conceptual tool? *Journal of Marriage and the Family, 41,* 15–26.

Nye, I. (1976). *Role structure and analysis of the family.* Newbury Park, Calif.: Sage.

O'Bryant, S. L. (1987). Attachment to home and support systems of older widows in Columbus, Ohio. In H. Z. Lopata (ed.), *Widows* (vol. 2). Durham, N.C.: Duke University Press.

Peplau, L. A., & Amaro, H. (1982). Understanding lesbian relationships. In W. Paul & J. D. Weinrich (eds.), *Homosexuality.* Newbury Park, Calif.: Sage.

Pines, A., & Kafry, D. (1977). Burnout and life tedium in three generations of professional women. Paper presented at the annual convention of the American Psychological Association, San Francisco.

Piotrkowski, C. S., Rapoport, R. N., & Rapoport, R. (1987). Families and work. In M. B. Sussman & S. K. Steinmetz (eds.), *Handbook of marriage and the family* (pp. 251–283). New York: Plenum.

Pleck, J. H., Staines, G. L., & Lang, L. (1980). Conflicts between work and family life. *Monthly Labor Review,* March, 29–32.

Quinn, W. H. (1983). Personal and family adjustment in later life. *Journal of Marriage and the Family, 45,* 57–73.

Rands, M., Levinger, G., & Mellinger, G. (1981). Patterns of conflict resolution and marital satisfaction. *Journal of Family Issues, 2,* 297–321.

Renshaw, J. R. (1976). An exploration of the dynamics of the overlapping worlds of work and family. *Family Process,* March.

Roberts, L. J., & Krokoff, L. J. (1990). Withdrawal, hostility, and displeasure in marriage. *Journal of Marriage and the Family, 52,* 95–105.

Rodgers, F. A., & Rodgers, C. (1989). Business and the facts of family life. *Harvard Business Review, 67,* 121–129.

Roff, L. L., & Klemmack, D. L. (1986). Norms for employed daughters' and sons' behavior toward frail older parents. *Sex Roles, 14,* 363–368.

Rogler, L. H., & Procidano, M. E. (1989). Heterogamy and marital quality in Puerto Rican families. *Journal of Marriage and the Family, 51,* 363–372.

Rossi, A. S. (1980). Aging and parenthood in the middle years. In P. B. Baltes & O. G. Brim (eds.), *Life-span development and behavior* (vol. 3). New York: Academic Press.

Rubin, L. B. (1976). *Worlds of pain: Life in the working-class family.* New York: Basic Books.

Rubin, L. B. (1980). The empty nest: Beginning or ending? In L. A. Bond & J. C. Rosen (eds.), *Competence and coping during adulthood* (pp. 309–331). Hanover, N.H.: University Press of New England.

Ryan, R. M., & Lynch, J. H. (1989). Emotional autonomy versus detachment: Revisiting the vicissitudes of adolescence and young adulthood. *Child Development, 60,* 340–356.

Salamon, S. (1977). Family bounds and friendship bonds: Japan and West Germany. *Journal of Marriage and the Family, 39,* 807–820.

Sarason, S. B. (1980). Individual psychology: An obstacle to comprehending adulthood. In L. A. Bond & J. C. Rosen (eds.), *Competence and coping during adulthood* (pp. 6–27). Hanover, N.H.: University Press of New England.

Sexton, C. S., & Perlman, D. S. (1989). Careers, gender roles, and perceived equity as factors in marital power. *Journal of Marriage and the Family, 51,* 933–941.

Spanier, G. B., Sauer, W., & Larzelere, R. (1979). An empirical evaluation of the family life cycle. *Journal of Marriage and the Family, 41,* 27–38.

Taylor, I. A. (1975). An emerging view of creative actions. In I. A. Taylor & J. W. Getzels (eds.), *Perspectives in creativity.* Chicago: Aldine-Atherton.

Tiedje, L. B., Wortman, C. B., Downey, G., Emmons, C., Biernat, M., & Lang, E. (1990). Role compatibility in women with multiple roles. *Journal of Marriage and the Family, 52,* 63–72.

U.S. Bureau of the Census (1989). *Statistical abstract of the United States, 1988.* Washington, D.C.: U.S. Government Printing Office.

Voydanoff, P. (1988). Work roles, family structure, and work/family conflict. *Journal of Marriage and the Family, 50,* 749–761.

Vuchinich, S. (1987). Starting and stopping spontaneous family conflicts. *Journal of Marriage and the Family, 49,* 591–601.

Wilensky, H. L. (1961). Orderly careers and social participation: The impact of work history on social integration in the middle class. *American Sociological Review, 26,* 521–539.

Wood, V., & Robertson, J. F. (1978). Friendship and kinship interaction: Differential effect on the morale of the elderly. *Journal of Marriage and the Family, 40,* 367–375.

Zeits, C. R., & Prince, R. M. (1982). Child effects on parents. In B. B. Wolman (ed.), *Handbook of developmental psychology* (pp. 751–770). Englewood Cliffs, N.J.: Prentice-Hall.

Chapter Thirteen

The integrating theme of later adulthood is the search for personal meaning. The love of peace became an urgent force in Picasso's personal philosophy during the 1940s.

Later Adulthood (60 to 75 Years)

For people born in 1987 in the United States, the life expectancy was 71.5 years for males and 78.3 for females (U.S. Bureau of the Census, 1989). The life expectancy of people born in 1920 was about 54 years. Major improvements in hygiene, nutrition, and medical technology have allowed more people to survive infancy and more to survive the period from 40 to 60. Thus more people actually experience a vigorous later adulthood today than was the case 60 years ago.

A discussion of aging in America must acknowledge the changing sex composition of the population at older ages. In 1985, 55% of those 65 to 69 years old were women; 61% of those 75 to 79 years old were women. This gender difference in longevity is observed in virtually all countries of the world, but the differences are accentuated in the developed countries (U.S. Bureau of the Census, 1987). The imbalance in the sex composition is much more noticeable today than it was 50 years ago, when there were just about as many men as women in the over-65 category (U.S. Bureau of the Census, 1983).

The curves in Figure 13.1 show the survival pattern for women born in 1900, 1960, and 1980. You can see that major gains in survival all across the life span were made from 1900 to 1960. However, the gains from 1960 and 1980 were primarily in the years after age 60. The three curves also include a life endurance estimate, Ω. This is the age to which one person in 100,000 can expect to survive. Life endurance for women increased from 105 in 1900 to 114 in 1980 (Meyers & Manton, 1984).

As the period of later adulthood becomes increasingly long and healthy, opportunities emerge to experience new relationships, develop new skills, and discover personal potential. We see the years from 60 to 75 as a period of continued psychological growth during which people must adapt to new roles and discover creative outlets for their leisure time as well as prepare themselves for the end of life.

The integrating theme of this life stage is a search for personal meaning. Upon entering this stage, adults begin to assert the competence and creativity attained during middle adulthood. As life progresses, motivations for achievement and power may give way to a desire for understanding—reminiscent of the toddler's need to know "why" and the later adolescent's need to challenge and experiment with life roles. The individual is still confronted with essential problems of definition and explanation during later adulthood. At this stage, adults may begin to apply the wealth of their life course experiences, their perspective on time, and their adaptation to life crises to a personally satisfying conceptualization of the question of life's meaning.

For some, the period of later adulthood ends in a state of physical or mental deterioration, or both, that impedes further psychological growth. The physical and psychological blows of poverty and hardship can be most damaging. The onset of senescence may result in a dramatic loss of memory, reasoning capacities, and problem-solving abilities, as well as an increase in fantasy activity, physical deterioration, and helplessness. For some, the chronic problems of aging cast a shadow of depression and hopelessness on the years of later adulthood. The chronic problems of aging may cause serious psychological and financial problems for children as they observe their parents' progressive decline. As a result of these changes, older adults may begin to feel alienated from their environment and discouraged about their severe loss of

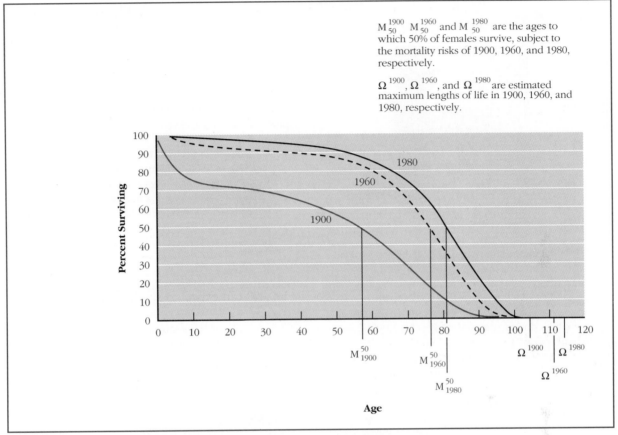

M_{50}^{1900} M_{50}^{1960} and M_{50}^{1980} are the ages to which 50% of females survive, subject to the mortality risks of 1900, 1960, and 1980, respectively.

Ω^{1900}, Ω^{1960}, and Ω^{1980} are estimated maximum lengths of life in 1900, 1960, and 1980, respectively.

Figure 13.1   Mortality Survival Curves for U.S. Females in 1900, 1960, and 1980

Source: G. C. Myers and K. G. Manton, "Compression of Mortality: Myth or Reality?" *Gerontologist, 24* (1984), 347. Reprinted by permission of the publisher.

capacities. Because of the extremes in intellectual competence, social involvement, and independence that differentiate the healthy older person from the seriously ill one, it is essential to keep physical and mental health in mind in thinking about the pattern of growth in later adulthood.

No matter what one's life condition, inward-turning, vigorous thinking about oneself and one's experiences can clarify the obstacles, hardships, and conflicts of daily existence. This is a difficult challenge, particularly as the full range of negative as well as positive events of a lifetime must be processed. People in all walks of life and at all income levels can achieve this sense of integrity through personal reflection on their experience. It is these people to whom others turn for a sense of wisdom and hope about life. Conversely, some people discover that what they have done is not to their liking, can find little meaning in life, and become scornful of other people's weaknesses. Such people can become overwhelmed by despair.

Box 13.1   The Introspections of Chester M. Pierce, M.D.

The themes that dominate the life stage of later adulthood—integrity, despair, and introspection—are very abstract. Students may have special difficulty understanding and empathizing with the intense and personally absorbing challenges that face adults during this time of life. In a great gesture of generativity, Dr. Chester M. Pierce has shared his introspections with us. Dr. Pierce is professor of education and psychiatry at Harvard University. He was founding chairman of Black Psychiatrists of America, and among his many outstanding accomplishments is membership in the National Academy of Sciences. Inspired by an invitation to lecture in honor of Dr. Solomon Carter Fuller, the first black psychiatrist in the United States, Dr. Pierce used the occasion to reflect on his own efforts to find meaning and a sense of unity in his life. He set the stage by describing the challenges that faced Dr. Fuller and how the legacy of Dr. Fuller's career helped him to cope with the realities of his own professional development as a psychiatrist.

No thinking Black person can gaze at the celebrated photo of Freud in his first visit to America, taken at Clark University in Worcester, Massachusetts, without knowing that Solomon Carter Fuller had overcome obstacles and resentments that did not affect the others in the photograph. In addition, one could be certain that unlike the others in the picture, Dr. Fuller, in spite of any achievement, would never be free to pursue his career without the burden of being suspect in the eyes of his peers in terms of ability, effectiveness, or efficiency. Finally, the Black viewer of the picture would know intuitively that throughout his career Dr. Fuller would have had to do more work for less reward and that at each instance of advancement he would have had to demonstrate superior qualifications and credentials than a White colleague aspiring for the same advancement.

In short, the unity that Dr. Fuller sought to bring to American psychiatry was accomplished

Developmental Tasks

Promoting Intellectual Vigor

Memory, reasoning, information, problem-solving abilities, and mental rigidity or fluidity all influence the adult's capacity to introspect, to assess a personal past history, and to plan for the future. How can we understand cognitive functioning and cognitive change in later life? We need to appreciate several problems in the study of this area in order to interpret ongoing research.

One problem is the distinction between age differences and age changes (Denney, 1982; Schaie, 1973). Let us say that in a cross-sectional study conducted in 1985, 70-year-olds performed less well than 40-year-olds. The difference may be clear, but it may not be a result of age alone. The 70-year-olds will have been born in the 1910s

Box 13.1 *(continued)*

under inestimable stress and duress. To this day all colored minority psychiatrists are beneficiaries of this legacy. Regrettably, to this day, all colored minority psychiatrists must continue to adapt to the same burdens that afflicted Solomon Carter Fuller.

What will be submitted by this lecture is that being Black in America means being stressed more because you are Black. Being a Black psychiatrist means you are stressed more because you are a Black psychiatrist. In the resolution of the psychological conflicts, all Blacks have a requirement to consolidate, integrate, and make sense of the diversity that being Black, and thereby marginal, brings with it in all interactions with the general society. Therefore there is a need to unify the diversity even as one struggles with the issue of when and how to unite.

Like Solomon Carter Fuller, Black psychiatrists today in their personal and professional lives operate in many circumstances of marginality and fractionation. Coordinating and controlling these operations, all of which are under the aegis of extra stress, may constitute the largest and most difficult developmental task for any Black citizen. Each citizen must order these operations according to his or her own perception of truth. [Pierce, 1989, pp. 297–298]

Later in this chapter we will return to Dr. Pierce's reflections as a way of clarifying how a person makes sense of a life of stresses, challenges, and achievements to arrive at a point of personal integrity.

Source: C. M. Pierce, "Unity in Diversity: Thirty-three Years of Stress." In G. L. Berry and J. K. Asamen (eds.), *Black Students*. Copyright © 1989 by Sage Publications, Inc. Reprinted by permission.

and the 40-year-olds in the 1940s. Differences in performance may well be a product of different educational opportunities, varying experiences with standardized tests, or other *cohort* factors rather than of age alone. For example, only 13% of men and 8% of women who were 65 years old or older in 1988 were college graduates. Educational attainment has changed over this century so that the younger cohorts are much more likely to have benefited from formal schooling at both the high school and college levels (U.S. Bureau of the Census, 1989). In any cross-sectional study of cognitive functioning, it is important to recognize the contribution of historical factors as well as possible developmental or aging factors that may contribute to observed differences in performance. Even in longitudinal studies that follow change across time, if only one cohort is sampled, it is impossible to tell whether changes from one period to the next are products of age and development or of particular resources and deficits characterizing that particular generation of subjects.

Whether measured cognitive abilities change with age depends largely on whether they have been cultivated and used frequently. This woman has been managing the books at home and at work for years, and is not likely to experience any decline in mathematical reasoning.

A second problem is the definition of abilities. *Cognitive functioning* is a very broad term that encompasses such varied abilities as vocabulary, problem solving, and short-term memory. It is very possible that the pattern of change in abilities with age depends on the abilities being tested. Some abilities are frequently used and have been developed to a high level of efficiency. For example, an architect is much more likely to retain abilities in the area of spatial relations and spatial reasoning than is someone whose lifework is not intimately connected with the construction and organization of spatial dimensions.

A third, and related, problem is the level of abstraction and the relevance of the tasks used to measure adult cognitive functioning. The definition of intelligence that is used in the design and application of most intelligence tests refers to capacities that are predictive of school-related success. The criteria for assessing adult intelligence are necessarily more heterogeneous than the ability to succeed in the school curriculum. There are reasons to believe that as people move through adulthood, their approach to the use of information and problem solving becomes modified by the contexts in which the individuals are most often involved (Labouvie-Vief & Schell, 1982).

Finally, factors associated with health are always intertwined with the functioning of older adults, although these factors are often not directly measured. In a longitudinal study of intelligence, Riegel and Riegel (1972) found that there were clear declines in performance among subjects who were to die before the next testing period. Vocabulary skills, which normally remain high or continue to show increases with age, are especially likely to decline in older subjects who will die within the coming few years (White & Cunningham, 1988). Thus at each older age the presence of subjects who may be approaching death will depress the average performance of the group as a whole.

In attempting to define intelligence in adulthood, several researchers have looked at the pattern of productivity in the work setting (Dennis, 1966; Lehman, 1953; Simonton, 1977). Special attention has been given to the relationship between creative achievement and age. The pattern that has been described is one of a fairly rapid rise to a peak in mid-career, followed by a gradual decline (Simonton, 1988). However, it is clear that opportunities for creative contribution persist throughout the career. What is more, as adults perceive that they may be approaching the end of their career, they may be especially inspired to make a distinctive statement. Thus last works or career "swan songs" are often marked by a profound simplicity and originality that set them apart from earlier work and illustrate a special facet of the person's creative potential (Simonton, 1989). Lehman reported that productivity of very high quality peaks when people are in their 30s. Work that is rated as "worthy" was observed to peak somewhat later and decline gradually. In considering total work productivity, Dennis identified the decade of the 40s as the most productive period. He differentiated patterns of productivity among a variety of professions. Among those he studied, the productivity of scholars in the humanities continued at a high level until the 70s, whereas the decline after age 40 was comparatively rapid for persons in the creative arts.

The role of older scholars and scientists is influenced by cultural values. For example, China has a shortage of scientists. Although the retirement age in China is 60, scientists who hold the title of professor can work in their laboratories until age 70. Those who have made unusual contributions may work after age 70, depending on their health. At the same time, there is an active attempt to advance the 45- to 55-year-old scientists by promoting them to leadership (Guangzhao, 1985). This climate encourages productivity throughout later adulthood.

Declining competence with age has been identified in a number of areas, including reaction time, visual-motor flexibility (the translation of visual information into new motor responses), and memory. Older subjects tend to respond more slowly in reaction-time tasks, indicating slowing in the information-processing phase as well as the response phase of many tasks (Strayer, Wickens & Braune, 1987). With regard to memory, Botwinick (1984) has described a gradual increase in the number of people whose memories decline at each age level. Short-term memory is more seriously affected by aging than long-term memory. Thus older subjects may find it more difficult to store newly acquired information and then retrieve it than younger subjects (Fozard & Poon, 1976; Reese, 1976). In studies of long-term memory, older subjects seemed to lose information in the short period right after learning but then to retain a high level of recall for the remaining material for up to 130 weeks (Fozard & Poon, 1976).

Memory functions are especially likely to be disrupted under conditions in which information is presented rapidly and contextual cues are absent. In a memory task involving the recall of five- and eight-word strings, older subjects (65 to 73) retained fewer words than younger subjects (18 to 22) when the word strings were presented at high speed and when they were not arranged in a meaningful sentence. Speed of presentation did not significantly reduce recall when the words were arranged in a normal semantic order (Wingfield et al., 1985).

In addition to actual declines in some kinds of memory performance, about 50% of older adults complain of memory problems. It is interesting to find that even after participating in programs designed to improve memory performance, these complaints persist (Scogin, Storandt & Lott, 1985). Anxiety and frustration over memory loss nag many older adults, even those whose memory performance has not dramatically declined.

Some research has focused on the ability of older adults to perform various Piagetian tasks, such as classification, conservation, and formal operational problem solving. In many areas, older adults perform less well than middle or young adults. Older subjects have been described as performing classification and problem-solving tasks in a more egocentric, animistic way than younger adults (Denney, 1982). In the area of conservation, however, the evidence is mixed. Some work has found that older adults do not handle the conservation-of-volume task as well as younger subjects but do perform other conservation tasks quite well. Other studies report no differences in conservation between younger and older subjects (Selzer & Denney, 1980). In one comparison, academic background rather than age was related to performance of formal operational problem solving. College-age men and women and college-educated men and women in the age range of 63 to 75 did equally well on tests of formal thought. However, those who had majored in natural/physical sciences while in college did better than those with social sciences and humanities backgrounds (Blackburn, 1984).

Research based on the standard Piagetian tasks has been criticized for its lack of relevance and familiarity for older subjects. In an attempt to control for the relevance of the task, Poon and Fozard (1978) studied the effect of the familiarity and datedness of objects on the time it took to name them. Some objects were clearly dated from the early 1900s. Others were contemporary items used in the 1960s and 1970s. The subjects in the age range of 60 to 70 named the dated objects faster than did the younger subjects. Younger subjects in the age range of 18 to 20 named the contemporary objects faster than did the older subjects. The implication of this research is that the performance of older subjects may be partly a product of their familiarity with the materials provided in the task.

In another approach to problem solving, ten older adults participated in constructing a set of practical problem-solving questions in order to help ensure their relevance for older adults (Denney & Pearce, 1989). One problem they posed was: "An elderly woman can drive her car to run errands except in the winter when the weather is bad. What should she do about getting groceries and other necessities when the weather is bad?"

Answers to this and other questions were rated on a scale of 1 to 4, depending on the number of safe and effective solutions offered. Those subjects in their 40s performed best. Subjects in their 50s, 60s, and 70s scored about the same, but slightly less well than those in their 30s and 40s, and about as well as those in their 20s. One could not conclude that problem-solving abilities showed a pattern of deterioration since this was not a longitudinal study. Perhaps one could conclude that even when the problems are authentic, older adults are not as likely to try to generate multiple solutions but to identify one or two solutions that have a good chance of succeeding.

John Horn (1979) has proposed that the course of mental abilities across the life span is not uniform. Some areas are strengthened, and others decline. He has made an especially strong case for differentiating *crystallized intelligence* (Gc) and *fluid intelligence* (Gf). Gc is the ability to bring knowledge accumulated through past learning into play in appropriate situations. Gf is the ability to impose organization on information and to generate new hypotheses. Both kinds of intelligence are required for optimal human functioning.

Gc and Gf can be identified as integrated structures in both young and later adulthood (Hayslip & Brookshire, 1985). However, Horn has argued that the two kinds of thinking draw on somewhat different neurological and experiential sources. Gc reflects the consequences of life experiences within a society. Socialization in the family, exposure to media, and participation in school, work, and community settings all emphasize the use and improvement of Gc. Gc increases with age, experience, and physical maturation. It remains at a high level of functioning throughout adulthood. Gf seems to be more characteristic of what we mean when we say that someone has a "good head on his [or her] shoulders." Finding a general relationship and applying it without having been schooled in that problem-solving area is an example of Gf, as is being able to approach new problems logically and systematically. Older adults do not spontaneously impose organization on new information. They are less likely than younger persons to attend to the incidental information or process-level learning that contributes to Gf. Horn has also hypothesized that Gf is more dependent on the specific number of neurons available for its functioning than is Gc. Thus neurological loss would be more damaging to Gf than to Gc.

Schaie and Hertzog (1983; Hertzog & Schaie, 1988) reported on the results of a 14-year longitudinal and cross-sectional study of adult intellectual development. Five mental abilities were measured: verbal meaning, spatial reasoning, inductive reasoning, number skills, and word fluency. The youngest subjects were in the age range of 25 to 39; the oldest were 67 to 81. In general, the longitudinal data showed less decrement with age than the cross-sectional data. The rate of decline in performance was most notable in all five areas after age 60. Decline in some areas, especially spatial and inductive reasoning, was notable during the decade of the 50s. The variation among all three groups in the sample remained quite stable. In other words, even though measured intelligence changes over time, the position of one person in relation to another remains about the same. Cohort differences favored the more recently born in the areas of spatial reasoning, inductive reasoning, and verbal meaning.

The quality of thought that is characteristic of older adults may also be a product of their environment. Skinner (1983) has described some possible environmental qualities that fail to reinforce systematic thinking or new ideas in aging people. Many people who live alone, for example, lack the diversity of social interaction that produces cognitive discrepancy and new concepts. Older people may be reinforced for talking about the past. Their recollections of early memories are interesting to students and younger colleagues. However, preoccupation with these reminiscences does not encourage thinking in new directions. Skinner claims that one is more likely to repeat oneself as one gets older. He suggests that it may be important for older adults to move into new areas of work in order to prevent repetition of old ideas. He believes that it is possible to analyze how the quality of one's thinking is being influenced by the circumstances of aging and also to identify interventions that can prevent the deterioration of cognitive abilities. For Skinner, these interventions include attempts to be sensitive to the signs of fatigue, planning for regular opportunities for stimulating verbal interactions with others, making careful outlines of written work to avoid distraction, and acting on ideas as they come to one's mind rather than counting on remembering them later.

We are left with the conclusion that the pattern of cognitive functioning in later adulthood is neither unidimensional nor stable. It is subject to environmental influences that may differentially affect adults who have experienced different historical conditions or different socioeconomic conditions. Although there is considerable evidence of decline in various aspects of functioning, the deterioration is not always of very great magnitude. In some areas, such as information and verbal skills, functioning remains at a high level. It does appear that cognitive functioning in later life is likely to become rather patterned, an outcome that may reflect the predictability and routineness of a low level of daily stimulation.

On the basis of extensive longitudinal research, K. Warner Schaie (1989) has identified six factors that are associated with retaining a high level of cognitive functioning in later adulthood:

- Absence of cardiovascular and other chronic diseases
- Favorable environment linked to high socioeconomic status
- Involvement in a complex and intellectually stimulating environment
- Flexible personality style at midlife
- High cognitive functioning of spouse
- Maintenance of level of perceptual processing speed

In this list we see evidence of the clear interplay of the somatic and the social systems as they contribute to ego functioning in the later years.

Redirecting Energy to New Roles and Activities

Role transition and role loss are present at every period of the life span. In later adulthood, however, convergence of role transitions is likely to lead to a revision of major life functions. Roles are lost through widowhood, retirement, and the deaths of friends. At the same time, new roles—grandparent, senior advisor, community leader, retiree—require the formation of new patterns of behaviors and relationships.

Grandparenthood

Within the course of family development, the role of grandparent may require a renewal of skills that have been stored in the attic along with the bottle sterilizer and the potty chair. Grandparents begin to renew their acquaintance with the delights of childhood, including diapering the baby, telling fairy tales, taking trips to the zoo, and having the pleasure of small helping hands with the baking, gardening, or carpentry.

These grandparents find pleasure in making sure that the children are safe and comfortable even while watching a parade pass by.

A person's skills, patience, and knowledge may be even more in demand in the grandparent role than they were in the parent role (Robertson, 1977).

People differ in the meaning they place on the grandparent role and in the way they enact it. In one of the first empirical studies of grandparenthood, Neugarten and Weinstein (1964) interviewed the grandmother and grandfather in 70 middle-class families. Five grandparenting styles were identified, each expressing a rather distinct interpretation of the grandparent role:

1. *Formal:* These grandparents were interested in their grandchildren but careful not to become involved in parenting them other than by occasional baby-sitting.
2. *Funseeker:* These grandparents had informal, playful interactions with their grandchildren. They enjoyed mutually self-indulgent fun with them.
3. *Surrogate parent:* This style was especially likely for grandmothers who assumed major child-care responsibilities when the mother worked outside the home.
4. *Reservoir of family wisdom:* This was an authoritarian relationship in which a grandparent, usually the grandfather, would dispense skills and resources. Parents as well as grandchildren were subordinate to this older authority figure.
5. *Distant figure:* This was a grandparent who would appear on birthdays and holidays but generally had little contact with the grandchildren.

It is clear from this list of grandparenting styles that the role prescriptions for the grandparent are ambiguous enough to permit wide differences in their enactment.

Most older adults take great satisfaction and pride in their grandchildren. Grandparenthood has a variety of personal meanings that contribute to the grandparent's overall sense of purpose and worth (Kivnick, 1983). Grandchildren symbolize an extension of personal influence that will most assuredly persist well beyond the grandparent's death. To this extent, grandchildren help older adults to feel more comfortable about their own death. Older adults see concrete evidence that some thread of their lives will persist into the future, giving a dimension of immortality to themselves and to the family ancestry that they represent (Mead, 1975).

In an analysis of the sources of vitality in later life, Erikson, Erikson, and Kivnick (1986) found that relationships with grandchildren played a critical role.

> *The major involvement that uniformly makes life worth living is the thought of and participation in their relationships with children and grandchildren. Their pride in their own achievement in having brought up their young, through thick and thin, and their satisfaction in the way these young have developed gives them, for the most part, deep gratification. With the arrival of grandchildren, they may identify themselves as ancestors, graduated to venerability. Listen to their voices as they trace their own ancestry and that of their children's traits: "She has her mother's fire, that first girl of ours. She has more energy and more projects than anyone. Come to think of it, my mother had that fire, too. And my wife's two grandmothers." "My son is a perfectionist, like me." "The kids are innately smart, like their father."* [p. 326]

Grandchildren also stimulate older adults' thoughts about time, the changing of cultural norms across generations, and the patterning of history. In relating to grandchildren as they grow up, they discover elements of the culture that remain stable. Certain stories and songs retain their appeal from generation to generation. Certain toys, games, and preoccupations of children of the current generation are remembered by grandparents from their own childhood. Grandparents may also become aware of changes in the culture that are reflected in new child-rearing practices; new equipment, toys, and games; and new expectations for children's behavior at each life stage. The communication that adults maintain with their grandchildren allows them to keep abreast of the continuities and changes in their culture as these are reflected in the experiences of childhood. Through their grandchildren, adults can avoid a sense of alienation from the contemporary world (Kahana & Kahana, 1970). The more involved grandparents are in the daily care and routines of their grandchildren, the more central they become to a young child's sense of security and well-being. This kind of importance is a benefit not only to the child but to the older adult's assessment of personal worth (Tomlin & Passman, 1989).

Some adults interpret the role of grandparent as an opportunity to pass on to grandchildren the wisdom and cultural heritage of their ancestry. In the process of fulfilling this role, older adults must attempt to find meaning in their experiences and to communicate that meaning to grandchildren in ways that the latter can understand. There are many avenues that grandparents select in order to educate their grandchildren. Storytelling, special trips, long walks, attending religious services, and working on special projects are all activities that allow grandparents some moments of intimacy with their grandchildren. During these times, grandparents can influence their grandchildren's thoughts and fantasies. The process of educating one's grandchildren involves a deep sense of investment in those experiences and ideals that one believes to be central to a fruitful life.

The many ways in which grandchildren can contribute to a feeling of well-being suggest that the absence of grandchildren or the failure to establish a relationship with grandchildren may easily become a source of despair for some adults. Many older people who have no children of their own find surrogate children in whom they can invest their energy. Those who are unable to establish an intimate relationship with any young children may find themselves growing out of touch with the content of contemporary culture and discouraged by the finality of their death.

Widowhood

The most difficult adaptation to a new role occurs when an adult loses a spouse. For many older people, this loss causes severe disruption as well as grief and depression. Although some adults remarry, many others remain unmarried and identify themselves as widows or widowers. In 1988, 14% of men and 79% of women 65 years old and over were widowed. Although most older widowers remarry, the vast majority of widows live alone (U.S. Bureau of the Census, 1989).

Widows must learn to function socially as well as in their own households without the presence of a marriage partner. Adaptation to this role requires resilience, creative problem solving, and a strong commitment to a belief in one's personal worth. Since the average woman is widowed at 56 and has a life expectancy of 78, she will be living in a new role status for at least 20 years (Lopata, 1973; O'Leary, 1977).

Widows are likely to experience a marked decrease in financial resources. They may have no marketable skills and feel insecure about entering the labor force. They may be uninformed or uneasy about using social service agencies to meet their needs. For most women, the loss of the husband is most keenly felt as a loss of emotional support: "He is most apt to be mentioned as the person the widow most enjoyed being with, who made her feel important and secure" (Lopata, 1978). The transition to widowhood can be especially difficult for those who had been caring for an ill partner, emotionally hoping for recovery yet observing constant decline (Bass & Bowman, 1990).

Despite the extreme pain and prolonged grief that accompany widowhood, most people cope with it successfully. Widows are likely to find support from children and friends. Over time, a widow's siblings, especially her sisters, can be a key source of emotional support as well as direct, instrumental assistance (O'Bryant, 1988). If widows do enter the labor force, they may discover a new domain of competence. Widows are likely to become more sensitive to their own needs and feelings and more compassionate toward others. Those widows who can transcend their losses can become more fully aware of the value of life and the need to live each moment to its fullest (Barrett, 1981).

Leisure Activities

Older adults commonly find that as the role responsibilities of parenthood decrease, they have more time and resources to devote to leisure activities. Different types of

In the hiking club, senior men enjoy outdoor exercise and companionship.

leisure activities are available for meeting a variety of psychosocial needs. In a study of the benefits of leisure activities, men and women aged 56 and over were asked to describe the sources of satisfaction found in their primary leisure activities (Tinsley et al., 1985). The six clusters of leisure activities and the primary benefits of each are listed in Table 13.1. The table suggests that different clusters of activities can meet different needs. It also provides some psychologically equivalent activities for adults who may be unable to continue a given activity or be uninterested in one but willing to try another.

One area not included in this list is physical exercise. Physical exercise is becoming a focus of leisure activity for more and more older adults, as its benefits are linked to health, self-esteem, and zest for life. People used to be very reluctant to encourage vigorous activity for older adults. They believed that a person who was unaccustomed to active physical exercise could be harmed by physical exertion. However, research on exercise in adulthood suggests quite the opposite interpretation. Not only can adults profit from a program of exercise but some of the negative consequences of a sedentary lifestyle can be reversed (DeVries, 1975). For example, Hopkins and her associates (1990) described a program in which women aged 57 to 77 participated in a low-impact aerobic dance class three times a week over 12 weeks. The program included stretching, walking, dance movements, large arm movements, and major leg-muscle movement. After 12 weeks the group showed improvement in cardiorespiratory endurance (walking half a mile as fast as possible); flexibility, muscle strength, body agility, and balance. A comparison group of women who did not participate showed stability or decline in all of these measures of fitness.

A person's exercise program should be developed in response to his or her level of fitness and ability to endure rigorous activity. The goal is a program that raises the heart rate more than 40% of the range from the resting rate to the maximum rate. For men in their 60s and 70s, this means raising their heart rates above 98 and 95,

Table 13.1 Leisure Activities and Their Psychological Benefits

Cluster	Primary Benefit
1. Playing cards Playing bingo Bowling Dancing	Companionship
2. Picnicking	Experiencing something new and unusual
3. Watching sports (not on TV) Watching television	Escape from the pressure of dealing with others
4. Raising houseplants Collecting photographs Collecting antiques Reading	Solitude and security
5. Knitting or crocheting Woodworking Ceramics	Expressiveness and recognition, but in a solitary context
6. Volunteer service Volunteer professional activities Attending meetings of social groups Attending meetings of religious groups	Intellectual stimulation, self-expression, and service

Source: Adapted from H. E. A. Tinsley, J. D. Teaff, S. L. Colbs, and N. Kaufman, "System of Classifying Leisure Activities in Terms of the Psychological Benefits of Participation Reported by Older Persons," *Journal of Gerontology,* (1985), *40* 172–178. Reprinted by permission of the publisher.

respectively. Rhythmic large-muscle activities, such as walking, jogging, running, and swimming, are the kinds of exercises most likely to lead to improvement in the cardiovascular-respiratory system.

Redirection of energy to new roles in later adulthood requires a degree of flexibility and resilience that often goes unnoticed in observations of older adults. Just imagine what life might be like 30 or 40 years from now. Will you be prepared to embrace the technology, lifestyle, or age role expectations that you will encounter during your own later adulthood? We are impressed with how readily most people adapt to new roles—especially those of retiree and widow—for which there is little early preparation or social reward.

Accepting One's Life

By later adulthood, evidence about one's successes and failures in the major tasks of middle adulthood—marriage, child rearing, and work—has begun to accumulate. Data from which to judge one's adequacy in these areas are abundant. As involvement in the child-rearing role decreases, adults have an opportunity to increase their focus on the degree of harmony in their marriage relationships. They can assess whether they have successfully responded to the changes in their relationships or whether their marriages have deteriorated with the departure of their children. In viewing their own children as mature adults, parents are able to determine whether they have helped them meet the challenges of intimacy, work, and child rearing with creativity and morality. In the work role, older adults can begin to estimate the degree to which their productivity has matched their abilities and the extent to which they have met their private goals for occupational accomplishment.

Individuals inevitably are vulnerable to some degree of discouragement about the limitations of their accomplishments. They must be able to accept the realities that present themselves and to realize that there is a necessary discrepancy between their accomplishments and their goals. The process of accepting one's past life as it has been can be a difficult personal challenge. One must be able to incorporate certain areas of failure, crisis, or disappointment into one's self-image without being over-burdened by a sense of inadequacy. One must be able to take pride in areas of achievement even when those accomplishments fall short of one's expectations.

One of the major themes in accepting one's life is figuring out what to make of the many indications of acceptance or rejection by others. In his reflections on this point, Dr. Pierce illustrates just how complicated it can be to understand the sources of one's feelings of being marginal, isolated, or part of the group.

> *The final lesson from these years . . . began at this time but took a decade for me to fathom. One of the first national committees on which I served was deciding who should join us. Many names were offered. All were rejected with the terse but mystifying statement, "He's not one of us."*
>
> *Who was "one of us" was baffling to me since at the table there were psychiatrists from rural and urban areas, psychoanalysts and state hospital administrators, men and women, researchers and practitioners, academicians and colored minority people. Years later, I realized what constituted "one of us."*
>
> *At that time, another group met. Invitees were told that continental breakfast would be available a half hour before the meeting was to start. Also they were told: (1) Bring your golf clubs, and (2) do not schedule your return flight before 5 p.m. the last day of the meeting.*
>
> *Only one person arrived with golf clubs. He had scheduled his return flight for 7 p.m. on the last day. His greatest blunder however was to arrive only five minutes earlier than the meeting was scheduled to start. By that point, "all of us" were on item three of the agenda. Almost predictably someone had said at 8:15 a.m., "We're all almost here, let's start." Further, predictably someone suggested we work extra hours rather than play golf, so that we could finish by noon rather than 5 p.m. on the last day. "All of us" had arranged early afternoon departures despite an admonition to the contrary.*
>
> *It hit me with monstrous impact that what is especially complicated about being Black in the U.S.A. is that, even while resolving whether acceptance signifies being welcomed or being tolerated, there are compounding subtle variables that must be factored into the resolution. The "one of us" incident taught me many things. Not the least tuition was that an inherent and considerable stress, in almost all situations in which there is some degree of acceptance, in either homoracial or heteroracial circumstances, is that we can never be sure how much acceptance depends on skin color and how much depends on interpreting what constitutes being "one of us."**

*Source: C. M. Pierce, "Unity in Diversity: Thirty-three Years of Stress." In G. L. Berry and J. K. Asamen (eds.), *Black Students.* Copyright © 1989 by Sage Publications, Inc. Reprinted by permission.

There appear to be a variety of responses to the challenge posed by this life task. Some older adults become extremely depressed in thinking about their past and resign themselves to a future of unhappiness. The illnesses, deaths, and personal crises of their past become dominant preoccupations. No current experiences can quite compensate for a general feeling of discouragement. Other older adults respond by becoming rigidly self-confident. They see their own lives as examples for younger people and are unable to tolerate any implication of failure. In encountering such adults, often one feels that they have developed a sense of self-righteousness at the expense of compassion. In order to protect their self-image, they reject all doubts and present an impression of total confidence.

Both of these strategies make it impossible for the older person to change during later adulthood. Another type of response is to accept the areas of disappointment or crisis but to put them in perspective with the spheres of personal achievements. For most adults, this approach would probably result in an overall balance tending toward pride rather than self-aggrandizement. A more flexible attitude toward one's life history allows one to conceive of new directions for growth and to feel optimistic about the possibility for success in these directions.

A number of investigators have raised questions about sources of life satisfaction and stress in later adulthood and their relation to perceptions of well-being. One especially intriguing question is whether people in their 60s and 70s feel "old" and just what that means. Most older adults do not perceive themselves as elderly (Kahana, Kahana & McLenigan, 1980). Those who do view themselves as old tend to have more difficulty adjusting to life than those who perceive themselves as middle-aged. Identification with the label "old" is associated with several life stresses, including poor health, reduced activity, widowhood, and reduced income level (Ward, 1977). The fear of growing old is also linked to lower levels of life satisfaction. Those adults over 55 who are quite worried about encountering illness, loneliness, social rejection, and poverty when they are old are also significantly less satisfied with the current quality of their lives (Klemmack & Roff, 1984). They may be chronic worriers.

Although it may not be adaptive for later adults to view themselves as old, it appears that it is also a sign of frustration to view oneself as much younger than one's real age. Montepare and Lachman (1989) asked subjects ranging from the teens to the 80s to describe the age that corresponded to the way they felt and the type of person whose interests and activities were most like theirs. Figure 13.2 shows the subjective age identities (dotted lines) in comparison with the actual ages of the male and female subjects. Younger subjects were likely to have a somewhat *older* subjective age identity. Older subjects were likely to have a *younger* subjective age identity, and the discrepancy was most noticeable among the oldest women. For younger men and women, having an older subjective age identity was associated with higher life satisfaction. For the oldest men, there was no relationship between subjective age and life satisfaction, but among the oldest women, those with the youngest subjective age had lower life satisfaction. At the older ages, those with the least discrepancy between their real and their subjective ages had the greatest satisfaction. Although it appears to be common for older adults to identify themselves as younger than they are, a major discrepancy between real and subjective age may reflect significant frustration over one's actual age and its constraints.

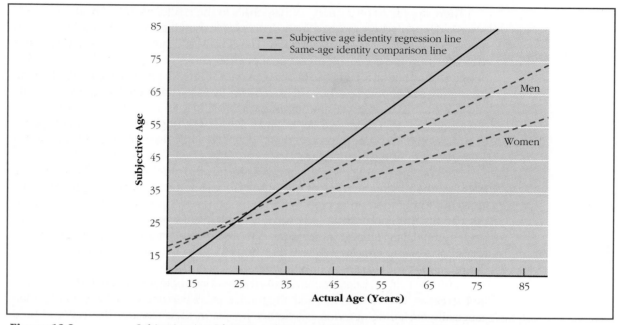

Figure 13.2

Subjective Age Identities of Men and Women Across the Life Span

Source: J. M. Montepare and M. E. Lachman, "'You're Only as Old as You Feel': Self-Perceptions of Age, Fears of Aging, and Life Satisfaction from Adolescence to Old Age," *Psychology and Aging,* (1989), *4* 75. Reprinted by permission of the author.

Flanagan (1978, 1980) generated a list of 15 areas of experience that contribute to life satisfaction from the open-ended responses of over 3,000 subjects:

1. Material well-being and financial security
2. Health and personal safety
3. Relations with spouse (girlfriend or boyfriend)
4. Having and raising children
5. Relations with parents, siblings, or other relatives
6. Relations with friends
7. Activities related to helping or encouraging other people
8. Activities related to local and national governments
9. Intellectual development
10. Personal understanding and planning
11. Occupational role
12. Creativity and personal expression
13. Socializing
14. Passive and observational recreational activities
15. Active and participatory recreational activities

Three nationally representative groups of subjects aged 30, 50, and 70 were asked to rate each area, telling how important it was for the quality of their lives and how well their needs in each area were being met. Three areas that were described as important by 80% of men and women at every age were health and personal safety, having and raising children, and personal understanding. A spouse or opposite-sex partner was very important to all but the oldest women, 57% of whom were widowed. Areas important to fewer than 70% of the sample at each age level were activities related to government, creativity and personal expression, socializing, and both passive and active recreational activities. Close friends increased in importance more for older women than for older men. Learning was less important for older than for younger subjects. Opportunities to learn were viewed as more adequate at each age, but the importance of learning decreased. In general, 85% of the 50- and 70-year-olds evaluated their overall quality of life as good, very good, or excellent. Flanagan estimated that most Americans felt good about their lives and were satisfied that their relevant needs were being met.

Demographic variables do not predict perceived life satisfaction adequately. A person's satisfaction with life remains fairly stable over the years despite losses of important roles and some decline in health (Costa et al., 1987). For older women, staying healthy, especially as it relates to being able to remain independent and not become a burden on others, is so central to feelings of well-being that other hopes and concerns seem to be minimized in light of that preoccupation. A 69-year-old woman described her situation as follows: "God's been good to me. My health is good. I can cut grass, climb ladders, and can paint. If you can do that at 69, that's pretty good, isn't it?" (Bearon, 1989, p. 774).

We all know people who have lived very difficult lives yet appear to be full of zest and enthusiasm. We also know people who appear to have had the benefits of many of life's resources yet are continually complaining about problems. In response to this reality, some researchers have looked to personality factors to predict subjective life satisfaction (Costa & McCrae, 1980; McCrae & Costa, 1983). A personality dimension described as *extraversion* is consistently associated with measures of well-being, happiness, and security. Extraversion includes such qualities as sociability, vigor, sensation seeking, and positive emotions. A personality dimension described as *neuroticism* is consistently associated with discouragement, unhappiness, and hopelessness. Neuroticism includes such qualities as anxiety, hostility, and impulsiveness. The implication is that real-life events are screened and interpreted through the filter of personality. Whether specific events will contribute to feelings of satisfaction or dismay will depend on how they are interpreted. Some people are more likely to be grumblers and others are more likely to be celebrants of life.

The research suggests five conclusions about accepting one's life during later adulthood:

1. Most adults are satisfied with their lives and with the way their needs are being met.
2. The age range from 30 to 50 is viewed by most people as the prime of life, though many in this range do not necessarily see the present as the prime of life.
3. The area of child rearing produces the most conflicts during adulthood. Child rearing is simultaneously an important source of satisfactions and a source of problems or stress.

Pablo Picasso, *La Joie de Vivre*, 1946. An adult finds value in life by seeing it as part of some larger, more abstract, infinite order. At age 65, Picasso creates this celebration of life, integrating many of his favorite themes, including sexuality, fertility, creativity, and mythology.

4. Satisfactions with parenting and work increase with age. In general, older adults do not tend to experience life as more stressful than do younger adults.
5. Life satisfaction is not tied solely to objectively measurable factors. It may well be a conceptual invention that is imposed on life events through the filter of personality.

Erikson (Erikson, Erikson & Kivnick, 1986) comments on the importance of trust for the acceptance of one's life.

> *The life cycle, however, does more than extend itself into the next generation. It curves back on the life of the individual, allowing, as we have indicated, a reexperiencing of earlier stages in a new form. This retracing might be described as a growth toward death, if that did not ring false as a metaphor. Maples and aspens every October bear flamboyant witness to this possibility of a final spurt of growth. Nature unfortunately has not ordained that mortals put on such a fine show.*
>
> *As aging continues, in fact, human bodies begin to deteriorate and physical and psychosocial capacities diminish in a seeming reversal of the course their development takes. When physical frailty demands assistance, one must accept again an appropriate dependence without the loss of trust and hope. The old, of course, are not endowed with the endearing survival skills of the infant. Old bodies are more difficult to care for, and the task itself is less satisfying to the caretaker than that of caring for infants. Such skills as elders possess have been hard won and are maintained only with determined grace. Only a lifetime of slowly devel-*

oping trust is adequate to meet this situation, which so naturally elicits despair and disgust at one's own helplessness. Of how many elders could one say, "He surrendered every vestige of his old life with a sort of courteous, half humorous gentleness"?   [p. 327]

Developing a Point of View About Death

It is inevitable that during later adulthood serious, frightening, and unhappy questions about death will fill the individual's thoughts. The stage of middle adulthood is the period in which most people lose their parents. During later adulthood, their peers die. These deaths are sources of psychological stress that involve adults in the emotional process of grief and mourning as well as in the cognitive strain of trying to accept or understand them.

The development of a perspective on death is a continuous process that begins in childhood and is not fully resolved until later adulthood. The earliest concern with death—during toddlerhood—reflects an inability to conceive of an irreversible state of lifelessness. Toddlers are likely to think that a person could be dead at one moment and "undeaded" the next. By middle school age, children have a rather realistic concept of death but are unlikely to relate that concept to themselves or to others close to them (Anthony, 1972).

People's thoughts about their own death do not become very realistic or focused until sometime during later adolescence. Before then, individuals have not yet established an integrated identity. Thus they are unlikely to project themselves into the distant future or to conceive of their own mortality. In the process of forming a personal identity, individuals ask questions about mortality, the meaning of life, and the possibility of life after death. During this stage, they begin to form a point of view about death. Because older adolescents are deeply preoccupied with their own uniqueness, they may tend to have a heightened sense of their own importance. They also see themselves at the very beginning of their adult lives. At this stage, death may be anticipated with great fear. Some adults never overcome this fear of death, which is associated with a deep narcissism and a sense of self-importance.

Young adults form intimate personal bonds that they expect to endure. One's concerns about death at this stage include some anxiety about the possible death of the other person and emerging feelings of responsibility for him or her. One's own death has greater consequences once one's personal fate is linked with that of another. Thus a point of view about death must involve some sense of being able to provide for one's partner or to feel confident that the partner can survive in one's absence. One's view of death broadens from a preoccupation with one's own mortality to an appreciation of one's relationships and interdependencies with other people.

During middle adulthood, people recognize that they have already lived about half of their lives. The issue of death becomes increasingly concrete as parents and older relatives die. At the same time, adults begin to have a larger impact on their families and communities. Increased feelings of effectiveness and vitality lessen the threat of death (Feifel & Branscomb, 1973; Fried-Cassorla, 1977). The degree to which individuals gain satisfaction from their own contributions to future generations will determine the extent of their anxiety about death during this stage. Achievement of a sense of generativity should allow adults to feel that their impact will continue to be felt even after death.

Ideally, during later adulthood the presence of ego concerns with respect to death should become minimal. Individuals come to accept their own lives as they have lived them and begin to see death as a natural part of the life span. Death no longer poses a threat to personal value, to potential for accomplishment, or to the desire to influence the lives of others. As a result of having accepted one's life, one can accept its end without fear or discouragement. This does not imply a willingness to die but an acceptance of the fact of death. Older adults can appreciate that the usefulness of their contributions does not necessarily depend on their physical presence (Kübler-Ross, 1969, 1972).

The evolution of a point of view about death requires some capacity to absorb the loss of one's close relatives and friends as well as to accept one's own death. The former task may be even more difficult than the latter in that the death of peers begins to destroy the social group of which the adult is a member. Losing one's friends and relatives means a loss of daily companionship, a shared world of memories and plans, and a source of support for values and social norms. The circumstances surrounding the deaths of others may also prove to be very frightening. One sees people suffer through long illnesses, die abruptly in the midst of a thriving and vigorous life, or die in an absurd, meaningless accident. In each instance, surviving adults must ask themselves about the value of each of these lives and subsequently about the value of their own life. They are also left with a growing set of possibilities in regard to the circumstances of their own death.

Our culture's rituals permit adults to cope with death-related anxiety. The elaborate arrangements for a burial service, the viewing of the body, the selection of a coffin or urn, gravestone, or cemetery site, and provision for care of the grave allow adults to work through the reality of their own death by focusing on aspects of it over which they can exercise some control. The details of a funeral and burial may not bring adults closer to an emotional acceptance of death, but they do impart some feeling of certainty about the events immediately following their own death. In fact, some people think of their funeral as a last social statement. All of the plans surrounding a death are designed to heighten the perception of the individual's social status and moral virtue. The event of death is a direct contradiction of the cultural values of activity, productivity, and individuality. In order to disguise the view of death as a final failure, individuals may attempt to maintain an illusion of competence by planning the circumstances of their own funeral.

Several investigators have considered the sources of personal anxiety about death and the changes in preoccupation with death at various ages. Although older adults seem to think about death more frequently then do young adults, they do not appear to feel more threatened by it. In a survey of over 400 adults in early, middle, and later adulthood, death was a more salient issue for the oldest (over-60) age group (Kalish & Reynolds, 1976). The oldest adults felt that they were more likely to die in the near future. They knew more people who had died and were more likely than younger subjects to have visited a cemetery or attended a funeral. The oldest adults were more likely to have made some specific arrangements related to their death, including the purchase of cemetery space, the writing of a will, and the making of funeral arrange-

Table 13.2 Fear of Death			
	Age		
	20–39	*40–59*	*60 +*
Afraid/terrified	40%	26%	10%
Neither afraid nor unafraid	21	20	17
Unafraid/eager	36	52	71
Depends	3	3	2

Source: R. A. Kalish and D. K. Reynolds, *Death and Ethnicity: A Psychocultural Study* (Los Angeles: University of Southern California Press, 1976), p. 209.

ments. Yet expressed fear of death was lowest in this oldest age group, and the percentage who said that they were unafraid of death or even eager for it was highest.

Fear of personal death is a natural, normal experience. Death can be feared for a variety of reasons, of which some relate to the actual process of dying and others to the consequences of dying. Concerns about the process of dying include fears of being alone, being in pain, having others see one suffering, or losing control of one's thoughts and body. Concerns about the consequences of dying include fears of the unknown, of loss of identity ("People will forget about me"), of the grief others will feel, of the decomposition of the body, and of punishment or pain in the hereafter (Florian & Kravetz, 1983; Conte, Weiner, & Plutchik, 1982).

Death does not seem to be as frightening to the old as to the young. Table 13.2 shows the responses of three age groups of adults to the following question: "Some people say they are afraid to die and others say they are not. How do you feel?" Admission of fear decreased with age and lack of fear or even eagerness to die increased. Bengston, Cuellar, and Ragan (1977) found a similar pattern in their survey of over 1,200 adults. Expressed fear decreased with age. The group aged 45 to 49 had the greatest fear of death and the group aged 70 to 74 had the lowest.

There may be several explanations for this finding. First, older people tend to be more religious and may find more comfort in the religious concepts of life after death. Second, older people may feel more accepting of their lives and the decisions they have made than younger people. This view is supported by the responses of subjects in the Kalish and Reynolds study to the following question: "If you were told that you had a terminal disease and that you had six months to live, how would you want to spend your time?" Older adults were more likely to concentrate on their inner lives or to continue their lives as they were. Young-adult and middle-aged subjects expressed more concern about their relationships with loved ones. The youngest subjects were most likely to want new experiences. The idea of death was viewed as less tragic and less disruptive to the old than to the young. A third explanation is that older people are more familiar with death. They have had more opportunities to experience the deaths of others. They have made more preparations for their own deaths. They realistically expect death in the near future. Death is less of an uncertainty. Many people who were over 60 in the mid-1970s never anticipated the healthy old age that they were enjoying. The years after 65 were seen as an unexpected bonus that their parents and grandparents did not enjoy.

Pablo Picasso, *Weeping Woman,* 1937. Bereavement is the emotional suffering that follows the death of a loved one. Avoiding the expression of grief tends to prolong the person's preoccupation with the loss.

Bereavement and Grief

Adults cope not only with their own illnesses and death but with those of their loved ones. The emotional suffering that follows the death of a loved one is called *bereavement.* It is commonly viewed as a major life stress accompanied by physical symptoms, role loss, and a variety of intense emotions, including anger, sorrow, anxiety, and depression. The stress of bereavement increases the likelihood of illness and even death among survivors. Among people who have lost a spouse, the more intense experiences of depression are felt by those who describe their marriage as very positive and vital. It is clear that this loss strikes at the core of an older adult's sense of attachment, social integration, and personal worth (Futterman et al., 1990). The depression and confusion accompanying grieving may decrease survivors' sensitivity to their own physical health. Those who are deep in mourning may have feelings of uselessness or emptiness that prevent them from seeking help for their own physical or emotional health problems. Some people try to cope with their grief by increasing their use of medication, alcohol, or tranquilizers, which can threaten their physical health. Loss of appetite and lack of sleep are other symptoms of grief that contribute to the whole pattern of increased vulnerability during this time.

In the face of bereavement, there is a need to "work through" the reality of the loss as well as the feelings that accompany it. The experience of the bereaved person is not very different from the experience of the person who is coping with his or her own death. Psychiatrist Erick Lindemann worked with many of the people whose relatives had died in the Coconut Grove fire in Boston. He described the normal grief reaction as involving three phases (Lindemann, 1944). First, the person must achieve "emancipation from bondage to the deceased." This "bondage" may include feelings of guilt about ways he or she had faulted or even harmed the dead person. Second, the person must make an adjustment to all the aspects of the environment from which the deceased is missing. Third, the person must begin to form new relationships. Lindemann found that one big obstacle to working through this grief was a desire to avoid the accompanying emotions and intense physical distress. According to his analysis, the strategy of avoiding grief only prolonged the subject's physical, mental, and emotional preoccupation with the dead person.

A Cultural Comparison

To appreciate how people cope with death, it is helpful to consider the cultural rituals that have emerged for structuring the response to death. Box 13.2, which describes the Amish way of death, illustrates the way in which death is openly incorporated into every aspect of life. The service and ritual are expressions of the belief in a spiritual immortality and a simultaneous recognition of separation. Families customarily care for their aging parents within their own homes. Dying persons are surrounded by their families, who provide reassurance of generational continuity. The bereaved family members receive help and care from community members for at least the first year after a family death. In one study, Amish families found six conditions especially helpful for coping with death:

(a) *the continued presence of the family, both during the course of the illness and at the moment of death;* (b) *open communication about the process of dying and its impact on the family;* (c) *the maintenance of a normal life-style by the family during the course of the illness;* (d) *commitment to as much independence of the dying person as possible;* (e) *the opportunity to plan and organize one's own death;* (f) *continued support for the bereaved for at least a year following the funeral, with long-term support given to those who do not remarry.* [Bryer, 1979, p. 260]

We are beginning to appreciate death as a meaningful component of the life course. Scientists are responding more realistically to the needs of the dying, to the process of grieving, and to the need for an ethic that will permit us to encounter death as a natural, dignified element of life. As we experience the deaths of others during adult life, our own lives are clarified. With each death we reflect on the quality of the relationship we have had with the person, the nature of his or her accomplishments, and the essential value or contribution of that life. The death of each loved or cherished person educates us about the meaning and value of our own life choices. It is with great admiration that we respond to those who confront their own death openly and with acceptance.

Summary

The life histories of older adults are enormously varied. Depending on life experiences, health, resources, education, family support, and cultural and religious orientation, later adulthood will be perceived and enacted differently by each person. The

Box 13.2   The Amish Way of Death

The importance that the Amish place on their funeral ceremonies is reflected not only in familiarity with death but also in an intensified awareness of community. As an Amish man reported in a family interview, "The funeral is not for the one who dies, you know; it is for the family." . . .

The Amish community takes care of all aspects of the funeral occasion with the exception of the embalming procedure, the coffin, and the horse-drawn wagon. These matters are taken care of by a non-Amish funeral director who provides the type of service that the Amish desire.

The embalmed body is returned to the home within a day of the death. Family members dress the body in white garments in accordance with the biblical injunction found in Revelation 3:5. For a man, this consists of white trousers, a white shirt, and a white vest. For a woman, the usual clothing is a white cape and apron that she wore at both her baptism and her marriage. At baptism a black dress is worn with the white cape and apron; at marriage a purple or blue dress is worn with the white cape and apron. It is only at her death that an Amish woman wears a white dress, with the cape and apron that she put away for the occasion of her death. This is an example of the lifelong preparation for death as sanctioned by Amish society. The wearing of white clothes signifies the high ceremonial emphasis on the death event as the final rite of passage into a new and better life.

Several Amish women stated that making their parents', husbands', or children's funeral garments was a labor of love that represented the last thing they could do for their loved ones. One Amish woman related that each month her aged grandmother carefully washed, starched, and ironed her own funeral clothing so that it would be in readiness for her death. This act appears to have reinforced for herself and her family her lifelong acceptance of death and to have contributed to laying the foundation for effective grief work for herself and her family. This can be seen as an example of the technique of preventive intervention called *anticipatory guidance* (Caplan, 1964, p. 84), which focuses on helping individuals to cope with impending loss through open discussion and problem solving before the actual death.

After the body is dressed, it is placed in a plain wooden coffin that is made to specifications handed down through the centuries. The coffin is placed in a room that has been emptied of all furnishings in order to accommodate the several hundred relatives, friends, and neighbors who will begin arriving as soon as the body is prepared for viewing. The coffin is placed in a central position in the house, both for practical considerations of seating and to underscore the importance of the death ceremonial.

The funeral service is held in the barn in the warmer months and in the house during the colder seasons. The service is conducted in German and lasts 1½ hours, with the same order of service as for every funeral. The guests view the body when they arrive and again when they leave to take their places in the single-file procession of the carriages to the burial place.

Source: Bryer, K. B. (1979). The Amish way of death. *American Psychologist, 34,* 255–261. Copyright 1979 by The American Psychological Association. Reprinted by permission of the author.

idea of developmental tasks that reflect similar themes for all older adults is bound to miss the vivid and complex reality of each person's experiences. Nevertheless, the tasks discussed here do reflect major themes that are likely to be confronted in the later years. These themes suggest new barriers to adaptation as well as new opportunities. Changes in memory and problem-solving skills may make the accomplishment of daily tasks a greater challenge. Role loss and the death of loved ones introduce needs for new kinds of support and changes in daily lifestyle. Most certainly they convey a very concrete message that a transition to a new period of the life span is under way.

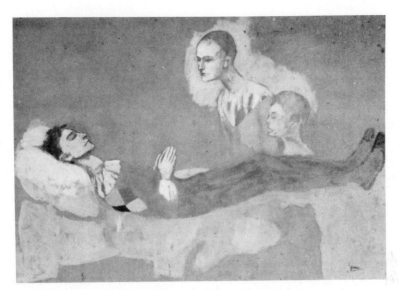

Pablo Picasso, *The Death of Harlequin,* 1905. When someone close to us dies, we reflect on the quality of our relationship with the person, the nature of the person's accomplishments, and the value or contribution of that life. Picasso painted this work in memory of Carlos Casagemas, who accompanied him from Barcelona to Paris in their youth. Casagemas committed suicide in 1901 when his love for a French model was rejected.

The tasks of older adults require a balance among investments in past, present, and future. There is an expectation that energy will be spent in the evaluative process of reviewing and accepting one's past achievements. However, this focus on the past will be balanced with the enactment of new roles and the resolution of new problems. The challenge of assessing the meaning of one's life is especially vital in addressing one's inevitable death. Here we see how the anticipation of a future life event can contribute to our present state, forcing us to a new level of thought and analysis that can have much broader implications for all spheres of functioning beyond that of coping with the event itself.

The Psychosocial Crisis: Integrity versus Despair

The attainment of integrity can come only after some considerable thought about the meaning of one's life. *Integrity,* as the term is used in Erikson's theory, refers to an ability to accept the facts of one's life and to face death without great fear. Older adults who have achieved a sense of integrity view their past in an existential light. They appreciate that their lives and their individuality are due to an accumulation of personal satisfactions and crises. They can accept this record of events totally, without trying to deny some facts or overemphasize others. Integrity is not so much a quality of honesty and trustworthiness, as we might use the term in daily speech, as it is an ability to integrate one's sense of past history with one's present circumstances and to feel content with the outcome.

The opposite pole of this crisis is *despair.* It is much more likely that adults will resolve the crisis of integrity versus despair in the negative direction than that infants will resolve the crisis of trust versus mistrust in the negative direction. For infants to experience trust, they must depend on the benevolence of a responsible caregiver who will meet their essential needs. In most cases, this caregiver is present and the infant learns to rely on him or her. In order to experience integrity, older adults must incorporate a lifelong sequence of conflicts, failures, and disappointments into their self-image. This in itself is a comparatively difficult process. In addition, older adults must face some degree of devaluation and even hostility from the social community. The negative attitudes expressed by family members, colleagues, and younger people toward the incompetence, dependence, or old-fashioned ways of older people may lead many of them to feel quite discouraged about their self-worth. The gradual deterioration of certain physical capacities, particularly the loss of hearing, impaired vision, and limited motor agility, feeds into the older person's sense of frustration and discouragement.

All of these factors are likely to create a feeling of regret about one's past and a continuous, haunting desire to be able to do things differently. The individual who resolves the crisis of later adulthood in the direction of despair cannot resist speculating about how things might have been or about what actions might have been taken if conditions had only been different. Thus despair makes an attitude of calm acceptance of death impossible. Either individuals seek death as a way of ending a miserable existence or they desperately fear death because it makes impossible any hope of compensating for past failures.

The Central Process: Introspection

In order to achieve a sense of integrity, the individual must engage in deliberate self-evaluation and private thought. The final achievement of a sense of integrity results from an ability to *introspect* about the gradual evolution of life events and appreciate the significance of each event in the formation of the adult personality. This state can be reached only through individual effort. One may even have to isolate oneself temporarily, shutting out the influences of potentially competitive or resentful associates.

As a product of his introspection, Dr. Pierce began to formulate an analysis of purpose that was embedded in his diverse life experiences, a sense of purpose that transcends the stresses of the many microaggressions to which Black Americans are exposed.

> *Meanwhile some other lessons or guidelines about racism have percolated from making analogies during these years. One, following studies on dog sled mushers who raced 1100 miles across Alaska, concerned the need for a clear goal. The mushers, despite organic brain signs at the end of the race, had been able to reach this goal without mishap. This seemed staggering. It suggested that, in spite of obstacles, having a clearly focused goal and informed resolution of conflicts would be valuable for Black's individual and community survival. This means that each Black, in our instance as Black psychiatrists, must do things to help Blacks and ourselves to make such resolutions and goal formulations.*

One consideration that seems important for Black professions to emphasize is service to the international community. Compared to White America we are in short supply of skilled and educated people. Compared to many countries of the world, especially third-world countries, Black America has a superabundance of skilled and educated people. Another opportunity to bring unity out of diversity would be for us to initiate more strong actions to bring our skill and education to other areas, even while we extend our slender resources to alleviate conditions in the U.S.A.

This view can be defended on the basis of historical and humanitarian needs. Also philosophically, due to our acquaintance with oppression, we might, as a group, find more ready congeniality to work on planetary projects. Politically, the model would help Blacks in the U.S.A. and help the country abroad. Psychologically, for those able to do it, it would be an avenue in which to utilize lofty aspirations and our willingness to sacrifice.

As a scouting report, it can be said that for a variety of reasons Black Americans are about to be recruited to wider efforts on a scale never before approached. Here is an instance where we should prepare for unity when our diversity is sought. *

One mode for engaging in self-evaluation is *reminiscence*. This process of nostalgic remembering allows adults to recapture some of the memorable events in their life histories. Reminiscence can be a playful recalling of a life adventure or a painful review of some personal or family crisis. The process of simple reminiscence has been described as comprising four elements: selection of an event or "story" to retell or review; immersion in the details of the story, including the strong emotions linked to the event; withdrawal from the past by distancing oneself from the event or comparing past and present; and bringing closure to the memory by summing up, finding some lesson, or making a general observation (Merriam, 1989). Through this kind of process, a person builds a mental and emotional bridge between the past and the present.

The process of reminiscence appears to lend continuity to older adults' self-concepts. They can trace the path of their own development through time and identify moments that were of central importance to the crystallization of their personal philosophies. We see reminiscence as an integrating process that has positive value for an eventual attainment of integrity. In excess, however, reminiscence can dominate reality. Some adults tend to dwell on sad events and allow earlier disappointments to preoccupy their current thoughts. In that case, their past lives take precedence over current circumstances. No new events can compete successfully with past memories for their attention. Under these conditions, realistic acceptance of their total life history is not possible.

Of course, the process of introspection will be affected by the selectivity of memory, the dominant value orientation, and the general quality of supportiveness or destructiveness in the social milieu. Given these contaminants of purely objective self-assessment, individuals must engage in repeated soul-searching efforts to sort out

---

Pablo Picasso, *Portrait of a Seated Man,* 1918. Later adulthood is viewed as a period of wisdom and stability. Through introspection and reminiscence, people discover meaning in their life stories.

their lives and come to terms with some of the discordant events that inevitably will be part of their history. They must determine whether the essential nature of their personal identity has survived through time. They must evaluate the quality of their close relationships and determine the degree to which they are able to meet the needs of others. They must identify those contributions that have represented a serious effort to improve the quality of other's lives. Finally, they must determine the extent to which their philosophy of life has been accurately translated into patterns of significant actions.

Ryff and Heincke (1983) used a psychosocial model to test the possible changes in personality configurations in later adulthood. Early, middle, and later adults were asked to respond to a variety of statements from three time perspectives—as they applied in the present, in the past during an earlier life stage, and in the future in a later life stage. Generativity was perceived by all age groups as being highest during middle adulthood, regardless of the respondent's ages. Similarly, integrity was perceived as being highest in later adulthood. Older adults rated themselves as being higher in integrity at present than they recalled having been in the past. Young and middle-aged adults expected to be higher on this dimension in the future than they were at present. This research suggests that people not only experience changes in the directions psychosocial theory would predict but also anticipate changes in those directions at various life stages. These expectations influence how one prepares for future life stages and evaluates them once they arrive.

The attainment of integrity ultimately is a result of thought. Adults' thoughts about their lives will generate a predominant stance toward their feelings of personal contentment and worth. The final outcome of this process of introspection is not a direct translation of the number of positive or negative events in one's life or the number of successes and failures in one's efforts to achieve. There are adults who have experienced grave, lifelong trauma or suffer from serious physical handicaps yet can maintain an attitude of contentment with their lot in life. There are other adults who view the past with great dissatisfaction and resentment although their lives have been comparatively conflict free. Resolving the conflict of integrity versus despair is a process of achieving an attitude of self-acceptance through private introspection.

Summary

The conflict of integrity versus despair is resolved through a dynamic process of life review and self-evaluation. Contemporary factors such as health, family relationships, and role loss or role transition are integrated with an assessment of one's past aspirations and accomplishments. Thoughts of the past may be fleeting or a constant obsession. Memories may be altered to fit contemporary events, or contemporary events may be reinterpreted to fit memories. The achievement of integrity is the culmination of a life of psychosocial growth. Psychologically speaking, it is the peak of the pyramid in that it addresses the ultimate question: How do we find meaning in life given the ultimate reality of death? Achievement of integrity in later adulthood inspires younger age groups to continue to struggle with the challenges of their own life stages.

☐ Applied Topic: Retirement

Retirement usually refers to one's status with respect to the paid labor force. One definition of retirement is that the person works less than full-time year round, and receives income from a retirement pension earned during earlier periods of employment (Atchley, 1977). Some people define retirement as the time at which people begin to receive social security or other pension benefits. However, retirement also refers to a psychological state—a sense of withdrawal from the job or the work organization and a new orientation toward work.

Of course, some people never retire. Some die before they reach retirement age. Some who are self-employed or whose work involves certain creative skills, such as acting, music, painting, or writing, simply continue to work well into their late adulthood. In fact, retirement is a relatively new opportunity from a historical perspective. At the turn of the century, almost 70% of men over the age of 65 were in the paid labor force, compared to 16% in 1984 (U.S. Senate, Special Committee on Aging, 1986). Men spend about 20% of their lives in retirement. As the period of healthy later adulthood expands for men, this proportion will certainly increase as well.

Recent cohorts of adults hold more positive views of retirement than did adults who reached retirement age during the 1940s and 1950s. At that time, most adults had not grown up in families in which parents had retired. They did not expect to have the opportunity to retire when they entered the labor market. Studies done on attitudes toward retirement during that period reflected sentiments of guilt and dread of

In many cultures, workers never retire, continuing their work as well as they can until they die. The old ones teach the young ones, passing the secrets of their craft from one generation to the next.

having nothing to do or of being paid (in the form of a pension) for doing nothing. Today most workers see retirement as an appropriate end to their work lives, a transition to which they are entitled. Postretirement perceptions tend to reflect a sense of optimism about life and satisfaction with the decision to retire. Many people perceive the decision to retire as one over which they have control and that will lead to positive consequences (Hendrick, Wells & Faletti, 1982).

Some people have more difficulty than others in adjusting to retirement. Three factors that seem to influence such adjustment include planning for retirement, perceptions of retirement, and the extent of income loss (Newman & Newman, 1983). Preparation for retirement involves a willingness to anticipate the changes that may occur in finances, family roles, daily activity, and social interactions after retirement, and to take some actions to address these changes. Ferraro (1990) names some items that reflect planning for the retirement years:

1. Build up your own savings.
2. Buy your own home.
3. Learn about pension and social security benefits.
4. Develop hobbies and other leisure-time activities.
5. Decide whether you want to move or continue to live where you are.
6. Prepare a will.
7. Make sure you'll have medical care available.
8. Move in with children or other relatives.

In a national survey of men aged 60 to 74, fewer than 4% were found to have participated in retirement preparation programs. Those workers who might benefit most from these programs, especially those with lower retirement income, are less likely to learn about or participate in them (Beck, 1984; Ferraro, 1990).

Perceptions of retirement involve a person's sense of relief or resentment regarding it. For many adults, work gives a structure to daily life. Moreover, salaries permit them to be independent and to maintain a sense of being socially valued. These adults may perceive retirement as rejection. It produces sentiments of uselessness. People whose work has brought them little satisfaction, however, can feel more effective and independent after they retire, as the following account makes clear.

> *This widowed man lives alone in a cabin in a sparsely populated, rural area. Throughout his working career, he held a variety of low-paying jobs that, in retrospect, neither required nor permitted real discipline or enterprise. He did not particularly like his jobs, and he was never viewed as performing them with particular success. For this man, retirement seems to signify not the loss of valuable structure, but his release from a series of rigid, repetitive demands that in and of themselves precluded inventiveness and enthusiasm. Retirement presents him with a new opportunity to reexperience the initiative that he now recalls as having characterized him until his midteens.*
>
> *This man has always enjoyed music. He has always loved listening to the radio and playing records. As an adolescent, he tinkered with radio equipment until the advent of transistors and integrated circuits. Over the years he has accumulated a collection of some two to three thousand 78 rpm records. Recognizing that plastic record disks are likely to warp or break, he has recently begun to copy them onto cassettes. He has removed his tape deck and large loudspeakers from their cabinet and strapped them to a mover's dolly, onto which he has built appropriate shelves. Each day, when he goes to the senior center for lunch, he wheels his movable entertainment center out to his pickup truck and brings his friends their favorite songs. This man has also begun to make his own TV dinners, using the partitioned trays on which his "meals on wheels" are delivered. He cooks large quantities of meat and vegetables and freezes them in these single-meal trays for easy access. The quality of this man's products is far from professional. In fact, his entertainment center looks rather slapdash, and the contents of his frozen meals do not always retain their flavor or texture when reheated. What is striking, instead, is the enthusiasm, the delight, and the pride with which he has devised his various projects. In each case he perceived a problem, combined his own ingenuity with the resources at hand to devise a solution that is satisfactory for his own needs, and created something that is usable, gives him pleasure, and remains a real source of personal pride.*   [Erikson, Erikson & Kivnick, 1986, pp. 181–182]

One of the attitudes associated with difficulty in adjusting to retirement is the Protestant ethic. People who adhere to this doctrine place great emphasis on hard work, achievement, and delay of gratification. Leisure activities and play are not considered worthwhile. One study found that retired adults who strongly endorsed the

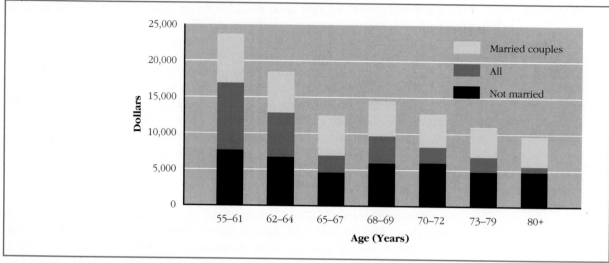

Figure 13.3   Median Annual Income by Marital Status and Age, 1980
Source: U.S. Bureau of the Census, *America in Transition: An Aging Society,* Current Population Reports
(ser. P-23, no. 128) (Washington, D.C.: U.S. Government Printing Office, 1983), p. 9.

Protestant ethic tended to engage in fewer daily activities. They also tended to perceive
these activities as lower in usefulness. A combination of these two factors was linked
to lower levels of satisfaction after retirement (Hooker & Ventis, 1984).

Finally, adjustment to retirement is especially difficult when it is associated with
a dramatic reduction in income. One can expect about a 25 to 30% reduction in
income after retirement. Although work-related expenses, taxes, and child-care expenses
may decrease, health and recreational expenses may increase.

Income loss is somewhat greater for those who retire before age 65 (Palmore,
Fillenbaum & George, 1984). Figure 13.3 shows the median annual income of adults
aged 55 to over 80 in 1980 by marital status and age. Older householders' annual
income is derived from social security (37%), earnings (25%), property (23%), and
pensions (13%). About 14% of all retired households receive income from at least
three sources—social security, private pensions, and other assets (Kart, Longino &
Ullmann, 1989). About 34% of households headed by someone 65 years old or older
had an annual income of less than $10,000 a year in 1987. Poverty is greater for older
minorities and those who live alone. At the other end of the scale, many of the richest
Americans are over 65. Among the 14 Americans listed as having wealth worth over
$1 billion in 1986, seven were over 65 years old. In 1987 about 20% of families headed
by someone over 65 had annual incomes of over $25,000 (U.S. Bureau of the Census,
1989).

Adjustment to retirement is expected to change with time. Atchley (1976) proposed three phases of adjustment: a honeymoon period, which is busy and positive;
a letdown phase, in which the meaning and structure of work are really missed; and
a reorientation phase, in which a stable life routine is established. In an attempt to

assess this model, one study grouped retired men into six six-month intervals from the date of retirement. Men in a period of 13 to 18 months after retirement were significantly more dissatisfied with life and had lower levels of physical activity than did those in the first six months after retirement. Later periods showed lower levels of satisfaction than in the first six months but not the marked depression of the 13-to-18-month period (Ekerdt, Bosse & Levkoff, 1985). These findings support the early euphoria idea as well as the notion of a letdown phase. The pattern and degree of recovery are not as clearly described in this research.

A Look Toward the Future of Retirement

The ongoing dialogue among older workers, retirees, and organizations is likely to result in the formulation of more varied, flexible alternatives to full retirement. More and more businesses are eliminating a mandatory retirement age. Preretirement plans, including phased retirement, part-time work, and reduced or redefined job expectations, are being devised. Exploration seems to be taking two directions at the same time. One looks at how to retain older workers in meaningful work roles. The other explores ways of permitting more flexible, earlier retirement (Gonda, 1981).

Several long-range concerns suggest a need to reexamine the "right to retirement" concept. First, prospects for a longer, healthier adulthood mean that a large proportion of the population will be out of the labor force for nearly one-third of their adult lives. With a reduced fertility rate, there may not be enough younger workers available to support this large nonworking population. Second, older adults who are well educated and who have enjoyed their work lives will want to continue some of the positive experiences of employment through constructive work. We are already beginning to sense some of this resistance in the attitudes of professionals in their 50s and 60s. In in-depth interviews with university professors, physicians, lawyers, business professionals, and social service professionals, over 35% were very negative about retiring and another 20% were ambivalent. One of those who was quite negative expressed it this way:

> *I'd probably try to get part-time teaching jobs, writing or editing, or research somewhere until I fall over. I mean really, I just can't imagine [retirement]. . . . This [teaching] is a rewarding activity. I don't banker to retire to the sun belt and sit around and contemplate my navel. I just couldn't do that.* [Karp, 1989, p. 752.]

Third, people who reenter the labor force during midlife or who make major midlife career changes will want to persist at these new activities in order to fulfill both personal and societal expectations for achievement (Horn, 1980; Ragan, 1980). Thus, just as the past few generations have begun to grow accustomed to retirement, the next generation of older adults may be finding ways to prolong their productive work lives.

☐ Chapter Summary

Variability in the patterns of adjustment during later adulthood results from the persistence of the individual's personality characteristics and the range of circumstances that can befall him or her. Certain regularities can be anticipated in the termination of old roles and the establishment of new ones. Consolidation of attitudes toward one's own life and toward the reality of one's own death can bring about a new perspective on life and lead to a more universalistic moral orientation.

It is critical that we be sensitive to the image that children, adolescents, young and middle-aged adults, and older adults themselves have of later adulthood. We should not underestimate the impact on a sense of well-being and optimism at every life stage of looking forward to a fulfilling later life. If the later years hold no promise, all earlier stages will be tinted with a sense of desperation. If the later years can be anticipated with eagerness for a new set of life experiences, we will be free at each earlier stage to experience our lives in a more confident and accepting manner.

References

Anthony, S. (1972). *The discovery of death in childhood and after.* New York: Basic Books.

Atchley, R. C. (1976). *The sociology of retirement.* New York: Halsted.

Atchley, R. C. (1977). *The social forces of later life.* Belmont, Calif.: Wadsworth.

Barrett, C. J. (1981). Intimacy in widowhood. *Psychology of Women Quarterly, 5,* 473–487.

Bass, D. M., & Bowman, K. (1990). The transition from caregiving to bereavement: The relationship of care-related strain and adjustment to death. *Gerontologist, 30,* 35–42.

Bearon, L. G. (1989). No great expectations: The underpinnings of life satisfaction for older women. *Gerontologist, 29,* 772–778.

Beck, S. H. (1984). Retirement preparation programs: Differentials in opportunity and use. *Journal of Gerontology, 39,* 596–602.

Bengston, V. L., Cuellar, J. B., & Ragan, P. K. (1977). Stratum contrasts and similarities in attitudes toward death. *Journal of Gerontology, 32,* 76–88.

Birren, J. E. (1974). Translations in gerontology—From lab to life: Psychophysiology and speed of response. *American Psychologist, 29,* 808–815.

Blackburn, J. A. (1984). The influence of personality, curriculum, and memory correlates on formal reasoning in young adults and elderly persons. *Journal of Gerontology, 39,* 207–209.

Botwinick, J. (1984). *Aging and behavior* (3rd ed.). New York: Springer.

Bryer, K. B. (1979). The Amish way of death: A study of family support systems. *American Psychologist, 34,* 255–261.

Caplan, G. (1964). Principles of preventive psychiatry. New York: Basic Books.

Conte, H. R., Weiner, M. B., & Plutchik, R. (1982). Measuring death anxiety: Conceptual, psychometric, and factor-analytic aspects. *Journal of Personality and Social Psychology, 43,* 775–785.

Costa, P. T., & McCrae, R. R. (1980). The influence of extraversion and neuroticism on subjective well-being: Happy and unhappy people. *Journal of Personality and Social Psychology, 38,* 668–678.

Costa, P. T., Zonderman, A. B., McCrae, R. R., Coroni-Huntley, J., Locke, B. Z., & Barbano, H. E. (1987). Longitudinal analyses of psychological well-being in a national sample: Stability of mean levels. *Journal of Gerontology, 42*(1), 50–55.

Denney, N. W. (1982). Aging and cognitive changes. In B. B. Wolman (ed.), *Handbook of developmental psychology* (pp. 807–827). Englewood Cliffs, N.J.: Prentice-Hall.

Denney, N. W., & Pearce, K. A. (1989). A developmental study of practical problem solving in adults. *Psychology and Aging, 4,* 438–442.

Dennis, W. (1966). Creative productivity between the ages of twenty and eighty years. *Journal of Gerontology, 21,* 1–8.

DeVries, H. A. (1975). Physiology of exercise. In D. S. Woodruff & J. E. Birren (eds.), *Aging: Scientific per-*

spectives and social issues. New York: Van Nostrand.

Ekerdt, D. J., Bosse, R., & Levkoff, S. (1985). An empirical test for phases of retirement: Findings from the normative aging study. *Journal of Gerontology, 40,* 95–101.

Erikson, E., Erikson, J., & Kivnick, H. (1986). *Vital involvement in old age.* New York: Norton.

Feifel, H., & Branscomb, A. (1973). Who's afraid of death? *Journal of Abnormal Psychology, 81,* 282–288.

Ferraro, K. F. (1990). Cohort analysis of retirement preparation, 1974–1981. *Journal of Gerontology, 45,* S25.

Flanagan, J. C. (1978). A research approach to improving our quality of life. *American Psychologist, 33,* 138–147.

Flanagan, J. C. (1980). Quality of life. In L. A. Bond & J. C. Rosen (eds.), *Competence and coping during adulthood* (pp. 156–177). Hanover, N. H.: University Press of New England.

Florian, V., & Kravetz, S. (1983). Fear of personal death: Attribution structure and relation to religious belief. *Journal of Personality and Social Psychology, 44,* 600–607.

Fozard, J. L., & Poon, L. W. (1976). *Research and training activities of the mental performance and aging laboratory (1973–1976).* Technical Report 76–02. Boston: Veterans Administration Outpatient Clinic.

Fried-Cassorla, M. (1977). Death anxiety and disengagement. Paper presented at the annual convention of the American Psychological Association, San Francisco.

Futterman, A., Gallagher, D., Thompson, L. W., Lovett, S., & Gilewski, M. (1990). Retrospective assessment of marital adjustment and depression during the first two years of spousal bereavement. *Psychology and Aging, 5,* 277–283.

Gonda, J. (1981). Convocation in work, aging, and retirement: A review. *Human Development, 24,* 286–292.

Guangzhao, Z. (1985). Retirement age for Chinese scientists. *Science, 230,* 738.

Hayslip, B., Jr., & Brookshire, R. G. (1985). Relationships among abilities in elderly adults: A time lag analysis. *Journal of Gerontology, 40,* 748–750.

Hendrick, C., Wells, K. S., & Faletti, M. V. (1982). Social and emotional effects of geographical relocation on elderly retirees. *Journal of Personality and Social Psychology, 42,* 951–962.

Hertzog, D., & Schaie, K. W. (1988). Stability and change in adult intelligence: 2. Simultaneous analysis of longitudinal means and covariance structures. *Psychology and Aging, 3,* 122–130.

Hooker, K., & Ventis, D. G. (1984). Work ethic, daily activities, and retirement satisfaction. *Journal of Gerontology, 39,* 478–484.

Hopkins, D. R., Murrah, B., Hoeger, W. W. K., & Rhodes, R. C. (1990). Effect of low-impact aerobic dance on the functional fitness of elderly women. *Gerontologist, 30,* 189–192.

Horn, J. L. (1979). The rise and fall of human abilities. *Journal of Research and Development in Education, 12,* 59–78.

Horn, J. L. (1980). On the future of growing old. Paper presented for a university lecture, University of Denver, Denver.

Kahana, B., & Kahana, E. (1970). Grandparenthood from the perspective of the developing grandchild. *Developmental Psychology, 3,* 98–105.

Kahana, B., Kahana, E., & McLenigan, P. (1980). *The adventurous aged: Voluntary relocation in the later years.* Paper presented at the meeting of the American Orthopsychiatric Association, Toronto.

Kalish, R. A., & Reynolds, D. K. (1976) *Death and ethnicity: A psychocultural study.* Los Angeles: University of Southern California Press.

Karp, D. A. (1989). The social construction of retirement among professionals 50–60 years old. *Gerontologist, 29,* 750–760.

Kart, C. S., Longino, C. F., & Ullmann, S. G. (1989). Comparing the economically advantaged and the pension elite: 1980 census profiles. *Gerontologist, 29,* 745–749.

Kivnick, H. Q. (1983). Dimensions of grandparenthood meaning: Deductive conceptualization and empirical derivation. *Journal of Personality and Social Psychology, 44,* 1056–1068.

Klemmack, D. L., & Roff, L. L. (1984). Fear of personal aging and subjective well-being in later life. *Journal of Gerontology, 39,* 756–758.

Kübler-Ross, E. (1969). *On death and dying.* New York: Macmillan.

Kübler-Ross, E. (1972). On death and dying. *Journal of the American Medical Association,* February.

Labouvie-Vief, G., & Schell, D. A. (1982). Learning and memory in later life. In B. B. Wolman (ed.), *Handbook of developmental psychology* (pp. 828–846). Englewood Cliffs, N.J.: Prentice-Hall.

Lehman, H. C. (1953). *Age and achievement.* Princeton, N.J.: Princeton University Press.

Lindemann, E. (1944). Symptomology and management of acute grief. *American Journal of Psychiatry, 101,* 141–148.

Lopata, H. Z. (1973). *Widowhood in an American city.* Cambridge, Mass.: Schenkman.

Lopata, H. Z. (1978). Widowhood: Social norms and social integration. In *Family Factbook*. Chicago: Marquis Academic Media.

McCrae, R. R., & Costa, P. T. (1983). Psychological maturity and subjective well-being: Toward a new synthesis. *Developmental Psychology, 19,* 243–248.

Mead, M. (1975). On grandparents as educators. In H. J. Leichter (ed.), *The family as educator.* New York: Teachers College Press.

Merriam, S. B. (1989). The structure of simple reminiscence. *Gerontologist, 29,* 761–767.

Meyers, G. C., & Manton, K. G. (1984). Compression of mortality: Myth or reality. *Gerontologist, 24,* 346–353.

Montepare, J. M., & Lachman, M. E. (1989). "You're only as old as you feel": Self-perceptions of age, fears of aging, and life satisfaction from adolescence to old age. *Psychology and Aging, 4,* 73–78.

Neugarten, B., & Weinstein, R. (1964). The changing American grandparent. *Journal of Marriage and the Family, 26,* 199–204.

Newman, B. M., & Newman, P. R. (1983). *Understanding adulthood.* New York: Holt, Rinehart & Winston.

O'Bryant, S. (1988). Sibling support and older widows' well-being. *Journal of Marriage and the Family, 50,* 173–183.

O'Leary, V. E. (1977). *The widow as female household head.* Paper presented at the annual convention of the American Psychological Association, San Francisco.

Palmore, E. B., Fillenbaum, G. G., & George, L. K. (1984). Consequences of retirement. *Journal of Gerontology, 39,* 109–116.

Pierce, C. M. (1989). Unity in diversity: Thirty-three years of stress. In G. L. Berry and J. K. Asamen (eds.), *Black Students.* Newbury Park, Calif.: Sage.

Poon, L. W., & Fozard, J. L. (1978). Speed in retrieval from long-term memory in relation to age, familiarity, and datedness of information. *Journal of Gerontology, 33,* 711–717.

Ragan, P. K. (1980). *Work and retirement: Policy issues.* Los Angeles: University of Southern California Press.

Reese, H. W. (1976). The development of memory: Lifespan perspectives. In H. W. Reese (ed.), *Advances in child development and behavior* (vol. 11). New York: Academic Press.

Riegel, K. F., & Riegel, R. M. (1972). Development, drop, and death. *Developmental Psychology, 6,* 306–319.

Robertson, J. F. (1977). Grandmotherhood: A study of role conceptions. *Journal of Marriage and the Family, 39,* 165–174.

Ryff, C. D., & Heincke, S. G. (1983). Subjective organization of personality in adulthood and aging. *Journal of Personality and Social Psychology, 44,* 807–816.

Schaie, K. W. (1973). Methodological problems in descriptive developmental research on adulthood and aging. In J. R. Nesselroade & H. W. Reese (eds.), *Life-span developmental psychology: Methodological issues.* New York: Academic Press.

Schaie, K. W. (1989). Perceptual speed in adulthood: Cross-sectional and longitudinal studies. *Psychology and Aging, 4,* 443–453.

Schaie, K. W., & Hertzog, C. (1983). Fourteen-year cohort-sequential analyses of adult intellectual development. *Developmental Psychology, 19,* 531–543.

Scogin, F., Storandt, M., & Lott, L. (1985). Memory-skills training, memory complaints, and depression in older adults. *Journal of Gerontology, 40,* 562–568.

Selzer, S. C., & Denney, N. W. (1980). Conservation abilities among middle-aged and elderly adults. *Aging and Human Development, 11,* 135–146.

Simonton, D. K. (1977). Creative productivity, age, and stress: A biographical time-series analysis of ten classical composers. *Journal of Personality and Social Psychology, 35,* 791–804.

Simonton, D. K. (1988). Age and outstanding achievement: What do we know after a century of research? *Psychological Bulletin, 104,* 251–267.

Simonton, D. K. (1989). The swan-song phenomenon: Last-works effects for 172 classical composers. *Psychology and Aging, 4,* 42–47.

Skinner, B. F. (1983). Intellectual self-management in old age. *American Psychologist, 38,* 239–244.

Strayer, D. L., Wickens, C. D., & Braune, R. (1987). Adult age differences in the speed and capacity of information processing: 2. An electrophysiological approach. *Psychology and Aging, 2,* 99–110.

Tinsley, H. E. A., Teaff, J. D., Colbs, S. L., & Kaufman, N. (1985). System of classifying leisure activities in terms of the psychological benefits of participation reported by older persons. *Journal of Gerontology, 40,* 172–178.

Tomlin, A. M., & Passman, R. H. (1989). Grandmothers' responsibility in raising two-year-olds facilitates their grandchildren's adaptive behavior: A preliminary intrafamilial investigation of mothers' and maternal grandmothers' effects. *Psychology and Aging, 4,* 119–121.

U.S. Bureau of the Census (1983). *America in transition: An aging society.* Current Population Reports (ser.

P-23, no. 128). Washington, D.C.: U.S. Government Printing Office.

U.S. Bureau of the Census (1987). *An aging world.* International Population Reports (ser. P-25, no. 78). Washington, D.C.: U.S. Government Printing Office.

U.S. Bureau of the Census (1989). *Population profile of the United States, 1989.* Current Population Reports (ser. P-23, no. 159). Washington, D.C.: U.S. Government Printing Office.

U.S. Senate, Special Committee on Aging (1986). *Aging America—trends and projections.* Washington, D.C.: U.S. Government Printing Office.

Ward, R. A. (1977). The impact of subjective age and stigma on older persons. *Journal of Gerontology, 32,* 227–232.

White, N., & Cunningham, W. R. (1988). Is terminal drop pervasive or specific? *Journal of Gerontology: Psychological Sciences, 43,* P141–P144.

Wingfield, A., Poon, L. W., Lombardi, L., & Lowe, D. (1985). Speed of processing in normal aging: Effects of speech rate, linguistic structure, and processing time. *Journal of Gerontology, 40,* 579–585.

Chapter Fourteen

Father Christmas is the perfect representative of the very old. He has all the benefits of extreme old age, but he is ever young in spirit; in fact, he is immortal.

Very Old Age (75 Until Death)

Pablo Picasso, whose works illustrate this book, lived to be 91 years old. When he was 79 he married Jacqueline Roque, with whom he enjoyed 12 years of married life. During the last 20 years of his life, he remained productive and energetic, persistently experimenting with new art forms and ideas.

Here are some other well-known people who achieved major accomplishments after 80 years of age (Wallechinsky, Wallace & Wallace, 1977):

At 100, Grandma Moses was still painting.

At 94, Bertrand Russell was active in international peace drives.

At 93, George Bernard Shaw wrote the play *Farfetched Fables*.

At 91, Eamon de Valera served as president of Ireland.

At 91, Adolph Zukor was chairman of Paramount Pictures.

At 89, Mary Baker Eddy was director of the Christian Science church.

At 89, Albert Schweitzer headed a hospital in Africa.

At 89, Arthur Rubenstein gave one of his greatest recitals in New York's Carnegie Hall.

At 88, Michelangelo did architectural plans for the Church of Santa Maria degli Angeli.

At 88, Pablo Casals was giving cello concerts.

At 88, Konrad Adenauer was chancellor of Germany.

At 85, Coco Chanel was the head of a fashion design firm.

At 84, W. Somerset Maugham wrote *Points of View*.

At 83, Alexander Kerensky wrote *Russia and History's Turning Point*.

At 82, Leo Tolstoy wrote *I Cannot Be Silent*.

At 81, Benjamin Franklin effected the compromise that led to the adoption of the U.S. Constitution.

At 81, Johann Wolfgang von Goethe finished *Faust*.

At 80, George Burns won an Academy Award for his performance in *The Sunshine Boys*.

We are entering a period of human experience in which increasing numbers of people are living to old age. In 1987, 5% of the population was 75 and over. This age group is expected to comprise 10% of the population in 50 years. In 1980, over 2 million people were 85 and over and 32,000 were 100 or more years old. The 85-and-over population is the fastest-growing age group in the United States. This group is expected to triple in size from 1980 to 2020 (U.S. Bureau of the Census, 1989b; U.S. Senate, Special Committee on Aging, 1986).

As more and more people live to be 75 and over, questions continue to be raised regarding the upper limit of the human life span. Meyers and Manton (1984) have demonstrated that the most enduring members of each new generation of aging adults appear to be living longer and longer. Life endurancy is the age to which one person in 100,000 can be expected to survive. Between 1900 and 1980, the age of the most enduring adults in the U.S. population increased from 105 to 111 for men and from 105 to 114 for women. Current evidence does not support the view of a fixed upper limit to the human life span.

As more people reach very old age, tasks and psychosocial competences emerge that have not yet been systematically delineated. We need to examine and understand the psychosocial competences and needs of this population in order to maintain the quality of their lives and help younger people form a picture of what they may expect as they get older.

The variations in life experiences and outlook among the very old are great. Neugarten (1981) has found it useful to distinguish between two groups of the very old, the old-old and the young-old. The old-old have "suffered major physical or mental decrements," which increase their dependence on health and social services. This group will grow as the number of adults over 75 increases. At present it forms a minority of the very old. The majority of people over 75 can be described as the young-old. They are competent, vigorous, and relatively healthy. They live in their own households and participate in activities in their communities.

Each new cohort of the very old will benefit from the information and technology that have been developed during this century. Those adults who will be over 75 in the year 2000 are quite likely to be high school graduates, to have benefited from many of the educational and health-related innovations of the mid–twentieth century, and to be even more vigorous than our current older population.

Jewett (1973) has described characteristics that are common among people whom he calls long-living, successful agers. His description is based on observations of 79 individuals between 87 and 103 years of age. These people are able to maintain social contacts that meet their needs and satisfy their interests. They pursue activities that challenge and intrigue them and that are consistent with their life goals. They are well able to adapt to changing events and life situations, a trait to which Jewett refers as an ability to "roll with the punches." They are religious in the broadest sense of the term. They have a well-developed sense of humor, and they enjoy life.

Schwartz, Snyder, and Peterson (1984) reported that the vast majority of long-living, successful agers are of average size and body structure. Their habits and life-styles (including patterns of exercise, working, playing, sleeping, diet, smoking, and use of alcohol, coffee, and other drugs) are characterized by moderation. They are less troubled by anxiety and enjoy relative freedom from accidents. These characteristics appear to be shared by people in the very old age group in a variety of cultures.

In an attempt to learn the secrets of longevity, Jim Heynen (1990) interviewed 100 people who were 100 years or older. He found wide variation in the lifestyles and philosophical perspectives of these centenarians. Here is some of the advice they offer on how to live a long life:

- "Mind your own business, have a good cigar, and take a shot of brandy."—*Brother Adelard Beaudet, Harrisville, R.I.*
- "I've lived long because I was so mean."—*Pearl Rombach, Melbourne, Fla.*
- "I always walked several miles a day. I'd talk to the flowers."—*Mary Frances Annand, Pasadena, Calif.*
- "Don't smoke before noon. Don't drink or smoke after midnight. The body needs 12 hours of the day to clear itself."—*Harry Wander, Boise, Idaho.*
- "I've been a tofu eater all my life; a mild, gentle man, never a worrier."—*Frank Morimitsu, Chicago.*

- "I picked my ancestors carefully."—*Stella H. Harris, Manhattan, Kan.*
- "Regular hours, taking it easy, smiling, whistling at the women when they walk by."—*John Hilton, Fort Lauderdale, Fla.*

The fact that an increasing number of people are reaching advanced years and that they share several characteristics leads us to hypothesize a new stage of psychosocial development that emerges at the upper end of the life span after one has exceeded the life expectancy for one's birth cohort. We call this stage *very old age.* This stage was not specifically identified in Erikson's original formulation of life stages. In his *Vital Involvement in Old Age* (1986), however, he began to characterize the dynamics of psychosocial adaptation in this period of life. With the encouragement of many colleagues who teach the human development course and are interested in dealing with this period, we have formulated a psychosocial analysis of development for the very old. We have drawn on research literature, firsthand reports, and personal observations of the very old to describe the developmental tasks, psychosocial crisis, and central process of this stage. Our intention is to discuss some of the most salient characteristics of life after 75 and to articulate what appears to be a psychosocial crisis peculiar to this period.

Developmental Tasks

Coping with the Physical Changes of Aging

There is no way to avoid the realization that one's body is not what it used to be.

> *With aging, as the overall tonus of the body begins to sag and innumerable inner parts call attention to themselves through their malfunction, the aging body is forced into a new sense of invalidness. Some problems may be fairly petty, like the almost inevitable appearance of wrinkles. Others are painful, debilitating, and shaming. Whatever the severity of these ailments, the elder is obliged to turn attention from more interesting aspects of life to the demanding requirements of the body. This can be frustrating and depressing.*   [Erikson, Erikson & Kivnick, 1986, p. 309]

There is a great deal of variation in fitness among people after age 70 as patterns of activity or inactivity, endurance or frailty, and illness or health take their toll. For most people, strength and capacity for moderate effort are about the same at age 70 as they were at age 40 (Marshall, 1973). However, older people are less resilient after a period of prolonged exertion. Their respiratory and circulatory systems usually degenerate to some extent, rendering them less capable of providing the heart and muscle tissue with oxygenated blood as quickly as they once could. One result is that sudden changes in posture may leave an older person feeling lightheaded. In order to adapt successfully to this kind of bodily change, the older person may find it

Recreational therapy can involve aerobic exercise. Very old people with limited mobility enjoy exercising their arms and upper bodies as they keep the ball bouncing and floating.

necessary to move more slowly and to change positions more deliberately. This observable change in the tempo of movement may be incorrectly interpreted as fatigue or weakness; in fact it is often a purposeful strategy for preventing dizziness.

Slowed metabolism reduces the need for calories, but there is a new risk. Reduction in food intake—particularly the elimination of foods such as milk—may cause essential vitamins and minerals to be missing from an older person's diet. Malnutrition can contribute to feelings of weakness and a lack of resilience. These effects may be mistakenly attributed to the aging process. In order to cope successfully with a diminished appetite, the very old person must become more conscientious in selecting foods that will provide the nutritional elements necessary for healthy functioning.

An increasing number of factors make it difficult to maintain a high level of physical fitness in later life. Figure 14.1 illustrates patterns of loss of bodily functions associated with age in six areas. For each body area, the level of functioning at age 30 is taken as 100% and losses are plotted in comparison with this level. As you can see, maximum breathing capacity suffers the greatest loss and brain weight changes the least. Most of the bodily changes begin in middle adulthood, but the rate of change appears to increase after age 60. The consequences of an inactive life, especially degeneration of muscle strength and obesity, contribute to an even greater decline in physical capacity, particularly after age 60.

Being consciously committed to the value of physical fitness is very important for adults. In order to face the later years in the best possible physical condition, adults must keep themselves in shape. Maintenance of optimal physical condition in very old age depends on being active in earlier periods of adulthood. Overweight people, as well as those of normal or below-normal weight, need to commit themselves to a program of physical activity and to realize that it is possible to continue a moderate level of physical activity throughout life.

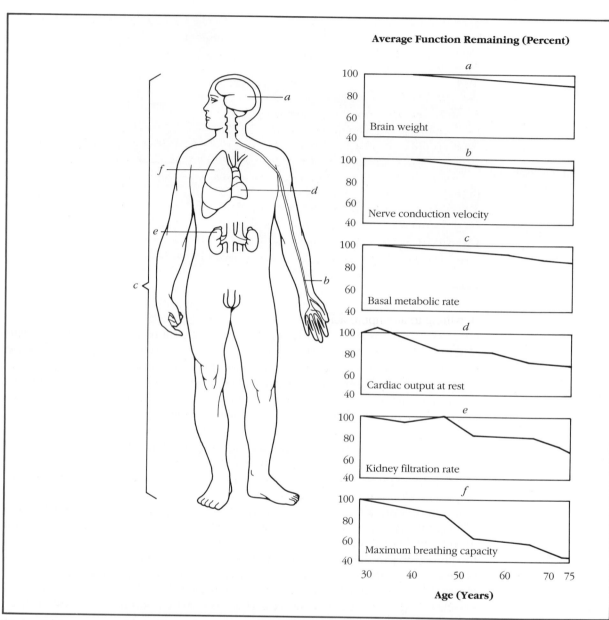

Figure 14.1   **Loss of Bodily Functions with Increasing Age**
Source: A. Leaf, "Growing Old," *Scientific American, 229,* 52. Copyright © 1973 by Scientific American, Inc.
All rights reserved.

With advancing age, some people tend to become more sedentary and to lose interest in physical activity. In order to maintain optimal functioning and retard the degenerative effects of aging, very old adults must continue to have frequent and regular opportunities for physical activity. A regular program of aerobic exercise, for example, can enhance cardiovascular functioning and reverse some of the effects of a sedentary adult lifestyle (Blumenthal et al., 1989). Older adults must make deliberate efforts to remain active despite reduced endurance and the likelihood of one or more chronic diseases that may interfere with mobility.

Behavioral Slowing

A change in functioning that is frequently cited during adulthood is reduced speed in responding to stimuli. Such *behavioral slowing* is observed in motor responses, reaction time, problem-solving abilities, memory skills, and information processing (Birren, Woods & Williams, 1980; Salthouse, 1985; Bashore, Osman & Heffley, 1989). Age-related slowing is more readily observable on complex tasks requiring mental processing than on routine tasks.

To explain why behavioral slowing occurs, biological, learned, and motivational factors have been suggested. At the biological level of analysis, there is evidence of the slowing of neural firing in certain brain areas, which could result in slower responses. Slowing may also be a product of learned cautiousness. With experience, people learn to respond slowly in order to avoid making mistakes. Finally, slow responses may be a product of a low level of motivation to perform a task. In experimental situations in which reaction time is being tested, adult subjects may be uninterested in the task and unwilling to attempt to achieve a high level of functioning.

The implications of the consequences of behavioral slowing are currently being examined. People who hold one point of view argue that even the slightest reduction in the speed of neural firing may result in reduced sensory and information-processing capacities. Slowness may reduce a person's chances for survival if a situation arises in which a sudden evasive action or immediate response is required. People pursuing another line of thinking point out that the actual magnitude of slowing observed in cognitive functioning (for example, 100 to 500 milliseconds in studies of memory) is so low that it may not seriously impair a person's ability to perform day-to-day tasks.

Since slowing occurs gradually, adults are able to compensate for it by making their environments more convenient or by changing their lifestyles. Slowing becomes more hazardous in situations that require the older adult to keep pace with a tempo that cannot be modified, as in the problems some older people encounter because of the amount of time given to cross a street at a green light. For many older adults and others with physical impairments, the amount of time the light stays green is insufficient to permit them to get to the other side of the street safely.

As older people recognize some situations in which they have trouble responding quickly, they must review the tempo of their day. The very old need to become more selective in their choice of activities so that they can allocate enough time for tasks most important to them and perform them to their own satisfaction. This means exercising greater control over their time and being less concerned about whether they are in harmony with the tempo of others.

Sensory Changes

Every sense modality—vision, hearing, taste, touch, and smell—is vulnerable to age-related changes. With age, greater intensity of stimulation is required to make the same impact on the sensory system that was once achieved with lower levels of

Table 14.1   Changes in Sensory Systems after Age 20

Age Group	Vision	Hearing	Taste and Smell
20–35	Constant decline in accommodation as lenses begin to harden at about age 20	Pitch discrimination for high-frequency tones begins to decline	No documented changes
35–65	Sharp decline in acuity after 40; delayed adjustment to shifts in light and dark	Continued gradual loss in pitch discrimination to age 50	Loss of taste buds begins
65+	Sensitivity to glare; increased problems with daily visual tasks; increases in diseases of the eye that produce partial or total blindness	Sharp loss in pitch discrimination after 70; sound must be more intense to be heard	Higher thresholds for detecting sour, salt, and bitter tastes; higher threshold for detecting smells, and errors in identifying odors

Source: Adapted from B. M. Newman and P. R. Newman, *Understanding Adulthood* (New York: Holt, Rinehart & Winston, 1983), p. 78.

stimulation. Some changes in the sensory systems of vision, hearing, taste, and smell are seen in Table 14.1. These changes begin in early adulthood, and their effects increase throughout the remainder of life.

Vision   Visual adaptation involves the ability to adapt to changes in the level of illumination. Pupil size decreases with age, so that less light reaches the retina. Older adults need higher levels of illumination to see clearly. It takes them longer to adjust from dark to light and from light to dark. Many older adults find that they are increasingly sensitive to glare. They may draw the shades in their rooms to prevent bright light from striking their eyes. Slower adaptation time and sensitivity to glare also interfere with night driving. Some of the visual problems that are noted by people over 75 are difficulty with tasks that require speed of visual performance, such as reading signs in a moving vehicle; a decline in near vision, which interferes with reading and daily tasks; and difficulties in searching for or tracking visual information (Kosnik et al., 1988).

Several physiological conditions can seriously impair vision and may result in partial or total blindness in old age. These conditions include cataracts, which are films covering the lenses, making them less penetrable by light; deterioration or detachment of the retina; and glaucoma, which is an increase in pressure from the fluid in the eyeball. Recent innovations have made cataract surgery much less stressful than it was in the past. In many cases, the hardened lens is removed and replaced with an artificial lens. In other cases, the person is fitted with contact lenses. Recovery of normal vision is now quite likely as long as the eyes are healthy in other respects (Clayman, 1989, pp. 240–241).

Loss of vision poses serious challenges to adaptation. It has the effect of separating people from contact with the world. Such impairment is especially linked with feelings of helplessness. Most older adults are not ready to cope with the challenge of learning to function in their daily world without being able to see. Loss of vision reduces activity level, autonomy, and the willingness to leave a familiar setting.

Hearing   Hearing loss increases with age. About 50% of people who are 85 years old or older say they have some hearing impairment (U.S. Bureau of the Census, 1989a). The most common effects of hearing loss are reduced sensitivity to both high-frequency and low-intensity (quiet) sounds and somewhat decreased ability to understand spoken messages. Certain environmental factors, including exposure to loud, unpredictable noise, and life injuries, such as damage to the bones in the middle ear, influence the extent of hearing loss.

Loss of hearing interferes with a basic mode of human connectedness—the ability to participate in conversation. Hearing impairment may be linked to increased feelings of isolation or suspiciousness. When hearing is diminished, a person may hear things imperfectly, miss parts of conversation, or perceive conversations as occurring in whispers rather than in ordinary tones.

The very old adult who is aware of these facts may be able to compensate intellectually for diminished auditory sensitivity. Knowing the people one is with and believing that one is valued in that group can help reassure a person about the nature of conversations and allay suspicions. Self-esteem plays an important part in this process. The older person with high self-esteem is likely to be able to make the intellectual adjustment needed for interpreting interactions and to request clarification when necessary. Such requests may even serve to stimulate greater interaction and produce greater clarity in communication. Older people with high self-esteem will insist that those who desire interaction consider their hearing impairment and face them as they speak.

Older people who have low self-esteem are likely to be more vulnerable to suspicions about the behavior of others because they doubt their own worth. They are more likely to perceive inaudible comments as attempts to ridicule or exclude them. These experiences contribute to feelings of rejection. They may produce irritability and/or social withdrawal.

Taste and smell   There are wide variations in the density of taste receptors among adult humans. With age, the number of taste buds decreases. Older adults have a higher threshold than young adults for detecting sour, bitter, and salt tastes. Some of this reduced sensitivity may be related to the impact of certain medications or poor oral hygiene. An especially important implication of insensitivity to salt is that older adults may add salt to their food and thereby aggravate hypertension (Spitzer, 1988; Miller, 1988). Older adults also require greater intensity to detect odors and are more likely to misidentify odors (Stevens & Cain, 1987). Changes in the senses of smell and taste may result in loss of appetite or disruption of normal eating habits. Loss of appetite (which may accompany illness and new medications), pain due to dental problems, and changes in the digestive system contribute to problems of malnutrition among the elderly.

These patterns of change are trends. They do not occur at the same rate in every person, nor does every person experience all of them. Older adults are much more diverse in their sensory acuity than young adults are.

You probably know older adults who are more vigorous and zestful than you are. You probably also know older adults who are painfully limited in their ability to function because of physical disabilities. Many factors can influence the progression

Pablo Picasso, *Portrait of Renoir, from a photograph,* 1919. For Renoir, severe arthritis became a major barrier to daily functioning. It is said that he would bind the paintbrush to his hand in order to continue his work.

of physical changes associated with aging, not the least of which is the level of fitness that was established and maintained during early and middle adulthood.

As a result of the various patterns of aging among this very old group, it is impossible to prescribe an ideal pattern of coping. What one hopes to achieve is a balance between self-sufficiency and a willingness to accept help that preserves as much as possible of the person's dignity and optimizes day-to-day mobility.

> *Appropriate dependence can be accommodated and accepted by elders when they realistically appraise their own physical capacities. One of our more practical elders simply states, "Of course, you're still interested in everything. But you don't expect yourself to do everything, the way you used to. Some things you just have to let go." However, inappropriate restriction can be, in its way, insulting and belittling. In describing his current life, one widowed man expresses both his refusal to accept restriction and his willingness to rely on appropriate assistance: "I can stay up here in the woods because I know if I really need help, my son will be here inside of three hours. Now, this deal with fixing my own water pipes, I'd have never tried that without my son so nearby, and I didn't even need him."* [Erikson, Erikson & Kivnick, 1986, pp. 309–310]

Illness and Health

Illnesses can be either acute or chronic. Acute illnesses usually begin suddenly and last a brief time. Some familiar acute illnesses are colds, measles, and flu. Chronic illnesses last a long time. They may be characterized by periods of intense illness

Table 14.2   Rate of Chronic Conditions for Adults 65–74 and 75 Years and Over, 1986

	Age	
Chronic Condition	*65–74*	*75+*
Heart conditions	250.0	319.4
High blood pressure (hypertension)	385.2	409.2
Varicose veins of lower extremities	76.2	71.9
Hemorrhoids	70.2	64.1
Chronic bronchitis	62.9	55.4
Asthma	46.4	36.3
Chronic sinusitis	168.6	170.7
Hay fever, allergic rhinitis without asthma	72.4	67.2
Dermatitis, including eczema	33.6	25.2
Diseases of sebaceous glands[b]	6.1[a]	7.2[a]
Arthritis	443.3	540.1
Trouble with:		
Ingrown nails	39.6	57.8
Corns and calluses	39.7	54.4
Dry (itching) skin	27.7	38.4
Diabetes	91.9	108.5
Migraine	21.3	20.1
Diseases of urinary system	58.3	92.3
Visual impairments	69.3	136.3
Cataracts	84.3	233.2
Hearing impairments	244.2	378.4
Tinnitus	83.2	88.3
Deformities or orthopedic impairments	158.4	195.7
Hernia of abdominal cavity	46.5	84.8
Frequent indigestion	43.3	35.6
Frequent constipation	51.2	83.9

[a]Figure does not meet standards of reliability or precision.

[b]Acne and sebaceous skin cyst.

Source: Adapted from U.S. Bureau of the Census, *Population Profile of the United States, 1989.* Current Population Reports, p-23, no. 159. (Washington, D.C.: U.S. Government Printing Office, 1989), p. 114.

followed by periods of remission, or they may grow progressively worse. Arthritis, hypertension, and diabetes are all chronic illnesses.

Over 80% of people over age 65 have at least one chronic condition, and multiple conditions are common. Table 14.2 shows the rate (persons per 1,000) of some chronic conditions among persons aged 65–74 and those aged 75 and older. About half of the people 85 and older say they cannot perform some major function because of a chronic illness. Nevertheless, more than 80% of the noninstitutionalized elderly over age 85 report being able to manage their basic daily living tasks, including eating, toileting, dressing, and bathing (U.S. Bureau of the Census, 1983, 1984).

One consequence of having to cope with chronic diseases is that perceptions of well-being and health change in later life. Rather than judging their health in terms of the absence of symptoms, many older adults are likely to say that they have "good days" and "bad days."

Box 14.1   Organic Brain Syndromes: Dementia

Organic brain syndromes are a major cause of institutionalization among the aged. These disorders can involve loss of memory for recent as well as past events; confusion or disorientation that renders the person unaware of the day of the week, the season of the year, or the city in which he or she lives; a loss of control over daily functions such as toileting, feeding, and dressing; and an inability to focus attention.

In some acute brain syndromes the onset of confusion is relatively sudden. Often this pattern is associated with a severe illness such as heart failure, alcoholism, or extreme malnutrition. In these cases, the symptoms of the brain syndrome often can be reversed if the accompanying illness can be treated. Supportive counseling, attention to diet, and skill training to reestablish control of daily functions can restore the person's previous level of adaptive behavior.

Chronic brain syndrome produces a more gradual loss of memory, reduced intellectual functioning, and an increase of mood disturbances, especially hostility and depression. Whereas a number of conditions can cause the acute brain syndrome, a smaller number of diseases are associated with chronic brain syndrome. Alzheimer's disease is the most common form of this syndrome, accounting for about 50% of the

dementias among the elderly (Jarvik & Kumar, 1984). The incidence of this disease increases with age, especially after age 70. The person experiences gradual brain failure over a period of seven to ten years. At present there is no treatment that will reverse the disease or slow its progress. Current treatments address specific symptoms, especially mood and memory problems.

As the number of older adults who experience Alzheimer's disease and related disorders grows, the plight of their caregivers has aroused increasing concern. Most Alzheimer's patients are cared for at home, often by their adult children. Caregivers often experience high levels of stress and depression as they attempt to cope with their responsibilities and as they assess the effectiveness or ineffectiveness of their efforts. The care of an older person with some form of dementia is fraught with problems and frustrations, but it also provides some opportunities for satisfactions and feelings of encouragement (Haley & Pardo, 1989). The "uplifts" and "hassles" frequently reported by caregivers give us some insight into the typical day-to-day experience of caring for a person who is suffering from this condition (Kinney & Stephens, 1989). First the uplifts:

Changes in functioning with advanced age   Do people generally experience rapid general decline after age 65 or 70? A longitudinal study of older adults helps to answer this question (Palmore, Nowlin & Wang, 1985). A group of older men and women who were studied in 1972 were interviewed again in the period from 1980 to 1983. The average age of the group at the time of follow-up was 81. Five areas were evaluated: social functioning, economic stability, mental health, physical health, and the ability to perform activities of daily living.

The group as a whole experienced no significant decline in social functioning or economic stability over the ten-year period. There were declines in mental and physical health and in the ability to perform activities of daily living. These declines were moderate. For example, for activities of daily living, the average rating on a 6-point scale dropped from 5.1—"Can perform all the usual instrumental and physical activities but at times this becomes a strain for the person, and he/she would welcome intermittent assistance with some of these"—to 4.1—"Can perform the usual instrumental and physical activities around home under usual circumstances, but requires

Box 14.1   *(continued)*

Seeing care recipient calm.
Pleasant interactions between care recipient and family.
Seeing care recipient responsive.
Care recipient showing affection.
Friends showing understanding about caregiving.
Family showing understanding about caregiving.
Care recipient recognizing familiar people.
Care recipient being cooperative.
Leaving care recipient with others at home.
Care recipient smiling/winking.
Being in care recipient's presence.
Receiving caregiving help from family.

Now the hassles:
Care recipient being confused/not making sense.
Care recipient's forgetfulness.
Care recipient's agitation.
Care recipient declining mentally.
Care recipient not cooperating.
Care recipient's bowel/bladder accidents.
Seeing care recipient withdrawn/unresponsive.
Dressing care recipient.
Bathing care recipient.
Assisting with care recipient's toileting.
Care recipient declining physically.

Care recipient not showing interest in things.
Care recipient not sleeping through the night.
Care recipient asking repetitive questions.*

    Two of the symptoms most difficult to manage are sleep disturbances and wandering. As cognitive functioning declines, the pattern of sleep deteriorates as well. The Alzheimer's patient sleeps only for short periods at a time, napping on and off during the day and night. Often the napping is accompanied by waking periods at night during which the person is confused, upset, and likely to wander away. Caregivers must therefore be continuously alert, night and day. When the disease reaches this level, family caregivers are most likely to find it necessary to institutionalize the patient (Wagner, 1984).

*Source: J. M. Kinney and M. A. P. Stephens, "Hassles and Uplifts of Giving Care to a Family Member with Dementia," *Psychology and Aging, 4,* 1989, 402–408. Reprinted by permission of the author.

assistance when additional or extraordinary demands are made such as for long distance travel, major shopping trips, large financial transactions, or during a crisis situation" (p. 247).

    There was also an impressive range in the ability to function among people in this sample. Some subjects showed marked declines in functioning over the ten-year period, while others actually showed improvements. Some factors assessed in the first period predicted level of functioning in the second. Women and blacks had lower levels of functioning after ten years. Those whose mental health scores were high in 1972 had higher social functioning ten years later. Those who were married maintained higher levels of functioning in most areas.

    The very oldest subjects showed the most marked declines in all areas, suggesting that deterioration may accelerate with increasing age. This finding may be a result of the greater interrelatedness of functioning among those over 80. For those who are very old, when one area of functioning declines, difficulties in many others emerge. For example, loss of a spouse may result in social withdrawal, loss of appetite, sleep

Maggie Kuhn, founder of the Gray Panthers, has structured her life in order to retain her functional independence. She continues to work as an advocate for those who cannot stand up for themselves.

disturbance, loss of energy, unwillingness to take medication, and reductions in physical activity. All of these changes can produce a rapid deterioration of the respiratory, circulatory, and metabolic systems.

Results of a longitudinal study of adults born between 1895 and 1919 extend the analysis of the pattern of aging and predictors of healthy functioning in later life (Guralnik & Kaplan, 1989). Data were collected in 1965 and again in 1984. Among the 841 individuals who made up the 1965 sample, 12.7% were assessed as high in functioning in 1984 and 46% as low to moderate in functioning; 41% had died. Comparisons between the high-functioning group and the others provided some indicators of demographic factors, chronic illness factors, and health or lifestyle factors that are associated with healthy aging. The factors most predictive of high functioning were a fairly high family income, absence of hypertension, absence of arthritis, absence of back pain, being a nonsmoker, having normal weight, and consuming a moderate amount of alcohol.

Despite our stereotypes of the very old, the level of functioning among adults 80 years old and older is surprisingly high. Figure 14.2 shows the percentages of men and women in a sample of over 1700 noninstitutionalized white adults 80 years old and over who could perform each of four functional indicators of physical ability.

Research of this type must be repeated on a variety of samples with different measures to clarify these patterns. Among people who survive into very old age, we see a need to keep individual differences clearly in mind. Further, we can expect that the need for assistance in daily living and mental or physical health care changes gradually during the decade of the 70s and may accelerate during the 80s and after.

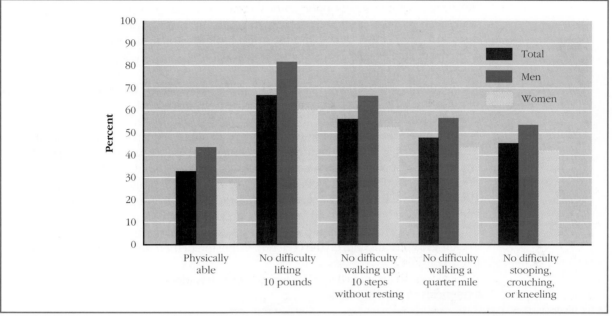

Figure 14.2   Physical Ability of Noninstitutionalized White Persons Aged 80 and Older, 1984 (percent)
Source: T. Harris, M. G. Kovar, R. Suzman, J. C. Kleinman, and J. J. Feldman, "Longitudinal Study of Physical Ability in the Oldest-Old," *American Journal of Public Health,* 79 (1989), 700. Reprinted by permission.

Developing a Psychohistorical Perspective

Through encounters with diverse experiences, decision making, parenting, and efforts to formulate a personal philosophy, adults reach new levels of conscious thought. Very old adults are more aware of alternatives. They can look deeply into both the past and the future. They recognize that opposing forces can exist side by side (Riegel, 1973). Through a process of creative coping, very old adults in each generation blend the salient events of their past histories with the demands of current reality. The product of this integration of past, present, and future is the formation of a *psychohistorical perspective.*

Think about what it means to have lived for 75 or more years. Those adults who were 80 years old in 1990 had lived through two world wars and the Great Depression by the time they were 35. They experienced the political leadership of 16 presidents. They adapted to dramatic technological innovations in communication, transportation, manufacturing, economics, food production, leisure activities, and health care. They have experienced striking changes in cultural and political values.

One consequence of a long life is the accumulation of experiences. A second consequence is the realization that change is a basic element of all life at the individual and social levels (Clayton & Birren, 1980). Sometimes these changes appear cyclical. Sometimes they appear to bring real progress. Within the framework of an extended life, very old adults have opportunities to gain a special perspective on conditions of continuity and change within their culture. In the process of developing a psycho-historical perspective, very old adults develop a personal understanding of stability and change, the effects of history on individual lives, and one's place in the chain of evolution.

We are all part of the process of psychosocial evolution. Each generation adds to the existing knowledge base and reinterprets the norms of society for succeeding generations. The very old are likely to be parents, grandparents, and great-grandparents. Many are seeing their lines of descent continue into the fourth generation, a generation that will dominate the 21st century. The opportunity to see several generations of offspring brings a new degree of continuity to life, linking memories of one's own grandparents to observations of one's great-grandchildren (Wentowski, 1985). We can expect the value of the oral tradition of history/storytelling to take on new meaning as the very old help their great-grandchildren feel connected to the distant past. We may also expect a greater investment in the future as the very old see in their great-grandchildren the concrete extension of their ancestry three generations into the future.

Erikson (Erikson, Erikson & Kivnick, 1986) has identified the emergence of these tendencies in the very old.

> *The elder has a reservoir of strength in the wellsprings of history and storytelling. As collectors of time and preservers of memory, those healthy elders who have survived into a reasonably fit old age have time on their side—time that is to be dispensed wisely and creatively, usually in the form of stories, to those younger ones who will one day follow in their footsteps. Telling these stories, and telling them well, marks a certain capacity for one generation to entrust itself to the next, by passing on a certain shared and collective identity to the survivors of the next generation: the future.* [p. 331]

Traveling Uncharted Territory: Life Structures of the Very Old

How should very old people behave? What norms exist to guide their social relationships or the structure of their daily lives? What does a healthy 85-year-old woman consider appropriate behavior, and what expectations do others have for her? When we talk about traveling uncharted territory, we are assuming that very old age is a time of life for which there are few age-specific social norms. The very old are creating their own definitions of this life stage (Keith, 1982). You may have heard the expression "Life begins at 80." One interpretation of this adage is that because there are so few norms for behavior and so few responsibilities when one reaches the period of very old age, one can do whatever one wants.

In an effort to describe the kinds of norms older adults use to guide their conduct, researchers asked older adults from New York City and Savannah, Georgia, to respond to six pictures similar to the two drawings in Figure 14.3 (Offenbacher & Poster, 1985). The responses to two questions were used to construct a code of conduct: "How do

Figure 14.3   Typical Drawings That Researchers Might Use to Establish Social Norms of the Very Old
Source: Drawings adapted from D. I. Offenbacher and C. H. Poster, "Aging and the Baseline Code: An Alternative to the 'Normless Elderly,'" *Gerontologist, 25* (1985), 527. Reprinted by permission of the publisher.

you think that people who know this person, such as family or friends, feel about him/her?" "How do you feel about this person?" Four normative principles were found in the responses:

1. Don't be sorry for yourself.
2. Try to be independent.
3. Don't just sit there; do something.
4. Above all, be sociable.

This code of conduct suggests that older people believe that being sociable, active, and independent constitutes doing a good job of living in later life. Of course, older adults are not the only people who value these qualities. However, these norms are very important as sources of self-esteem for this age group. They promote a sense of vigor and a shield against feelings of depression or discouragement.

The themes "Don't be sorry for yourself" and "Don't just sit there" suggest that the very old continue to see their lives as precious resources not to be wasted away in self-pity and passivity. The emphasis on activity as opposed to meditation reflects the Western cultural value of a sense of agency. Thinking is not as highly valued as action. Doing things, having an impact, and receiving the feedback that action stimulates provide the keys to successful living. Although the results of this research cannot be taken as the final word on the norms that govern the behavior of all very old adults, they are an important first step in understanding the structure that very old people impose on their lives.

The fact that older adults must carve out new patterns for adapting to later life is demonstrated in two specific areas of functioning: living arrangements and gender-role definition.

Living Arrangements

The pattern of living arrangements for most people changes noticeably after age 75. Before then, the majority of later adults have lived in family households, mostly as married couples. Among householders over age 75, 58% live in nonfamily households—that is, they live either alone or with a nonrelative. The percentage of older women who live alone after age 75 has been increasing steadily until now they are the norm among elderly women. In 1965, 30% of women over 75 lived alone; in 1987, 51% lived alone (U.S. Bureau of the Census, 1989a). Older women are less likely to live with other family members after the death of their spouse than they were in the past. Further, feelings of subjective well-being appear to be high among older widows who live alone (Alwin, 1984).

One implication of these trends in living arrangements is that increasing numbers of very old women are establishing a new single lifestyle in which they function as heads of households. This does not mean that they are not in need of social interaction and support services. However, they are often relieved of the responsibilities of caring for spouses who are ill. Depending on their own health, they may be freer to direct their time and interests toward their own friends, grandchildren, hobbies, and activity preferences than they have been at any other time in their lives.

The pattern of elderly women living alone is similar in Canada, the United Kingdom, and the United States, but less than 10% of Japanese women aged 65 and over live alone. Most live with relatives in three-generation households. Among those 85 and over, only 5 or 6% live alone. In most developing countries, families provide housing and care for the very old. Although people may not experience the same degree of longevity in these countries, there is a clear pattern of elderly widows living with their sons or daughters (U.S. Bureau of the Census, 1987).

The majority of very old men—about 70%—are married and live with their spouses. Only 24% are widowed. In contrast, 23% of very old women are married and 68% are widowed. Widowed men are much more likely to remarry, and they tend to do so quickly. However, remarriage among the very old is still a new frontier. Sexual and social stereotypes inhibit some older people from considering remarriage. Too, potential financial consequences may make remarriage undesirable. A widow may lose her husband's pension or her social security benefits if she remarries. Some older couples cope with this problem by living together instead of marrying. Those who do remarry usually view the new relationship quite positively. One older woman described her new marriage as follows: "We're like a couple of kids. We fool around—have fun. We go to dances and socialize a lot with our families. We enjoy life together. When you're with someone, you're happy" (Rosenfeld, 1978, p. 56).

Interstate migration   Although most older adults remain in their home communities, the trend toward interstate migration has increased over the past three decades (Flynn et al., 1985). In the period from 1975 to 1980, 1.6 million adults over the age of 60 moved their residence across state lines. We cannot determine how many of these adults were in the very old age group. However, we can infer that many of these older interstate migrants will live out their lives in communities in which they did not grow up, work, or raise their children. They are pioneers, establishing new friendships, community involvements, and lifestyles. Another significantly large group of older adults returns to their birth state after they retire. New York, California, and Florida have an especially strong pull for their native sons and daughters (Rogers, 1990).

About 60% of all older migrants move to ten states. In 1980, more than 25% of all interstate migrants over age 60 moved to Florida. This trend has had a dramatic impact on the housing, health, and social service resources of many Florida communities.

Housing options Differences in lifestyle, health, interest, ability to perform daily activities, marital status, and income enter into the very old person's preference for housing arrangements. Housing for the elderly—sometimes referred to as *retirement housing*—has expanded dramatically, and developers have experimented with a great variety of housing configurations that are intended to meet the special needs of particular aging populations. These options range from inner-city hotels for those with minimal incomes to sprawling luxury villages with apartments, medical clinics, and sponsored activities (see Table 14.3).

We know of people who have visited a number of retirement communities and evaluated the options of various housing arrangements before they were really ready to make a housing change. The advice of one of our retired professional colleagues is to anticipate the move into a retirement setting and live there before one is seriously restricted by declining health. That way, one will become more easily integrated into the social network of the residents and be more likely to receive help from neighbors when one needs it. Some older adults maintain two residences, one in a warm climate and one in a cooler climate. There are mobile home parks for older adults who want to spend the winter months in a warm climate but do not want to invest in an expensive second residence. Two of our dearest colleagues devised a particularly creative arrangement through which they lived in three locations: they spent the summer and autumn at their university-based residence, the winter in Mexico, and the spring in Washington, D.C., where they volunteered their time with a government agency working on issues related to aging.

Institutional care On any given day, about 5% of adults over 65 live in nursing homes and other group-care settings. The rate of institutionalization increases from about 2% of those 65 to 74 years old to 23% of those 85 and over. These rates, based on one moment in time, underestimate the risk of having to spend some time in a nursing home during one's later life. The lifetime probability of spending some time in a nursing home is estimated to be between 25 and 50%, depending on the technique used to make this projection. About 75% of those in nursing homes do not have spouses. The likelihood of being in a nursing home increases when there is no family member who can help an older person manage his or her daily living needs (U.S. Senate, Special Committee on Aging, 1986).

We tend to think that once people are admitted to a nursing home, they stay there until they die. However, there is actually a high annual turnover among nursing home residents. Often a person will enter a nursing home for a period of convalescence

Table 14.3 Six Types of Group Retirement Housing

The first site is a *retirement hotel* in downtown Los Angeles. Many older hotels in the downtown section of the city have lost popularity in recent years and in order to maintain reasonable occupancy, some have specialized as senior citizen hotels. This ordinarily involves little adjustment, since by this time the hotel would already be occupied primarily with senior citizens. At this retirement hotel, two meals are provided daily and all dwelling units are single rooms. There is a recreation room in the basement, and on a mezzanine a lounge, a game room, and a TV room.

The second site is a *rental retirement village*—not fitting the popular stereotype of country club living for the elderly, but rather providing apartments with few added frills. Federal financing was involved. The site, located in a suburban area, has about 80 single-story buildings. In addition to the dwelling units, the site includes a large central building containing administrative offices, a cafeteria-assembly room, a library, doctor's clinic, recreation room, activity rooms, and a lounge. Also on the site is a small grocery store.

The third site, a type growing in prominence in many areas of the country, is a *single high-rise building* in an urban area, assisted by a federal program making direct loans to churches and other nonprofit organizations, at a much lower interest rate than they could otherwise obtain. All dwelling units are apartments. The building contains lounges and a recreation room.

The next two sites are *retirement villages.* The first is located in a semi-arid mountain-desert area of southern California. Dwellings are mostly single family houses, with a few garden apartments. Besides a shopping center, there are extensive on-site recreational facilities, including golf, swimming, and specifically designed activities buildings or areas.

The fifth site, with a cooperative financial arrangement and 40-year mortgages, is a somewhat more *luxurious retirement village* in northern California. All dwellings are apartments (one to three bedrooms)—referred to as "manors." On the site are a medical clinic, golf course, swimming pools, clubhouses, and buildings or areas for arts and crafts, games, meetings, and classes. Nurses are on duty at the clinic at all times, and there is a visiting nurse service as well. Group health insurance is available.

The sixth site is a church-sponsored *life-care home,* licensed by the State Department of Social Welfare to give personal care and protective service. An FHA-insured mortgage is involved. (The site also has a medical unit on the premises, although the design of the present study excludes residents therein.) All meals are provided. The location is a college town in urban southern California. An attractive feature of this site is the availability of three different types of dwelling unit, cottages, apartments, and rooms, to be occupied according to the individual's decreasing ability to care for himself. A central building houses the dining room, lounges, and activity rooms.

Source: S. R. Sherman (1971). The choice of retirement housing among the well-elderly. *Aging and Human Development, 2,* 119–120. Reprinted by permission.

after hospitalization and then return home. Nursing homes and housing for the very old have adapted to the changing needs of their clients over the past 20 years. Many nursing homes are part of a *continuing-care retirement community.* These residential settings offer housing and medical, preventive health, and social services to residents who are well at the time they enter the community. Once admitted, they are guaranteed nursing care if they become ill or disabled (Cohen, Tell & Wallace, 1988).

In trying to cope with a spouse who had Alzheimer's disease, Mr. G. decided to move to a continuing-care retirement community. He lived in the minimal-care residential part of the community, and his wife lived in a full-service unit. With this arrangement, he could remain close to his wife without having full responsibility for her care. This solution relieved Mr. G. of many of the financial burdens he had encountered in trying to care for his wife at home. The move also prevented Mr. G. from

In a continuing care community people have the security of knowing that they can remain in the same residential setting even if their needs for health care increase significantly.

becoming socially isolated, a concern of many very old adults who are caring for aging parents or spouses.

At present, about half the states are establishing community-based long-term health-care programs to provide medical and social services to those who are chronically ill and are eligible for institutionalization but who nevertheless live in the community. These programs provide relief for family members and friends who are trying to care for the very old, and they bring comfort to the very old clients who prefer to remain in their homes. These programs also offer flexibility by providing needed services and modifying them as a person's condition changes.

Long-term home health-care programs are experimental. They evolve in response to the patterns of need that emerge in a community and the quality of services available. As the programs develop, their emphasis tends to shift from providing services to those who would otherwise be institutionalized to preventing institutionalization among a high-risk population (Birnbaum et al., 1984; Branch & Stuart, 1984).

Gender-Role Definitions

Another aspect of traveling uncharted territory is the way in which very old adults view masculinity and femininity. How do the very old define gender roles? How does gender influence behavior? Do very old adults make the same distinctions as college-age populations in regard to the behaviors appropriate or desirable for men and women?

Some researchers have reported a transformation of sex-role orientation during midlife. Men become more nurturant and women become more assertive (Gutmann, 1964). As women encounter widowhood and a long period of singlehood, some may become increasingly alienated from a view of themselves as sexual beings. Others may become more liberated, taking an active role in seeking out intimate relationships

(Long, 1980). It makes sense to expect that as one's physical appearance changes, the criteria one uses to judge attractiveness also change. The very old are less likely than early and middle adults to view the changes of aging as unattractive (Wernick & Manaster, 1984; Ross et al., 1989). Conceptions of gender can be expected to change on three levels: psychological, social, and physical.

In an attempt to clarify the question of how gender is conceptualized, researchers asked a group of older adults to complete the Bem Sex Role Inventory (Windle & Sinnott, 1985). This inventory has been widely used to assess masculinity, femininity, and androgyny in adolescent and young-adult populations. Twenty adjectives associated with femininity, 20 associated with masculinity, and 20 neutral adjectives are rated for their accuracy in describing the person. The inventory is constructed in such a way that masculinity and femininity can be measured as two separate, uncorrelated dimensions. For example, a woman might receive high scores in both masculinity and femininity.

The responses of the older adults did not form separate masculinity and femininity scales. For the men, the adjectives were divided into eight clusters: feminine (sympathetic, shy, understanding), sensitive (compassionate, warm), resourceful, achievement-oriented, leadership, bitter, dominant, and kind. For the women, the adjectives fell into nine clusters: resourceful, feminine, achievement-oriented, dominant, bitter, adventurous, self-reliant and nurturant, involved with others, and assertive and loyal. These conceptions are summarized in Table 14.4.

The common dimensions of personality as perceived by older men and older women are feminine, resourceful, achievement-oriented, bitter, and dominant. In addition, older men identify leadership, sensitivity, and kindness as definitive dimensions of personality, while older women identify adventurousness, self-reliance and nurturance, involvement with others, and assertiveness and loyalty. The unique male categories have to do with personal dimensions related to orientations toward other people. The categories that are unique to female respondents involve degree of independence from and relationship to others and excitement. Women do not tend to view adventurousness, assertiveness, and self-reliance as qualities that go together and are necessarily associated with masculinity, and men do not tend to view sensitivity and kindness as connected traits that are necessarily linked to femininity, as younger raters tend to do.

This research suggests that the concept of gender becomes more differentiated in later life than it is in earlier stages. Very old adults do not tie a large number of adjectives into one integrated conception of masculinity or femininity. Personality organization takes on a multidimensional quality in which such concepts as sensitivity and kindness or dominance and assertiveness are treated as separate factors rather than as elements in one integrated gender-role conceptualization. Further, men and women do not use identical strategies for organizing these concepts.

Although older men and women may have more differentiated views of gender and personality than younger people do, they still tend to be tied to many of the sex-role standards of their historical cohort. For example, older women are likely to believe that the only kinds of relationships that are possible between men and women are romantic or courtship relationships (Adams, 1985). Few very old women have friendships with very old men—partly because few older men are available but also

Table 14.4 Personal Characteristics as Derived from Responses of Very Old Adults to the Bem Sex Role Inventory	
Very Old Men	*Very Old Women*
* Feminine: Sympathetic	* Resourceful
Shy	* Feminine
Understanding	* Achievement-oriented
Sensitive: Compassionate	* Dominant
Warm	* Bitter
* Resourceful	Adventurous
* Achievement-oriented	Self-reliant and nurturant
Leadership	Involved with others
* Bitter	Assertive and loyal
* Dominant	
Kind	

*Characteristics perceived by both men and women.
Source: Derived from M. Windle and J. D. Sinnott, "A Psychometric Study of the Bem Sex Role Inventory with an Older Adult Sample," *Journal of Gerontology, 40* (1985), 336–343. Reprinted by permission of the publisher.

because most older women have no models for independent friendship relationships with men. During their early and middle adult years, their friendships with men were formed while they were part of a couple or were mediated by some other situation, such as a work setting.

Today's very old adults are also likely to be uncomfortable about dating. Although most current research on aging confirms that older adults have sexual needs and are able to be sexually active, most older women do not readily integrate sexuality into their single lifestyles. They are members of a generation that did not feel comfortable about open sexuality outside of the marriage relationship. Once they are single again, they find it difficult to become involved in sexual relationships.

Many men among the current cohort of the very old also behave in accordance with the sex-role standards of their young adulthood. Although women far outnumber men at advanced ages, men still seem to prefer to remarry rather than play the field, although they have become a very scarce and valuable commodity. The norm of serial monogamy guides these men's behavior. Many men are probably motivated by a desire to continue to be taken care of as well as to satisfy their sexual needs.

We can envision some change in these patterns as contemporary generations of early, middle, and later adults enter very old age. Because so many more adult women are in the workplace, they have more experience with male colleagues. Changing sexual norms have already led many more adults to experience nonmarital sexual relationships. Acceptance of new sexual relationships in later life is more likely because many adults will have experienced more sexual relationships in earlier years of adulthood. The high divorce rate of the last 20 years means that in the future many more older women will have had the experience of developing a single lifestyle that includes a network of both male and female friends. We can expect that future groups of older

Pablo Picasso, *Luncheon on the Grass, after Manet,* 1970. These very old men appear to be carrying on their afternoon visit undisturbed by the presence of the nude women. The role and expression of sexuality in very old age are called into question in this drawing.

adults will be more comfortable about cross-sex relationships—both those involving romance and those involving friendship.

Summary

The three developmental tasks of very old adults are coping with the physical changes of aging, developing a psychohistorical perspective, and traveling uncharted territory with respect to standards of behavior and lifestyle. A key to the life decisions and behaviors of the very old lies in their health status. Chronic conditions begin to pose major barriers to activity, social interaction, and independence. Although many older people are quite capable of meeting their own daily needs, the rate of decline in health appears to accelerate after age 80. Further, many of those who are still strong and vigorous are involved in the care of a more frail spouse or other family member. Coping successfully with increasing limitations and declining physical health becomes one of the major areas of accomplishment for the very old.

Another consequence of living a very long time is that it provides a unique psychohistorical perspective. Older adults have the opportunity to integrate the concept of change into their interpretations of life events. They can also appreciate the impact of historical events on individual lives. Potentially they provide an important generational bridge, introducing wisdom and continuity among past, present, and future to those with whom they interact.

The very old are freed from age-related normative constraints at the same time that they are restricted by the new physical limitations on mobility, sensory information, and self-sufficiency. Living arrangements and gender-role definitions are two areas in which the very old find their lives changing. Coping requires them to create their own codes of conduct with which to keep their lives meaningful and vigorous.

The Psychosocial Crisis: Immortality versus Extinction

By the end of later adulthood, most people have developed a point of view about death. They have confronted their fears of death and overcome them. If they have achieved a sense of integrity, they believe that life makes sense. The achievement of integrity brings a sense of personal dignity about the choices they have made and the goals they have achieved without despair for the failures, missed opportunities, or misfortunes that may have occurred. Thus armed, the very old can accept the end of life and view it as a natural part of the life span. They are capable of distilling wisdom from the events of their lives and from their successes and mistakes.

However, the very old are faced with a new challenge. All of us struggle with a certain disbelief about our own mortality. Even though we know that death is a certainty, an element of human thought prevents us from facing the full realization of death and makes us continue to hope for immortality. This quality may be adaptive in that people who have a sense of hope cope better than those who do not. With advancing age, a conflict builds between the acceptance of death and the intensifying hope for immortality. The very old struggle to find meaning in their survival.

We have argued that the very old have a unique appreciation of change. They begin to sense themselves as links in a long, fluid chain of historical and biological growth and change. The positive pole of this crisis is a confidence in the continuity of life, a transcendence of death through the development of a symbolic sense of immortality.

A sense of *immortality* can be achieved and expressed in five ways (Lifton, 1973). First, one can live on through one's children, sensing a connection and attachment to the future through their lives and those of their offspring. This type of immortality may be extended to include devotion to one's country, to one's social organizations or groups, or to humankind.

Second, one can believe in an afterlife or in a spiritual plane of existence that extends beyond one's biological life. Most religious traditions have a concept that describes a state of harmony with natural forces such that one endures beyond earthly life.

Third, one can achieve a sense of immortality through one's creative achievements and one's impact on others. Many people find great comfort in believing that they are part of a chain of positive influences on the lives of others. This sense of immortality is clearly tied to the achievement of a sense of generativity in middle adulthood. Those adults who have made a strong commitment to improving the quality of life for future generations during middle adulthood are likely to see evidence of this effort by the time they reach very old age.

Fourth, one may develop the notion of participation in the chain of nature. In death, one's body returns to the earth and one's energy is brought forth in a new form.

Fifth, one may achieve a sense of immortality through what Lifton (1973) describes as *experiential transcendence*:

Pablo Picasso, *Head of Harlequin,* 1970. At age 89, the artist portrays himself once again as Harlequin: sensual, clever optimistic, and innocent.

> *This state is characterized by extraordinary psychic unity and perceptual intensity. But there also occurs . . . a process of symbolic reordering. . . . Experiential transcendence includes a feeling of . . . "continuous present" that can be equated with eternity or with "mythical time." This continuous present is perceived as not only "here and now" but as inseparable from past and future.*   [p. 10]

This concept of immortality is independent of religion, offspring, or achievement. It is an insight derived from moments of rapture or ecstasy in which all that one senses is the power of the moment. In these experiences, life and death dissolve and all that remains is continuous being.

The five ways of attaining a sense of immortality are summarized in Table 14.5.

The negative pole of this crisis is a sense of being bound by the limits of one's own life history. In place of a belief in continuous existence and transformation, there is a resignation to the end of life as an end to motion, attachment, and change. One

Table 14.5   **Five Ways of Attaining a Sense of Immortality**
Live on through children and grandchildren.
Believe in afterlife or spiritual plane of existence.
Make a positive impact on others through creative achievements.
Become integrated in the chain of nature.
Achieve a sense of experiential transcendence—a feeling of continuous presence.

Box 14.2 Erikson on Aging

The Eriksons' advice on aging suggests the achievement of a level of experiential transcendence.

With aging, there are inevitably constant losses—losses of those very close, and friends near and far. Those who have been rich in intimacy also have the most to lose. Recollection is one form of adaptation, but the effort skillfully to form new relationships is adaptive and more rewarding. Old age is necessarily a time of relinquishing—of giving up old friends, old roles, earlier work that was once meaningful, and even possessions that belong to a previous stage of life and are now an impediment to the resiliency and freedom that seem to be requisite for adapting to the unknown challenges that determine the final stage of life.

Trust in interdependence. Give and accept help when it is needed. Old Oedipus well knew that the aged sometimes need three legs; pride can be an asset but not a cane.

When frailty takes over, dependence is appropriate, and one has no choice but to trust in the compassion of others and be consistently surprised at how faithful some caretakers can be.

Much living, however, can teach us only how little is known. Accept that essential "not-knowingness" of childhood and with it also that playful curiosity. Growing old can be an interesting adventure and is certainly full of surprises.

One is reminded here of the image Hindu philosophy uses to describe the final letting go—that of merely being. The mother cat picks up in her mouth the kitten, which completely collapses every tension and hangs limp and infinitely trusting in the maternal benevolence. The kitten responds instinctively. We human beings require at least a whole lifetime of practice to do this. The religious traditions of the world reflect these concerns and provide them with substance and form. [Erikson, Erikson & Kivnick, 1986, pp. 332–333]

has no faith in the ideas of connection and continuity but rather a great fear of *extinction*—a fear that death brings nothingness.

The following quotations from a study of very old men suggest the range in sentiment along the dimension of immortality versus extinction (Rosenfeld, 1978, p. 10). About 28% were described as having low morale and made statements such as the following: "I feel I'm a forgotten man. I don't exist anymore. . . . I don't feel old . . . I'm just living out my life." About 25% were stoic but not especially positive about their condition: "You know you're getting old. You have to put your mind to it and take it as it comes. You can't get out of it. Take it gracefully." Almost half found their lives to be full and rewarding: "I go home with my cup overflowing. There are so many opportunities to do things for people. These are the happiest days of my life."

The Central Process: Social Support

Social support has been defined as information leading people to believe that they are cared for and loved, are esteemed and valued, and belong to a network of communication and mutual obligation (Cobb, 1979). *Social support* is a broad term that includes the quantity and interconnectedness or web of social relationships in which a person is embedded, the strength of those ties, the frequency of contact, and the extent to which the support system is perceived as helpful and caring (Bergman et al., 1990). For the very old, social support plays a major role in maintaining well-being and fostering the possibility of transcending the physical limitations that accompany aging.

Social support contributes to health and well-being in three ways (House, 1985). First, because social support involves meaningful social relationships, it reduces isolation. People who have intimate companions in later life have higher levels of life satisfaction. They feel valued and, in turn, valuable. Second, the presence of caring, familiar others provides a flow of affection, information, advice, transportation, assistance with meals and daily activities, finances, and health care—all critical resources (Stephens & Bernstein, 1984). Third, the presence of a support system tends to reduce the impact of stressors and to protect people from some of the consequences of serious illnesses. The support system often serves to encourage an older person to maintain health-care practices and to seek medical attention when it is needed. Mental and physical health tend to be positively related to involvement in meaningful, supportive social relationships (House, 1985).

Very old people are likely to experience declines in physical stamina. They may also have limited financial resources. In order for the very old to transcend the limitations of their daily living situations, they must be convinced that they are embedded in a network of social relationships in which they are valued. Their value cannot be based solely on a physical exchange of goods and services. It must be founded on an appreciation of their dignity and a history of reciprocal caring.

The value of reciprocity in both emotional and caregiving support is very strong in our culture. People want and expect to be able to give about the same as or more than they receive. Most older adults continue to see themselves as involved in a reciprocal, supportive relationship with their friends. They may expect to receive more care from their children when they are ill than they will provide. By shifting to a life-span perspective, however, they can retain a sense of balance by seeing the help they receive now as comparable to the help they gave at earlier life stages (Ingersoll-Dayton & Antonucci, 1988). When very old people are highly valued, it is not so important that they reciprocate in the exchange of tangible resources. Wisdom, affection, joie de vivre, and a positive model of surviving into old age are intangible resources that are highly valued by members of the very old person's social support network. Being valued may also mean that the very old person's advice and conversation are adequate exchange for some of the services and assistance provided by family and friends.

Of course, being an integral part of a social system does not begin in later life. It has its origins in infancy with the formation of a mutual relationship with a caregiver. Social support systems are extended in childhood and early adolescence through identification with a peer group and in early and middle adulthood through marriage, child rearing, and relationships with co-workers and adult friends. In later life, family members are usually the primary sources of social support, especially one's spouse, children, and siblings.

For very old people, especially women, the likelihood of living alone is quite high. After the death of a spouse, men and women must realign their social support systems from among relationships that include their adult children, friends, relatives, neighbors, and new acquaintances in order to satisfy their needs for interaction and companionship. Very old adults who are childless and those who have no surviving children or siblings are especially vulnerable to ending their lives in isolation (Hays, 1984).

For many older adults, religious participation provides an additional source of social support. Older adults are likely to describe themselves as more religious in their beliefs and their behavior than younger adults. The place of religion in the lives of the very old is especially significant for black Americans. Blacks are more likely than whites to attend religious services regularly, even at advanced ages. They are more likely to describe themselves as very religious, a characterization that reflects the frequency of their private prayer, their strong emotional commitment, and their frequent religious reading. Religious involvement among elderly blacks is not predicted by income or education (Taylor, 1986).

Ethnic identity itself can become an important vehicle for social support in later life (Cool, 1987). Ethnic identity can provide a variety of sources of nonfamilial support, from a loose network of associations to membership in formal clubs and organizations. Members of an ethnic group may feel a strong sense of community as a result of their shared exposure to past discrimination, their realization of common concerns, and their sense of responsibility to preserve some of the authenticity of their ethnic identity for future generations. Participation in such a support network can be another vehicle for contributing wisdom gained through life experiences to those who will follow. Insofar as members of ethnic groups have felt somewhat marginal to the larger society in the past, their mutual support in later life can protect them from some of the negative stereotypes that the society imposes on the very old.

Summary

We view involvement in a social support system as an essential ingredient in the achievement of a sense of immortality for the very old. The social support system confirms the value of very old people, providing direct evidence of their positive impact on others and a sense of embeddedness within their social communities. The social support system of the very old usually includes adult children. Positive interactions with children contribute to the sense of living on through one's offspring and their descendants. Interactions with members of the social support system, especially those that are marked by feelings of warmth, caring, and celebration, may be moments of experiential transcendence. These are times at which a very old person feels the fullness and joy of existence that transcends physical and material barriers.

☐ Applied Topic: Meeting the Needs of the Frail Elderly

We certainly cannot accept the idea that people will survive to a very old age simply to live out their lives in conditions of poverty, isolation, chronic illness, and recurring hospitalization. Yet we know that at present about 10% of people over age 80 suffer from some form of senile dementia. Forty-five percent of those over age 65 are limited in their daily activity because of one or more chronic conditions. Of those who are in nursing homes, only half have surviving children and many express sentiments of real loneliness (Rosenfeld, 1978). Many other very old adults live alone in a community, trying to preserve their autonomy with minimal financial resources. Still others who are married struggle to care for ailing spouses while their own physical resilience declines.

In thinking about the frail elderly, it is helpful to distinguish between optimal ability level and actual ability (Denney, 1982; Gottesman, Quarterman & Cohn, 1973). *Optimal ability* is what we are capable of doing when we are motivated and well prepared. *Actual ability* is the way we usually perform. At every period of life, there is some gap between what we might be capable of doing and our actual level of performance. However, there may also be some real limits to the optimal level of performance. For example, we might say that a middle-school-age boy is not as strong as he might be if he exercised more and used his muscles in more concentrated effort. However, even after exercise and training, his optimal strength would still be less than that of an adolescent who has experienced the increase in muscle mass that accompanies puberty.

We need to ask whether aging itself imposes limits on the optimal performance level of the very old or whether it is the environment and the expectations of others that reduce effective functioning. In tests of hearing, for example, older adults often show reduced sensitivity to high-frequency and low-intensity sounds. However, the hearing tests themselves impose a certain barrier to performance. Older people are cautious about making errors. They tend to say they have heard a tone only if they are absolutely certain that they have. In one study, older subjects were instructed to take a chance and respond even if they were not completely sure about having heard the tone. Their hearing tests showed significant improvement over normal testing conditions (Rees & Botwinick, 1971).

The goal of providing services or community resources to the frail elderly should be to enhance a realistic level of performance. We should not try to get 80-year-olds to live the lives of teenagers or people in their 50s. We should not attempt to minimize the true limitations that older adults may be encountering. Many very old adults move slowly, have difficulty hearing or seeing, or experience reduced strength and endurance in approaching daily tasks. They may experience some forgetfulness or confusion about events. They may feel less confident in decisions about financial matters or less trusting of new professionals, such as doctors, lawyers, accountants, and home maintenance personnel.

Many very old adults resist assistance from human service professionals because they do not understand the purposes of their services. For example, some very old adults will not apply for food stamps even though they may qualify for this form of assistance. They have lived life with an ethic of self-sufficiency, and they simply cannot accept what they perceive to be "welfare" or "something for nothing."

Most community mental health agencies provide counseling services for the elderly. However, this is a service that many older adults do not understand and do not perceive as very important. Consequently, it is one that they infrequently use. The current cohort of older adults has not been socialized to use the assistance of mental health professionals in coping with what we might consider normal life stresses such as grief, isolation, and chronic pain. Programs need to take into account the physical, educational, and attitudinal characteristics of the aging population. Then efforts must be made to educate the very old about the services that are offered.

While we do not want to underestimate the limitations of the elderly, neither do we want to overestimate them. We do not want to take away the supports that help very old adults sustain their independence or overreact to their physical or intellectual limitations. We see this tendency in the responses of some adult children to their aging parents. Once the children realize that their parents are not functioning at the same high level of competence that they enjoyed previously, they move toward a role reversal. They may infantilize or dominate their parents. They may insist on taking over all financial matters or attempt to relocate their parents to a more protective housing arrangement. Little by little, they take away all their parents' decision-making responsibilities.

Although children may view such actions as being in the parents' best interests, they may fail to take the parents' own preferences into account. For example, adult children tend to overemphasize the importance of health and financial considerations for their parents and overlook the significance of familiar housing in preserving the companionship and daily support that are critical to their parents' sense of well-being (Kahana, 1982). Adult children may also fail to realize how important decision-making tasks and responsibility for personal care are to the maintenance of their parents' personality structures. In mutually satisfying relationships between adult daughters and their aging mothers, the daughters make sure that mothers are consistently involved in decisions that affect their lives, even when the mothers are heavily dependent upon their daughters for daily care (Pratt et al., 1989).

In many nursing homes, there is a similar tendency to reduce or eliminate expectations of autonomy by failing to give residents any responsibilities for planning or performing the activities of daily life. Routine chores such as cooking, cleaning, shopping for groceries, doing laundry, planning meals, answering the phone, paying bills, and writing letters all give older adults the sense that life is going along as usual. Replacing these responsibilities with unstructured time may subject very old people to more stress than continuing to expect some forms of regular contribution to daily life. Paid work assignments and structured daily responsibilities are activities that an institutional setting can provide in order to help maintain a high level of social and intellectual functioning among the residents.

Supporting the optimal functioning of frail elderly people requires an individualized approach. Each person has a unique profile of competences and limitations. For some, the physical environment presents the greatest barriers to optimal functioning. A person who cannot walk without fear of falling, who cannot see well, or who cannot grasp objects because of arthritis may need to have modifications in the home that will compensate for these limitations. Many creative strategies have been introduced that permit people with serious physical disabilities to retain an optimal level of autonomy in their homes.

For some very old adults, the quality of the neighborhood presents the greatest barrier to optimal functioning. Older people may be afraid of vandalism, theft, or other forms of neighborhood crime. They may need transportation, emergency med-

Table 14.6   Critical Distances of Neighborhood Services for the Elderly

Service	Critical Distance	Maximum Recommended Distance
Bus stop	On site to 3 blocks	1 block
Outdoor area	On site to 3 blocks	3 blocks
Laundromat	On site	On site
Grocery store	1–10 blocks	6 blocks
Supermarket	1–10 blocks	6 blocks
Bank	1–10 blocks	6 blocks
Post office	1–3 blocks	3 blocks
Department store	1–3 blocks	3 blocks
Cleaners	1–11 blocks	6 blocks
Senior center	On site	On site
Beauty/barber	On site to 10 blocks	10 blocks
Physician	1–10 blocks	10 blocks
Butcher shop	1–10 blocks	6 blocks
Snack bar	1–10 blocks	10 blocks
Public library	On site to 10 blocks	10 blocks
Dentist	1–10 blocks	10 blocks
Eye doctor	1–10 blocks	10 blocks
Foot doctor	Indeterminate	10 blocks
Center (for all ages)	Used as senior center	On site
Movie	Indeterminate	10 blocks
Church/synagogue	Indeterminate	Indeterminate[a]
Bar	No importance	No importance

[a]Critical distance indeterminate because of high percentage of persons who do not use and only small number who do use.

Source: R. Newcomer, "An Evaluation of Neighborhood Service Convenience for Elderly Housing Project Residents," in P. Suedfeld and J. Russell (eds.), *The Behavioral Basis of Design*, p. 304. Copyright © 1976 by McGraw-Hill, Inc. Reprinted by permission.

ical services, and convenient social settings. Table 14.6 summarizes the results of a study on the importance and critical distance of neighborhood services for the very old. The *critical distance* is the limit beyond which a very old person would find the service inaccessible. Of course, one must keep in mind that the critical distance may vary with the topography. Climbing two blocks up a steep hill may be more difficult for a very old person than four blocks of flat walking. Interventions at the community level may be necessary to meet the safety, health, and social needs of some older adults who want to remain in their communities.

For other very old adults, the absence of meaningful interpersonal relationships is the greatest barrier to optimal functioning. The role of the informal social support system cannot be underestimated in meeting the needs of the frail elderly. Children, spouses, other relatives, and neighbors are all important sources of help. Within communities, very old people are themselves likely to provide significant help to agemates who may be ill, bereaved, or impaired in some way. Older adults prefer not to have to ask for help. However, they are much better off if they have someone to

Meaningful interpersonal relationships are a key ingredient in promoting optimal development in the frail elderly.

turn to than if they have no one. It is hypothesized that the reason so many institutionalized older adults feel lonely is that they were socially isolated before they entered the institutions. In other words, older people with family or friends to whom they can turn are less likely to need long-term institutional care.

Finally, people can do a lot for themselves to promote a fulfilling later life. For example, Thomas Szasz (1982) has described the *psychiatric will,* an instrument in which people can declare what kinds of assistance they are and are not willing to accept in their very old age. Adults can express their positions on receiving psychiatric treatment, conditions under which they would accept institutionalization, and the kinds of responsibilities that they would like their children or other executor of their affairs to exercise for them.

Very old adults can alter the structure of their environment to enhance a sense of well-being. They may move to a warmer climate, to homogeneous-age communities, or to more modest homes or apartments for which they will have fewer maintenance responsibilities. They may select some family and friendship relationships that they can sustain through frequent interaction, mutual help giving, and shared activities. They may participate in activities in community settings, including churches, senior centers, libraries, and volunteer organizations, in which they will retain a sense of social connectedness. As at earlier ages, very old people make certain choices that direct the course of their lives and influence their overall level of adjustment.

The following case illustrates the importance of psychological attitude in allowing a person with serious physical problems to play a meaningful role in a social setting for the frail elderly. Mr. Z.'s outlook helps him maintain his vitality and express his love of life:

> *Mr. M. L. Z. is an eighty-nine-year-old white male of Eastern European origin. He lives in a midsized nursing home in the Middle West. Many of his daily activities revolve around his circulating among the facility's residents, chatting, playing cards, reading to them, and "fetching things." Most important, Mr. Z. carries his old battered violin about with him and at the drop of a hat will play a tune or break into song in a surprisingly strong, clear, melodic voice. He claims to be able to sing songs in any one of seven languages, and with the least encouragement will try out several for anyone who will listen.*
>
> *Mr. Z is small (5'3"), frail-looking, and completely bald. He has facial scars and wears extremely thick-lensed glasses. He seems to be known and well-liked by practically all residents and staff of the facility in which he resides, and by many visitors there as well.*
>
> *He recalls a colorful history. He "escaped" his homeland at the tender age of fifteen and a half to avoid compulsory military service, and fled to Russia. There he was inducted into the army, and was subsequently sent off to duty in Siberia, where he lived for about six years. After another tour of duty in a border patrol he deserted, made his way across Europe, and eventually came to the United States. Here he took odd jobs, educated himself, and in time "got into show business"; he became a vaudeville prompter. In time his contacts in entertainment took him around the world. Yet time took its toll.*
>
> *He tells of marrying a woman with whom he lived for "almost forty years." They had no children and she died some fifteen years ago. Following her death, he began to experience a series of physical difficulties. An operation for cataracts left him with the need for very thick glasses. At one time he had a toupee made, which he has not worn for some time. One leg was amputated because of a diabetic condition and he now wears a prosthetic leg. In addition, he wears a hearing aid, false teeth, and, for the last year, a heart pacer. Several years ago he experienced what he calls a "small stroke," which left him "mixed up" for a few days. But he "worked this out," he reports, by "walking a lot," an activity in which he engages frequently.*
>
> *Mr. Z. says he has never smoked and drinks only on "occasions" or holidays, and then only to a limited degree. He scorns food fads, and eats "mostly" fresh fruits and "lots of vegetables"; he loves fish and drinks lots of tea.*
>
> *Despite all his troubles, Mr. Z. maintains what is apparently a cheerful, optimistic view of life and circumstances, while he pursues his "hobby" of energetically helping his fellow residents keep their spirits up and their interests high.*
>
> *He is very highly regarded and seen as filling a very important role in his nursing home as a story-teller and entertainer.* *

In summary, the quality of life for the frail elderly depends on three factors: (1) the specific nature and timing of the health-related limitations that accompany aging;

---

*A. N. Schwartz, C. L. Snyder, and J. A. Peterson, *Aging and Life: An Introduction to Gerontology*, 2nd ed., pp. 33–34. Copyright © 1984 by Holt, Rinehart and Winston. Reprinted by permission.

(2) the availability of appropriate resources within the home, family, and community to help compensate for or minimize those limitations; and (3) the selective emphasis that the person gives to some life experiences over others as being central to well-being.

☐ Chapter Summary

In attempting to describe the psychosocial development of the very old, we are drawn to concepts that have a strong non-western philosophical flavor. We have introduced such concepts as psychohistorical perspective, experiential transcendence, immortality, and social support—themes that reflect the need to assume a long-range perspective on life and its meaning. The concept of time changes with advanced age so that the continuity of past, present, and future becomes clearer. With the attainment of a deep confidence in being meaningfully integrated into an effective social system, the very old can find pleasure in the natural flow of events without concern for the accumulation of material goods or the need to exercise power.

The actual quality of daily life for the very old is influenced to a great extent by health-related factors. The daily activities of many older adults are restricted by one or more chronic diseases. On the other hand, the majority of the very old continue to live in their own households and to perform tasks of daily living independently. A key to the ability of the very old to retain their independence lies in whether or not they are integrated into effective social support networks. A support system provides help, resources, meaningful social interaction, and a psychological sense of being valued. Those who are isolated are more likely to face the ends of their lives bound to the tedium of struggling with physical limitations and resenting their survival. Those who survive within a support system can transcend the real limitations of their health, finding comfort and continuity in their participation in a continuing chain of loving relationships.

References

Adams, R. G. (1985). People would talk: Normative barriers to cross-sex friendships for elderly women. *Gerontologist, 25,* 605–611.

Bashore, T. R., Osman, A., & Heffley, E. F., III (1989). Mental slowing in elderly persons: A cognitive psychophysiological analysis. *Psychology and Aging, 4,* 235–244.

Bergeman, C. S., Plomin, R., Pedersen, N. L., McClearn, G. E., & Nesselroade, J. R. (1990). Genetic and environmental influences on social support: The Swedish adoption/twin study of aging. *Journal of Gerontology: Psychological Sciences, 45,* 101–106.

Birnbaum, H., Burke, R., Swearingen, C., & Dunlop, B. (1984). Implementing community-based long-term care: Experience of New York's long-term home health care program. *Gerontologist, 24,* 380–386.

Birren, J. E., Woods, A. M., & Williams, M. V. (1980). Behavioral slowing with age: Causes, organization, and consequences. In L. W. Poon (ed.), *Aging in the 1980s.* Washington, D.C.: American Psychological Association.

Blumenthal, J. A., Emery, C. F., Madden, D. J., George, L. K., Coleman, R. E., Riddle, M. W., McKee, D. C., Reasoner, J., & Williams, R. S. (1989). Cardiovascular and behavioral effects of aerobic exercise training in healthy older men and women. *Journal of Gerontology: Medical Sciences, 44,* M147–M157.

Branch, L. G., & Stuart, N. E. (1984). A five-year history of targeting home care services to prevent institutionalization. *Gerontologist, 24,* 387–392.

Clayman, J. L. (1989). *The American Medical Association encyclopedia of medicine.* New York: Random House.

Clayton, V. P., & Birren, J. E. (1980). The development of wisdom across the life span: A reexamination of an ancient topic. In P. B. Baltes & O. G. Brim, Jr. (eds.), *Life-span development and behavior* (vol. 3, pp. 104–135). New York: Academic Press.

Cobb, S. (1979). Social support and health through the life course. In M. W. Riley (ed.), *Aging from birth to death*. Boulder, Colo.: Westview.

Cohen, M. A., Tell, E. J., & Wallack, S. S. (1988). The risk factors of nursing home entry among residents of six continuing care retirement communities. *Journal of Gerontology: Social Sciences, 43,* S15–S21.

Cool, L. E. (1987). The effects of social class and ethnicity on the aging process. In P. Silverman (ed.), *The elderly as modern pioneers*. Bloomington: Indiana University Press.

Denney, N. W. (1982). Aging and cognitive changes. In B. B. Wolman (ed.), *Handbook of developmental psychology* (pp. 807–827). Englewood Cliffs, N.J.: Prentice-Hall.

Erikson, E., Erikson, J., & Kivnick, H. (1986). *Vital involvement in old age*. New York: Norton.

Flynn, C. B., Longino, C. F., Jr., Wiseman, R. F., & Biggar, J. C. (1985). The redistribution of America's older population: Major national migration patterns for three census decades, 1960–1980. *Gerontologist, 25,* 292–296.

Gottesman, L. E., Quarterman, C. E., & Cohn, G. M. (1973). Psychosocial treatment of the aged. In C. Eisdorfer & M. P. Lawton (eds.), *The psychology of adult development and aging*. Washington, D.C.: American Psychological Association.

Guralnik, J. M., & Kaplan, G. A. (1989). Predictors of healthy aging: Prospective evidence from the Alameda County study. *American Journal of Public Health, 79,* 703–708.

Gutmann, D. L. (1964). An exploration of ego configurations in middle and later life. In B. L. Neugarten (ed.), *Personality in middle and later life*. New York: Atherton.

Haley, W. E., & Pardo, K. M. (1989). Relationship of severity of dementia to caregiving stressors. *Psychology and Aging, 4,* 389–392.

Harris, T., Kovar, M. G., Suzman, R., Kleinman, J. C., & Feldman, J. J. (1989). Longitudinal study of physical ability in the oldest-old. *American Journal of Public Health, 79,* 698–702.

Hays, J. A. (1984). Aging and family resources: Availability and proximity of kin. *Gerontologist, 24,* 149–153.

Heynen, J. (1990). *One hundred over one hundred*. Golden, Colo.: Fulcrum.

House, J. S. (1985). Social support. *LSA, 8* (Winter), 5–8

Ingersoll-Dayton, B., & Antonucci, T. C. (1988). Reciprocal and nonreciprocal social support: Contrasting sides of intimate relationships. *Gerontology, 43,* S65–S73.

Jarvik, L. F., & Kumar, V. (1984). Update on diagnosis. Update on treatment. *Generations,* 7–11.

Jewett, S. (1973). Longevity and the longevity syndrome. *Gerontologist, 13,* 91–99.

Kahana, B. (1982). Social behavior and aging. In B. B. Wolman (ed.), *Handbook of developmental psychology* (pp. 871–889). Englewood Cliffs, N.J.: Prentice-Hall.

Keith, J. (1982). *Old people as people: Social and cultural influences on aging and old age*. Boston: Little, Brown.

Kinney, J. M., & Stephens, M. A. P. (1989). Hassles and uplifts of giving care to a family member with dementia. *Psychology and Aging, 4,* 402–408.

Kosnik, W., Winslow, L., Kline, D., Rasinski, K., & Sekuler, R. (1988). Visual changes in daily life throughout adulthood. *Gerontology, 43,* P63–P70.

Leaf, A. (1973). Growing old. *Scientific American, 229,* 44–53.

Lifton, R. J. (1973). The sense of immortality: On death and the continuity of life. *American Journal of Psychoanalysis, 33,* 3–15.

Long, J. L. (1980). Female sexuality through the life span. In P. B. Baltes & O. G. Brim, Jr. (eds.) *Life-span development and behavior* (vol. 3, pp. 208–252). New York: Academic Press.

Marshall, W. A. (1973). The body. In R. R. Sears & S. Feldman (eds.), *The seven ages of man*. Los Altos, Calif.: William Kaufman.

Meyers, G. C., & Manton, K. G. (1984). Compression of mortality: Myth or reality? *Gerontologist, 24,* 346–353.

Miller, I. J., Jr. (1988). Human taste bud density across adult age groups. *Journal of Gerontology: Biological Sciences, 43,* B26–B30.

Neugarten, B. L. (1981). Growing old in 2020. *National Forum, 61,* 28–30.

Newman, B. M., & Newman, P. R. (1983). *Understanding adulthood*. New York: Holt, Rinehart & Winston.

Offenbacher, D. I., & Poster, C. H. (1985). Aging and the baseline code: An alternative to the "normless elderly." *Gerontologist, 25,* 526–531.

Palmore, E. B., Nowlin, J. B., & Wang, H. S. (1985). Predictors of function among the old-old: A 10-year follow-up. *Journal of Gerontology, 40,* 244–250.

Pratt, C. C., Jones, L. L., Shin, H., & Walker, A. J. (1989). Autonomy and decision making between single older women and their caregiving daughters. *Gerontologist, 29,* 792–797.

Reese, J. N., & Botwinick, J. (1971). Detection and decision factors in auditory behavior of the elderly. *Journal of Gerontology, 26,* 133–136.

Riegel, K. F. (1973). Dialectic operations: The final period of cognitive development. *Human Development, 16,* 346–370.

Rogers, A. (1990). Return migration to region of birth among retirement-age persons in the United States. *Journal of Gerontology: Social Sciences, 45,* S128–S134.

Rosenfeld, A. H. (1978). *New views on older lives.* Rockville, Md.: National Institute of Mental Health.

Ross, M. J., Tait, R. C., Grossberg, G. T., Handal, P. J., Brandeberry, L., & Nakra, R. (1989). Age differences in body consciousness. *Journal of Gerontology: Psychological Sciences, 44,* P23–P24.

Salthouse, T. A. (1985). Speed of behavior and its implications for cognition. In J. W. Birren & K. W. Schaie (eds.), *Handbook of the psychology of aging* (pp. 400–426). New York: Van Nostrand Reinhold.

Schwartz, A. N., Snyder, C. L., & Peterson, J. A. (1984). *Aging and life: An introduction to gerontology* (2nd ed). New York: Holt, Rinehart & Winston.

Sherman, S. R. (1971). The choice of retirement housing among the well elderly. *Aging and Human Development, 2,* 119–120.

Spitzer, M. E. (1988). Taste acuity in institutionalized and noninstitutionalized elderly men. *Journal of Gerontology: Psychological Sciences, 43,* P71–P74.

Stephens, M. A. P., & Bernstein, M. D. (1984). Social support and well-being among residents of planned housing. *Gerontologist, 24,* 144–148.

Stevens, J. C., & Cain, W. S. (1987). Old-age deficits in the sense of smell as gauged by thresholds, magnitude matching, and odor identification. *Psychology and Aging, 2,* 36–42.

Szasz, T. S. (1982). The psychiatric will: A new mechanism for protecting persons against "psychosis" and psychiatry. *American Psychologist, 37,* 762–770.

Taylor, R. J. (1986). Religious participation among elderly blacks. *Gerontologist, 26,* 630–636.

U.S. Bureau of the Census (1983). *America in transition: An aging society.* Current Population Reports (ser. P-23, no. 128). Washington, D.C.: U.S. Government Printing Office.

U.S. Bureau of the Census (1984). *Demographic and socioeconomic aspects of aging in the United States.* Current Population Reports (ser. P-23, no. 138). Washington, D.C.: U.S. Government Printing Office.

U.S. Bureau of the Census (1987). *An aging world.* International Population Reports (ser. P-95, no. 78). Washington, D.C.: U.S. Government Printing Office.

U.S. Bureau of the Census (1989a). *Statistical abstract of the United States, 1989.* Washington, D.C.: U.S. Government Printing Office.

U.S. Bureau of the Census (1989b). *Population profile of the United States, 1989.* Current Population Reports (ser. P-23, no. 159). Washington, D.C.: U.S. Government Printing Office.

U.S. Senate, Special Committee on Aging (1986). *Aging America—trends and projections.* Washington, D.C.: U.S. Government Printing Office.

Wagner, D. R. (1984). Sleep. *Generations,* Winter, 31–36.

Wallechinsky, D., Wallace, I., & Wallace, A. (1977). *The book of lists.* New York: Morrow.

Wentowski, G. J. (1985). Older women's perceptions of great-grandmotherhood: A research note. *Gerontologist, 25,* 593–596.

Wernick, M., & Manaster, G. J. (1984). Age and the perception of age and attractiveness. *Gerontologist, 24,* 408–414.

Windle, M., & Sinnott, J. D. (1985). A psychometric study of the Bem Sex Role Inventory with an older adult sample. *Journal of Gerontology, 40,* 336–343.

Variations in Life Expectancy

The five tables in this appendix contain information about variations in life expectancy. In Tables 1 and 2 we focus on the effects of birth year, sex, and race. In Table 1, information about the average remaining lifetime for persons aged 65, 70, and 80 in six birth cohorts indicates the likelihood of reaching very old age. In Table 2, we consider life expectancy for more recent cohorts, and look at separate data for black and other nonwhite races.

Table 1 Average Remaining Lifetime at Various Ages by Sex and Race, 1900 to 1978

Exact Age, Race, and Sex	1978*	1968	1954	1939–1941	1929–1931	1900–1902
All Classes						
At birth	73.3	70.2	69.6	63.6	59.3	49.2
65 years	16.3	14.6	14.4	12.8	12.3	11.9
75 years	10.4	9.1	9.0	7.6	7.3	7.1
80 years	8.1	6.8	6.9	5.7	5.4	5.3
White						
Male:						
At birth	70.2	67.5	67.4	62.8	59.1	48.2
65 years	14.0	12.8	13.1	12.1	11.8	11.5
75 years	8.6	8.1	8.2	7.2	7.0	6.8
80 years	6.7	6.2	6.3	5.4	5.3	5.1
Female:						
At birth	77.8	74.9	73.6	67.3	62.7	51.1
65 years	18.4	16.4	15.7	13.6	12.8	12.2
75 years	11.5	9.8	9.4	7.9	7.6	7.3
80 years	8.8	7.0	7.0	5.9	5.6	5.5
Black and Other Races†						
Male:						
At birth	65.0	60.1	61.0	52.3	47.6	32.5
65 years	14.1	12.1	13.5	12.2	10.9	10.4
75 years	9.8	9.9	10.4	8.2	7.0	6.6
80 years	8.8	8.7	9.1	6.6	5.4	5.1
Female:						
At birth	73.6	67.5	65.8	55.6	49.5	35.0
65 years	18.0	15.1	15.7	13.9	12.2	11.4
75 years	12.5	11.5	12.0	9.8	8.6	7.9
80 years	11.5	9.3	10.1	8.0	6.9	6.5

*Provisional figures for all classes in 1980 are as follows: at birth, 73.6 years; at age 65, 16.4 years; at age 75, 10.4 years; at age 80, 8.2 years. (Source: National Center for Health Statistics. *Monthly Vital Statistics Report.* Vol. 29. No. 13. September 17, 1981.)

†Black only for 1929–1931 and 1900–1902.

Note: From *Demographic and Socioeconomic Aspects of Aging in the United States* (p. 59) by the U.S. Bureau of the Census, 1984. (Current Population Reports Series P-23, No. 138), Washington, D.C.: U.S. Government Printing Office.

Table 2   Expectation of Life at Selected Ages by Race and Sex: Death-Registration States, 1900–1902, and United States, 1959–1961, 1969–1971, 1979–1981, 1986, and 1987

| Life Table Value, Period, and Age | Total | White | | All Other | | | |
| | | | | Total | | Black | |
		Male	Female	Male	Female	Male	Female
Expectation of life							
At birth:							
1987	75.0	72.2	78.9	67.3	75.2	65.2	73.6
1986	74.8	72.0	78.8	67.2	75.1	65.2	73.5
1979–81	73.88	70.82	78.22	65.63	74.00	64.10	72.88
1969–71	70.75	67.94	75.49	60.98	69.05	64.10	72.88
1959–61	69.89	67.55	74.19	61.48	66.47	60.00	68.32
1900–1902	49.24	48.23	51.08	—	—	32.54	35.04
At age 1 year:							
1987	74.7	71.9	78.5	67.4	75.3	65.5	73.8
1986	74.6	71.7	78.4	67.4	75.1	65.5	73.7
1979–81	73.82	70.70	77.98	66.01	74.31	64.60	73.31
1969–71	71.19	68.33	75.66	62.13	70.01	61.24	69.37
1959–61	70.75	68.34	74.68	63.50	68.10	—	—
1900–1902	55.20	54.61	56.39	—	—	42.46	43.54
At age 20 years:							
1987	56.3	53.6	59.9	49.2	56.7	47.3	55.3
1986	56.2	53.4	59.9	49.1	56.6	47.3	55.3
1979–81	55.46	52.45	59.44	47.87	55.88	46.48	54.90
1969–71	53.00	50.22	57.24	44.37	51.85	43.49	51.22
1959–61	52.58	50.25	56.29	45.78	50.07	—	—
1900–1902	42.79	42.19	43.77	—	—	35.11	36.89
At age 65 years:							
1987	16.9	14.9	18.8	14.3	17.8	13.5	17.1
1986	16.8	14.8	18.7	14.1	17.7	13.4	17.0
1979–81	16.51	14.26	18.55	13.83	17.60	13.29	17.13
1969–71	15.00	13.02	16.93	12.87	15.99	12.53	15.67
1959–61	14.39	12.97	15.88	12.84	15.12	—	—
1900–1902	11.86	11.51	12.23	—	—	10.38	11.38

Source: National Center for Health Statistics (1990). Vital Statistics of the United States, 1987, vol. 11, Mortality, Part A. Washington, D.C.: Public Health Service Table A.

In Table 3 we compare the average lifetimes of men and women in the fifty states. Numerous regional factors are associated with longevity, including variations by state in financial and health care resources, education, exposure to environmental hazards, and lifestyle. The data may also reflect genetic patterns in members of regional subgroups.

Table 3   Average Lifetime in Years, By Sex and States: 1979–1981

State	Both Sexes Number	Rank	Male	Female	State	Both Sexes Number	Rank	Male	Female	State	Both Sexes Number	Rank	Male	Female
U.S.	73.88	(x)	70.11	77.62	KS	75.31	8	71.60	78.99	ND	75.71	5	72.09	79.68
AL	72.53	45	68.28	76.79	KY	73.06	41	69.14	77.12	OH	73.49	35	69.85	77.06
AK	72.24	46	68.71	76.87	LA	71.74	50	67.64	75.89	OK	73.67	¹31	69.63	77.81
AZ	74.30	21	70.46	78.34	ME	74.59	19	70.78	78.41	OR	74.99	14	71.35	78.77
AR	73.72	29	69.73	77.83	MD	73.32	38	69.71	76.83	PA	73.58	34	69.90	77.16
CA	74.57	20	71.09	78.02	MA	75.01	13	71.27	78.46	RI	74.76	18	70.96	78.33
CO	75.30	9	71.78	78.80	MI	73.67	¹31	70.07	77.29	SC	71.85	49	67.56	76.12
CT	75.12	12	71.51	78.57	MN	76.15	2	72.52	79.82	SD	74.97	16	71.03	79.21
DE	73.21	40	69.56	76.78	MS	71.98	48	67.64	76.39	TN	73.30	39	69.15	77.47
DC	69.20	(x)	64.55	73.70	MO	73.84	¹27	69.92	77.72	TX	73.64	33	69.70	77.67
FL	74.00	¹23	70.08	77.98	MT	73.93	25	70.47	77.68	UT	75.76	4	72.38	79.18
GA	72.22	47	68.01	76.35	NE	75.49	6	71.73	79.29	VT	74.79	17	71.06	78.49
HI	77.02	1	74.08	80.33	NV	72.64	44	69.26	76.48	VA	73.43	36	69.60	77.27
ID	75.19	10	71.52	79.15	NH	74.98	15	71.43	78.42	WA	75.13	11	71.74	78.57
IL	73.37	37	69.55	77.13	NJ	74.00	¹23	70.48	77.39	WV	72.84	43	68.86	76.93
IN	73.84	¹27	70.16	77.46	NM	74.01	22	69.91	78.34	WI	75.35	7	71.86	78.87
IA	75.81	3	72.00	79.60	NY	73.70	30	70.02	77.18	WY	73.85	26	69.95	78.20
					NC	72.96	42	68.60	77.35					

(x) Not applicable. ¹ Florida and New Jersey share the same rank of 23; Indiana and Missouri share the same rank of 27; Michigan and Oklahoma share the same rank of 31. Therefore, the numbers 24, 28, and 32 are omitted in order for the states to total 50.

Source: U.S. National Center for Health Statistics, *U.S. Decennial Life Tables for 1979–81, Vol. II, State Life Tables* (each state), August 1985.

In Tables 4 and 5 we provide cross-cultural data on longevity. In Table 4, consistent patterns in gender differences are indicated in nineteen developed countries. In Table 5, the impact of economic and educational development on longevity is viewed from a global perspective.

Table 4   Life Expectancy at Birth and at Age 65, by Sex, for Various Countries: Various Years from 1970 to 1978

Country and Year	Male		Female		Excess of Female over Male	
	At Birth	At Age 65	At Birth	At Age 65	At Birth	At Age 65
Austria, 1977	68.5	NA	75.6	NA	7.1	NA
Czechoslovakia, 1977	67.0	NA	74.1	NA	7.1	NA
Denmark, 1977–78	71.5	13.7	77.5	17.1	6.0	3.4
Finland, 1978	68.5	12.3	77.1	16.2	8.6	3.9
France, 1977	69.7	13.2	77.8	17.2	8.1	4.0
Germany, West, 1976–78	69.0	12.6	75.6	16.2	6.6	3.6
Hungary, 1978	66.6	12.2	73.3	14.9	6.7	2.7
Italy, 1970–72	69.0	13.3	74.9	16.2	5.9	2.9
Netherlands, 1977	72.0	13.9	78.4	18.0	6.4	4.1
Norway, 1977–78	72.3	14.3	78.6	17.7	6.3	3.4
Sweden, 1974–78	72.2	14.1	78.1	17.5	5.9	3.4
England and Wales, 1974–76	69.6	NA	75.8	NA	6.2	NA
Yugoslavia, 1970–72	65.4	12.4	70.2	14.4	4.8	2.0
New Zealand, 1970–72	68.6	NA	74.6	NA	6.0	NA
Israel, 1978	71.5	14.2	75.8	15.7	4.3	1.5
Japan, 1976	72.2	NA	77.4	NA	5.2	NA
Canada, 1970–72	69.3	13.7	76.4	17.5	7.1	3.8
United States, 1978	69.5	14.0	77.2	18.4	7.7	4.4
USSR, 1971–72	64.0	NA	74.0	NA	10.0	NA

NA = Not available.

Note: From *Demographic and Socioeconomic Aspects of Aging in the United States* (p. 70) by the U.S. Bureau of the Census, 1984 (Current Population Reports Series P-23, No. 138), Washington, D.C.: U.S. Government Printing Office.

Table 5   Life Expectancy by Continent and Region, 1988, and Projections for 2000

Continent and Region	Life Expectancy (Years)	
	1988	2000
World total	61.3	65.0
More developed regions	73.3	75.6
Less developed regions	59.5	63.6
Percent of world	(x)	(x)
Africa[1]	52.7	57.7
Asia	61.0	65.3
More developed regions	77.8	78.5
Less developed regions	60.7	65.0
East Asia	69.4	73.1
South Asia	57.3	62.4
Latin America[1]	66.8	70.4
Middle America[1]	67.8	71.4
Caribbean[1]	65.8	69.0
South America[1]	66.5	70.2
Northern America[2]	75.5	76.9
Europe[2]	74.3	75.9
Soviet Union[2]	68.9	73.2
Oceania	69.2	71.2
Australia and New Zealand[2]	75.9	76.9
Less developed regions	59.0	62.6

[1]Less developed regions

[2]More developed regions

Note: Regional classification is based on factors including industrial development, literacy rates, gross reproduction rates, and per capita income.

Source: U.S. Bureau of the Census (1989). *Statistical Abstract of the United States: 1989 (109th ed.)*. Washington, D.C.: U.S. Government Printing Office. Table 1402.

GLOSSARY

abasement   A lowering in rank, office, prestige, or esteem.

abdominal cavity   The area between the lower border of the ribs and the upper border of the thighs. The abdominal cavity includes organs of both the digestive and urinary systems.

abortion   Termination of a pregnancy before the fetus is capable of surviving outside the uterus.

accommodation   (a) In Piaget's theory of cognitive development, the process of changing existing schema in order to account for novel elements in the object or the event. (b) In vision, changes in the curvature of the lens in response to the distance of the stimulus.

achievement motivation   Internal state of arousal that leads to vigorous, persistent, goal-directed behavior when an individual is asked to perform a task in relation to some standard of excellence and when performance will be evaluated in terms of success and failure.

acoustic   Pertaining to the quality of sounds.

acquired immunodeficiency syndrome (AIDS)   A deficiency of the immune system due to infection with the human immunodeficiency virus.

acute illness   Illness that begins suddenly and lasts a brief time, such as a cold.

adaptation   The total process of change in response to environmental conditions.

adaptive self-organization   The process by which an open system retains its essential identity when confronted with new and constant environmental conditions. It creates new substructures, revises the relationships among components, and establishes new, higher levels of organization that coordinate existing substructures.

adaptive self-regulation   Adjustments made by an operating system in which feedback mechanisms identify and respond to environmental changes in order to maintain and enhance the functioning of the system.

adult executive   Family pattern in which all the adults in the household participate in decision making.

advocate   A person who pleads another's cause.

affect   Emotion, feeling, or mood.

affiliative behavior   Actions intended to form positive, affectionate bonds with others.

age-graded expectation   An assumption that someone should do something because of how old he or she is.

agency   Viewing the self as the originator of action.

aggression   Hostile, injurious, or destructive behavior.

alcoholism   An addiction to alcohol; excessive and compulsive use of alcohol.

alienation   Withdrawal or separation of people or their affections from an object or position of former attachment.

allele   The alternate state of a gene at a given locus.

alliances   Bonds or connections between families, groups, or individuals.

Alzheimer's disease   The most common form of chronic brain syndrome involving gradual brain failure over a period of 7 to 10 years.

ambiguity   Uncertainty or confusion of meaning.

ambivalence   A state of having simultaneous conflicting feelings about a person, object, or event.

amino acids   Organic acids that are the basic building blocks of proteins.

amniocentesis   The surgical insertion of a hollow needle through the abdominal wall and into the uterus of a pregnant woman to obtain fluid for the determination of sex or chromosomal abnormality of the fetus.

amniotic sac   A thin membrane forming a closed sac around the embryo and containing a fluid in which the embryo is immersed.

647

anal stage   In Freud's psychosexual theory, the second life stage, during which the anus is a primary source of sexual satisfaction. Issues of willfulness and order are central to this stage.

androgeny   The capacity to express both masculine and feminine characteristics as the situation demands.

anesthetic   A substance that produces loss of sensation with or without loss of consciousness.

animosity   Ill will or resentment.

anomaly   Irregularity, something that is inconsistent with the normal condition.

anorexia nervosa   An emotional disorder in which the person loses the ability to regulate eating behavior; the person is obsessed with a fear of being overweight and avoids food or becomes nauseous after eating.

anoxia   A medical term that means complete absence of oxygen within a tissue, such as the brain or a muscle, causing disruption in cell metabolism and cell death unless it is corrected within a few minutes.

antecedent   A preceding event, condition, or cause.

antibodies   Substances that neutralize toxins and destroy harmful bacteria or viruses in the bloodstream.

anxiety   A painful or apprehensive uneasiness of mind, usually over an impending or anticipated problem.

Apgar rating   Assessment of the newborn based on heart rate, respiration, muscle tone, response to stimulation, and skin color.

aptitude   Potential for learning and future performance of a skill.

arbitrary   Selected at random and without logical reason.

artificial insemination   Injection of donor sperm into a woman's vagina to promote conception.

aspiration   A strong desire to achieve something.

assimilation   In Piaget's theory of cognitive development, the process of incorporating objects or events into existing schema.

assumption   A fact, statement, or premise that is considered true and that guides the underlying logic of a theory.

attachment   The tendency to remain close to a familiar individual who is ready and willing to give care, comfort, and aid in time of need.

attachment behavioral system   A complex set of reflexes and signaling behaviors that inspire caregiving and protective responses in adults; these responses shape a baby's expectations and help create an image of the parent in the child's mind.

attachment patterns   Three distinct behavioral patterns of attachment that are characteristic of infants and seem to lead to different patterns of attachment formation in later relationships. 1. *Secure attachment:* confidence in a caregiver, permitting exploration of the environment with little protest over brief separations; 2. *Anxious–avoidant attachment:* expectation that requests for comfort will be rejected, reflected in considerable distress at separation, and rejection of caregiver's efforts to interact or soothe after separation; 3. *Anxious–resistant attachment:* expectation of unpredictable behavior from caregiver, leading to distress at separation, caution in the presence of strangers, erratic exploratory behavior, and apparent desire for closeness with caregiver combined with anger at caregiver.

attribution   The act of ascribing a quality or characteristic to someone else or to oneself.

auditory acuity   The ability to recognize sounds of varying pitch and loudness.

auditory system   The body parts and neural connections related to hearing.

authoritarian   A style of decision making in which the leader assumes total responsibility for making decisions and assigning responsibility. The authoritarian leader or parent expects obedience from everyone in a lower status position.

authority   A person who has power and influence and who is seen by others as the legitimate decision maker.

authority structure   An influence and decision-making system of relationships in business, government, education, and families.

autonomous morality   A more mature moral perspective in which rules are viewed as a product of cooperative agreements.

autonomy   The ability to behave independently, to do things on one's own.

autosomal   A chromosome other than a sex chromosome.

avoidance conditioning   A kind of learning in which specific stimuli are identified as painful or unpleasant and are therefore avoided.

Babinski reflex   A response in which toes extend and fan out when the sole of the foot is gently stroked. This reflex is a sign of an immature nervous system. Eventually, a stroke on the sole of the foot makes one's toes curl down.

bar mitzvah In the Jewish religion, a ceremony celebrated at age 13 to mark a boy's entry into adult status (bas mitzvah for girls).

basal metabolism Amount of energy used at rest.

behavioral slowing Age-related delay in the speed of response to stimuli.

behavior modification The use of concepts from learning theory, especially reinforcement, repetition, and association, to alter behavior.

bereavement The emotional suffering that follows the death of a loved one.

bilingualism The ability to speak two languages fluently.

biological adaptation A process whereby species evolve that have characteristics most suitable to the conditions of the environment.

birth order The order in which children in a family were born.

breathing capacity Oxygen capacity and efficiency of the lungs.

burn out A feeling of worthlessness brought about through prolonged exposure to work conditions that are frustrating, emotionally draining, and threatening.

cajole To persuade with flattery and humor.

care The commitment to be concerned.

career Occupation(s) or profession(s) followed as a lifework.

case study A research method consisting of an in-depth description and analysis of a single person, family, or group.

categorization The process of arranging, classifying, or describing by labeling or naming.

causal agent A person or object that makes something happen.

causality The relation between a cause and an effect.

cell differentiation A process whereby cells take on specialized structures related to their function.

cell nucleus The part of the cell that contains the material essential to reproduction and protein synthesis.

central process The dominant context or mechanism through which the psychosocial crisis is resolved.

cerebellum A part of the brain located in the back; the area that coordinates muscle activity and equilibrium.

cerebral cortex The layer of gray matter in the brain that serves to coordinate central nervous system functions.

cerebrum The upper part of the brain; the seat of conscious mental processes.

cervix The narrow lower end of the uterus, which forms the beginning of the birth canal.

cesarian delivery Delivering a newborn by lifting it out through an incision in the uterine wall.

chromosome One of the rodlike bodies of a cell nucleus that contain genetic material and that divide when the cell divides. In humans there are 23 pairs of chromosomes.

chronic illness Illness that lasts a long time. It may begin suddenly and recur or become progressively more serious.

chronological Arranged in the order of time.

chronological age The number of years and months since birth.

circular reaction In cognitive development, the infant's use of familiar actions to achieve familiar results.

circumcision Removing the foreskin that covers the glans of the penis.

classical conditioning A form of learning in which a formerly neutral stimulus is repeatedly presented with a stimulus that evokes a specific reflexive response. After repeated pairings, the neutral stimulus elicits a response similar to the reflexive response.

classification The action of grouping objects according to some specific characteristics they have in common, including all objects which show the characteristic and none which do not.

climacteric The period of menopause for women and a parallel period of reduced reproductive competence for men.

clinical studies Research conducted on populations who are or have been treated for a problem, or who are waiting to be treated.

clique A small exclusive group of people.

codominance A condition in which both genes at a specific allele contribute to the characteristic that is expressed, as in AB blood type.

cognition The capacity for knowing, organizing perceptions, and problem solving.

cognitive behaviorism The study of those cognitive dimensions related to understanding a person's ability to learn and perform tasks.

cognitive differentiation   The act of adding additional units of information, which increases the complexity of a concept.

cognitive map   An internal mental representation of the environment.

cognitive representation   Scheme, mental image.

cognitive style   A characteristic way of analyzing problems and organizing events.

cognitive theory   An analysis of the quality of thought and changes in thought at various stages of development.

cognitive unconscious   The range of mental structures and processes that operate outside awareness but play a significant role in conscious thought and action.

cohabitation   A relationship in which a man and woman live together but are not married.

cohort   In research design, a group of subjects who are studied during the same time period.

cohort sequential study   A research design that combines cross-sectional and longitudinal methods. Cohorts consist of participants in a certain age group. Different cohorts are studied at different times. New cohorts of younger groups are added in successive data collections to replace those who have grown older. This design allows the analysis of age differences, changes over time, and the effects of social and historical factors.

coitus   Sexual intercourse.

colloquial   Used in familiar or informal conversation.

combinatorial skills   The ability to perform mathematical operations, including addition, subtraction, and multiplication. These skills are acquired during the stage of concrete operational thought.

communication skills   All those skills involved in accurately expressing one's thoughts to others and in accurately interpreting the meaning of communications from others.

competence   The exercise of skill and intelligence in the completion of tasks.

competence (sense of)   The sense that one is capable of exercising mastery over one's environment.

competence motivation   The desire to exercise mastery by effectively manipulating objects or social interactions.

competition   A contest between rivals.

compulsions   Repetitive ritualized actions which serve as mechanisms for controlling anxiety.

concrete operational thought   In Piaget's theory, a stage of cognitive development in which rules of logic can be applied to observable or manipulatable physical relations.

conditional reward   A positive consequence that occurs when a specific condition or standard is met.

conditioned response   A response that is evoked by a stimulus as a result of repeated, systematic association.

conditioned stimulus   A stimulus that evokes a response as a result of repeated, systematic association.

confidence   A conscious trust in oneself and in the meaningfulness of life.

conformity   Behavior in accordance with some specified standard or expectation.

congenital   Existing from the time of birth.

congruence model   A model of sex role identity which suggests that it is most adaptive for males to adopt a strong masculine sex role and for females to adopt a strong feminine sex role.

connotation   The images and ideas suggested by a word rather than the specific object or action to which the word refers.

conscious   The kind of mental activity of which one is aware.

consensus   General agreement.

conservation   The concept that physical changes do not alter the mass, weight, number, or volume of matter. This concept is acquired during the concrete operational stage of cognitive development.

consonantal sounds   Sounds made by the consonants as opposed to the vowels.

context   The set of circumstances or facts that surround a person, event, or situation.

contextual dissonance   Discrepancy between a characteristic of the individual and norms related to that characteristic within the community, for example being one of few poor children in a middle-class school.

contextualization of learning   Offering instruction in ways that first draw upon a child's existing experiences, knowledge, and concepts, and then expand them in new directions.

contingent relationship   The effect of a behavior consistently producing a specific outcome.

contingent roles   Roles that serve to define the behaviors of adjacent role groups, as parent-child, or student-teacher.

continuing-care retirement community Nursing homes for the elderly that offer housing, medical, and social services to residents who are well when admitted, and that guarantee nursing care to residents who become ill or disabled.

contour The edge or line that encompasses or defines a shape or object.

contraceptive A method of preventing conception or impregnation.

contractions Tightening of the uterine muscles during childbirth.

control group The subjects in an experiment who do not experience the manipulation or treatment and whose responses or reactions are compared with those of subjects who are treated actively to determine the effects of the manipulation.

conventional morality A stage of moral reasoning described by Kohlberg in which right and wrong are closely associated with the rules created by legitimate authorities, including parents, teachers, or political leaders.

cooperation Working or acting together for a common purpose or benefit.

coping Active efforts to respond to stress. Coping includes gathering new information, maintaining control over one's emotions, and preserving freedom of movement.

core pathologies Destructive forces that result from severe, negative resolutions of the psychosocial crises.

corollary Something that follows naturally from a previous statement.

correlation A measure of the strength and direction of the relationship among variables.

creativity The willingness to abandon old forms or patterns of doing things and to think of new ways.

critical period A time of maximum sensitivity to or readiness for the development of a particular skill or behavior pattern.

crossing-over Interchange of genes or chromosome segments.

cross-sectional study A research design in which the behavior of subjects of different ages, social backgrounds, or environmental settings is measured once to acquire information about the effects of these differences.

crystallized intelligence Skills and information that are acquired through education and socialization.

cultural continuity A smooth transition from the role expectations of childhood through adolescence and adulthood.

cultural determinism The theoretical concept that culture shapes individual experience.

cultural discontinuity Discrete expectations associated with each stage or period of life.

cultural norms Shared expectations held by members of society for one another's behavior.

cultural relativism A premise of cultural anthropology that the meaning of a specific ritual or norm must be interpreted in light of the values and goals of the culture.

culture The concepts, habits, skills, arts, technology, religion, and government of a group of people during a specific period.

cumulative relation In heredity, when the allelic states in a single pair of genes combine to influence a trait.

curriculum The courses offered by an educational institution.

day care A variety of programs and settings designed to care for infants and young children on a daily basis.

decentering Gaining some objectivity over one's own point of view; reducing the dominance of one's subjective perspective in the interpretation of events.

defense mechanism A technique, usually unconscious, that attempts to alleviate the anxiety caused by the conflicting desires of the id and the superego in relation to impulses (e.g., repression, denial, projection).

deference Courteous or respectful regard for the wishes of another.

delay of gratification The ability to postpone receiving a reward or having pleasure until a later time.

dementia Disorders, either acute or chronic, that have various causes and results, some reversible and some irreversible, and that involve serious impairment or loss of intellectual capacities, control of bodily functions, and personality integration.

democratic A style of decision making in which the leader involves all group members in reaching a decision. The democratic leader expects all members to share responsibility for decisions that are made.

dependent variable A factor that is defined by a subject's responses or reactions, and that may or may not be affected by the experimenter's manipulation of the independent variable.

depression   A state of feeling sad, often accompanied by feelings of low personal worth and withdrawal from relations with others.

deprivation   The state of being without something one needs.

depth perception   The ability to recognize and judge depth.

desensitize   To provide repeated exposure to a specific stimulus so that it no longer has its original impact, as in desensitization to violence through repeated television viewing.

despair   Feeling a loss of all hope and confidence.

developmental stage   A period of life dominated by a particular quality of thinking or a particular mode of social relationships. The notion of stages suggests qualitative changes in competence at each phase of development.

developmental tasks   Skills and competences that are acquired at each stage of development.

dialect   A form of language that differs from the standard in pronunciation, grammar, and word meaning.

diaphragm   The dome-shaped sheet of muscle that divides the thorax (chest) from the abdomen. The diaphragm is attached to the spine, ribs, and sternum.

differential responsiveness   Responding more intensely or with greater attentiveness to some stimuli than to others.

diffidence   The inability to act, due to overwhelming self-doubt.

dilatation   Condition of being stretched open beyond normal limits.

discipline   A strategy for punishing or changing behavior.

disclosure   Revealing confidential information, ideas, feelings, or fantasies.

disdain   A feeling of scorn for the weakness and frailty of oneself or others.

disengagement theory   A theory describing later adulthood that suggests that psychological adjustment is associated with withdrawal from social roles and social relationships.

dissident   Differing in some way.

dissociation   Dissolving the ties, no longer associating together.

diuretics   Drugs that increase the production of urine.

diversity   Variety, differences.

division of labor   Splitting the activities needed to accomplish a task between participants.

DNA   Deoxyribonucleic acid. DNA molecules are the chemical building blocks of chromosomes found in the cell nucleus.

dominance   The personal characteristic of asserting oneself in relation to others and of trying to control others.

dominance hierarchy   A social ordering with the most controlling and assertive people at the top and the more submissive people at the bottom.

dominant gene   A form of a gene that is always expressed in the phenotype when the gene is present, as in the example of Rr for tongue rolling.

double bind   A kind of interaction that carries both an accepting and rejecting message.

doubt   A sense of uncertainty about one's abilities and one's worth.

Down's syndrome   A chromosomal irregularity in which the child has an extra chromosome. The condition results in mental retardation.

dramatic role playing   Taking on a role in fantasy play.

dual-career marriage   A marriage in which both partners have high-powered professional, technical, or administrative careers.

dual-earner marriage   A marriage in which both partners work to earn money.

dyadic relationship   A two-person relationship.

early adolescence   The period of psychosocial development that begins with the onset of puberty and ends around 18 years of age, usually with graduation from high school.

early adulthood   The period of psychosocial development that begins in the early twenties and ends in the early thirties.

early school age   The period of psychosocial development that begins when the child enters school around the age of five and ends around the age of seven.

effacement   The shortening of the cervical canal.

efficacy   The power to produce effects.

efficiency   The quality of accomplishing what is undertaken with little waste of time or energy.

egalitarian   Marked by the treatment of others as peers and equals out of a belief in human equality.

ego   In psychoanalytic theory, the mental structure that experiences and interprets reality. The ego includes most cognitive capacities, including perception, memory, reasoning, and problem solving.

egocentric empathy Recognizing distress in another person and responding to it as if it were your own.

egocentrism The perception of oneself at the center of the world; the view that others and events base their behavior on or occur as a result of one's own perceptions.

ego ideal A set of positive standards, ideals, and ambitions that represent the way a person would like to be.

ego processes All those processes necessary for thinking and reasoning, for example, memory.

ego satisfaction Sources of job satisfaction which bring a sense of personal accomplishment, pride, or power, or meet other inner motives and goals.

ego strength The soundness of the individual's personality.

Electra conflict In Freud's psychosexual theory, the central conflict of the phallic stage for a girl, when she desires intimacy with her father and expresses hostility toward her mother.

electronic fetal heart rate monitoring Continuous monitoring of fetal heart rate using an electronic amplification device.

embryo The developing human individual from the time of implantation to the end of the eighth week after conception.

embryology A branch of biology that studies the nature and development of embryos.

emotions States of feeling.

empathy The capacity to recognize and experience the emotional state of another person.

empty nest The time when children leave the home.

emulate To try to equal or excel.

enactive attainment Personal experiences of mastery.

endogenous Growing from within.

enhancement Making something more attractive.

enuresis Bed wetting beyond the age when toilet training is usually completed.

enzyme Complex proteins produced by living cells that act as catalysts for biochemical reactions.

epigenetic principle A biological plan for growth such that each function emerges in a systematic sequence until the fully functioning organism has developed.

epinephrine An adrenal hormone.

equilibrium In Piaget's theory, the balance every organism strives to attain in which organized structures (sensory, motor, or cognitive) provide effective ways of interacting with the environment.

equivalence In cognitive theory, the concept that two objects of the same size and shape remain the same in quantity even though the shape of one of them is changed.

estrogen The major female sex hormone.

ethics Principles of conduct founded upon a society's moral code.

ethnic group identity Knowing that one is a member of a certain ethnic group; recognizing that aspects of one's thoughts, feelings, and actions are influenced by ethnic membership; and taking the ethnic group values, outlook, and goals into account when making life choices.

ethnicity Traits, background, allegiance, or association that are associated with an ethnic group.

ethnic subculture The cultural values and behavioral patterns characteristic of a particular group in a society that shares a common ancestry; memories of a shared historical past; and a cultural focus on symbolic elements that distinguish the group from others.

ethology The comparative investigation of the biological bases of behavior from an evolutionary perspective, to determine the proximal causes of behavioral acts, the relative contribution of inheritance and learning to these acts, and the adaptive significance and evolutionary history of different patterns of behavior within and across species.

euphoria A sense of well-being and expansiveness.

Eurocentric Considering Europe and Europeans as focal to world culture, history, economics, philosophy, morality, and so on.

evaluation A determination of the worth of one's skill in a particular behavior.

evolution A theory that accounts for the changes from one species to another as well as modifications within species over time.

exclusivity A shutting out of others for elitist reasons.

exhibition Showing one's talents or skills publicly; attracting attention to oneself.

expansion Elaborating on a child's expression by adding more words.

expectations Views held by oneself or by others about what would be appropriate behavior in a given situation or at a given stage of development.

expediency Most efficient way of achieving the desired end.

experiential transcendence   A way of experiencing immortality through achieving a sense of continuous presence.

experimental group   The subjects who experience the manipulation or treatment in an experiment.

experimentation   A method of research that is conducted under repeatable and highly controlled conditions, in which some variable or group of variables are systematically manipulated while others are held constant; used to assess cause-and-effect relationships.

expressive   Using language to communicate thoughts and feelings.

extended family   The family group that includes family members other than the nucleus of parents and children.

external ear canal   The visible part of the ear, which collects and transmits sound.

extinction   In classical conditioning, the reduction of an association when the unconditioned stimulus is not presented.

extinction   The negative pole of the psychosocial crisis of very old age in which it is feared that the end of life is the end of all continuity.

extrinsic satisfaction   Sources of job satisfaction including salary, other financial benefits, working conditions, or special privileges.

facilitate   To make easier.

fallopian tube   The tube, extending from the uterus to the ovary, in which fertilization takes place.

false labor   Uterine contractions that do not indicate the start of the birth process.

family constellation   The many variables that describe a family group, including the presence or absence of mother and father, sibling number, spacing, and sex, and the presence or absence of extended family members in the household.

family day care   A child-care arrangement in which a person cares for several children in his or her own home, often along with the person's own children.

family executive   A family pattern in which all people in the household participate in decision making.

family of origin   The family to which one is born.

family of procreation   The family one begins as an adult.

fantasy   A form of symbolic thought that is not restrained by the limits of reality.

fast mapping   Forming a rapid, initial, partial under-standing of the meaning of a word by relating it to the known vocabulary and restructuring the known-word storage space and its related conceptual categories.

fear of loss of love   A motive for parental identification in which the child tries to be like the parent in order to preserve a sense of closeness with the loved parent.

feedback   Information about how a particular activity is being carried out that returns to a central control mechanism. Feedback may be automatic information from muscles about a physical activity or evaluative information from a teacher about academic performance.

fertility   The capacity to reproduce.

fertilization   The penetration of an egg by a sperm.

fetal alcohol syndrome   A condition of the fetus involving central nervous system disorders, low birth weight, and malformations of the face; the condition is associated with heavy use of alcohol by mothers, especially during the last trimester of pregnancy.

fetoscopy   Examination of the fetus through the use of a fiberoptic lens.

fetus   The unborn infant. Usually the term *fetus* refers to infants between 12 weeks of gestational age and birth.

fiberoptic lens   A bundle of very thin transparent glass or plastic fibers that transmit light by internal refractions.

fidelity (I)   The ability to freely pledge and sustain loyalties to others.

fidelity (II)   The ability to freely pledge and sustain loyalties to values and ideologies.

filial obligation   The responsibilities of adult children for their aging parents.

fixation   In psychoanalysis, a preoccupation with the issues and tasks of a particular stage of development; an inability to progress to more mature stages.

fixed action pattern   A genetically guided sequence of complex highly patterned behavior, such as nest building or mating, that is characteristic of a particular species and is prompted or triggered by a specific stimulus pattern that signals or releases the innate behavior pattern.

fluid intelligence   The ability to impose organization on information and to generate new hypotheses.

forebrain   The front section of the three primary divisions of the brain in the embryo of a vertebrate; the part of the adult brain derived from this tissue.

formal operations   In Piaget's theory, the final stage of cognitive development characterized by reasoning, hypothesis generating, and hypothesis testing.

frail elderly   Older people who may have delicate health, one or more inactivating chronic conditions, and possibly some form of dementia.

frame of reference   The events or point of view that influence one's judgments.

fraternal twins   Children born at the same time who developed from two different ova.

frustration   Dissatisfaction derived from unmet needs.

full-term baby   A baby who has developed in utero for the complete gestational period of 9 months or approximately 36 weeks.

functional autonomy of motives   In Allport's theory, the notion that behaviors may initially be performed because of specific motives, but may continue because the person enjoys them and/or finds them useful in new ways.

gamete   A mature germ cell involved in reproduction.

gender   The sex of the person.

gender label   Words that identify one's gender, as boy, girl, man, or woman.

gene   The fundamental physical unit of heredity. A gene is a linear sequence of nucleotides along a segment of DNA that carries the coded instructions for synthesis of RNA, which, when translated into protein, leads to hereditary character.

gene pool   Genetic information contained in the genes of the population or culture which provides the ancestry for an individual.

generativity   The capacity to contribute to the quality of life for future generations. A sense of generativity is attained toward the end of middle adulthood.

genetic anomalies   Neurological or physical abnormalities that have a genetic cause.

genetic engineering   The development and application of scientific methods, procedures, and technologies that allow direct manipulation of genetic material in order to alter the hereditary traits of a cell, organism, or population.

genetic fingerprinting   Study of individual genetic characteristics.

genetics   The study of heredity.

gene transfer   The insertion of copies of a gene into living cells in order to induce synthesis of the gene's product; the desired gene may be microinjected into the cell directly, or it may be inserted into the core of a virus by gene splicing and the virus allowed to infect the cell to replicate the gene in the cell's DNA.

genitalia   The reproductive organs, especially the external ones.

genital stage   In Freud's psychosexual theory, the final life stage, during which the genitals are the primary source of sexual satisfaction and in which sexual impulses are directed toward members of the opposite sex.

genome   A full set of chromosomes that carries all the inheritable traits of an organism.

genotype   The hereditary information contained in the cells. Genotype may or may not be observable in the phenotype (see **phenotype**).

gerontologist   A professional who deals with aging and the problems of the aged.

gestation   The period of carrying a fetus from conception to birth.

gestational age   The age of the fetus from the time of conception.

Glick effect   Statistical evidence of lack of persistence which relates dropping out of high school or college with a high probability of divorce.

global empathy   Distress experienced and expressed as a result of witnessing someone else in distress.

grammar   Rules for the arrangement of words and phrases in a sentence and for the inflections that convey gender, tense, and number.

grasp reflex   An automatic involuntary movement present at birth that disappears as the nervous system matures. Any object placed in the infant's palm will be firmly grasped.

grief   Deep sorrow resulting from a loss.

group identity   The positive pole of the psychosocial crisis of early adolescence in which the person finds membership in and value convergence with a peer group.

group play   An early form of game, such as Ring around the Rosie or London Bridge, in which winning or losing is not as important as the ritualized behavior.

growth rate   The amount of growth that occurs during a given period of time.

guilt   An emotion associated with doing something wrong or anticipating doing something wrong.

habituation   A form of adaptation in which the child no longer responds to a stimulus that has been repeatedly presented.

hedonic   Pertaining to pleasure.

hedonistic behavior   Pleasure-seeking behavior.

hemophilia   A sex-linked hereditary disease in which blood clots very slowly.

heredity   The qualities and potential transmitted genetically from one generation to the next.

heterogeneous   Having different qualities.

heteronomous morality   A child's moral perspective in which rules are viewed as fixed and unchangeable.

heterosexual relationships   Associations and friendships with members of the opposite sex.

heterozygous   Characterized by the presence of different alleles of a particular gene at the same locus.

hindbrain   The rearmost section of the three primary divisions of the brain in the embryo of a vertebrate; the part of the adult brain derived from this tissue, including the medulla oblongata, the pons, and the cerebellum.

holophrase   A word functioning as a phrase or sentence.

homeostasis   A relatively stable state of equilibrium.

Homo erectus   An extinct species of early humans, dating from 1.7 million years ago, characterized by upright stature and a well-evolved postcranial skeleton with a smallish brain, low forehead, and protruding face. This species has a larger skull, with a different shape than *Homo habilis,* but a smaller brain than *Homo sapiens.* The tools used by Homo erectus were more complex than those used by Homo habilis but less complex than the tools used by Homo sapiens. Homo erectus is the first species known to have controlled fire.

homogeneous   Sharing the same qualities.

Homo habilis   An extinct species of upright East African hominid, dating from about 1.5 million to more than two million years ago, which had some advanced human-like characteristics, including the ability to use the hands skillfully as well as some stone tools.

Homo sapiens   The species of bipedal primates to which modern humans belong, characterized by a brain capacity that averages 1400 cubic centimeters (85 cubic inches) and by dependence upon language and complex manufactured tools. In the "candelabra" model, we evolved gradually from *Homo erectus* ancestors. In the "Noah's Ark" theory, we evolved separately from Homo erectus and expanded rapidly, whereas Homo erectus underwent rapid extinction.

homozygous   Characterized by the presence of matched alleles of a particular gene at the same locus.

hope   An enduring belief that one can attain one's essential wishes.

horizontal career movements   Changes that represent the same level of attainment at a more personally comfortable work setting.

hormones   A group of chemicals, each of which is released into the bloodstream by a particular gland or tissue and has a specific effect on tissues elsewhere in the body.

hue   The property of light by which the color of an object is classified as red, blue, green, or yellow in reference to the spectrum.

human immunodeficiency virus (HIV)   The cause of AIDS, it gains access to the body through the bloodstream and attacks the brain, sometimes causing damage and dementia.

hypothesis   A tentative proposition that can provide a basis for further inquiry.

hypothetico-deductive reasoning   A method of reasoning in which a hypothetical model based on observations is first proposed and then tested by deducing consequences from the model.

id   In psychoanalytic theory, the mental structure that expresses impulses and wishes. Much of the content of the id is unconscious.

ideal self   A view of the self as one would wish it to be.

identical twins   Children born at the same time who developed from the same ovum.

identification   A psychological mechanism in which the people attempt to enhance their own self-concept by incorporating some of the valued characteristics of important others such as parents into their own behavior.

identification with the aggressor   A motive for parental identification in which the child tries to be like the parent in order to prevent injury or rejection from the parent.

identity   In cognitive theory, the concept that an object is still the same object even though its shape or location has been changed.

identity achievement   Individual identity status in which, after crisis, a sense of commitment to family, work, political, and religious values is established.

identity confusion   The negative pole of psychosocial crisis of later adolescence in which a person is unable to integrate various roles or make commitments.

identity foreclosure   Individual identity status in which a commitment to family, work, political, and religious values is established prematurely, without crisis.

idiosyncratic Marked by a characteristic peculiarity of personal habit, temperament, or personality structure.

illusion of incompetence Expressed by children who perform well in academic achievement tests, yet perceive themselves as below average in academic ability and behave in accordance with this perception.

imaginary companion A fantasized character created by a child's symbolic capacities.

imitation Repetition of another person's words, gestures, or behaviors.

immortality The positive pole of the psychosocial crisis of very old age in which the person transcends death through a sense of symbolic continuity.

immunity A state of protection by the immune system against a disease or diseases. Immunity is present from birth and is the first line of defense against the vast majority of infectious agents.

imprinting A process whereby an animal comes to follow a large object, usually its mother, at some point after birth.

impulse Internal psychological drive for certain types of behavior such as aggressive or sexual impulses.

impulse control Control of internal psychological drives for particular types of behavior.

incentive Something that motivates one to act, such as a reward for succeeding.

incest Sexual relations between people so closely related that they are forbidden by law to marry.

independence Self-government; a state of not being subject to the control of others or not relying on others for support.

independent variable A factor that is manipulated in an experiment, and the effects of the manipulation measured.

individual identity The commitment to a personal integration of values, goals, and abilities that occurs as personal choices are made in response to anticipated or actual environmental demands at the end of adolescence.

individuation The process of becoming a unique and distinct person.

induction A form of discipline that points out the consequences of a child's actions for others.

industry A sense of pride and pleasure in acquiring culturally valued competences. The sense of industry is usually acquired by the end of the middle childhood years.

inertia A paralysis of thought and action that prevents productive work.

infancy The period of psychosocial development that begins when the child is born and ends when the child is approximately two years old.

infanticide Killing infants.

inference (a) The act of moving from one proposition, statement, or judgment considered to be true to another whose truth is believed to follow from the first. (b) The act of moving from statistical sample data to generalizations, usually with calculated degrees of certainty.

inferiority A sense of incompetence and failure which is built on negative evaluation and lack of skill.

infertility Inability to conceive or carry a fetus through the gestational period.

inflections Word endings that indicate tense and number.

in-group A group of which one is a member; contrasted with **out-group.**

inhibition A psychological restraint that prevents freedom of thought, expression, and activity.

initiative The ability to offer new solutions, to begin new projects, or to seek new social encounters; active investigation of the environment.

innate Present at birth.

innate behavior Existing from birth; inborn; hereditary.

inner ear An extremely intricate series of structures deep within the skull. The front part is concerned with hearing; the rear part is concerned with balance.

inoculation An injection, usually to prevent disease, that stimulates the production of antibodies.

inordinate Exceeding reasonable limits.

insight In Piaget's theory of cognitive development, the last phase of sensorimotor intelligence in which children solve problems by thinking over the possible solutions and selecting the correct one to try.

instinct An inherited and largely unalterable tendency of an organism to make a complex specific response to environmental stimuli.

instrumental Guiding behavior toward solving problems and accomplishing tasks.

instrumental conditioning A form of associational learning in which the behaving organism emits responses that are shaped into the desired response by reinforcement. Once the desired response occurs it is strengthened by continued reinforcement.

integrity   The ability to accept the facts of one's life and to face death without great fear. The sense of integrity is usually acquired toward the end of later adulthood.

intellectual flexibility   A person's ability to handle conflicting information, to take several perspectives on a problem, and to reflect on personal values in solving ethical problems.

interdependence   (a) Marked by all the elements in a system relying on one another for their continued growth. (b) Systems that depend on each other.

internalization   A process in which the values, beliefs, and norms of the culture become the values, beliefs, and norms of the individual.

intersubjectivity   A shared repertoire of emotions which enable infants and their caregivers to understand each other and create shared meanings; they can engage in reciprocal, rhythmic interactions, appreciate state changes in one another, and modify their actions in response to emotional information about one another.

interview   A research method in which subjects are questioned about various aspects of their lives, including their feelings and thoughts.

intimacy   The ability to experience an open, supportive, tender relationship with another person without fear of losing one's own identity in the process of growing close. The sense of intimacy is usually acquired toward the end of early adulthood.

intonation   Rise and fall in pitch during speech.

intrapsychic   Occurring within the psyche, mind, or personality of an individual.

intravenous (feeding)   Introduction of a substance into a vein.

intrinsic motivation   A drive to behave in a certain way that comes from within the person.

introspection   Deliberate self-evaluation and examination of private thoughts and feelings.

introvert   Focused inward upon the self.

in utero   In the uterus.

in vitro   In an artificial environment.

in vivo   Biological processes occurring or caused to occur within the living body of a plant or animal.

irregular verbs   Verbs that do not conform to the usual pattern of inflection; for example, sell, sold; see, saw.

irritability   The ease with which stimuli cause disruption or pain.

isolation   A crisis resolution in which situational factors or a fragile sense of self leads a person to remain psychologically distant from others.

isolation   The state of being alone.

kibbutz   An Israeli community in which members share the ownership of all property and the profits from production. Children are reared communally.

labor   The period of involuntary contractions of the uterine muscles that occurs prior to giving birth.

lactation   Presence and secretion of milk that automatically occurs in the breasts of the mother of a newborn infant.

laissez-faire   A style of leadership in which the leader permits members to make their own decisions as they see fit.

language perception   The ability to recognize sounds and differentiate among sound combinations before the meanings of these sounds are understood.

latency   The time that elapses between a signal to act and the act itself.

latency stage   In Freud's psychosexual theory, the fourth life stage, during which no significant conflicts or impulses are assumed to rise. Superego development proceeds during this period.

latent learning   Learning about the contextual or background information that surrounds the information or task that is the target of attention.

later adolescence   The period of psychosocial development that begins around the time of graduation from high school and ends in the early twenties.

later adulthood   The period of psychosocial development that begins in the early fifties and ends with death.

launching period   The time in family life during which children leave home.

leading crowd   A group of students identified in James Coleman's research as leaders in the high school who tend to associate with one another and who make up the top group in the social hierarchy of the student culture.

learning   Any relatively permanent change in thought and/or behavior that is the consequence of experience.

learning set   A general strategy for problem solving.

learning theory   A set of principles that account for changes in behavior at every stage of life, usually focusing on ways in which controlled changes in the environment produce predictable changes in behavior.

lexicon   The vocabulary of a language.

life careers Activities in particular domains that last for a significant amount of time during one's life, such as the parenting career.

life course Individual life patterns as they are expressed in a social and historical time period.

life crisis An unusual level of stress and tension that occurs during one's life, including psychosocial crises and events in one's life that cause tension, such as the death of a parent.

life endurancy The age to which one person in 100,000 can be expected to survive.

life expectancy The average number of years from birth to death as based on statistical analyses of the length of life for people born in a particular period.

life review A process of recalling significant life events, accomplishments, and difficulties from earliest memories up to the present.

life span The length of an individual's existence.

lifestyle A relatively permanent structure of activity and experience, including the tempo of activity, the balance between work and leisure, and patterns of family and social relationship.

lightening The stage of pregnancy in which the movements of the fetus are first felt by the pregnant woman.

linguistic system Combination of vocabulary, grammar, phonetics, and language customs.

literacy The state of being able to read and write.

loneliness A feeling of sadness related to being alone; failing to meet one's needs for companionship.

longitudinal study A research design in which repeated observations of the same subjects are made at different times, in order to examine change over time.

long-term memory The encoding and storing of events for recall at a much later time.

love An emotion characterized by a capacity for mutuality that transcends childhood dependency.

love withdrawal A form of discipline in which parents express disappointment or disapproval and become emotionally cold or distant.

malnutrition A condition of ill health that results from faulty or inadequate food intake.

mammal Any vertebrate of the class Mammalia, which nourishes its young with milk from the mammary glands, is more or less covered with hair, and (with the exception of the egg-laying monotremes) gives birth to live young.

masculinity model A model of sex-role identity which suggests that a masculine sex-role orientation is most adaptive for females as well as for males.

mastery Competence or skill.

mastery (sense of) A self-conceptualization that one has acquired certain competence, skill, or control over one's environment.

matched groups sampling In which two or more groups of subjects who are similar on many dimensions are selected as the sample for an experiment. The effects of different treatments or manipulations are determined by comparing the behavior of these groups.

maternal deprivation Lack of opportunities for interaction with a mother or primary caregiver.

maturation rate The rate at which certain personal, biological, and behavioral characteristics emerge and develop in an individual through the process of growth.

means-end relationship A sensorimotor scheme for the causal connection between certain actions and certain consequences.

medulla A part of the brain just above the spinal cord that controls life-sustaining functions such as breathing, blood pressure, and heart rate.

meiosis An aspect of cell division resulting in the number of chromosomes in gamete-producing cells being reduced to one half.

memory The power and process of recalling and reproducing what has been learned or experienced. It can be exercised as short-term memory and long-term memory.

menarche The beginning of regular menstrual periods.

menopause The ending of regular menstrual periods.

mental age One's age as measured by an intelligence test. Usually, mental age is determined by the level of difficulty of the questions the child can answer correctly.

mental image A form of representational thought which involves the ability to hold the picture of a person, object, or event in one's mind even in the absence of the stimulus itself.

mental operations A transformation, carried out in thought rather than action, which modifies an object, event, or idea.

mentor A trusted counselor or guide.

metabolization The process by which energy is provided for vital processes and activities and new material is assimilated to repair the waste, through the chemical changes in living cells.

metacognition Thinking about one's own thinking, including what individuals understand about their reasoning capacities and about how information is organized, how knowledge develops, how reality is distinguished from belief or opinion, how to achieve a sense of certainty about what is known, and how to improve understanding.

methodology Particular techniques used to conduct a research investigation.

midbrain The middle of the three primary divisions of the brain in the embryo of a vertebrate, or the part of the adult brain derived from this tissue; also called the mesencephalon, it is the topmost part of the brain stem, situated above the pons.

middle adulthood The period of psychosocial development that begins in the early thirties and ends in the early fifties.

middle school A school containing grades 5 through 8.

middle school age The period of psychosocial development that begins at about age 8 and ends when the child enters puberty.

mistrust A sense of unpredictability in the environment and suspicion about one's own worth. Experiences with mistrust are most critical during infancy.

mitochondrial DNA DNA from mitochondria, rich in proteins, fats, and enzymes, which are found outside the nucleus of a cell and produce energy for the cell through cellular respiration. The DNA is passed on solely through the mother and can be used to trace genetic lineage.

mobility Ability to engage in movement.

model In social learning theory, the one who is imitated.

modeling Demonstrating behaviors that can be imitated by others.

molecule The smallest part of a substance that retains the properties of the substance.

monozygotic twins Twins who develop from a single fertilized egg. These twins have identical genetic characteristics.

moral judgments Cognitive decisions about right or wrong behavior which involve an underlying rationale.

moral prescriptions Positive rules for valued behavior.

moral prohibitions Rules to suppress negatively valued behavior.

moral script The culture's expectations about valued and devalued behaviors for children of each age and in each social context.

morphological abnormalities Damage to body form and structure.

mortality The quality of life that involves one's eventual death.

mortality (infant) The number of deaths per 100,000 of liveborn infants.

motherese The simplified, redundant style of speaking used by adults and older children so that they are more likely to be understood by a child who is learning language.

motive Something that causes a person to act.

motor functions Bodily movement of both voluntary and reflexive types.

multiparas A woman who has borne two or more children or who is pregnant for the second time.

muscle tonus A level of moderate contraction that is present in normal muscles.

mutual adaptation Two or more people changing in response to each other.

mutuality Ability of two people to meet each other's needs and share each other's concerns and feelings.

myelination The formation of a soft, white, fatty material called myelin around certain nerve axons, to serve as an electrical insulator that speeds nerve impulses to muscles and other effectors.

narcissistic Extremely self-absorbed and self-loving.

naturalistic observation A research method in which subjects' behavior is observed and described as it occurs in its natural setting without experimental intervention.

natural selection A process whereby those individuals best suited to the characteristics of the immediate environment are most likely to survive and reproduce.

need Physical or psychological requirement for well-being.

negative identity A clearly defined self-image that is completely contrary to the cultural values of the community.

negativism Refusal to comply with others' requests.

neighborhood The physical area and the residents of the area where one lives.

neonatal Affecting the newborn, especially during the first month of life.

nerve conduction velocity Speed of neural firing.

neural tube The hollow longitudinal tube formed by

infolding and subsequent fusion of the opposite ectodermal folds in the vertebrate embryo.

neurological development Growth of the nervous system.

neuron A nerve cell with specialized processes that is the fundamental functional unit of nervous tissue.

nondisjunction An event occurring during cell division, in which both chromosomes of a pair go to the same new cell. Nondisjunction results in chromosomal irregularities, including Down's syndrome.

normative Conforming to an average pattern.

norms Collective expectations, or rules for behavior, held by members of a group or society.

nostalgia A wistful or sentimental yearning for return to some past period.

nuclear family A household grouping that includes the mother, father, and their children.

nurturance The tendency to attempt to care for and further the growth and development of another.

obesity A condition characterized by being excessively fat.

object permanence A scheme acquired during the sensorimotor stage of development in which children become aware that an object continues to exist even when it is hidden or moved from place to place.

object relations The component of ego development that is concerned with the self, self-understanding, and self–other relationships.

observation A research method in which behavior is watched and recorded.

observational learning Changes in thought or behavior that result from watching others.

obsessions Persistent repetitive thoughts which serve as mechanisms for controlling anxiety.

occupational career The pattern of participation in the labor market.

occupational status A hierarchy of status among large groups of occupations which reflects their relative power, influence, and respect among members of the society.

Oedipal conflict In Freud's psychosexual theory, the central conflict of the phallic stage, in which the boy has strong desires for the mother, strong aggressive feelings toward his father, and strong fears of castration by the father.

old-old Among the very old, those who have suffered major physical or mental decrements.

ontogenesis The course of development.

operant conditioning A form of learning in which new responses are strengthened by the presentation of reinforcements.

operational definition In research, the way an abstract concept is defined in terms of how it will be measured.

optimal ability The level of performance of which one is capable at the highest levels of motivation and preparation.

oral stage In Freud's psychosexual theory, the first life stage, during which the mouth is the primary source of sexual satisfaction. Issues of self-concept and personal worth are important at this stage.

organic brain syndromes Disorders involving memory loss, confusion, loss of ability to manage daily functions, and loss of ability to focus attention.

organ inferiority In Adler's theory, a strong sense that some organ of one's body is weak and inferior. The person becomes preoccupied with thoughts of this weakness.

outcome variables Dimensions that are viewed as the consequence of a particular intervention or experimental manipulation.

out-group A group that competes with one's own group; contrasted with **in-group.**

ovum An egg; the female germ cell.

palate The roof of the mouth, separating the mouth from the nasal cavity.

paradox A statement that may appear to be opposed to common sense, yet is true.

peer A person belonging to the same group, often on the basis of age or grade.

peer pressure Expectations and demands to conform to the norms of one's peer group.

perception The recognition and organization of sensory experiences.

perceptual gestalts The recognition and integrated organization of sensory experiences in such a way as to perceive a whole.

perineum The area between the anus and the back of the vagina.

peristalsis Successive waves of involuntary contraction passing along the walls of the intestine or other hollow muscular structure, forcing the contents onward.

permissive Marked by a relatively easygoing and tolerant discipline technique that allows the child's desires to be asserted.

personal constructs   In George Kelly's theory, personal points of view about the world through which a person interprets both psychological and social events.

personal history   The life events that occur during an individual's development.

personality consolidation   The strengthening of personality through a process of self-examination, increasing awareness, crisis, and personal development.

person-environment fit   The fit between the person's needs, skills, and interpersonal style and the characteristics of the environments in which the person participates.

perspective taking   The ability to consider a situation from the point of view of another person or angle.

phallic stage   In Freud's psychosexual theory, the third stage of development, during which the Oedipal and Electra conflicts occur.

phenotype   Observable characteristics that result from a particular genotype and a particular environment.

phenylketonuria (PKU)   A genetic disease that restricts intellectual development if it is not treated.

phobia   An intense, irrational fear.

phonetics   The sound system of a language.

phylogeny   The evolutionary chain of species associated with a particular plant or animal.

physical prowess   Physical ability and skill.

physiological   Characteristic of normal physical and chemical functions of the body.

pitch   The range of high to low sounds.

placenta   The vascular organ that connects the fetus to the maternal uterus and mediates metabolic exchanges.

plasticity   The capability of being molded.

pleasure principle   The desire to experience pleasure and avoid pain through the immediate discharge of impulses that guide the functioning of the id.

polygamy   A family organization in which a spouse may have more than one mate.

population   All units for potential observation.

postconventional morality   In Kohlberg's stages of moral reasoning, the most mature form of moral judgments. Moral decisions are based on an appreciation of the social contract which binds members of a social system and on personal values.

postpartum depression   A period of sadness that may be experienced by the mother after giving birth and that appears to be related to hormonal activity.

power assertion   A discipline technique involving physical force, harsh language, or control of resources.

precarious   Characterized by a lack of stability or security.

preconscious   Absent from but capable of being readily brought into consciousness.

preconventional morality   In Kohlberg's stages of moral reasoning, the most immature form of moral judgments. Moral decisions are based on whether the act has positive or negative consequences, or whether it is rewarded or punished.

precursor   Forerunner, the substance from which another organ is formed.

preoperational thought   In Piaget's theory of cognitive development, the stage in which representational skills are acquired.

press   Steady push or demand.

pre-term baby   A baby who is born before the full gestational period.

primal wishes   Very early needs and desires.

primary process   The seemingly unorganized mental activity, characteristic of the id and the unconscious, that occurs in dreams, fantasies, and related processes. Characterized by an absence of negatives, a here-and-now focus, and symbolic flexibility.

primate   Any of various omnivorous mammals of the order Primates, including the three suborders Tarsioidea (tarsiers), Prosimii (lemurs, loris, and their allies), and Anthropoidea (humans, great apes, gibbons, Old World monkeys, and New World monkeys). Distinguished by varied locomotion, use of hands, and flexible, complex behavior involving a high level of cultural adaptability and social interaction.

prime adaptive ego qualities   Mental states that form a basic orientation toward the interpretation of life experiences; new ego qualities emerge in the positive resolution of each psychosocial crisis.

primiparas   A woman who has borne one child or who is pregnant for the first time.

primitive causality   An understanding of cause and effect acquired by infants which is based solely on sensory and motor experience, not symbolic logic.

proactive   Initiating action, as opposed to reactive.

probability   The likelihood that something will happen.

procreation   To give birth to offspring.

progesterone   A hormone related to pregnancy.

projection The attribution of one's own ideas, feelings, wishes, or attitudes to other people.

projective technique Method for measuring aspects of personality by asking a person to make responses to ambiguous stimuli.

prompting Urging a child to say more about an incomplete expression.

prosocial behavior Positive social behavior such as helping another person.

Protestant ethic A code of values that emphasizes hard work, achievement, and delay of gratification.

proximity Close, nearby.

psychiatric will A document that explains the kinds of psychiatric treatment a person is or is not willing to accept in very old age.

psychohistorical perspective An integration of past, present, and future time with respect to personal and societal continuity and change.

psycholinguistics The study of language as it is affected by psychological factors.

psychosexual theory Freud's theory of psychological development, which proposed that cognitive, emotional, and social growth were associated with predictable changes in sexual sensitivity during childhood. This theory is sometimes called psychoanalytic theory.

psychosocial crisis A predictable life tension that arises as people experience some conflict between their own competences and the expectations of their society.

psychosocial environment The influence of culture, values, resources, demands, competences, and motives that are embedded in the structure of the social and physical environment.

psychosocial evolution The contribution of each generation to the knowledge and norms of the society.

psychosocial moratorium A period of free experimentation before a final identity is achieved.

psychosocial theory A theory of psychological development that proposed that cognitive, emotional, and social growth were the result of the interaction between social expectations at each life stage and the competences that people bring to each life challenge.

psychotemporal perspective Sense of time as it is affected by psychological factors.

puberty The period of physical development at the onset of adolescence when the reproductive system matures.

punishment A penalty or negative experience imposed on a person for improper behavior.

purpose The ability to imagine and pursue valued goals.

quickening Sensations of fetal movement, usually during the second trimester of fetal growth.

radius of significant relationships The groups of important people in one's life; the breadth and complexity of these groups change over the life span.

random Characteristic of a situation in which each event of a set of events is equally likely to occur.

random sampling A method for choosing the sample for a study in which each member of the population under investigation has an equal chance of being included.

rapport Harmony and understanding in a relationship.

reaction range The range of possible responses to environmental conditions that is established through genetic influences.

reaction time The time that lapses between the signal to make a response and the response itself.

reality principle The motivating force or mechanism by which the ego protects the person by preventing id impulses from being gratified until a socially acceptable form of expression can be found.

receptive language The ability to understand words.

recessive gene A form of a gene that is expressed in the phenotype only when a similar allele is present. In combination with a dominant gene the characteristics associated with the recessive gene are masked.

reciprocal interactions Interactions in which the behavior of each participant influences the responses of the other.

reciprocity A scheme describing the interdependence of related dimensions, such as height and width or time and speed.

redundant Using more words than are necessary to convey meaning.

reference group A group with which an individual identifies and whose values the individual accepts as guiding principles.

reflex An involuntary response to a simple stimulus.

reflexive self-concept Berstein's concept of the influence of language on shaping a self-concept that is sensitive to social relationships and roles.

reinforcement In operant conditioning, the positive consequence that follows a given behavior.

reinforcement patterns   The frequency and timing with which reinforcements are presented.

rejectivity   The unwillingness to include certain others or groups of others in one's generative concerns.

releasing stimulus   An odor, color, movement, sound, shape, pattern of events, or relationship among any of these that elicits the performance of a fixed action pattern in a particular species.

reliability   The consistency of a test in measuring something.

reminiscence   Process of thinking and/or telling about past experiences.

repertoire   A list of abilities, skills, and full range of performance possible.

representational skill   Skills learned in the preoperational stage, including mental imagery, symbolic play, symbolic drawing, imitation, and language, that permit the child to represent experiences or feelings in a symbolic form.

repression   A defense mechanism that involves pushing unacceptable anxiety-provoking impulses, memories, thoughts, or feelings into the unconscious.

repudiation   Rejection of roles and values that are viewed as alien to oneself.

research design   A plan for conducting research that includes the method for gathering data, the sample selected to participate in the study, the frequency with which data are to be gathered, and the statistical techniques that are to be used in analyzing the data.

resilience   The capacity to recover from stress.

respiratory distress syndrome   An acute lung disease of the newborn. It occurs primarily in premature babies and babies born to sick mothers, and is characterized by rapid breathing, flaring of the nostrils, inelastic lungs, and other physical malformations that may cause serious breathing problems.

response   A behavior that follows a particular stimulus event.

response repertoire   The range of behaviors that a person or animal is capable of performing.

responsiveness   Reacting readily to another's request or need.

retina   The light-sensitive membrane lining the back of the eye on which images are cast by the cornea and lens.

retrospective study   A research design in which sub-jects are asked to report on experiences they had earlier in their lives.

reversibility   A scheme describing the ability to undo an action and return to the original state.

reward   A positive consequence that follows desired behavior.

reward structure   The pattern of positive consequences that occurs within an institution, a classroom, or a family group to encourage particular behaviors.

ribs   The flat curved bones that form a framework for the chest and a protective cage around the heart, lungs, and other organs.

risk   To expose to danger with a possibility of loss or injury.

rite of passage   A ritual associated with a crisis or a change of status (for example, marriage for an individual).

ritual   A formal and customarily repeated act or series of acts.

RNA   Ribonucleic acid; a compound that conveys the information in the DNA strands to the cytoplasm in order to stimulate the production of specific amino acids.

role   A set of behaviors that have some socially agreed-upon functions and for which there exists an accepted code of norms, such as the role of teacher, child, or minister.

role compatibility   Partners in a relationship approach situations in a manner that works well; their behaviors and responses complement one another.

role diffusion   The negative pole of the psychosocial crisis of later adolescence in which the person cannot make a commitment to any unified vision of the self.

role enactment   Patterned characteristics of social behavior that one performs as a result of being in a specific role.

role expectations   Shared expectations for behavior that are linked to a social role.

role experimentation   The central process for the resolution of the psychosocial crisis of later adolescence, which involves participation in a variety of roles before any final commitments are made.

role prescription   The specific behaviors and norms associated with a particular role.

role reversal   Assuming the behaviors of a person in a reciprocal role, as when a child acts toward his or her parent as a parent.

role strain   The conflict and competing demands made by several roles that the person holds simultaneously.

role-taking abilities   Skills related to understanding and enacting the roles of others.

rooting   An infant reflex in which the baby's head turns toward the direction of the cheek that is stimulated.

saline solution   A solution containing salt.

sample   The group of people who have been selected to participate as subjects in a research project.

sampling   A method of choosing subjects in a study.

sanction   A negative consequence that occurs when a standard or rule has been violated.

schedules of reinforcement   The frequency and regularity with which reinforcements are given.

scheme   In Piaget's theory, the organization of actions into a unified whole, a mental construct.

school phobia   A strong, irrational fear of some aspect of the school situation, interpreted in psychoanalytic theory as an expression of a child's reluctance to leave the mother.

scientific process   A process for building a body of knowledge involving observation, theory construction, operationalizing the theory, testing the theory, evaluating and revising the theory.

secondary process   The conscious mental activity and logical thinking controlled by the ego and influenced by environmental demands.

secular trend   A tendency observed since approximately 1900 for more rapid physical maturation from one generation to the next, probably as a result of favorable nutrition, increased mobility, and greater protection from childhood diseases.

sedentary   Sitting still much of the time.

self-concept   The characteristics and attributes one applies to oneself.

self-control   The ability to control impulses and the ability to control events.

self-disclosure   The ability to communicate personal information and feelings to someone else.

self-efficacy   A sense of confidence that one can perform the behaviors that are demanded in a specific situation.

self-encodings   Evaluations and concepts related to information about oneself.

self-esteem   The evaluative dimension of the self that includes feelings of worthiness, pride, and discouragement.

self-theory   An organized set of ideas about the self that is accumulated through daily interactions.

semantic contingency   The immediate matching of an adult's utterance to the content or topic of a child's verbalization.

semicircular canals   The three curved tubular canals in the labyrinth of the inner ear that are concerned with balance.

semiotic thinking   The understanding that one thing can stand for another.

senescence   The process of becoming old.

sensitive period   A span of time during which a particular skill or behavior is most likely to develop.

sensitivity (of caregiver)   Attentiveness to an infant's state, accurate interpretation of the infant's signals, and well-timed responses that promote mutually rewarding interactions.

sensorimotor intelligence   In Piaget's theory of development, the first stage of cognitive growth during which schema are built on sensory and motor experiences.

sensorimotor play   Sensory exploration and motoric manipulation that produce pleasure.

sensory deprivation   The relative absence of all forms of stimulation.

sensory functions   The responses of the body and nervous system to a variety of stimuli; vision, hearing, taste, smell, and touch.

sensory receptors   Millions of microscopic structures throughout the body that collect information about the external environment or the body's internal state. Receptors are attuned to particular stimuli, and fire when excited.

sensory stimulation   Events that have an impact on any of the sense receptors, including sounds, sights, tasks, or tactile stimuli.

separation anxiety   Feelings of fear or sadness associated with the departure of the object of attachment.

serial monogamy   Having one intimate relationship at a time as opposed to having several at once.

sex education   An organized curriculum focusing on the biological, psychological, cultural, and interpersonal aspects of love, sexuality, and reproduction.

sex-linked characteristic   Characteristics for which the allele is found on the sex chromosomes.

sex-role identification   The integration of knowledge about one's gender, awareness of cultural expectations associated with each sex, identification with the like-sex parent, and preference for one's sex role.

sex-role preference A positive value for the expectations and norms held for a specific gender group.

sex-role standards Attributes held by the culture for males and females. These attributes can include both precepts and sanctions.

sex-typed Marked by a trait, characteristic, or behavior that is seen as associated with either men or women by a large number of people.

sexual differentiation Sexual organs take on their unique male and female structure.

shame An intense emotional reaction to being ridiculed or to a negative self-assessment.

shaping In behavior modification, altering behavior by reinforcing progressively closer approximations of the desired behavior.

sibling Brother or sister.

sign Something that represents something else, usually in an abstract, arbitrary way; for example, a word for an object.

single-adult executive Family pattern in which one adult in the household makes the major decisions.

skull plates Making up the bony skeleton of the head, they serve to protect the brain and other organs.

social attachment A strong, affectionate bond that develops between infants and their caregivers.

social clock Orderly and sequential changes that occur with passage of time as individuals move from adolescence through adulthood and old age.

social cognition Concepts related to understanding interpersonal behavior and the point of view of others.

social competence The skills involved in making friends, maintaining friendships, and enjoying the benefits of close peer relations.

social convention Socially accepted norms and regulations that guide behavior.

social cooperation Working in a collaborative mode with one or more other people.

social desirability The quality of a person's responding or behaving in ways that are viewed as acceptable or proper by others.

social integration Being comfortably involved in meaningful interpersonal associations and friendship relations.

socialization The process of teaching and enforcing group norms and values to the new group members.

social learning theory A theory of learning that emphasizes the ability to learn new responses through observation and imitation of others.

social milieu The environment, especially the people, the norms, and the cultural expectations in one's surroundings.

social perspective taking The capacity to recognize the point of view held by others, especially when it differs from one's own.

social referencing The process by which infants use facial features and verbal expressions as clues to the emotional responses of another person, often the mother, and as information about how to approach an unfamiliar, ambiguous situation.

social role theory The theory that emphasizes participation in varied and more complex roles as a major factor in human development.

social support Information leading people to believe that they are cared for and loved, that they are esteemed and valued, and that they belong to a network of communication and mutual obligation.

societal processes All those processes through which a person becomes integrated into society, for example cultural rituals.

socioeconomic status One's ranking on a number of social and financial indicators, including years of education, kind of work, and salary.

solicitude Attentive care and protectiveness.

somatic processes All those processes necessary for the functioning of the biological organism, for example the sensory capacities.

sonar An apparatus that can detect objects under water through the use of reflected sound waves.

soothability The ability to regain a calm state following irritation or pain.

sperm The male germ cell.

sperm bank A facility where sperm are donated and frozen for use in artificial insemination.

spontaneous ejaculation A discharge of semen without deliberate manipulation.

stagnation A lack of psychological movement or growth during middle adulthood which may result from self-aggrandizement or from the inability to cope with developmental tasks.

status Relative social prestige or rank.

stethoscope An instrument for listening to sounds in the body, particularly those made by the heart or lungs.

stimulus   Any change in the energy of the environment that has the potential to influence a perceiver.

stimulus generalization   The capacity for similar stimuli to evoke the same response.

stranger anxiety   Feelings of fear or apprehension in the presence of unfamiliar people, especially during infancy.

strange situation   A standard laboratory procedure designed to describe patterns of attachment behavior. A child is exposed during a 20-minute period to a series of events that are likely to stimulate the attachment system. Child and caregiver enter an unfamiliar laboratory setting; a stranger enters; the caregiver leaves briefly; and the caregiver and infant have opportunities for reunion while researchers observe child, caregiver, and their interactions.

stratified sampling   A method for choosing the sample for a research study in which subjects are selected from a variety of levels or types of people in the population.

subjective age identity   The age one feels oneself to be, based on perceived similarity to people of this age.

subjective reality   The way things appear from the person's point of view.

sublimation   Channeling energy from unconscious wishes into socially acceptable behaviors.

subordinate   Being in a lower, submissive rank.

substantive complexity   The degree to which one's work requires thought, independent judgment, and frequent decision making.

succorance   Giving help or relief.

superego   In psychoanalytic theory, the mental function that embodies moral precepts and moral sanctions. The superego includes the ego ideal, or the goals toward which one strives, as well as the punishing conscience.

surrogate mother   Woman who conceives and bears a child for an infertile couple.

survey   A research method in which carefully worded questions are asked of a large number of respondents, either orally or in writing.

symbol   An object, image, or word that represents something. A symbol can be a word that represents an object, as *chair,* or an object that represents a concept, as a dove.

symbolic drawing   Drawings that represent a specific thought.

symbolic play   Imaginative or pretend activities that express emotions, problems, or roles.

synchronize   To coincide or agree in time.

syntax   The rules for ordering words in a specific language.

system   A combination of things or parts, forming a complex or unitary whole and functioning as a unit.

taboo   Proscribed by society as improper or unacceptable.

tactile stimulation   Any stimuli that evoke a response from the sensory receptors in the skin. Touching, tickling, pinching, and rubbing are examples.

talent   Areas of skill or competence.

teachable moments   The times when a person is maturationally most ready to learn a new skill.

technology   A technical method of achieving a practical purpose.

telegraphic speech   Two-word sentences, used by children, that omit many parts of speech but convey meaning.

temperament   Innate characteristics that determine the person's sensitivity to various sense experiences and his or her responsiveness to patterns of social interaction.

temporal association   Events that occur together or close together in time.

teratogens   Agents that might produce malformations during the formation of organs and tissues.

test   Groups of questions or problems that usually indicate and measure abilities, potentials, or psychological characteristics.

testosterone   A hormone that fosters the development of male sex characteristics and growth.

thalamus   An area of the brain near the pituitary gland that integrates sensory information and relays it to the cortex.

theory   A logically interrelated system of concepts and statements that provides a framework for organizing, interpreting, and understanding observations, with the goal of explaining and predicting behavior.

toddlerhood   The period of psychosocial development that begins around the age of two and ends around the time the child enters kindergarten.

toxemia   The presence of toxins produced by bacteria in the bloodstream.

trauma   In psychoanalytic theory, an emotional shock that has long-lasting psychological consequences.

trial-and-error learning   A mode of learning in which the solution is discovered by observing the consequences of each response.

trimester   A period of three months during the nine months of pregnancy.

trust   An emotional sense that both the environment and oneself are reliable and capable of satisfying basic needs.

ultrasound   A technique for producing visual images of the fetus in utero through a pattern of deflected sound waves.

unconditioned response   A response that is evoked by a stimulus prior to opportunities for learning; sometimes described as a reflexive response.

unconditioned stimulus   A stimulus that evokes a response prior to opportunities for learning.

unconscious   In Freud's psychosexual theory, a reservoir of wishes, needs, and fantasies that influence behavior but of which we are not normally aware.

underachievement   A term describing students who perform below the level of their ability.

uniformitarianism   A principle that states that the same laws of nature apply uniformly across time.

uterus   In the female reproductive system, the hollow muscular organ in which the fertilized ovum normally becomes embedded and in which the developing embryo and fetus is nourished and grows.

validity   The extent to which a test measures what it is supposed to measure.

value   A principle or quality that is intrinsically desirable.

variables   Dimensions that can have a number of different values.

venereal disease   Any infection transmitted by sexual intercourse.

verbal persuasion   Encouragement from others.

verbatim   Word for word; using the exact words.

vernix caseosa   A coating of dead cells and oil that covers the skin during fetal development.

vertical career movements   Promotions, the attainment of higher positions, or changes to more prestigious organizations or institutions.

vicarious   An experience achieved through the imagined participation in events that happen to another person.

visual acuity   The ability to detect visual stimuli under various levels of illumination.

visual tracking   Following an object's movement with one's eyes.

vocabulary   A list of the words a child uses and understands.

vocalizations   Any sounds or utterances a child makes.

voluntary movement   Movement that is guided by a person's conscious control.

volunteer sampling   In which subjects for a study are selected from volunteers.

will   The determination to exercise free choice and self-control.

willfulness   Wanting to have your own way.

wisdom   The detached yet active concern with life itself in the face of death.

withdrawal   Becoming socially and emotionally detached.

work clock   Timetable of expectations for the progression of work life.

young-old   Among the very old, those who remain healthy, vigorous, and competent.

zygote   The developing individual formed from two gametes.

Name Index

Subject Index

Photo Credits

CHAPTER OPENER PHOTOS
2, 34, and **68,** © 1991, ARS, New York/SPADEM; **128,** Collection, The Museum of Modern Art, New York. Gift of Mrs. Bertram Smith. © 1991, ARS, New York/SPADEM; **184, 236,** and **284,** © **1991,** ARS, New York/SPADEM; **328,** Courtesy of The National Gallery of Art, Washington, D.C. Rosenwald Collection. © 1991, ARS, New York/SPADEM; **366, 414, 460,** and **510,** © 1991, ARS, New York/SPADEM; **562,** Courtesy of The Galerie Louis Leiris, Paris. © 1991, ARS, New York/SPADEM; **602,** © 1991, ARS, New York/SPADEM.

COLOR INSERT PHOTOS: PRENATAL PERIOD AND BIRTH
16-WEEK-OLD FETUS, © Lennart Nilsson, *A Child Is Born,* Dell Publishing Company; FERTILIZATION, Francis Leroy, Biocosmos/Science Photo Library/Photo Researchers; CELL DIVISION, © Petit Format/Nestle/Science Source/Photo Researchers; THE EGG, © Petit Format/Nestle/Science Source/Photo Researchers; 5½-WEEK AND 8-WEEK EMBRYO, 4½-MONTH AND 5½-MONTH FETUS, © Lennart Nilsson, *A Child Is Born,* Dell Publishing Company; ULTRASOUND, © Alexander Tsiaras/Science Source/Photo Researchers; 2 BABIES, © Larry Hamill; HOME BIRTH, © Suzanne Arms-Wimberley.

COLOR INSERT PHOTOS: FAMILY LIFE ACROSS CULTURES
PUEBLO INDIAN FAMILY, © Gale Zucker; ALL OTHERS, © Larry Hamill.

TEXT PHOTOS
CHAPTER ONE. 15, 21, and **26,** © Gale Zucker.
CHAPTER TWO. 38 (left to right), Jon Erikson, Richard Schoenbrun, Brown Brothers, National Library of Medicine; **46,** University of Chicago; **47,** © 1991, ARS, New York/SPADEM; **52,** Amazon Photos; **54,** © 1991, ARS, New York/SPADEM; **55,** © Gale Zucker; **57,** Paul Koby.
CHAPTER THREE. 72 (both), M. F. W. Tweedie/Photo Researchers; **73,** Library of Congress; **74,** Mark Newman/Tom Stack & Associates; **81,** © Gale Zucker; **83** and **85,** © 1991, ARS, New York/SPADEM; **89,** © Gale Zucker; **92,** © 1991, ARS, New York/SPADEM; **96** (top left and right), © 1991, ARS, New York/SPADEM; (bottom left) Courtesy of The Philadelphia Museum of Modern Art. A.E. Gallatin Collection. © 1991, ARS, New York/SPADEM; **100** and **108,** © Gale Zucker; **110,** Courtesy of The Los Angeles County Museum of Art. © 1991, ARS, New York/SPADEM; **116** and **121,** © Gale Zucker.
CHAPTER FOUR. 132, Omikron/Science Source/Photo Researchers; **137,** © 1991, ARS, New York/SPADEM; **146,** © Gale Zucker; **153,** Footprints courtesy of Christopher and Lisa Drakes and Stanford Hospital; **159,** © Gale Zucker; **161,** © 1991, ARS, New York/SPADEM; **165,** © Gale Zucker; **176** (both), Amazon Photos.
CHAPTER FIVE. 186, © Gale Zucker; **189, 193,** and **197,** Amazon Photos; **201** (left), John Ficara/Woodfin Camp & Associates; (right) © Larry Hamill; **202,** Courtesy of Diana Rosenstein, M. A. and Harriet Oster, Ph.D.; **208,** © 1991, ARS, New York/SPADEM; **211, 213,** and **216** (both), Amazon Photos; **219,** © 1991, ARS, New York/SPADEM; **225,** © Larry Hamill; **227,** © 1991, ARS, New York/SPADEM.
CHAPTER SIX. 239, Courtesy of The Yale University Art Gallery. Gift of Stephen Carlton Clark. © 1991, ARS, New York/SPADEM; **241,** © Larry Hamill; **253,** Amazon Photos; **256,** © Gale Zucker; **258,** © 1991, ARS, New York/SPADEM; **261,** © Larry Hamill; **266,** Amazon Photos; **269,** © Gale Zucker; **273,** Amazon Photos; **275** and **276,** © Gale Zucker.
CHAPTER SEVEN. 289, © 1991, ARS, New York/SPADEM; **295,** © Larry Hamill; **297,** Amazon Photos; **299,** © 1991, ARS, New York/SPADEM; **301** and **305,** © Gale Zucker; **309,** © 1991, ARS, New York/SPADEM; **310,** © Larry Hamill; **313,** © Gale Zucker; **316,** Courtesy of The Fogg Art Museum, Harvard University, Cambridge, Massachusetts. Bequest of the Collection of Maurice Wertheim, class of 1906. © 1991, ARS, New York/SPADEM; **319,** © Gale Zucker.

CHAPTER EIGHT. 332, Amazon Photos; **335,** © Gale Zucker; **340,** Courtesy of The National Gallery of Art, Washington, D.C. Chester Dale Collection. © 1991, ARS, New York/SPADEM; **341,** © Larry Hamill; **343,** Amazon Photos; **346,** © 1991, ARS, New York/SPADEM; **349,** © Larry Hamill; **354** and **357,** © Gale Zucker; **360,** Collection, The Museum of Modern Art, New York. Abby Aldrich Rockefeller Fund. © 1991 ARS, New York/SPADEM.

CHAPTER NINE. 370, © 1991, ARS, New York/SPADEM; **372,** © Gale Zucker; **373,** Courtesy of The Albright-Knox Art Gallery, Buffalo, New York. Fellows for Life Fund, 1926. © 1991, ARS, New York/ SPADEM; **376,** © Gale Zucker; **379,** © 1991, ARS, New York/SPADEM; **382,** © Gale Zucker; **384,** Amazon Photos; **389** and **395,** © Gale Zucker; **400,** © 1991, ARS, New York/SPADEM; **402,** © Gale Zucker; **403,** Amazon Photos.

CHAPTER TEN. 417, Amazon Photos; **420,** Collection, The Museum of Modern Art, New York. Nelson A. Rockefeller Bequest. © 1991, ARS, New York/SPADEM; **423,** © Gale Zucker; **424,** Collection, The Museum of Modern Art, New York. Gift of Mrs. Simon Guggenheim. © 1991, ARS, New York/SPADEM; **426** and **431,** © Gale Zucker; **436,** Amazon Photos; **439,** © 1991, ARS, New York/SPADEM; **441** and **443,** © Gale Zucker; **445,** Courtesy of The Metropolitan Museum of Art. Gift of Mr. and Mrs. John L. Loeb, 1960. (60.87). © 1991, ARS, New York/SPADEM; **451,** © Gale Zucker.

CHAPTER ELEVEN. 472, Amazon Photos; **476,** © 1991, ARS, New York/SPADEM; **480,** © Gale Zucker; **481,** Amazon Photos; **485,** © Larry Hamill; **487** (both), © Gale Zucker; **491,** Courtesy of the Baltimore Museum of Art: The Cone Collection, formed by Dr. Claribel Cone and Miss Etta Cone of Baltimore, Maryland. BMA 1950.272. © 1991, ARS, New York/SPADEM; **497** and **501,** © 1991, ARS, New York/ SPADEM; **503,** © Gale Zucker.

CHAPTER TWELVE. 514, © 1991, ARS, New York/SPADEM; **516,** © Gale Zucker; **522,** Courtesy of The Albright-Knox Art Gallery, Buffalo, New York. Room of Contemporary Art Fund, 1941. © 1991, ARS, New York/SPADEM; **526,** David M. Grossman/Photo Researchers; **529,** © Gale Zucker; **534,** © 1991, ARS, New York/SPADEM; **536,** © Gale Zucker; **537** and **539,** © Larry Hamill; **547,** © Gale Zucker; **549, 553,** and **557,** © 1991, ARS, New York/SPADEM.

CHAPTER THIRTEEN. 566, Courtesy of Dr. Chester M. Pierce; **567,** Clark University Archives; **568,** Amazon Photos; **573,** © Larry Hamill; **576,** © Gale Zucker; **582, 586, 589,** and **592,** © 1991, ARS, New York/SPADEM; **594,** © Larry Hamill.

CHAPTER FOURTEEN. 607, © Gale Zucker; **612,** © 1991, ARS, New York/SPADEM; **616,** Bettye Lane/Photo Researchers; **623,** Amazon Photos; **626** and **628,** © 1991, ARS, New York/SPADEM; **635,** © Gale Zucker.